Travel Discount Coupon

This coupon entitles you to special discounts when you book your trip through the

TRAVEL NETWORK ®
RESERVATION SERVICE

**Hotels ♦ Airlines ♦ Car Rentals ♦ Cruises
All Your Travel Needs**

Here's what you get: *

♦ A discount of $50 USD on a booking of $1,000** or more for two or more people!

♦ A discount of $25 USD on a booking of $500** or more for one person!

♦ Free membership for three years, and 1,000 free miles on enrollment in the unique Travel Network Miles-to-Go® frequent-traveler program. Earn one mile for every dollar spent through the program. Redeem miles for free hotel stays starting at 5,000 miles. Earn free roundtrip airline tickets starting at 25,000 miles.

♦ Personal help in planning your own, customized trip.

♦ Fast, confirmed reservations at any property recommended in this guide, subject to availability.***

♦ Special discounts on bookings in the U.S. and around the world.

♦ Low-cost visa and passport service.

♦ Reduced-rate cruise packages and special car rental programs worldwide.

Visit our website at http://www.travelnetwork.com/Frommer or call us globally at 201-567-8500, ext. 55. In the U.S., call toll-free at 1-888-940-5000, or fax 201-567-1838. In Canada, call at 1-905-707-7222, or fax 905-707-8108. In Asia, call 60-3-7191044, or fax 60-3-7185415.

* To qualify for these travel discounts, at least a portion of your trip must include destinations covered in this guide. No more than one coupon discount may be used in any 12-month period, for destinations covered in this guide. Cannot be combined with any other discount or promotion.
**These are U.S. dollars spent on commissionable bookings.
***A $10 USD fee, plus fax and/or phone charges, will be added to the cost of bookings at each hotel not linked to the reservation service. Customers must approve these fees in advance. If only hotels of this kind are booked, the traveler(s) must also purchase roundtrip air tickets from Travel Network for the trip.

Valid until December 31, 1998. Terms and conditions of the Miles-to-Go® program are available on request by calling 201-567-8500, ext 55.

ZEA234

Frommer's ®
7th Edition

NEW ZEALAND
FROM $50 A DAY

The Ultimate Guide to Comfortable
Low-Cost Travel

by Elizabeth Hansen
Assisted by Richard Adams

Macmillan • USA

ABOUT THE AUTHORS

Elizabeth Hansen has lived and worked in both Australia and New Zealand. She is the author of *Bed and Breakfast New Zealand, The Women's Travel Guide to New Zealand, Frommer's Australia, Frommer's Australia from $50 a Day,* and *Frommer's San Diego.* In addition to writing and speaking about her two favorite destinations, Elizabeth also enjoys consulting with travelers who are headed down under. **Richard Adams** is a photographer (see the back cover of this book) as well as co-researcher, navigator, and map enthusiast. When Elizabeth and Richard are not traveling, they live in La Jolla, California.

MACMILLAN TRAVEL

A Simon & Schuster Company
1633 Broadway
New York, NY 10019

Find us online at **www.frommers.com**

Copyright © 1998 by Simon & Schuster, Inc.
Maps copyright © by Simon & Schuster, Inc.

"Waltzing on the Track at Christmas," "Captain Crayfish's South Sea Saturday Night," and "Parlez-vous Kiwi?" copyright © 1995 by Elizabeth Hansen. Reprinted by permission.

MACMILLAN is a registered trademark of Macmillan, Inc.
FROMMER'S is a registered trademark of Arthur Frommer. Used under license.

ISBN 0-02-861408-9
ISSN 1045-9111

Editor: Alicia Scott
Production Editor: Lori Cates
Design by Michele Laseau
Digital Cartography by Roberta Stockwell and Ortelius Design

SPECIAL SALES

Bulk purchases (10+ copies) of Frommer's and selected Macmillan travel guides are available to corporations, organizations, mail-order catalogs, institutions, and charities at special discounts, and can be customized to suit individual needs. For more information write to: Special Sales, Macmillan General Reference, 1633 Broadway, New York, NY 10019.

Manufactured in the United States of America

Contents

1   **The Best of New Zealand from $50 a Day   1**

   1   The Best Things to See & Do   1

   2   The Best Affordable Adventures   3

   3   The Best Experiences for Serious Thrill-Seekers   4

   4   The Best Multiday Treks   4

   5   The Best Short Walks   5

   6   The Best Trout Fishing   6

   7   The Best Bird Watching   7

   8   The Best Views   7

   9   The Best Museums   8

  10   The Best Places to Experience Maori Culture   8

  11   The Best Moderately Priced Accommodations   9

  12   The Best Places to Stay on a Shoestring   10

  13   The Best Moderately Priced Restaurants   11

  14   The Best Dining Bargains   12

  15   The Best Craft Shopping   13

  16   The Best of New Zealand After Dark   13

2   **Getting to Know New Zealand   15**

   1   The Lay of the Land   18

   2   The Natural World   19

   ★   *Geological Fault or Maui's Fish: How New Zealand Came to Be*   20

   ★   *Oh Deer!*   22

   3   History 101   22

   4   New Zealand Today   27

   5   The Maori Language   28

   6   A Taste of New Zealand: From Mussels to Meat Pies   29

   7   New Zealand's Literary Traditions   30

3   **Planning an Affordable Trip to New Zealand   32**

   1   How This Guide Can Save You Money   32

   2   Visitor Information & Entry Requirements   33

   ★   *Tying the Knot in New Zealand*   34

   3   Money   35

4 45 Money-Saving Tips   35

★ *The New Zealand Dollar, the U.S. Dollar &*
   the British Pound   36

★ *What Things Cost in Auckland*   37

5 When to Go   40

★ *New Zealand Calendar of Events*   43

6 Finding an Affordable Place to Stay   46

7 Shopping for New Zealand's Best Buys   48

8 Health & Insurance   49

★ *Start Packing: What to Bring & What to Wear*   50

9 Tips for Travelers with Special Needs   51

★ *Manuka Honey: An Affordable & Delectable Souvenir*   52

10 Getting There Without Going Broke   54

11 Getting Around Affordably   57

12 Suggested Itineraries   64

★ *Fast Facts: New Zealand*   65

4   The Active Vacation Planner   69

1 Tramping   69

★ *Staying Safe & Healthy in the Great Outdoors*   72

★ *A Christmas Waltz on Milford Track*   81

2 Fishing   82

3 Boating & Other Water Sports   84

4 Playing Golf   85

5 Skiing & Snowboarding   86

6 Cycling   87

7 More Guided Tours, Outfitters & Package Deals   87

5   Auckland   89

1 Orientation   92

★ *TOURISTOP: The Budget Traveler's Best Friend*   93

2 Getting Around   95

★ *Cheap Thrills: What to See & Do for Free in Auckland*   96

★ *Fast Facts: Auckland*   98

3 Affordable Accommodations   99

★ *Family-Friendly Accommodations*   105

4 Great Deals on Dining   110

5 Exploring Auckland: What to See & Do   117

★ *Taking in the Views*   118

★ *Especially for Kids* 126

6 Outdoor Activities & Spectator Sports 126

7 Shopping 127

8 Auckland After Dark 130

9 Easy Side Trips from Auckland 131

6 Farther Afield from Auckland 136

1 The Bay of Islands 136

★ *Stalking the Elusive Kiwi* 143

2 The Coromandel Peninsula 153

3 The Waikato: Waitomo and Cambridge 162

7 Rotorua & The Bay of Plenty 167

1 Tauranga: Beaches & Boats 167

2 Rotorua 172

★ *Cheap Thrills: What to See & Do for Free (or Almost) in Rotorua* 176

8 Gisborne & Hawkes Bay 192

1 Gisborne 193

2 Hawkes Bay 199

★ *Getting to Know the Gannets* 202

9 Lake Taupo & Beyond 209

1 Taupo 209

★ *Cheap Thrills: What to See & Do for Free in Taupo* 212

★ *Golfing for Dollars* 216

2 Tongariro National Park 222

★ *For the Love of Pihanga* 223

3 Wanganui 226

4 New Plymouth: Gateway to Egmont National Park 237

10 Wellington 237

1 Orientation 240

2 Getting Around 242

★ *Fast Facts: Wellington* 243

3 Affordable Accommodations 244

4 Great Deals on Dining 247

5 Exploring Wellington: What to See & Do 251

★ *Cheap Thrills: What to See & Do for Free in Wellington* 255

6 Outdoor Activities 257

7 Shopping 258

8 Wellington After Dark 258

9 Wairarapa: A Side Trip from Wellington 260

11 Marlborough, Nelson, the West Coast & Wanaka 262

1 Picton & Blenheim 262

2 Nelson & Beyond 270

★ *Abel Tasman National Park* 275

★ *Todd's Valley: "Free" Room & Board* 280

3 Westport: Adventure Center of the West Coast 284

4 Greymouth & Lake Brunner 286

5 Hokitika: Greenstone, Glowworms & Gold 293

★ *Gazing at Glowworms* 295

6 Franz Josef and Fox Glaciers 300

7 Wanaka: Gateway to Mt. Aspiring National Park 308

12 Queenstown, Fiordland & Mount Cook 314

1 Queenstown 316

★ *Cheap Thrills: What to See & Do for Free in Queenstown* 318

2 Te Anau 333

3 Milford Sound 339

4 Mount Cook 343

13 Southland 348

1 Invercargill 348

★ *A Carvery Treat* 353

2 Stewart Island 354

★ *Captain Crayfish's South Sea Saturday Night* 357

14 Dunedin 359

1 Orientation 359

2 Getting Around 362

★ *Fast Facts: Dunedin* 363

3 Affordable Accommodations 364

4 Great Deals on Dining 368

5 Exploring Dunedin: What to See & Do   371

6 Outdoor Activities   377

7 Shopping   378

8 Dunedin After Dark   378

9 En Route to Christchurch   380

15   Christchurch   382

1 Orientation   382

2 Getting Around   386

★ *Fast Facts: Christchurch*   387

3 Affordable Accommodations   388

4 Great Deals on Dining   392

★ *Family-Friendly Restaurants*   394

5 What to See & Do in Christchurch   396

★ *Cheap Thrills: What to See & Do for Free in Christchurch*   397

6 Outdoor Activities   402

7 Shopping   404

8 Christchurch After Dark   404

9 Side Trips from Christchurch   406

Appendix   410

A Kiwi /Yankee Glossary   410

★ *Parlez-vous Kiwi?*   411

A Glossary of Kiwi Menu Terms   412

The Metric System   413

Index   415

List of Maps

New Zealand at a Glance   16

New Zealand's Outdoor
   Recreational Areas   70

New Zealand's Best Hikes:
   Marlborough, Nelson &
   Beyond   76

New Zealand's Best Hikes:
   Queenstown & Fiordland   79

Greater Auckland   90

Central Auckland   100

Devonport   123

Farther Afield from
   Auckland   137

Rotorua & Environs   173

Greater Rotorua   175

Lake Taupo Region   211

Wellington   238

Te Papa Museum of
   New Zealand   252

Marlborough, Nelson &
   Beyond   264

Central Nelson   271

World Heritage Highway   301

Queenstown & Fiordland   315

Central Queenstown   319

Southland   349

Dunedin   360

Christchurch   384

For Rick, for being there—again.

ACKNOWLEDGMENTS

The author gratefully acknowledges the assistance of the New Zealand Tourism Board and Qantas Airways. I am also thankful for the hospitality offered by New Zealand's most gracious hosts. I also appreciate the input from the numerous readers who have taken the time to share their experiences with me. My assistant, Suzanne Osborne, is much appreciated, too.

AN INVITATION TO THE READER

When researching this book, I discovered many wonderful places—hotels, restaurants, shops, and more. I'm sure you'll find others. Please tell us about them so we can share the information with your fellow travelers in upcoming editions. If you were disappointed with a recommendation, we'd love to know that, too. Please write to:

Frommer's New Zealand from $50 a Day
Macmillan Travel
1633 Broadway
New York, NY 10019

AN ADDITIONAL NOTE

Please be advised that travel information is subject to change at any time—and this is especially true of prices. We therefore suggest that you write or call ahead for confirmation when making your travel plans. The authors, editors, and publisher cannot be held responsible for the experiences of readers while traveling. Your safety is important to us, however, so we encourage you to stay alert and be aware of your surroundings. Keep a close eye on cameras, purses, and wallets—all favorite targets of thieves and pickpockets.

WHAT THE SYMBOLS MEAN

✪ Frommer's Favorites

Our favorite places and experiences—outstanding for quality, value, or both.

The following abbreviations are used for credit or charge cards:

AE	American Express	JCB	Japan Credit Card
BC	Bankcard	MC	MasterCard
DC	Diners Club	V	Visa

FIND FROMMER'S ONLINE

Arthur Frommer's Outspoken Encyclopedia of Travel (www.frommers.com) offers more than 6,000 pages of up-to-the-minute travel information—including the latest bargains and candid, personal articles updated daily by Arthur Frommer himself. No other Web site offers such comprehensive and timely coverage of the world of travel.

The Best of New Zealand from $50 a Day

I hardly recognize New Zealand these days. The little country I first visited in 1975 has really grown up. Gone are inconvenient shopping hours, pesky liquor-licensing laws, and limited public transportation. Travelers today can browse through craft shops seven days a week, enjoy a glass of wine at an inexpensive cafe, and easily hop from downtown Wellington to the beaches of Kapiti Coast via electric train. Also gone are the days when motels and hotels were the only lodging options. Now travelers can stay at cozy B&Bs, where amiable hosts provide not just a roof and a morning meal, but useful travel advice, too.

In short, New Zealand has become a visitor-friendly destination, where people can enjoy all of the spectacular outdoor activities that New Zealanders have cherished for generations—hiking or "tramping," skiing, boating, fishing, biking, surfing, sailing, and even skydiving. Plus, you can do it all for less now since, over the last 10 years, New Zealand's streamlined infrastructure has created more than 80 new visitors centers throughout the country, where staffers book accommodations and tours and provide essential travel information at no charge. Even better, it probably won't cost you a dime to explore New Zealand's phenomenal landscapes—admission to almost all of the nature reserves and national parks maintained by the Department of Conservation is now free.

Even though New Zealand has changed a lot since I first stepped off the plane in Auckland 22 years ago, I'm happy to report that its most important character traits have stayed the same: It's still the most beautiful country on the face of the earth, and New Zealanders are still the nicest people you'll ever meet.

I look forward to sharing my New Zealand with you. I've evaluated and inspected, compared prices, and sampled the soup. With all that in mind, here's my list of favorite New Zealand places and experiences:

1 The Best Things to See & Do

- **The Auckland Museum:** Located right in the Auckland Domain, surrounded by sweeping lawns and flower gardens, this museum has exhibits covering every aspect of Maori culture, from 82-foot war canoes to live folk concerts—it's a great place to come before setting out to explore the rest of New Zealand. Don't miss the panoramic views of the harbor from the front steps. See chapter 5.

- **The Puhoi Pub:** This is one of New Zealand's most interesting old public-licensed hotels. Even though the beer isn't free, the history is, and it couldn't be better—old photos, saddles, and farm implements hang from the walls. Take a look inside and then do what the locals do: Order a pitcher of Lion Red and lounge on the lawn. The town of Puhoi is just off State Highway 1, about an hour's drive north of Auckland. See chapter 5.

- **Hot Water Beach:** The Coromandel boasts some of New Zealand's best beaches and Hot Water is one of them. If you hit it 2 hours before or after low tide, you can dig a hole in the sand and make your own spa pool. See chapter 6.

- **Craters of the Moon** (Wairakei): Just north of Lake Taupo, this thermal area—unlike the ones around Rotorua—is free. You'll see and hear bubbling mud pools and watch steam rising from cracks and fissures. The eerie landscape definitely lives up to its name. See chapter 9.

- **The Wairakei Geothermal Power Station:** Witness the awesome power of steam at this remarkable sight just north of Taupo. It was the second place in the world to convert wet steam into energy—the Italians were first. You can drive through the steamy valley where more than 100 bores have been drilled. The lively visitors center has great exhibits and shows a rather compelling video highlighting local geothermal activity—and it's all free. See chapter 9.

- **Te Papa Museum of New Zealand** (Wellington): When it opens in 1998, this will be the nation's first bicultural museum. Maori history will be told side-by-side with Pakeha (New Zealanders of European descent) history. I recently toured the construction site—hard hat and all—and looked at the plans for the museum's exciting exhibits. I was blown away. See chapter 10.

- **Wine Tasting:** It's a popular activity throughout New Zealand, but wines from the Marlborough District are especially notable. If you have your own wheels, it doesn't cost a thing to taste the vintages and visit the many wineries in and around Blenheim—my favorites are Cellier Le Brun and Cloudy Bay. See chapter 11.

- **The Milford Road:** This road winds its way between Te Anau and Milford Sound and passes stunning scenery. Waterfalls, lofty peaks, and running streams make this one of New Zealand's most memorable drives. Many misinformed folks try to tackle this drive in a day trip from Queenstown, but I highly recommend starting in Te Anau. Otherwise, you'll spend almost 9 hours sitting in the car or bus. See chapter 12.

- **The Dunedin Public Art Gallery:** Now ensconced in its new quarters in the center of town, this admission-free gallery holds more than 40 works by Frances Hodgkins, who was born in Dunedin and is considered the finest painter in New Zealand's history. A large collection of works from the Guggenheim was exhibited here in 1997. See chapter 14.

- **The Wizard of Christchurch:** This guy is a local institution. Too outrageous for an ordinary soapbox, he stands on a ladder in Cathedral Square Monday through Friday at 1pm and shares his opinions with the crowd that gathers to see him. In case you tire of his semantics, other free Christchurch activities include strolling along the peaceful Avon River or admiring the inside of the famous cathedral. See chapter 15.

- **The Botanic Gardens:** Located in Christchurch's Hagley Park, these gardens are recognized as some of the best in the world. If you have time, walk around for awhile and then stop for a picnic lunch. The Avon River's duck population is on hand to keep you company. See chapter 15.

2 The Best Affordable Adventures

- **Skiing an Active Volcano:** It's not something you can do just anywhere, but fortunately you can do it every winter (June through October) on Mount Ruapehu in Tongariro National Park, just south of Lake Taupo on the North Island. There are two popular ski areas on this 9,227-foot active volcano: Whakapapa and Turoa. See chapter 4.
- **Sailing on the Hauraki Gulf:** Cruising these waters near Auckland has always been fun, but now there's an extra treat: You can watch Team New Zealand and the America's Cup challengers get ready for the real deal in 2000. My favorite skipper, Reg (G. R.) Eggers, lives on Waiheke Island and captains a 36-foot *Lidgard* sailboat—he'll be happy to take you out for a spin. See chapter 5.
- **Swimming with Dolphins:** You can do it in the Bay of Islands, and you can bet it'll be an unforgettable experience. You can't touch the dolphins, but you can get up-close and personal—the gentle creatures seem as curious about us as we are of them. Several tour operators in the area provide transportation and equipment (snorkel, fins, and mask). See chapter 6.
- **Playing Golf, New Zealand Style:** If you've come all the way here, you might as well play by the local rules. For example, at the Purangi Golf & Country Club, on the North Island's Coromandel Peninsula, if you hit a sheep on the course, you get another shot. On other courses there are treacherous steam vents to avoid, as well as the more conventional water hazards and sand traps. Visitors can hire (rent) clubs at almost all Kiwi courses. See chapters 4 and 6.
- **Sea Kayaking on the Marlborough Sounds:** This is fast becoming one of New Zealand's most popular outdoor activities. For the best experience, go with the **Marlborough Sounds Adventure Company** in Picton, on the South Island. Their 1-day guided trips come complete with a naturalist, so you learn about local plants and animals while paddling the pristine waters. They also offer a unique twilight paddle with a barbecue dinner, and multiday trips. See chapter 11.
- **Whale Watching:** This is another one of New Zealand's cheaper thrills, especially if you hit the waters around Kaikoura on the South Island, where a pod of giant sperm whales often feeds unusually close to shore from April to August. You can spot them from the water on a boat or from the air, but book well ahead. See chapter 11.
- **Cave Rafting:** If donning a wet suit and hard hat and floating through dark caves on an inner tube is your kind of thing, there are plenty of places in New Zealand to do it—it's actually an unusual and exciting experience. First-timers and families with young children should go with **Norwest Adventures** (☎ 03/789-6686) in Westport on the South Island; but more daring, hardier souls will be better off with **Wild West Adventure Tours** (☎ 03/768-6649) in nearby Greymouth. You can also go cave rafting in and around Waitomo on the North Island. Keep your eyes peeled for glowworms! See chapters 6 and 11.
- **Canoeing:** You can do it all over New Zealand—and you should at least once—but one of the best spots is Okarito Lagoon (near Whataroa) on the South Island. It's a huge wetland with shallow waters and tidal flats, and a perfect place for bird watching. Rent a boat and oars from **Okarito Nature Tours** (☎ 03/753-4014). See chapter 11.
- **Flightseeing Over the Glaciers:** This is bound to be one of your most cherished New Zealand memories. Helicopters take off from the Fox and Franz Josef townships, fly various routes over the glaciers, and—weather permitting—land right on them so you can get out and walk around. At Mount Cook, small fixed-wing

planes head up to the Tasman Glacier and do the same thing. It's a bit pricey, but definitely worth the extra bucks. See chapters 11 and 12.

3 The Best Experiences for Serious Thrill-Seekers

- **Bungy Jumping:** Today it's as closely associated with New Zealand as the kiwi. You can do it in Taupo (on the world's first purposely built bungy platform); in Hanmer Springs, in Queenstown (the world's first bungy site); and several other places. It isn't exactly an inexpensive endeavor, but you can certainly watch for free. See chapters 9 and 12.
- **Jet Boating:** This is a thrill-a-minute adventure sport that got its start on the Shotover River gorge near Queenstown, which is still one of the best places to do it. Expert drivers send you flying through rushing rapids and between huge boulders. **The Shotover Jet Company** (☎ 03/442-8570) in Queenstown is the premier outfitter; however, they also run Huka Jet near Taupo—same boats, same trip time for NZ$20 (US$14) less per person. The Taupo trip isn't as scary because you aren't careening through a canyon, but it's still a pretty wild ride. For folks who want to combine jet boating and eco-touring, **Dart River Jet Safari** (☎ 03/442-9992) in Queenstown offers a great package. See chapters 9 and 12.
- **Abseiling:** Also known as rappelling, this sport involves descending steep cliff faces on ropes. It's perfectly safe, provided you are with an operator that knows what he's doing and is fairly compulsive about the condition of the equipment. That's why I think you should go with **Norwest Adventures** (☎ 03/789-6686) in Westport on the West Coast. They bill their trip "the adrenaline buzz of a lifetime" but also have a good safety record. See chapter 11.
- **Helihiking or Walking on Glaciers:** This is an incredible adventure, but you must be physically fit. Between the two, helihiking is less strenuous because the helicopters lift you over the steepest part and plop you down on the glacier where your hike begins. But this still isn't an activity for wimps—the glacier ice is steep. I recommend you undertake either of these activities at Fox Glacier, rather than Franz Josef, because that's where **Alpine Guides** (☎ 03/751-0825) is based, and they're the best. (Sorry if this sounds too opinionated, but losing a reader down a crevasse would just ruin my whole day.) See chapter 11.
- **White-Water Rafting:** The rushing rivers around Queenstown have long been associated with rafting, but this isn't the only area in New Zealand where you can experience the rush of whipping through wild rapids, not to mention the inevitable spills and chills. Waitomo and the West Coast of the South Island are other popular rafting spots. Stick with a qualified operator—I've listed the best and safest ones in regional chapters throughout this guide. See chapter 12.

4 The Best Multiday Treks

- **The Queen Charlotte Walkway:** Hike through lush coastal forest and around secluded coves and inlets in the Marlborough Sounds area. It takes 4 days to cover the whole thing, but independent walkers can do just a day or two. A guided walk, where packs are moved by boat, is also available. See chapter 4.
- **The Abel Tasman Coast Track:** This one starts and ends in Abel Tasman National Park at the north end of the South Island and has beautiful shoreline views. One-day walks are possible, but hikers who do the whole trail take 3 to 5 days to cover the 51 kilometers (32 miles). This is an easy walk to do independently, but guides are available. See chapter 4.

- **The Heaphy Track:** It takes 4 to 6 days to get from the junction of the Brown and Aorora rivers, across tussock-covered flats, and finally to the wild sea on the West Coast. You have to carry your own gear, though, because guided hikes are not available. See chapter 4.
- **The Milford Track:** This stretch in Fiordland has often been called "the finest walk in the world," and, having done it, I'd have to agree. The 54-kilometer (33-mile) trail follows the Clinton and Arthur valleys and crosses Mackinnon Pass, and the scenery is simply unforgettable. See chapter 4.
- **The Hollyford Track:** This course follows the Hollyford River as it makes its way out to Martin's Bay on the southwest coast of the South Island. This is one of the few Fiordland tracks that can safely be walked in winter; the trek takes about 4 days. See chapter 4.
- **The Routeburn Track:** You can either start in Fiordland and end near Glenorchy, just outside of Queenstown, or vice versa. Either way you'll cross the Harris Saddle, which affords magnificent views. The track takes 2 to 3 days to complete and guided trips are available. See chapter 4.

5 The Best Short Walks

- **Auckland's Waterfront:** It's fun to stroll along Tamaki Drive as it winds its way from the city to St. Heliers. As you pass through seaside suburbs, you'll share the footpath with in-line skaters and joggers; watch for windsurfers plying the waves nearby. See chapter 5.
- **Rainbow Falls:** To get here, start near the old Stone Store in Kerikeri in the Bay of Islands region. The grade is easy—if you can walk from one end of a shopping mall to the other, you can do this hike, also known as the Kerikeri River Walk. It takes 2 hours round-trip. See chapter 6.
- **Mount Maunganui:** Adjacent to Tauranga, this summit soars 252 meters (819 feet) high. It takes a couple of hours to climb to the top, where you'll relish magnificent ocean views. You can also walk the 3.5 kilometers (2.17 miles) around the base, which takes less than an hour. After your walk, soak or swim in one of the hot saltwater pools at the base of mountain. See chapter 7.
- **Te Kuri Farm Walkway:** This track crosses some private land on the northern outskirts of Gisborne, which was donated by local resident Murray Ball, creator of *Footrot Flats* and other cartoons. It is a 2- to 3-hour loop that includes a climb to a panoramic vista at 230 meters (747^1/$_2$ feet). See chapter 8.
- **Mount Egmont:** Also called Taranaki by the Maori, this beautiful cone-shaped peak on the North Island's west coast was once an active volcano. There are lots of great hiking trails (over 180 miles) that crisscross Egmont National Park. You can get to the summit and back in a day. See chapter 9.
- **Carew Falls Walk:** Located near Lake Brunner, this hike starts just beyond the Lake Brunner Lodge and winds through a podocarp forest that looks like an illustration from a children's book of fairy tales. Ferns of all sizes and shapes grow among moss-covered trees and granite boulders. The savvy traveler will allow time to sit in the forest, perhaps with a picnic lunch, and watch the fantails flitting between trees. See "Greymouth" in chapter 11.
- **Lake Matheson:** This alpine lake near the township of Fox Glacier, on the West Coast of the South Island, is often pictured on postcards with Mount Cook and Mount Tasman reflected on its surface. To see this view yourself, go early in the morning when there's less wind. You can walk around this serene body of water any time of the day—it takes about 1^1/$_2$ hours. See chapter 11.

- **The Blue Pools Track:** This is just one of the short walks you can take from the scenic World Heritage Highway, which follows the West Coast as it proceeds over Haast Pass. You'll tramp though a beech forest to deep blue pools that are full of trout in fall and winter. The Department of Conservation has installed helpful plant-identification plaques and a wooden-decked swing bridge along the way. See chapter 11.
- **The Rob Roy Glacier Trek:** This bush walk in Mt. Aspiring National Park offers an excellent view of the glacier; the trip takes 5 hours round trip and can be done independently or with **Edgewater Adventures** (☎ **03/443-8311**). See chapter 11.
- **A Day on the Routeburn Track:** Even though the famous Routeburn is a multiday affair, it's possible to just walk the last (or first, depending which way you're coming from) day of it. You'll start and return to Glenorchy, outside of Queenstown, and you can do it independently or with a guide. See chapter 12.

6 The Best Trout Fishing

- **Lake Rotorua:** It's one of the most scenic spots you'll find for catching a trout. But keep in mind that the license you buy for the rest of New Zealand will not cover you here. Also, before you bait your hook, you should probably know that the catch-and-release ethos is alive and well here—and throughout New Zealand—and there are lots of restrictions. See chapters 2 and 7.
- **Lake Taupo:** It's almost synonymous with trout and easily one of the world's best places for hooking both the rainbow and brown varieties. You can become part of the "picket fence" of people fishing from shore, or hire a boat and head out into the lake. Like Rotorua, Taupo issues its own licenses. See chapters 4 and 9.
- **The Tongiriro River:** Near the little town of Turangi, at the south end of Lake Taupo, this river is a good spot for frugal fishers. A couple of the "fly shops" in the area might even give you free advice, which you'll need because the techniques used in New Zealand are different than those used in other parts of the world. See chapter 4.
- **Tekapo River:** The adjacent canals and nearby lakes here offer your best chance of catching a trout without a guide—this is important for budget-minded travelers to keep in mind because fishing guides in New Zealand get paid almost as much as lawyers in California. The Tekapo River area is accessed from the towns of Omarama or Twizel. See chapter 4.
- **Lake Te Anau:** This is the second-largest lake in New Zealand and one of the five areas in the country where you can fish year round—the others are Lake Brunner, Lake Wakatipu, the Rotorua district, and Lake Taupo. Otherwise, rivers and streams are open for brown and rainbow trout fishing from October to April. Some local restrictions apply. See chapter 4.
- **Lake Brunner:** Just east of Greymouth, this lake is the home base of one of the country's best guides. If you've saved some splurge money for fishing, I suggest you stay at Lake Brunner Lodge and let Ray Grubb take you out for a day. Hooking a big one here could be one of your fondest New Zealand memories. See chapter 4 and 11.

7 The Best Bird Watching

- **Tiritiri Matangi:** This small island in the Hauraki Gulf has been designated as a native bird sanctuary—I once saw the rare takehe here, a flightless bird at one time thought to be extinct. To get to Tiritiri Matangi, take Fuller's "Twin Island Explorer," a combination of their Waiheke Island ferry from Auckland and a sailing excursion with Reg Eggers. See chapter 5.

- **The Miranda Shorebird Centre:** Located on the Sea Bird Coast about an hour from the Auckland Airport, this is the first overnight stop in New Zealand for many enthusiastic birders. Wrybills and dotterels are just two of the 60 or so species in the area. See chapter 5.
- **The Aroha Island Ecological Centre** This nature area near Kerikeri in the Bay of Islands is one of the best places in the country to see a kiwi in its natural surroundings. Despite its name, the reserve is not an island, but a pleasant patch of bush where those who stay overnight have a good chance of seeing one of the famous flightless birds. See chapter 6.
- **Cape Kidnappers:** This remarkable Hawkes Bay preserve is home to a colony of some 6,000 gannets. The sanctuary is open to the public from late October to April, but the best time to view these large birds is from early November to late February. Several tour operators make trips here, but you can also access the colony by walking (for free) along the beach at low tide. See chapter 8.
- **White Heron Sanctuary:** Catch a glimpse of both white herons (*kotuku*), who nest at this sanctuary from November to February, and Royal Spoonbills. To get here, start in Whataroa on the West Coast, where you'll take a 40-minute jet boat ride to the sanctuary, then walk along a boardwalk through native bush to a hide (blind) for bird viewing. The scenery is an added bonus here. See chapter 11.
- **Royal Albatross Colony:** Located on the Otago Peninsula near Dunedin, this is the only mainland nesting site of the albatross. Unfortunately, the colony wasn't too lucky during the 1997 season—the big birds made 10 nests, but none within the viewing area. It's only the second time in 25 years that this has happened, and everyone's keeping their fingers crossed for the coming seasons. See chapter 14.

8 The Best Views

- **Savage Memorial Park** (Auckland): It's simply one of my favorite vistas in the whole country. You can see the whole harbor—almost always dotted with white sailboats—and the distant gulf islands. It might be a bit windy, but the view is breathtaking. The park itself is named after Michael Joseph Savage, the first Labour Prime Minister of New Zealand who was in office from 1935 until his death in 1940. See chapter 5.
- **One Tree Hill** (Auckland): This summit offers a view of the city as well as the bustling harbor beyond. It's named for the lone pine tree growing on the hill's highest point, and the joke around town is that the landmark almost became "none tree hill" when a Maori activist took a hatchet to the tree in 1996. One Tree Hill Domain is accessed through Cornwall Park—a true urban oasis where sheep graze on the grass-covered slopes of extinct volcanoes. See chapter 5.
- **Kaiti Hill Lookout** (Gisborne): Enjoy a panoramic view of Poverty Bay, the city, its harbors and rivers. There's a statue of Captain Cook here—it's not a good likeness, but the sight of this English seaman against the backdrop of bright blue sky and water is still rather moving. At the bottom of the hill there's a memorial on the spot where Cook first stepped ashore. See chapter 8.
- **Te Mata Peak** (Hawkes Bay): It looks like a sleeping giant from the distance, but if you take the windy drive to the 1,310-foot summit you'll be rewarded with a 360-degree view and the sense that you're sitting on top of the world. See chapter 8.

- **Knight's Point View Point:** This vista on the West Coast between Fox Glacier and Haast provides a lofty 180-degree ocean view. The coast here looks much like California's Big Sur—beautiful big waves crash against looming cliffs, and native plants cling to barren hillsides. It's scenic spots like this that helped the area earn its World Heritage designation. See chapter 11.
- **The Skyline Gondola:** Hop on board and ascend Bob's Peak in Queenstown in a matter of minutes. En route and at the top, passengers are treated to stellar views of Lake Wakatipu and The Remarkables, which are the mountains bordering the lake. The best time to ride the gondola is at sunset when the play of light is brilliant. See chapter 12.

9 The Best Museums

- **The New Zealand National Maritime Museum:** This gem is located on the waterfront in Auckland, close to Viaduct Basin where the competitors for the 2000 America's Cup hang out. Exhibits at this interactive museum deal with everything from early Polynesian exploration on outriggers to the country's state-of-the-art yacht designs. The scow *Ted Ashby* goes out twice daily and is one of the best and cheapest ways for visitors to see the harbor. See chapter 5.
- **The Auckland Museum:** Located right in the Domain, this museum contains a treasure-trove of Maori artifacts. Be sure to notice the portraits by the well-known New Zealand artist C. F. Goldie, who captured on canvas the ornate tattoos of Maori chieftains. The "Weird and Wonderful" program provides great hands-on activities for children ages 2 to 12. See chapter 5.
- **Te Papa Museum of New Zealand** (Wellington): This grand new museum is scheduled to open in 1998. A "Mountains to Sea" area will be highlighted by the skeleton of a blue pigmy whale, and "Awesome Forces" features exhibits on volcanoes and earthquakes. In the virtual reality section you can bungy jump without actually taking the plunge. See chapter 10.
- **The International Antarctic Centre:** Christchurch has long been the gateway to Antarctica, and finally there's a place where people can share the experience of life on the frozen continent. The displays and audiovisuals here are really remarkable—I especially like the amateur video made by one of the researchers for his family. See chapter 15.

10 The Best Places to Experience Maori Culture

- **Auckland:** This quintessential New Zealand city has one of the best collections of Maori artifacts, including an 82-foot war canoe and a full-scale meeting house—all displayed in the Auckland Museum. The best way to experience the Maori way is to enjoy a *hangi* dinner and concert on an actual *marae*, but if your time is limited—and it probably will be—you should attend one of the museum's Maori concerts, given twice daily. See chapter 5.
- **The Bay of Islands:** A Maori group here called **Heritage Tours** (☎ 09/ 402-6288) offers an opportunity to experience the native culture and swim with dolphins—all on the same cruise. The half-day trip starts with a traditional challenge on the dock, followed by a *hongi* greeting, in which you touch noses with the hosts. See chapter 6.
- **Rotorua:** This used to be the place where visitors queued up to get into a hangi dinner–Maori concert hosted by one of the big hotels. You can still attend one of these dinner shows, but I recommend that you do something more authentic.

Rotoiti Tours (☎ 07/348-8969) offers hangi dinners and concerts on maraes (courtyards surrounding Maori meetinghouses), and the residents of Ohinemutu put on a nightly concert at their meetinghouse. See chapter 7.

- **Taupo** (NI): This resort town is home to the Tuwharetoa tribe, and visitors can make arrangements to go fishing, bush-walking, or horse trekking with a local Maori as your guide—the tribe has exclusive access to some of the best wilderness areas in the Taupo district. Make arrangements through **Tuwharetoa Tourism** (☎ 07/378-0254). See chapter 9.

11 The Best Moderately Priced Accommodations

- **Ascot Parnell** (Auckland; ☎ 09/309-9012): This is one of the most popular places to stay in the city, so book early if you want to bed down in one of the 11 rooms. It's a bed and breakfast–type inn with a great location in Parnell, surrounded by cafes, shops, and lots of attractions. The owners, Bart and Therese Blommaert, couldn't be nicer or more helpful. See chapter 5.
- **Mercury Bay Beachfront Resort** (Whitianga; ☎ 07/866-5637): Located on the Coromandel Peninsula, this refuge enjoys a perfect seaside location. All eight units have a sitting area and cooking facilities, as well as at least one bedroom and bathroom. There's a spa pool in the garden and the hosts happily provide beach equipment. See chapter 6.
- **Namaste Point** (Rotorua; ☎ 07/362-4804): This magical spot is located 20 minutes outside of Rotorua in a residential neighborhood right on the edge of Lake Rotoiti. Here Gillian Marks offers three spacious, modern units with kitchenettes that she stocks with breakfast ingredients. The gracious hostess also supplies a canoe, dinghy, and paddle boat for guests who want to get out on the water. See chapter 7.
- **Te Ana Farm** (Rotorua; ☎ 07/333-2720): Just south of Rotorua, this is one of the most popular farmstays on the North Island, so if you want to stay here, be sure to reserve well ahead. Hosts Heather and Brian Oberer get rave reviews for their hospitality and Heather's incredible gourmet meals. See chapter 7.
- **The Gables** (Picton; ☎ 03/573-6772): Here you have a cozy B&B where hosts Dick and Ann Smith go out of their way to make guests feel welcome. All three rooms are attractively furnished and have private baths. Scrambled eggs with salmon is the specialty of the house at breakfast. See chapter 11.
- **Teichelmann's Central Bed & Breakfast** (Hokitika; ☎ 03/755-8232): As the name indicates, this B&B is all about location, so close to banks, restaurants, attractions, and the bus station. Feel free to contact owners Russell Wenn and Julie Collier in cyberspace before you go—they're very helpful when it comes to itinerary planning for the West Coast. King-size beds are an added bonus in most of the six rooms here. See chapter 11.
- **Jade Court Motor Lodge** (Hokitika; ☎ 03/755-8855): This is a spacious motel, where all 18 units come with cooking facilities, three of them with spa baths. Owners Frank and Karen Bradley keep their place in immaculate condition. See chapter 11.
- **Matai Lodge** (Whataroa; ☎ 03/753-4156): This farmstay is located on a 350-acre property outside of Whataroa where sheep and dairy cattle graze in the paddocks. In spite of the scenic surroundings, the real attraction here is the hosts: Glenice and Jim Purcell are two of the country's kindest Kiwis. See chapter 11.
- **The Briars** (Omarama; ☎ 03/438-9615): This is a rural homestay about an hour's drive from Mount Cook—it's the perfect place to overnight if you're on

your way to Mount Cook, especially if you leave Te Anau or Queenstown later than you expected. Marylou and Don Blue welcome guests year round to their attractive, modern house furnished with antiques, lots of books, and a collection of Mackenzie Country paintings. See chapter 12.

- **Fendalton House** (Christchurch; ☎ 03/355-4298): Pam Rattray mollycoddles her guests and serves the best breakfast in New Zealand at this cozy B&B, which is a 5-minute drive or 20- to 30-minute walk to the city center. All three of her rooms come with *en suite* (attached) bathrooms. See chapter 15.
- **Hambledon** (Christchurch; ☎ 03/379-0723): This sprawling historic home is just a short walk from the city center. Jo and Calvin Floyd offer spacious suites in the mansion, a self-contained flat (apartment) in the coachhouse, and attractive rooms in the gatehouse. A stay here will never be forgotten. See chapter 15.

12 The Best Places to Stay on a Shoestring

- **The North Shore Caravan and Holiday Park** (Auckland; ☎ 09/419-1320): This place offers tent sites, motorhome sites, cabins, and motel units with low rates. All the facilities are kept in spic-n-span condition and downtown Auckland is 20 minutes away by bus. See chapter 5.
- **The Warkworth Inn** (Warkworth; ☎ 09/425-8569): It may not look it, but this historic hotel is almost 150 years old. None of the rooms has attached bathrooms, but each has a sink and tea- and coffee-making facilities. See chapter 5.
- **Peak View Farm** (Havelock North; ☎ 06/877-7408): Named for the view it affords of Te Mata Peak (see "Best Views," above), this old homestead is situated on 25 acres of land, complete with sheep. The tariff includes room and breakfast, but Keith and Dianne Taylor offer home-cooked dinners at an extra charge—it's not surprising that about 80% of their guests take advantage of this option. See chapter 8.
- **Club Nelson** (Nelson; ☎ 03/548-3466): Yes, it's a hostel, but not your ordinary hostel. Linley Rose and Peter Richards offer dorm rooms, shared rooms, and double rooms in an historic 1902 house set on 2¹/₂ acres with a pool and tennis court. See chapter 11.
- **YMCA in Christchurch** (Christchurch; ☎ 03/365-0502): This place is cheap, clean, and ideally located across from the Arts Centre and near the Botanic Gardens—some rooms even overlook the gardens. You can get a private single or double with bathroom, phone, TV, and tea- and coffee-making facilities, or stay in one of the big bunk rooms. Either way, it's one of the best deals in town. See chapter 15.
- **Pear Drop Inn** (Christchurch; ☎ 03/329-6778): At this countryside homestay, about 20 minutes outside Christchurch, Brenda Crocker makes full use of the 2¹/₂ acres, which are dotted with flower gardens, fruit trees, organic vegetable gardens, and even a pond. She makes her own relish, chutney, and jam and uses her fresh produce to whip up breakfast and dinner. Staying here is like staying with "relies," or relatives. See chapter 15.
- **Mount Vernon Lodge** (Akaroa; ☎ 03/304-7180): This rustic retreat on the Banks Peninsula, east of Christchurch, offers several types of accommodation from cabins and cottages to standard double rooms. It's a great spot for families—kids will love the swimming pool, not to mention the free-roaming lambs and chickens. See chapter 15.

13 The Best Moderately Priced Restaurants

- **Vino-Vino Bar & Cafe** (Waiheke Island; ☎ 09/372-9888): This charming cafe serves the best pumpkin soup I've ever tasted. The rest of the menu features interesting New Zealand twists like hot roast lamb on rye with beetroot-and-mint chutney. Choose from 17 New Zealand beers, 9 imported beers, and numerous wines by the bottle or glass. There's an open fire in winter and outdoor seating on a sunny deck in summer. See chapter 5.
- **Sirocco** (Rotorua; ☎ 07/347-3388): Their wonderful Mediterranean dishes incorporate fresh New Zealand ingredients: vegetarian ravioli, thin-cut scotch fillet, and *cotoleta Milano* (lamb cutlet, tomato, and olive tapenade). The cafe itself is located in an old house that's been "done up" by the current owners. See chapter 7.
- **Rutland Arms Inn** (Wanganui; ☎ 06/347-7677): Located in a hotel dating from 1846, this cafe/bar feels like an upscale pub; farm implements and horse brasses hang on the walls, and the cuisine is English, with a nice selection of British beers. See chapter 9.
- **One Red Dog** (Wellington; ☎ 04/384-9777): This is a friendly, relaxed spot with good service and good food. The cuisine spans the globe but includes several tasty Italian specialties such as pizza, pasta, and calzones (try the "Elvis was an Alien" calzone, filled with chicken marinated in honey, ginger, and orange zest, with mushrooms, onion and roasted red capsicum). One Red Dog is affiliated with the Loaded Hog microbrewery, whose beers are served up nice and cold here. See chapter 10.
- **Broccoli Row** (Nelson; ☎ 03/548-9621): A seafood and vegetarian cafe where diners sit at tables in a large outdoor courtyard or in one of two cozy rooms inside. Broccoli Row's chalkboard menu changes daily, but might feature something like snapper filets baked with ginger, grapefruit, and spring vegetables. See chapter 11.
- **The White House** (Wanaka; ☎ 03/443-9595): This place would look more at home in the Greek Islands than on the South Island—there aren't too many whitewashed buildings with blue window frames in these parts. The cuisine is a blend of both: fresh New Zealand produce brought to life with delicious Mediterranean flavors. Not the least expensive spot in town, but easily the best. See chapter 11.
- **Giuseppe's Gourmet Pizza and Pasta Bar** (Queenstown; ☎ 03/442-5444): A welcome exception to the pricey dining scene in Queenstown. Located in a quiet suburb, Giuseppe's caters to locals and prepares superb meals at down-to-earth prices. I love the bruschettas, pizzas, and creative pastas. See chapter 12.
- **Kepler's Family Restaurant** (Te Anau; ☎ 03/249-7909): After a long day, tired travel writers, like weary travelers, don't want to sit through a protracted meal. Kepler's was the perfect spot for me one such day. The service was as good as my roast lamb dinner, which was served with three fresh vegetables and a glass of red wine. See chapter 12.
- **Dux de Lux** (Christchurch; ☎ 03/366-6919): It's just as fun to hang out here as it is to eat. Located in the historic Arts Centre, "the Dux" serves imaginative vegetarian food and a few seafood dishes. You can eat inside or at a table in the courtyard. See chapter 15.

14 The Best Dining Bargains

- **Stone Oven Bakehouse & Cafe** (Devonport; ☎ 09/446-1065): Located right on Auckland's North Shore, this is a great place to hole up with a pile of postcards. Plenty of goodies are baked on the premises—everything from breads to apple and berry strudel—and the management doesn't mind if you just want to sip coffee or tea and hang out. Lunch is good, too—mostly pizzas, sandwiches, and salads—but if a picnic is more what you had in mind, you can get your supplies here, too. See chapter 5.
- **Atlas Power Cafe & Bar** (Auckland; ☎ 09/360-1295): This little restaurant on Ponsonby Road is my favorite in an area known as the "cafe capital of New Zealand." They serve *pinchos*, which are small meals eaten like tapas. I had salmon mousse on crostini, topped with three huge smoked mussels. See chapter 5.
- **Kebab Kid** (Auckland; ☎ 09/373-4290): This Parnell Road place serves a hearty pita pocket filled with marinated lamb for just NZ$6.75 (US$4.40), and other Greek and Middle Eastern favorites are similarly priced. It's a casual spot popular with the twenty-something crowd, but everyone will feel welcome. See chapter 5.
- **La Casa Italiana** (Devonport; ☎ 09/445-9933): This little quick-food counter on the Devonport Ferry Wharf is one of my favorite places to eat. You can dive into a delicious, standard-size Super La Casa pizza for NZ$8.50 (US$5.95). This is a popular spot for commuters who use the ferry for their daily trip into Auckland. See chapter 5.
- **Karmic Enchilada** (Coromandel; ☎ 07/866-7157): This place, located in a small town on the Coromandel Peninsula, looks like a throwback to the '60s. Fruit smoothies are served in quart-size Mason jars and chili chicken enchiladas are the house specialty. See chapter 6.
- **Replete Food Company Delicatessen & Cafe** (Taupo; ☎ 07/378-0606): We're talking super-cheap eats here. I discovered this place on my last trip down under and couldn't believe how good the food was for the money: You can have a multicourse lunch here for less than NZ$10 (US$7). I was so impressed that I did a bit of snooping around and learned that owner Greg Hefferman was formerly the head chef at exclusive Huka Lodge, just out of town. Now he's not only creating wonderful food here, but also running a cooking school and writing a cookbook. See chapter 9.
- **Gourmet Lane** (Wellington): Located in Wellington's BNZ Centre, this food court is like all others: It's a boon to budget travelers. Main courses run NZ$5 to NZ$6 (US$3.25 to $3.90), and there's even sporadic lunchtime entertainment. See chapter 10.
- **The Smelting House Cafe** (Greymouth; ☎ 03/768-0012): It's a cute little spot, but pretty trendy for the West Coast—in fact, locals didn't quite know what to make of it. Eventually overseas visitors introduced the concept of "hanging out" here, and now it's enjoyed by locals and travelers alike. Owners Margaret and Brian Weston, who are a former dietitian and a doctor, turn out wholesome homemade meals like a broccoli, mushroom, and sausage calzone or roast chicken with a mushroom and wine sauce. See chapter 11.
- **The Bank** (Dunedin; ☎ 03/477-4430): It really was the ANZ Bank until 1993, but now it's a licensed cafe offering light lunches and dinners for NZ$5 to $7 (US$3.25 to $4.55). See chapter 14.
- **Main Street Cafe & Bar** (Christchurch; ☎ 03/365-0421): This place serves tasty vegetarian cuisine at rock-bottom prices. You could have a filling portion of

spinach-and-mushroom lasagna or cheesy bean casserole here for the price of an entree (appetizer) in more posh restaurants. The desserts are to die for—especially the carrot cake. See chapter 15.

15 The Best Craft Shopping

- **Parnell:** An inner suburb of Auckland, this is a good area to look for everything from handknitted jumpers (sweaters) to local wood crafts. Don't miss the colonial-style **Parnell Village Shops**—a really charming cluster connected by plant-filled patios, wooden decks, and even a little bridge. See chapter 5.
- **The Bay of Islands:** There's no shortage of souvenirs and gift shops here; however, two shops stand out when it comes to good quality crafts at reasonable prices. **The Cabbage Tree** (☎ 09/402-7318), in Paihia, sells pottery, wood crafts, and original paintings and prints. Over in Russell, **Dalrymples** (☎ 09/403-7630) sells sheepskins, handknits, leathergoods, and the like. See chapter 6.
- **The Coromandel Peninsula:** Go to the visitor centers, either in Thames, the Coromandel township, or Whitianga, and pick up a copy of "The Coromandel Craft Trail," which will show you the way to studios, workrooms, and shops throughout the area. The **True Colours Craft Co-op** in Coromandel township is one of the best. See chapter 6.
- **Cambridge:** This cute little town in the Waikato District is on the way from Hamilton to Rotorua. Stop here and check out the **Cambridge Country Store** (☎ 07/827-8715) where New Zealand crafts are sold. The prices aren't the best, but the selection is. See chapter 6.
- **Nelson:** Located at the tip of the South Island, this city is famous for its craft industry. You can browse through the region's pottery shops and even watch artisans work at the **Höglunds Glassblowing Studio** (☎ 03/544-6500)on Korurangi Farm near Richmond. See chapter 11.
- **Christchurch:** Its claim to fame is the historic **Arts Centre,** which houses a dozen or so craft shops in an area called the Galleria. I recently bought a piece of pottery here and the woman who took my money and wrapped the gift was the artist. On the weekends (and on some Fridays during the summer), there's a great craft market here. See chapter 15.

16 The Best of New Zealand After Dark

- **The Loaded Hog** (Auckland; ☎ 09/366-6491): This is one of the city's few microbreweries and one of my favorite watering holes. It occupies a *beaut possie* (an enviable location) adjacent to Viaduct Quay, home to the America's Cup compounds. The place really gets rocking Thursday through Saturday nights when a DJ plays dance music and the line to get in snakes out the door and around the corner. See chapter 5.
- **Surrender Dorothy** (Auckland): Located on Ponsonby Road, this is one of Auckland's most popular gay nightspots. The famous Hero Parade, celebrating gay and lesbian life, takes place on Ponsonby Road in late February or early March. **The Staircase** (known locally just as "The Case"), on Karangahape Road, is another happening homosexual hangout. See chapter 5.
- **Smash Palace** (Gisborne; ☎ 06/867-6967): You have to see it to believe it. Started as the tasting room for the Parker Methode Champenoise winery, this glorified tin shed, located in an industrial area out by the airport, now has bicycles hanging from the ceiling, old license plates and hubcaps on the walls, and a DC-3 sticking up out of the roof. Owner Phil Parker will happily pour

complimentary tastes of his Classical Brut or First Light Reds, or you can enjoy locally brewed beer and pizza. See chapter 8.

- **Rose & Shamrock** (Havelock North; ☎ **06/877-2999**): This is a great Irish-style pub in the Hawkes Bay region where locals gather to sip on suds and have a good old time. An open fire is usually roaring under the beautiful mahogany mantel, and posters depicting pastoral scenes of Ireland adorn the walls. There's sometimes live entertainment—I enjoyed an evening of Morris dancing on my last visit. The tasty pub grub will only enhance an evening here. See chapter 8.
- **The Court Theatre** (Christchurch; ☎ **03/366-6992**): This is quite possibly New Zealand's best theater. I've seen many plays here—ranging from Tom Stoppard to Shakespeare—and have never been disappointed. Located in the Arts Centre, where atmosphere oozes from the Gothic stone buildings, The Court presents a variety of comedies and dramas throughout the year. Call or e-mail the theater before your trip to see what will be playing while you're in town. See chapter 15.
- **The Christchurch Casino** (Christchurch; ☎ **03/365-9999**): This casino, the first in New Zealand, is so much nicer than its Auckland counterpart: One is dingy and depressing; the other positively sparkles. I don't think gambling is a good pastime for travelers on a budget, but it's fun to wander around and watch for free. See chapter 15.

Getting to Know New Zealand 2

In travel, as in life, it's a good idea to know where you're going. Success comes not to those who wander around aimlessly, but to those who do their homework and plan ahead.

You probably already know at least two things about New Zealand: That it's incredibly beautiful and that there are lots of sheep. *National Geographic* and other travel publications have made this pretty clear over the past several decades.

You may, however, be operating under two common misconceptions. The first is that New Zealand and Australia are close neighbors and so have similar climates and cultures—this one's particularly popular among Americans. But, in fact, while the two countries are both in the Southern Hemisphere, they are actually 1,600 kilometers (about 1,000 miles) apart. And, they're also two very different places. Australia tends to be hot and dry while New Zealand is temperate and—yes—wet. Australia's landscape features brilliant reds and oranges ringed by splendid white beaches and deep blue waters; on the other hand, New Zealand offers the striking contrast of lush semitropical rain forests, cascading waterfalls, playful geysers, and miles of glorious coastline winding in and out of island-studded bays and harbors.

The people are different in both countries, too. Although both nations were colonized by the British, Australia was originally just a place for prisoners—New Zealand has always been England's other pasture. Plus, Oz's harsh conditions have fostered a resilient population that tends not to take things too seriously, while New Zealanders are, for the most part, more reserved and soft-spoken. And while Australia is multicultural, New Zealand has only recently begun to encourage ethnic immigration. If there's one thing that both nations do share, though, it's a love of sports, and a strong rivalry exists between them.

The second common misconception—and I wish I had a nickel for every time I've heard this one—is that New Zealand is "like the U.S. 20 years ago." This may have been true in the '70s, but it just isn't so today. More than 85% of Kiwis live in urban areas and they use PCs, cellular phones, ATMs, and all the other trappings of the '90s just as much—or more—than the rest of the world. Yes, many households still dry laundry on a line in the backyard, but that's not because they don't have electric dryers; it's because they like this method better.

New Zealand at a Glance

North Island

Cape Reinga
North Cape
Mangonui
Kerikeri
Kaitaia
Bay of Islands
Poor Knight's Island
Whangarei
Dargaville
Warkworth
Kaiparu Harbour
Orewa
Auckland
Thames
Ngaruawahia
Hamilton
Pirongia Forest Park
Waitomo
Pureora Forest Park
Taupo
Lake Taupo
Turangi
Tongariro National Park
New Plymouth
Cape Egmont
Mt. Egmont 2518 m
Egmont National Park
Whanganui National Park
Taihape
Wanganui
Feilding
Palmerston North
Woodville
Foxton
Levin
Waikanae
Lower Hutt
Wellington
Upper Hutt
Masterton
Tararua Forest Park
Haurangi Forest Park

Pacific Ocean

Great Barrier Island
Coromandel Peninsula
Whitianga
Coromandel Forest Park
Kaimaimamaki Forest Park
Hauraki Gulf
Bay of Plenty
Tauranga
Hicks Bay
East Cape
Raukumara Forest Park
Opotiki
Whakatane
Ruatoria
Rotorua
Lake Rotorua
Te Urewera National Park
Whirinaki Forest Park
Huiarau Mts.
Gisborne
Kaimanawa Forest Park
Wairoa
Kaweka Forest Park
Napier
Hawke's Bay
Ruahine Forest Park
Hastings
Kaimanawa Mts.

Tasman Sea

Cook Strait

North Island
South Island

1 10 12 14 16 25 3 30 43 45 4 1 1 52 58 53 35 36 50

South Island

Legend

ⓘ Information

Abel Tasman
National Park

Tasman Bay

Marlborough Sounds

Cook Strait

Kahurangi
National Park

Motueka

Nelson

Picton ⓘ

Karamea

Tasman Mts.

61

Blenheim

Westport

69

63

1

Nelson Lakes
National Park

65

Kaikoura Mts.

Paparoa
National Park

Reefton

Hanmer
Forest Park

Greymouth

7

Lake Sumner
Forest Park

Hanmer Springs

Hokitika ⓘ

1

Franz Josef Glacier

Arthur's Pass
National Park

Kaiapoi

Westland
National Park

Mt. Cook National Park

72

ⓘ

Christchurch

Fox Glacier ⓘ

Mount Cook
3754 m

Methven

75

6

Lake Tekapo

Akaroa

Lake Pukaki

8

Lake Tekapo

Ashburton

Haast

Twizel ⓘ

Canterbury Bight

Timaru

Mount Aspiring
National Park

Lake Wanaka

Pacific Ocean

Milford Sound

83

Tasman Sea

Wanaka

89

Cromwell

Oamaru

Doubtful Sound

Queenstown

85

Alexandra

1

Lake Wakatipu

Palmerston

Garvie Mts.

8

Lake Te Anau

Te Anau

ⓘ

Dunedin

**Fiordland
National Park**

Lake Manapouri

Roxburgh

94

96

Gore

1

Milton

99

1

Invercargill

0   58 mi
      93 km

N

Foveaux Strait

Oban

Stewart Island

17

Impressions

All people think that New Zealand is close to Australia, or Asia, or somewhere, and that you cross to it on a bridge. But that is not so. It is not close to anything but lies by itself out in the water. It is nearest to Australia, but not near. The gap between is very wide. It will be a surprise to the reader, as it was to me, to learn that the distance from Australia to New Zealand is really twelve or thirteen hundred miles, and that there is no bridge.

—Mark Twain, after a visit to the South Pacific at the end of last century

What *is* old-fashioned about New Zealand—and this is the reason I love this country so much—is that no one takes the issues of fairness, honesty, decency, and human rights lightly. People are still a high priority here, and there's a real focus on family and genuine hospitality.

1 The Lay of the Land

New Zealand is composed of two major islands—the North Island and the South Island—plus little Stewart Island pointing off toward Antarctica. It's bounded on the north and east by the South Pacific Ocean, on the west by the Tasman Sea, and on the south by the Southern Ocean. From tip to tip, the whole country measures about 1,600 kilometers (about 1,000 miles), although at its widest it's no more than 280 kilometers (174 miles) across. Because of its shape, the Maoris named New Zealand *Aotearoa,* the land of the long white cloud.

New Zealand is about the same size as the British Isles or Japan, or the U.S. state of Colorado, and it's about two-thirds the size of California. The population totals 3.6 million—with 952,000 New Zealanders in Auckland; 331,000 in the capital of Wellington; 324,000 in the South Island's largest city, Christchurch; and 113,000 in Dunedin. Hamilton, with 156,000 inhabitants, is the largest inland city.

THE NORTH ISLAND

The terrain north of Auckland is marked by rolling green hills dotted with sheep and cows, vast pastures interspersed with tracts of characteristic ponga ferns, cabbage trees, and plumey toi toi. The **Bay of Islands,** birthplace of New Zealand, is rich in history and is a haven for sailors and anyone itching to hook a marlin. The west side of **Northland** has the country's largest remaining stand of kauri trees.

The city of **Auckland,** the largest urban area, is built on a series of dormant volcanoes, which provide great views of the city's impressive harbor.

New Zealand is part of the Pacific "Rim of Fire," and there are large areas of continuing thermal activity, predominantly on the North Island. **Lake Taupo** fills a huge crater formed during a volcanic eruption that took place in A.D. 186. South of Taupo, three active volcanoes—Ruapehu, Ngauruhoe, and Tongariro—are located in **Tongariro National Park.** Quiet for 8 years, Ruapehu erupted in 1995 and again in 1996, pretty much ruining that year's ski season. The bubbling mud pools and spouting geysers around **Rotorua** are further evidence of the country's steamy nature. While Maori people live all over the North Island, their biggest concentration is in the Rotorua/Taupo area.

On the east coast of the North Island, **Hawkes Bay** enjoys a mild climate and is a major fruit-growing and wine-producing region. **Wellington,** the nation's capital, is perched on the southern edge of the North Island; it's New Zealand's hilliest city and, thus, closely resembles San Francisco.

THE SOUTH ISLAND

The sometimes turbulent **Cook Strait** separates the North Island from the South Island. On its southern shore the **Marlborough Sounds** are a maze of azure bays and inlets. The top of the South Island, from Picton to Farewell Spit, is rimmed by beautiful beaches.

The South Island is sparsely populated (two-thirds of New Zealanders live north of Lake Taupo) and dominated by the Southern Alps, which cover more territory than the entire country of Switzerland. Of the peaks, **Mount Cook,** which the Maori named Aorangi (the cloud piercer), is the highest. To the south and east of Mount Cook are lakes that have been harnessed for electric power. Sprawling sheep stations characterize this area. On the **West Coast,** in a zone so ecologically important that it's now a **World Heritage Area,** Fox and Franz Josef glaciers stretch toward the sea. **Fiordland** is where you'll find the sounds—Milford, Doubtful, and others. The fern-covered wilderness in this area can be, and frequently is, crossed on the country's famous multiday walking tracks. On the east coast of the South Island, **Christchurch** is the garden capital of the country, and **Dunedin** is New Zealand's university town. Christchurch retains a slightly English atmosphere—most homes are surrounded by tidy gardens; school boys wear short pants and striped blazers; and the river Avon winds lazily through the city. Dunedin, on the other hand, is reminiscent of Scotland and boasts magnificent stone buildings.

Located off the tip of the South Island, **Stewart Island** is a sparsely populated area that's popular with bush walkers.

2 The Natural World

In the northern quarter of the North Island, you'll find the surviving stands of tall, stately **kauri trees,** whose hardwood trunks—unblemished by knots or other imperfections—were so prized for shipbuilding by early settlers. Fortunately, planting is now under way to replace these magnificent trees.

During December and January, North Island cliffs and lake shores are a mass of scarlet when the *pohutukawa* (or Christmas tree) bursts into bloom, while its kinsman, the *rata,* is doing likewise down on the South Island. Much like its relative, the pohutukawa, the rata tree comes alive with brilliant red flowers around Christmastime. In early spring, the *kowhai,* which makes no distinction between north and south but grows almost everywhere, is a profusion of large golden blossoms. The *totara* has always been much loved by the Maori, who find its light, durable timber just right for making canoes, as well as wood carvings. Then there are the pines, including the *rimu* (red), *matai* (black), *kahikatea* (white), and *Dacrydium laxifolium* (pigmy). And the beeches—red, black, and silver. Almost all are evergreen, and seasonal color changes are subtle.

New Zealand also has a wide array of flowering plants, a full 80% of which are not to be found anywhere else in the world. The undisputed queen of blossoms has to be the world's largest buttercup: the **Mount Cook lily.** There are almost 60 varieties of **mountain daisies,** plus a curious **"vegetable sheep,"** which grows in mountainous terrain and has large, cushiony blooms that look like sheep even when you take a close look. Bright orange-and-yellow **"red hot pokers"** look like just that. Up to a dozen fringed, saucer-shaped white blooms adorn a single flower stalk of the *hinau,* and the golden *kumarahou* bloom has been used over the years in medicinal herb mixtures.

The **kiwi,** of course, is the flightless bird that has come to symbolize New Zealand. Wingless and about the size of a chicken, it lives in hollow trunks or holes in the

Geological Fault or Maui's Fish: How New Zealand Came to Be

Geologists say that New Zealand's islands are the relatively young remnants of a continental mass separated by violent shifts in the earth's crust. Its location on a major fault line accounts for frequent earthquake activity, volcanic mountains, the drowned glacial valleys of Fiordland, and the string of mountain ranges that stretches (with a few interruptions) from the alpine peaks of the South Island up to the blunted headland at Cape Reinga.

The Maori, however, have their own version of how New Zealand came to be. According to their legend, way back in the days of the gods and demigods, a woman named **Taranga** threw her frail fifth son into the sea because she felt the infant was too weak to survive. He was rescued by **Rangi,** the Sky Father, who raised him through childhood, then returned him to his mother, complete with magical powers and the enchanted jawbone of his grandmother. The overjoyed Taranga doted on her restored son, **Maui,** so much that his brothers soon became jealous. Not only was Maui their mother's favorite, but he pulled off astonishing feats like snaring the sun in the pit from which it rose each morning, then smashing its face with that all-powerful jawbone until it was too weak to do anything but creep across the sky. This provided the people with longer days in which to fish and, thus, elicited abundant gratitude and respect for young Maui.

When he set off to fish, Maui always snagged the biggest catch, while his nonmagical brothers barely brought home enough to feed their families—much to the consternation of their wives, who duly complained to Maui. With a condescending (and irritating) wave of his hand, Maui promptly promised his sisters-in-law one load of fish so large it would spoil before they could eat it all. They were delighted, but their husbands were frustrated, angry, and determined to beat Maui with one last fishing expedition, which they launched at dawn.

ground, emerges only at night to forage for insects and worms with a long curved beak that has nostrils at its tip, and emits a shrill, penetrating screech. Kiwis are very rare, but it's not uncommon for bush walkers to see a **weka**—also known as a woodhen. Although flightless, it can run very fast. If you hear a series of pure bell-like sounds pouring through the forest air, it's likely to be the song of the lovely **bellbird.** Only slightly different in sound is the handsome **tui,** black birds with white tufts under their necks. You'll probably also see **fantails** in the bush. They munch on the insects that walkers stir up. Around swampy areas, those ear-piercing screams you hear in the night will be coming from the **pukeko,** a dark blue hen-sized creature with an orange peak. He prefers walking to flying, but can fly if pressed. And the forest-dwelling **morepork's** call (often heard at dusk or after dark) may give you a start—it sounds just like its name. The graceful **gannet** is found only on offshore islands, with one exception, Cape Kidnappers near Napier. There are **white herons** at Okarito, a unique **albatross** colony out from Dunedin, and **penguins** in many spots around the country.

Down in the mountains of the South Island there's a mountain parrot that's as bold as the kiwi is shy. The **kea** nests among the rocks, but keeps an eye on the main roads and is quick to check out newcomers. It's not unusual, for instance, to see as many as three of these birds camped alongside the road to Milford Sound. If you stop, keep a sharp eye on them. They are quick to steal jewelry or other shiny objects and attack other targets, like rubber windshield wipers, with their strong curved beaks.

The clever (and probably obnoxious) Maui hid under the flooring mats of his brothers' canoe, armed with a special fishhook whose point was fashioned from a chip of the precious jawbone. It wasn't until they were well out to sea that he appeared, sending his brothers into a rage. However, they grumpily agreed with Maui when he assured them that their luck would turn if they'd only sail out of sight of any land.

Sure enough, they soon filled the canoe with fish. It became so full, in fact, that they began to take on water, and the brothers suggested returning home. But the arrogant Maui insisted they sail still farther into the unknown waters and he calmly produced his magic hook. The brothers then sailed on—bailing and complaining—until at last Maui struck his nose until it bled, smeared his blood on the hook as bait, and threw his line overboard while chanting an incantation for the "drawing up of the world."

What Maui hooked turned out to be a gigantic fish, as large as the gable of a *whare runanga* (meeting house), whose very size rendered it *tapu* (sacred). With the fish came the large wedge of land we know today as New Zealand's North Island. Maui, respectful of the tapu, quickly departed for home to get a priest, leaving his brothers with strict orders not to cut up the fish until his return. He was no sooner out of sight than they started scaling and cutting the huge fish.

The gods were much angered, and they set that great fish to lashing about, throwing cut-up chunks in all directions—which is a perfect explanation for the existence of the North Island's mountains and offshore islands. And though we may call it the North Island, any Maori knows it's really Te Ika a Maui, "the Fish of Maui."

The South Island is actually Maui's canoe, with Stewart Island as its anchor stone. And up in Hawkes Bay, that famous fishhook has been transformed into Cape Kidnappers.

Savvy campers and trampers are careful to keep their gear well beyond the reach of the mischievous kea.

As curious as birds are here, none of them holds a candle to the **tuatara,** a reptilian "living fossil" whose prehistoric ancestors became extinct 100 million years ago. Shaped like a miniature dinosaur, complete with a spiny ridge down the back and a thick tail, it's protected by law and confined to offshore islets.

New Zealand has no native land mammals. Before there were humans here, the land was covered by tall trees, beautiful ferns, and birds that never learned to fly because there was nothing to flee.

When the Maori arrived, they brought dogs and rats and hunted native birds for food and feathers, which they made into cloaks. An early tribe hunted the giant moa, a relative of the ostrich and emu, into extinction. Good old Captain Cook added to the confusion when he released a pig, whose wild descendants still wander about. But, the British colonists did the greatest damage to New Zealand wildlife when they chopped down huge tracts of native trees to create pastures, and then imported red

Factoid

In New Zealand, there are 3.6 million people and 48 million sheep—that translates into 13.3 sheep for every human resident!

Oh Deer!

Homesick British colonists imported a number of animals to New Zealand. Some of these, like sheep and cattle, became the country's economic backbone. Others, such as rabbits, had no predators to contend with and so multiplied and became a serious threat to farmers. Six rabbits could—and often did—eat as much grass as one sheep. In 1893, 16 million rabbit skins were exported, but it wasn't until the Rabbit Destruction Council resorted to large-scale trapping and poison airdrops after World War II that the problem was brought under control.

The tale of the imported deer is even stranger. First introduced for sport in 1851, they also multiplied and caused widespread erosion by damaging and devouring back-country vegetation. Amateur hunters couldn't keep the population under control, so the government paid professional cullers to do the job—many of whom used helicopters to locate and shoot the deer.

During a visit to New Zealand in the late 1970s, I was invited to go flying with an American helicopter pilot who was culling deer on the west coast of the South Island. I took the spotter's seat, but—push come to shove—failed to report any sightings. Shoot Bambi? Not me.

Imagine my surprise when I returned to New Zealand a few years later and found deer being treated like members of the royal family. It seems someone had figured out that Asians would pay top dollar for antler velvet, from which they make medicine and aphrodisiacs. Deer farms sprang up everywhere and are today a major component of the agricultural industry. Venison and skins are exported to Western Europe and several Asian nations, but antler velvet is still the most-prized commodity.

deer and rabbits so they would have something to hunt. (For a sense of New Zealand before the colonists cleared the land, rent the movie *The Piano*.) Without predators, the deer and rabbits multiplied at alarming rates and are, today, subjects of eradication programs. The colonists also brought opossum, hedgehogs, weasels, stoats, and, of course, sheep and cows.

The one ecological error the British didn't make involves snakes—the country doesn't have any. So when you're walking in the bush, don't worry about where you put your foot down. Nor are there any predatory animals. In fact, there's only one poisonous spider, the Katipo, and it's rarely found anywhere except on a few scattered sand dunes. Travelers aren't likely to come across a Katipo—it'll be black with an orange or yellow stripe on the back. If you do, it will probably be on the western beaches of the North Island.

3 History 101

Dateline
- **950** Estimated date of first New Zealand landfall by Maori.
- **Mid-1300s** First major influx of Maori settlers.

continues

EARLY MAORI SETTLEMENT   When it comes to New Zealand's first inhabitants, there's more than one theory as to how they got settled here. The Maori legend tells of Kupe, who sailed from Hawaiki, the traditional homeland of the Polynesians, around A.D. 950. Even legend doesn't tell us exactly where Hawaiki was located in the vast South Pacific, but present-day authorities believe it belonged to the

Society Islands group that includes Tahiti. One tale of Kupe's adventures goes like this: He murdered the carver named Hoturapa, took the man's wife and canoe, and set off on a long voyage, which eventually brought them to the place he named Aotearoa, meaning "land of the long white cloud." Another says that Kupe was pursuing a mammoth octopus when he stumbled onto New Zealand. Historians have further explanations, for example, that the first Maori canoes to reach New Zealand came by accident, after having been blown off course at sea.

During the 12th century, two more Maori canoes are said to have touched the shores of Aotearoa. A young Polynesian, Whatonga, was swept out to sea during canoe races, and his grandfather, Toi, went to find him. When the two were reunited somewhere in the Whakatane region in the Bay of Plenty, they found people already living there. The newcomers intermarried with the "Moa Hunters," who hunted a tall, wingless bird by that name. Nothing more is known about these settlers, and they are sometimes referred to as the Archaic Maori. Descendants of the two Polynesian paddlers and the Moa Hunters now form the basis of two present-day Maori tribes.

It wasn't until the mid-14th century that Maori arrived in great numbers—they came from Hawaiki to escape the tribal warfare that had erupted in the wake of overpopulation and severe food shortages. According to Maori tradition, seven ocean-going canoes sailed in a group, which has come to be known simply as "the fleet." Others sailed in groups of one or two; some came singly. Upon hitting land, canoe groups kept together, settling in various parts of the country, and it is to these seven canoes that most modern-day Maori trace their roots.

By the time "the fleet" arrived, the moa had been hunted to extinction, along with other bird species, such as giant rails, swans, and geese. There were, however, large supplies of fish and seafood as well as berries and a few other edible plants, which were supplemented by such tropical plants as taro, yams, and kumara (a kind of sweet potato) that the settlers had brought from Hawaiki. Dogs and rats had also made the voyage and became an important source of protein. The cultivation of these imported vegetables and animals gradually led to an agricultural society in which the Maori lived in permanent villages centered around a central *marae* (village common or courtyard) and *whare runanga* (meeting house). This is where the distinctive Maori art forms of wood carving and tattooing evolved, along with their strong sense of

- **1642** Abel Tasman becomes first European to sight the South Island.
- **1769** Capt. James Cook begins 6-month mapping of North and South Islands.
- **1773** Cook's second visit to New Zealand.
- **1777** Cook's third and final visit to New Zealand.
- **1792** First sealers and whalers arrive in New Zealand waters.
- **1814** First Christian missionary, Rev. Samuel Marsden, arrives in Bay of Islands.
- **1833** James Busby named as "British Resident" under jurisdiction of New South Wales.
- **1839–43** New Zealand Company sends out 57 ships carrying 19,000 settlers.
- **1840** Treaty of Waitangi with Maori chiefs signed in Bay of Islands.
- **1844** Maori Chief Hone Heke chops down British flagpole in Bay of Islands, beginning a 20-year revolt centered around land rights.
- **1852** New Zealand Constitution Act passed by British Parliament.
- **1860s** Discovery of gold on South Island's west coast and North Island's east coast, creating several boomtowns.
- **1860–81** Second Maori War over land rights.
- **1882** Refrigeration introduced; first shipment of lamb to England.
- **1893** Voting rights extended to women.
- **1914–18** 100,000 New Zealanders join Australia—New Zealand Army Corps to fight in World War I; New

continues

Zealand loses more soldiers per capita than any other nation.

- **1939** New Zealand enters World War II.
- **1947** Statute of Westminster adopted by government; New Zealand gains full independence from Britain.
- **1951** New Zealand ratifies Australia–New Zealand–United States (ANZUS) mutual security pact.
- **1960s** New Zealand begins monitoring radioactivity in region as France accelerates nuclear testing in its Polynesian possessions.
- **1965** New Zealand troops sent to Vietnam.
- **1973** Britain joins European Economic Community (Common Market), with subsequent disastrous reduction in imports from New Zealand.
- **1981** A tour by the South African rugby team causes violent protest in New Zealand.
- **1982** As a move against deep economic recession, New Zealand signs Closer Economic Relations (CER) agreement with Australia.
- **1984** Labour Government begins comprehensive reform and deregulation of New Zealand's economy.
- **1985** All nuclear-armed and nuclear-powered vessels banned from New Zealand ports; Greenpeace's *Rainbow Warrior* sunk by French intelligence agents in Auckland harbor, killing a crew member.
- **1986** New Zealand competes in the America's Cup races for the first time.

continues

family loyalty and harmony with the environment. The culture was truly thriving when Captain James Cook first encountered New Zealand's Maori.

ABEL TASMAN & DUTCH DISCOVERY   The first recorded sighting of New Zealand by Europeans came on December 13, 1642, when Abel Tasman, scouting new trade territory for the Dutch East India Company, spied what he described as "a great high, bold land" on the west coast of the South Island. Sailing north in his two tall-masted ships, the *Heemskirk* and *Zeehaen,* he entered Golden Bay on December 18 and met the Maori before even reaching land: As the two ships anchored in the peaceful bay, several Maori war canoes put out from shore and the paddlers shouted hostile challenges. The next day the Maori attacked a cockboat rowing between Tasman's ships, killing four sailors. A dismayed Tasman fired at the retreating canoes and put out to sea. For many years afterward, lovely Golden Bay was known as Murderer's Bay.

As it turned out, this was Tasman's only glimpse of the Maori since bad weather forced him to proceed up the west coast of the North Island. He failed to find a suitable landing spot, so he left what he charted as a vast southern continent to sail on to Tonga and Fiji. So if it weren't for bad weather and the hostile Maori on that December day, the first European exploration of New Zealand would almost certainly have been Dutch. However, that distinction was left for an Englishman more than a century later.

ENTER CAPTAIN COOK   When Captain James Cook left England in 1768 on the 368-ton bark *Endeavour,* he was under orders from George III to sail to Tahiti to observe the transit of the planet Venus across the sun, a once-a-century happening. But the Yorkshireman carried "secret additional orders," which he opened only when his initial duty was accomplished. King George had told him to sail southwest in search of the "continent" reported by Abel Tasman. If he found it uninhabited, he was to plant the English flag and claim it for the king; if not, his instructions were to take possession of "convenient situations"—but only with the consent of the indigenous people. Cook was also supposed to study the soil, examine the flora and fauna, and make charts of the coastal waters.

On October 7, 1769, Nicholas Young, son of the ship's surgeon, spotted New Zealand from his perch in the mast. Naming the headland (in the Gisborne area) Young Nick's Head, Captain Cook sailed into a crescent-shaped bay and put down anchor. A rather kindly man, Captain Cook made every effort to cultivate Maori friendship, communicating by way of a young Tahitian chief named Tupea who had come along as both a guide and an interpreter. Even though the Maori understood Tupea, they remained hostile. They wouldn't accept Cook's gifts or permit him to take food and water to his men on the ships. Disappointed and bitter, Cook weighed anchor after he claimed the country for King George. Consequently, he named the beautiful bay Poverty Bay because, as he noted in his journal, "it afforded us not one thing we wanted."

Sailing north, Cook rounded the tip of the North Island and went on to circumnavigate both islands during the next 6 months, charting the terrain with amazing accuracy, missing only such details as the entrance to Milford Sound (which is quite invisible from the open sea) and the fact that Stewart Island was not a part of the mainland (he mistakenly believed Foveaux Strait to be a bay). In addition, he recorded the flora and fauna and brought back sketches of the indigenous people, who grew more friendly as word of the gift-bearing *Pakeha* (fair-skinned men) spread. He also recorded details of Maori customs and described the "Indians" as "a brave, open, warlike people." Even today, the journal he kept so meticulously makes fascinating reading.

Captain Cook returned to New Zealand for a month in 1773 and again in 1777. Until his death at the hands of indigenous people in Hawaii on February 14, 1779, he ranged the length and breadth of the South Pacific, sailing as far north as the Arctic Circle and as far south as Antarctica. He and the *Endeavour* have, in fact, become as much a part of New Zealand legend as those early Maori chiefs and their mighty canoes.

THE BRITISH ARE COMING Sealers began arriving in 1792 and virtually stripped South Island waters of its flourishing seal colonies, and by 1820 they moved on to more profitable waters. Whalers, too, discovered rich hunting grounds in New Zealand

- **1987** The New Zealand yacht *KZ-7* wins the World Championship in Sardinia; at home, the sharemarket crashes.
- **1990** New Zealand hosts the Commonwealth Games and the visit of Elizabeth II adds to the festivities commemorating the 150th anniversary of the Treaty of Waitangi.
- **1991** Relations between the United States and New Zealand, strained by the 1985 antinuclear ban, begin to thaw.
- **1993** New Zealand celebrates 100 years of women's suffrage.
- **1994** The decade of belt-tightening starts to pay off and New Zealand's economy is declared one of the world's most competitive; South African rugby team tours New Zealand without protest.
- **1995** Team New Zealand wins the America's Cup; Mt. Ruapehu erupts for the first time in 8 years; New Zealand's population reaches 3.5 million; economic growth continues.
- **1996** Mt. Ruapehu erupts again. Ash clouds disrupt air travel throughout much of the country.
- **1997** Maoris demand return of Crown lands; racial tensions increase. Maori activist damages the America's Cup.

waters and arrived in droves. Oil vats soon dotted the Bay of Islands, which was a safe place to anchor. Their unscrupulous methods were much like those of the sealers, and New Zealand's coastal waters were no longer a natural haven for the mammoth animals. But unlike the sealers, the whalers started bringing in other Western evils: a population of escapees from Australia's penal colonies, ex-convicts, runaway sailors, and a motley collection of "beachcombers." They holed up in the Kororareka settlement, now known as Russell; their grogeries (drinking spots), brothels, and lawlessness earned it the nickname "hellhole of the Pacific." Ships that would have normally called in at the port stayed away in fear.

Legitimate traders and merchants, attracted by the wealth of flax, the abundance of trees for shipbuilding, and the lucrative trading of muskets and other European goods with the Maori, were little better than the sealers and whalers in respecting the country's natural resources. Great forests were felled with no eye to replanting; luxuriant bushlands disappeared in flames to clear land; and when commercial value was placed on the Maori's tattooed and preserved heads, even the native population was threatened for a time as chiefs eager to purchase muskets lopped off more and more heads of both friends and foes. The latter was a short-lived trade, but it was quite lively while it lasted.

The immigration of Europeans, mostly from Great Britain, had a devastating impact on Maori culture. Most destructive were the introduction of liquor, muskets, and European diseases against which the Maori had no immunity. Muskets intensified the fierce intertribal warfare—tens of thousands were killed off by the fire-spouting sticks until muskets became so common that no one tribe had superiority in terms of firepower; by 1830 Maori chiefs began to realize that the weapon was destroying all of their tribes.

Missionaries also began to arrive during this period, spearheaded by the Rev. Samuel Marsden, who arrived in the Bay of Islands in 1814 and preached his first sermon to the Maori on Christmas Day with the help of a young chief he had befriended. He preached a practical brand of Christianity; and when his duties as chaplain to the convicts in Sydney, Australia, demanded his return, he left behind a carpenter, a shoemaker, and a schoolteacher to instruct the Maori. Most missionaries who followed were of the same Christian persuasion and were responsible for the following: putting the Maori language in writing (largely for the purpose of translating and printing the Bible); establishing mission schools (by the 1840s large numbers of Maori could both read and write); and upgrading agricultural methods through the use of plows and windmills.

On the religious front, their progress was slow—to their credit, they were determined not to baptize any Maori until he or she had a full understanding of the Christian faith—and it was some 11 years before they had their first Maori convert. By the late 1830s, however, Maori were ready to accept the concept of a god of peace, undoubtedly influenced greatly by the vastly changed nature of warfare since the coming of the musket. They were also a literal-minded, practical people, much impressed by the missionaries' ability to cure diseases that Maori healers couldn't and by their resistance to tribal witchcraft. Christianity was, in fact, the beginning of the end of many aspects of Maori society that had existed for centuries.

As the number of British immigrants in New Zealand grew, so too did lawlessness, with much harm done to both Maori and settlers. The missionaries complained to the British government, which was by no means anxious to recognize the faraway country as a full-fledged colony, having already experienced difficulties with America and Canada. As a substitute, in 1833 the Crown placed New Zealand under the jurisdiction of New South Wales and sent James Busby as "British Resident," with full responsibilities for enforcing law and order, but he was completely ineffectual.

THE TREATY OF WAITANGI   Back in Britain, the newly formed New Zealand Company began sending out ships to buy land from the Maori and establish permanent settlements. Their methods were questionable, to say the least, and caused increasing alarm in London. It must be noted, however, that between 1839 and 1843 the New Zealand Company sent out 57 ships carrying 19,000 settlers, the nucleus of a stable British population. In 1839 Captain William Hobson was sent to New Zealand by the government to sort things out, and by catering to the Maori sense of ceremony (and some mild arm-twisting), he arranged an assembly of chiefs at the Busby residence in the Bay of Islands. There, on February 6, 1840, the famous Treaty of Waitangi, after lengthy debate, was signed with much pomp.

The treaty guaranteed the Maori "all the Rights and Privileges of British Subjects" in exchange for their acknowledgment of British sovereignty, while granting the Crown exclusive rights to buy land from the Maori. The fact that many of the chiefs had no idea of the treaty's meaning is clear from one chief's later explanation that he had merely signed a receipt for a blanket sent by the queen as a gift! Nevertheless, 45 of the Maori chiefs at the assembly did sign, and when it was circulated around the country, another 500 also signed. Instead of easing tensions, however, the Treaty of Waitangi ushered in one of the bloodiest periods in New Zealand's history.

The British were eager to exercise their exclusive right to purchase Maori land, and while some chiefs were just as eager to sell, others wanted only to hold on to their native soil. As pressures forced them to sell, the Maori soon revolted and when Chief Hone Heke (ironically, the first to sign the treaty) hacked down the British flagpole at Kororareka (Russell) in 1844, it signaled the beginning of some 20 years of fierce battles.

The Maori, always outnumbered and outarmed, won the unqualified respect and admiration of the British as brave and masterful warriors. The British, on the other hand, were regarded with the same degree of respect by the chiefs, who had not expected that the Pakeha could put up any sort of real fight. At last the British emerged as victors, but the seizure of their land is still the subject of debate today.

4 New Zealand Today

If you read the newspaper while you're down under, you'll feel right at home. Politics, the economy, and racial strife are on the front page nearly every day. Below I've highlighted some of the hot issues in New Zealand in recent decades.

NO NUKES, PLEASE   From the mid-1960s on, New Zealanders have stood tough against nuclear energy. They protested, and eventually stopped, a proposed nuclear power plant, which the government wanted to build at Wiri in the greater Auckland area. They have also passionately protested French nuclear testing in the Pacific. In 1985 a Greenpeace ship, the *Rainbow Warrior,* was sunk by French intelligence agents in Auckland Harbor, killing a crew member. The same year, all nuclear-armed and -powered ships were banned from Kiwi ports, including those of the U.S. Navy. This violated the ANZUS Treaty among Australia, New Zealand, and the United States, and caused a rift between Washington and Wellington. To some extent, this situation still exists, although the Clinton government has indicated it may restore full diplomatic relations.

ROGERNOMICS   From its inception, New Zealand's economy has relied heavily on overseas trade. For many years the country exported meat, wool, and dairy products to Great Britain and used the profits to support social legislation such as old-age pensions, child-welfare programs, free university education, and generous unemployment programs. New Zealand was in many respects a "welfare state."

However, in 1973 Great Britain joined the European Common Market, and the aftermath was disastrous to New Zealand's economy. Without a buyer for their products, prices fell and so did the Kiwi standard of living. Efforts to diversify were mildly helpful. Moslem butchers were brought into the freezing works (slaughterhouses) so that New Zealand meat could be sold to Middle Eastern countries; farmers diversified and started raising deer and goats; trading partnerships in Asia were established;

Impressions

The longer I live the more I turn to New Zealand, I thank God I was born in New Zealand. A young country is a real heritage, though it takes time to recognize it. But New Zealand is in my very bones.

—Katherine Mansfield, 1922

forestry, fishing, horticulture, and manufacturing efforts were increased; and the number of sheep on the land declined from 72 million in 1983 to the present low of 48 million.

Finally, in 1984 the Labour Government instituted comprehensive economic reform, under the leadership of Roger Douglas. The reforms are thus referred to as "Rogernomics," and they include the removal of subsidies on agriculture, financial deregulation, removal of many import controls, tax reform, privatization of state assets, and the floating of the exchange rate.

Over the next 10 years, everyone struggled to adjust to the changes, and by 1994 it was clear that the decade of belt-tightening had paid off. New Zealand now has one of the strongest economies in the world, and Kiwi economists are regularly invited overseas to tell other countries how they achieved this economic miracle.

Through it all, New Zealanders have retained their egalitarian and humanitarian approach, but it's clear that with the new free-market economy New Zealand is no longer the homogeneous place it once was. For the first time, there are "haves" and "have nots," and this concerns many citizens.

KIWI POLITICS   New Zealand is a parliamentary democracy, headed by Queen Elizabeth II; the governor-general is her representative, and the prime minister and members of Parliament are locally elected. The two main political parties are National and Labour, and the current government is a coalition of the National party and New Zealand First, a smaller, secondary party. The opposition includes the Labour party and the other two minor parties: Alliance and Act. The current prime minister is Jim Bolger. In the capital city of Wellington, all government business is conducted in the Beehive—a building named for its shape.

RACIAL TENSIONS   For many years the descendants of New Zealand's original inhabitants, the Maori, and the Pakeha colonists coexisted peacefully in a relationship earmarked by mutual respect. No one can agree on what caused the situation to change, but the fact remains that New Zealand now is experiencing a period of racial tension. The Waitangi Tribunal of 1987 gave the Maori the right to petition the Government for the return of land taken from them as a result of the Treaty of Waitangi in 1840. While there is a general willingness to meet just claims, some Pakehas grumble that the Government is being too soft and is virtually giving away the country. Others support reconciliation. The situation is not dissimilar to the Mabo Decision in Australia, which allows Aborigines to lay claim to tribal land.

5 The Maori Language

Living in a predominantly European culture, the Maori were forced by circumstance and education to use the English language and came very close to losing their own colorful and vivid language. However, thanks to the growth of *kohanga reo,* or language nests, thousands of Maori preschoolers and parents are learning the beautiful Maori language from tribal elders, and the dialect is being heard more and more in homes, schools, universities, on the radio, and on the evening TV newscasts.

While you're in New Zealand, you'll always be surrounded by Maori words and phrases, in both names of places and names of objects that are always identified by their Maori names. It's a lot more fun to travel around New Zealand if you know, for example, that *roto* is the Maori word for "lake" and *rua* is the word for "two"—hence the name Rotorua. Keep in mind that in the Maori language some words may be both singular and plural—words like *Maori, Pakeha,* and *Kea* never need an *s* to denote the plural (like the English words deer and fish).

Here's a helpful list of the most commonly used prefixes and suffixes for place names:

Ao	Cloud
Ika	Fish
Nui	Big, or plenty of
Roto	lake
Rua	Cave, or hollow, or two (Rotorua's two lakes)
Tahi	One, single
Te	The
Wai	Water
Whanga	Bay, inlet, or stretch of water

These are other frequently used words:

Ariki	Chief or priest
Atua	Supernatural being, such as a god or demon
Haka	Dance (war, funeral, etc.)
Hangi	An oven made by filling a hole with heated stones; and the feast roasted in it
Karakia	Prayer or spell
Kaumatua	Elder
Kereru	Wood pigeon
Kumara	Sweet potato
Mana	Authority, prestige, psychic force
Marae	Courtyard, village common
Mere	War club made of greenstone (jade)
Pa	Stockade or fortified place
Pakeha	Caucasian person; primarily used to refer to those of European descent
Poi	Bulrush ball with string attached, twirled in action song
Tangi	Funeral mourning or lamentation
Taonga	Treasure
Tapu	Under religious or superstitious restriction ("taboo")
Tiki	Human image, sometimes carved of greenstone
Whare	House

6   A Taste of New Zealand: From Mussels to Meat Pies

The star of Kiwi cuisine, as far as I'm concerned, is **seafood**—always fresh and of a wide variety. **Bluff oysters** are a treat—they're large and tangy, with a strong taste of the sea. Then there are the tiny whitebait, usually served in fritters, sometimes crisply fried. The **crayfish,** like New Zealand rock lobster, may be more expensive than other seafood, but they're worth every penny. And a fish with which I'm on a first-name basis—the **John Dory**—is as sweet and succulent as any I've ever tasted. New Zealand **green-lipped mussels** are one of several species of mussels—the tastiest in my opinion.

Up in the north parts of the North Island you can sometimes find **toheroa soup,** a delicacy made from a small shellfish much like a cockle that's served in a rich chowder. **Trout,** of course, abound in New Zealand rivers and lakes, but they're not sold commercially (seems Kiwis adhere to the theory that for such a sporting fish, it would be a deep indignity to be eaten by anyone who hadn't landed it in a fair fight).

Lamb is something else you should try while you're down under. Lots of restaurants serve it these days, but the best roast lamb meals (usually accompanied by garden-fresh veggies) are still to be found on the dinner table at farmstays.

Dairy products, too, play a featured role in the New Zealand diet, and you'll know why after your first taste of rich, creamy milk, butter, and ice cream. New Zealand cheeses are also delicious and relatively inexpensive. A loaf of Vogel bread (rich whole-grain bread that you'll find in almost any health-food store and many supermarkets), a selection of cheeses, and some fresh fruit make the perfect picnic lunch.

You'll find **meat pies** everywhere—from lunch counters in railway and bus stations to pubs to take-out shops. These thick-crusted little pies filled with chunks of meat and gravy can be delicious if they're homemade, with light, flaky crusts and just the right combination of mild spices and herbs. Keep an eye out for the "homemade" sign, which will be more prevalent than you might imagine—avoid the tasteless factory-made pies whenever possible.

The traditional New Zealand dessert is **pavlova** (named after the prima ballerina Anna Pavlova): a large meringue shaped like a cake, baked slowly at a low temperature to form a crusty outside and a tender inside. The top is usually filled with whipped cream and fruit (kiwifruit when available)—don't leave New Zealand without experiencing pavlova.

BEER & WINE

Beer is the closest thing to a national drink in New Zealand, and you'll have to do a bit of sampling to find your favorite brew—friends of mine spend a lot of time debating the merits of **DB** (Dominion Breweries), **Lion, Steinlager,** and a few others. If you're a dedicated beer drinker or have a large party, you'll save money by ordering a "jug of draft," which holds about five 8-ounce glasses.

Every year, New Zealand's vineyards produce better and better **wines.** McWilliams, Montana, Mission, Corbans, and Penfolds—big companies that started producing bulk wine about 30 years ago—have now been joined by boutique wineries that yield small amounts of world-class vintages. My favorite wineries to visit are in the **Marlborough District** around Blenheim: Hunter's, Cloudy Bay, and Cellier Le Brun—the only *méthode champenoise* specialist in the country.

The **Hawkes Bay** region also produces some great chardonnays and cabernets that compare favorably with their Napa Valley counterparts. I particularly like the Reserve Chardonnay from Clearview Winery near Havelock North. While, in general, New Zealand's white wines are of a higher standard than its reds, Te Mata in the Hawkes Bay area has produced some award-winning cabernet sauvignons.

7 New Zealand's Literary Traditions

Short-story writer **Katherine Mansfield** and novelist **Janet Frame** are two of New Zealand's literary giants. Both have written from the perspective of a love-hate relationship with their native country, as did poet/satirist **A. R. D. Fairburn.** The work of **James K. Baxter,** New Zealand's most gifted poet, concerns religion and social injustices. **Dame Ngaio Marsh** was an internationally known mystery writer. And the late **Sylvia Ashton-Warner** was both a respected novelist and an educator.

Novelist and naturalist **Peter Hooper** celebrates the South Island's West Coast, where he lives and teaches, interweaving legend and myth with historical fact. **Maurice Gee** is one of the country's most popular contemporary novelists, and **Maurice Shadbolt** is another favorite storyteller.

In recent years more and more quality literature has emerged from the Maori community. Writing in English, such authors as **Keri Hulme, Rowley Habib, Witi Ihimaera,** and **Patricia Grace** have brilliantly brought the Maori experience in New Zealand to life.

Keri Hulme won the prestigious Booker Prize for *The Bone People,* which takes place on the West Coast. This is a spooky tale of a child's strange and hurtful past. Collections of Katherine Mansfield's short stories include *Prelude, Bliss and Other Stories* and *The Garden Party and Other Stories.* And you may want to read Alan Duff's *Once Were Warriors,* which deals with poverty and violence in a Maori family (or see if you can rent the movie). Maurice Gee's *Going West* is set in Auckland and Wellington.

Bulibasha, by Witi Ihimaera, provides a look at Maori sheep-shearing gangs on the North Island's east coast. *Tomorrow We Save the Orphans* by Owen Marshall is a collection of short stories. *An Angel at My Table,* by Janet Frame, was made into a movie directed by Jane Campion.

3 Planning an Affordable Trip to New Zealand

New Zealand has so many places to explore, things to do, sights to see—it can be bewildering to plan your trip with so much vying for your attention. Where to start? That's where we come in. In the pages that follow you'll find everything you need to know to plan your ideal trip.

1 How This Guide Can Save You Money

You may be wondering if it's really possible to experience all that New Zealand has to offer on just $50 a day. You bet it is! First, though, there're a few things I need to explain about how our "dollar-a-day" budget concept works. Remember that this amount is in U.S. dollars—at press time, US$50 is equivalent to NZ$71.50. We assume that two adults are traveling together and that between the two of you, you have at least NZ$143 (US$100) to spend. The cost of sightseeing, transportation, and entertainment are extra, but we have plenty of hot tips on those activities as well.

This could be divvied up as follows: NZ$85 (US$59.50) for a double room, NZ$8 (US$5.60) per person for lunch, NZ$16 (US$11.20) each for dinner, and about NZ$5 (US$3.50) each for breakfast. Tea, coffee, milk, and sugar are provided free in all New Zealand lodgings, with the possible exception of hostels and motor camps. And, of course, should you wish to take advantage of the cooking facilities found in most Kiwi motels, your lunches and dinners will cost much less than the price above; and if you stay at B&Bs, breakfast will be included in the tariff.

Now I'm certainly not implying that the $50-a-day premise works only for two people traveling together. Absolutely not. Most of my trips to New Zealand have been solo ventures, so I'm keenly aware of the needs of single travelers. Since most motel rates are priced as doubles, rooms can get expensive for single travelers. B&Bs and hostels tend to be a better deal for those on their own in New Zealand.

The accommodations and dining figures I quoted above are for moderately priced options. The average B&B homestay or guest house costs about NZ$85 (US$59.50) a night for a double *with breakfast*. Motel rates range from NZ$70 to NZ$120 (US$49 to $84) without breakfast. Staying at one of the country's hostels, much more attractive than most European varieties, can bring your lodging costs down to NZ$16 to NZ$18 (US$11.20 to U.S.$12.60) per person a night; a camp site or spot in a motorhome camp would be even less. Because our title is *from* $50 A Day, I've also included options for travelers with a more flexible budget—these are listed under the "Worth a Splurge" heading in the regional chapters and include some unique inns and picturesque country lodges.

As for dining, the NZ$16 (US$11.20) I've suggested for dinner will get you a main course and a nonalcoholic beverage at most of New Zealand's cafes and moderately priced restaurants. It's even less expensive to eat at food courts, fish-and-chips shops, delis, and modest ethnic places where NZ$5 (US$3.50) will definitely fill you up. As mentioned above, you can also save money by cooking at your motel or in the shared kitchen at your hostel. At lunchtime, I suggest you do as the locals do and picnic.

2 Visitor Information & Entry Requirements

VISITOR INFORMATION

NEW ZEALAND TOURISM BOARD   Once you've decided to go to New Zealand, the first thing you should do is contact the nearest **New Zealand Tourism Board** and ask them to send you a complimentary copy of their *New Zealand Vacation Planner*. This magazine-type guide is published once a year and includes general information on the country to get you started. Their official Web site is at **www.nztb.govt.nz**.

Here's a list of North American offices of the New Zealand Tourism Board: 501 Santa Monica Blvd., Suite 300, Santa Monica, CA 90401 (☎ **800/388-5494** in the U.S, or 310/395-7480; fax 310/395-5453); and 888 Dunsmuir St., Suite 1200, Vancouver, BC, V6C 3K4 (☎ **800/888-5494** in Canada only, or 604/684-2117).

Other locations include Level 8, 35 Pitt St., Sydney, NSW 2000, Australia (☎ **02/247-5222**); New Zealand House, Haymarket, SW1Y 4TQ, London, England (☎ **0171/973-0360**); Friedrichstrasse 10–12, 60323 Frankfurt am Main, Germany (☎ **069/9712-1110**, fax 069/9712-1113); and 3414 Jardine House, 1 Connaught Place, Central, Hong Kong (☎ **852/526-0141**).

VISITOR INFORMATION NETWORK   When you arrive in New Zealand, you'll find more than 80 local visitor information offices around the country. These are staffed by helpful people who can make accommodation and tour bookings, give advice on local dining options, provide maps, and answer questions. They also sell phone cards and postage stamps. Always keep your eyes peeled for the identifying green "*i.*" You'll find local Visitor Information Network addresses listed for each destination in this book. They're also listed in the *New Zealand Vacation Planner* (see above).

While you're traveling in New Zealand, tune in to Tourist Information FM radio, which provides travel information 24 hours a day on 88.2 FM.

WEB SITES   The Internet provides a wealth of travel information on New Zealand. Here's a list of sites that I've checked out and highly recommend:

- **The New Zealand Tourism Board (www.nztb.govt.nz)**   Their page provides basic information on things like government and environment, plus lots of regional highlights.
- **New Zealand on the Web (nz.com/NZ)**   Another good resource with tons of travel information.
- **New Zealand Travel Reservation Centre (nz.com/webnz/tpac/nz)**   Basic travel information is provided, plus bookings for airline tickets, coach and train tickets, car rentals, accommodations, and all kinds of activities and tours.

Tying the Knot in New Zealand

New Zealand's natural beauty and relaxed lifestyle may just convince you and your loved one that it's time to tie the knot. Should this happen and you want to waste no time getting hitched, the procedure is fairly simple. A list of "Celebrants" can be found in the Yellow Pages under "Justice Department," or you can contact a local District Court. One of you must go to a Registrar of Marriages and fill out a form of the intended marriage. After 3 days, the Registrar will issue a license good for 3 months. Minors under 20 must have their parents' permission. If you have been married before, you will need to show proof of the dissolution of the marriage. For further information, contact a New Zealand Consulate or Embassy (see above).

- **Travel Gay New Zealand (nz.com/webnz/tpac/gaynz)**   This page is part of the New Zealand Travel Reservation Centre site(above); it's got good travel advice for gay and lesbian visitors.
- **Heritage Inns (nz.com/HeritageInns)**   You'll find all of the B&Bs associated with Heritage Inns here, including photos and contact information.

ENTRY REQUIREMENTS

PASSPORTS   You'll need a passport to get into New Zealand, and it must be valid for no less than 3 months beyond the date you plan to return home. It's a good idea to make two photocopies of the identification page of your passport (the one with your photo), as well as any other travel documents, then leave one copy at home and carry the other with you. You'll save yourself a lot of hassle in case you and those vital papers part company, and you need them replaced. The photocopies will not serve as valid documents, but they'll provide the necessary information to get new ones without a lot of red tape.

VISAS   If you're staying for less than 3 months, you won't need a visa (provided that you don't intend to work, study, or undergo medical treatment) if you're a citizen of the United States, Canada, Great Britain (British citizens are allowed to stay 6 months), Australia, Austria, Belgium, Brunei, Denmark, Finland, France, Germany, Greece, Iceland, Indonesia, Italy, Japan, Korea (South), Liechtenstein, Luxembourg, Malaysia, Malta, Monaco, Nauru, the Netherlands, Portugal, Singapore, Spain, Sweden, Switzerland, Thailand, or Tuvalu.

If you wish to stay beyond the limits stated above, or if your nationality is not listed, consult your nearest New Zealand Embassy, High Commission, or consulate for information on obtaining the appropriate visa.

Americans who want to stay longer than 3 months may obtain a visa application from the **New Zealand Embassy,** 37 Observatory Circle NW, Washington, DC 20008 (☎ **202/328-4880,** fax 202/667-5227) or the **New Zealand Consulate-General,** 12400 Wilshire Blvd, Suite 1150, Los Angeles, CA 90025 (☎ **310/207-1605,** fax 310/207-3605). There's no fee, but you'll need a photograph.

Canadian residents should contact the **New Zealand High Commission,** Ottawa Metropolitan House, Suite 727, 99 Bank St., Ottawa, Ontario K1P 6G3 (☎ **613/238-5991,** fax 613/238-5707).

For information on working or living in New Zealand, inquire at one of the consulates or write to the **New Zealand Immigration Service,** P.O. Box 27-149, Wellington, NZ, for current regulations.

OTHER ENTRY REQUIREMENTS   Visitors must have three things before entering New Zealand: a confirmed outward or round-trip ticket; enough money for their New Zealand stay— NZ$1,000 (US$700) per person per month (credit or charge cards are acceptable as evidence of funds); and the necessary documents to enter the next country on their itinerary or to reenter the country from which they came. I've never been asked to show any of these things upon arrival in the country, but I did have to flash my Amex card once when I was already in New Zealand and wanted to get an extension on my 3-month visa.

CUSTOMS   Please save yourself a lot of embarrassment and don't bring any fruit or plants into New Zealand—the country has strict regulations about this issue.

There is no Customs duty on any personal items you bring into the country and intend to take with you. New Zealand's duty-free allowances are: 200 cigarettes or 250 grams (about 8 oz.) of tobacco or 50 cigars; 4.5 liters of wine or beer (equivalent to six 750-ml bottles); one bottle of spirits or liqueur (up to 1,125 ml/about 2¹/₂ pints); and goods totaling NZ$700 (US$490) that were purchased for your own use or for a gift. If you plan to take in anything beyond those limits, contact the embassy or consulate office nearest you, *before* you arrive.

3 Money

You shouldn't have any trouble at all with New Zealand's currency: The **New Zealand dollar (NZ$)** is based on the decimal system with 100 cents to the dollar. There are coins in denominations of 5, 10, 20, and 50 cents and $1 and $2, as well as banknotes in $5, $10, $20, $50, and $100 amounts.

On my last trip to New Zealand I carried traveler's checks, a couple of different credit cards, and an ATM card. I only used one credit card (Visa) and the ATM card. I kept thinking I'd cash the **traveler's checks,** but I never seemed to be able to get to a bank during open hours, and I didn't stay in hotels with money-changing facilities. **ATMs,** also known in New Zealand as **banks-in-a-wall,** are available throughout the country and are the most convenient way to go, in spite of the minimal fee added by my bank at home. My Wells Fargo Bank ATM card works in the Cirrus system used by the Bank of New Zealand. Other banks accept ATM cards in the Plus system. If you intend to use ATMs while down under, ask your bank for a directory of locations where you can use your card. You probably won't need very much cash because most businesses accept **credit and charge cards.** MasterCard and Visa are the most popular; American Express and Diner's Club are also widely accepted.

4 45 Money-Saving Tips

AIR TRAVEL

1. Travel to New Zealand during the off-season—April through August—when airlines offer their lowest fares. You'll also get cheaper fares if you fly on certain days of the week—at press time, Monday, Tuesday, and Wednesday were the best days.
2. Take advantage of the free stopovers allowed on many airfares to New Zealand. So along with exploring New Zealand, you could stop over in Tahiti, the Cook Islands, Western Samoa, Tonga, Fiji, or Hawaii at no extra cost.
3. Book your flight early to take advantage of advance-purchase fares.
4. Look into airline package deals that include a rental car or accommodations. One of the best air-land deals is offered by **Sunmakers Travel Group** (☎ 800/841-4321 in the US). You get round-trip airfare and a 7-day Thrifty car rental,

The New Zealand Dollar, the U.S. Dollar & the British Pound

For U.S. Readers At this writing $1 US = approximately NZ$1.43 (or NZ$1 = 70¢), and this was the rate of exchange used to calculate the dollar values given in this book (rounded up to the nearest nickel).

For British Readers At this writing £1 = approximately NZ$2.38 (or NZ$1 = 42p), and this was the rate of exchange used to calculate the pound values in the accompanying table.

Note: International exchange rates fluctuate from time to time depending on political and economic factors. Thus the rates given in this table may not be the same when you travel to New Zealand.

NZ$	U.S.$	U.K.£	NZ$	U.S.$	U.K.£
0.25	0.18	0.10	15	10.50	6.30
0.50	0.35	0.21	20	14.00	8.40
0.75	0.53	0.32	25	17.50	10.50
1	0.70	0.42	30	21.00	12.60
2	1.40	0.84	35	24.50	14.70
3	2.10	1.26	40	28.00	16.80
4	2.80	1.68	45	31.50	18.90
5	3.50	2.10	50	35.00	21.00
6	4.20	2.52	60	42.00	25.20
7	4.90	2.94	70	49.00	29.40
8	5.60	3.36	80	56.00	33.60
9	6.30	3.78	90	63.00	37.80
10	7.00	4.20	100	70.00	42.00

plus car insurance, for little more than the cost of an airline ticket. **Qantas Vacations USA** (☎ **800/641-8772** or 310/322-6359), affiliated with Qantas Airways, usually has some good package deals too.

5. If you fly **Qantas Airways** (☎ **800/227-4500** in the U.S. and Canada), you can earn frequent-flyer mileage credit with Alaska Airlines, American Airlines, British Airways, Continental Airlines, and US Airways. And, more importantly, you can purchase your ticket on Qantas with frequent-flyer miles from any of the above airlines.

6. You can find some pretty good deals on flying within New Zealand. **Air New Zealand** (☎ **800/262-1234** in the US) and **Ansett New Zealand** (☎ **800/366-1300** in the US and Canada), the two major carriers in New Zealand, give significant discounts to holders of VIP (backpackers) cards and YHA (Youth Hostel Association) members. Plus both offer valuable air passes like Air New Zealand's **Explore New Zealand Airpass**—you purchase three to eight flight coupons for a set price; for NZ$495 (US$346.50) you get three coupons for three sep-arate flights, good for 60 days from the date of your first flight. But, *they must be purchased before you reach New Zealand!*

What Things Cost in Auckland	U.S. $
While the cost of a home or a car varies quite a bit from place to place within New Zealand, prices for the items visitors purchase are pretty much the same throughout the country.	
Airport bus to city center (Air Bus, one way)	US$7
Rates for two at Auckland Central Backpackers (cheap)	US$25.90
Double at Epsom Homestay B&B (affordable)	US$56
Double at Aachen House (pricey)	US$94.50
Dinner for one at Kebab Kid (cheap)	US$4.90
Dinner for one at Portofino (affordable)	US$11.20
Dinner for one (pricey)	US$21
Cappuccino at La Bocca	US$2.10
Postcard stamp (to anywhere overseas)	US$.70
Roll of Kodacolor film, 36 exposures	US$5.60
Petrol (gas), per liter	US$.64
Pint (20 ounces) of beer at The Loaded Hog	US$3.36
Movie ticket	US$7

ACCOMMODATIONS

7. Keep in mind, when planning your itinerary, that dining and lodging cost more in New Zealand's major cities than in other parts of the country; prices are slightly higher on the North Island than on the South Island.

8. Take advantage of the **free** services offered at the more than 80 Visitor Information Network offices all over New Zealand—these services include booking accommodations.

9. Stay at bed-and-breakfasts, where the rates include breakfast, not to mention personalized attention.

10. Don't overlook the inexpensive motel units and apartments located in motor camps and campgrounds throughout New Zealand.

11. New Zealand hostels—both private ones and those affiliated with Hostelling International—are a lot nicer than their European and American counterparts. Plus, hostels usually have private rooms with twin or double beds, in addition to the traditional dorm-style bunk rooms.

12. Do a farmstay. Staying at a New Zealand farm is not only a memorable experience, it's also a dollarwise option for budget travelers. Breakfast is included, plus many hosts offer a free tour of their properties, transportation to and from the airport or bus/rail station, and plenty of free travel advice.

13. Throughout New Zealand, many vacation homes, known as *baches* or *cribs*, are available for rent when the owners aren't using them. This can be a really good value choice for budget travelers, especially families.

14. Most goods and services in New Zealand are subject to a 12.5% GST tax. When requesting a room rate, always ask whether the GST is included.

15. Whenever you reserve a room or other accommodations, ask about discounted long-stay rates, off-season rates, corporate rates, senior-citizen rates, weekend packages, or auto-club discounts. Also, moteliers and B&B hosts often build a travel agent's commission into their tariffs, so ask if there's a discount for direct booking.

DINING

16. Remember that B&B homestays, farmstays, guest houses, and inns offer complimentary coffee and tea, and often breakfast is included.

17. Ask your B&B hosts for some good-value dining recommendations in the area.

18. Cooking dinner or "picnicking" in your motel room is a thrifty alternative to dining out, and picnic lunches are a great way to take advantage of New Zealand's natural beauty. Save on motel and hostel breakfast costs by picking up a stash of muffins and fresh fruit at a supermarket, especially if you're going to be on the road that day.

19. Eat at restaurants that allow you to bring your own wine, and buy your wine at wholesale liquor stores, which are prevalent throughout New Zealand (inquire about store locations at local visitors centers).

20. Many B&B and farmstay hosts offer home-cooked dinners to guests at an extra cost; these meals are usually a great deal and, more often than not, prove to be a memorable travel experience.

21. Kiwis rarely tip—and you shouldn't either.

22. When dining out, keep in mind that in New Zealand breads and side dishes cost extra. And don't feel you have to order a main course. Many locals order an "entree" (first course here) and a salad or side of fresh vegetables.

RENTING A CAR

23. A rental car can be a huge money saver, despite the high costs up front. Having a car will spare you the per-person fares for day trips by coach and rail, which can add up fast. Plus, it can carry you to scenic nature reserves and other places where there are lots of free outdoor activities.

24. In cities, calculate whether it's cheaper to take local tours or rent a car for sightseeing. Also, if you're without a car, take city buses or walk instead of getting a taxi.

25. If you rent a car for inter-city transportation, you'll save money by getting a small vehicle that gets good gas mileage. Make sure your car-rental agreement includes unlimited free kilometers, and remember that standard or stick-shift cars use less petrol (gas) than automatics.

26. Check the rates offered by local, independent car rental companies in New Zealand—they're usually less expensive than the internationally known companies. One of the best is **Maui Rentals** (☎ **800/351-2323** in the U.S.), which has a fleet of modern cars at low rates and offices in Auckland and Christchurch.

27. If you're booking a one-way contract, ask whether there are any drop-off charges and confirm the time of day the car is due to avoid late charges.

28. Before you leave for New Zealand, check whether your car insurance from home will cover you down under. If it does, you'll save money by declining the rental agency's insurance.

29. If you're a member of an auto club, take your membership card with you to New Zealand; it'll entitle you to Automobile Association (AA) member discounts on some accommodations and attractions, plus excellent free maps.

PUBLIC TRANSPORTATION

30. Coaches (buses) are the most affordable way to travel in New Zealand. **InterCity Coaches** and **Mount Cook Landline**—two of New Zealand's biggest coach lines—offer a 30% discount to card-holding members of YHA (Youth Hostel Association) and VIP (a group of backpacker hostels), as well as those over age 60. Mount Cook Landline's **Explorer Coach Passes** is also a good-value option—7 days of travel in a 30-day period for NZ$335 (US$234.50). **Newmans Coach Lines,** another national bus company, gives discounts to anyone over 50 and offers a valuable **Auckland/Wellington Stopover Pass.** For just NZ$95 (US$66.50) passholders can travel any route between these two cities (without backtracking) over a 14-day period.

31. The combination bus-rail or bus-rail-ferry **Travelpasses** offered by InterCity Coaches, Tranz Scenic passenger trains, and **The Interislander** ferries, are also worth checking out.

32. Trains are also a good and relatively cost-efficient way to travel in New Zealand. **Tranz Scenic** (☎ 0800/802-802 in New Zealand) trains are quite comfortable, and they run along coastlines and mountain gorges with fantastic views, which are sometimes hidden from highways that run farther inland or on higher ground. Tranz Scenic offers some dollarwise packages that include both train travel and accommodations, plus a 20% discount for students; a 30% discount for YHA and Backpacker cardholders and Golden Age (over 55); and some Saver Fares and Super Saver fares, which are 30 to 50% less for travel at off-peak times (outside of school holidays and summer season).

33. **Kiwi Experience** (☎ 09/366-1665) and the **Magic Travellers Network** (☎ 09/358-5600) provide inexpensive coach transportation for "independent adventurous travelers" (meaning backpackers). These private inter-city shuttles provide an affordable alternative to the big national bus lines on some routes between major cities.

OUTDOOR ACTIVITIES, SIGHTSEEING & OTHER FUN STUFF

34. B&B hosts are a great resource for finding affordable outdoor guides with whom they're personally familiar. They'll also recommend great local spots for fishing, hiking, swimming, or whatever it is you want to do.

35. Throughout New Zealand—while traveling along the highway—keep your eyes peeled for dark green signs with gold letters. These indicate **Department of Conservation nature reserves.** As a minimum, they're great picnic spots with no admission charges, and often have walking tracks through scenic bushland.

36. If you're fit and adventurous, you can walk the country's famous hiking trails without a guide—it's *a lot* cheaper. You can get good trail maps from the Department of Conservation.

37. If you want to catch a film in New Zealand, go on Monday or Tuesday night, when most local cinemas charge only NZ$6 (US$4.20)—the regular price is NZ$9 to NZ$10 (US$6.30 to US$7).

38. Remember to ask for VIP, YHA, auto club, senior citizen, or whatever discount is appropriate at sightseeing attractions and tours.

39. In Auckland, arm yourself with either the money-saving **Explorer Bus** ticket or the **BusAbout Pass,** which offer the cheapest way to travel between all the major attractions (see "Getting Around," in chapter 5).

SHOPPING

40. Buy souvenirs in local department stores rather than at tourist traps, which often hike up their prices so that they can give kickbacks to tour guides who bring them business.

41. When shopping for gifts to take home, consider buying tea, shortbread biscuits (cookies), honey, or kiwifruit jam—all of which you can buy for next to nothing at a local supermarket.

42. Purchases sent overseas are not subject to New Zealand's 12.5% Goods and Services Tax.

43. Buy New Zealand books at one of the many national Automobile Association (AA) offices scattered throughout the country. Members of auto clubs around the world receive discounts and can also get free road maps.

TELEPHONES

44. Long-distance calls within New Zealand are expensive. The cheapest time to phone is between 10pm and 7am. The next-best time is during the "economy" period: Monday through Friday from 7 to 8am and 6 to 10pm; Saturday, Sunday, and holidays from 7am to 10pm.

45. The cheapest way for overseas visitors to call home is to use Country Direct numbers.

5 When to Go

In New Zealand, seasons correspond with the Southern Hemisphere, and are thus opposite of those in North America and Europe. There really isn't a bad season to travel, so your own schedule and interests should set your timing priorities. One important thing to remember, however, is that during Kiwi holiday times, accommodations can be very tight. So if you plan to come between mid-December and the end of January, when New Zealand families are traveling about their country on annual "hols," or during the Easter, April, July, or September–October midterm school holidays (see "Holidays," below, for specific dates), reservations are an absolute must.

THE SEASONS

SPRING   September, October, and November. This is one of the best times to visit, when the countryside is bright with blossoming fruit trees and brand-new baby lambs. Springtime is also a favorite season among camera buffs because pastures, lush and green from winter's rain, are often framed by snow-capped mountain peaks. Gardens throughout New Zealand are blooming with bright colors, especially those with rhododendrons.

SUMMER   December, January, and February. New Zealanders are pretty preoccupied with beaches and boats during these months, and resorts are booked solid. Even walking tracks and mountain huts are crowded. With enough advance planning, you could share these sun-filled days with the locals, but you'll pay top dollar for everything you do. Personally, I'd stay home until the kids go back to school at the end of January, although the thought of summer berries—especially raspberries—does make this season a tempting one.

FALL   March, April, and May. This is a great time for budget travelers to visit New Zealand because the cheapest airfares are available from April through August. In addition, the weather is pleasant and just cool enough in southern parts of the country to remind you that winter is on its way, while in the Bay of Islands region and elsewhere in the north, midday and early afternoons are still shirt-sleeve warm. Poplars are a brilliant gold, and more subtle foliage changes can be seen in the forests. One of the things I like best about traveling during March is buying fresh fruit from the side of the road. Around Cromwell in the South Island you can buy bags of delicious "stone fruit," (peaches, apricots, plums, and the like) for a fraction of what they'd cost elsewhere in the world. In the North Island look for kiwifruit and apples. Just remember those Easter and April school holidays, when accommodations bookings may be tight.

WINTER   June, July, and August. While the weather isn't the best, this is also a great time for budget travelers to roam around New Zealand. You won't need to prebook lodging (except during the 2-week school holiday in July), and you should get some great off-season rates on rooms and cars. Of course, you won't get deals in the ski areas—this is their high season. When I think of winter in New Zealand, I visualize wonderful bowls of piping hot pumpkin soup, sitting in front of cozy fires, and shopping for handknit woolen sweaters. These items are sold year round, but the best bargains are available during the cool months when the locals, not just overseas visitors, are buying them.

WEATHER

Weatherwise, you're safe to visit New Zealand any time of the year. Temperatures are never extreme, although I've experienced days when they were. One thing to keep in mind, however, is that on a visit that takes you to both islands, you'll be going from a subtropical climate at the northern tip of the North Island to a cooler (and sometimes downright cold) climate on the South Island. Your best bet is to do as the locals do and dress in layers.

There isn't a specific rainy season, but chances are you'll experience some showers while you're here—it's what makes the country appear so green. The West Coast of the South Island can experience up to 100 inches or more of rain a year on its side of the Southern Alps, while just over those mountains to the east, rainfall will be a moderate 20 to 30 inches. Rain is also heavier on the west coast of the North Island, with precipitation on the whole ranging from 40 to 70 inches annually. Milford Sound is probably the wettest place in the country—and also perhaps the most beautiful—with an annual downpour of 365 inches. But fortunately, it doesn't rain every day or all day long.

New Zealand's Average Temperature and Rainfall

Temperatures reflected are daily average (°C/°F).
Rainfall reflects the daily average in millimeters/inches (mm/in) and are accurate within 1mm.

		Summer	Fall	Winter	Spring
Bay of Islands	Max. Temps	25/77	21/70	16/61	19/66
	Min. Temps	14/57	11/52	7/45	9/48
	Rainfall	7/0.28	11/0.44	16/0.64	11/0.44
Auckland	Max. Temps	24/75	20/68	15/59	18/65
	Min. Temps	12/54	13/55	9/48	11/52
	Rainfall	8/0.32	11/0.44	15/0.6	12/0.48
Rotorua	Max. Temps	24/75	18/65	13/55	17/63
	Min. Temps	12/54	9/48	4/39	7/45
	Rainfall	9/0.36	9/0.36	13/0.52	11/0.44

		Summer	Fall	Winter	Spring
Wellington	Max. Temps	20/68	17/63	12/54	15/59
	Min. Temps	13/55	11/52	6/43	9/48
	Rainfall	7/0.28	10/0.4	13/0.52	11/0.44
Nelson	Max. Temps	22/72	18/65	13/55	17/63
	Min. Temps	13/55	8/46	3/37	7/45
	Rainfall	6/0.24	8/0.32	10/0.4	10/0.4
Westport	Max. Temps	22/72	17/63	13/55	15/59
	Min. Temps	12/54	10/50	5/41	8/46
	Rainfall	12/0.48	14/0.56	15/0.6	16/0.64
Christchurch	Max. Temps	22/72	18/65	12/54	17/63
	Min. Temps	12/54	8/46	3/37	7/45
	Rainfall	7/0.28	7/0.28	7/0.28	7/0.28
Mount Cook	Max. Temps	20/68	14/57	8/46	14/57
	Min. Temps	9/48	4/39	-1/30	4/39
	Rainfall	12/0.48	13/0.52	13/0.52	14/0.56
Queenstown	Max. Temps	22/72	16/61	10/50	16/61
	Min. Temps	10/50	6/43	1/34	5/41
	Rainfall	8/0.32	8/0.32	7/0.28	9/0.36
Invercargill	Max. Temps	18/65	15/59	11/52	15/59
	Min. Temps	9/48	6/43	1/34	5/41
	Rainfall	13/0.52	14/0.56	12/0.48	13/0.52

As for sunshine, you'll find more in the northern and eastern areas of both islands, especially in the Bay of Islands and the Nelson/Marlborough Sounds area. Frost and snow in the North Island are mainly confined to high country spots like Mount Egmont/Taranaki and the peaks of Tongariro National Park.

HOLIDAYS
NATIONAL PUBLIC HOLIDAYS

New Year's Day	January 1	**ANZAC Day**	April 25
New Year's Holiday	January 2	**Queen's Birthday**	first Mon in June
Waitangi Day	February 6	**Labour Day**	last Mon in October
Good Friday	varies	**Christmas Day**	December 25
Easter	varies	**Boxing Day**	December 26
Easter Monday	varies		

REGIONAL HOLIDAYS
These holidays are always observed on Monday. If the date falls on a Friday or weekend, it is observed the following Monday. If it falls earlier in the week, it is observed on the preceding Monday.

Wellington	January 22	**Taranaki**	March 31
Auckland	January 29	**Hawkes Bay**	November 1
Northland	January 29	**Marlborough**	November 1
Nelson Region	February 1	**Westland**	December 1
Otago	March 23	**Canterbury**	December 16
Southland	March 23		

Readers Recommend

"In all my overseas travels I have never seen a country as geared for tourists as New Zealand and what a beauty! It was a holiday of a lifetime and, of course, gorgeous weather was the cherry on top."

—Margaret Shephard, Pietarmaritzburg, South Africa.

SCHOOL HOLIDAYS

Midterm school holidays last for 2 weeks, and December holidays last 6 weeks (through the end of January). That's when Kiwi families are on the move, so be sure of your reservations during those months. The next scheduled school holidays are December 18, 1997 to January 25, 1998; April 10 to 26, 1998; July 4 to 19, 1998; and September 26 to October 11, 1998.

NEW ZEALAND CALENDAR OF EVENTS

More information on special events can be found in the regional chapters of this book.

January

○ **Auckland Anniversary Day Regatta,** Auckland. The "City of Sails" hosts this annual colorful sailing event, which attracts both local and international folks. It's fun to watch from shore or one of several lofty viewpoints. Last Monday in January. Call ☎ 09/308-9141 for details.

• **Summer City Festival,** Wellington. A wide range of daily cultural, entertainment, and recreational events in the capital city. Including a Mardi Gras, Teddy Bear's Picnic, and Summer City Valentine's night. January and February. Call ☎ 04/801-3222 for details.

• **Fiordland Summer Festival Weekend,** Te Anau. The festivities here include a celebrity debate, a rodeo, garden tours, and harness racing in the main street, as well as arts and crafts, food stalls, and street entertainment. Early to mid-January. Call ☎ 03/249-7959 for details.

• **Wellington Cup Racing Meeting,** Wellington. Leading horse-racing event (galloping), which is held in conjunction with the **National Yearling Sales.** Late January. Call ☎ 04/801-4000 for details.

• **Harvest Hawkes Bay Wine and Food Festival,** Hawkes Bay. This festival provides an opportunity to sample local wines and food in all in one place. Late January–early February. Call ☎ 06/879-7603 for details.

February

• **Bay of Islands Arts Festival,** Bay of Islands. This festival offers a diverse program featuring every kind of art form—from drama to painting. Held annually since 1992, it attracts over 5,000 people every year. Early February. Call ☎ 09/405-0090 for details.

• **Waitangi Day Celebrations,** Bay of Islands. New Zealand's national day, celebrating the signing of the Treaty of Waitangi. February 6. Call ☎ 09/402-7308 for details.

• **Martinborough Country Fair,** Martinborough. Popular gathering of crafts artisans from around the country. First Saturday in February. Call ☎ 06/306-9043 for details.

○ **Garden City Festival of Flowers,** Christchurch. Garden visits, floating gardens, floral carpets in the "Garden City" of the South Island. Mid-February for 10 days. Call ☎ **03/379-9629** for details.

• **Devotion Festival,** Wellington. This is New Zealand's second largest annual gay and lesbian event. Only the Hero Parade in Auckland is bigger (see below). February 14, 1998 and mid-Feburary to mid-March 1999. Call ☎ **04/801-4000** for details.

• **Ford Art Deco Weekend,** Napier. This "not-too serious celebration" includes wining, dining, dancing, jazz, vintage cars, special walks and tours, and much more. Most participants dress in 1920s and 1930s fashions. Third weekend in February. Call ☎ **06/835-0022** for details.

• **World Dragon Boat Festival,** Wellington. Dragon boats are modified Chinese long boats that are used for racing with a crew of 20 paddlers, one drummer or caller who sets the stroke speed, and a steerer. Every year teams from all over the world come to compete in these colorful races. February 17–22, 1998 and weekend of February 21, 1999. Call ☎ **04/471-0205** for details.

• **Hero Parade and Party,** Auckland. This is the country's largest annual gay and lesbian event. Now in its eighth year, festivities include film, theater, cabaret, dance, and sport. The festival culminates with a street parade and all-night dance party. Late February (Festival February 7–21, 1998. Parade and party February 21, 1998). Call ☎ **09/307-1057** or send an e-mail to **maxsam.xtra.co.nz** for details.

• **Devonport Food & Wine Festival,** Devonport. Held on the Windsor Reserve near the Ferry Wharf in Auckland's most picturesque North Shore community. Entertainment includes jazz, classical, and opera. All proceeds go to charity. Late February (February 21–22, 1998). Call ☎ **09/446-0688** or 09/445-3011 for details.

○ **Golden Shears,** Masterton. This international shearing contest lasts for 3 days and includes wool handling, and lamb and goat shearing. Masterton is located in the Wairarapa District northeast of Wellington. Late February to early March. Call ☎ **06/378-7373** for details.

March

• **Ngaruawahia River Regatta,** Turangawoewoe Marao, Ngaruawahia. Held on the Waikato River near Hamilton. Includes *waka*(canoe) races, Maori cultural performances. Early March. Call ☎ **07/839-3580** for details.

• **ECNZ Wild Foods Festival,** Hokitika. Wild pig, venison, possum pâté, goat, all sorts of wild herbs, honey, and fish from local waters star in this 1-day West Coast celebration. Great fun. March. Call ☎ **03/755-8322** for details.

• **Savile Polo Cup,** Clevedon Pologround, Clevedon (south of Auckland). One of New Zealand's oldest sporting trophies, the Savile pits domestic teams against international contenders. Late February to early March. Call ☎ **09/236-0670** for details.

○ **Round the Bays Run, Auckland.** Runners from around the South Pacific participate in this 8km (about 5-mile) run, ending with a barbecue in one of the city's parks. Late March (March 29, 1998). It's fun to watch. Call ☎ **09/525-2166** for details.

April

• **Rugby Season,** countrywide. April through September. Matches take place on weekends in small towns and every city. Contact the **New Zealand Rugby Football League Inc. (☎** 09/524-4013**)** or the **New Zealand Rugby Football Union (☎** 04/499-4995**)** for details.

- **Arrowtown Autumn Festival,** Arrowtown. Week of market days, miners' band, and street entertainment celebrating the gold-mining era. The week after Easter. ☎ **03/442-4100** for details.
- **Royal New Zealand Easter Show,** Auckland. Held at the Expo Centre, it annually attracts more than 1,000 competitors and incorporates elements of an agricultural and pastoral show including halls with produce, a merry-go-round, equestrian events, etc. At least 15,000 to 20,000 Kiwis attend. Easter weekend. Call ☎ **09/638-9969** for details.

May
- **Fletcher Challenge Marathon,** Rotorua. Full marathon run around Lake Rotorua. Serious competition. Early May. Call ☎ **07/348-8448** for details.
- **Bay of Islands Country Music Festival,** Bay of Islands. This festival draws musicians from all around New Zealand. There's also at least one international act each year. Second weekend in May. Call ☎ **09/404-1063** for details.

June
- **Wanaka Winter Wonderland,** Wanaka and Treble Cone Ski Field. Skiing events during this winter carnival include the Rip Curl Heli Challenge, the Merrell Classic Telemark Race, the ETA Ripples NZ Extreme Snowboarding Challenge, the NZFSA Mogul Tour, the Cardrona Snowboard Cup, and the Virgin Vodka NZ Snowboard Masters. Late June to early October. Call ☎ **03/443-1233** for details.

July
- **Queenstown Winter Festival,** Queenstown. Boisterous, fun-filled celebration of winter season, with ski events and street entertainment. Late June. Call ☎ **03/442-4100** for details.

August
- **Bay of Islands Jazz and Blues Festival,** Bay of Islands. Held at various places around Paihia and Russell at night and during the day. Early to mid-August. Call ☎ **09/402-7547** for details.

September
- **Bay of Islands Wine and Food Festival,** Bay of Islands. Set on the picturesque grounds of the Quality Resort Waitangi. Features top New Zealand wine and food exhibitors and great entertainment. Last weekend in September. Call ☎ **09/402-7557** for details.

October
- **Rhododendron Week,** Dunedin. Fun-filled days highlighted by garden tours and cultural events to celebrate this city's magnificent displays of rhododendron blooms. Mid-October. Call ☎ **03/474-3300** for details.

November
- **Cricket Season,** countrywide. November through April. Cricket has been played in New Zealand since the 1830s and is the oldest organized sport in the country. If you're interested in knowing more about the sport or catching a match, contact **The National Cricket Museum in Wellington** (☎ **04/385-6602**).
- **Whangamomona Republic Day,** Whangamomona. Passports are issued and entry visas sold to visitors when borders are closed around this self-styled republic, which was formed after boundary changes moved Whangamomona from the Taranaki region to that of Wanganui-Manawatu. All sorts of street entertainment and food stalls, with proceeds going to charity. Nearest Saturday to November 1. Contact ☎ **06/759-6080** for details.

- **Toast Martinborough,** Martinborough. Annual food and wine festival. Mid-November. Call ☎ **06/306-9043** for details.
- **Christchurch A & P Show,** Christchurch. This agricultural and pastoral show is the South Island's largest and includes thoroughbred and standard-bred racing. Even those who don't attend watch the running of the New Zealand Cup on TV. Second week in November. Call ☎ **03/379-9629** for details.
- **Ellerslie Flower Show,** Auckland. Held at the Auckland Regional Botanic Garden, this is New Zealand's premier garden and outdoor living event. Includes complete gardens, the latest in barbecues, and outdoor furniture. November. Call ☎ **09/309-7875** for details.

December
- **Horse Racing (NZ Derby, Queen Elizabeth Auckland Handicap, and others),** Auckland. Check locally for specific dates of individual events during the month. Call ☎ **09/366-6888** for details.

6 Finding an Affordable Place to Stay

Where you stay in New Zealand will influence your whole impression of the country. Because I want you to love my home-away-from-home the way I do, I've put together some tips for choosing accommodations. Some terms can be confusing down under, and I want to make sure you pick the right digs, and pay the right price.

HOTELS

In New Zealand, *hotel* refers to modern tourist hotels and older public-licensed hotels. The former are usually outside the reach of budget travelers (unless it's time for a splurge), but the latter can be a good value. This is particularly true in small towns, where pubs offer a small number of rooms—generally with shared bathrooms down the hall. As reader P. A. McCauley of Baltimore, Md., points out: "For those who are on a budget but don't have backpacking gear, they can be a life-saver."

MOTELS & MOTOR INNS

In New Zealand, motel rooms, known as "units," usually come with cooking facilities and a living room, known as a "lounge," and a bedroom. Even if there aren't cooking facilities, you'll always find an electric kettle or "jug," tea, coffee, milk, sugar, etc., and usually a small refrigerator. The majority of rooms have TVs and telephones and on-premises laundry facilities. Motel rates range from NZ$70 to NZ$100 (US$49 to US$70) single or double. A motel room without a separate bedroom is called a bed-sitter (studio).

Motor inns are basically upscale motels, often with a restaurant on the premises.

BED-&-BREAKFASTS

This is the most confusing term, because it means something different in nearly every country. In New Zealand, properties offering lodging and breakfast for one set price include homestays, farmstays, guesthouses, and inns.

HOMESTAYS   Many New Zealand families open their homes to visitors, sometimes because they have a few spare rooms while their kids are in boarding school, and sometimes because they just love meeting people. Homestays are a wonderful way to meet people and see how they live. More often than not, your hosts will prove to be a great resource for information and advice about local attractions and restaurants; the breakfasts are usually very good, and home-cooked dinners (when they're offered) are an especially good value. The average homestay, not booked through an agency,

Readers Recommend

"While not critical, you might want to alert North American readers traveling in winter about the lack of central heat in most motels. The standard space heater warms up the main room, but my wife kept complaining about towels that never dried in a damp, chilly bathroom. No reason not to go, but if you really want your comforts, stick to a hotel."
                                   —Ira & Sharon Silverman, Rockville, Md., USA.

costs NZ$80 (US$56) for a double and NZ$60 (US$42) for a single. Some of the best homestay B&Bs in New Zealand got together and formed a group called **Hospitality Hosts.** Ask Dick Smith at The Gables, 20 Waikawa Rd., Picton (☎ 03/573-6772, fax 03/573-8860) to send you a copy of their brochure.

For information on bed-and-breakfasts in New Zealand and details on how to order the book, *A Guide to Bed & Breakfast Australia & New Zealand,* check out this Web site: **http://www.cyberlink.com.au/bedbreakfast**. Another good source of character accommodations is the booklet *Off the Beaten Track in New Zealand.* You might want to order the 1998 edition from Greenstone Press, Motukiekie Rocks, R.D. 1 Runanga, Westland, New Zealand. The cost is NZ$15 per copy (which in cludes postage within New Zealand); for overseas postage add NZ$4.

FARMSTAYS   Basically, this is a homestay on a New Zealand farm. But it's also an ideal opportunity to enjoy the beautiful Kiwi countryside and learn what life in New Zealand is all about, including what it takes to raise sheep, cattle, and even kiwifruit.

In addition to the specific farmstays recommended in this book, several companies will help you find a farm. It's much more expensive to book a farmstay through one of the agencies below than to book directly with a property described in this book. I'm only telling you about these companies in case you want to do a farmstay in a particular area in which I have no farms listed. The two agencies below can book you in farms all over the country. **New Zealand Farm Holidays,** P.O. Box 256, Silverdale, Auckland, New Zealand (☎ 09/307-2024, fax 09/426-8474). The cost, including dinner and breakfast, begins at about NZ$82 ($57.40) per person. **Hospitality Plus, The New Zealand Home & Farmstay Co. Ltd.,** P.O. Box 56175, Auckland 3, New Zealand (☎ 0800/109-175 in New Zealand, or 09/810-9175; fax 09/810-9448), also offers homestays and farmstays from NZ$60 (US$42) per person for bed and breakfast, to NZ$100 (US$70) for dinner, bed, and breakfast; dinners without accommodation cost NZ$50 (US$35) per person for three courses, including wine.

GUEST HOUSES   Offering good value and modest prices, guest houses have simply furnished rooms (often without *en suite* or attached bathrooms), and there's almost always a guest lounge with a TV and tea- and coffee-making facilities. Guest houses cost about NZ$85 (US$59.50) for a double and NZ$60 (US$42) for a single. For more information, contact **New Zealand's Federation of Bed & Breakfast Hotels, Inc.,** 52 Armagh St., Christchurch, New Zealand (☎ 03/366-1503, fax 03/366-9796).

BED-&-BREAKFAST INNS   These inns, with their attractive furnishings and superb morning meals, are my personal favorite type of accommodation in New Zealand. They cost a bit more—up to NZ$160 (US$112) or more for a double and NZ$100 (US$70) or more for a single—but I'd rather skimp in other places and splurge on a wonderful B&B. As with homestays and farmstays, the hosts are helpful and gracious, but in the case of most New Zealand inns, you get a bonus of historic ambience and old-world charm. Sometimes it's hard to tell the difference between a homestay bed-and-breakfast and a bed-and-breakfast inn; generally inns have more rooms than homestays and guests have less interaction with the hosts. All of the B&Bs associated with **Heritage Inns** can be found on their web site at **nz.com/HeritageInns**. You can also request one of their brochures from Ann Davies at Birchwood, R.D. 3, Clevedon, Auckland, New Zealand (☎ **09/292-8729,** fax 09/292-8555).

HOLIDAY HOMES & COUNTRY LODGES

When they're not being used by their owners, **holiday homes** throughout New Zealand can be rented by the night or longer. Known as *baches* (or *cribs* on the South Island), these are very good value for independent travelers. You can buy *Baches & Holiday Homes to Rent,* which lists the details on over 500 properties, from bookstores or the AA in New Zealand—or contact Mark and Elizabeth Greening, P.O. Box 3107, Richmond, Nelson, New Zealand (☎ and fax **03/544-4799,** e-mail **greening@nelson.planet.org.nz**). The price is NZ$19.95 (US$13.97).

Country Lodges originally catered to hunters and other sport-minded folks; nowadays they've become exclusive haunts where gourmet meals are as important as fishing. These lodges are generally outside a frugal traveler's realm, but I've included a few in this book in case there's room for a splurge in your budget.

HOSTELS

Even if you've never done the hostel thing before, you may want to try it in New Zealand. In addition to big, dorm-style rooms, most hostels offer private singles and doubles. Hostels are great for budget travelers who don't mind communal kitchens and shared bathrooms.

For information on YHA hostels, see "For Students," in "Tips for Travelers with Special Needs," later in this chapter. Also keep in mind that in New Zealand, **YHA hostels** are open 24 hours a day and do not impose curfews or duties—and having a glass of wine with your meal is quite acceptable. Kitchens at these hostels are fully equipped.

Other popular hostels are part of the **VIP network.** While you don't need a VIP card, it'll get you a discount at any of the network's 60+ hostels, plus other significant discounts on transportation (see "Getting Around," later in this chapter). VIP Discount Cards cost NZ$25 (US$16.25) and are valid for 12 months. Contact **Backpackers Resorts of New Zealand Ltd.,** Box 991, Taupo, New Zealand (☎ and fax **07/377-1157**) for details. Hostels cost about NZ$16 to NZ$18 (US$11.20 to US$12.60) per person.

MOTOR CAMPS

Motor camps aren't just for those traveling by campervan (RV) or with a tent; they also have cabins, flats, and motel units. All of these are "self-contained"—with a kitchen and bathroom. Only motel units are serviced—meaning they get daily maid service, and occupants of cabins sometimes have to supply their own linens. Campers share communal kitchens and bathrooms.

7 Shopping for New Zealand's Best Buys

Calling all shoppers! You're going to love browsing through Kiwi craft shops and galleries. Artisans abound and they create beautiful—and useful—items to take home as gifts and mementos.

Woodcrafts include bowls, carvings, goblets, and other wares made from the country's native timbers. Look for *rimu, kauri,* and *matai* pieces. You'll also find lots of **pottery,** especially around Nelson where there are more than 60 full-time potters and 400 hobbyists. **Handblown glass** pieces are also for sale—and you can watch the glassmakers work their magic at studios near Nelson and in Hokitika.

Of course, in this nation of 48 million sheep, there are lots of **wool** sweaters, slippers, and the like. Best of all, these items are usually handknit with the name of the craftperson sewn into the garment—a special touch. Also, don't overlook one of my favorite items: **spencers** are wool undershirts worn for warmth in this country where central heating is still not a given. The spencer I wear the most came from Ballantyne's Department Store in Christchurch, but I've also bought plenty of them for friends at The Woolshed in Taupo; spencers usually run about NZ\$47 (US\$32.90) for a woman's long-sleeved variety. **Sheepskins,** which can be used as rugs or wall hangings, are every traveler's favorite thing to buy in New Zealand, and they're a real bargain here too; you can get one for about NZ\$90 (US\$62.95).

If you're going on to Australia after leaving New Zealand, buy your sheepskin here—they're much less expensive. Sheepskin car seat covers are also popular purchases, as are sheepskin-lined apres ski footwear.

On the West Coast and in other parts of the country you'll have several opportunities to watch **greenstone** carvers at work. The early Maori made war clubs, pendants, and adzes from this indigenous nephrite jade. Today much of the jewelry reflects the Maori influence. Deposits of jade are mined in New Zealand on the West Coast of the South Island. The greatest number of greenstone factories are in Hokitika, but you can buy the jewelry and other items at stores through-out the country. Nephrite jade doesn't have high inherent value; the value's in the artistry. You'll also see jewelry made from **carved bone** and *paua* (abalone) shell.

When you're looking for gifts and mementos, don't overlook grocery store items. Tea, kiwifruit jam, and local honey will all be appreciated. If you buy souvenir videos, remember that the U.S., Canada, and Japan use the NTSC system and New Zealand, Australia, Europe, and the UK use the PAL system.

8 Health & Insurance

BEFORE YOU GO

HEALTH PRECAUTIONS   If you take any form of medication, it's a good idea to bring along prescriptions (written in the generic form, not the brand name) from your doctor in case you need refills. This also applies to prescriptions for eyeglasses or contact lenses.

INSURANCE   Check to be sure your property insurance is in good order, meaning make sure your premium payments are up-to-date and that you have full coverage for fire, theft, and so on (this policy may cover a lost camera or the like down under). You should also find out whether your health insurance policy covers you when you're out of the country. If it doesn't, check with your insurance carrier about temporary medical coverage for the duration of your trip. Most travel agents can arrange this, along with travel-delay or cancellation and lost-luggage insurance.

IN NEW ZEALAND

STAYING HEALTHY   Medical facilities here are excellent and health care is top-notch. The ailments that frequently plague visitors in New Zealand are **sunburn** and

Start Packing: What to Bring & What to Wear

First things first: No matter when you plan to go or what you plan to do, dress in New Zealand is, for the most part, informal.

When you visit will, of course, play a big part in your packing decisions—remember that the seasons correspond with the Southern Hemisphere. There are, however, few temperature extremes—either in the subtropical tip of the North Island or in the cooler South Island. Auckland, for example, has an average midsummer maximum temperature of 73°F, with a midwinter average high of 56°F. Queenstown's summer average maximum is 72°F, with a winter high of 50°F. Generally, you can look for mild days in the Bay of Islands, and cool to cold days down in the Southern Alps. The best way to dress in New Zealand is to do what the locals do: Dress in layers!

One item I wouldn't be without during a winter visit is my **spencer**—a lightweight lambswool undershirt I bought on one of my first trips to New Zealand. I'd suggest that after arrival you buy one in the lingerie section of a department store (such as Ballantynes in Christchurch, where I got mine) or in a specialty store (such as the Woolshed in Taupo).

What you plan to do will also determine what you bring. New Zealand offers some of the best tramping in the world, so if that's your kind of thing, bring suitable clothing: a sturdy pair of hiking boots, a backpack, and a water bottle. If most of your tramping will be with an organized trek on the glaciers, you won't need boots and a heavy coat —both will be provided by your guide.

Now here's a bit of advice about space. I've often returned from New Zealand with an overstuffed suitcase that was nice and light when I left: I doubt you're going to be able to resist buying those terrific natural-wool sweaters (especially the handknits), so I'd suggest leaving all your sweaters at home and picking up one or two in New Zealand to wear during your trip. In warm weather, men will, no doubt, be tempted to adopt the universal Kiwi male dress of walking shorts, high socks, and a short-sleeve shirt—all of which you can pick up after arrival. You'll find yourself wearing some of your nicest souvenirs before you even leave the country.

Here are a few other essentials for any trip to New Zealand: a washcloth in a plastic bag since they're seldom furnished in New Zealand motels; dual-voltage appliances (such as a hair dryer); adapter plugs for New Zealand's three-pronged outlets; insect repellent; prescriptions for your medications (in generic, not brand-name, form) or glasses or contact lenses; a small calculator or currency converter; a flashlight if you'll be driving after dark; cassette tapes if you'll be driving a lot; a camera and more film than you think you'll need.

Sports enthusiasts may want to bring favorite fishing rods, golf clubs, or skis, all of which are allowed through Customs; however, these are readily available for rent in New Zealand if you don't feel like lugging that sort of stuff along. Many fishing guides furnish equipment, and you can rent clubs at most golf courses. If you're staying in hostels, you might bring along a sleeping bag or sheets and a pillowcase; blankets and linens can be rented, though.

sandfly bites, both of which are preventable. Standard bug repellent works against sandflies. It's also important to stay covered up when they're around. These pesky bugs are prevalent in coastal areas throughout the year, as well as along river banks and lake fronts. Basically, the closer you get to the water, the more sandflies you'll encounter.

9 Tips for Travelers with Special Needs

FOR TRAVELERS WITH DISABILITIES

New Zealand is a good destination for disabled travelers. Its cities are easy to explore on wheelchair, and public transportation is equipped to carry disabled passengers; plus, it's possible for disabled travelers to participate in many outdoor activities. Recognizing that wheelchair travelers, as well as their companions, are all too often excluded from older motels and B&Bs because of narrow doors, steps, and inaccessible bathrooms, New Zealand's accommodations industry has encouraged new designs. Since 1975 every new public building and every major reconstruction in the country has been required to provide reasonable and adequate access for the disabled. Accommodations with five or more units must provide one or more accessible facilities.

Driving in New Zealand is possible for the physically handicapped traveler since **Budget Rent a Car** offers vehicles especially adapted to meet the needs of disabled drivers. You can get advance information through the **New Zealand Tourism Board,** 501 Santa Monica Blvd., Suite 300, Santa Monica, CA 90401 (☎ **800/388-5494,** or 310/395-7480 in the U.S.), or at the other locations listed in "Visitor Information" at the beginning of this chapter.

General information and news for disabled travelers are also available from the **Travel Industry and Disabled Exchange (TIDE),** 5435 Donna Ave., Tarzana, CA 91356 (☎ **818/343-6339).** You can also contact **Nautilus Tours,** operators of tours for the disabled, at this address and phone number. The **New Zealand Disability Resource Centre,** 840 Tremaine Ave., Palmerston North, New Zealand (☎ **06/356-2311,** fax 06/355-5459) can also provide visitor information.

FOR GAY & LESBIAN TRAVELERS

New Zealanders aren't homophobic the way many Americans are. They tend to have more of a live-and-let-live attitude. Most of country's gay and lesbian scene, however, is centered around Auckland and Wellington. The two largest gay festivals on New Zealand's calendar occur in late February and early March every year: Auckland's **Hero Party and Street Parade** and Wellington's **Devotion Festival.** Both are pride celebrations and last about 2 weeks, during which there are film, theater, cabaret, dance, and sporting events culminating with a street parade and all-night dance party (the party and parade are on the last day). The Devotion Festival follows the Auckland event. (These are timed to precede the huge Gay and Lesbian Mardi Gras in Sydney, Australia.)

You can get up-to-date information on the festivals, as well as social clubs, tours, and accommodations for gay and lesbian travelers, from the Web site, **Travel Gay New Zealand,** at nz.com/webnz/tpac/gaynz.

The **International Gay Travel Association (IGTA),** P.O. Box 4974, Key West, FL 33041 (☎ **800/448-8550** for voice mail, or 305/292-0217), is an international network of travel-industry businesses and professionals who encourage gay and lesbian travel. Membership costs US$125 a year, plus a one-time fee of US$100. Check out the IGTA Web site at **www.rainbow-mall.com.**

Manuka Honey: An Affordable & Delectable Souvenir

Sometimes its not *what* you buy, but *where* you buy it that makes a difference. I became interested in manuka honey (made from pollen gathered from manuka trees—the same plant that produces tea tree oil) during my last trip to New Zealand. It's one of nature's medicinal miracles and can be used for a multitude of purposes (sort of a New Zealand aloe). It's even been proven to have antibiotic properties— you can put it in tea or eat it off a spoon for a sore throat, put it on cuts, scrapes, and abrasions to help healing, and rub it into your skin to improve elasticity. Many older people buy it in the biggest tubs available and rub it into their skin on a regular basis; consequently, they have the softest skin I've ever felt. Jars of honey are available at specialty and gift shops all over New Zealand, but I also found it in Woolworth's and other supermarkets in similar packaging at a fraction of the cost.

For comparison's sake I've listed the prices I found in March of 1997 for a 500g jar of manuka honey:

Woolworth's (Taupo)	NZ$4.62
Woodcraft (Taupo)	NZ$5.65
NZ Corner (Taupo)	NZ$6.95
The Honey Hive (Taupo)	NZ$7.50
Alpine Guides Shop (Fox Glacier)	NZ$8.20

A word of caution: Honey cannot be taken into Australia, so if that's your next stop, I'd ship the honey home.

Above & Beyond Tours (☎ 800/397-2681) specializes in planning trips to New Zealand and Australia for gay and lesbian travelers.

FOR SENIORS

Accommodations discounts for those over 60 are becoming more and more frequent in New Zealand. You're much more likely to get a deal if you make the booking yourself, not through an agent.

Some sightseeing attractions offer senior-citizen prices—so, again, inquire when you pay your admission fee and make sure you have some form of photo identification. Anyone over age 60 is entitled to a 30% discount on Inter-City and Mount Cook coaches and Tranz Scenic trains. Newmans Coaches gives a 30% discount to those over age 50. Members of the **American Association of Retired Persons (AARP)** (☎ 202/434-2277) are eligible for discounts on some car rentals and hotels.

FOR SOLO TRAVELERS

Much of my traveling in New Zealand has been done alone, and I can tell you from firsthand experience that this is a great place to do it. Everyone is very friendly, and B&B hosts go out of their way to make you feel at home. You may end up spending a day sightseeing with someone you met at your B&B or hostel, an especially good place to meet other solo travelers. Of course, you won't want to take off on a long trek in the mountains by yourself or wander around city streets late at night— New Zealand still enjoys a relatively low rate of violent crime, but you shouldn't push your luck.

Some bed-and-breakfast accommodations charge significantly less for one person than for two. We only list room rates for double rooms throughout this book, so single travelers should inquire about singles rates at individual lodgings.

FOR FAMILIES

Go ahead, bring the kids! New Zealand is great destination for a memorable family vacation. Even in these changing times, the family unit is still very much the core of Kiwi life, and visiting families are welcomed with open arms. And, unlike many other cultures, New Zealanders don't frown on children in restaurants. Families are welcome in all motels, on farmstays, and in hostels. But, do keep in mind that many of the better B&Bs do not accept children because they're located in homes full of priceless antiques and they're trying to sell a quiet, adult ambience.

You'll have no trouble keeping the kids amused. There are plenty of beaches, and New Zealand's adventures—kayaking, sailing, hiking, skiing, swimming with dolphins, whale watching—are all family-friendly activities. Older children can also experience the thrills of rafting, jetboating, and bungy jumping (with parental approval). And the good news is that virtually every sightseeing attraction in New Zealand admits children at half price, and many have family prices as well. When it's time for an adults-only evening, most B&Bs, motels, and hotels can arrange for a baby-sitter.

An increasingly popular way for families to experience New Zealand is the farmstay—children and parents alike enjoy walking the fields with the farmer and, more often than not, lend a helping hand with the farm chores. For the city-bred, that's a real treat. See "Finding an Affordable Place to Stay," above, for information on staying at a farmhouse.

Bringing an entire family to New Zealand can be a costly affair, but there are ways to cut corners. Motel units usually come complete with kitchen facilities, and preparing your own meals comes in handy when there are multiple mouths to feed. If the thought of cooking and washing up isn't appealing, think again. Shopping for groceries in New Zealand—be it in small neighborhood "dairies" or supermarkets much like those at home—is actually fun. You'll see many familiar products, plus a host of unfamiliar brands, plus fresh meats, fruits, and vegetables.

You might also consider using New Zealand's excellent YHA hostel accommodations. There's no additional membership requirement for children under 18 traveling with adult family members. Since not all hostels have suitable rooms—and since those that do, have them in limited numbers—you should write for their handbook (see "For Students," below) and book as far in advance as possible.

FOR STUDENTS

Students should know about **S.T.A. Travel** (also known as the Student Travel Network), with its U.S. West Coast headquarters at 7202 Melrose Ave., Los Angeles, CA 90046 (☎ **800/777-0112** in the most of the U.S., 213/934-8722 in California, or 212/627-3111 in New York; 0171/361-6123 in London; 604/681-9136 in Vancouver; 03/9349-2411 in Melbourne). It offers discounted international airfares on the major carriers for students under 26. These favorable rates sometimes extend to recent graduates or faculty members. The New Zealand headquarters is at 10 High St., Auckland (☎ **09/309-0458**). You can also check out their Web site at **www.sta-travel.com**.

If you're planning on staying in cheap digs throughout the country, join **Hostelling International–American Youth Hostels (HI-AYH),** 733 15th St. NW, Suite 840, Washington, DC 20005 (☎ **202/783-6161,** fax 202/783-6171, e-mail hiayhserv@hiayh.org). HI-AYH membership cards give you access to 55 HI–New Zealand hostels, plus many travel and sightseeing discounts. Membership costs US$10 for students ages 17 or younger, US$25 for those 18 to 54, and US$15 for ages 55 and older; you can purchase one by telephone with a Visa or MasterCard.

Should you arrive in New Zealand without a membership card, you may obtain an **International Guest Card** costing NZ$4 (US$2.80) per night or NZ$24 (US$16.80) for your entire stay. International Guest Cards can be obtained at HI–New Zealand hostels or YHA Travel in Auckland (51 High St.), Wellington (corner of Cambridge Terrace and Wakefield Street), and Christchurch (173 Gloucester Street, at the corner of Manchester). For more information, contact **YHA New Zealand,** P.O. Box 436, Christchurch (☎ **03/379-9970,** fax 03/365-4476, e-mail yhagenq@yha.org.nz).

YHA members can buy travel insurance at discounted rates in New Zealand, and they receive discounts on domestic flights offered by Air New Zealand and Ansett New Zealand; InterCity, Mount Cook, and Newmans coachlines, as well as Tranz Scenic trains are also discounted for YHA members. For details, contact YHA New Zealand at the address above.

One of the leading tour operators for students and others ages 18 to 35 is **Contiki Holidays,** 300 Plaza Alicante, Suite 900, Garden Grove, CA 92640 (☎ **800/266-8454** in the U.S., fax 714/740-0818, e-mail ContikiUSA@aol.com). For details, see "Getting There Without Going Broke," below.

Another good travel agency for the 18-to-35 crowd is **Council Travel,** also known as Council on International Education Exchange, which has offices in most U.S. Cities and on many college campuses. (Head office: 205 E. 42nd St., New York, NY 10017; ☎ **212/822-2600**). Look in your local phone book or call ☎ **800/226-8624** or 888-COUNCIL in the U.S. They specialize in budget airfares, Hostelling International cards, work abroad and language programs, and dollarwise rail and bus passes. They can also supply you with an **International Student Identity Card,** which will get you discounts on airfares, bus tickets, car rentals, and admission to attractions. You must, however, arm yourself with this valuable document before you leave home. There are too many discounts to list here, but all are included on Council Travel's Web site at **www.ciee.org**. The cost is US$19 and you can obtain the card from any of the 47 Council travel offices or one of the 550 college campuses that issue cards across the United States. There's also a Teacher Identity Card.

10 Getting There Without Going Broke

In this section I'll be dealing with the single largest item in any budget for New Zealand travel—the cost of getting there. While not nearly as costly as it once was, transportation across the South Pacific is the first financial hurdle in your planning. Once you arrive, you'll have a number of options as to how much or how little to spend on transportation around New Zealand.

BY PLANE

You *could* go by ship, of course—one of the luxury liners that sail maybe twice a year, or a freighter making stops all across the Pacific—but for most of us the only practical way to go is by air.

You're going to have to do some heavy-duty pretrip research on airfares to New Zealand. Fares vary seasonally and different airlines have different types of fares. Your first task should be to study the fare options, decide which one best suits your needs, then either phone the airlines directly, call one of the air consolidators listed below, or visit a qualified travel agent.

THE AIRLINES

Qantas Airways, Air New Zealand, and United Airlines provide service to New Zealand from the United States. Qantas, Air New Zealand, Canadian International

Airlines, and Air Pacific bring visitors from Canada. Qantas, Air New Zealand, and British Airways provide transportation from the U.K. and Europe.

Of these, I prefer to fly **Qantas** because of its unblemished safety record. The airline has twice been awarded the Cumberbatch Trophy for "outstanding contributions to air safety." The wonderful in-flight service is another reason to pick Australia's favorite carrier. Where else do coach-class passengers enjoy free cocktails, free headsets, free wine or beer with dinner, and receive amenity kits that contain toiletries and slipper socks? They even distribute printed menus, a courtesy other airlines reserve for business class and above. I also love their ergometrically designed seats, which are the most comfortable in the industry. Plus, by flying Qantas I earn American Airlines frequent-flyer mileage credit. Qantas' other mileage partners are Alaska Airlines, British Airways, Continental Airlines, and US Airways. Check out Qantas's Web site at **http://www.qantas.com.au**.

These are the principal airlines offering service to New Zealand:

- **Air New Zealand:** (☎ **800/262-1234** in the U.S. and Canada, Web site: **www.airnz.com**)
- **Air Pacific:** (☎ **800/227-4446** in Canada)
- **British Airways:** (☎ **800/247-9297** in the U.S. and Canada)
- **Canadian Airlines International:** (☎ **800/426-7000** in the U.S., **800/ 665-1177** in Canada)
- **Qantas:** (☎ **800/227-4500** in the U.S. and Canada, Web site at **www.qantas.com.au**)
- **United Airlines:** (☎ **800/241-6522** in the U.S. and Canada)

FINDING A GOOD AIRFARE

Below I've listed a number of ways to find affordable flights to and from New Zealand. Remember, the sample fares that I've quoted here are not set in stone—these figures can change in a matter of days as airlines rush to introduce new and more competitive prices. Use the following as a guide, then shop around carefully.

Note: When you leave New Zealand, you'll have to pay a departure tax of NZ$20 (US$14) from Auckland; NZ$25 (US$17.50) from Christchurch.

SEASONAL SAVINGS   When you travel can have a real impact on your airline costs. Low season runs from April through August; shoulder season includes March and September through November; and peak season is December through February, when fares are sky-high.

FOR FREQUENT FLYERS   Don't overlook the possibility of getting a free ticket through your frequent-flyer or mileage club. Domestic carriers have partner airlines that fly to New Zealand: For instance, American Airlines is partners with Qantas. Members of American's AAdvantage Program accrue AA frequent-flyer miles not only every time they fly that airline but also every time they use their American Airlines/ Citibank credit card (1 mile for each dollar spent). Mileage credits can be used to fly to New Zealand on Qantas.

AIR CONSOLIDATORS   One way to get a cheap ticket to New Zealand is to go through a wholesaler that buys up quantities of seats from the airlines and sells them to consumers at discounted prices. One of the best of these is ✪ **Airmakers** (☎ **800/ 248-8593** in the U.S.). Another possibility is **Discover Wholesale Travel, Inc.** (☎ **800/576-7770** in California, 800/759-7330 elsewhere in the U.S., fax 714/ 833-1176). Another company is **Pacific Destination Center** (☎ **800/227-5317** in the U.S., or 714/960-4011). Check with each to see what they're offering when you want to go.

STOPOVERS   As I've said previously, getting to New Zealand can hardly be called cheap. However, if you choose one of the fare classifications that permit en-route stopovers, you'll be purchasing transportation to multiple destinations for the same fare you would pay to get to New Zealand only.

PROMOTIONAL & APEX FARES   Every airline comes up with annual special bargain fares for limited time periods. Savings can be considerable, although many times there are restrictions you must meet to qualify for the fare. Before you make reservations be sure to check for any of these fares.

At the present time, Qantas' least expensive ticket from Los Angeles to Auckland is the **Super Apex,** which costs US$925 round trip. To get this, you have to purchase your ticket 21 days ahead, fly on a Wednesday during the low season (see "Seasonal Savings," above), and stay no less than 7 days and no more than a month. If you travel during low season, but not on Wednesday, the fare is US$987. In shoulder season the Super Apex costs US$1131 on Wednesday and US$1182 on other days. In peak season, the Super Apex costs US$1337 on Wednesday or US$1388 otherwise. This is a nonchangeable ticket and a 50% cancellation penalty applies. No stopovers are permitted. If you want to stay more than 1 month, you could use a **Custom Apex** ticket, which requires a 14-day advance purchase and a stay of 7 days to 3 months. This costs US$1054 on Wednesday in low season, US$1115 the rest of the week; US$1260 or US$1311 in shoulder season; or US$1466 or US$1517 in peak season. One free stopover is permitted and a 35% cancellation penalty applies. It costs US$75 to change the ticket within 14 days of departure. For an additional amount, the Custom Apex can permit a stay of up to 6 months. The **Excursion Fare** permits stays of up to 1 year and costs US$1708 in low season, US$1914 in the shoulder season, and US$2120 in the peak season.

PACKAGE DEALS   There are several excellent package plans on the market that offer good value to the budget traveler. In addition to air travel, they include transportation, lodging, and some sightseeing discounts. (See also the dollarwise adventure packages described in chapter 4.)

One of the best **fly/drive** deals is offered by ✪ **Sunmakers Travel Group,** 100 W. Harrison, South Tower #350, Seattle, WA 98119-4123 (☎ **800/841-4321** in the U.S., or 206/216-2900). Their package includes round-trip airfare and 7 days Thrifty car rental, plus car insurance for little more than the cost of an airline ticket. Sunmakers also offers a **Basic New Zealand Package** that includes airfare, a 6-night hotel pass, and 7 days car rental at an incredibly low price. Call them for details.

Qantas Vacations USA, 300 Continental Blvd., Suite 610, El Segundo, CA 90245 (☎ **800/641-8772** in the U.S., or 310/322-6359 , fax 310/535-1057), and **Qantas Vacations Canada,** 5353 Dundas Street West, Suite 505, Etobicoke, Ontario M9B 6K5 (☎ or **800/268-7525** in Canada, fax 416/234-8569), offers good deals, too.

Mount Cook Tours, 1960 Grand Ave., Suite 910, El Segundo, CA 90245-5038 (☎ **800/468-2665**) offers both escorted package tours and self-drive vacation packages.

For those in the 18-to-35 bracket, **Contiki Holidays,** 300 Plaza Alicante, Suite 900, Garden Grove, CA 92840 (☎ **800/266-8454** in the U.S., fax 714/740-0818, e-mail ContikiUSA@aol.com), offers great New Zealand holidays. You'll travel with a group on these trips, but they're not like the typical group tours—schedules allow for ample free time. Transportation and accommodations are perfectly adequate, and activities include beachside barbecues, whitewater rafting, and ballooning. In short, these are fun tours that appeal to young, lively travelers.

BY SHIP

While cruise ships aren't a budget mode of transportation, there is the possibility of traveling on a freighter that takes paying passengers. A company called **TravLtips,** Box 580188, Flushing, NY 11358 (☎ **800/872-8584**) specializes in freighter travel. They publish a magazine devoted to the subject; subscriptions cost US$20 per year.

11 Getting Around Affordably

Now comes one of the most important decisions you'll have to make concerning your trip to New Zealand. Will you drive from point to point? Take the train? Or utilize one of the coach (bus) companies that provide service on both major and minor routes within the country? Consider your options carefully. I've done the homework for you below.

BY PLANE

There are basically two players in the domestic air travel game in New Zealand. **Air New Zealand** operates National and Link service, as well as Mount Cook Airline. **Ansett New Zealand** is the other major airline, although several other small airlines fly internal routes. Schedules are frequent and convenient, and the equipment is modern and comfortable. All domestic flights are nonsmoking.

DISCOUNT FARES WITHIN NEW ZEALAND

Both airlines mentioned below give significant discounts to holders of **VIP** (backpackers) cards and **YHA** members.

AIR NEW ZEALAND For those whose time is limited (or those who simply want to vary their modes of travel), the **Explore New Zealand Airpass** offered by Air New Zealand (☎ **800/262-1234** in the U.S.) is a good deal. You purchase three to eight flight coupons for a set price. For NZ$495 (US$346.50) you purchase three coupons good for any three of their 460 daily flights; six coupons cost NZ$990 (US$693). Fares for children 2 to 14 are two thirds of the adult fare. These coupons (good for 60 days from the date of your first flight and accepted on all Air New Zealand National, Link, and Mount Cook Airline services) *must be purchased before you reach New Zealand* and be bought in conjunction with international travel. You don't have to reserve individual flights, however, until you actually reach New Zealand, and unused coupons may be turned in for a refund before you leave for home.

ANSETT NEW ZEALAND The other alternative is to take advantage of the deals offered by **Ansett New Zealand** (☎ **800/366-1300** in the U.S. and Canada). These include the **New Zealand Airpass,** which is priced similarly to Air New Zealand's Explore New Zealand Airpass above; the **Scenic Standby Airpass,** which allows unlimited travel on a standby basis; and the **Student/Backpacker Budget Airpass** for those carrying an International Student Identity Card, a YHA membership card, or a Backpackers International card.

BY COACH (BUS)

For the budget traveler, coaches (buses) offer a comfortable and cost-effective way of getting around New Zealand. Consider the following: You get to rub elbows with New Zealanders; on many of the coaches, drivers give an excellent commentary on the countryside; and you don't need to worry about driving on the left, reading maps, or getting lost. Smoking is not permitted on these coaches and there are frequent stops for tea and refreshments en route.

DEALS ON COACH FARES

The three major coach companies in New Zealand are **InterCity, Mount Cook Landline,** and **Newmans,** all of which offer point-to-point tickets and discount passes.

You should know that **all coach and rail journeys must be booked in advance during peak travel periods (summer and holidays).** Outside of these months, reservations are not usually necessary, but it's better to book ahead if you can—especially if there's just one bus a day to your destination.

NEWMANS COACH LINES   With an extensive service network on the North Island only, **Newmans Coach Lines** (☎ 09/309-9738 in Auckland) offers a 30% discount to holders of YHA cards, New Zealand Backpackers Passes, and the Independent Traveller Discount Cards. A 30% discount is also given to anyone over 50, and a 30% discount is offered to valid full-time students (or anyone with an International Student Identity Card). However, their best deal is the **Auckland/ Wellington Stopover Pass.** For just NZ$95 (US$66.50) passholders can travel any route between these two cities (without backtracking) over a 14-day period. The pass is also good on the Waitomo Wanderer Bus Service.

INTERCITY   Probably the most popular bus company, **InterCity** (☎ 09/357-8400 in Auckland) gives a 20% discount to students and a 30% discount to anyone over 60, YHA members, and VIP (backpackers) card holders. They offer a number of regional passes. For instance, the **West Coast Passport** costs NZ$114 (US$79.80) and is good for 3 months on the route from Nelson to Queenstown. The **North Island Value Pass** is also good for 3 months and costs NZ$95 (US$66.50). InterCity coaches are also included in the **Travelpass.**

MOUNT COOK LANDLINE   Mount Cook (☎ 0800/800-287 in New Zealand, or 800/468-2665 in the U.S.) gives a 30% discount to all the cardholders mentioned above and anyone over age 60. Mount Cook operates on both islands, but service is more extensive on the South Island.

Mount Cook's New Zealand Explorer Coach Pass

Travel Days	Duration of Pass	NZ$	US$
7 days	30-day	NZ$335	US$234.50
10 days	60-day	NZ$400	US$280.00
15 days	60-day	NZ$464	US$324.80
25 days	90-day	NZ$544	US$380.80
33 days	90-day	NZ$699	US$489.30

Also included with this pass is a one-way air sector or return ferry trip across Cook Strait. Children are charged half price.

THE TRAVELPASS   **InterCity Coachlines,** in partnership with **Tranz Scenic** passenger trains and **The Interislander** ferries, offers two good-value passes:

The **3 in 1 Travelpass** provides unlimited rail, coach, and ferry travel.

Travel Days	Duration of Pass	NZ$	US$
5 days	10 days	NZ$350	US$245
8 days	3 weeks	NZ$470	US$329
15 days	5 weeks	NZ$590	US$413
22 days	8 weeks	NZ$690	US$422.50

The **4 in 1 Travelpass,** which includes an Ansett New Zealand flight.

Travel Days	Duration of Pass	NZ$	US$
5 days	10 days	NZ$580	US$406
8 days	3 weeks	NZ$700	US$490
15 days	5 weeks	NZ$820	US$574
22 days	8 weeks	NZ$920	US$644

For a small surcharge, passholders can also use the Lynx Cook Strait ferries. Children ages 5 to 15 are charged two thirds of the cost of an adult pass. Additional flight sectors for adults can be purchased for NZ$230 (US$161) each; for children for NZ$155 (US$108.50). For more information call **Travelpass New Zealand** (☎ 09/ 357-8455,** fax 09/366-4406).

ALTERNATIVE BUSES AND SHUTTLES

For young adventurous types who want more than just transportation between cities and towns, **Kiwi Experience** (☎ 09/366-1665) and the **Magic Travellers Network** (☎ 09/358-5600) provide a cross between a standard coach and a tour. Popular with backpackers, they travel over a half dozen preset routes, and passengers can get off whenever they like and pick up the next coach, days or even weeks later. The coaches stop at scenic spots along the way for bush walking, swimming, and sometimes even a barbecue. Prices vary according to the route, but typically cost NZ$370 to NZ$480 (US$259 to US$336) to cover both islands in no less than 11 to 15 days, or as little as NZ$130 (US$91) for a short Auckland–Taupo return loop. Passes are valid for 6 months.

Another alternative for getting around is offered by numerous private companies that run minibus shuttles between cities. Some of these are listed in the regional chapters of this book. You can also find them in the Yellow Pages or through visitor information centers.

BY TRAIN

Tranz Scenic (☎ 0800/802-802 in New Zealand) operates eight long-distance train services in New Zealand. This is a fun way to get around, especially if you switch it up with some other form of transportation. New Zealand's trains are quite comfortable, and they run along coastlines and mountain gorges with fantastic views, which are sometimes hidden from highways that run farther inland or on higher ground.

Below are the major rail services in New Zealand and their fares:

AUCKLAND–WELLINGTON The *Northerner,* a night train, has reclining airline-style seating, plus a licensed buffet car where drinks and food are served. The one-way fare is NZ$109 (US$76.30).

The day trip is via the *Overlander,* and you'll hear an informative commentary as you pass through fern forests, sacred Maori burial grounds, and volcanic peaks. Free morning and afternoon tea is served by hostesses and stewards, who also provide newspapers and magazines and will take orders for drinks to be served at your seat. The one-way fare is NZ$129 (US$90.30).

AUCKLAND–TAURANGA The *Kaimai Express* makes this trip for NZ$49 (US$34.30) via the scenic Waikato region.

AUCKLAND–ROTORUA The *Geyserland* carries passengers from the big city to the heart of Maori culture and thermal activity. The train leaves Auckland at 8:20am and arrives in Rotorua at 12:25pm. The fare is NZ$59 (US$41.30).

CHRISTCHURCH–PICTON   If you take the ferry across Cook Strait, you can catch the *Coastal Pacific* to Christchurch. The train departs Picton at 1:40pm and arrives in Christchurch at 7pm. The fare is NZ$65 (US$45.50). Book a "throughfare" (ferry/train) ticket for the best deal.

CHRISTCHURCH–DUNEDIN–INVERCARGILL   The *Southerner* makes this run, one train in each direction. A buffet car serves drinks and food. You're given an illustrated map of the route, which passes some spectacular coastal scenery as well as pastoral scenes of grazing sheep and wheat fields. The one-way fare is NZ$107 (US$74.90).

CHRISTCHURCH–GREYMOUTH   The *TranzAlpine,* New Zealand's most popular train, travels between Christchurch and Greymouth via the beautiful scenery of Arthur's Pass National Park. The train departs Christchurch at 9am and arrives in Greymouth at 1:25pm. The one-way fare is NZ$74 (US$51.80); there are also day excursions. See chapter 15.

The trains described above are all quite modern. They're carpeted, attractive, and well heated, air-conditioned, and ventilated.

Tranz Scenic offers the following discounts: 20% for students, 30% for YHA and Backpacker cardholders and Golden Age (over 55). They also offer a limited number of Saver Fares and Super Saver fares, which are 30 to 50% less for travel at off-peak times (outside of school holidays and summer season).

BY CAR

New Zealand is a driver's paradise. You can wander at will over roads that (outside the larger cities) carry light traffic. Better yet, you can stop to take a closer look at an inviting seascape or lush fern forest. When lunchtime arrives, you can picnic at a scenic overlook.

New Zealand roads are exceptionally well maintained, except for a few mountainous stretches on the South Island, and I'll tell you where they are in the regional chapters of this book. Renting a car might sound expensive to some budget travelers, but it can save you a lot of money in the long run because you'll avoid paying per-person fares for day trips by coach or rail, which can really add up.

FINDING A REASONABLE RENTAL RATE

Of course, the big multinational car-rental companies are everywhere in New Zealand, but I've searched out some smaller firms with lower prices and more personal service.

One of the best bargains I've been able to unearth is through **Maui Rentals** (☎ **800/351-2323** in the U.S.), which provides the latest-model cars—all under 8 months old—at low daily rates ranging from NZ$35 to NZ$117 (US$24.50 to US$81.90), depending on the size car you rent (from 2- to 10-passenger vehicles) and the time of the year you're traveling. That price includes unlimited mileage, but insurance is about NZ$15 (US$10.50) extra per day. Because Maui has offices in Auckland and Christchurch, they don't charge extra if you pick up your car on one island and drop it off on the other. They also have terrific rates for campervans (more about that later). To book, call the number above or contact them directly at **Maui Rentals,** 36 Richard Pearse Dr., Mangere, Auckland (☎ **09/275-3013;** fax 09/275-9690); or 530–544 Memorial Ave., Christchurch (☎ **0800/651-080** in New Zealand, or 03/358-4159; e-mail nzinfo@maui-rentals.com). Both locations are open daily from 7am to 6pm and provide courtesy airport shuttle service. Check out their Web site at **www.maui-rentals.com**., e-mail zinfo@maui-rentals.com.

The Automobile Association

"We came to the conclusion that we could get better rental-car deals by waiting until we were there and not trying to make arrangements from the States. Of course, we were not traveling in high season either. . . . We found the AA in New Zealand was exceptional in giving us timely and plentiful information that helped make our trip very enjoyable."

—W. Svirsky, Longwood, Fla., USA.

"We rented a car through the AA in Auckland. Don't forget your American AAA card as I did! The lady at the Auckland AA found us a rental for NZ$70 a day; if I had had my AAA card, it would have been NZ$35 to NZ$40, she said."

—V. Wright, Gig Harbor, Wash., USA.

Recently, I had a really good experience with **Avon/Percy Rent A Car,** 166 St. Asaph St., Christchurch (☎ **0800/7368-2866** (RENT AVON) in New Zealand, or 03/379-3822; fax 03/365-5651). I contacted them after reader Diane Morand wrote a glowing report, and I have to agree they certainly were helpful. Avon has offices throughout New Zealand, and they don't add a surcharge for one-way hires. Because they don't have counters at airports, they'll meet your flight—a nice touch. Rates range from NZ$58 to NZ$88 (US$40.60 to US$61.60) a day depending on what car you want. This includes unlimited kilometers.

Other possibilities include **Affordable Rental Cars,** 12 Kenyon Ave., Mt. Eden, Auckland (☎ **0800/454 443** in New Zealand, or 09/630-1567; fax 09/630-3692). Daily rates here range from NZ$35 to NZ$38 (US$24.50 to US$26.60) off-season (May through September) and are NZ$45 (US$31.50) the rest of the year. Minibuses cost more. These prices include GST (Goods and Services Tax), insurance, unlimited mileage, airport transfers, and maps.

Another good alternative to the higher-priced multinational companies is **Apex Car Rentals,** 160 Lichfield St., Christchurch (☎ **03/379-6897;** fax 03/379-2647; e-mail rentals@southern.co.nz; Web site www.southern.co.nz/rental), which offers late-model cars from NZ$49 (US$34.30) per day (all-inclusive).

North Harbour Rent A Car, 175 Wairau Road, Auckland (☎ **03/444-7777;** fax 03/444-7099) has new and late-model cars from NZ$33 (US$23.10) per day.

Nearly all New Zealand car-rental firms offer unlimited-mileage rates, a decided plus for budget travelers. You can also save a bundle by declining the insurance, but don't do this unless you're sure your car insurance at home covers you in New Zealand. When you're quoted a rate, always ask if GST (12^{1}/$_{2}$%) is included and if there are charges for one-way hires.

If you decide to go with one of the big guys—**Avis** (☎ **800/331-1084** in the U.S.); **Budget** (☎ **800/472-3325** in the U.S., or 800/267-8900 in Canada); **Hertz** (☎ **800/654-3001** in the U.S., or 800/263-0600 in Canada); **Thrifty** (☎ **800/367-2277** in the U.S. and Canada)—you can reserve in advance through U.S. offices. Daily costs average from about NZ$100 (US$70) for economy models up to NZ$150 (US$105) for larger models. All offer reductions for longer rental periods.

ALTERNATIVES TO RENTING A CAR

TOURIST BUY BACK If you're staying in New Zealand for an extended period of time, you may be interested in the guaranteed tourist buy-back plan offered by **North Harbour Hyundai,** 175 Wairau Rd., Takapuna (☎ **09/444-7795;** fax 09/444-7099). This car dealership on Auckland's North Shore sells used Toyotas, Nissans, Hondas, and similar cars to visitors with a written agreement to purchase the vehicle after a stipulated time period. You might, for instance, buy a 10-year-old car for NZ$5,000 (US$3,500), drive it for 3 months, and sell it back for NZ$3,000 (US$2,100). Cars come with a nationwide warranty and the owner pays insurance.

CARPOOLING   Another alternative to renting a car is getting a lift from someone who's going your way. **Travelpool (09/307-0001** in Auckland) puts people who want a ride in touch with those who have a car and vice versa. The system operates throughout the country. The person getting a ride pays a small commission and something toward gas, which works out to cost about half the price of a bus ticket.

DRIVING RULES & MAPS

You must be at least 21 to rent a car in New Zealand, and you must possess a current driver's license that you've held for at least 1 year from the United States, Australia, Canada, the United Kingdom, and a few other countries, or an International Driving Permit. You drive on the left and must—by law—buckle that seat belt when the car is moving. The speed limit on the open road is 60mph (100kmph); in congested areas, towns, and cities it's 30mph (50kmph). Drive with extreme caution when an area is signposted **LSZ** (Limited Speed Zone). Signposting, incidentally, is very good throughout the country—there's little chance of losing your way. Also, be aware that drinking-and-driving laws are strictly enforced—the fact that you're a visitor doesn't exempt you from responsibility here. And, be forewarned—New Zealanders are very aggressive drivers. Just keep your cool and you'll be fine. Fuel prices vary from area to area but are currently about NZ 89¢ (U.S. 62¢) per liter (that's about US$2.36 per gallon).

MAPS   You'll be given a set of maps when you pick up your rental car, and if you're a member of the Automobile Association in the United States, Australia, Britain, or some European countries, you'll have reciprocal privileges with the New Zealand AA, which includes their detailed maps, plus "strip maps" of your itinerary and comprehensive guidebooks of accommodations (some of which give discounts to AA members). Be sure to bring your membership card from home. One of the best maps of New Zealand is issued by the **New Zealand Automobile Association** at 99 Albert St., Auckland (☎ **09/377-4660**); 343 Lambton Quay, Wellington (☎ **04/ 473-8738**); or 210 Hereford St., Christchurch (☎ **03/379-1280**). **Wises Mapping,** 360 Dominion Rd., Mt. Eden, Auckland (☎ **09/638-7146**), also issues an excellent map, which is available at newsstands and bookshops throughout New Zealand, too.

BY TAXI

Taxi stands are located at all terminals and on major shopping streets of cites and towns. You cannot hail one on the street within a quarter mile of a stand. Taxis are on call 24 hours a day; their telephone numbers are in local directories, though there's an additional charge if you phone for one. Rates vary from place to place, but all city taxis are metered (in smaller localities there's often a local driver who'll quote a flat fee). Drivers don't expect a tip just to transport you, but if they handle a lot of luggage or perform any other special service, it's very much in order. See regional chapters for specific taxi companies to call throughout New Zealand.

BY RV OR MOTORHOME

If you want to take advantage of New Zealand's budget motor camps—or if you're simply an RVer at heart—**Maui Rentals** (☎ 800/351-2323 in the U.S.), **Mount Cook Line** (☎ 800/468-2665 in the U.S.), and **Newmans** (☎ 09/302-1582 in Auckland) offer minivans and motorhomes at seasonal prices ranging from NZ$80 to NZ$150 (US$56 to US$105) for two berths; NZ$95 to NZ$210 (US$66.50 to US$147) for a midsize vehicle; and NZ$130 to NZ$235 (US$91 to US$164.50) for larger ones. For reservations, call one of these companies; vehicles can be also be booked at local branches of these firms throughout New Zealand. See section 6, "Finding an Affordable Place to Stay," earlier in this chapter for details on what New Zealand motor camps are like.

BY INTERISLAND FERRY

Try to plan a crossing of Cook Strait on the **Wellington—Picton ferry** in at least one direction while you're in New Zealand. You'll get a look at both islands from the water, as well as the near-mystical Marlborough Sounds. The crossing is one of New Zealand's best travel experiences.

The Interislander (☎ 0800/802-802 in New Zealand, or ☎ 04/498-3000; fax 04/498-3090; fax 0800/101-525 in New Zealand) ferry operates every day year round. You can choose from four or five departure times, and the crossing takes about 3 hours. The standard fare is NZ$44 (US$30.80) for adults, half that for children 4 to 14 (kids under 4 are free). **Economy, Sailaway Saver, and Super Saver fares** offer 15% to 50% discounts, but they require an advance purchase and are frequently not available in periods of peak travel, so you would be wise to book your crossing well in advance. There are also reduced-price **Family Saver** and **Senior-Saver** (over 60) fares. If you're traveling by train or InterCity coach, ask about the cost-effective "throughfares." Bicycles can be taken on the ferry for an additional charge of NZ$12 (US$8.40). The standard rate for taking a car, minibus, or caravan with you is NZ$160 (US$112), but discounted fares are available. Campervans and motorhomes cost up to NZ$190 (US$133), and the same discounts are available if you make arrangements far enough in advance. *If you plan to transport a car by ferry, you need a confirmed reservation.* Without it, your trip could be delayed by a day or more.

You'll travel on The Interislander on either the *Arahura* or the *Aratika*, each of which has a licensed bar, cafeteria, TV lounge, information bureau, and shop. They also have a family lounge with toys to keep young children amused during the voyage; video and movie theaters; a recliner lounge; and a work room. Crossings can be a lot of fun, with passengers strolling the decks (whatever you do, don't go inside until you've witnessed Wellington's lovely harbor from the railing).

The Lynx (same telephone and fax numbers as above) is a faster Cook Strait ferry service that operates only in peak travel periods—mostly December through March. The crossing takes about 1³/₄ hours and costs NZ$59 (US$41.30) for passengers and NZ$190 (US$133) for cars. It makes three round-trips daily.

Warning: The swells in Cook's Strait can be a little unsettling on a rough day. If you're subject to a queasy stomach at sea, best pick up something from the pharmacy before embarking. *Another tip:* If you don't want to miss a minute of the beautiful scenery or the chance of seeing friendly schools of dolphins, take along a picnic lunch to eat outside under the sky.

12   Suggested Itineraries

Deciding how long to stay and where to go can be a problem, because New Zealand has so much to see and do that you'll have a hard time fitting in everything. But it is possible to plan itineraries that give you a good sampling of New Zealand life.

HIGHLIGHTS

Below is a list of places that shouldn't be missed. Keep them in mind when planning your trip to New Zealand. The "golden triangles"—the routes often followed by big tour groups—are **Auckland–Waitomo–Rotorua** on the North Island and **Christchurch–Queenstown–Mt. Cook** on the South Island. Surely you can be more creative than that.

NORTH ISLAND

Auckland gets short-shrifted by too many visitors. There are tons of fun things to do here. The **Bay of Islands** is really lovely, but I'd stay in either Russell or Kerikeri—Paihia is starting to feel too touristy. **Rotorua** is way past *starting* to feel touristy, but go there anyway because you can experience Maori culture, see lots of thermal activity, and watch a sheep show. It's a tough call to decide between **Hawkes Bay** and **Taranaki/New Plymouth,** and you probably can't do both because they're on opposite sides of the North Island. There's great walking on Mt. Egmont/Taranaki, and the rhododendron gardens in New Plymouth are beautiful in the spring. On the other hand, Hawkes Bay has wineries and gannets. **Wellington** also gets missed by way too many people, but I think the new Museum of New Zealand will draw more attention to the country's capital.

SOUTH ISLAND

I love **Christchurch,** probably because I'm somewhat of a garden junkie, and Dunedin because of its old university feel. I think **Queenstown** is overrated, overpriced, and overcrowded, but I adore the **West Coast** and the **World Heritage** area. **Nelson** is a great place for shopping for crafts and flopping on the beach, and the **Marlborough Sounds** are one of New Zealand's best-kept secrets. Notice I haven't mentioned **Milford Sound** and **Mt. Cook?** I know they're on everybody's must-see list, and they are both very beautiful, but there are so many wonderful places in this country that I prefer to skip the ones where I'll run into lots of tour buses.

ONE POSSIBILITY: THE PACIFIC COAST HIGHWAY

This isn't a real highway with a number, but rather a route devised to lead you along the coast of the North Island from Auckland to Napier in the Hawkes Bay region. Pick up a map at the visitor center in Auckland or any other visitor center along the way. The Pacific Coast Highway will lead you around the Coromandel Peninsula, the Bay of Plenty, and the East Cape, to Gisborne and then Hawkes Bay. If you follow this route, you'll see some of the country's best scenery. The map also delineates a dozen walks you can do along the way and gives information on the key points of interest.

IF YOU NEED HELP

If you really get stuck while planning your trip to New Zealand, contact **Tailored Travel,** Thorpe, RD 2, Wakefield, New Zealand (☎ **03/543-3825;** fax 03/543-3640; e-mail Tailored@Nelson.Planet.org.nz, Web site nz.com/webnz/nzct). This is a small business run by Robert and Joan Panzer. They do an especially good job for people with special needs: When we last spoke, he was creating an itinerary for a traveler who needs dialysis three times a week.

I'm also available to consult with people planning a trip or needing to know about New Zealand for other reasons. I especially enjoy creating custom itineraries for first-time travelers. Reach me by e-mail at **ehansen298.@aol.com** or by snail mail at **P.O. Box 1721, La Jolla, CA 92038,** or by fax 619/454-8868.

SUGGESTED ITINERARIES

If You Have 1 Week

Touring the North Island Only

Day 1   Arrive in Auckland in the early morning; sightsee in the afternoon.

Day 2   Do a day trip from Auckland to one of the gulf islands or out to the West Coast.

Day 3   Drive to Rotorua (356km/221 miles) via Cambridge and the Waikato. En joy the area.

Day 4   Full day of sightseeing; Maori concert or hangi in evening.

Day 5   Drive up to Whitianga on the Coromandel Peninsula via Tauranga and Mt. Maunganui. Enjoy the beach.

Day 6   Take a day to enjoy the Coromandel.

Day 7   Drive back to Auckland via Coromandel township and Thames. Stop on the Sea Bird Coast for fish and chips. Early evening departure for overseas destination.

Touring the South Island Only

Day 1   Arrive in Auckland in the early morning; fly to Christchurch; sightsee in the afternoon.

Day 2   Sightsee in Christchurch: Botanic Gardens and Antarctic Visitor Centre. Walk along (or punt) the Avon.

Day 3   Day trip to go whale watching at Kaikoura.

Day 4   Day trip to nearby Banks Peninsula; stay overnight on a sheep farm.

Day 5   Drive along the east coast from Christchurch to Dunedin (362km/225 miles about 5 hours), across part of the Canterbury Plains and through the seaside town of Timaru and the "White Stone City" of Oamaru.

Day 6   Entire day of sightseeing in Dunedin, with drive or tour-bus excursion to the Otago Peninsula to see Larnach Castle, Southlight Wildlife, and the Royal Albatross Colony.

Day 7   Sightseeing in the morning; midafternoon flight to Auckland, arriving in time for your evening overseas departure.

If you have 2 weeks

Combine these two itineraries

If you have 3 weeks

Follow the two itineraries as above and add a week of driving up the West Coast and visiting Nelson and the Marlborough Sounds.

FAST FACTS: New Zealand

American Express   The American Express Travel Service office is at 101 Queen St., Auckland (☎ **09/379-8240**). Other agencies (mostly travel-agent offices) around the country are located in Christchurch, Dunedin, Lower Hutt (near Wellington), Napier, Nelson, Queenstown, Rotorua, Wellington, and Whangarei. They accept mail for clients (you're a client if you have an American Express card or traveler's checks), forward mail for a small fee, issue and change traveler's checks, and replace lost or stolen traveler's checks and American Express cards.

Business Hours Banks in international airports are open for all incoming and outgoing flights; others are open from 9am to 4:30pm Monday through Friday. Shops are usually open from 9am (sometimes 8am) to 5:30pm Monday through Thursday, until 9pm on either Thursday or Friday. Increasingly, shops are open all day Saturday; most shops are closed Sunday.

Camera/Film Film is expensive in New Zealand, so bring as much as you can with you. You're not limited by Customs regulations, just by baggage space. Most brands are available in larger cities. There is also same-day developing service in most cities.

Cigarettes You can bring in 200 cigarettes per person, as allowed by Customs regulations. Most brands for sale in New Zealand are English or European, although more and more American brands are appearing on the market.

Climate See "When to Go," earlier in this chapter.

Crime See "Safety," below.

Currency See "Money," earlier in this chapter.

Customs See "Visitor Information & Entry Requirements," earlier in this chapter.

Driving Rules See "Getting Around," earlier in this chapter.

Drugstores Pharmacies observe regular local shop hours, but each locality usually will have an Urgent Pharmacy, which remains open until about 11pm every day except Sunday, when there will be two periods during the day when it's open.

Electricity New Zealand's voltage is 230 volts, and plugs are the three-pin type. If you bring a hair dryer, it should be a dual-voltage one, and you'll need an adapter plug. Many B&Bs and other types of lodging provide hair dryers these days. Most motels and some B&Bs have built-in wall transformers for 110-volt, two-prong razors, but if you're going to be staying in hostels, cabins, homestays, or guesthouses, better bring dual-voltage appliances.

Embassies/Consulates In Wellington, the national capital, you'll find embassies for the United States and Canada, as well as the British High Commission (see "Fast Facts: Wellington" in chapter 10). In Auckland you'll find consulates for the United States, Canada, and Ireland (see "Fast Facts: Auckland" in chapter 5).

Emergencies Dial ☎ **111** anyplace in New Zealand for the police, an ambulance, or to report a fire. Should you need a doctor, either consult the nearest visitor information office or prevail on your motel or B&B host to direct you to one. Even most small towns have medical centers.

Holidays See "When to Go," earlier in this chapter.

Information See "Visitor Information & Entry Requirements," earlier in this chapter.

Language English is spoken by all New Zealanders—Maori and Pakeha. You'll hear Maori spoken on some TV and radio programs and in some Maori settlements.

Liquor Laws The minimum drinking age is 20 in pubs, 18 in licensed restaurants or with parent or guardian. Children are allowed in pubs with their parents.

Mail   New Zealand post offices will receive mail for you and hold it for one month. Just have it addressed to you c/o *Poste Restante* at the Chief Post Office of the city or town you'll be visiting. American Express will receive and forward mail for its clients. Allow 10 days for delivery from the United States. It costs NZ$1.50 (US$1.05) to send an airmail letter to the United States or Canada and NZ$1.80 (US$1.26) to the United Kingdom or Europe. Overseas airmail postcards and aerograms cost NZ$1 (US 70¢). "Fast Post" mail within New Zealand costs NZ80¢ (US 56¢) per card or letter.

Maps   Get free maps from AA offices around the country by showing your home-country membership card. Rental-car firms furnish a map with every car rented.

Newspapers/Magazines   New Zealand has no official national newspapers, although a large percentage of Kiwis read the *New Zealand Herald,* published in Auckland. *The Dominion* (Wellington) and *The Press* (Christchurch) are also widely read.

Passports   See "Visitor Information & Entry Requirements," earlier in this chapter.

Pets   Because of its dependence on a disease-free agricultural environment, New Zealand has strict restrictions on the importation of animals. If you must bring a pet, check first with the Ministry of Agriculture and Fisheries, P.O. Box 207, Wellington, or any New Zealand embassy or consulate. And be prepared to quarantine Fido or Kitty in Hawaii for several months.

Radio/TV   The BCNZ (Broadcasting Council of New Zealand) is the major broadcaster in New Zealand, operating TV Channel 1 and TV Channel 2, and Radio New Zealand. The majority of TV productions come from Britain and America. For current scheduling, check the listings in daily newspapers. And to hear the country's beautiful national anthem, "God Defend New Zealand," sung in both English and Maori, tune in to Channel 1 at sign off time.

Rest Rooms   There are "public conveniences" strategically located and well signposted in all cities and many small towns. You'll find public rest rooms at most service stations. Local **Plunket Rooms** are a real boon to mothers traveling with small children, for they come with a "Mother's Room," where you can change diapers and do any necessary tidying up. The Plunket Society is a state-subsidized organization, which provides free baby care to all New Zealand families, and their volunteers are on duty in the Plunket Rooms—no charge, but they'll welcome a donation.

Taxes   There's a 12.5% Goods and Services Tax (GST). And be sure to save enough New Zealand currency to pay the departure tax of NZ$20 (US$13) from Auckland and NZ$25 (US$17.50) if you depart from Christchurch.

Telephone/Fax   The country code for New Zealand is **64.** When calling New Zealand from out of the country, you must first dial the country code, then the city code (for example, 03, 09, 06), but without the zero. The telephone area code in New Zealand is known as the STD (subscriber toll dialing). To call long distance within New Zealand, dial the STD—**09** for Auckland and Northland, **07** for the Thames Valley, **06** for the East Coast and Wanganui, **04** for Wellington, or **03** for the South Island—then the local number. (If you're calling from outside New Zealand, omit the "0.") For operator assistance within New Zealand, dial **010;** for directory assistance, **018.** There are three main kinds of public telephones in New Zealand: card phones, credit-card phones, and coin phones.

The most economical way to make international phone calls from New Zealand is to charge them to an international calling card (they're available free from your long-distance company at home, so get one before you go). All calls, even international ones, can be made from public phone booths (long-distance calls made from your hotel or motel often have hefty surcharges added). To reach an international operator, dial **0170;** for directory assistance for an international call, dial **0172.** You can also call home using Country Direct numbers. These are **000-911** for the U.S.; **000-944** for British Telecom (operator); **000-912** for British Telecom (automatic); **000-940** for UK Mercury; **000-919** for Canada; **000-996** Australia-Optus; **000-961** Australia-Telstra.

Local calls cost NZ20¢ (US13¢). Reader W. Svirsky of Longwood, Fla., found the use of card phones almost mandatory because in many areas the only public phones were card phones. "Fortunately," he wrote, "the magnetic-strip PhoneCards are available just about everywhere in NZ$5 (US$3.25), NZ$10 (US$6.50), NZ$20 (US$13), and NZ$50 (US$32.50) denominations. The digital readout on the phones shows the current value of the card and the decrease in value as you use the phone."

You'll find fax facilities at many hotels, motels, and B&Bs, as well as in some local post offices, Visitor Information Network offices, and photocopy centers.

Time   New Zealand is located just west of the international dateline, and its standard time is 12 hours ahead of Greenwich mean time. Thus when it's noon in New Zealand, it's 7:30am in Singapore, 9am in Tokyo, 10am in Sydney; and—all the previous day—4pm in San Francisco, 7pm in New York, and midnight in London. In New Zealand, daylight saving time starts the first weekend in October and ends in mid-March.

Tipping   Most New Zealanders don't tip wait persons unless they've received extraordinary service—and then only 5 to 10%. I suggest you follow suit. Also, I'd give taxi drivers about 10% and porters NZ$1 or $2, depending on how much luggage you have.

Tourist Offices   See "Visitor Information & Entry Requirements," earlier in this chapter.

Visas   See "Visitor Information & Entry Requirements," earlier in this chapter.

Water   In cities and towns, you can drink away—New Zealand tap water is pollution free and safe to drink anywhere you develop a thirst. In the bush, you should boil, filter, or chemically treat water from rivers and lakes to avoid contracting *giardia* (a waterborne parasite that causes diarrhea).

The Active Vacation Planner 4

When it comes to outdoor and recreational activities, it's tough to beat New Zealand. This relatively small country is clean and green and offers so many perfect places and opportunities to get outdoors, from serene sojourns in the bushland to exhilarating excursions in the mountains. So stretch your legs, take a deep breath, and experience the beautiful forests, majestic fiords, and secluded beaches. You'll be in good company, too: Kiwis consider recreation a way of life and welcome visitors to join them.

This chapter covers New Zealand's most popular active vacation choices, providing you with details on the best places to do what you want to do and the best contacts for information, equipment, guides, and supplies. Of course, it's only a sampling of what New Zealand offers. I've covered all the biggies like tramping (hiking) and skiing, but you can also enjoy more offbeat sports like paragliding, caving and cave rafting, mountain biking, mountaineering, horse trekking, rock climbing, abseiling, hunting, and just plain running. Information on these options is included in the regional chapters of this book.

For more details on active vacation experiences and how to plan them, contact the New Zealand Tourism Board nearest you (see "Visitor Information" at the beginning of chapter 3) for a copy of the 28-page **"Naturally New Zealand Holidays"** brochure. If the tourism board is out of stock, contact **Naturally New Zealand Holidays,** P.O. Box 34-703, Auckland, New Zealand 1330 (☎ **09/480-0580,** fax 09/480-0282). This booklet is an excellent catalog of low-impact adventure trips.

Another good but more expensive resource is *New Zealand Outside, The Annual & Directory* from Southern Alps Publications Ltd., P.O. Box 737, Christchurch, New Zealand (☎ **03/326-7516,** fax 03/326-7518; e-mail mary@outside.nz.com). The directory costs NZ$19.95 (US$13.95), plus NZ$15 (US$10.50) for economy postage or NZ$21 (US$14.70) for air mail.

1 Tramping (Hiking)

Call it what you will—hiking, bushwalking, trekking—tramping is one of the best and most popular ways to experience natural New Zealand. The pristine forests, clear blue lakes, sparkling rivers, and fern-filled valleys found throughout the country inspire

New Zealand's Outdoor Recreational Areas

North Island

Cape Reinga
North Cape
Mangonui
Kaitaia
Kerikeri
Bay of Islands
Poor Knight's Island
Whangarei

Pacific Ocean

Dargaville
Warkworth

Kaiparu Harbour

Great Barrier Island
Coromandel Peninsula

Hauraki Gulf

Orewa
Auckland
Whitianga
Coromandel Forest Park

Thames
Kaimaimamaki Forest Park

Bay of Plenty

Hicks Bay
East Cape
Raukumara Forest Park

Ngaruawahia
Hamilton
Tauranga
Opotiki
Ruatoria
Whakatane

Pirongia Forest Park
Rotorua

Lake Rotorua

Waitomo

Whirinaki Forest Park

Huiarau Mts.

Te Urewera National Park

Pureora Forest Park
Taupo
Gisborne

Lake Taupo

Turangi
Kaimanawa Forest Park
Wairoa

Tongariro National Park

Kaimanawa Mts.

Kaweka Forest Park

New Plymouth

Cape Egmont
Mt. Egmont 2518 m
Napier
Hawke's Bay

Egmont National Park
Whanganui National Park
Taihape
Hastings

Ruahine Forest Park

Wanganui

Palmerston North
Feilding
Woodville

Foxton
Levin

Waikanae

Tararua Mts.

Masterton
Tararua Forest Park

Lower Hutt
Wellington
Upper Hutt
Haurangi Forest Park

Cook Strait

Tasman Sea

North Island

South Island

70

Legend

- *i* Information
- 🎿 Skiing
- 🎿 Heliskiing
- 🚣 Kayaking
- 🚴 Cycling
- ⛵ Sailing
- 🎣 Fishing
- 🤿 Diving
- 🏄 Surfing

South Island

Tasman Bay

Marlborough Sounds

Abel Tasman National Park

Kahurangi National Park

Motueka

Nelson

Picton

Karamea

Blenheim

61

Westport

69

63

Nelson Lakes National Park

Kaikoura Mts.

65

Paparoa National Park

Reefton

Hanmer Forest Park

Tasman Sea

Greymouth

7

Hanmer Springs

Hokitika

1

Arthur's Pass National Park

Kaiapoi

Franz Josef Glacier

Westland National Park

Mt. Cook National Park

72

Christchurch

i Fox Glacier

Mount Cook 3754 m

Methven

75

Akaroa

6

Lake Tekapo

Ashburton

Lake Pukaki

Canterbury Bight

Haast

8

Lake Tekapo

Twizel

Timaru

Mount Aspiring National Park

Lake Wanaka

03

Pacific Ocean

Milford Sound

Wanaka

89

Oamaru

Cromwell

85

1

Doubtful Sound

Queenstown

Alexandra

Palmerston

Lake Wakatipu

Lake Te Anau

8

Garvie Mtns.

Te Anau

i

Dunedin

Fiordland National Park

Lake Manapouri

Roxburgh

94

Milton

96

Gore

1

99

Invercargill

Foveaux Strait

0   58 mi / 93 km

N

Oban

Stewart Island

Staying Safe & Healthy in the Great Outdoors

Even in relatively safe New Zealand, you need to take precautions if you're going to be spending a lot of time outdoors. While "Godzone," as the New Zealanders refer to their homeland, doesn't have snakes and other predatory animals, you could get into a scary situation if you aren't properly prepared. Here are some helpful hints to consider before heading off:

- **Emergencies**   For emergencies anywhere in the country dial ☎ **111.**
- **Weather**   Although New Zealand has a mild climate, the weather can change quickly at any time of the year, especially in the high country. Before setting off into the forests and mountains, be sure you have a good topographical map, high-energy foods, water, warm clothing, and rain gear.
- **Giardia**   In the bush you should boil, filter, or chemically treat all water from rivers and lakes to avoid contracting this waterborne parasite, which causes diarrhea.
- **Getting Lost**   Trampers must register their intended route and estimated time and date of return with the Department of Conservation (DOC) office closest to the area in which they plan to trek. This is vitally important, because if DOC doesn't know you're out there, they won't know to look for you in the event that you are lost or injured. Likewise, to avoid any unnecessary searches being launched, let the DOC know immediately when your hike is over so they don't consider you missing.
- **Sandflies**   In wetter areas, particularly in Fiordland, sandflies can be a pest, but they can be effectively controlled by use of an insect repellent. If you are bitten, a topical application of hydrocortisone ointment or tea tree oil will help relieve the itching. If the bites are really bothering you, stop in a chemist shop (drugstore) and pick up an over-the-counter antihistamine.
- **Sun**   New Zealand's clear, unpolluted atmosphere produces some pretty strong sunlight. Be prepared to wear a broad-brimmed hat, sunglasses, and lots of SPF 15+ sunscreen if you plan to be out in the sun for more than 15 to 20 minutes.

even the most dedicated couch potatoes to explore on foot. Some stroll. Others stride. It really doesn't matter. The experience—the sights, sounds and smells—is all the same.

The **Department of Conservation** maintains more than 8,000 kilometers (about 5,000 miles) of tracks (trails) in New Zealand, as well as more than 900 backcountry huts for sleeping and shelter. These are found in 13 national parks and numerous scenic reserves and are used frequently by locals—tramping has long been a favorite Kiwi pastime.

If you'd like to include some walks on your itinerary, you need to decide whether you'll do one of the country's famous multiday walks or a couple of shorter strolls, depending on your level of fitness and the amount of time you can spare. Next you need to decide whether you'll be a freedom (independent) walker or with a guide. Independent walkers can sleep in lodges or huts with bunk beds, cooking facilities, and toilets, but they must carry their own sleeping bag, food, and cooking utensils. These overnight huts are staffed, should you need any assistance or advice along the way.

In any case, remember that tramping is best in New Zealand from late November through April, when temperatures are most moderate. From May to October the trails through alpine regions are difficult—and possibly dangerous—due to snow. Be sure to check the seasonal weather information in chapter 3 before planning a hiking holiday and remember to bring comfortable shoes or boots, a day pack, a water bottle, sunglasses, a torch (flashlight), a hat, and—of course—a good map.

SHORT WALKS   Lack of time and energy don't have to keep you from enjoying a wonderful Kiwi bushwalk. Even in cities, there are scenic tracks. I'll tell you about some of them in the pages that follow (my favorites are listed in chapter 1, "The Best of New Zealand"), and visitor information offices and regional Department of Conservation offices can furnish brochures highlighting the best walks in their area. You'll also spot other places to stroll while on the highway—keep your eyes peeled for dark green signs with gold letters. They indicate Department of Conservation nature reserves. At a minimum, they're great picnic spots, and often they offer walking tracks through scenic bushland.

Just remember to wear appropriate footwear; don a hat, sunglasses, and some sunscreen; and carry a water bottle on warm days. Depending on your interests, you may also want to bring binoculars for bird watching, a sketch pad, a camera, or a journal. If you're in doubt about the difficulty of a given trail, ask a local—or be prepared to turn back if the going gets too rough. Hiking trails in New Zealand are generally very well maintained and offer frugal travelers the country's best bargain.

HIKING SAFARIS   Besides straight-up single-track hiking, New Zealand also has popularized **hiking safaris,** like those offered by **New Zealand Nature Safaris,** 52 Holborn Dr., Stokes Valley 6008, Wellington, New Zealand (☎ **04/563-7360** or 025/360-268; fax 04/563-7324; e-mail nzns@globe.co.nz; Web site www.cybermagic.co.nz/nz-safari-tours). This company runs three multiday minibus trips that incorporate hiking, camping, kayaking, swimming, and nature observation—and keep you strictly off the beaten track. The best news is that these trips are a super value: The 9-day **Northern Exposure** costs NZ$585 (US$410) per person, and the 10-day **West Coast Wilderness** and **Secret South Safari** each costs NZ$650 (US$455). Readers Tracy and Jamie Morton of Atlanta, Georgia, USA, said "Thanks for including New Zealand Nature Safaris in your guide. What a gem of a find for two folks on a conservative budget, who love the outdoors and an 'off the beaten track' adventure."

Keen walkers could also look into trips to New Zealand offered by **Country Walkers,** P.O. Box 180, Waterbury, VT 05676-0180 (☎ **800/464-9255** in the U.S.; fax 802/244-5661; e-mail ctrywalk@aol.com; Web site www.countrywalkers.com/countrywalkers/homepage.htm).

MULTIDAY WALKS   New Zealand's wonderful multiday walks are justifiably famous. The well-maintained trails provide views of incredible scenery and, because many can be done as a guided walk, they are accessible to people of all fitness levels. Everyone has their own opinion of which track is the best, but the Department of Conservation has identified eight Great Walks in New Zealand: the **Waikaremoana** and **Tongariro Crossing and Ruapehu Circuit** on the North Island; the **Abel Tasman Coast Walk** and the **Heaphy, Routeburn, Milford,** and **Kepler Tracks** on the South Island; and the **Rakiura Track** on Stewart Island. (For my personal favorites, see "The Best Multiday Treks" and "The Best Short Walks" in chapter 1.)

Certainly one of the most splendid walks is the 4-day Milford Track in Fiordland National Park, which draws trekkers from around the world, but there are those who will tell you that the Routeburn, Hollyford, Abel Tasman, or Heaphy are just as good. If you'd like to strike out on your own, contact the **Department of Conservation,** P.O. Box 10-420, Wellington, New Zealand (☎ 04/471-0726, fax 04/471-1082). They maintain visitor centers throughout the country. Freedom walkers (independent hikers) need to secure hut passes or tickets and register their hiking plans (known as "intentions") before setting out. At press time, freedom walkers only needed to make advance reservations for walking the Milford Track and the Routeburn. Facilities along other trails are on a first-come, first-serve basis. Families receive a 30% discount on accommodation in Department of Conservation huts, but the DOC advises against children under 10 attempting any of the strenuous multiday hikes.

Author's note: Having said that, I walked the Milford Track with a family who carried their 13-month-old daughter in a backpack, while their 7-year-old son skipped ahead of us most of the way.

You can make a reservation for a guided walk through the operators listed under the various hikes below. These companies provide accommodation in huts (sometimes with hot showers and "real" beds), all meals, and the services of a naturalist/guide. Walkers carry a minimum amount of gear.

NEW ZEALAND'S BEST HIKES
MARLBOROUGH, NELSON & BEYOND
Queen Charlotte Walkway

Walking is nearly as popular as boating in the Marlborough Sounds. While there are numerous tracks near Picton, the hands-down favorite is the Queen Charlotte Walkway. Under the watchful eye of the **Department of Conservation** (☎ 03/573-7582, fax 03/573-8362), this 67km (42-mile) track passes through lush coastal forest, around coves and inlets, and along ridges offering spectacular views of the Queen Charlotte and Kenepuru Sounds.

The trail stretches from Ship Cove to Anakiwa, and walking from one end to the other takes 4 days. However, you needn't walk the whole track. The Queen Charlotte offers two unusual options: the possibility of walking only part of the trail (1-day walks are possible) and accommodation in cabins, rustic lodges, and homestays along the way. (Read about Craglee Homestay under "Affordable Accommodations," in chapter 11.) Access to Ship Cove is by boat or float plane, and you can start or finish the walk at many different points along the way. You can do the walk with friends or with a guide. And—this is the best part—you don't have to carry your pack. It can be transported by boat from one point to another while you enjoy an unweighted walk.

Duration/Distance: 4 days/67km (42 miles)
Start: Ship Cove (Marlborough Sounds)
End: Anakiwa (Marlborough Sounds)
Open: Year-round. Guided walks given November through May only.
Contact Information: For an independent walk, contact **Department of Conservation,** Picton Field Centre, Picton, New Zealand (☎ 03/573-7582, fax 03/573-8362). There is a camping fee of NZ$4 (US$2.80) per night, or lodgings are available at various price levels. Transfers are available from **The Cougar Line,** P.O. Box 238, Picton (☎ 03/573-7925, fax 03/573-7926), which will drop you off, transfer your pack, and pick you up when you want to return. Similar services are offered by **Endeavour Express,** Rural Bag 434, Picton (☎ 03/579-8465).

For a guided walk, contact **The Marlborough Sounds Adventure Company,** P.O. Box 195, Picton, New Zealand (☎ 03/573-6078, fax 03/573-8827). They offer a **Four-Day Queen Charlotte Sound Walking Adventure** that includes boat transfers, a knowledgeable guide, bunk-bed accommodation, good meals, and hot showers. The cost for the 4-day package covering 45km (28 miles) from Ship Cove to Punga Cove is NZ$750 (US$525) per person.

Abel Tasman Coast Track

This walk is well known for its views of gorgeous shoreline. You pass through coastal forests and walk along beautiful beaches. Access to Marahau is by bus or boat. Launches make it convenient to do 1-day walks. Buses pick you up at the end of the trail. See also the box "Abel Tasman National Park" in chapter 11.

Duration/Distance: 3 to 5 days/51km (32 miles)
Start: Marahau (Abel Tasman National Park)
End: Wainui Bay (Abel Tasman National Park)
Open: Year-round. Guided walks given year-round.
Contact Information: For independent walks, contact the **Department of Conservation,** King Edward and High streets (P.O. Box 97), Motueka, New Zealand (☎ 03/528-9117, fax 03/528-6751). There is a NZ$20 (US$14) per night hut fee and NZ$6 (US$4.20) per night camping fee—plus transfers. Rates higher mid-October through mid-April. Lower prices for children.

For guided walks, contact the **Abel Tasman National Park Enterprises,** 234 High St., Motueka (P.O. Box 351), Nelson, New Zealand (☎ 0800/221-888 or 03/528-7801; fax 03/528-6087; e-mail enquiries@abeltasman.co.nz; Web site webnz.com/AbelTasman). A 3-day package costs NZ$625 (US$438); the 5-day package costs NZ$895 (US$626.50). Lower prices for children.

Heaphy Track

This exciting walk takes you from the junction of the Brown and Aorere rivers, across tussock-covered flats, and finally to the wild sea on the West Coast. Bus and taxi transfers are available to both ends of the track.

Duration/Distance: 4 to 6 days/77km (48 miles)
Start: Brown Hut (Kahurangi National Park)
End: Kohaihai River mouth (Kahurangi National Park)
Open: Year round.
Contact Information: For independent walks, contact the **Department of Conservation,** 1 Commercial St. (P.O. Box 53), Takaka, New Zealand (☎ 03/525-8026, fax 03/525-8444). There is a NZ$12 (US$8.40) per night hut fee; NZ$6 (US$4.20) per night camping fee—plus transfers. Lower prices for children.

Guided walks are not available.

QUEENSTOWN & FIORDLAND

Independent walkers are required to have reservations for walking the Milford and Routeburn tracks below. These can be made through the **Department of Conservation, Great Walks Booking Desk–Fiordland National Park Visitor Centre,** P.O. Box 29, Te Anau, New Zealand (☎ 03/249-8514, fax 03/249-8515). Bookings should be made as early as possible, as the number of people allowed on each track is limited and the demand—especially from mid-December through January—is great.

Routeburn Track

Both Queenstown and Te Anau are starting points for this famous walk, a 3-day/2-night, 39km (24-mile) trek that takes you right into the heart of unspoiled forests, along river valleys, and across mountain passes. It's a soul-stirring experience, and suitable for ages 10 and up—you should be at a good level of physical fitness.

New Zealand's Best Hikes: Marlborough, Nelson & Beyond

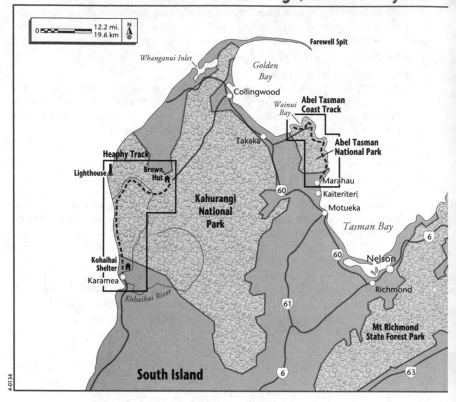

On this track you'll cross the Harris Saddle and pass through parts of both Mount Aspiring and Fiordland national parks. Bus transfers are available to the start of the track and from the finish. Along the way are waterfalls, forested valleys, and spectacular mountain scenery.

Duration/Distance: 2 to 3 days/39km (24 miles). The Routeburn can be walked in either direction.

Start/Finish: Routeburn Shelter, 75km (47 miles) from Queenstown via Glenorchy

Alternate Start/Finish: "The Divide" Shelter, 80km (50 miles) from Te Anau on the Milford Road

Open: Late October through mid-April.

Contact Information: For independent walks, contact the **Department of Conservation Great Walks Booking Desk,** Fiordland National Park Visitor Centre, P.O. Box 29, Te Anau, New Zealand (☎ **03/249-7924,** fax 03/249-7613). There is a NZ$28 (US$19.60) per night hut fee (lower price for children); NZ$9 (US$6.30) per night camping fee—plus transfers. Advance reservations required.

For guided walks, contact **Routeburn Walk Limited,** P.O. Box 568, Queenstown, New Zealand (☎ **03/442-8200,** fax 03/442-6072; reservations ☎ 03/249-7411 ext. 8063), which offers a 2-night/3-day package. You'll be bused from Queenstown to "The Divide" (on the Milford Road), then walk to Lake McKenzie, across the Harris Saddle, past the Routeburn Falls, and on to meet the coach that returns you to

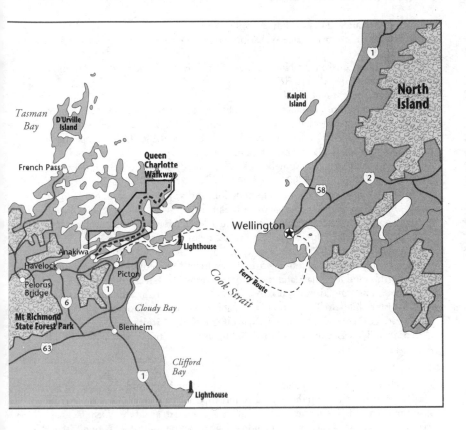

Queenstown. Along the way, comfortable lodges are provided for overnight stops, and you'll be treated to some of the most spectacular views in New Zealand. The cost is NZ$950 (US$670) for adults and NZ$850 (US$595) for children under 15. Costs include all transport, meals, and accommodation. Treks depart regularly from November through April. You should reserve as far in advance as possible, since this track is very popular with New Zealanders, and groups are limited in size.

It's also possible to combine the Routeburn Track and the Greenstone Valley Track into a 6-day/5-night excursion called **The Grand Traverse** (see below).

Greenstone Valley Track

This walk also takes you through scenes of natural beauty that will form lifetime memories. It follows an ancient Maori trail used by tribes who passed through the valley en route to rich greenstone lodes near Lake Wakatipu. The trail you'll walk, however, was actually cut by Europeans in the late 1800s as they opened up a route between Lake Wakatipu and Martins Bay on the Fiordland coast. Since the track passes through a valley, it is somewhat less demanding than the Routeburn Walk, but certainly no less beautiful. You'll pass Lake Howden and Lake McKellar and follow the Greenstone River through deep gorges and open valley land to Lake Wakatipu. Boat transfers are available to/from Elfin Bay. The Greenstone Track can be walked in either direction or linked with the Routeburn or Caples track for a 4- or 5-day round trip. (See "The Grand Traverse," below.)

Duration/Distance: 2 days/40km (25 miles)
Start/Finish: Elfin Bay on Lake Wakatipu, 86km (53 miles) from Queenstown via Glenorchy
Alternate Start/Finish: Lake Howden near "The Divide" Shelter, 80km (50 miles) from Te Anau on the Milford Road
Open: November through April.
Contact Information: For independent walks, contact the **Department of Conservation,** Fiordland National Park Visitor Centre, P.O. Box 29, Te Anau, New Zealand (☎ **03/249-8514,** fax 03/249-8515). There is a NZ$8 (US$5.60) per night hut fee—plus transfers. Lower price for children.

For guided walks, contact **Routeburn Walk Limited,** P.O. Box 568, Queenstown, New Zealand (☎ **03/442-8200;** fax 03/442-6072; reservations ☎ 03/249-7411 ext. 8063). They provide overnight accommodation, and as you relax at night, there are books on hand to tell you about many of the plants and wildlife you've seen during the day's walk. The expert guides can also relate tales of the Maori and how they once lived when they walked this valley. The 3-day/2-night walk costs NZ$950 (US$670) for adults, NZ$850 (US$595) for ages 10 to 15; children under 10 not allowed.

The Grand Traverse is a 6-day/5-night excursion that follows the Routeburn Track northbound for 3 days and then crosses over to the Greenstone Valley Track for 3 days. The guided walk costs NZ$1,250 (US$880) for adults, NZ$1,150 (US$810) for children. This option is available only between November and April each year. You can book through **Routeburn Walk Limited,** P.O. Box 568, Queenstown, New Zealand (☎ **03/422-8200;** fax 03/442-6072; reservations ☎ 03/ 249-7411 ext. 8063).

Hollyford Track

The Hollyford is a relatively flat track that follows the Hollyford River out to the coast at Martins Bay. It can be walked round-trip, or one way with an optional fly out from Martins Bay. Another option is to use a jet boat to avoid the "Demon Trail" section. This is one of the few Fiordland trails that can be walked year-round (there are no alpine crossings).

Duration/Distance: 4 days/56km (35 miles) one way
Start: Hollyford Camp, 9km (6 miles) off Milford Road
Finish: Martins Bay (optional fly out or walk back)
Open: Year-round. Guided walks given October through April only.
Contact Information: For independent walks, contact the **Department of Conservation,** Fiordland National Park Visitor Centre, P.O. Box 29, Te Anau, New Zealand (☎ **03/249-7924,** fax 03/249-7613). There is a NZ$4 (US$2.80) per night hut fee—plus jet boat, optional fly out, and bus transfer. Lower price for children.

For guided walks, contact the **Hollyford Valley Guided Walk,** P.O. Box 360, Queenstown, New Zealand (☎ **0800/832-226** in New Zealand, or 03/442-3760;

Impressions

The Routeburn and Greenstone are two of the most superb walking areas in the world. Dense rain forest with excellent tracks, sparkling lakes, mighty peals, and remote passes supply a sense of challenge without too great a feeling of danger. Well-equipped and comfortable lodges guarantee a good night's rest, and experienced guides ensure a safe journey. These walks are an experience that anyone will always remember.
                                    —Sir Edmund Hillary, conqueror of Mount Everest

New Zealand's Best Hikes: Queenstown & Fiordland

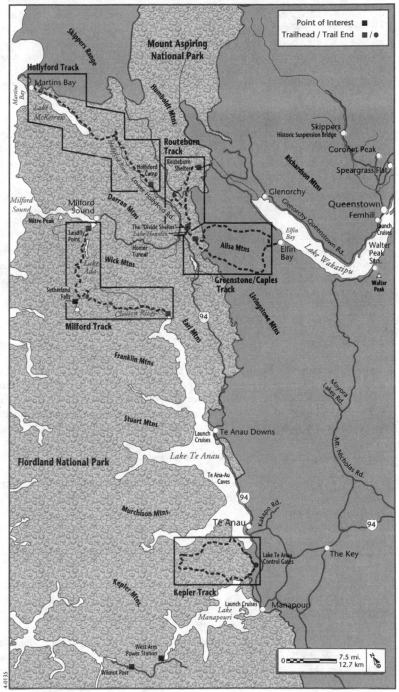

Point of Interest ■
Trailhead / Trail End ■ / ●

Mount Aspiring National Park

Skippers Range

Hollyford Track

Martins Bay

Lake McKerrow

Skippers
Historic Suspension Bridge

Coronet Peak

Humboldt Mtns

Routeburn Track

Speargrass Flat

Hollyford Camp

Routeburn Shelter

Richardson Mtns

Glenorchy

Milford Sound

Milford Sound

Darran Mtns

Lower Hollyford Rd.

Queenstown

Fernhill

Mitre Peak

The "Divide Shelter"
Lake Howden

Elfin Bay

Launch Cruises

Sandfly Point

Ailsa Mtns

Walter Peak Stn.

Wick Mtns

Homer Tunnel

Lake Ada

Glenorchy Queenstown Rd.

Lake Wakatipu

Elfin Bay

Walter Peak

Sutherland Falls

Greenstone/Caples Track

Clinton River

Livingstone Mtns

Milford Track

Earl Mtns

94

Franklin Mtns

Mavora Lakes Rd.

Stuart Mtns

Mt. Nicholas Rd.

Launch Cruises

Te Anau Downs

94

Fiordland National Park

Lake Te Anau

Te Ana-Au Caves

94

Murchison Mtns

Kakapo Rd.

Te Anau

The Key

94

Lake Te Anau Control Gates

Kepler Mtns

Kepler Track

Launch Cruises

Manapouri

Lake Manapouri

West Arm Power Station

0   7.5 mi.
     12.7 km

Wilmot Pass

4-0135

79

fax 03/442-3761; e-mail hvwalk@voyager.co.nz; Web site nz.com/webnz/ Queenstown/HVWalk.htm). They offer warm, comfortable lodges with hot showers and real beds. Cooks prepare breakfast and dinner. If your time and energy are *really* limited, you could fly to and from Martins Bay and overnight at the lodge without doing any walking. This costs NZ$395 (US$276.50) per adult and NZ$350 (US$245) per child under 15. The 3- to 5-day walking package costs NZ$950 to NZ$1,150 (US$665 to $805). Less for children.

Kepler Track

The 67km (42-mile) Kepler Track is a circular trail starting and ending at the Lake Te Anau outlet control gates. It takes 4 days to complete, and en route trampers traverse beech forests and a U-shaped glacial valley and walk along the edges of lakes Te Anau and Manapouri. Shuttle bus and boat transfers service this track.

Duration/Distance: 3 to 4 days/67km (42 miles)
Start: Lake Te Anau Control Gates
Finish: Lake Te Anau Control Gates
Open: Late October through mid-April.
Contact Information: For independent walks, contact the **Department of Conservation,** Fiordland National Park Visitor Centre, P.O. Box 29, Te Anau, New Zealand (☎ **03/249-7924,** fax 03/249-7613). There is a NZ$15 (US$10.50) per night hut fee; NZ$6 (US$4.20) per night camping fee—plus transfers. Lower prices for children.

At press time, guided walks weren't offered but were under consideration.

✪ Milford Track

Most dedicated trampers consider the world-famous Milford Track the finest anywhere in the world. Four days are required to walk the 54 kilometers (33 miles) from Glade Jetty at Lake Te Anau's northern end to Sandfly Point on the western bank of Milford Sound. To walk the pure wilderness is to immerse yourself in the sights, sounds, smells, and feel of nature left to itself—it's nearly impossible to emerge without a greater sense of the earth's rhythms. It's a walk closely regulated by park authorities, both for the safety of hikers and for the preservation of this wilderness area, yet there is no intrusion on individual response to nature once you begin the journey.

You set out from Te Anau Downs, 27¹/₂km (17 miles) north of Te Anau township, where a launch takes you to the head of the lake. Then the track follows the Clinton River, climbs over the Mackinnon Pass (1,073 meters/3,520 ft.), and provides a view of Sutherland Falls. Along the way are alpine meadows, beautiful views, and many waterfalls. At Sandfly Point, another launch ferries you across Milford Sound. Upon arrival, you may decide to spend the night at Milford or to return to Te Anau, but reservations are a must, whichever you choose.

Duration/Distance: 4 days/54km (33 miles)
Start: Lake Te Anau (Te Anau Downs)
End: Sandfly Point, near Milford Sound
Open: Late October through mid-April.
Contact Information: For independent walks, contact **Department of Conservation Great Walks Booking Desk,** Fiordland National Park Visitor Centre, P.O. Box 29, Te Anau, New Zealand (☎ **03/249-8514,** fax 03/249-8515). Reservations are accepted from early November to mid-April for the following tramping season, which runs from mid-October to mid-April. No more than 24 people are booked to start the walk on any given day, and applications begin coming in early for specific days.

A Christmas Waltz on Milford Track

As the launch glided across Lake Te Anau toward the head of the Milford Track, those of us on board sipped tea and tried to eye one another without being too obvious. My Kiwi friend, Donald, and I sat together amid our companions: a Kiwi family (a husband and wife, their 13-month-old daughter and 7-year-old son, and the husband's teenage brother) and seven Australian university students. It was the day before Christmas, and here I was, 7,000 miles from home and about to start a 4-day hike with 12 strangers and someone I'd only known for a short time.

I made plans to walk the Milford Track 5 months earlier when I visited New Zealand during my summer vacation. I met Donald on that trip, and he convinced me that to really see his country, I needed to spend some time "in the bush." Being a red-blooded Kiwi, Donald had thought we should hike independently, not in an organized group: "Groups have running hot and cold water in all their lodges and clean beds every night. You wouldn't want that, would you?"

"Oh, no, of course not," I'd assured him. Then I wondered how I was going to tell this guy that the most I ever walk is from one end of a shopping mall to the other.

I prepared for the trip by trekking up and down the hills around my home in California in a pair of borrowed hiking boots. By the time Christmas vacation came along, I felt like John Muir.

Our first hut, Clinton Forks, was 5 miles from the boat landing, and it started raining as we left. The Australians took off at a jog and were quickly out of sight. We crossed the bridge over the Clinton River and followed a "bush track" through a beautiful beech forest. It stopped raining, and sunlight glittered on the leaves.

We walked and talked, stopped for a "brew up" (a trailside tea party), and took lots of photos, so it was mid afternoon before we arrived at the hut. If I'd seen our spartan lodgings before the forest beauty had mellowed me, I might've been upset. As it was, I hesitated a moment—then began unloading my pack.

That night we dined on sausages and pooled our food supplies—Donald had loaded up on dehydrated Surprise brand peas, and there were plenty to go around. The Aussies, however, preferred a diet of Fosters Lager and generous portions of whisky. About halfway through their first case of beer they broke into song: traditional carols, tunes from *Godspell,* and an occasional chorus of "Waltzing Matilda." Other Christmas Eves had been more elegant, but none more enjoyable.

In the morning we watched in delight as the 13-month-old girl presented her parents with a unique gift by taking her first steps across the hut.

We walked the 8 miles to Mintaro Hut, passing from the light greens of beech and fern to darker trunks resembling a scene from a Gothic fairy tale. We picnicked near some rapids, with waterfalls cascading over granite cliffs. Except for a few brief showers, the weather held during the day, but then rain turned to hail just as we spotted the hut. We dressed for Christmas dinner in hiking gear and feasted on rehydrated beef Stroganoff and more Surprise peas, accompanied by a fine New Zealand wine. Near the end of dinner, one of the Aussies stepped outside and returned with the news that it was snowing.

Thousands of miles from home, I was in an isolated wilderness hut on Christmas night and was sure I'd never been happier. Donald scattered the rest of the peas on the hut's steps for the birds, and we climbed into our sleeping bags. The last thing I remember hearing as I drifted off was a faint chorus of "Waltzing Matilda."

The cost is NZ$212 (US$148.40) and includes huts and transportation. Lower prices for children.

For guided walks, contact the **Milford Track Guided Walk,** P.O. Box 185, Te Anau, New Zealand (☎ **03/249-7411** ext. 8063, fax 03/249-7590), which offers an excellent guided walk that includes guides, cooked meals at the overnight lodges, and accommodations at each end of the trek. Walkers carry day packs only. From December 1 to March 13 (the peak season), fees run NZ$1,586 (US$1,110.20) for adults and NZ$844 (US$590.80) for children for a 5-night/6-day package (beginning and ending in Te Anau). There is also a package that includes a flight to Queenstown from Milford Sound. This costs NZ$1,710 (US$1,197) per adult and NZ$945 (US$661.50) per child. From November 2 to November 30 and from March 14 to April 10 (the dates vary slightly every year), the Te Anau back to Te Anau package costs slightly less—NZ$1,489 (US$1,042.30) for adults and NZ$844 (US$590.80) for children; with the optional flight to Queenstown it costs NZ$1,595 (US$1116.50) for adults and NZ$945 (US$661.50) for children.

2 Fishing

For general information about fishing in New Zealand, contact the **New Zealand Fish and Game Council,** P.O. Box 13-141, Wellington 4, New Zealand (☎ **04/ 499-4767,** fax 04/499-4768). The **New Zealand Professional Fishing Guides,** P.O. Box 16, Motu, Gisborne, New Zealand (☎ **06/863-5822,** fax 06/863-5844), may also be helpful. If you'd like assistance in planning a New Zealand fishing holiday, contact **The Best of New Zealand Fly Fishing,** 2817 Wilshire Blvd., Santa Monica, CA 90403 (☎ **800/528-6129** in the U.S., or 310/998-5880; fax 310/829-9221). This travel agency specializes in angler activities. In any case, ask them for a free copy of their 48-page brochure *The Best of New Zealand Fly Fishing* (which includes information on saltwater fishing).

FRESH-WATER FISHING

New Zealand has a reputation as being a great place for **trout fishing,** and, in fact, from October through April it is the world's best place to fish for wild brown trout.

Angling for **rainbow** and **brown** trout can put dinner on the table, but these days more and more fishing people are opting for catch and release. In any case, you'll have

Readers Recommend

Urewera True Adventure—Fishing Rafting & Outdoor Adventures, R.D.1, Golf Road, Murupara, New Zealand (☎ **07/366-5827**). *"Murray & Lynnette Downie, a hospitable young couple and proprietors of the business, welcomed us to their farm with warmth and enthusiasm. Our cabin was clean, comfortable, and nicely appointed. Lynnette's meals were superb, and Murray took us for the best fishing we have ever experienced. The scenery alone was enough to warrant the trip. The river was solitary and peaceful except for the frequent interruptions made by the huge rainbow and brown trout rising from the water hooked to our lines. Whether it be for a guided fishing or hunting trip or simply a delightful rafting adventure in a beautiful wild part of New Zealand, one cannot beat the stay we had here. The costs were quite reasonable too; food and lodging was NZ$50 (US$35) per person per night with an additional charge of NZ$275 (US$193) for fishing, which included guide service and all equipment. Our trip was arranged through The Best of New Zealand Fly Fishing."*

—Lois Scaff, La Crescenta, California, USA.

The ova for New Zealand's rainbow trout were introduced from the Russian River in California in 1883 and 1884. Brown trout are native to Europe but were introduced to New Zealand from Tasmania in 1867.

a great day out in the open. Rotorua and Taupo are trout-fishing centers, but it's conceivable that you could fish nearly any river or lake in the country and come up with a trout. The season is long—from the first Saturday in October through the end of April. During this time all rivers and streams are open for brown and rainbow trout, but local restrictions may apply. There are several areas where you can fish year-round, including the **Rotorua District** and **Lake Taupo** on the North Island and **Lake Te Anau, Lake Brunner,** and **Lake Wakatipu** on the South Island. The **Tongiriro River,** near Turangi, is one of the prime trout-fishing rivers in the world, and May to October is the best time to be there. The rainbow and brown trout here average 4.5 pounds. May to October is also a good time to fish lakes Taupo and Rotorua.

Fishing licenses are available from fishing tackle and sports shops on a daily, weekly, monthly, or seasonal basis. These are good for the whole of New Zealand, except Taupo and Rotorua, which have their own licenses.

Both the North Island and the South Island have trout in streams and lakes, but salmon fishing is limited to the South Island. The **Rakaia River** near Ashburton is a favorite spot, and January through March is prime time.

SALTWATER AND BIG-GAME FISHING

Writer Zane Grey called the Bay of Islands the "angler's El Dorado" because of its plentiful big-game fishing. In fact, deep-sea fishing comes into its own along some 500 kilometers (about 300 miles) of the North Island's coastline. Waters less than an hour from shore hold such trophies as **marlin, shark** (mako, thresher, hammerhead, tiger), and five species of **tuna, broadbill,** and **yellowtail.** The season runs from mid-January through April, and you'll find well-equipped bases at the Bay of Islands, in Whitianga on the Coromandel Peninsula, and in Tauranga and Whakatane in the Bay of Plenty. No license is required.

Light-tackle spin fishing for **kahawai, snapper, shark,** and others is excellent anywhere along the New Zealand coast. No license is required.

A NOTE ON FISHING GUIDES: DO YOU REALLY NEED ONE?

I'm not sure how they justify it, but fishing guides in New Zealand charge up to NZ$600 (US$420) a day for one or two people. Sure, they supply all equipment and lunch—and well they should for that price. You'll find the names of specific guides under many "Outdoor Activities" headings in the regional chapters of this book. If you decide to splurge on a fishing experience, you should stay at Lake Brunner Lodge (see "Greymouth" in chapter 11) and let Ray Grubb or one of his staff take you to where the big ones are biting. They charge NZ$430 (US$301) per guide per day for one or two people. In any case, make your plans well in advance. The good guides are booked up early.

I wouldn't blame you if you decided to go it alone. If that's the case, your best chance for catching a brown or rainbow trout without a guide in the South Island summer is in the Tekapo River and canals or any of the lakes in that vicinity. These places are accessed from Omarama or Twizel (south and east of Mt. Cook). You may also have good luck anytime of year in the Tongariro River near Turangi (at the south end of Lake Taupo). The nice people at the Creel Tackle Shop or the Turangi Fly

Shop rent equipment and might even give you some free advice—which you'll need because fishing techniques in New Zealand are very different from those used in other parts of the world. As a minimum, you'll need to talk to a local. If you're bringing your own gear, bring a 6 or 7 weight 4-piece fly rod and reel. You won't wear waders November through March, and you can hire them in winter.

3 Boating & Other Water Sports

New Zealanders love the water. Anytime they're not working in an office or on a farm, you'll find them in the water or on the water. Visitors, too, can participate in all kinds of aquatic adventures. Beaches abound in the Bay of Islands, in the Gisborne area, in the Marlborough Sounds area, around Nelson, and in many other places throughout the country.

BOATING

Of course, boating is a major summer pastime (December through February) in a country surrounded by water. There are countless possibilities—from exploring the thousands of secluded inlets and tranquil bays to sailing to uninhabited islands, even heading out to the high seas.

Auckland, known as the City of Sails, is said to contain more boats per capita than any other city in the world. Once you see the Waitemata Harbour dotted with white sails on a Sunday afternoon, you'll have no trouble believing me.

SAILING   Sailing is extremely popular in and around the Auckland harbor and the adjacent Hauraki Gulf. Other beautiful places to sail are the Bay of Islands and the Marlborough Sounds.

Both **bareboat and skippered charters** are available. If this interests you, contact **Moorings Rainbow Yacht Charters,** Opua Wharf, Opua, Bay of Islands, New Zealand (☎ **09/402-7821,** fax 09/402-7546); or **Waiheke Island Yacht Charters** (in the Auckland vicinity), 32 Palm Rd., Palm Beach, Waiheke Island, New Zealand (☎ **09/372-9579** or 025/764-753, fax 09/372-9580). Other reliable operators include **Marlborough Sounds Charters Ltd.,** P.O. Box 71, Picton, New Zealand (☎ or fax **03/573-7726**); and **Charter Link,** The Marina, Half Moon Bay, Auckland, New Zealand (☎ **09/535-8710,** fax 09/537-0196).

For more information on sailing, contact the **New Zealand Yachting Federation,** P.O. Box 909000 AMSC, Auckland, New Zealand (☎ **09/303-2360,** fax 09/373-5897).

CANOEING & KAYAKING   If paddling is more your speed, you'll find a lot of kayaking and canoeing enthusiasts in New Zealand. Sea kayaking is popular in the Bay of Islands, in the Hauraki Gulf, around the Coromandel Peninsula, in the Marlborough Sounds, and even in Milford Sound. The Rangitikei River, between Wanganui and Palmerston North, is ideal for those who prefer river paddling.

For more information, contact **Coastal Kayakers,** P.O. Box 325, Paihia, Bay of Islands, New Zealand (☎ **09/402-8105,** fax 09/403-8550); **Auckland Canoe Centre,** 502 Sandringham Rd., Auckland, New Zealand (☎ **09/815-2073,** fax 09/815-2074); or **Marlborough Sounds Adventure Co.,** P.O. Box 195, Picton, New Zealand (☎ **03/573-6078,** fax 03/573-8827).

JETBOATING   More of a thrill-seeker's sport, jetboating presents yet another way of getting out on the water. You go zipping around like you would in a speedboat; the only difference is that jet boats are designed to cruise through shallow waters. Invented by South Island farmer Bill Hamilton in the 1950s, these craft operate all over the world. In New Zealand, favorite places to zoom include the Huka River near Lake Taupo and the Shotover and Kawarau rivers near Queenstown, although most of the major rivers in both the North and South Islands have jetboat operations as well.

WHITE-WATER RAFTING   The best places to go rafting are the North Island's challenging Wairoa and Mohaka rivers. The Kaituna River, near Rotorua, is popular because of its wild drops. In Queenstown, operators offer action-packed trips on the Shotover and Kawarau rivers. Rafting is a year-round activity in New Zealand, with wet suits and warm clothing required for winter months. Operators give instruction and provide equipment and transfers to and from the launch point.

OTHER WATER SPORTS: FROM SURFING TO SCUBA DIVING

If you're a surfer, you probably know that Raglan, on the North Island (due west of Hamilton), is a truly hot surfing spot. And it isn't the only place to ride the waves.

SURFING & WINDSURFING   If you're in search of waves, head to the waters around the Bay of Plenty—according to a Kiwi friend, Mount Manganui offers the best surf on any New Zealand beach. Other spots include Taylor's Mistake—a primo surfing area at Sumner near Christchurch—and Port Waikato south of Auckland. If you arrive in New Zealand without a board, inquire at the nearest visitor information center about where you can rent one.

For **windsurfing,** head to Oakura, near New Plymouth, which offers world-class windsurfing and surfing; Wellington is also a great spot for boardsailing.

SCUBA DIVING   The best places in New Zealand for getting underwater are the Bay of Islands and the waters around Northland's Poor Knights Islands. Visibility here ranges from 66 to 230 feet in the best months—February through June. It gets pretty cold, but hardy folks even dive in Milford Sound and at Stewart Island. Be sure to bring proof of certification with you.

Feel like a wreck? The remains of the *Rainbow Warrior* lie on the white-sand bottom among Northland's Cavalli Islands (see "Paihia" in chapter 6 for info on how to get there), and the Russian cruise ship *Mikhail Lermontov* sits where it sunk in the Marlborough Sounds.

For details on diving, contact **Paihia Dive,** Williams Road, Paihia, Bay of Islands, New Zealand (☎ **09/402-7551,** fax 09/402-7110); the **Dive Industry of New Zealand,** P.O. Box 875, Auckland, New Zealand (☎ **09/849-5896,** fax 09/849-3526), or the visitor center in Picton (see chapter 11).

4 Playing Golf

New Zealand is a nation of golfers. A recent survey by the New Zealand Golf Association found that 512,000 Kiwis play at least one round of golf a year. There are approximately 400 private and public courses that offer duffers and pros myriad opportunities to grip it and rip it. Members of overseas clubs are granted guest privileges at most private clubs. Equipment and a "trundler" or motorized cart can be rented. And while fishing is a pricey pastime, greens fees in New Zealand are well below the world's average. Here you'll pay anywhere from NZ$6 to NZ$40 (US$4.20 to US$28) for 18 holes on a good course; and up to NZ$70 (US$49) for the country's top links.

The best time to play golf in New Zealand is from October to April, when temperatures range from 60 to 70°F, but die-hards play year-round. You may find courses crowded on weekends, much less so during the week.

The Auckland area has 36 courses, including **Titirangi,** in the western suburbs, and **Muriwai,** a true links course located 40 minutes west of the city. In Rotorua, the **Arikikapakapa** course is dotted with geothermal activity (steam vents and boiling mud pools), which makes the course as tricky to play as it is to pronounce. One of the most outstanding courses in the country is the **Wairakei International Golf Course** located in Wairakei Tourist Park, near Taupo. Wellington's **Paraparaumu Beach Golf Club** has been rated one of the world's top 50 Courses by *Golf Digest* magazine.

On the South Island, you'll find **Russley** and **Shirley** in Christchurch. Russley is parklike, its fairways lined by pine trees, while Shirley is more open but no less demanding. **Balmacewan,** in Dunedin, is the oldest course in New Zealand, founded in 1871, while **St. Clair** is noted for its magnificent pines and spectacular ocean views.

For more information contact the **New Zealand Golf Association,** P.O. Box 11-842, Wellington, New Zealand (☎ **04/472-2967,** fax 04/499-7330). For golf packages, you might want to contact **New Zealand Golf Excursions USA, Inc.,** 2141 Rosecrans Ave., #1199, El Segundo, CA 90245 (☎ **800/622-6606** in the U.S., fax 310/322-4972) or **Kiwi Golf Tours** (☎ **800/873-6360**).

5 Skiing & Snowboarding

New Zealand attracts dedicated skiers like a magnet—its "down under" ski season (usually late June through September or October) allows those from the Northern Hemisphere to hit the slopes year-round. In addition to 13 conventional ski areas, the country offers something you can't do anywhere else: At **Mount Cook** you fly by ski plane or helicopter to the 8,000-foot-high head of the Tasman Glacier and ski down the 8.5-mile run. While this is hardly an activity for beginners—and not exactly a budget activity—it does provide advanced skiers with a memorable, worth-a-splurge experience.

SKIING

On the North Island, the two major commercial ski fields are ✪ **Whakapapa** and ✪ **Turoa,** both on the slopes of Mount Ruapehu in Tongariro National Park. Ruapehu, with a simmering crater lake, is an active volcano that soars some 9,200 feet high, making it the North Island's highest peak. Ruapehu erupted in 1995 and again in 1996—both prevented the opening of the ski fields. **Whakapapa** (☎ **07/892-3738,** fax 07/892-3732), the largest ski field, offers a range of facilities for beginners to the most advanced. **Turoa** (☎ **06/385-8456**), on Mount Ruapehu's south side, is appreciated for its long spring season lasting into late October or early November.

On the South Island, **Mt. Hutt ski field,** P.O. Box 14, Methven, New Zealand (☎ **03/302-8811,** fax 03/302-8697, e-mail patrol@chch.planet.co.nz; Web site www.mtcook.co.nz), located only 1¹/₂ hours from Christchurch, offers both traditional downhill skiing and heliskiing.

Farther south are four ski areas that lure both New Zealanders and overseas visitors to the Southern Lakes Ski Region between Queenstown and Wanaka. You can take your pick from the internationally respected **Remarkables, Cardrona, Treble Cone,** and **Coronet Peak.** Among them, they offer downhill skiing, cross-country skiing, and heliskiing. All have good trails for beginner, intermediate, and expert skiers. Coronet Peak is 18km (11 miles) from Queenstown; The Remarkables (named for the colors the peaks turn at sunset) are 23km (14 miles) from town. Between them they operate rope tows, platters, and T-bars, as well as double, triple, and quad chair lifts. Both ski areas offer ski rental, ski lessons, and fast-food restaurants. Coronet Peak has a licensed restaurant as well. Mount Cook Landline operates shuttle buses to both ski areas from Queenstown. Cardrona is 57 km (35 miles) from Queenstown, but only 33 km (20 miles) from Wanaka; Treble Cone is 28km (17 miles) past Wanaka. Ski buses to the Cardrona and Treble Cone slopes operate daily in winter.

Near Wanaka, **Waiorau Nordic** (☎ **03/443-7541**) offers 35 kilometers (22 miles) of trails from July to October.

Lift-ticket prices in New Zealand range from NZ$35 to NZ$58 (US$24.50 to US$40.60); ski, boot, and pole rentals cost from NZ$25 to NZ$35 (US$16.25 to US$19.50); and lessons are available from about NZ$25 (US$17.50) for a half-day group class. Costs for kids are lower.

For further information on skiing, you can contact the **New Zealand Ski Council,** P.O. Box 27-501, Wellington, New Zealand (☎ **04/499-4995,** fax 04/ 499-8136).

SNOWBOARDING

The top **snowboarding** destinations in New Zealand are **Turoa** in the North Island and **Treble Cone** and **Cardrona** in the South Island. **Temple Basin Ski Area** in Arthur's Pass National Park, 2 hours from Christchurch, is another good place. **Helisnowboarding** is offered in the Southern Lakes Region.

6 Cycling

Cycle touring is popular with New Zealand visitors because it provides a great way to see the wonders of the country at a relaxed pace. The South Island's West Coast is probably the area most frequently covered, though it's possible to cycle almost anywhere. Two other good areas are Christchurch and the Canterbury Plains.

SAFETY TIPS Wherever you cycle, please remember that helmets are compulsory, and that mountain biking is prohibited in national parks. Cyclists are not permitted on motorways (freeways). Always ride on the left, and remember that traffic turning left gives way to everything on the right. At night, make sure you have a functioning white front light and red rear light and reflector.

RENTALS If you don't want to go on an organized tour, and aren't planning on bringing your bike with you, **Adventure Cycles,** P.O. Box 91-296, Auckland 1030, New Zealand (☎ **0800/335-566** in New Zealand, or 09/309-5566; fax 09/ 309-4211), offers rentals and sales with a guaranteed buy-back plan. They are also part of an association of 24 operators that can provide organized activities.

TOURS Several operators organize cycling trips in New Zealand. You might want to contact **New Zealand Pedaltours,** P.O. Box 37-575, Parnell, Auckland, New Zealand (☎ **09/302-0968,** fax 09/302-0967). They offer trips on both the North and the South islands, which last anywhere from 4 to 19 days. The back-up vehicle allows everyone to cycle as much as they wish each day, with the option of riding in the vehicle at any time. Accommodations are in small country inns, lodges, and hotels.

7 More Guided Tours, Outfitters & Package Deals

In addition to the operators and outfitters mentioned above, all the companies below offer good-value deals. If you finish reading this section and still haven't found what you're looking for, send for a copy of *New Zealand Outside, The Annual &*

Directory. Ordering instructions are on the first page of this chapter, as is info on the catalog "Naturally New Zealand Holidays." Both are very helpful.

The ❂ **Sunmakers Travel Group,** 100 W. Harrison, South Tower #350, Seattle, WA 98119-4123 (☎ **800/841-4321** in the U.S., or 206/216-2900), offers two good deals for adventurous travelers. The first, the **"Summer Traverse,"** is a 10-day expedition that uses foot, raft, canoe, kayak, mountain bike, and horseback to move through the South Island's diverse landscapes. All guides are fully qualified, and equipment is top-quality. Accommodations include a farmstay, camping, and hotels. The Summer Traverse begins and ends in Christchurch and costs from US$1,538 per person based on double occupancy; this trip is land only. Sunmakers also offers a dollarwise **"Extreme Deal,"** which features skiing in the South Island's top ski fields. The package, which costs from US$1,879 per person based on double occupancy, includes round-trip airfare, accommodations, lift tickets, transfers, and daily minivan shuttle to the mountain of your choice.

Mount Cook Tours, 1960 Grand Ave., Suite 910, El Segundo, CA 90245-5038 (☎ **800/468-2665** in the U. S., fax 310/640-2823 in the U.S.; **800/999-9306** in Canada; **1800/221-134** in Australia; or **0800/800-737** in New Zealand), operates the skiplanes at Mt. Cook; owns The Remarkables and Coronet Peak ski fields; and offers a number of good-value ski packages that include accommodations, lift tickets, and transfers to and from the slopes. Contact them at one of the above numbers. If the skiing bug should bite you after you're in New Zealand, head for one of Mount Cook Line's local Travel Centres, which are located throughout the country.

Mount Cook Tours also offers a number of Walking Track Vacations, including the Milford Track Guided Walk, The Grand Traverse, the Routeburn Walk, the Greenstone Valley Walk, and others.

American Wilderness Experience, 2820-A Wilderness Place, Boulder, CO 80301-5454 (☎ **800/444-0099** or 303/444-2622 in the U.S., fax 303/444-3999), offers trips to national parks and the World Heritage Area; they include walking, rafting, and wildlife observation.

Te Urewera Adventures of New Zealand, Ruatahuna, Private Bag 3001, Rotorua, New Zealand (☎ **07/366-3969,** fax 07/366-3333) is one of two companies offering outdoor experiences in a remote wilderness area southeast of Rotorua (the other one is highlighted above in "Readers Recommend"). Te Urewera Adventures offers 1- to 5-day horse trekking trips, 3- to 7-day camping/tramping experiences, and guided fishing adventures. Horse treks are available year-round; camping/tramping is available November to March; fishing is in the Whakatane watershed. Hosts Whare and Margaret Biddle do a great job.

Arriving in Auckland: The City of Sails

New Zealand's largest city is a rapidly evolving metropolis. Auckland's long been the country's most populous urban center, but it's only recently developed a sense of style and palpable energy. The skyline now boasts the tallest tower in the Southern Hemisphere, and inner-city pubs have given way to chic sidewalk cafes. The harbor remains as gorgeous as ever and, in spite of commercial construction, numerous large, leafy parks still provide oases around the edges of the downtown area.

All of this development continues to attract new arrivals—about 25% of the nation's population now lives here and thousands are coming each year. In addition to New Zealanders of European descent, Auckland also has the largest Polynesian population of any city in the world and has recently welcomed noticeable numbers of Asian residents. These ethnic groups give "the city of sails" a cosmopolitan feel not found in other Kiwi centers.

Auckland's international airport is most often the overseas visitor's introduction to New Zealand, and many new arrivals pick up a car and turn south—or north to the Bay of Islands. In doing so they miss an integral part of the nation. Auckland isn't typical of New Zealand anymore than New York or Los Angeles are typical of the United States or Sydney is typical of Australia—but it does have a lot to offer. Savvy travelers should plan to spend several days here before heading out to explore the rest of the country.

The city straddles a narrow isthmus with excellent harbors on either side. The land here was created by the activity of some 60 volcanoes over a period of more than 50,000 years. According to Maori legends, giants inhabited this area in the days before the Moa-Hunters. Europeans arrived in Auckland in 1839, and when the Treaty of Waitangi was signed in 1840, negotiations with the Maori transferred the isthmus to British ownership. The flag was hoisted on September 18, 1840, an event marked annually by the Anniversary Day Regatta (celebrated in January because of better sailing conditions). The thriving town served as New Zealand's first capital until 1864, when the seat of government was transferred to Wellington because of its central location.

Today's Auckland is nestled among those volcanic peaks, which have now settled into gently rounded hills, minor mountains, and sloping craters. North Head and Bastion Point stand like sentinels

Greater Auckland

GREATER
AUCKLAND

A&P Showgrounds **7**
Auckland Domain **3**
Auckland Zoo **2**
Avondale Racecourse **1**
Devonport Ferry **4**
Ellerslie Racecourse **8**
Howick Colonial Village
   (Pakuranga) **10**
Kelly Tarlton's Southern Ocean
   Adventure **6**
One Tree Hill
   and Cornwall Park **9**
Parnell Rose Gardens **5**
Rainbow's End Adventure Park **11**
Waitakere Ranges **12**
Winery Region **13**

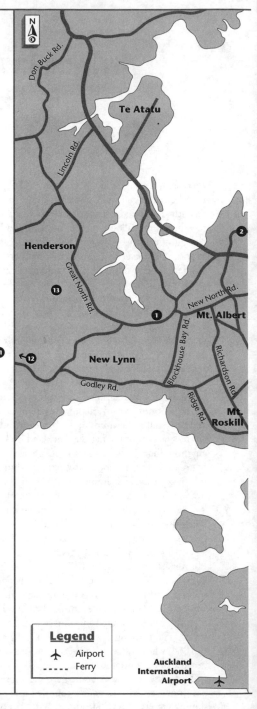

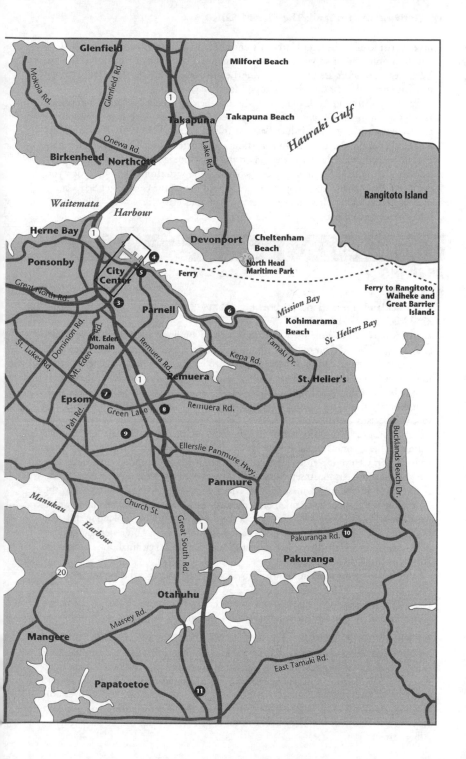

Glenfield

Milford Beach

Mokoia Rd.

Glenfield Rd.

1

Takapuna

Takapuna Beach

Hauraki Gulf

Onewa Rd.

Birkenhead

Northcote

Rangitoto Island

Waitemata

Harbour

Herne Bay

1

Devonport

Cheltenham Beach

Ponsonby

4

City Center

5

Ferry

North Head Maritime Park

Great North Rd.

3

Parnell

Ferry to Rangitoto, Waiheke and Great Barrier Islands

St. Lukes Rd.

Dominion Rd.

Mt. Eden Domain

6

Mission Bay

Kohimarama Beach

St. Heliers Bay

Remuera Rd.

Tamaki Dr.

Kepa Rd.

Mt. Eden Rd.

1

Remuera

St. Helier's

Epsom

7

Green Lane

8

Remuera Rd.

Pah Rd.

9

Ellerslie Panmure Hwy.

Bucklands Beach Dr.

Manukau

Harbour

Panmure

Church St.

Great South Rd.

1

Pakuranga Rd.

10

20

Pakuranga

Otahuhu

Massey Rd.

Mangere

East Tamaki Rd.

Papatoetoe

11

on either side of Waitemata Harbour's entrance. Rangitoto Island, the result of an eruption only 700 or so years ago, sits in majestic splendor just offshore. Mount Eden's eastern slopes are marked by Maori earthworks, and One Tree Hill is a significant archeological site where a large Maori *pa* (fort) once existed.

When you arrive in Auckland, you'll see that the city is busy sprucing up in preparation for hosting the America's Cup in the year 2000. The competitors' compounds are under construction in Viaduct Basin at the west end of the central business district. Other ambitious plans include turning Quay Street, which runs along the harbor, into a pedestrian thoroughfare and creating an underground transport center for coaches and trains at Britomart Place. What will the waterfront look like when you get there? Will the building projects be completed before the Challenger Series starts in November, 1999? These are the questions anxious city officials are asking themselves as we go to press.

1 Orientation

ARRIVING
BY PLANE

The **Auckland International Airport** lies 21km (13 miles) south of the city just behind Manukau Harbour.

As soon as you've gone through Immigration you'll get your first taste of Kiwi hospitality. Hosts and hostesses wearing blue vests are available to answer questions, show you the way to complimentary luggage trolleys (carts), and give general arrival information. These volunteers are mostly retired people who "work" at the airport simply because they like helping others—they're very sweet and don't accept tips. You'll breeze through Customs provided you read chapter 3 and didn't bring any food—especially fruit.

The facilities in the International Terminal include: Avis, Hertz, and Budget counters (these companies also have counters in the domestic terminal); a Visitor Information Centre (open for all flight arrivals); a Maui Campers rental desk; and the check-in counters for Ansett New Zealand and Air New Zealand domestic flights. If you're connecting to a domestic flight, check your luggage here and then enjoy the 10-minute walk (about half a mile) or free shuttle bus to the domestic terminal, where there are two separate areas for Air New Zealand and Ansett New Zealand in different buildings. (The domestic terminal has rental showers in case you're feeling grotty.) The City of Sails Cafe & Bar is also in the International Terminal, as is a Bank of New Zealand Currency Exchange.

The **Visitor Information Centre** provides luggage storage; the fee for 24 hours is NZ$3 (US$2.10) for hand luggage, NZ$7 (US$4.90) for large items, and NZ$5 (US$3.50) per suitcase. They also sell phone cards, have maps, make accommodation bookings, and provide tons of brochures on sightseeing options.

GETTING INTO TOWN   The **Airbus** (☎ **09/275-9396,** fax 09/275-9394) transports passengers between the airport and the Downtown Airline Terminal. You can pick up the Airbus near the baggage claim areas in both airport terminals. The fare is NZ$10 (US$7) one way, NZ$16 (US$11.20) round-trip (NZ$7/US$4.90 one way and NZ$12/US$8.40 round-trip for YHA, VIP, students, and seniors over 60). If you're staying at a city hotel on the direct route, the driver will drop you off upon request. The **Downtown Airline Terminal** is at 86–94 Quay St., at the corner of Albert Street.

TOURISTOP: The Budget Traveler's Best Friend

Since 1978, Otto and Joan Spinka have operated Touristop, located in Auckland's Downtown Airline Terminal, 86–94 Quay St. (☎ 09/377-5783, fax 09/377-6325). This knowledgeable couple specializes in offering bookings for accommodations, tours, rental cars, sightseeing tours, harbor cruises, and just about anything else associated with New Zealand—wide travel at the best possible price. They are also agents for all nationwide coachline networks, with coaches departing nearby. They issue one- and multiday coach passes, as well as all backpacker coach passes. They even offer international airfares at "unbeatable prices," and there's never any booking fee. They're open daily from 7:30am to 6pm. Otto provides luggage storage for travelers, and you'll also find magazines, maps, phone cards, film, candies, coins, and a nice selection of New Zealand souvenirs here, too—but most of all, you'll find a helping Kiwi hand.

Taxi fares between the airport and the city center run about NZ$35 (US$24.50) on weekdays, a little higher on weekends and at night. Auckland Co-op Taxi (☎ 09/300-3000) is one recommendable company.

Direct minibus transport between the airport and B&Bs, hotels, and motels is supplied by **Super Shuttle** and **Shuttle Link** (☎ 09/275-1234) for NZ$15 (US$10.50) per person one way; add NZ$5 (US$3.50) for each additional person traveling in a group. If you plan to take the shuttle to the airport, reserve at least 2 hours before you want to travel.

Drivers will find spacious parking lots in front of both terminals.

BY TRAIN OR BUS

Tranz Scenic trains arrive and depart from the **Auckland Railway Station,** just east of the city center on Beach Road (☎ 0800/802-802 in New Zealand). **InterCity** and **Newmans** buses arrive and depart from the **Sky City Coach Terminal** on Hobson Street (☎ 09/357-8400). **Mount Cook** coaches arrive and depart from the **Downtown Terminal** on Quay Street (☎ 0800/800-287 in New Zealand). *Note:* The train and bus depots will be moving to a new underground transport center at Britomart Place at some point in the future—perhaps even during the life of this edition. Call the numbers above for information.

VISITOR INFORMATION

There are two centrally located **Auckland Visitors Centres:** one at 299 Queen St., at Aotea Square; and one at 1 Queen St., Queen Elizabeth II Square (☎ 09/366-6888, fax 09/366-6893). Both are open Monday through Friday from 8:30am to 5:30pm and Saturday, Sunday, and public holidays from 9am to 5pm. Stop by and pick up free brochures and free advice on accommodations, sightseeing, or ongoing transport. Look for a copy of *Auckland A–Z,* Auckland's *What's On,* and the *Auckland Tourist Times* (which are also distributed free by many hotels) for a listing of current daytime and nighttime happenings. The **North Shore Visitor Information Centre,** 49 Hurstmere Rd., Takapuna (☎ 09/486-8670, fax 09/486-8562), is open Monday through Friday from 9am to 5pm, Saturday, Sunday, and public holidays from 10am to 3pm; and the **Visitor Information Centre** at the Auckland Airport International Terminal (☎ 09/275-6467, fax 09/256-8942) is open daily from 5am until the last flight arrives.

For information before leaving home, you can e-mail the visitors centers at **visitor@auckland.tourism.co.nz**; their mailing address is P.O. Box 7048 Wellesley Street, Auckland, New Zealand.

Other useful information services: The **Department of Conservation Centre** (☎ **09/303-1530**) has details on walks, campgrounds, the gulf islands, and national parks. DOC and the **Regional Parks Information Centre** (☎ **09/303-1530**) share space in the Ferry Building on Quay Street; they're open Monday through Friday, March through October; Monday through Saturday during February and November; and daily in December and January. They are closed Christmas Day, Boxing Day, New Year's Day, and Waitangi Day (February 6).

The **Auckland City Government** has a Web site at **www.akcity.govt.nz**.

SPECIAL EVENTS

✪ **Auckland Anniversary Day Regatta**   The "City of Sails" hosts this annual colorful sailing event, which attracts local and international entrants. It's fun to watch from shore or one of several lofty viewpoints. Last Monday in January. Call ☎ **09/366-6888** for details.

Round the Bays Run   This event is great fun, with runners from around the South Pacific participating in this 8km (about 5-mile) run, ending with a barbecue in one of the city's parks. Late March (March 29, 1998). Call ☎ **09/525-2166** for details.

Devonport Food & Wine Festival (Devonport)   Twenty wineries from around the country participate; it costs NZ\$10 (US\$7) for the tasting glass, which can be used both days. Entertainment includes jazz, classical music, and opera. Held in the Windsor Reserve near the Ferry Wharf. Late February (February 21 to 22, 1998). It starts at 11am both days, finishing at 6pm on Saturday and 5pm on Sunday. All funds raised go to charity. Call ☎ **09/446-0688** or 09/445-3011 for details.

Ellerslie Flower Show   Held at the Auckland Regional Botanic Garden, this is New Zealand's premier garden and outdoor living event. Includes complete gardens, the latest in barbecues, and outdoor furniture. November. Call ☎ **09/309-7875** for details.

Hero Parade and Party   This is the country's largest gay and lesbian event. Now in its eighth year, festivities in Auckland include film, theater, cabaret, dance, and sport. The festival culminates with a street parade and all-night dance party. Late February (February 7 to 21, 1998. Parade and party February 21, 1998). Call ☎ **09/307-1057,** or send an e-mail to maxsam.xtra.co.nz for details.

Horse Racing (NZ Derby, Queen Elizabeth Auckland Handicap, and others)   Check locally for specific dates of individual events during the month. Call ☎ **09/366-6888** for details.

Royal New Zealand Easter Show   Held at the Expo Centre, it annually attracts more than 1,000 competitors and incorporates elements of an agricultural and pastoral show with fresh produce stalls, a merry-go-round, equestrian events, and more. At least 15,000 to 20,000 Kiwis attend. Easter weekend. Call ☎ **09/638-9969** for details.

CITY LAYOUT

Central Auckland is surrounded by districts that have become cities in their own right—people may *work* in the inner city, but when evening comes, they're off to wider spaces. And the homeward journey will take them over at least one of the many bridges (they cross the harbor, rivers, creeks, and bays) and possibly onto the speeding motorway that runs north–south through the city. That motorway can be a blessing for the visitor unfamiliar with the territory and driving on the left, because it virtually eliminates the possibility of losing your way when you set out for the Bay of Islands, Rotorua, or other major points.

Main Arteries & Streets

The city itself is fairly straightforward. The main street is **Queen Street,** which ends in Queen Elizabeth Square at **Quay Street.** Quay Street runs along the Waitemata harbor front. At the other end of Queen Street is **Karangahape Road** (pronounce it "Ka-ranga-happy," or simply call it "K Road" as Aucklanders do), a mere 2km (1¼ miles) from Quay Street. Within that area you'll find most of the city's shops, restaurants, nightspots, and hotels, as well as bus, rail, and air terminals.

You can find a street map of Auckland at the **Visitor Information Centre** or at the **Automobile Association** (if you remembered to bring your home-country membership card). The AA map is the better one.

NEIGHBORHOODS IN BRIEF

Parnell An inner suburb that lies just east of Auckland Central. The cafes and shops here make this a great area for a stroll punctuated by morning or afternoon tea.

Mission Bay and St. Heliers These attractive waterfront suburbs have views of Waitemata Harbour and Rangitoto Island. There's a footpath along the shore for walkers and joggers.

Remuera Known locally as "Remmers," this is Auckland's most affluent suburb. It's where the "ladies who lunch" live, and real estate carries big price tags.

Mt. Eden and Epsom Both are inner suburbs with older homes and established gardens. Each has a small shopping area.

Herne Bay and Ponsonby These are inner suburbs to the west of Auckland Central; they were once considered undesirable but are now popular among the city's yuppies, who are restoring the neighborhoods' fine old homes. Ponsonby is the cafe capital of New Zealand and hosts some of Auckland's most interesting little eating spots. It is the Bohemian quarter as well as the city's gay area.

North Shore City This area is really an amalgam of several small towns: **Devonport, Takapuna, Birkenhead,** and others. They lie beyond the north end of the Harbour Bridge and are popular places to live as well as visit. You can access these towns by bus, car, and ferry. Devonport is the most popular with visitors because of the easy access by ferry.

Mangere Home to Auckland International Airport; don't be surprised if you hear local folks substituting the name of the suburb for the name of the airport—"What time are you due out at Mangere?"

Otara This neighborhood to the south is home to Auckland's growing cosmopolitan population, where Pacific Islanders constitute 45%, Maori 26%, Europeans/Anglos 23%, and Asians, Indians, and others 6%.

2 Getting Around

BY BUS

The Link is the newest addition to Auckland's public transport system, and these white buses provide the most convenient way to move around the central city. The Link travels in a loop (in both directions—a complete circuit takes an hour) that

Cheap Thrills: What to See & Do for Free in Auckland

In addition to the activities listed below, peruse *The Herald* for ideas of offbeat, free, and inexpensive things to do. When we were last in Auckland my husband saw an ad for "Wings & Wheels" (a 2-day show of vintage cars and planes), which was lots of fun *for him.*

- **Taking in the Views**   It won't cost a thing to drive or walk to the top of any or all of the million-dollar view points, located throughout the "City of Sails" (see my favorites below).

- **Exploring the Auckland Museum**   It's one of the country's best, and admission to the permanent collection is always free. Other free museums include the Auckland Art Gallery, New Zealand's oldest and largest, and The Royal New Zealand Navy Museum in Devonport.

- **Touring the Lion Brewery**   You can go on a free tour of the "Home of New Zealand's finest beers" on Tuesdays and Thursdays at 10:30am and 2pm. It's about 1¹/₂ hours long and culminates with free tastings of Steinlager, Lion Red, and other favorites. It's best to book in advance (☎ 09/377-8840).

- **Enjoying a Free Concert**   During the summer, you can catch one in the Winter Garden and the Band Rotunda in The Domain, at Aotea Square, and in Tahaki Reserve on Mt. Eden. For times and dates, pick up a flyer at the Visitor Centre or, before you go, contact **Auckland City, Music in Parks,** Private Bag 92 516, Wellesley Street, Auckland (☎ 09/379-2020, fax 09/571-3757).

- **Participating in Cornwall Park's Summer Programme**   Free guided walks, band concerts, and craft displays are all part of the fun from December through March at the park. For information, contact the **Huia Lodge Visitor Centre,** P.O. Box 26072, Epsom, Auckland (☎ 09/630-8485, fax 09/524-6433).

- **Parking It**   All of Auckland's beautiful and well-maintained parks and gardens—the Parnell Rose Garden, Dove Myer Robinson Park, Cornwall Park, and The Domain—are open to the public free of charge and are perfect spots for a picnic. The Winter Garden and Fernz Fernery in The Domain are open November through March from 9am to 5:30pm, and April through October from 9am to 4:30pm. Enjoy a picnic, stroll around, or just take a load off and do some people-watching.

- **Driving Along the Water**   Tamaki Drive starts in the city and follows the coastline out to the suburb of St. Heliers. This is a popular jogging and in-line skating route, but when I'm short of time (or energy) I drive—slowly—watching the sailboats and windsurfers on the harbor. The Michael Savage Memorial Park, above Tamaki Drive, is another of Auckland's great vistas.

- **Browsing Through Shops along Parnell Road**   I could easily spend the better part of a day here looking at New Zealand–made crafts, especially if I stopped for a lunch break in one of the area's many charming cafes. My favorite shops are those clustered together in the colonial-style Parnell Village.

- **Spending a Day in Devonport**   I love taking the ferry to this seaside suburb. The view of the Auckland skyline from the water is fantastic, and it's fun to watch the sailboats jockey for position in the harbor. If you have time, go up to the lofty lookout points on either Mount Victoria or North Head. Hit the village for an inexpensive lunch at the Stone Oven Bakehouse & Cafe.

includes Queen Elizabeth II Square, Railway Station, Parnell, Newmarket, Karangahape Road, Ponsonby, and Queen Street. It operates every 10 minutes Monday through Friday from 6am to 6pm; every 30 minutes Monday through Thursday from 6 to 10pm (to 11pm on Friday); and Saturday, Sunday and public holidays from 7am to 11pm. The fare is NZ$1 (US 70¢); you can even use your Yellow Bus Company's BusAbout Pass or Family Pass on The Link (see below). For more information call **Rideline** (☎ **0800/10 30 80** in New Zealand).

The **Yellow Bus Company,** which is the intracity bus system run by the City of Auckland Transportation Company, is good and reaches most city highlights. You can pick up timetables from **The Bus Place,** on Victoria Street West; the **Downtown Bus Terminal,** on Commerce Street; or the **visitor centers** listed earlier. For schedules, fares, and routes, call **Rideline** (☎ **0800/10 30 80** in New Zealand).

Fares are by zone, running from NZ60¢ to NZ$6.60 (US42¢ to US$4.62). Children 4 to 15 are charged half fare, and children under 4 ride free. Exact change is not needed. If you're going to be using the buses a lot, you can purchase a 1-day **BusAbout Pass** for unlimited bus travel at NZ$8 (US$5.60) for adults or NZ$4 (US$2.80) for children. There's also a **Family Pass** for NZ$12 (US$8.40). Buy them on the buses or at the Downtown Bus Terminal.

One word of caution when you're planning evening activities: Auckland buses stop running at 11:30pm (or earlier depending on the route) Monday through Saturday and 8pm or so on Sunday. So if you're going to stay out late, plan on taking a taxi home.

The **Yellow Bus Company's Inner-City Shuttle** (it's the one painted yellow, with a red band and the destination "000 Street Car") runs Monday through Friday every 10 minutes from the Railway Station along Customs Street, up Queen Street to Karangahape Road, then back to the station by way of Mayoral Drive and Queen Street for a fare of NZ40¢ (US28¢)—no matter how far you ride.

The **Explorer Bus** (☎ **09/360-0033**) is a double-decker tourist bus departing from the Ferry Building at Quay Street on the hour from 9am to 4pm daily. It's sponsored by United Airlines, and their name is emblazoned all over the bus—you can't miss it. There are drop-offs and pickups at eight major Auckland attractions, and in general it's a convenient way to get around for 1 day on a set fare of NZ$15 (US$10.50).

Airport and sightseeing buses depart from the Downtown Airline Terminal on Quay Street.

BY TAXI

Taxi stands are at all terminals and on the corner of Customs Street West at Queen Street, or you can phone for a taxi (☎ **09/300-3000**). At flag fall, the fare is NZ$2 (US$1.40), with the meter rising NZ$1.50 (US$1.05) per kilometer. Waiting time costs NZ44¢ (US31¢) per minute.

BY BICYCLE

Well, I suppose you *could.* Still, with Auckland's up-and-down terrain, it might be pretty tiring. Bikes are, of course, wonderful for harbor-front rides and a few other level stretches, but all in all, you're better off on foot or using the bus. Still, if biking's your thing, you can rent one from **Adventure Cycles,** 1 Fort Lane (☎ **0800/ 335-566** in New Zealand, or 09/309-5566; fax 09/309-4211). Rates are NZ$15 to $25 (US$10.50 to US$17.50) a day and include helmet, lock, water bottle, maps, and other bicycle paraphernalia.

BY CAR

Driving in Auckland can be a real hassle. My best advice is to park the car and use the bus system as much as possible. If you must drive into the city, you can park the car for the day in lots (called "car parks" hereabouts) operated by the City Council. They're on Beresford Street, just off Karangahape Road; near the waterfront on Albert Street, west of Queen; on Victoria Street, just east of Queen; Britomart, off Customs Street to the east of Queen Street; downtown to the east of Queen Street; downtown to the west of Queen Street with an entrance from Customs Street West; Civic Underground on Mayoral Drive; and Victoria Street East. All are open 24 hours daily, and rates are quite reasonable.

Author's note: Don't pick up a car at the airport when you first arrive in New Zealand if you're exhausted and have never driven on the left before. It isn't hard to drive on the left, but it's easier to learn if your eyes are open. Go to your hotel and take a nap and see about having the car delivered later in the day.

BY BOAT

The **Devonport Ferry** departs regularly from Queen's Wharf on Quay Street (☎ 09/ 367-9125). The round-trip (return) fare is NZ$7 (US$4.90). There are also a couple of dollarwise multitrip passes. Riding the Devonport Ferry is really one of the most memorable Auckland experiences—in other words, you shouldn't miss it. For more details, see "Exploring Auckland: What to See and Do" below.

You could also travel around the harbor on **Fuller's Harbor Explorer** (☎ 09/ 367-9111), which goes to Devonport, Kelly Tarlton's Southern Oceans Adventure, and Rangitoto Island. This all-day boat pass costs NZ$22 (US$15.40) for adults, half price for children.

FAST FACTS: Auckland

Airlines   **Qantas** flights can be booked at 154 Queen St. (☎ **09/357-8900,** or 0800/808-767 in New Zealand). Contact **Air New Zealand** at Air New Zealand Travel Centres (☎ **0800/737-000** in New Zealand). For flight arrival information, dial ☎ **09/357-3030;** for departure information, ☎ **09/367-2323.**

American Express   You'll find the American Express Travel Services office at 101 Queen St. (P.O. Box 2412), Auckland (☎ **09/379-8243**).

Area Code   Auckland's STD (area) code is **09.**

Baby-sitters   Most hotels and motels can furnish baby-sitters. Also, **Freemans Bay Child Care,** Pratt Street (☎ **09/376-7282**), will provide daytime child care and help in arranging baby-sitters for the evening in Auckland.

Currency Exchange   Cash traveler's checks and exchange any other currency at city-center banks and most neighborhood branches. Hotels and restaurants will usually cash traveler's checks in another currency, but you'll get a much better rate at banks. A currency exchange in the Ferry Building on Quay Street is open daily.

Dentist   For emergency and/or after-hours dental service, call **Auckland Accident & Emergency Clinic** at ☎ **09/520-6609;** open Monday through Saturday from 8am to 11pm, Sunday until 10pm.

Disabled Services   For information on ramps, toilets, car parks, telephones, and a showroom with equipment for people with disabilities, contact the **Disability Resource Centre,** 14 Erson Ave. (P.O. Box 24-042), Royal Oak, Auckland (☎ **09/625-8069,** fax 09/624-1633).

Doctor   For emergency medical service, call ☎ **09/524-5943** or 09/579-9909; for emergency ambulance service, dial ☎ **111.**

Embassies/Consulates   All embassies are in Wellington, the national capital (see "Fast Facts: Wellington" in chapter 10). Auckland has consulates of the **United States,** at 4th floor General Building, Shortland and O'Connell streets (☎ **09/ 303-2724,** fax 09/366-0870); **Canada,** at 48 Emily Place (☎ **09/309-3690,** 09/ 307-3111); and **Ireland,** in the Dingwall Building at 87 Queen St. (☎ **09/302-2867**).

Emergencies   Dial ☎ **111.**

Fax   Fax facilities are available through hotels, motels, and many B&Bs, as well as in the main post office (see "Post Office," below).

Hospitals   The major hospitals are **Auckland Hospital,** Park Road, Grafton (☎ **09/379-7440**); **Green Lane Hospital,** Green Lane Road, Epsom (☎ **09/ 638-9909**); and the **National Women's Hospital,** Claude Road, Epsom (☎ **09/ 638-9919**).

Lost Property   Contact the Central Police Station (☎ **09/379-4240**) or any local police station.

Luggage Storage/Lockers   There are "left luggage" facilities at the Visitor Information Centre in the International Terminal of Auckland Airport. The fee for 24 hours is NZ$3 (US$2.10) for hand luggage, NZ$7 (US$4.90) for large items, and NZ$5 (US$3.50) per suitcase. **Touristop,** located in Auckland's Downtown Airline Terminal, 86–94 Quay St. (☎ **09/377-5783,** fax 09/377-6325), provides luggage storage for NZ$1 (US70¢) per bag, per day. They're open daily from 7:30am to 6pm.

Newspapers/Magazines   The *New Zealand Herald* is the daily paper. The *Sunday Star, Sunday Times,* and *Sunday News* are Sunday-morning publications.

Police   In an emergency, dial ☎ **111.** For other matters, call the Central Police Station (☎ **09/379-4240**).

Post Office   The Chief Post Office (CPO), in the CML Mall, on Queen Street at Wyndham Street, is open Monday through Thursday from 8:30am to 5pm (until 6pm on Friday), and Saturday from 9am to noon. For *Poste Restante* pickup, go to the Post Shop in the Bledisloe Building on Wellesley Street. There is a conveniently located Post Shop in the Downtown Shopping Centre on Quay Street at Queen Elizabeth II Square.

Religious Services   Go to the Holy Trinity Cathedral (Anglican), Parnell Road, Parnell; the Tabernacle (Baptist), 429 Queen St.; the Aotea Chapel (Methodist), opposite Town Hall; St. Andrews (Presbyterian), 2 Symonds St.; the Meeting House (Society of Friends/Quaker), 113 Mt. Eden Rd., Mt. Eden; or St. Patrick's Cathedral (Roman Catholic), 43 Wyndham St.

Taxes   The national 12.5% Goods and Services Tax (GST) applies across the board.

Telephone   See "Telephone" under "Fast Facts: New Zealand," in chapter 3.

Weather Information   For Auckland regional forecasts, call ☎ **009-9909** (it's a 24-hour service, but not a free call).

3 Affordable Accommodations

You'll find the most affordable lodgings outside of the city center. The hotels in the central business district cater to folks on expense accounts, not those of us on a

Central Auckland

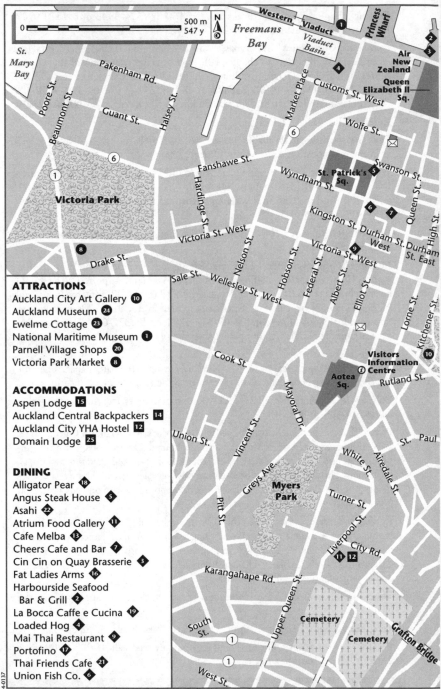

0 — 500 m / 547 y
N

Freemans Bay
St. Marys Bay

Western
Viaduct
Viaduct Basin
Princess Wharf
Air New Zealand
Queen Elizabeth II Sq.

Pakenham Rd.
Market Place
Customs St. West

Poore St.
Beaumont St.
Guant St.
Halsey St.

Wolfe St.

Fanshawe St.
Swanson St.
St. Patrick's Sq.
Wyndham St.
Queen St.

Victoria Park

Kingston St.
Durham St. West
Durham St. East
High St.

Hardinge St.
Victoria St. West
Victoria St. West

Drake St.
Nelson St.
Hobson St.
Federal St.
Albert St.
Elliot St.
Lorne St.
Kitchener St.

Sale St.
Wellesley St. West

ATTRACTIONS
Auckland City Art Gallery ⑩
Auckland Museum ㉔
Ewelme Cottage ㉓
National Maritime Museum ❶
Parnell Village Shops ⑳
Victoria Park Market ❽

ACCOMMODATIONS
Aspen Lodge ⑮
Auckland Central Backpackers ⑭
Auckland City YHA Hostel ⑫
Domain Lodge ㉕

DINING
Alligator Pear ⑱
Angus Steak House ❺
Asahi ㉒
Atrium Food Gallery ⑪
Cafe Melba ⑬
Cheers Cafe and Bar ❼
Cin Cin on Quay Brasserie ❸
Fat Ladies Arms ⑯
Harbourside Seafood Bar & Grill ❷
La Bocca Caffe e Cucina ⑲
Loaded Hog ❹
Mai Thai Restaurant ❾
Portofino ⑰
Thai Friends Cafe ㉑
Union Fish Co. ❻

Cook St.

Visitors Information Centre
Rutland St.

Aotea Sq.

Mayoral Dr.
Vincent St.
Greys Ave.

St. Paul
White St.
Airedale St.

Myers Park
Turner St.

Union St.
Pitt St.

Liverpool St.
City Rd.
⑪ ⑫

Karangahape Rd.
Upper Queen St.

South St.
Cemetery
Cemetery
Grafton Bridge

West St.

4-0137

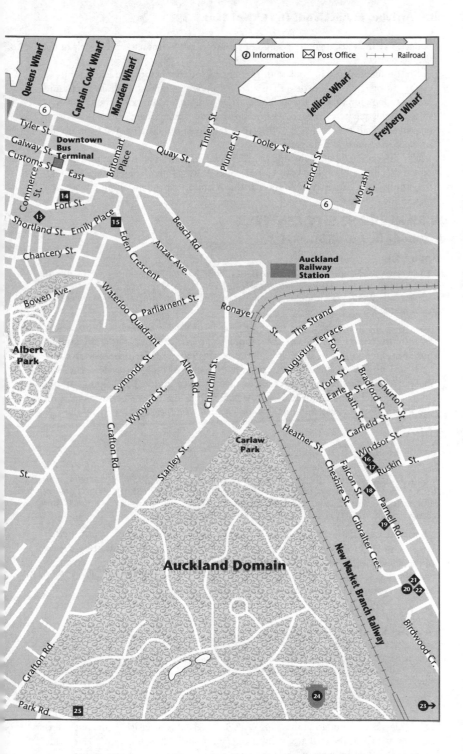

Legend:
- ⓘ Information
- ✉ Post Office
- ┝┿┿┥ Railroad

Queens Wharf
Captain Cook Wharf
Marsden Wharf
Jellicoe Wharf
Freyberg Wharf

⑥

Tyler St.
Galway St.
Customs St.
Commerce St.
Downtown Bus Terminal
East
Britomart Place
Quay St.
Tinley St.
Plumer St.
Tooley St.
French St.
Morash St.
⑥

Fort St.
14
13
Shortland St.
Emily Place
15
Eden Crescent
Beach Rd.
Anzac Ave.
Chancery St.

Auckland Railway Station

Bowen Ave.
Waterloo Quadrant
Parliament St.
Ronaye St.
The Strand
Augustus Terrace
Fox St.
York St.
Earle St.
Bradford St.
Bath St.
Churton St.
Garfield St.

Albert Park

Symonds St.
Wynyard St.
Allen Rd.
Churchill St.
Heather St.
Windsor St.
16
17
Ruskin St.
18
Falcon St.
Cheshire St.

Grafton Rd.
Stanley St.
Carlaw Park
19
Parnell Rd.
Gibralter Cres.

St.

Auckland Domain

New Market Branch Railway

21
20 22

Birdwood Cr.

Grafton Rd.
Park Rd.
25
24
23→

budget. I've included a good selection of suburban B&Bs, motels, and hostels in the listings below.

I recommend that you book your first night's lodging before you leave home—I can think of few things worse than arriving anywhere after a 12-hour flight and having to look for a room. If you should arrive without a room reservation, however, turn immediately to the nearest visitor information center (there's one in the International Arrivals Building at the airport). Just keep in mind that you'll be in no position to shop around for a great deal.

The rates quoted below include the 12.5% GST. Almost all of the properties except those "In or Near The City Center" offer at least some free parking, although the number of spaces may be limited. If this is important to you, inquire when you make your reservation.

IN OR NEAR THE CITY CENTER
A BUDGET BED & BREAKFAST

Aspen Lodge

62 Emily Place, Auckland. ☎ **09/379-6698.** Fax 09/377-7625. 26 rms (none with bathrm). NZ$69 (US$48.30) double, including breakfast. Lower rates May–Sept. AE, BC, DC, JCB, MC, V. Bus: It's a short walk from the Downtown Bus Terminal and the rail station, where you can pick up the Link.

This small, neat establishment is a short walk from Queen Street in the city center and also from the main rail and bus station. The rooms are small but clean, and the breakfasts are more than adequate. Several readers have criticized the spartan decor here, so I now recommend the Aspen only to dedicated budget travelers. Facilities include tea- and coffee-making equipment and a guest laundry. The helpful staff can arrange car and camper-van rentals, as well as sightseeing tours. Aspen Lodge is on the airport shuttle route, and there's good city bus service nearby.

A MOTEL

Domain Lodge

155 Park Rd., Grafton, Auckland. ☎ **09/303-2509.** Fax 09/358-0677. 30 units (all with bathrm). TV TEL. NZ$84.38 (US$59.07) bed-sitter (studio) for 1, NZ$95.63 (US$66.94) bed-sitter for 2; NZ$106.88 (US$74.82) one-bedroom unit for 2; NZ$129.38 (US$90.57) one- or two-bedroom unit for up to 4. Additional person NZ$11.25 (US$7.88) extra. Full breakfast is available for NZ$7.50 (US$5.25). AE, BC, DC, MC, V. Use public bus.

Overlooking the 200-acre Domain (Auckland's giant park), this conveniently located lodge is owned by the Auckland Division of the Cancer Society (patients being treated at Auckland Hospital stay free), and superior digs are offered to the public on an as-available basis, including bed-sitter units. All units have tea and coffee facilities. Best of all, your room rates go directly to the Cancer Society.

A PAIR OF HOSTELS

✪ Auckland Central Backpackers

9 Fort St., Auckland. ☎ **09/358-4877.** Fax 09/358-4872. Web site http://www.acb.co.nz. 120 rms (none with bathrm). NZ$18 (US$12.60) single in dorm; NZ$42 (US$29.40) double; NZ$14 (US$9.80) bunk (no linens). Breakfast available NZ$5–$8 (US$3.50–$5.60). MC, V. Bus: Many nearby.

This centrally located hostel gets rave reviews from readers (and my mate Simon Irvine from Christchurch) and won the New Zealand Tourism Board's top award for best budget accommodation in 1994. With 308 beds, this place isn't tiny, but guests still comment that the staff are "helpful and courteous." All beds except 20 are made up with sheets and duvets. A bar, restaurant, movie theater, travel agency, barbecue,

Internet services, and convenience store are located on-site. Auckland Central Back-packers is a VIP hostel.

Auckland City YHA

HostelCity Rd. and Liverpool St., Auckland. ☎ **09/309-2802**. Fax 09/373-5083. E-mail auck.hostel@yha.org.nz. 150 beds (none with bathrm). NZ$19 (US$15.40) per person for YHA members in dorm, NZ$22 (US$15.40) per person double/twin rm, Non YHA members add NZ$4 (US$2.80) per person, per night. MC, V. 24-hour airport shuttle service. Bus: All Queen St. buses.

Centrally located off Queen Street, this is one of Auckland's top hostels. Separate male and female bathrooms are provided on each floor. All rooms are attractive and comfortable enough and most have a good view of the harbor; a few family units are available too. There's a guest lounge and a separate TV lounge, as well as a good moderately priced restaurant and laundry facilities. You can arrange early check-in or late check-out if you need to, and the friendly 24-hour staff can also book accommodations and tours for your next destination, including discounts. This is a YHA hostel.

IN HERNE BAY
A GUESTHOUSE

Heathmaur Lodge

75 Argyle St., Herne Bay, Auckland. ☎ **09/376-3527**. Fax 09/360-0308. 18 rms (9 with bathrm). NZ$60 (US$42) double without bath, NZ$75 (US$52.50) double with bath, NZ$90 (US$63) double with bath and harbor view. Lower rates for weekly stays in winter. BC, DC, MC, V. Bus: no. 16 or no. 5 on Jervois Rd or catch The Link at College Hill.

Located in a quiet neighborhood, this old white frame house dates from 1911—it was originally built for the Laidlaw family (founders of Farmers Trading Company). Accommodations are on three levels, and there's no lift (elevator). Don't expect cookie-cutter quarters here: Number 11 on the second level (first floor) has a great water view and a sink, but no toilet or shower; number 1 on the top floor has a view of the harbor bridge, a double bed, a sink, and a private toilet and shower right across the hall; number 5 on the top floor has a double and single bed, a harbor view, tea and coffee facilities, and a tiny en suite (attached) bathroom. Trendy Ponsonby Road cafes are about a 15-minute walk away. Some rooms can have a telephone on request, but there's a pay phone on the premises, too. The TV lounge is quite attractive for a budget guest house, with a pool table in a separate room. This place feels like a home away from home for folks who don't mind a little deferred maintenance. Families are welcome.

IN MT. EDEN AND EPSOM
SUPER-CHEAP SLEEPS

Epsom Homestay

10 Ngaroma Rd., Epsom, Auckland. ☎ **09/625-7336**. 2 rms (both with bathrm). NZ$70–$80 (US$49–$56) double. Rates include breakfast. Dinner (available upon request) NZ$30 (US$21) extra. V. Use public bus.

Janet and Jim Millar's bungalow is almost 80 years old. One of the rooms here has a private sitting area with extra bedding for families (The Millars' grandchildren are frequent and welcome visitors, so little ones are no problem.) All other rooms are spacious and comfortable. There's a path at one end of the street leading directly to Maungakiekie (One Tree Hill Domain). Both experienced travelers, the Millars enjoy talking about travel with their guests. Early arrivals are welcome. There's nearby bus service into the city center.

FOR A FEW EXTRA BUCKS

Bavaria Bed and Breakfast Hotel

83 Valley Rd., Mount Eden, Auckland. ☎ **09/638-9641.** Fax 09/638-9665. 11 rms (all with bathrm). NZ$99–$105 (US$69.30–$73.50) double. Rates include breakfast. AE, BC, MC, V.

In a quiet residential area on the western slope of Mount Eden, close to restaurants, shops, and banks, the Bavaria is owned and operated by Rudi and Ulrike Stephan, who came to New Zealand as visitors and stayed on to become permanent residents. The colonial-style house is surrounded by private gardens, and the guest rooms—singles, doubles, and family size—are spacious and attractively furnished. The TV lounge opens to a sun deck, and the sunny breakfast area overlooks the gardens. The Bavaria is located 2km (1 mile) from the city center and 15 minutes from the airport; a bus stop is nearby too.

Mt. Eden Motel

47 Balmoral Rd., Mount Eden, Auckland. ☎ **09/638-7187.** Fax 09/630-9563. 25 units (all with bathrm). TV TEL. NZ$75–$85 (US$52.50–$59.50) unit for 1, NZ$85–$100 (US$59.50–$70) unit for 2. Additional person NZ$12 (US$7.80) extra. Seventh consecutive night free.AE, BC, CB, DC, JCB, MC, V. Public bus.

Only a short, pleasant walk from Mount Eden and the suburb's shopping district, this motel is set back from the road in a residential part of town, eliminating any possible traffic noise. In fact, with off-street parking just outside your unit, you can forget driving into the city, since there's good bus service just a few minutes away. There are one- and two-bedroom units, as well as bed-sitters (studios) with double and twin beds, all with full kitchens and radios. Some units sleep up to eight people, and nonsmoking rooms are available. Facilities include an outdoor pool, an indoor Jacuzzi, a guest laundry, a car wash, and a barbecue area. Breakfast is available, and there are many restaurants nearby. Laurel and Bruce Waters, the owner/operators, will help with your sightseeing and ongoing itinerary.

Ranfurly Evergreen Lodge Motel

285 Manukau Rd. (near Ranfurly Rd.), Auckland. ☎ **09/638-9059.** Fax 09/630-8374. 12 units (all with bathrm). TV TEL. NZ$90–$95 (US$63–$66.50) unit for 1 or 2. Extra person NZ$14 (US$9.80). AE, BC, DC, MC, V. Public bus.

This two-story motel has a pleasant setting of manicured lawn, roses, and hedges. Each of the one-bedroom units accommodates two to five people and has one full window wall. The rooms are nicely decorated, and come equipped with color TV and electric blankets. There's a guest laundry, as well as car-wash facilities, and a shopping center is just 100 yards away. Although the units have kitchens, a continental breakfast is available for NZ$6 (US$4.20). On the direct airport bus route, the lodge is 5km (3 miles) from the city center; a public bus stops at the door.

IN PARNELL

Chalet Chevron Bed & Breakfast Hotel

14 Brighton Rd., Parnell, Auckland. ☎ **09/309-0290.** Fax 09/373-5754. 12 rms (all with bathrm). TEL. NZ$108–$120 (US$75.60–$84) double. Rates include breakfast. AE, DC, MC, V. Bus: The Link.

David and Fae England, the enthusiastic and informative hosts, have a genuine interest in their guests' comfort—and their Auckland experience. The guest rooms are pleasant and comfortable, and there is one family room. Three rooms have bathtubs and the rest have showers. Four rooms offer delightful sea views. A TV is provided in the lounge. The hotel is a short walk from Parnell Village, and there's good bus service to the city center.

Family-Friendly Accommodations

Epsom Homestay *(see p. 103)*   The downstairs garden suite in this 80-year-old bungalow is perfect for families—it has a private sitting area with extra bedding. Your hosts, the Millars, often have their grandchildren on the premises, so little ones are no problem. Plus, there's nearby bus service to the city center.

Green Glade Motel *(see p. 107)*   Kids will love swimming at nearby beaches and romping through the pine forest behind this motel. Plus, there are eight one- and two-bedroom units that have complete kitchens, five units with tea and toast facilities, and laundry facilities on the premises.

Karin's Garden Villa *(see p. 108)*   The large lawn here is a perfect place for kids to stretch their legs, and the beach is just minutes away. The bright, airy two-story studio cottage has a double bed, a sofa sleeper, cooking facilities, a telephone, and a shower, making it ideal for families.

WORTH A SPLURGE

✪ Ascot Parnell

36 St. Stephens Ave., Parnell, Auckland 1. ☎ **09/309-9012.** Fax 09/309-3729. Web site nz.com/HeritageInns/AscotParnell. 11 rms (all with bathrm). TEL. NZ$125 (US$88) double. Additional person NZ$40 (US$28) extra for adults and children. Not suitable for children under 6. Rates include breakfast. AE, BC, DC, MC, V. Bus: The airport bus stops in front; The Link bus service is 1 block away.

This bed-and-breakfast is one of Auckland's most pleasant inns, and it's also conveniently located—only a short walk from Parnell Road, where there are myriad shopping and dining options, and a hilly walk (about 1½ miles) from the city center. The grounds feature a gigantic century-old pin oak that's registered as a "historic tree." The house dates from 1910 and, under the loving care of Bart and Therese Blommaert, it maintains an informal elegance. The guest rooms are spacious, each with an individual decor; one family room will accommodate up to four. The whole place is absolutely spotless. Request a ground-floor room if you want to avoid climbing the stairs. I like room 8, which has both a queen bed and a single bed with dusty rose bedspreads, a little alcove with a table and chairs (a good place to stash luggage), and a view over the garden of the city center. There's a pretty breakfast room and a TV lounge. Complimentary coffee, tea, and juice are available in the lounge, and beer and cold drinks are for sale here too—they're in the fridge and you pay on an honor system. Off-street parking is another bonus. I've had nothing but good reports from readers who've stayed here, many of whom praise the hosts' friendly, personalized travel advice. And I have to agree: Bart and Therese couldn't be nicer or more helpful. Because the Ascot Parnell is so popular, reserve as far in advance as possible.

IN REMUERA
SUPER-CHEAP SLEEPS

Raceway Motel

67 St. Vincent Ave., Remuera, Auckland. ☎ **09/524-0880** or 09/524-0155. Fax 09/520-0155. 10 units (all with bathrm). MINIBAR TV TEL. NZ$75 (US$52.50) unit for 1 or 2. AE, MC, V. Take the Greenlane exit on the motorway toward Ellerslie Racecourse and it's the second left.

In a tranquil spot that's still close to the city center, this motor lodge is near Ellerslie Racecourse and Alexandra Park, only a short walk from a good shopping center and licensed restaurants. All units have complete kitchens and radios, and there's a guest laundry, as well as covered parking. Cots and highchairs are available, and both continental and cooked breakfasts are available through room service. Public bus transportation is nearby.

FOR A FEW EXTRA BUCKS

Sedgwick Kent Lodge

65 Lucerne Rd., Remuera, Auckland. ☎ **09/524-5219.** Fax 09/520-4825. E-mail sklodge@ibm.net. 4 rms (all with bathrm). TV. NZ$100–$155 (US$70–$109) double. Rates include breakfast. AE, MC, V.

I envy the lucky readers who stay in this beautifully restored turn-of-the-century homestead. It looks like something out of *Architectural Digest,* and Louisa Hobson-Corry entertains in Martha Stewart style. There's kauri (native timber) paneling in the bathrooms, and superior-quality linens on all beds. Breakfast is served in front of the fireplace during the winter and on the patio in summer. Louisa is happy to take visitors shopping in Parnell, and her husband, Cliff, likes to lead walks in the Waitakere Ranges. Two spa pools, a piano, a fax, a computer, and a very friendly cat named Oscar are all available for guests' enjoyment.

WORTH A SPLURGE

✪ Aachen House

39 Market Rd., Remuera, Auckland. ☎ **09/520-2329,** or 0800/AACHEN in New Zealand; mobile phone 021/670-044. Fax 09/524-2898. 9 rms (all with bathrm). TEL. NZ$135–$250 (US$95–175) double. Rates include cooked breakfast. Located 4km (2¹/₂ miles) from downtown, with bus service a block away; from the airport, take the shuttle.

Hosts Joan and Greg McKirdy have lived in Jakarta, Fiji, and Hong Kong, and when they returned to New Zealand, they brought home the antiques and paintings from their foreign homes. These help to create the genteel ambience that prevails at this special B&B. The breakfast room, with its lace tablecloths, rotunda ceiling, and heated marble floor, resembles an Edwardian tea house. The lounge has a crystal chandelier, instant hot water for tea and coffee from a brass tap, and a collection of antique porcelain in glass-fronted cabinets. There are high ceilings throughout the historic house—each with decorative plaster friezes. One bedroom is wheelchair accessible and overlooks the garden. I think the Gardenia Room upstairs is the best deal; it has a window bench and twin beds that convert into a king. The Victorian Suite has a four-poster bed and its own balcony overlooking the park. Smoking is not permitted in the house, and this place isn't recommended for children under 16.

IN DEVONPORT AND BEYOND

If you choose to sleep in this charming seaside suburb, consider buying a ferry pass: either the 10-trip (NZ$26/US$18.20 adult, NZ$12/US$8.40 child) or the weekly pass (NZ$23/US$16.10). Otherwise, each return (round-trip) to the city will cost you NZ$7 (US$4.90) per adult and NZ$3.50 (US$2.45) per child. **Super Shuttle** provides the best transportation to Devonport from the airport.

CAMPGROUNDS & CABINS

✪ North Shore Caravan and Holiday Park

52 Northcote Rd., Takapuna, Auckland (P.O. Box 36139, Auckland 9). ☎ **09/419-1320** or 09/418-2578. Fax 09/480-0435. 7 motel rms (all with bathrm), 29 cabins, 8 tourist flats, 150 caravan and tent sites. NZ$80 (US$56) double rm; NZ$37–$55 (US$25.90–$38.50) cabin for 2; NZ$64.50 (US$45.15) flat for 1, NZ$73 (US$51.10) flat for 2; NZ$18 (US$12.60) caravan/tent site for 1, NZ$25 (US$17.50) caravan/tent site for 2. Additional adult in caravan/tent site

NZ$12.50 (US$8.80), additional child NZ$7 (US$4.90) extra. AE, MC, V. Frequent bus service nearby; 20 minutes to central Auckland.

A member of the "Top 10 Group of Holiday Parks," this spot boasts a first-rate location, accessible to downtown Auckland via the Harbour Bridge. All communal facilities, including the kitchen, are kept very clean. I particularly like the pink Italian tile baths. Other facilities include a large laundry with dryers and a TV room. There's a Pizza Hut next door. The cabins are basic, sleep up to four people, and have sinks (with hot and cold running water), refrigerators, toasters, cutlery, and an electric kettle. You provide your own bedding and share communal kitchen and bathroom facilities.

SUPER-CHEAP SLEEPS

Cheltenham-by-the-Sea

2 Grove Rd., Devonport, Auckland. ☎ or fax **09/445-9437.** 5 rms (1 with bathrm). NZ$65–85 (US$45.50–59.50) twin or double without bath, NZ$110 (US$77) queen with bath. Rates include breakfast. No credit cards.

Joyce and Harry Mossman's large home is set amid shade trees and a spacious lawn, only a minute from Cheltenham Beach and just a little farther from shops, restaurants, and bus transportation. The hosts offer one room with a queen bed and en suite (attached) bathroom; the other rooms (one double, one triple, one twin, and one single) share two other bathrooms. Joyce and Harry prefer to have only a couple of these rooms in use at any time, "otherwise we lose the personal touch." There's a TV in the lounge. The Mossmans' home is a 20-minute walk or less than a 10-minute drive to the ferry wharf, and they can and will arrange local tours for you.

Green Glade Motel

27 Ocean View Rd., Northcote, Auckland. ☎ **09/480-7445.** Fax 09/480-7439. 13 units (all with bathrm). A/C TV TEL. NZ$78.75–$90 (US$55.15–$63) unit for 1 or 2. Best Western discounts available. AE, DC, MC, V. The owner will pick you up at the Downtown Airline Terminal.

The Green Glade is run by owner Geoff Calvert, who knows his country well and maintains a tour desk to assist guests with trip planning. There are eight one- and two-bedroom units with complete kitchens, plus five units with tea and toast facilities. All have modern furnishings and a cheerful decor, with a radio, central heating, and electric blankets. Affiliated with Best Western, the motel has a pool, heated spa pool, and guest laundry facilities. A continental or a hot breakfast is available for a small additional charge. A real bonus is the forested public reserve just back of the motel, great for peaceful walks. Restaurants, a golf course, beaches, and shopping centers are all nearby. The motel is on the North Shore, across the Harbour Bridge, 8km (5 miles) from the city center. There's good public bus transportation to the center of Auckland.

✪ Ducks Crossing Cottage

58 Seabreeze Rd., Devonport, Auckland. ☎ and fax **09/445-8102.** TV. 3 rms (2 with bathrm). NZ$75 (US$52.50) double without bath, NZ$90 (US$63) double with bath. Rates include breakfast. No credit cards.

You'll get lots of personal attention from hosts Peter and Gwenda Mark-Woods—Kiwi hospitality reigns here. She's a jolly, sweet woman and a retired nurse. The modern home (built in 1994) is surrounded by cottage gardens. A window bench in the lounge catches the sun and is a great place to hole up with a book. One room has a king bed (which converts to twins) and a private bathroom. The most spacious room is the upstairs queen room, which has a balcony and en suite (attached) bathroom. There is also a small double that shares a bathroom with the hosts. All rooms have TVs (an unusual feature for a homestay B&B) and quilts made by Gwenda herself. Ducks Crossing is located across the street from Waitemata Golf Club and just off Lake Road, the main drag into and out of Devonport. A little traffic noise now and then is the only drawback. It's a 25-minute walk to the ferry, but hosts gladly "run people down." Look for the ducks—crossing.

MODERATELY PRICED OPTIONS

Devonport Villa Inn
46 Tainui Rd., Devonport, Auckland. ☎ **09/445-8397**. Fax 09/445-9766. E-mail dvilla@ihug.co.nz. Web site www.devonportvillainn.co.nz. 7 rms (all with bathrm). NZ$135–$185 (US$95–$126) double. Rates include full breakfast. AE, MC, V. The hosts will pick up arriving guests at the ferry.

Winner of the 1997 New Zealand Tourism Award for Hosted Accommodation, this is a delightful base from which to do your exploration of the area. Hosts Yvonne Lambert and Philip Brown make guests feel welcome and provide them with sightseeing information as well as ideas for onward travels. In addition, Yvonne serves delicious breakfasts that include homemade muffins and muesli (granola). The house is a restored villa dating from 1903. Each room has a high ceiling, an armoire made from native timbers, a quilt made by Yvonne's sister, and fresh flowers. Guests are welcome to enjoy the lounge and dining room; some even buy fish-and-chips from a nearby shop and bring them to the inn for supper. Crab Apple, their lovely cat, is only too happy to help clean up the leftovers. Devonport Villa is a 20-minute walk from the wharf, but a minibus meets every ferry and transports guests to the inn for NZ$1 (US 70¢). Cheltenham Beach is 2 minutes' walk away. No smoking is permitted in the villa.

The Esplanade Hotel
1 Victoria Rd., Devonport, Auckland. ☎ **09/445-1291**. Fax 09/445-1999. 11 rms (all with bathrm), 7 suites. TV TEL. NZ$140–$160 (US$98–$112) double; NZ$210 (US$147) suite for 1 or 2. Additional person NZ$25 (US$17.50) extra. AE, BC, DC, MC, V.

This lovely old Edwardian-style hotel has recently been renovated. It's situated at the water end of Devonport's main street, only steps from the ferry wharf. The front rooms have wonderful views. The suites are out of the range of the cost-conscious traveler (unless you feel like splurging), so I recommend that you stay in a standard room and enjoy the prime location and historic ambience. Reader Jennie Fairlie from Queensland, Australia sums up her stay here this way: "I was fortunate enough to stay in a front room and greatly enjoyed the magnificent view of the harbor with ships of all sizes passing by, the activity at the Ferry Terminal, the smells and sounds of people eating at the many sidewalk cafes, and the children swimming and the dogs playing in the park opposite. The restaurant at the hotel is first-class."

Karin's Garden Villa
14 Sinclair St., Devonport, Auckland. ☎ or fax **09/445-8689**. 4 rms (1 with bathrm), 1 studio cottage. NZ$95 (US$66.50) double without bath, NZ$115 (US$81) double with bath; NZ$125 (US$88) studio cottage (without breakfast, 3-night minimum). Rates include continental breakfast. Dinner NZ$20 (US$14) extra. MC, V. Take the airport shuttle, or the host will meet you at the ferry.

Karin Loesch's homey old villa has a large lawn and fruit trees at the end of a cul-de-sac, just a few minutes' walk from the beach, golf, restaurants, shops, and the bus line. She and her two teenage children are multilingual and welcome visitors, especially families, from all over the world. Guests can use the laundry and use the kitchen to cook their own meals or enjoy Karin's dinners, which are extra. Breakfast includes "good German coffee." The bright, airy two-story studio cottage has a double bed, a sofa sleeper, cooking facilities, a telephone, and a shower. The ferry wharf is a 20-minute walk away.

✪ Villa Cambria

71 Vauxhall Rd., Devonport, Auckland. ☎ **09/445-7899**. Fax 09/446-0508. Web site nz.com/webnz/bbnz/vcambria.htm. E-mail villacambria@xtra.co.nz. 3 rms (all with bathrm), 1 garden loft (with bathrm). NZ$120–$150 (US$84–$105) double; NZ$160 (US$112) garden loft, NZ$180 (US$126) garden loft with honeymoon package. Rates include breakfast. AE, MC, V. Take the Super Shuttle to the door from the airport; the hosts provide a courtesy transfer from the ferry.

Hosts Clive and Kate Sinclair welcome guests with open arms. The house was built in 1904 and is surrounded by landscaped grounds and gardens. The lounge is furnished with antiques, and breakfast, which includes fresh home-baked goodies, is served on a kauri kitchen table. The Garden Loft is spacious and has its own balcony, microwave, fridge, sink, and a few kitchen utensils—young children are welcome to stay in the loft, but not the house. All rooms have a decanter of port and tea- and coffee-facilities, and laundry facilities are available on the premises. The Sinclairs are very helpful with arranging onward bookings and planning local sightseeing. Plus, Clive's a member of the local golf club (Waitemata), and he'll play with guests or set up tee times for them. There are fewer rules and formalities here than in some B&Bs, but the surroundings are just as lovely.

WORTH A SPLURGE

The Peace & Plenty Inn

6 Flagstaff Terrace, Devonport, Auckland. ☎ **09/445-2925**. Fax 09/445-2901. Web site nz.com/HeritageInns/Peace&Plenty/index.html. E-mail hyland@voyager.co.nz. TEL. 6 rms (all with bathrm). NZ$210 (US$147) double, NZ$275 (US$193) "Atea Suite." Rates include full breakfast. AE, DC, MC, V.

Hosts Carol and Bruce Hyland have lived and traveled in various parts of the world, and they called on their worldly experiences when it came time to restore and decorate the house that's now their inn. The Bahama Room acknowledges the islands where they lived on their boat; Canada is a tribute to Bruce's nationality; and Provence is simply a favorite destination. The house was built in 1888 for the manager of a kauri timber mill and so is built of the prized (and pricey) native wood. Each room is outfitted with superb linens, fluffy robes, decanters of port, tea- and coffee-facilities, and toiletries; fresh flowers abound. Carol's breakfasts include homemade yogurt and muesli (granola), as well as free-range eggs and edible flowers. Complimentary tea, coffee, sherry, and cookies are always available in the lounge, and breakfast can be served in bed on request at no extra charge—it's not surprising that this is a very popular honeymoon destination. The Garden Suite, the only room where children are allowed, has a TV and a private entrance. Smoking is not permitted. Peace & Plenty is less than a block from the ferry landing and Victoria Road restaurants (guests receive a 10% discount at several local restaurants), and it's a gorgeous house with lots of Martha Stewart–type touches. The rates are high, but you get what you pay for. *One caveat:* There's a tiny bit of noise from the street.

IN NEARBY CLEVEDON

✪ Birchwood Country Bed & Breakfast

R.D.3. Clevedon, Auckland. ☎ **09/292-8729**. Fax 09/292-8555. 3 rms (1 with bathrm). NZ$135 (US$95) queen without bath, NZ$150 (US$105) queen with bath, NZ$160 (US$112) king with en suite (attached) bathrm. Rates include full breakfast. AE, MC, V. Located 30 minutes' drive from the airport, 45 minutes from the city.

This gorgeous home is situated on 200 acres in a farming area south of Auckland. The interiors are right out of a magazine, with matai floors, oriental rugs, fine china, and lots of fresh flowers. Hosts Ann and Mike Davies bought the farm 20 years ago and restored the house, which dates from 1887. Period furnishings enhance the historic ambience. The largest bedroom has a king bed and en suite bathroom; the other two are smaller, have queen beds, and share a bathroom. All have robes, toiletries, first-class bed and bath linens, and ceiling fans. There's a real country kitchen with the original pot-belly stove, and breakfast features delicious homemade muffins, fresh fruit from their orchard, and free-range eggs. Evening meals aren't served, but there are some restaurants in the area (see "Great Deals on Dining," below). Guests can enjoy the swimming pool in the garden, play tennis, or watch the 240 dairy cows being milked. Or if you're staying here from November through April, you may be able to catch a local polo match. Slippers are kept by the front door for guests' use (shoes aren't allowed on the polished wood floors). Be sure to get good directions to this B&B, especially if you're arriving at night—the roads are dark. There's no smoking in the house; children under age 12 are not accepted; and there's no wheelchair access.

4　Great Deals on Dining

Eating out in Auckland can be just about anything you want it to be. There are scads of small, attractive, and moderately priced cafes; a wide range of cuisine at reasonable prices; and an impressive array of posh restaurants serving international dishes. They're scattered all over the city, but there are interesting concentrations along Parnell Road in Parnell and Ponsonby Road in Ponsonby.

When you're dining in restaurants, be careful when you order. You can double your bill by asking for bread and a side salad—items that are usually included with every main course in the United States. And don't feel compelled to tip. Kiwis do only when the service has been exceptional.

FOOD COURTS & OTHER DINING COMPLEXES　You can really stretch your travel dollars and save some precious sightseeing time by heading to one of the city's food courts, where NZ$5 (US$3.50) will surely fill you up. In Auckland, one of the most popular ones is located on the second level of the **Downtown Shopping Centre** at Queen Elizabeth II Square on Quay Street. It's open daily, Monday through Thursday from 7am to 6pm, Friday from 7am to 8pm, and weekends from 7am to 4pm. **Food Alley** on Albert Street, across from the Stamford Plaza Hotel, is another good one. Nine different kinds of ethnic cuisines are represented; it's open daily from 10am to 10pm, and it's licensed to serve alcohol.

There's also a food court in the Atrium Shopping Centre on the west side of Elliott Street between Victoria and Wellesley near the Visitor Centre. At the **Atrium Food Gallery** you'll find everything from McDonald's to pastas, kebabs, roast meals (chicken and other meats), Chinese, sushi, a bakery, and coffee shops. Prices for meals range from NZ$5 to NZ$9 (US$3.50 to US$6.30); it's open Monday through Thursday 7am to 6pm, Friday 7am to 9pm, Saturday 7am to 6pm, and Sunday 7:30am to 6pm.

Victoria Park Market, on Victoria Street West (☎ **09/309-6911,** fax 09/ 377-8954) has an International Food Court (open daily 9am to 6pm), as well as several licensed cafes and a McDonald's. This is an especially appealing place on weekends when you can enjoy low-cost dining (NZ$4 to $6/US$2.80 to $4.20 for a meal), plus free entertainment.

IN OR NEAR THE CITY CENTER
SUPER-CHEAP EATS

✪ Cafe Melba
33 Vulcan Lane (between High and O'Connell sts.), Auckland. ☎ **09/377-0091.** Fax 09/529-1209. Reservations not accepted. Main courses NZ$6.50–$13.50 (US$4.60–9.50). AE, BC, DC, MC, V. Daily 7am–7pm. MODERN NEW ZEALAND.

This inner-city hideaway is located in a tiny cobblestone lane that runs between two 19th-century buildings. I recommend you sit outside and watch the parade of passersby. Chris Upton, the British owner/manager, spent 4 years working his way around the world on the *QEII*. He also used to manage one of New Zealand's top country lodges. Now he's busy putting Melba's on the map. Breakfast (which, with the exception of a few items, is served all day) ranges from chunky toasted muesli with summer fruits and natural yogurt to the Melba Grill—bacon and eggs on five-grain toast with sausages, herbed potatoes, tomato, and mushrooms. For lunch you might try a pasta dish like smoked chicken, pinenuts, and mushrooms tossed with pesto and pasta (all pasta dishes come with a salad). Or go with a gourmet sandwich like grilled eggplant, capsicum (bell pepper), and goat cheese on toasted country bread with sundried tomato pesto. If you just want to stop by for a glass of wine in the afternoon, don't be surprised if they give you a plate of bread and dips—remember, you can't have alcohol in a restaurant without food service.

Cheers Cafe & Bar
12 Wyndham St., just off Queen St. ☎ **09/309-8779.** Reservations not required. Main courses NZ$9–$14.50 (US$6.30–$10.20). AE, DC, MC, V. Daily 11am–1am. CAFE.

This licensed cafe in the city center is a bright, airy place with lots of blond wood, greenery, and a fountain. The tempting menu includes chicken or beef satay on basmati rice with spicy peanut sauce, stir-fried lamb with garlic and mint, fresh fish fillets or steaks (choose either blackened or baked with beurre blanc), and chicken thighs pan-fried with tomato pesto and fresh chiles. You can also order nachos, a burger, an omelet, or a variety of pastas. Cheers is well known for its inventive cocktails, vast beer selection, and its cellar of local and imported wines. There are also some "Alcohol-Free Cocktails," featuring freshly squeezed juice drinks. Happy hour is Monday through Friday from 5 to 6pm, Saturday and Sunday from 11am to 6pm.

FOR A FEW EXTRA BUCKS

Angus Steak House
35 Albert St., at Swanson St. ☎ **09/379-7815.** Reservations recommended. Steak and salad bar NZ$21.60 (US$15.12). AE, DC, JCB, MC, V. Mon–Fri noon–2pm; daily 5–11pm. STEAKHOUSE.

This centrally located Auckland favorite serves up generous portions of great food at reasonable prices. Main courses include seven kinds of steak, chicken, or ham. All prices include a trip to the plentiful salad bar. Since the entrees are so big, many couples split one and pay NZ$6.80 (US$4.40) extra for the second person's trip to the salad bar. The wooden tables are a little too close together and the low-beamed ceiling in the cellar a little low—tall travelers should be careful. Beer and wine are available, or you can bring your own.

Mai Thai
57B Victoria St. W., near Albert St. ☎ **09/303-2550.** Fax 09/521-4494. Reservations recommended. Main courses NZ$12.50–$21.50 (US$8.40–$15.10). AE, MC, V. Mon–Fri noon–3pm; Mon–Sat 6–10:30pm. THAI.

This is one of the best Asian restaurants in Auckland. Although it's a bit small, Mai Thai is big on service. The decor and ambience here are peaceful, a real breath of fresh air in the heart of the city center. Thai servers proffer their country's traditional cuisine—some of which is very spicy. The house specialty is prawn and fish cakes, and the tom yum goong (spicy prawn soup) is also quite tasty. It's fully licensed for liquor, and the wine list is surprisingly good—or you can bring your own.

WORTH A SPLURGE

✪ Cin Cin on Quay Brasserie & Bar

In the Ferry Building, 99 Quay St. ☎ **09/307-6966.** Reservations recommended for lunch. Main courses NZ$21.90–$28.50 (US$15.33–$19.95). AE, BC, DC, JCB, MC, V. Breakfast Sat–Sun 8–11am; lunch and dinner daily 11am–1am; snacks Fri–Sat until 3am. Bar is open late. NEW ZEALAND/PACIFIC.

This stylish waterfront restaurant in the old Ferry Building is a hit among ferry-goers, of course, plus Aucklanders who know how many awards Cin Cin has won. A wood-burning pizza oven, mesquite grill, and open kitchen are a few of the unusual features inside, where the chef oversees a menu that includes Italian, French, Chinese, and Japanese touches. The large bar serves drinks outside all day, specializing in imported beers and wines by the glass. Inside, marble floors add a touch of elegance to the large casual dining area, marked by bright colors. Upstairs, there's mezzanine dining in a more formal setting. Light meals and snacks (like pizza) are also served.

Harbourside Seafood Bar & Grill

Upstairs in the Ferry Building (above Cin Cin on Quay), 99 Quay St. ☎ **09/307-0486** or 09/307-0556. Fax 09/307-0523. Reservations recommended. Main courses NZ$24–$35 (US$16.80–$24.50). AE, BC, DC, JCB, MC, V. Mon–Sat 11:30am–10pm, Sun 9:30am–10pm. Closed Christmas Day. SEAFOOD.

This stylish bilevel restaurant on the waterfront is right in the city center and has a terrific view of the harbor. You can sit inside or out—if you sit inside, ask for a table by a window. The decor is modern with a marbled entrance, paintings, dividing screens, and a crayfish tank. Seafood dishes have won plenty of kudos, and there's an extensive wine list. The menu features a charcoal-grilled seafood platter, pan-fried John Dory, and baked salmon fillet. My favorite is the risotto: prawns, scampi, scallops, squid, mussels, and fish tossed with a Tuscan sauce. Four token meat dishes are offered for those who don't eat fish. An excellent brunch is served on Saturday, Sunday, and holidays. It's fully licensed, too.

Union Fish Company

41 Albert St. ☎ **09/309-6593** or 09/379-6745. Reservations required. Main courses NZ$20–$24 (US$14–$16.80). AE, DC, MC, V. Mon–Fri noon–2:30pm; daily 5:30–10pm. SEAFOOD.

Many Aucklanders consider this the best place for Japanese-style seafood. Choose your own crayfish from a bubbling tank and the chef will prepare it any way you like. Or select from specialties like sashimi, Bluff oysters, Nelson salmon (fresh or smoked), scallops, green-lipped mussels, or the daily fresh catch. And don't worry, it's fully licensed.

IN PONSONBY

Ponsonby, the Cafe Capital of New Zealand, is Auckland's Bohemian quarter, and dozens of inexpensive little cafes line both sides of Ponsonby Road. Competition in this area is fierce, which luckily for us keeps prices down.

✪ Atlas Power Cafe & Bar

285 Ponsonby Rd., Ponsonby. ☎ **09/360-1295.** Reservations accepted. Meals NZ$7–$13.50 (US$4.90–$9.50). AE, BC, DC, MC, V. Daily 7:30am–10pm. ECLECTIC.

"Pinchos" are small meals enjoyed like tapas, but bigger. On a recent visit, my husband and I each ordered one to start. I had the salmon mousse on crostini with three delicious, huge smoked mussels in their shells; my husband went with penne pesto aïoli salad with crostini and chicken. Both were great and cost only NZ$9 (US$6.30) apiece. We were too full to order anything else, so it turned out to be a great bargain. The service is very friendly—the waitress chatted both with us and passersby. The coffee here is really good, too. They roast and grind their own beans on the premises. Sit inside or, if weather permits, on the sidewalk. The cafe is fully licensed.

IN PARNELL

Parnell Road has a lively dining scene. Things get interesting at Heather and Garfield streets and continue up St. Stephens Avenue. There are bars, cafes, take-out joints, delis, lots of fine restaurants, and two wine stores for BYO meals—a good way to shave a few bucks off the bill. I suggest you roam the area for a while before deciding where to eat. In addition to the places listed below, you might try **The Fat Ladies Arms,** on Parnell Road (corner of Windsor Street), Parnell (☎ **09/358-2688**), where you can get good pub grub—steak, seafood, chicken, curry, and rice plates for NZ$8 to NZ$9 (US$5.60 to US$6.30). It's open daily.

Saints of Parnell Pastry Shop, 227 Parnell Rd., Parnell (☎ **09/379-0571**) is a good place to buy picnic fare, which you could take over to Parnell Rose Garden or Auckland Domain—both nearby. Lunch here is less than NZ$4 (US$2.80) per person. They have everything from quiches and sandwiches to cakes and cookies.

Tip: Even if you don't eat at one of the restaurants in the Parnell Village Shops, walk through to the patio at the back of the cluster and look at the view of the Auckland Museum in The Domain—it's especially impressive at night.

SUPER-CHEAP EATS

Kebab Kid

363 Parnell Rd., Parnell. ☎ **09/373-4290**. Fax 09/366-6418. Light meals NZ$6–$7 (US$4.20–$4.90). AE, DC, MC, V. Sun–Mon noon–10pm, Tues–Thurs and Sat noon–11pm, Fri noon–2am. Bus: The Link. GREEK/MIDDLE EASTERN.

This is a very popular, very casual place. The twenty-somethings that run Kebab Kid have set up half a dozen wooden tables in a small room where you can enjoy good, cheap Greek eats—they even provide magazines to read while you wait. You might enjoy *charwarma,* a toasted whole-meal bun with spiced lamb, lettuce, tomatoes, and sauces; or grilled chicken in pita bread with tsatsiki sauce. There's also a selection of Moroccan salads, hummus, tsatsiki with pita, and falafel for two. You order at the counter, and meals are prepared in the open kitchen in a corner of the room. The baklava comes with "hokey pokey" ice cream, New Zealand's favorite flavor—vanilla ice cream with chunks of hard candy. This is a nonalcoholic environment—you can't buy it or bring it. Take-out is also available.

FOR A FEW EXTRA BUCKS

Alligator Pear

211 Parnell Rd., Parnell. ☎ **09/307-2223.** Fax 09/625-0659. Reservations not essential. Main courses NZ$13–$20 (US$9.10–$14). AE, DC, MC, V. Tues–Sun 5:30pm–late. Bus: The Link. MEDITERRANEAN/NEW ZEALAND.

This basement restaurant feels like a European taverna. The owners are chef Errol Syme, a Kiwi, and maitre d' Brian Aitchison, a Scotsman. Both the decor and menu reflect the various places they've vacationed, including the Mediterranean, Egypt, North Africa, Greece, and Spain. The blackboard menu lists daily specials—on my last trip I had a tasty good pumpkin and sausage soup. All main dishes come with a signature pear-shaped potato croquet, and dinner is followed by an alligator-shaped chocolate. This restaurant is not as trendy as other places on the street, but it offers good food at reasonable prices. In case you're wondering: an "alligator pear" is what the English call an avocado. It's BYO here—pick up a bottle of wine at nearby Glengarry's.

La Bocco Caffe e Cucina

251 Parnell Rd., Parnell. ☎ **09/375-0083.** Reservations accepted. Lunch NZ$9.50–$16 (US$6.70–$11.20), dinner main courses NZ$16–$21.50 (US$11.20–$15.10). AE, BC, DC, MC, V. Daily 9am–11pm. Bus: The Link. ITALIAN.

This is a cute little spot for dessert, coffee, or a light Italian meal. It's known locally as a place to enjoy good coffee and good conversation. Inside seven tables and a long black leather bench along one wall create a cozy coffeehouse ambience. There are a few tables outside on a well-used brick patio; four stools on the sidewalk are served through an open window on "fine" days. There is no smoking inside. The Midnight Chocolate Cake is "a killer" and large enough to share several ways. They're fully licensed.

Portofino

156 Parnell Rd., Parnell. ☎ **09/373-3740.** Reservations not accepted. Main courses NZ$10.50–$19.50 (US$7.40–$13.70). AE, DC, MC, V. Sun–Thurs 11am–11pm, Fri–Sat 11am–11:30pm. Bus: The Link. ITALIAN.

This small, licensed restaurant is very popular and, as a result, very noisy. People wait on the footpath (sidewalk) for a table to open up so they can savor the pizzas, pastas, and other traditional Italian meat dishes. It's under the same ownership as the equally popular Portobello across the street.

Thai Friends Cafe & Restaurant

311 Parnell Rd., in the Parnell Village Shops, Parnell. ☎ **09/373-5247.** Reservations recommended, especially Thurs–Sat nights. Main courses NZ$14–$20 (US$9.80–$14); takeaway NZ$12–$15 (US$8.40–$10.50). AE, BC, DC, MC, V. Mon–Sat noon–3pm, daily 6–10:30pm. Bus: The Link. THAI.

Both indoor and outdoor seating are available at this very popular restaurant, but budget travelers would be wise to get takeaway from the window at the front of the building. You can eat it at a table right there on the patio or go around back to one of the wooden tables on the rear porch, which has a great view of the Auckland Museum. The window is open daily from noon to 10:30pm. It's less expensive only because you're not dining in. But if you do decide to spend the extra money, you can sit inside one of the conventional tables or on the floor with your legs extended through a recess—it's an interesting set-up that you have to see for yourself. The cafe is fully licensed.

IN MISSION BAY

Kelly's Cafe
23 Tamaki Dr., Orakei (at Kelly Tarlton's Southern Oceans Adventure). ☎ **09/528-5267**. Fax 09/528-2004. Reservations accepted. Breakfast NZ$4.50–$11.50 (US$3.15–$8.10). Lunch main courses NZ$6–$14.50 (US$4.20–10.20). AE, BC, DC, MC, V. Daily 8am–6pm. INTERNATIONAL.

This licensed cafe (self-service with a blackboard menu) is built out over the water at Kelly Tarlton's Southern Oceans Adventure. It's great on a hot day—the windows fold out of the way to let the sea breeze in, and the view couldn't be better. I could sit here all day watching the windsurfers and sailboats. It's a great place for breakfast, lunch, or tea. Breakfast fare includes fruit smoothies, toasted bagels, omelettes, or a mixed grill. Lunch is "filled sandwiches"; salads such as smoked chicken and melon, seafood pasta, Greek salad, and chargrilled veggies; and a selection of hot dishes. They also serve a range of coffees and teas. Renovation is planned for mid-1997, and they hope to start opening for dinner after January, 1998.

IN DEVONPORT AND BEYOND
Super-Cheap Eats

Catch 22 Fish Shop
19 Victoria Rd., Devonport. ☎ **09/445-2225**. Reservations not accepted. Average meal NZ$4–$5 (US$2.60–$3.25). No credit cards. Sun–Mon noon–8pm, Tues–Thurs 9:30am–8pm, Fri 9:30am–9pm, Sat 10:30am–8pm. FISH-AND-CHIPS.

I realize that this is a fish shop, not a restaurant, but I'm including it because you might want to buy fish-and-chips and take them across the road to Windsor Re serve—I can't think of a better picnic spot. However, don't buy the paua fritters; my husband and I did and ended up feeding them to a golden retriever with an indiscriminate palate. Catch 22 sells juice and cold sodas but no alcohol

La Casa Italiana
Shop 9, the Devonport Ferry Wharf, Devonport. ☎ **09/445-9933**. Reservations not accepted. Main courses NZ$7–$10 (US$4.90–$7). No credit cards. Daily 10am–8pm. PIZZA/PASTA.

This little quick-food counter on the Devonport Ferry Wharf is one of my favorite places to eat. Delicious pizzas come in two sizes and with a choice of 13 toppings. On a recent lunch visit, my husband and I shared a standard-size Super La Casa (tomato, cheese, mushrooms, ham, salami, bacon, capers, prawns, olives, and more) for NZ$15 (US$10.50). There are tables and chairs nearby—inside and outside. La Casa's owners are brothers Tony and Jafar, who immigrated to New Zealand 9 years ago. They make their pizza dough and all the desserts on the premises. Cappuccino and espresso are available, as is wine.

Stone Oven Bakehouse & Cafe
12C Clarence St., Devonport. ☎ **09/446-1065**. Reservations not necessary. Main courses NZ$3–$9 (US$2.10–$6.30). No credit cards. Daily 6:30am–7:30pm. CAFE.

This is a one of my favorite places to hang out. There's a play area at one end for children and a sitting area with lounge furniture that's perfect for holing up with a stack of postcards. But once you get a whiff of the freshly baked breads, it won't be long before you're at the counter ordering. For lunch, try a large slice of ham or veggie pizza, a sandwich, steak-and-cheese pie, or a salad with a roll. All of the baked goods are made on the premises and they're wonderful, especially the apple and berry strudel. There are lots of tables inside and a few outside. It's also fully licensed.

For a Few Extra Bucks

Monsoon Cafe Restaurant

71 Victoria Rd., Devonport. ☎ **09/445-4263**. Reservations accepted. Main courses NZ$13.50 (US$9.50). AE, MC, V. Daily 5pm–11pm. THAI/MALAYSIAN.

The decor here is contemporary, with tables topped in faux black marble and black upholstered chairs; the walls have been sponge-painted terra-cotta with black wainscoting. Main courses include "From the Wok," mixed vegetables and tofu with sesame seeds, flavored with coriander; "From the Curry Pot," chicken and pumpkin in a green curry sauce; and noodle dishes like pad Thai, rice noodles with shrimp, egg, and crushed peanuts. Takeaway will save you NZ$3 (US$2.10) on each dish. Peace & Plenty guests (see "Affordable Accommodations," above) receive a 10% discount. If you want beer or wine, you have to bring it yourself.

Moderately Priced Options

Carpe Diem

49 Victoria Rd., Devonport. ☎ **09/445-7732**. Reservations accepted. Main courses NZ$10.80–$24.80 (US$7.55–$17.35). BC, DC, MC, V. Mon 9am–5pm, Tues–Thurs and Sun 9am–10pm, Fri–Sat 9am–11pm. MODERN NEW ZEALAND.

This cafe is popular with both locals and visitors. The food is good and the casual decor appealing enough. For lunch you might have a salad of mache leaves with grilled feta, sun-dried tomatoes, croutons, and hazelnut oil dressing; homemade soup with grilled bruschetta; or Thai-flavored chicken wok fry with cashew nuts on jasmine rice. Dinner main courses include rack of lamb with pistachio herb crust, sweet baby onions, and a rosemary jus, or potted chicken fricassee with wild mushrooms and red-wine sauce. Depending on the time of day, you might prefer just to have a cappuccino or espresso and one of their great desserts. It's fully licensed, but you can bring your own wine.

Skoozi of Devonport Bar & Bistro

14 Victoria Rd., Devonport. ☎ **09/445-8743**. Reservations accepted. Lunch NZ$9.50–$15.50 (US$6.70–10.90); dinner main courses NZ$10.50–$20 (US$7–$14). AE, BC, DC, MC, V. Daily 10:30am–10pm or later. MODERN NEW ZEALAND.

This casual bar and bistro is housed in the former Bank of New Zealand building, which dates from the 1930s. The brunch and midday menu is served from 10:30am to 4pm; a "more substantial" menu starts at 4pm. I suggest you have a "First Flavour" and then share a pizza—all this will cost about NZ$20.50 (US$14.40) per person. First Flavours might include mussel and olive cannelloni with pesto and melted Havarti; chargrilled niçoise salad; or jalepēno, butternut, and feta strudel. Pizzas might come topped with rosemary roasted lamb, kumara and hipi-ti (goat cheese); or duck, forest mushrooms, and sun-dried tomatoes. You can eat inside or outside on the sidewalk. They're fully licensed. Peace & Plenty guests (see "Affordable Accommodations," above) receive a 10% discount.

Worth a Splurge

Porterhouse Blue

58 Calliope Rd., Devonport. ☎ **09/445-0309**. Fax 09/446-0078. Reservations recommended. Main courses NZ$18.50–$25 (US$13–$17.50). AE, BC, DC, MC, V. Mon–Sat 6:30–10pm. CALIFORNIA/FRENCH.

Porterhouse Blue was recently voted "one of the Top 100 Restaurants in New Zealand." An open fire and candles contribute to the cozy atmosphere here, as do lots of green plants, terra-cotta–colored walls, and a pretty stained-glass window. The menu includes boned leg of rabbit, braised lamb shanks, ocean-fresh fish, and wild venison medallions. I only wish they didn't charge NZ$2 (US$1.40) per person for bread. On the other hand, the restaurant offers free transportation within Devonport. If you take the ferry over from the city, someone will meet you at the wharf if you call ahead. It's fully licensed, or you can bring your own booze. *Budget tip:* Save NZ$10/US$7 or more by picking up your wine at the **High Flying Grapes,** 101 Victoria Rd. (☎ 09/445-9189).

LUNCH & DINNER CRUISES

This is a terrific way to explore Auckland's spectacular harbor, especially in the evening when the city lights are reflected along the shoreline. **The Pride of Auckland Company,** in the Downtown Airline Terminal at the corner of Quay and Albert streets (☎ 09/373-4557, fax 09/377-0459), offers a lunch cruise for about NZ$49 (US$34.30) per person and a dinner trip for NZ$110 (US$77), which I think is exorbitant. They'll offer a 15% discount if you show them this *Frommer's* guide, but in my opinion, it's still too pricey.

A more affordable way to dine afloat is to put together a picnic and go out on **Fuller's Harbour Explorer,** or go back and forth on the **Devonport Ferry.** Gather your goodies from the Stone Oven Bakehouse in Devonport, Saints of Parnell Pastry Shop in Parnell, or the food court in Auckland's Downtown Shopping Centre (see above).

5 Exploring Auckland: What to See & Do

Auckland has a lot to offer visitors, and it's unfortunate that many overseas travelers deplane here and start driving without even checking out the city. In addition to the places described below, I'd also take a look at the "Easy Side Trips from Auckland" section at the end of this chapter.

TIPS ON HOW TO SPEND YOUR TIME

Below I've suggested what I would see and do as a first-time visitor to Auckland, depending on how many days I had to spend here. This certainly isn't an itinerary for everyone, just a way to show you what the highlights are and how to experience them in a limited amount of time—without running yourself ragged.

Day 1   You should spend at least half the day to see and fully appreciate the Auckland Museum. In the afternoon, I'd go with Kelly Tarlton's Southern Oceans Adventure.

Day 2   Spend it on the waterfront. Visit the National Maritime Museum on Hobson Wharf and check out the America's Cup berths under construction nearby.

Day 3   Take the ferry over to Devonport, on Auckland's North Shore, and spend the day exploring its charming streets, which are lined with colonial-style bungalows; I'd also opt for a picnic lunch at one of the nearby beaches.

Day 4   Take a side trip to Waiheke Island or the Waitakeres.

Day 5   Visit the ancient Maori fort on One Tree Hill or take a harbor cruise; then plan an afternoon of shopping at Victoria Park Market or the stores along Parnell Road.

THE AUCKLAND MUSEUM & OTHER TOP ATTRACTIONS

Before you set out to explore Auckland, arm yourself with the money-saving **Explorer Bus** ticket or a **BusAbout Pass** for traveling between major attractions (see "Getting Around," earlier in this chapter).

Taking in the Views

There're so many spectacular view points in and around Auckland, all of which offer picture-perfect panoramas of the city skyline, the harbor, and the coastal islands beyond. Before you leave, you should experience at least two or three different ones, perhaps even make a picnic out of one of them. Here's a list of my favorites:

- **Mt. Eden**   With or without binoculars, the view is nothing short of spectacular from this summit, Auckland's highest point. An extinct volcano, which was fortified by the Maori, Mt. Eden looks down on the city, both harbors, and the Hauraki Gulf. Mt. Eden Domain is accessed via Mt. Eden Road. The only drawback here is that several tour buses stop here and the fumes can get to be a bit much. Therefore, if you have to pick between here and One Tree Hill (below), head for the Hill even though the view of the city is better from Mt. Eden.

- **One Tree Hill**   The obelisk and the single pine tree on this peak are visible from everywhere in the city. Like Mt. Eden, this was once a Maori pa (fort/settlement) dating from about the 14th century. A plaque on the monument gives a thumbnail sketch of early Maori history. The Obelisk is a "permanent record of [Sir John Logan Campbell's] admiration for the achievements and character of the Great Maori people." However, this landmark nearly became "None Tree Hill" in 1996 when a Maori activist took a hatchet to the tree. It's been saved, but not without considerable effort. You'll note it's now well protected by an iron fence. The view from the top is spectacular. Hearty types run, cycle, and walk up here. The peak is accessed through Cornwall Park, and as you wind up to the top you'll see grazing sheep and volcanic craters. The adjoining parkland is great for long walks.

- **Savage Memorial Park**   This park, located above Tamaki Drive, is one of my favorite view points in New Zealand. From here you can see the harbor—almost always dotted with white sailboats—and the gulf islands. It might be a windy spot, but the view is fantastic. One of my favorite memories of Auckland is standing here during the Anniversary Day Regatta (the last Monday in January) when the harbor was alive with colorful international sailing craft. The park was named after Michael Joseph Savage, the first Labour Prime Minister of New Zealand from 1935 until his death in 1940.

- **North Head Maritime Park, Devonport**   Unlike the three view points mentioned above, North Head provides a look back at the city from the North Shore. While you're here take time to explore the old military fort with its tunnels and gun sites. They were placed here to protect the harbor from advancing navies. North Head is a 25- to 30-minute walk from the village of Devonport, or you can take a bus. This is a good view point for watching the Team New Zealand and challenger yachts make their way from Viaduct Quay to the America's Cup course.

- I haven't seen it, but by the time you get there, Auckland's new **Sky Tower** will offer another great viewpoint. This structure, at 330 meters (1,082 feet), will be the tallest tower in the Southern Hemisphere. When it's finished, there will be four observation decks, including the spectacular Sky Deck (360° seamless glass platform), plus knee-knocking views through glass floors.

Auckland Museum

Auckland Domain. ☎ **09/309-0443,** or 09/306-7067 for recorded information. Permanent collection, admission by donation; Maori concert, NZ$7 (US$4.90); Weird and Wonderful, NZ$1 (US 70¢). Charges for other special exhibitions may apply. Daily 10am–5pm. Closed Good Friday and Christmas Day. Bus: 635 from the Downtown Bus Terminal. Free parking.

A visit to this museum is a virtual must on any Auckland itinerary. You'll gain a full appreciation of the Maori culture, which you will be exposed to when traveling to other parts of the country. The imposing gleaming-white building, surrounded by the sweeping lawns and flower gardens of The Domain, houses the world's largest collection of Maori artifacts, providing you with a rich background from which to understand the Maori of today. Be sure to pick up a free guide map as you enter the museum.

In the **Maori Court,** the most impressive exhibit is probably the 82-foot war canoe chiseled from one enormous totara trunk and covered with intricate, symbolic carvings. You'll see that same artistic carving in the 85-foot meetinghouse, whose painted rafters and carved and painted wall panels are a wonder of red, black, and white scrollwork. The wall panels also feature tribal-motif carvings interspersed with traditional woven flax patterns. The meetinghouse sits between two storehouses raised on stilts to protect community goods from predators. Also on display are gorgeous feather cloaks (each feather knotted in by hand) once worn by high-ranking men, as well as jade tikis. Look for the greenstone *mere* (war club), such a lordly weapon that it was reserved only for the slaying of the highest-ranking captives (who considered it an honor to meet their end with such a club). Also, be sure to check out the Maori portraits, the life's work of famed New Zealand artist C. F. Goldie, a Pakeha (New Zealander of European descent).

Twice daily at 11am and 1:30pm, **Maori concerts** bring to life the culture and history of New Zealand's native people. These performances include action songs, a poi ball demonstration, and an explanation of the use of greenstone and making *piu piu* (flax) skirts. Guided tours of the Maori gallery take place 45 minutes before every show.

The Museum is currently undergoing an extensive refurbishment program aimed at revitalizing all its galleries and displays. The first of these areas, the **Scars on the Heart** exhibit, is located on the second level of the building. It tells the story of New Zealand in conflict, from the Land Wars in the 1840s to its present-day peacekeeping operations. There's a similar plan for level 1: It's going to feature a journey through New Zealand's natural flora, fauna, marine life, and bird life (due to open November 1998).

If you're traveling with youngsters ages 2 to 12, I suggest that you take them to **Weird and Wonderful,** a children's discovery center that provides a wealth of imaginative hands-on experiences.

Elsewhere in the museum are the **Hall of South Pacific Art,** the **Hall of Asian Art,** the **Pacific Canoe Hall,** native bird displays (including that giant moa exhibit), and much, much more.

The shop near the entrance of the museum is one of my favorite places to buy publications on Maori art and New Zealand flora and fauna, as well as reproductions and replicas of some of the exhibits. Consider looking here for inexpensive mementos to carry home. There's also a cafe (open from 10am to 4:30pm), which serves sandwiches, salads, desserts, and beverages.

Author's note: Be sure to experience the view from the front of the museum. Most bus tours drop you at the door and you miss the sweeping panorama of the harbor across to Devonport, Rangitoto, and beyond. Go to the back where there's a wide lawn and a good view of One Tree Hill to the south and the downtown skyline (dominated by the new Sky Tower) to the north—it's a photo opportunity you won't want to miss.

❍ New Zealand National Maritime Museum

Hobson Wharf, Quay St. ☎ **09/373-0800.** Fax 09/377-6000. Admission NZ$10 (US$7) adults, half price for children 5–17 (under 5 free); NZ$20 (US$14) family ticket. AE, DC, MC, V. Daily 9am–5pm. Free parking.

Allow plenty of time for your visit here; there's *a lot* to see and do. I'd suggest an hour at the least, but it really deserves 3 or 4 hours. Encompassing 1,000 years of maritime history, this interactive museum tells the story of the early Polynesian explorers, the immigrant ships that brought "new" New Zealanders from many countries, and the yachting successes of a nation obsessed by the sea. The Big Boat, *KZ-1,* is out front. Inside, visitors can sit in oral-history chairs, trace their ancestors on computers, and note the amazingly accurate map created of Captain Cook's first voyage to New Zealand in 1769. Be sure to notice the Moth Class dinghy designed by Kiwi schoolboy Bruce Farr—now one of the world's leading yacht designers—and don't skip the audiovisual presentation in the theater near the entrance. The scow *Ted Ashby* provides half-hour rides daily at 12:30 and 2:30pm for an additional charge of NZ$7 (US$4.90)—it's the least-expensive harbor cruise you'll find. There's a free guided tour daily, a good museum store, and a cafe for lunch or tea.

Kelly Tarlton's Southern Oceans Adventure

Orakei Wharf, 23 Tamaki Dr., Orakei. ☎ **09/528-0603.** Admission NZ$18 (US$12.60) adults, NZ$9 (US$6.30) children 4–12, free for children under 4; special rates for family groups and senior citizens. AE, BC, CB, DC, JCB, MC, V. Daily summer (Oct 1–Mar 31) 9am–9pm, winter (Apr 1–Sept 30) 9am–6pm. Transportation: Mission Bay city bus, Explorer Bus, or Fuller's Harbour Explorer. Free parking.

This was the inspiration and final project of the late Kelly Tarlton, the famed diver whose New Zealand legacy also includes the outstanding Museum of Shipwrecks in the Bay of Islands (see chapter 6). On this adventure, you'll be transported to an underwater environment by way of a moving walkway that passes through a clear tunnel surrounded by hundreds of native New Zealand fish—without getting wet. It's just like an real dive—you'll move over a sandy ocean bottom, through forests of waving seaweed, into mysterious underwater caves, and along rocky reefs. Look for sea creatures ranging from tiny seahorses to the leggy octopus, and don't miss the magnificent shark tank with its toothy inhabitants and huge stingrays.

In the **Antarctic Encounter** you get a taste of the coldest, windiest, and driest continent on earth. Wander through a replica of Captain Scott's Hutt and hop aboard a Haaglund's "snow cat," which transports you across the ice to live King and Gentoo penguins and other Antarctic creatures. There's good wheelchair access from the parking lot, and Kelly's Cafe offers snacks and buffet meals at reasonable prices. (See "Great Deals on Dining," above.)

Auckland Art Gallery

Kitchener and Wellesley sts., at the intersection of Albert Park. ☎ **09/309-0831** for recorded information. Admission free to main building; fees for touring various exhibitions; New Gallery NZ$3 (US$2.10) adults, NZ$1 (US 70¢) children. Daily 10am–5pm.

New Zealand's oldest and largest art gallery, this is one of the most active art museums in the South Pacific. The Main Building focuses on historical works. Its permanent collection ranges from European masters to contemporary international art, plus the most comprehensive collection of New Zealand fine art in the country. Works by New Zealand artists date from 1770 to the present and include a display of fine Maori portraits. The Gallery Cafe offers refreshment, and there's good browsing in the bookshop. Free guided tours are given daily at 2pm. In the New Gallery the focus is on contemporary New Zealand art, including the McCahon room, which features the work of Colin McCahon, one of New Zealand's most respected artists. Within the building you'll find a restaurant, bookshops, antique print shop, and cafe bar. Free guided tours are given daily at 1pm.

MORE MUSEUMS & A ZOO

Auckland Zoo

Motions Rd., Western Springs. ☎ 09/378-3819. Infoline, 09/378-1620. Admission NZ$11 (US$7.70) adults, NZ$6 (US$4.20) children 5–15, free for children under 5; NZ$28.50 (US$20) family ticket for 2 adults and up to 4 children. Group discounts available. AE, BC, DC, JCB, MC, V. Daily 9:30am–5:30pm (last admission 4:15pm). Closed Christmas Day. Bus: 45, leaving every 10 minutes from Customs St. Free parking.

One of the few places to observe the kiwi, that flightless bird that has become New Zealand's national symbol, is the Nocturnal House here at the zoo. The birds are exhibited daily in natural bush settings, which resemble a moonlit forest floor. You can watch them foraging, their long beaks seeking food in the leaf-covered ground. Don't plan a quick run out to the zoo just to look at the kiwis, however—more than 2,000 other birds, mammals, fish, and reptiles (representing some 200 species) will entice you from one area to another in the beautifully tended park surroundings. For instance, you can also take a look at the tuatara, Earth's oldest reptile. The zoo's newest exhibits include a rain forest, the Galapagos tortoise enclosure, and a sea life center.

Ewelme Cottage

14 Ayr St. ☎ 09/379-0202. Admission NZ$3 (US$2.10) adults, accompanied children free, unaccompanied N7$2 (US$1.40). Wed Sun 10:30am–noon and 1–4:30pm. Closed Good Friday and Christmas Day. Bus: 635, 645, or 655 from the Downtown Bus Terminal.

This cottage was built by the Rev. Vicesimus Lush (somehow, I find humor in that surname for a minister) and named for Ewelme Village in England. It has been authentically preserved, right down to 19th-century furnishings and as much of the original wallpaper as could be salvaged. It's worth a look.

Howick Historical Village

Lloyd Elsmore Park, Bells Rd., Pakuranga. ☎ 09/576-9506. Admission NZ$9 (US$6.40) adults, NZ$4 (US$2.80) children 17 and under, NZ$20 (US$14) family of 2 adults and 2 children. Mid-Mar to Dec 24, daily 10am–4pm; Dec 26 to mid-Mar, daily 10am–5pm. Drive 30 minutes on the Pakuranga Hwy. Bus: Howick and Eastern bus to Fortunes Rd., Pakuranga.

More than 25 buildings in a flowering garden setting take you back to village life in colonial New Zealand. Based on the local military, the village faithfully depicts the 1840–80 period. There's a good cafe on the premises.

Museum of Transport and Technology, and New Zealand Science Centre

825 Great North Rd., Western Springs. ☎ 09/846-0199. Admission NZ$8 (US$5.60) adults, NZ$4 (US$2.80) senior citizens and children; NZ$17 (US$11.90) family ticket for 2 adults and up to 4 children under 18. Daily 10am–4pm. Closed Christmas Day. Bus: 145 from Customs St. East.

There's a fascinating collection of vehicles, trains, trams, aircraft, steam engines, and pioneer artifacts at the MOTAT, as it's best known. Here you'll find New Zealand's only full-time publicly operating tramway, including Auckland's first electric tram (circa 1902). In the Pioneers of Aviation Pavilion, special tribute is paid to Richard Pearse, who on March 31, 1902, flew an aircraft on the South Island. Life in 1840–90 New Zealand is re-created in the Victorian Village, where the church is still used for weddings and christenings. There are several places to eat on the grounds, but the 120-year-old Colonial Arms Restaurant is rather special, serving Devonshire teas and á la carte meals. The museum is just 3 miles from the city center.

PARKS & GARDENS

✪ **The Auckland Domain,** bounded by Grafton Road, Park Road, Titoki Street, and the railway line, is a lovely green expanse near the city center. This is a perfect place for picnics, and there are walking paths and massive sweeping lawns. Ducks swim on ponds formed by natural springs. If you're interested in plants, don't miss the **Winter Garden** and the **Fernery,** both contained in glass houses. Admission is free. The Winter Garden is open daily from 10am to 4pm. If you're here on a summer Sunday you might want to enjoy a free concert sponsored by Auckland City, Music in Parks, from 4:30 to 6pm. For information call ☎ **09/379-2020** or fax 09/571-3757. The stately Auckland Museum, the focal point of The Domain, is described above.

Cornwall Park is a true urban oasis (enter from Green Lane). Information is available at the **Huia Lodge Visitor Centre,** P.O. Box 26 072, Epsom, Auckland (☎ **09/630-8485,** fax 09/524-6433). The **Cornwall Park Restaurant,** P.O. Box 21-102, Royal Oak, Auckland (☎ **09/630-2888,** fax 09/630-2867), is a nice cafe with inside or outside seating. Both are located in the park before you start the ascent up **One Tree Hill** and are open daily from 10am to 4pm. Lunch ranges from NZ$10.50 to NZ$16.50 (US$7.40 to $11.60); snacks or tea are NZ$3 to NZ$5 (US$2.10 to $3.50). American Express, Bankcard, Diners Club, MasterCard, and Visa are accepted at the cafe. For more information on the park, see "One Tree Hill" in "Taking in the Views," above.

The **Parnell Rose Garden,** on Gladstone Road in Parnell (☎ **09/307-0136** or 09/302-1252), is a delightful place to stop if you're in town when roses are blooming (November through March). Thousands of traditional roses are set in color-coordinated beds. Admission is free and the park is open daily until sundown. Take bus 702 from the Downtown Bus Terminal, or the Explorer Bus.

After sniffing the roses you might want to continue your walk through the rest of **Dove Myer Robinson Park.** Go to the northeast side of the park for a great view of the harbor, Devonport, and Rangitoto Island. On your way you'll pass the memorial to the members of the New Zealand services in Korea 1950–53, presented by the Korean Embassy. Note the huge pohutukawa tree (New Zealand Christmas Tree) across from the memorial. This is a great point from which to watch the Anniversary Regatta and will be good for watching the America's Cup boats go out to the racecourse.

DASHING OFF TO DEVONPORT
TAKING THE FERRY

One of the nicest ways I know to see Auckland, and a very pleasant alternative to the pricey harbor cruises, is a ride on the ✪ **Devonport Ferry.** Usually you'll be aboard the zippy catamaran *Kea,* but from time to time the much-beloved and semiretired steam ferry MV *Kestrel* makes the journey. As the city recedes, you'll witness big-city development first hand. The old red-brick Ferry Building with its clock tower stands in marked contrast to streamlined high-rises, while the new Sky Tower and the stately white Auckland Museum look down on it all with the dignity born of historical perspective. You'll pass the naval base; then if you plan it right and return in the evening, you'll catch the sparkling city lights. Get the ferry (☎ **09/367-9125**) at the Queens Wharf terminal on Quay Street (its North Shore destination is Devonport), leaving every half hour (on the hour and half hour) from 7am to 7pm and every hour (on the hour) from 7 to 11pm daily. The round-trip fare is NZ$7 (US$4.90). If you're planning on spending a lot of time in Devonport or if you're staying over here and

Devonport

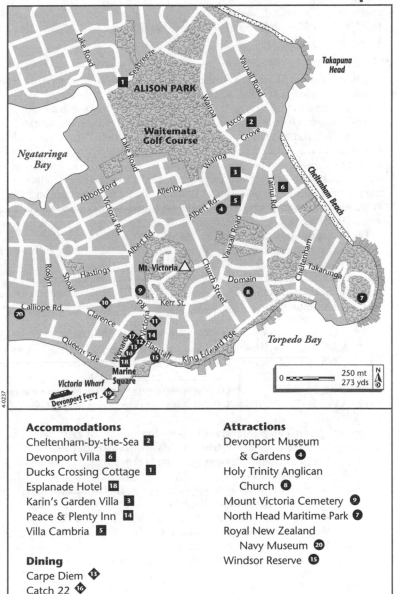

Accommodations

Cheltenham-by-the-Sea **2**
Devonport Villa **6**
Ducks Crossing Cottage **1**
Esplanade Hotel **18**
Karin's Garden Villa **3**
Peace & Plenty Inn **14**
Villa Cambria **5**

Dining

Carpe Diem **13**
Catch 22 **16**
La Casa Italiana **19**
Monsoon Cafe Restauarnt **12**
Porterhouse Blue **10**
Skoozi of Devonport Bar & Bistro **11**
Stone Oven Bakehouse & Cafe **17**

Attractions

Devonport Museum
   & Gardens **4**
Holy Trinity Anglican
   Church **8**
Mount Victoria Cemetery **9**
North Head Maritime Park **7**
Royal New Zealand
   Navy Museum **20**
Windsor Reserve **15**

commuting to Auckland, you might want to buy a ferry pass: either the 10-trip (NZ$26/US$18.20 adult, NZ$12/US$8.40 child) or the weekly pass (NZ$23/ US$16.10).

IN TOWN

The little suburb of Devonport is where the Maori say their great ancestral canoe Tainui first touched land in this area, somewhere around the 14th century. You'll see a stone memorial to that event on the grassy strip along the King Edward Parade fore-shore—the bronze sculpture is an orb topped by a korotangi (weeping dove), one of the birds the Maori brought with them from their homeland. There are four white-sand beaches in Devonport, as well as **Mount Victoria,** which sits near the business center and is now topped by a harbor signal station (great views from up there). You can also walk up to **North Head** and explore the old military fort with its tunnels and gun sites, or let **Devonport Tours** (☎ 09/357-6366) take you there on a 1-hour minibus tour. The cost is NZ$22 (US$15.40) for adults, half price for children. Prebooking is essential.

The **Visitor Information Centre** (☎ 09/446-0677) is located near the ferry land-ing in the library at the water end of Victoria Road. Stroll along **King Edward Pa-rade** and admire the beach and view of Auckland. Before long you'll come to the Masonic Hotel, built in 1866, at the corner of Church Street. Just across the way, **Art by the Sea** (☎ 09/445-6665, fax 09/445-6667) is in what was once the Duder Brothers' mercantile store; it's open daily from 10am to 5pm. The crafts of New Zealand artists are sold.

Other good places to shop include **The Glass House,** 61 Victoria Rd. (☎ 09/445-0377); look for the Tony Sly pottery. I also really like **Flagstaff Gallery,** 25 Victoria Rd. (☎ 09/445-1142), where most of the works of art are by New Zealand artists and they will ship your purchases. (Remember: You don't pay GST on things shipped out of the country.) You may also find some interesting items at **Abigail's Country Store,** 43 Victoria Rd. (☎ 09/445-3072). Many shops in Devonport are open 7 days a week

The **Devonport Village Market** is held the first Sunday of every month from 10am to 3pm. There are entertainment, 70 stalls of quality crafts, food booths, and more. It takes place at the Devonport Community House, 32 Clarence St., Devonport (☎ 09/445-7684).

It's not imperative, but you may want to visit the **Royal New Zealand Navy Mu-seum** on Spring Street (☎ 09/445-5186, fax 09/445-5046), 5 blocks from the ferry wharf. It's open daily from 10am to 4:30pm, and admission is free. You also might like to visit the **Devonport Museum and Gardens,** at 31-A Vauxhall Rd. (☎ 09/ 445-2661), between 2 and 4pm on weekends. Devonport is full of interesting houses that survive from the 1800s and early 1900s—no. 9 Mays St. is a marvel of cast-iron decoration, and virtually every house on Anne Street is a museum piece. The **Espla-nade Hotel,** one of the first things you'll see as you debark from the ferry, dates from 1902.

If you should decide to stay for dinner, there are an increasing number of good cafes and restaurants in Devonport (see "Great Deals on Dining," earlier in this chapter).

ORGANIZED TOURS & CRUISES

You can book several half- and full-day tours of the city and its environs at the **Visi-tors Information Centre.** The half-day tours (morning or afternoon) cover sightseeing highlights, and an all-day tour usually includes the eastern and western suburbs, the zoo, and vineyards. Half-day tours run about NZ$36 (US$25.20) for adults, half that for children.

Bush & Beach Ltd., P.O. Box 3479, Shortland Street, Auckland (☎ **09/478-2882,** or 0800/4-BEACH in New Zealand; fax 09/478-2882), are outdoor specialists offering a range of small-group (one- to eight-passenger) tours around Auckland's west coast via minibus. Led by experienced guides, the tours are flexible and focus on the unique aspects of each route. One half-day tour (12:30 to 5pm) includes surf beaches, and a subtropical rain forest, with time to explore and refreshments; the full-day tour (9:30am to 5pm) is available August through April only and includes beaches, the rain forest, a gannet colony (sea birds with a wingspan of up to 2 meters), plus a chance to relax and enjoy a glass of wine at a local vineyard. Lunch and refreshments are included. The half-day costs NZ$55 (US$38.50) and the full-day is NZ$89 (US$62.30). YHA and VIP cardholders receive a 10% discount.

Auckland's premier ecotour is the **Twin Island Explorer,** 32 Palm Rd., Palm Beach, Waiheke Island (☎ **025/764-753** or 09/372-9579, fax 09/372-9580), a trip to Tiritiri Matangi Island in the Hauraki Gulf. My husband and I took this excursion when we were last in New Zealand and loved it. Our adventure started with a Fuller's ferry ride to Waiheke Island where we met Reg Eggers at the dock with his 36-foot yacht (sailboat), the *Lidgard*. We then took a 2-hour sail to Tiritiri Matangi Island and passed by the America's Cup course (where *Black Magic* and others were practicing). Upon arrival at the island, which is 3km (1.86 miles) long and 1.5km (.93 miles) wide, Reg led us on a hike through ancient native forests, along beaches, and across land that was cleared for farming in 1850. The last farming lease expired in 1971, and in 1984 a group of volunteers started a program for replanting 200,000 native trees—the idea being if they could re-create native forests, it would help to revive populations of native birds, which have nearly disappeared. While on the island, we admired the plant life in the bush, enjoyed the view of other Hauraki Gulf islands, and watched for rare native birds. The North Island saddleback, takahe, and stichbird are only found on offshore islands because on the mainland they've been killed off by imported mammals. There are 190 takahe left in New Zealand, and 19 of these are on Tiritiri Mantangi. We stopped for a picnic lunch at the lighthouse before sailing back to Waiheke Island. The cost is NZ$65 (US$45.50) from Waiheke Island and NZ$85 (US$59.50) from Auckland, and it was one of the highlights of our trip. Reg is a delightful companion and a font of information on native plants and animals. He's a DOC-accredited guide as well as an experienced sailor. Bring your own lunch.

Author's note: If you're coming from Devonport to Waiheke Island, you have to go via Auckland, but Fuller's will give you credit for your Devonport–Auckland ticket, so you pay the same as someone traveling from Auckland to Waiheke.

HARBOR CRUISES

You'll no doubt want to explore the harbor, which is a beautiful body of water and the focal point of the city. There are lots of ways to do this. Some cruises, like those offered by the **Pride of Auckland,** are overpriced and definitely not for budget travelers. Your best bet is taking the 10-minute ferry ride to Devonport, but if that just isn't enough for you, **Fuller's Auckland,** Quay Street (☎ **09/367-9102** for information, 09/367-9111 to book), has a wide variety of cruises around the harbor. The best deal, in my opinion, is the **Coffee Cruise** or **Harbour Explorer.** It's NZ$20 (US$14) for adults and NZ$10 (US$7) for children. You have a choice of either taking a continuous 1^1/2-hour cruise, enjoying coffee and seeing the sights, or you can get an all-day Explorer Pass and get on and off at Devonport, Kelly Tarlton's

---

Especially for Kids

Don't forget the **Weird and Wonderful** children's discovery center at the Auckland Museum and Kelly Tarlton's **Southern Ocean Adventure,** both of which are listed above. See also the description for Rainbow's End Adventure Park, below.

Southern Oceans Adventure, or Rangitoto Island along the way. It also passes the Harbour Bridge. You can disembark and reboard the next boat or return on any Devonport Ferry. Fuller's also offers cruises to Rangitoto Island and Waiheke Island and a cruise-and-vineyard tour to Waiheke Island that includes a wine tasting. The latter lasts a half a day and the price is about NZ$45 (US$31.50). Call for current schedules and prices, then buy tickets at the downtown waterfront ticket office in the Ferry Building. They also run longer cruises to Great Barrier Island.

In addition to the Devonport Ferry and the dollarwise Fuller's trips, the **New Zealand National Maritime Museum** offers a great deal: twice a day the scow *Ted Ashby* takes passengers on a 30-minute trip around the harbor. This only costs NZ$7 (US$4.90) in addition to the regular admission to the museum.

Rainbow's End Adventure Park

Great South and Wiri Station rds., Manukau City. ☎ **09/262-2044.** Infoline, 09/262-2030. All-day Super Pass (including all rides), NZ$30 (US$21) adults, NZ$20 (US$14) children 4–13, free for children under 4; Mini Pass (including 3 rides), NZ$15 (US$10.50), plus NZ$5 (US$3.50) for each additional ride. AE, DC, MC, V. Daily 10am–5pm, during January 10am–10pm. Closed Christmas Day. Free parking. Catch Cityline bus to Manukau City. It stops within sight.

This leisure park boasts all sorts of action rides, video games, mini-golf, and a roller coaster. The kids—of any age—will love it!

GETTING TO KNOW THE LOCALS

One of Auckland's (and indeed, New Zealand's) very best attractions is offered by the **Auckland Tourist Hospitality Scheme,** and it doesn't cost a penny. Do this at the beginning of your trip if possible—it will give more meaning to every Kiwi contact you make hereafter. This group of enthusiastic volunteers will arrange for you to spend a morning, afternoon, or evening with an Auckland family for absolutely no other reason than to have an opportunity to talk with locals in an informal, relaxed environment—in their homes. It's a great way to learn about New Zealand daily life firsthand and to exchange views from our different parts of the world. They'll try to match you by profession or hobby from among the 80 Auckland families who participate. They don't arrange overnight stays—just friendly visits. You can call them when you arrive, or better yet, write in advance to any of the following: Mrs. Polly Ring, 775 Riddell Rd., Glendowie, Auckland 5 (☎ **09/575-6655**); Mrs. Jean Mahon, 2/17 Arundel St., Hillsborough, Auckland (☎ **09/624-3398**); Mrs. Eve Williamson, 170 Cook St., Howick, Auckland (☎ **09/535-8098**); Mrs. Valerie Blackie, Flat 3, 16 Orakau Ave., Epsom, Auckland (☎ **09/625-9373**); and Mrs. Meryl Revell, 60 Prince Regent Dr., Half Moon Bay, Auckland (☎ **09/535-5314**).

6 Outdoor Activities & Spectator Sports

OUTDOOR ACTIVITIES

CYCLING   You can rent a bike from **Adventure Cycles,** 1 Fort Lane (☎ **0800/335-566** in New Zealand, or 09/309-5566; fax 09/309-4211). Rates are NZ$15 to

$25 (US$10.50 to $17.50) a day and include helmet, lock, water bottle, maps, and other bicycle paraphernalia. I don't think Auckland is the best place for biking, but if you want to take a ride, I'd follow Tamaki Drive along the waterfront to St. Heliers.

GOLF   Golfers will find themselves welcome at some 30 courses in the Auckland area. For details, contact **Auckland Visitor Golf Association** (☎ and fax **09/522-0491**) Monday through Thursday from 9am to 5pm, and ask for the name of the course nearest you and current greens fees. (Also see "Playing Golf" in chapter 4.)

SAILING   Reg Eggers of **New Zealand Sailing Safaris,** 32 Palm Rd., Palm Beach, Waiheke Island (☎ **025/764-753** or 09/372-9579, fax 09/372-9580), offers 4- and 8-hour sailing trips at a great bargain. Reg is an incredibly interesting and well-informed skipper. The cost for 4 hours is NZ$45 (US$31.50) per person; an 8-hour trip is NZ$65 (US$45.50) per person.

SWIMMING   Accessible from Tamaki Drive (frequent bus service from the Downtown Bus Terminal), Judges Bay, Okahu Bay, Mission Bay, Kohimarama, and St. Helier's Bay beaches are popular inner-harbor swimming venues. It's a good idea to check on tidal conditions before heading out—call the Visitor Information Centre (☎ **09/366-6888**).

TENNIS   The **Stanley Street Tennis Stadium** has racquets and balls for rent. For reservations, call ☎ **09/373-3623.**

WALKING   If you have the time, don your Reeboks and head to the Waitakeres—the ranges west of Auckland (see "Easy Side Trips from Auckland," below). Within the city, my favorite stroll is along **Tamaki Drive,** which follows the shoreline from the city center through numerous seaside suburbs. In the past, I've enjoyed walking along the harbor front from the Maritime Museum past the Ferry Building to Kings Wharf, but I'm afraid that during the life of this edition this is going to be a messy construction zone, so I can't really recommend that you do it. If you feel the need to *really* stretch your legs, follow the lead of the locals and hike up to the top of Mt. Eden or One Tree Hill.

SPECTATOR SPORTS

HORSE & DOG RACING   Both **horse and greyhound racing** are popular Auckland pastimes, and you can check up on race meets during your visit by calling the 24-hour **Recorded Racing Information Service** (☎ **09/520-7507**).

RUGBY   Check with the Visitor Information Centre for current schedules of New Zealand's famous **All Black rugby team.** Rugby Season, countrywide, is April through September. For match information contact **New Zealand Rugby Football League Inc.** (☎ **09/524-4013**) or **New Zealand Rugby Football Union** (☎ **04/499-4995**).

7 Shopping

Queen Street is the major shopping street. The bottom end looks kind of down-at-the-heels, but the stores and atmosphere at the top end are better. Auckland's late shopping night (when the shops stay open later) is Friday. In addition to the city center, some of the best shopping is along Parnell Road. The **Parnell Village Shops** are a really charming collection of shops connected by plant-filled brick patios, wooden decks, and even a little bridge. Park-type benches dotted throughout provide a respite for weary shoppers, and there are views of downtown and the Auckland Museum from the rear of the complex. There are other shops along Parnell Road between York Street and St. Stephens Avenue.

The other good shopping cluster is **Victoria Park Market,** Victoria Street West (☎ **09/309-6911,** fax 09/377-8954). This is a lively gathering place for shoppers interested in fashion (new and used), wood items, glassware, candles, T-shirts, Chinese herbs, greeting cards, jewelry, hats, backpacks, and day packs. While it's not as upscale as Parnell Village, it's a fun, funky hangout popular among locals, especially on weekends when there's free entertainment. There is an International Food Court as well as several fully licensed cafes. It's an appealing place for low-cost dining—a meal will only set you back about NZ$4 to NZ$6 (US$2.80 to $4.20). It's open daily from 9am to 6pm (cafes have later hours). Closed Christmas Day.

Located in the inner suburb of Newmarket is **Two Double Seven Shopping Center,** 277 Broadway. This is one of Auckland's newest shopping complexes. Housed in a sprawling, five-story, block-long building, the center houses specialty stores that sell sportswear, jewelry, giftware, music, high-fashion shops, plus an international food court. Drivers will find a covered parking area, and others can take any bus number beginning with 30 or 31 and marked Onehunga or Favona, departing from Victoria Street East (just off Queen Street, outside the A.M.P. Insurance Building).

DEPARTMENT STORES   A **David Jones Department Store,** a favorite Australian emporium, is under construction in Quay Park Mall on the Auckland waterfront and Harrods of London will soon open in the international terminal at Auckland Airport.

DUTY-FREE SHOPPING   At **Alders Duty Free Stores,** they stock a variety of international brands, as well as New Zealand handcrafts and souvenirs. All purchases will be held until your departure from the country. They have three locations in Auckland at Auckland International Airport (☎ **09/275-6893**), 25 Victoria St. W. (☎ **09/308-9014**), and 25 Queen St. (☎ **09/358-1111**).

Customhouse, 22 Customs St. W., is a beautifully restored old building that dates from 1888. It will soon be home to three levels of duty-free shopping.

LOCAL MARKETS   **Devonport Village Market** is held at Devonport Community House, 32 Clarence St., Devonport, on the first Sunday of every month from 10am to 3pm. For information call ☎ **09/445-7684.**

The **Clevedon Craft and Produce Market** (☎ **09/527-6228**) is held the second and fourth Sunday of every month.

SPECIALTY SHOPPING

Author's note: If you have a store mail your purchases out of the country, you'll save yourself the 12.5% GST (Goods and Services Tax). You do have to pay postage, but still, it's like getting the shipping free—and you don't have to carry souvenirs and mementos around for the rest of your trip.

CRAFTS

Auckland has several good places to shop for local crafts. In addition to the shops listed below, there is a good crafts shop at the Auckland Museum (see "Exploring Auckland: What to See & Do," above).

Elephant House

237 Parnell Rd., Parnell. ☎ **09/309-8740.** Mon–Fri 9:30am–6pm, Sat–Sun 10am–5pm during the summer; in the winter they close at 5pm during the week. AE, BC, DC, MC, V. Bus: The Link.

This large shop features lots of New Zealand crafts and is located just steps off Parnell Road, down a picturesque little walkway (follow the elephant footprints) and surrounded by patios of used brick, timber, and lots of plants. Everything they sell is made in New Zealand. Items include honey, handmade clothing, dried flowers, products made from native wood (rimu, kauri, matai), pottery, and jewelry. This is a co-operative and the prices are right.

Wood'n You

171 Parnell Rd., Parnell. ☎ **09/373-3550.** Mon and Sat 10am–4:30pm, Tues–Fri 10am–5pm. AE, BC, DC, MC, V. Bus: The Link.

As the name implies, this store has all kinds of wooden things—bowls, goblets, games, picture frames, decorative boxes—all hand-crafted.

Woolly For You

237 Parnell Rd., Parnell. ☎ **09/377-5437.** Mon–Fri 10am–5pm, Sat–Sun 10am–4pm. AE, BC, DC, JCB, MC, V. Bus: The Link.

If it's wool you're looking for, this is where to come. They carry knitwear, sheepskins, toys, and slippers—all of which are made in New Zealand. Some of the hand-knit items carry the name of the person who made them. As you might expect with handcrafts, these items are not inexpensive: sweaters range from NZ$80 to NZ$400 (US$56 to US$280).

LEATHER

Leather Fashions Ltd.

530 Ellerslie/Panmure Hwy., Panmure, Auckland. ☎ **09/527-3779** or 09/570-4789. Fax 09/527-3779. Mon–Fri 8:30am–5pm and Sat 10am–3pm.

This shop has won accolades from budget travelers over the years for its reasonable prices. It sells all sorts of leather and suede apparel and handbags, in classic as well as trendy designs including sheepskin. They furnish complimentary taxi service from the city center, accept all major credit cards, and will gladly ship overseas.

SHEEPSKIN

Breen's Sheepskins

Southpac Tower, 6 Customs St. W., Auckland. ☎ **09/373-2788.** Daily 9am to 10pm. Major credit cards accepted.

Breen's claims to have the largest range of sheepskins in New Zealand. The wide variety of styles, colors, and prices combined with the assortment of coats and jackets, rugs in several sizes, bed underlays (wonderful for a good night's sleep), car seats, boots, hats, and so on kept me interested for an entire morning. This shop was established 28 years ago, and Grant Barlow and his staff can offer good advice and guidance for what may well be some of your most valued purchases in the country.

VINTAGE CLOTHING

Nu to U

373 Parnell Rd. (between the Kebab Kid and Cathedral Restaurant), Parnell. ☎ **09/377-9235.** Mon–Fri 10am–5pm and Sat 10:15am–3:30pm. BC, MC, V. Bus: The Link.

This is a good place to buy recycled women's and children's clothing and accessories (or maybe drop off those items you regret bringing from home). All clothes sold here are less than 3 years old.

WINE

All wine shops in New Zealand are closed on Sunday (however, you can buy wine from vineyards on Sundays). If you're going to a BYO restaurant, you might want to buy your wine at the following shop.

Glengarry

164 Parnell Rd., Parnell. ☎ **09/358-1333.** Mon–Wed 9am–9pm; Thurs, Fri, and Sat from 9am to 10pm. AE, BC, DC, MC, V. Bus: The Link.

Glengarry is part of a nationwide chain of 18 stores (15 are in Auckland) that offer competitive prices. They sell wines from New Zealand, Australia, Chile, Spain, Portugal, France, Germany, and South Africa. It's a much better deal than Áccént On Wine, down the street. There's also a Glengarry in Devonport.

8 Auckland After Dark

For current cultural and entertainment events in Auckland, contact the **Bass Booking Agency,** Aotea Centre (☎ 09/307-5000), which provides easy credit-card booking with next-day courier ticket delivery. They can also make bookings around the country—a good way to save time and avoid disappointment. In addition to the listings here, you'll find current goings-on in the *Tourist Times.*

THE PERFORMING ARTS

For cultural offerings that include dance, concerts, and theater, check out what's happening at the **Aotea Centre,** 299 Queen St. at Aotea Square (☎ 09/307-5060); the ASB Theatre here seats 2,240. The **Watershed Theatre,** on Customs Street West (☎ **09/358-4028,** fax 09/357-6706), is a legitimate theater offering fringe dramatic works. Adult tickets are NZ$25 to NZ$29 (US$17.50 to US$20.30); on Mondays they're NZ$20 (US$14). **Sky Theatre,** at Harrahs at Sky City (☎ **0800/SKYCITY** [759-2489]), usually features big floor shows imported from Las Vegas. Tickets are NZ$30 to NZ$40 (US$21 to US$28); packages with dinner are available.

THE PUB & CLUB SCENE

High Street in the city center has a high concentration of little bars that attract a younger crowd. **Parnell Road** in Parnell has more sophisticated cafe-bars, and **Ponsonby Road** and **K Road** are the center of gay and lesbian nightlife.

Live music is on tap Friday and Saturday evenings at the **Queen's Head,** 396 Queen St. (☎ **09/302-0223,** fax 09/302-0533), a pretty pub that serves inexpensive light meals. It's open from 11am to 11pm Sunday through Thursday, until 1am on Friday and Saturday. The original facade of a hotel dating from 1890 has been retained—a small architectural jewel that escaped the bulldozer.

The **Shakespeare Tavern,** at the corner of Albert and Wyndham streets (☎ **09/373-5396**), is New Zealand's first pub brewery. Eight beers are made on-site and served in the Bard Lounge. Pub grub is offered in Hathaway's Brasserie. Shakespeare Tavern is open daily from noon to midnight. A handle of beer costs NZ$3.80 (US$2.66).

My favorite Auckland watering hole is ✪ **The Loaded Hog,** on Viaduct Quay, 104 Quay St., near Customs Street West (☎ **09/366-6491,** fax 09/366-6495). This is one of the city's few microbreweries, and it enjoys a waterfront location near Hobson Wharf. It's open Monday through Wednesday from 11am to 1am, Thursday through Saturday from 11am to 4am, and Sunday from 10am to 1am. Free brewery tours are given from 2 to 4pm on Saturday. Farm implements hang from the walls, bar stools and chair seats are covered in either red or blue plaid, and there are wood floors. Large windows overlook the dock, where the America's Cup berths are located. A DJ spins on Thursday through Saturday nights, and the line to get in snakes out the door and around the corner. If you decide to eat here, light meals are available for NZ$5 to NZ$7 (US$3.50 to US$4.90) and main courses cost NZ$10.50 to NZ$14 (US$7.40 to US$9.80).

Kitty O'Brien's Tavern, 2 Drake St. (☎ **09/303-3936**), is another spot you might enjoy. This Irish pub offers music nightly with a band every Friday and Saturday. Stand-up comics also sometimes appear here. All New Zealand beers are served, as well as Guinness. Kitty's opens at 11am every day but Sunday, when it opens at noon. Closing time is midnight Monday through Wednesday, 2am Thursday through Saturday, and 1am on Sunday. A handle (20-oz. mug) of standard New Zealand draft beer will set you back NZ$3.80 (US$2.66).

A CASINO

Harrah's Sky City Casino, corner of Victoria and Federal sts., Auckland (☎ **09/ 912-6000,** or 0800/888-711 in New Zealand), opened with great fanfare, but everyone I've spoken to agrees it doesn't live up to its advance billing. Frankly, I think the interior is downright depressing. If you must gamble, wait until you get to the much more attractive Christchurch Casino. Harrah's has 97 gaming tables, a keno lounge, 1,050 slot machines, and restaurants and bars. Harrah's Club—a European style casino-within-a-casino with a strict dress code (collar, tie, and jacket for men; business or evening attire for women)—and is located on the third floor. Open daily 24 hours. Gamblers must be at least 20 years of age.

GAY & LESBIAN CLUBS

The gay area of Auckland is concentrated around **Ponsonby Road** and **"K" Road.** The 2-week Hero Festival culminates in a parade, which is held every February or March on Ponsonby Road, and a street party featuring international DJs on three dance floors.

Some of the more popular gay and lesbian clubs include ✪ **The Staircase Cabaret** (known locally just as **"The Case"**), 340 Karangahape Rd. (☎ 09/377-0303); **The Legend Bar Limited,** 335 Karangahape Rd. (☎ 09/377-6062); **S.P.Q.R. Cafe & Bar,** 150 Ponsonby Rd. (☎ **09/360-1710**); and ✪ **Surrender Dorothy,** 3/175 Ponsonby Rd. (☎ **09/376-4460**).

10 Easy Side Trips from Auckland

Wineries, ranges, the gulf islands, and beaches all lie within a comfortable day trip of Auckland. They can be visited as part of an escorted tour or independently.

WAIHEKE ISLAND

Waiheke Island is a sparsely populated retreat just 35 minutes from the city by ferry and a great place for hiking, kayaking, and cycling. Seventy percent of the hilly island is farmland, and it has a permanent population of 6,000, 700 of whom commute into Auckland daily. Alternative lifestyles flourish here. Oneroa, the main village, is a 15-minute walk from the ferry. Call **Fuller's** (☎ **09/367-9111**) for information on their *Quickcat* service to Waiheke Island.

The ✪ **Twin Island Explorer** (☎ **025/764-753**) provides an interesting tour to Tiritiri Matangi that leaves from Waiheke Island (see "Organized Tours and Cruises," earlier in this chapter).

WHERE TO STAY

Gulf Haven

49 Great Barrier Rd., Enclosure Bay, Waiheke Island. ☎ **09/372-6629.** Fax 09/372-8558. Web site nz.com/webnz/bbnz/haven.htm. 2 rms (neither with bathrm), 2 studio apts (both with bathrm). NZ$80–$95 (US$56.75–$67) double; NZ$155 (US$112) studio apts (2-night minimum on weekends). Double rates include continental breakfast. Breakfast NZ$8 per person extra in studio units. BC, MC, V. The hosts pick up guests from the ferry.

I don't use superlatives loosely, but I have to tell you that the gardens surrounding this homestay are drop-dead gorgeous. Not only do the gardens surround the house, but they fill terrace after terrace between the house and the rocky coastline about 100 feet below. Luckily, hosts Alan Ramsbottom and Lois Baucke have large windows throughout their quiet, modern home, so the view is always accessible. The rooms are clean and comfy, but not fancy.

They'll pick you up at the ferry. Visitors who don't have a car, but would like to explore more, can join the rural letter carrier when she makes her rounds (☎ 09/372-9166) for NZ$15 (US$10.50). No smoking is permitted inside the house, and children are not accepted.

Palm Beach Backpackers Lodge

54 Palm Rd., Palm Beach, Waiheke Island. ☎ **09/372-8662.** Fax 09/379-2084. 16 dorm, twin, single, and double rms (most without bathrm), 16 campsites. NZ$20 (US$14) per person double; NZ$15 (US$10.50) dorm bed; NZ$10 (US$7) per person campsite. The ferry from Auckland takes 35 minutes; then there's a free bus to Palm Beach.

Located just 50 yards from the water's edge, this is an ideal spot for activity-oriented guests. Sea kayaking, sailing, horseback riding, mountain biking, fishing, snorkeling, and bushwalks all start from here. There's even a nudist beach nearby, plus barbecues, kitchen facilities, storage lockers, and a TV room. The rooms themselves are the basic motel varieties.

WHERE TO EAT

✪ Vino-Vino Bar & Cafe

Oceanview Mall, Oneroa, Waiheke Island. ☎ **09/372-9888.** Reservations not accepted. Snacks NZ$3–$8 (US$2.50–$5.60); lunch or dinner NZ$7.50–$12 (US$5.30–$8.40). AE, BC, DC, MC, V. Mon–Thurs 11am–10pm, Fri–Sat 11am–11pm, Sun 11am–8pm. MODERN NEW ZEALAND.

This wine bar/cafe has four things going for it: a menu that's actually fun to read, a great atmosphere, a wonderful view, and most importantly, good food. I stopped in here recently and had the best pumpkin soup I've ever tasted. Other menu offerings include Vino's hot roast lamb on rye with beetroot-and-mint chutney, white-onion and rosemary pizza bread with cheese, egg, and green-olive pâté (try this), and salad with sesame-tofu balls and peanut-and-coriander dressing. There's an open fire in winter and outdoor seating on a sundeck in summer. A dozen wines are available by the glass (more by the bottle), and Guinness is on tap.

RANGITOTO ISLAND

Rangitoto is another popular day-trip destination. The volcanic island has miles of walking tracks and offers great views of Auckland and the Hauraki Gulf. There are also pohutukawa forests, fern groves, and a black-backed-gull colony. **Fuller's** (☎ **09/367-9111**) *Manu* provides regular service and Fuller's also offers a ferry/guided safari package.

WEST OF AUCKLAND: WINERIES, BEACHES & MORE

To the west of Auckland are numerous **wineries** that welcome visitors for free tours and tasting. For a complete list, pick up the brochure "Winemakers of West Auckland" at the Visitor Information Centre.

The **Arataki Visitor Centre,** Scenic Drive, Waitakere Ranges (☎ **09/817-7134,** fax 09/817-5656), is the best source of information in the area. Stop by and view their video and other informative displays on the local natural environment.

The **Waitakere Ranges** are also west of Auckland and, along with the **surf beaches** at Piha and Muriwai, present another day-trip destination. Bushwalking, scenic drives, board surfing, hang gliding, and picnicking are all popular activities here. The **gannet colony** at Muriwai Beach is one of only two mainland nesting sites in the world. **Bush & Beach Ltd.** (☎ 09/478-2882, or 0800/4-BEACH in New Zealand; fax 09/478-2882), also conducts tours of the area (see "Organized Tours & Cruises," earlier in this chapter).

THE HIBISCUS COAST/KOWHAI COAST

Located 48km (30 miles) north of Auckland, the Hibiscus Coast comprises the communities of Silverdale, Whangaparaoa, Orewa, Waiwera, and Puhoi. It only takes about 45 minutes by car to drive here from central Auckland. For folks with limited time, a trip up here provides a great glimpse into rural New Zealand life. It's also a convenient stop en route to the Bay of Islands. InterCity coaches and Auckland city buses provide regular service.

Tourist information is available from the **Hibiscus Coast Information Centre,** 214A Hibiscus Coast Hwy. (next to the Kentucky Fried Chicken), Orewa (☎ 09/ 426-0076, fax 09/426-0086). This office is open from 10am to 5pm Monday through Friday and from 10am to 4pm on weekends (Monday through Friday during summer they open at 9am); the office is closed Christmas Day. The **STD (area code)** for the Hibiscus Coast is **09.**

WHAT TO SEE & DO

Few things are as relaxing as soaking in the **Waiwera Thermal Pools,** State Highway 1 (☎ 09/302-1684). Nineteen indoor and outdoor pools are kept at 28° to 45°C (80° to 115°F), and there are private pools as well as larger ones—also a water slide. The complex is open daily from 9am to 10pm. It costs NZ$12.50 (US$8.80) for adults and NZ$7.50 (US$5.30) for children up to age 14; NZ$32 (US$22.40) for a family. If you forgot yours, a shop on the premises sells "togs" (swimsuits).

It's a slight detour off the highway, but if history interests you, take a look at the ✪ **Puhoi Hotel,** or "pub" as it's known. The two-story white frame building holds the district's first liquor license, issued in 1879. Farm implements and saddles are suspended from the walls, and the place is a treasure trove of old photos. If history doesn't interest you, you could do as the locals do on a sunny day: Order a pitcher of Lion Red and lounge on the lawn.

You might also stop by the town of **Warkworth,** once the center of extensive saw milling of kauri spars to furnish masts for the Royal Navy. There are the remains of several Maori *pas* (fortified villages) in the area. About 7km (4 miles) away, at the coastal town of **Sandspit,** you can take a launch to Kawau Island to visit **Mansion House,** the restored home of Gov. George Grey.

WHERE TO STAY

Angel Valley

42 Manuel Rd. (R.D. 2), Silverdale. ☎ and fax **09/426-6175.** 2 rms (none with bathrm), 1 studio (with bathrm). NZ$70 (US$49) double; NZ$90 (US$63) self-contained unit for 2. Rates include breakfast. Dinner NZ$20 (US$14) extra. MC, V. Courtesy pick-up from Silverdale.

This country homestay affords you a chance to wake up to sheep outside the window and admire a spectacular view of rolling green hills. Ute Engel lives on this 4-acre farmlet, 5 minutes off State Highway 1. She offers two rooms in her cozy no-smoking home and an adjacent studio unit with cooking facilities. She only takes one party at a time so the in-home guests have their own bathroom. The hostess is a very sensitive and caring person, and the atmosphere at Angel Valley is noticeably peaceful. Children are welcome, but stairs make this homestay a poor choice for less mobile people. Vegetarian meals are available.

Marco Polo Backpackers Inn
2d Hammond Ave., Hatfields Beach, Orewa. ☎ **09/426-8455.** 6 rms with 24 beds (no rooms with bathrm). NZ$25 (US$17.50) single; NZ$34 (US$21) double; NZ$14 (US$9.80) bed in a dorm; NZ$8 (US$5.60) per person tent site. MC, V. Bus: 894 or 895 from Platform 5A in Auckland Downtown Bus Terminal; ask bus driver to stop at Marco Polo.

Hosts Jan and Marleen Bastiaanssen get rave reviews from guests for their friendliness and helpfulness. They even organize coastal walks and volleyball games on the beach. This hostel, just north of Orewa, offers a fully equipped kitchen and a homey atmosphere.

○ The Warkworth Inn
Queen St., Warkworth. ☎ **09/425-8569.** Fax 09/425-9696. 8 rms (none with bathrm). NZ$58.50 (US$40.95) double. Rates include continental breakfast. AE, BC, DC, MC, V.

This is one of New Zealand's best bargains. All quarters in this 132-year-old property have tea- and coffeemaking facilities, sinks, clocks, and heaters. High ceilings are all that belie the otherwise youthful appearance of the accommodations. Guests share a TV lounge opening onto a veranda. There's a restaurant on the premises, and bistro meals are available in the bar. Although this inn is in the town center, little traffic noise exists because Highway 1 bypasses Warkworth—however, this could be a noisy spot on Friday night when there's a band in the bar.

EN ROUTE TO THE BAY OF ISLANDS
If your next stop after Auckland is the Bay of Islands, you'll most likely drive through the city of **Whangarei.** We found a nice picnic or rest stop at **Whangarei Falls.**

EN ROUTE TO THE COROMANDEL PENINSULA
THE PACIFIC COAST HIGHWAY
As mentioned in chapter 3, the Pacific Coast Highway isn't a "highway," but a scenic route that follows the coastline from Auckland to Hawkes Bay—it was purposely planned for visitors. If you travel this way from Auckland to Thames, you'll go through the Sea Bird Coast. This east-coast road is also the way cyclists travel since they aren't allowed on the motorway.

THE SEA BIRD COAST
This wading bird habitat rings the upper reaches of the Firth of Thames (an inlet off the Hauraki Gulf) with the most significant and protected parts between Miranda and Kaiaua. The area attracts thousands of migratory wading birds both from New Zealand and abroad. Bar-tailed godwits breed in northeastern Siberia and spend their

Readers Recommend
Town Basin in Whangarei. *"On the way north to the Bay of Islands, there is a lovely marina called the Town Basin, which appears to be the center for arts and crafts in the area as well as home to some delightful cafes and licensed bistros. It was lovely to sit watching the boats while sipping a drink outside under one of the umbrellas."*
—Christine Jenkinson, Sundbury, Victoria, Australia.

summers in New Zealand. Some New Zealand dotterels and wrybills (unique New Zealand species) live here year-round, but winter brings half the world's population of wrybills (there are about 5,000 worldwide). This is also a huge feeding area for Alaskan migrants (they're here mid-September to mid-March). The Sea Bird Coast is located 90km (55.8 miles) southeast of Auckland.

For Serious Birders

✪ Miranda Shorebird Centre

On the Pacific Coast Hwy., R.D.1, Pokeno, (P.O. Box 90-180, Auckland Mail Centre). ☎ and fax **09/232-2781**. Free admission (donation appreciated). AE, BC, DC, MC, V.

Miranda is on the west coast of the Firth of Thames. This is a popular spot for bird watchers. A blackboard list of rare birds seen recently is updated daily. If you decide to overnight here, it's very cheap. A small flat with en suite (attached) bathroom and kitchen costs NZ$45 (US$31.50) for a double; the four bunkrooms, which sleep four to six people, are NZ$15 (US$10.50) each, per person. There are shared facilities and a shared kitchen for the bunk rooms. If you stay here, bring bedding (only a limited amount of bed and bath linen can be rented at the Centre), your own food, and a swimsuit—there's swimming/soaking at the Miranda Hot Pools (☎ **0800/ 468-777** in New Zealand) daily from 9am to 9pm.

WHERE TO EAT

In addition to the restaurant listed below, you might like to stop in Pipiroa and visit **The Pipiroa Country Kitchen,** State Highway 25, Pipiroa (R.D.1, Ngatea, Hauraki Plains, 2852) (☎ and fax **07/867-7599**). This country tearoom also has a seasonal blackboard menu and special weekend treats They're open Monday through Thursday from 10am to 4:30pm, Friday through Sunday, and public holidays from 10am to 8pm. Both eat-in and takeaway are available.

Kaiaua Fisheries Licensed Seafood Restaurant & Takeaways

East Coast Rd., Kaiaua. ☎ **09/232-2776**. Reservations not accepted. NZ$1.80–$2.80 (US$1.30–$1.96) per piece of fish. MC, V. Daily 9am–9pm. FISH-and-CHIPS.

Owners Graham and Christine Blackwell won the national title of "The Best Fish & Chip Shop" in 1995. They catch and sell their own fish, and you choose the type you want: hoki, John Dory, flounder, or red snapper. Usually one order of chips (NZ$1.50/US$1.05) is enough for two people. If you come on a weekend, be prepared to queue to give your order at the counter and then wait for your number to be called when your order is ready. There is also a restaurant here, but the takeaway is more fun. There are a few tables inside, picnic benches outside, or you can take your meal across the road and eat on the waterfront.

6 Farther Afield from Auckland

From Auckland, many visitors head south to Waitomo and its glow-worms, then on to Rotorua where Maori culture is alive and well. It's not a bad idea to include these places on your itinerary; the silent glow of Waitomo's grotto and Rotorua's thermal steaminess are certainly significant and there's plenty of coverage on them later in this book. But I also hope that you'll consider a detour north to the Bay of Islands, a beautiful region drenched in New Zealand history, or perhaps you'll at least head a bit off the beaten path to the Coromandel Peninsula. These areas are too often overlooked by overseas visitors, although much loved by Auckland-area residents. The Coromandel Peninsula, which juts out between the Hauraki Gulf and the Pacific, is rich in unspoiled terrain, and its coastline is incredibly beautiful.

1 The Bay of Islands

233km (145 miles) N of Auckland

For New Zealanders, this is where it all began—"civilization" disguised as British culture, that is. But long before Capt. James Cook anchored the *Endeavour* off Motuarohia Island in 1769, Maori civilization existed here in perfect harmony with nature (but often at considerable *disharmony* with their tribal neighbors). Maori history tells of the arrival of Kupe and Ngahu from Hawaiki, then of Whatonga and Toi, and later of the great chiefs Ruatara, Hongi Hika, and Tamati Waaka Nene. It glorified the waterfront settlement at Kororareka, already well established when Captain Cook appeared and gave the region its Pakeha name. Be that as it may, New Zealand's modern history also begins here in the Bay of Islands.

British settlers first set foot on New Zealand soil in 1804, and a whole litany of British "firsts" follows that date: in 1814, the first Christian sermon (today, you'll find a large Celtic cross memorial planted on that very spot, a stretch of beach on the north side of Rangihoua Bay); in 1820, the first plow was introduced; in 1831, the first European marriage; in 1835, the first printing press; in 1839, the first bank; and in 1840, a post office, Customs House, and official treaty between the British and Maori chieftains. After that, British civilization was here to stay.

The Bay of Islands you'll encounter today is a happy blend of history and natural beauty, which make it (as any resident is quick to

Farther Afield from Auckland

tell you) "the best spot in the country to live—or play." And play they do. Recreation is king up here. Imagine a deeply indented coastline whose waters hold some 144 islands, most with sandy stretches of beach. Imagine clear blue waters teeming with sportfish like the kingfish (yellowtail). Imagine, too, a climate with average winter temperatures ranging from 7 to 16°C (45 to 61°F) and summer temps of 14 to 25°C (57 to 77°F).

However, you won't find any local transportation systems except for the delightful little ferry that delivers schoolchildren, business people, visitors, and freight from one shore to the other. Nor will you find any sort of wild nightlife. The Bay of Islands is for soaking up sun, sea, and fresh air, and for putting the frenetic pace of big-city life on hold.

ESSENTIALS
GETTING THERE

BY PLANE   Eagle Airways (☎ 0800/737-000 in New Zealand) has daily flights between Auckland and Kerikeri, with a shuttle bus into Paihia. Make reservations through Air New Zealand.

BY COACH (BUS)   Both **InterCity** (☎ 09/357-8400 in Auckland) and **Northliner Express** (☎ 09/307-5873 in Auckland) have daily bus service between Auckland and Paihia or Kerikeri. Both companies charge NZ$42 (US$29.40) one way. Northliner offers a 30% discount to backpackers and anyone over age 50.

InterCity gives a 30% discount to YHA members, VIP (backpacker) card holders, and anyone over age 60.

BY CAR It's an easy, beautiful drive to the Bay of Islands from Auckland. Along the way you'll pass through rolling green hills dotted with sheep and cows, and you'll see lots of huge ponga ferns and pine trees, as well as cabbage trees, poplars, and toi toi. The coastal views and tranquil beaches are also gorgeous. You might want to stop along the Hibiscus Coast, in Warkworth, or Whangarei (see "Easy Side Trips from Auckland" and "En Route to the Bay of Islands" in chapter 5). You may want to take the longer route through the kauri forest on the west coast (see "En Route to Auckland, by Way of the West Coast," below). The straight shot from Auckland can be accomplished in 3 hours, but I suggest you forget about hurrying and enjoy your introduction to Northland.

Note: If Russell is your destination, you'll need to take the car ferry at Opua. The ferry that shuttles back and forth from Paihia carries only pedestrians. (See "By Ferry," below.)

BY TOUR Several companies in Auckland offer 1-, 2-, and 3-day tours to the Bay of Islands. For good value and personal service, you might want to contact Henry and Lorna at **Best Deal Sights** (☎ **09/818-7799**).

GETTING AROUND

BY CAR Driving is easy and parking seldom a problem in the Bay of Islands. If you arrive via air or bus, **rental cars** are available through **Budget Rent-A-Car,** in the Paihia Holiday Shoppe, corner of Selwyn and Williams roads, in the ASB Bank Building, Paihia (☎ **09/402-8568**).

ON FOOT You can walk to everything in Russell and Paihia—both towns are small and distances short between attractions. It's when you move from the Paihia/Russell area to Kerikeri that you will need wheels.

BY BUS The Bay of Islands doesn't have a public bus service; however, **Kerikeri Bus Line** (☎ **09/407-7135** or 025/404-893) operates between Kerikeri, Opua, Paihia, and Waitangi Monday through Friday. One-way tickets cost NZ$1 to $4 (US70¢ to $2.80) adult, NZ 50¢ to $2 (US 35¢ to $1.40) for children; round-trips are NZ$5 to $6 (US$3.50 to $4.20) adult, NZ$2.50 to $3 (US$1.75 to $2.10) for children.

BY TAXI The **Island Water Taxi** (book at the Visitor Information Centre) offers 24-hour service, and fares depend on the time of day and number of passengers.

BY FERRY If you stay in Russell but want to eat or hang out in Paihia, you'll have to take the little ferry that connects the two places. The ferry is the only inexpensive way to get from one shore to another (well, there is a roundabout drive, but it takes much too long). The ferry runs at hourly intervals beginning at 7am (on the hour from Russell, on the half hour from Paihia) and ending at 7:30pm (from Paihia). In summer, crossings are extended to 10:30pm. Fares are NZ$6 (US$4.20) round trip for adults, NZ$3 (US$2.10) for children 5 to 15; children under 5 free. You'll soon have that schedule firmly fixed in your mind—it's important to be on the same side of the water as your bed when the service shuts down! If you should find yourself stranded, however, all is not lost—you'll just have to take one of the more expensive water taxis.

About 15 minutes south of Paihia, at **Opua,** there's a flat-bottom car ferry for drivers that crosses the narrow channel to Okiato Point, a 10-minute drive from Russell. Crossings are every 10 minutes from 6:40am to 9pm, and the one-way fare for car and driver is NZ$7 (US$4.90) plus NZ$1 (US70¢) for each adult passenger, half price for children.

VISITOR INFORMATION

You'll find the **Bay of Islands Information Centre** on Marsden Road on the waterfront (P.O. Box 333) in Paihia (☎ **09/402-7345;** fax 09/402-7314; e-mail paivin@nzhost.co.nz). The staff can arrange accommodations throughout the Bay of Islands—bed-and-breakfast, motel unit, motor camp, or tent site. They also keep up-to-the-minute information on all sightseeing and other activities. The office is staffed daily from 8am to 5pm during winter, to 7pm during the summer. They can't book flights, the Cook Strait ferry, or trains, however. For this you will need to go to the **Paihia Holiday Shoppe,** corner of Selwyn and Williams Road, Paihia (☎ **09/ 402-7811,** fax 09/402-7812).

There isn't an information center in Kerikeri; the best bet is to get information from the one in Paihia. You can also get Kerikeri information from the following Web site: http://www.kerikeri.co.nz.

The STD **(telephone area code)** for the Bay of Islands is **09.**

SPECIAL EVENTS

You may want to plan your itinerary so that you're in the Bay of Islands when these events are in full swing:

Bay of Islands Arts Festival   This festival offers a diverse program featuring every kind of art form, from drama to painting. Held annually since 1992, it attracts over 5,000 people every year. Early February. Call ☎ **09/405-0090** for details.

Waitangi Day Celebrations   Locals celebrate the signing of the Treaty of Waitangi in 1840. February 6. Call ☎ **09/402-7308** for details.

The Bay of Islands Country Music Festival   It draws musicians from all around New Zealand. There's also at least one big international act each year. Second weekend in May. Call ☎ **09/404-1063** for details.

The Bay of Islands Jazz and Blues Festival   This one's held at various venues around Paihia and Russell and runs night and day. Early to mid-August. Call ☎ **09/ 402-7547** for details.

The Bay of Islands Wine and Food Festival   Set in the picturesque grounds of the Quality Resort Waitangi, this festival features top New Zealand wine and food exhibitors and great entertainment. Last weekend in September. Call ☎ **09/402-7557** for details.

ORIENTATION

There are three distinct areas in the Bay of Islands: **Paihia/Waitangi, Russell,** and **Kerikeri.**

PAIHIA & WAITANGI   This is the hub for the region's commercial and tourist action. There are lots of hostels and motels, places to eat, and tour booking agencies. The access from Auckland is easy and it's easy to get around without a car. All of the tours and cruises start here. It is a short (1.61km/1 mile) walk to **Waitangi** where the historic Treaty House is located. In Paihia, the main drag is Marsden Road It runs along the waterfront. Williams Road is a one-way street perpendicular to the coast. This is the major commercial area.

RUSSELL   If you're into either fishing or history, you'll want to be based in **Russell,** located on a peninsula across the inlet from Paihia. Most of the charter boats in the area are anchored here and Russell is also the first capital of New Zealand, so there's no shortage of historic buildings and sites to explore. There are plenty of good accommodations to choose from, and it's easy to get around without a car. It's also quieter than Paihia and convenient because most cruises stop here. Access is by ferry, so it feels isolated, which can be a plus or minus, depending on your travel needs and interests.

KERIKERI   It takes about 20 minutes to drive from Paihia to Kerikeri, a thriving fruit-growing region that's also known for its arts and crafts. The pace here is relaxed and decidedly noncommercial. The area has recently been "discovered" by wealthy New Zealanders and folks from overseas who are building magnificent homes and supporting local performing arts. Most of the attractions here are natural ones—swimming, kayaking, sailing, walking, and so forth. The area also has a lot of good restaurants.

OUTDOOR ACTIVITIES

BEACHES   There are beaches galore for good swimming from November through March. They're lined up all along the town waterfronts, and delightful little coves with curving strands are just awaiting your discovery down almost any side road along State Highway 10 headed north—if you pass through privately owned land to reach the water, you may be asked to pay a small fee, something like NZ$1 (US 70¢).

FISHING   Light-line fishing is affordable, and the Visitor Information Centre in Paihia can furnish a list of fishing charters available, as many come and go. Most supply rods and bait and run 3- to 5-hour trips. I'd also recommend asking your hosts where you are staying for names and numbers of good fishing guides and charter companies.

GOLF   You can arrange to play on the beautiful 18-hole waterfront course at Waitangi Golf Course. The greens fees are NZ$25 (US$17.50) per person for 18 holes; clubs are available for hire.

KAYAKING   Contact **Coastal Kayakers,** Pahia Waterfront (Box 325), Paihia (☎ 09/402-8105, fax 09/404-0291). They provide full instruction, so no experience is necessary. Paddle to a deserted island, visit the mangrove forest, and challenge a waterfall. A half day (about 4 hours) costs NZ$40 (US$28) and includes complimentary tea and coffee; bring your own lunch.

SAILING   Contact Mike and Debbie at **Gungha New Zealand Cruises,** R.D.1, Kerikeri (☎ 09/407-7930, fax 09/407-9794). They take a maximum of 12 people at a time on their 14-meter (45^{1}/2-ft.) sailboat *Gungha,* where you can help sail the boat or just relax and enjoy the scenery. Dolphins, penguins, and seabirds are often fluttering about. A full day of sailing including lunch and transfers is NZ$65 (US$45.50) per person.

SCUBA DIVING   There's some pretty good underwater exploration to be done in these waters. **Paihia Dive, Hire and Charters Ltd.,** on Williams Road (☎ 09/402-7551, fax 09/402-7110), can provide all equipment and arrange dives. Paihia Dive offers trips to the wreck of the *Rainbow Warrior* three times a week. **Matauri Kat Charter** (☎ 09/405-0525) does this trip daily.

WALKING   The Bay of Islands is rich in excellent scenic and historic walks. The park rangers below or the Visitor Information Centre in Paihia can furnish details of all trails, as well as a very good booklet called **"Walking in the Bay of Islands Maritime and Historic Park"** (which costs NZ$1). Go by the Park Visitor Centre in Russell (P.O. Box 134; ☎ 09/403-7685, fax 09/403-7649) or the Ranger

Station in Kerikeri (P.O. Box 128; ☎ 09/407-8474) for trail maps and assistance. There are also beautiful campsites, some of them on uninhabited islands in the bay, with nominal per-night fees. You must reserve with the park rangers at Russell—you might write ahead and ask for their free useful brochure, "Huts and Camping." Send US$1 for each booklet to cover postage.

The **Kerikeri River Walk** is an easy 1-hour walk to ✪ **Rainbow Falls.** This delightful trail starts in the car park next to the Stone Store. The grade is easy and the round trip takes about 2 hours. Along the way you'll pass Fairy Falls. It's also possible to drive to the top of Rainbow Falls, but I hope you'll consider doing the walk because it's really lovely.

EXPLORING THE TOWNS
PAIHIA/WAITANGI

If you're interested in history, the **Treaty House** in Waitangi should be at the top of your sightseeing list; it's the birthplace of modern New Zealand.

Treaty House
Waitangi National Reserve, Waitangi. ☎ 09/402-7437. Fax 09/402-8303. Admission NZ$7 (US$4.90) adults, free for children. Daily 9am–5pm.

It was on the grounds (near the flagpole) of this Georgian-style house that the British Crown succeeded in having its first treaty ratified by enough chieftains to assure its acceptance by major Maori leaders throughout the country. Set in parklike grounds, this was the home of James Busby from 1832 to 1880, and its broad lawn was the scene of the colorful meeting of Pakeha and Maori during the treaty negotiations over 150 years ago on February 6, 1840. Inside, there's a museum display of a facsimile of the treaty written in Maori, an exhibition on James Busby and his family, other mementos of those early days, and rooms with period furnishings. An audiovisual presentation of the treaty's history may be seen at the Visitors Centre. You'll also see one of the most magnificent whare runangas (meetinghouses) in the country, constructed for the 1940 centennial celebration; it contains elaborately carved panels from all the Maori tribes in New Zealand. Just below the sweeping lawn, on Hobson's Beach, there's an impressive 117-foot-long **Maori waka** (war canoe), also made for the centennial, from three giant kauri trees.

If your visit coincides with the February 6 celebration of **Waitangi Day**, you'll find the center of activity is the Treaty House lawn—scene of the Waitangi Treaty signing, with a re-creation of that event, lots of Maori song and dance, and Pakeha officials in abundance, dressed to the nines in uniforms of yesteryear and today. The Royal New Zealand Navy is usually there in force, as are crowds of vacationing Kiwis. Book way ahead, then get set to join the crowds.

Kelly Tarlton's Museum of Shipwrecks
Near the Paihia–Waitangi Bridge. ☎ 09/402-7018. Admission NZ$6 (US$4.20) adults, NZ$2.50 (US$1.75) children 6–16 years old. Open daily 10am–5pm. Closed Christmas Day.

Located on a three-masted bark, the *Tui*, this museum shows off fine treasures from the many ships that have perished in the waters off New Zealand. The late Kelly Tarlton, a professional diver, made treasure hunting in nearby waters his life's work. Beside each display of treasure he brought up from the deep, there's a photograph of the ship from which it was recovered. There's a continuous slide show depicting Kelly going about his work underwater, and realistic sound effects of storms, the creaking of timbers, and the muffled chant of sea chanteys. A cafe is open during the day. There's also a restaurant for nighttime dining.

RUSSELL

Russell is a veritable concentration of historical sites. It was here that the great Maori leader Hone Heke burned everything except mission property at a time when most of what was there should have been burned in the interest of morality and environmental beauty, since the town seethed with all sorts of European vices, diseases, and injustices against the indigenous people. The old Anglican church and headstones of sailors buried in its graveyard bear to this day bullet holes from that long-ago battle.

On the highest elevation in Russell stands the **flagstaff** Hone Heke chopped down four times in defiance of British rule. It is reached by auto or on foot, and the lookout up there affords one of the best views of the bay.

Bay of Islands Maritime Park Headquarters and Visitors Centre

The Strand, on the waterfront in Russell. ☎ **09/403-7685.** Fax 09/403-7649. Free admission. Mon–Fri 8:30am–4:30pm, Sat–Sun 9am–4:30pm, closes at 5pm November through May.

Stop here and watch the 15-minute audiovisual presentation *The Land Is Enduring* to get a grasp of the Maori and English history of this area. The center, operated by the Department of Conservation, has camping information and maps and sells a variety of books, prints, cards, T-shirts, sweatshirts, and local Heritage Trail guides.

Pompallier

The Strand, on the waterfront in Russell. ☎ **09/403-7861.** Fax 09/403-8588. Admission NZ$5 (US$3.50) adults, free for children. BC, MC, V. Daily 10am–5pm. Closed Christmas Day.

This house was built in 1841 by the French Bishop Pompallier for the Roman Catholic Mission to house a printing press used from 1842 to 1849 to print religious documents in the Maori language. That press is still here today, and there's also a working tannery and a book bindery. Tours are given at 10:15am, 11:15am, 1:15pm, and 3:15pm.

Russell Museum

York St., Russell. ☎ and fax **09/403-7701.** Admission NZ$2.50 (US$1.75) adults, NZ50¢ (US 35¢) children. Daily 10am–4pm.

This local history museum records the earliest years of Maori-European contact. Highlights are the one-fifth-scale model of the Captain Cook's *Endeavour,* the Hansen-King Collection of historic costumes, and the 10-minute video on Russell's beginnings.

Christ Church

At Church St. and Robertson Rd., Russell. Free admission. Daily 9am–5pm.

Dating from 1836, this is not only the oldest surviving church in New Zealand but also the oldest building in the country still used for its original purpose. Among those who contributed funds for its construction was Charles Darwin, who visited New Zealand on *The Beagle* while making the observations that resulted in *The Origin of Species.* The church has been the site of numerous turning points in history, including Captain Hobson's proclamation prior to the signing of the Treaty of Waitangi. Be sure to notice the needlepoint pew cushions crafted by local residents.

KERIKERI

You may very well want to base yourself here. As a minimum, take the time to make the 20-minute drive to this small town that figured prominently in the country's early history. It holds the oldest masonry building in New Zealand, the **Stone Store,** on Kerikeri Rd., built between 1832 and 1835 as a mission supply center. At press time the Stone Store is closed for renovation but it should be open by the time you get there. **Kemp House,** New Zealand's oldest surviving building, is adjacent to the

Stalking the Elusive Kiwi

Visitors who come to New Zealand thinking they're going to see the kiwi bird are apt to be disappointed. The country doesn't have many of the hen-sized brown birds, and the ones they do have are downright shy. The ✪ **Aroha Island Ecological Centre,** located 12km (7.4 miles) outside of Kerikeri at Rangitane, was established to educate the public about its feathered icon. The exhibit area is open daily from 9:30am to 5:30pm except Wednesday, and admission is free. Visitors are welcome to picnic on the grounds, and kayaks and canoes are for rent at NZ$2 (US$1.40) per hour.

Your best bet for seeing a kiwi in the wild is to stay overnight at the Aroha Island Ecological Centre. You can camp in a lovely spot down by the water for NZ$7.50 (US$5.25) per person or stay in Aroha's cottage or twin-bedded room. The cottage rents for NZ$60 (US$42) most of the year and NZ$75 (US$52.50) in the height of summer. It sleeps up to five in single beds and has a full kitchen, TV, and en suite bathroom. The twin-bedded room also has an en suite bathroom and a veranda with a view of the Kerikeri Inlet. It costs NZ$85 (US$59.50) for two people with breakfast. Campers may well pass a kiwi on their way to the loo during the night. Those staying in the cottage or room will have to sit outside and wait. In any case, there's no way you can miss the loud screech of the male and the softer squawk of the female. Whether you stay here or not, please drive carefully at night in this area. Cars and dogs account for the majority of kiwi deaths. Bookings can be made by calling ☎ **09/407-5243,** fax 09/407-5246, or writing to Private Box 541, Kerikeri.

Stone Store. (After you've toured these two places, stop by the **Stone Store Cafe and Restaurant** for a snack or a meal.)

Rewa's Village, located in the Stone Store basin, is an authentic reconstruction of a pre-European Maori kainga (fishing village). Built in 1969, this kainga is the same as if it had been here when the missionaries first came to New Zealand. Because it is an unfortified kainga, Rewa's Village has no elaborate carved gateway or buildings. A video here tells of the founding of Kerikeri in 1819 and the significance of Kororipo Pa (the fort that was across the river) and the mission buildings.

For information on the **Kerikeri River Track** to Rainbow Falls, see "Outdoor Activities," above.

Kerikeri is also an arts-and-crafts center, and you can watch many of the artisans at work in their small shops. The **Kerikeri Art & Craft Trail** takes you to 17 studios within a few kilometers of Kerikeri. Member locations are designated by yellow triangles. Pick up a map at area businesses. They also have a Web page at www.northland.ac.nz/artcraft.

A SIDE TRIP TO CAPE REINGA

If time permits, I heartily recommend the road trip to ✪ **Cape Reinga**—the northernmost point on the North Island. There's something intriguing about being at the very top of New Zealand (and if you visit Stewart Island down south, you'll have seen the country from stem to stern). And besides, there's a mystical aura about the cape, since the Maori believed that it was from a gnarled pohutukawa tree in the cliffs here that souls jumped off for the return to their Hawaiki homeland after death.

You can do this trip in your rental car, but the advantage of going on a tour bus is that it will travel along the hard-packed golden sands of the **Ninety-Mile Beach** (which measures 52 miles at low tide) on the return trip south. Private vehicles are not allowed on the beach. It's a tough call: You'll save money by going in your rental car, but it is really fun to ride along the beach. I'll leave the decision to you, but keep in mind that if you drive, it's 7 hours round trip from the Bay of Islands to Cape Reinga and back. If that sounds like too long of a day, you might go up to the Cape and then back only as far Kaitaia or Ahipara, stay overnight there, and then proceed back to Auckland via the west coast (see "En Route to Auckland by Way of the West Coast" later in this chapter). Kaitaia has a **YHA Hostel** at 160 Commerce St., Kaitaia (☎ **09/408-1840**) and the **Siesta Homestay** is located in Ahipara (see "Affordable Accommodations," below).

You might also want to plan your trip so that you pass through the town of Mangonui at either lunch or dinner time. The **Mangonui Fish Shop & Takeaways** on Beach Road (☎ and fax **09/406-0478**) is one of the best fish-and-chips shops in New Zealand.

ORGANIZED TOURS AND CRUISES

There's a wealth of sightseeing to be done on land in the Bay of Islands, but nothing compares with the bay itself. All those islands are set in water so sheltered that it's known to mariners as one of the best hurricane anchorages in the South Pacific. And if you do no other sightseeing during your stay, you should take one of the **bay cruises** that circumnavigate these islands. There's the 4-hour ✪ **Cape Brett cruise,** with its impressive passage through the **"Hole in the Rock"** when the weather is right; the cost is from NZ$50 (US$35) for adults, NZ$25 (US$17.50) for children.

Then there's the longer (5¹/₂-hour) ✪ **Cream Trip,** which retraces the route used in years gone by to collect cream for market from the islands and inlets around the bay. Along this route, your knowledgeable skipper will point out Captain Cook's first anchorage in 1769; the spot where Rev. Samuel Marston preached the first Christian sermon on the beach; island locales of violence, murder, and cannibalism; and Otehei Bay, on Urupukapuka Island, which was the site of Zane Grey's camp so well written of in his *The Angler's El Dorado*. The price of the Cream Trip is NZ$65 (US$45.50) for adults, NZ$33 (US$23.10) for children.

Maori owned and operated, **Bay of Island Heritage Tours Ltd.,** Maritime Building, Marsden Rd. (P.O. Box 96), Paihia, Bay of Islands (☎ **09/402-6288**), offers a ✪ **Dolphin & Whale Watch, Swim with the Dolphins** tour. It starts with a Maori *powhiri* (welcome), which includes a *taki* (challenge) and a *karanga* (call of welcome) on the wharf, a *hongi* (touching of noses) as you board, and Maori blessing (*karakia*) on board. No guarantee you'll see dolphins or whales, but your chances are pretty good. If you don't see any, you can come back again for free. There are no resident dolphins in this area; the ones seen are just passing through. Out on the water, one of the Maori gives a talk about the cultural significance of the dolphins (dolphins collect spirits of dead people and guide them to heaven) and Maori history in the area. Once dolphins are sighted everyone gets a mask, snorkle, and fins and gets in the water to swim with the gentle, curious creatures. You can't touch them, but you do get up-close-and-personal. There's another swim stop on the way back, as well as a lesson in how to do a haka (Maori challenge), and some Maori guitar playing and singing. Bring a towel, your swimsuit, and sunscreen. A hot shower and wet suits are provided in winter. The whole trip lasts 4 hours and costs NZ$85 (US$59.50) for adults and NZ$45 (US$31.50) for children.

Heritage Tours also offers a **Paihia Mini Tour,** a 1-hour guided tour of Paihia, Mount Bledisloe, and Haruru Falls daily at 9:30am and 2pm; a **Waitangi Treaty Grounds** 1¹/₂-hour guided tour daily at noon; **guided fishing trips; Whanau Homestay,** where you can experience the hospitality of a Maori family firsthand; and **Manu Kai Huia,** a shop featuring quality Maori arts and crafts. Company owners Nina, Arapeta, and Lawrence Hamilton are members of the Ngapuhi tribe; their direct ancestor Pomare II signed the Treaty of Waitangi in 1840.

Other companies also offer the swim-with-dolphins experience, but they lack the Maori insight. Fuller's Northland calls their trip **Dolphin Encounters** (NZ$85/US$59.50 for adults, NZ$45/US$31.50 for children). Fuller's (below) offer a 10% discount for a family and 15% off to backpackers.

Fuller's (☎ **0800/653-339** in New Zealand, **09/402-7421** in Paihia, **09/403-7866** in Russell) is the largest and most visible tour operator in the Bay of Islands. **Kings** (☎ **0508/888-282** in New Zealand, or 09/402-8288) conducts similar trips for slightly lower prices. They both offer the coach trip I mentioned above to **Cape Reinga via Ninety-Mile Beach.** The trips leave Paihia at 7:30am, return at 6:30pm, and cost from NZ$60 (US$42) for adults, from NZ$51 (US$35.70) for children.

SHOPPING

If you decide to take some time to browse around the shops in the area, there are several good choices. Go to **Dalrymples,** The Strand, Russell (☎ **09/403-7630**), where Peter Dalrymple keeps an assortment of good-quality gifts and souvenirs at reasonable prices. He also stocks handknit pullovers, leather jackets, and sheepskins. Over on the Paihia side, **The Cabbage Tree** (☎ **09/402-7318,** fax 09/402-8106) has two locations, one on Williams Road and the other on the wharf in the Maritime Building. Here you'll find good-quality carved bone and jade, pottery, hand-blown glass, original art, jewelry, and wood crafts. In Kerikeri, follow the **art and craft trail** mentioned above and make your purchases directly from their creators. Kerikeri is also a great area for browsing through **garden nurseries,** and you can buy **local fruit** from roadside stands where orchardists leave an honesty box for your use.

AFFORDABLE ACCOMMODATIONS

The Bay of Islands has plenty of affordable places to stay. Most are of modest size, earning a moderate but adequate income for couples or families who seem far more interested in their guests' having a good time than in charging "what the traffic will bear." Rates do fluctuate according to season, however, with a slight increase during holidays and a slightly higher jump December through February. During these peak periods, it is absolutely essential to reserve well in advance, since the Bay of Islands is tops on just about every Kiwi family's holiday list, and many book from year to year.

Several readers have suggested that staying on the Paihia side of the bay is more convenient because of late-night crossing difficulties. Having stayed in Paihia, Kerikeri, and Russell, I have to agree, but I still prefer Russell because it's less touristy. Kerikeri is great, but not as convenient for catching bay cruises.

The rates quoted below include the 12.5% Goods and Services Tax.

IN AND NEAR RUSSELL

Arcadia Lodge

Florence Ave., Russell. ☎ **09/403-7756.** Fax 09/403-7657. 9 rms. NZ$80 (US$56) double bed & breakfast unit; NZ$20 (US$14) per person in 3-person dorm rm. BC, V.

Jolene Bosanquet and Peter Heays own this lodge, which has three double and two single rooms upstairs for bed and breakfast guests. The four attractive dorm units are spotless and comfortable, and have great views of the bay—they're an extension of the main house. Each is a self-contained unit with linen and kitchen and will sleep three adults. The kitchen is available for B&B guest use, and complimentary tea and coffee are included in room rates. There are also a dinghy and old bikes for guests to use, and the hosts put on a weekly barbecue. This is a very popular place with budget travelers, both in New Zealand and among overseas travelers who've heard about it by word of mouth, so it's a good idea to book ahead if you can. The lodge is located on the outskirts of town.

Aimeo Cottage

Okiato Point Rd. (R.D. 1), Russell. ☎ and fax **09/403-7494.** 1 rm (with bathrm), 1 self-contained unit (with bathrm). NZ$85 (US$59.50) double, extra person NZ$15 (US$10.50). Rates include cooked breakfast. Dinner NZ$20 (US$14) per person. No credit cards. Courtesy pick-up from Paihia, NZ$30 (US$21) per carload from Kerikeri and Whangarei.

Annie and Helmuth Hormann arrived in New Zealand by way of Tahiti on their 35-foot sailboat. Their home, located near the Opua car ferry, has a fabulous water outlook and is sprinkled with Tahitian artifacts. She works at the Duke of Marlborough Hotel (see below), and he's home during the day. (A native of Berlin, the host refers to their picnic table as his "beer garden.") They offer one double room with bathroom and one self-contained apartment with bathroom and kitchen, which is a great bargain. A restaurant, gallery, and store are within walking distance.

✪ Ounuwhao–Harding House

Matauwhi Bay, Russell. ☎ and fax **09/403-7310.** 4 rms (1 with bathrm), 1 self-contained cottage. NZ$85–$95 (US$59.50–$67) B&B double without bath, NZ$100–$125 (US$70–$88) B&B double with bathrm. Cottage NZ$150 (US$105) for up to 4 people; breakfast available for NZ$10 (US$7) per person. MC, V. Closed June–July. Courtesy pick-up from Russell Wharf.

No, I haven't misspelled the name of this B&B—it's pronounced "oo-noo-*fow*" and it means "fighting with spears." Allan and Marilyn Nicklin bought this 1894 house in Dargaville and had it shipped here by land and sea. Only Kiwis would be so industrious! Their efforts are evident: The house has high ceilings, tall windows, imported English floral tile in the bath, and beautiful wallpaper throughout. Guests enjoy the lounge where a TV, tea- and coffeemaking facilities, and a fireplace are available to them. Three rooms have sinks; all have quilts, cushions, and curtains made by Marilyn, plus brass headboards. In the words of reader Meg Gammon of Kailua, Hawaii, "It is perfect in every way." No smoking is permitted in the house.

✪ Wairoro Park

P.O. Box 53, Russell. ☎ **09/403-7255.** 7 chalets (all with bathrm). TV TEL. NZ$80 (US$56) chalet for 2. Minimum charge of NZ$200 (US$140) per chalet during the Christmas holidays. Additional person NZ$12 (US$8.40) extra for adults, NZ$6 (US$4.20) extra for children. BC, MC, V. Go about a mile from the ferry, then turn left on a hilly dirt road and follow the signs.

The hospitality here could probably be labeled Kiwi-Dutch-English, since owner Yan Boerop is Dutch, his wife, Beryl, is English, and they're both now dyed-in-the-wool Kiwis. They've settled in on the Russell side of the Opua car ferry in an absolutely idyllic setting of some 160 acres on the shores of a sheltered bay cove. They use a great many of those acres to run cattle, and in the midst of an orchard just steps away from the beach, they have three two-story A-frame chalets and three one-bedroom luxury chalets. The first level of each holds a large lounge and fully equipped kitchen. There are two bedrooms upstairs, and when you include the three divans in the lounge, these units actually accommodate up to eight people. Facilities include a covered carport and decks with gorgeous views. A large three-bedroom chalet is set on its own

18 acres of bushland, with private water access and marvelous sea views—call for rates and availability. The Boerops thoughtfully provide a dinghy or motorboat, a 12-foot catamaran, two kayaks, and a windsurfer at no charge for guests. Regulars book from one holiday season to the next—which means, of course, that it's a good idea to write as far in advance as possible, no matter when you're coming.

For a Few Extra Bucks

The Duke of Marlborough Hotel

The Strand (P.O. Box 191), Russell. ☎ **09/403-7829.** Fax 09/403-7828. 29 rms (all with bathrm), 2 suites. TV TEL. NZ$95–$150 (US$67–$105) double; NZ$200 (US$140) suite. Lower rates off-season. DC, MC, V.

The Duke of Marlborough has watched generations of residents and visitors come and go from its waterfront perch since it opened as New Zealand's very first hotel in the late 19th century. It's survived three major fires and been rebuilt three times. Grand it may be—stuffy it isn't. Just a few steps from the Russell wharf, the covered veranda is the natural gathering place for fishermen at the end of the day. The conversation tends to be lively, attracting locals as well as hotel guests. The Duke, in fact, could be called the social hub of Russell (if Russell could, in fact, be said to have a social hub).

Regulars come back to the Duke year after year for its old-worldliness and also for the comfortable rooms. Some beds have wicker headboards, the floors are carpeted, the walls are wood paneled, and tea- and coffeemaking facilities are available in each room. There's a dining room serving all meals, a TV lounge, a charming guest lounge with wicker furniture, a colonial-style bar, and a fireplace.

IN PAIHIA

Campgrounds & Cabins

Bay of Islands Holiday Park

Lily Pond, Puketona Rd. (P.O. Box 393), Paihia. ☎ and fax **09/402-7646.** 200 tent sites, 100 powered sites, 3 on-site caravans, 11 cabins, 2 tourist flats, 66-bed lodge. NZ$9.50 (US$6.70) per person site; NZ$37 (US$25.90) double, cabin or on-site caravan; from NZ$60 (US$42) double tourist flat. Additional adult NZ$8 (US$5.60) extra. Lower rates off-season. DC, MC, V.

This is a big place, offering a communal kitchen and bath, laundry facilities, linen rental, a camp store, a games room, and a children's playground. It's about 4 miles to the beach and boat ramp and 5 miles to Paihia. The hosts are Linda Stewart and Maurice Biddington.

Super-Cheap Sleeps

Centabay Backpackers Hostel

Selwyn Rd., Paihia. ☎ **09/402-7466.** Fax 09/402-8145. 3 units (all with bathrm), 18 rms (none with bath). NZ$50–$75 (US$35–$52.50) double in studio unit; NZ$39 (US$27.30) double/twin share; NZ$16 (US$11.20) per dorm bed. Family and group rates available in low season. MC, V. Free parking. Courtesy pick-up from bus terminal.

Readers Recommend

Villa Helios, 44 Du Fresne Place, Russell. ☎ and fax **09/403-7229.** *"Gai and Bob Tuxford's B&B is high on the cliff at Tapeka Point with views of the bay and islands that take your breath away. I could visualize her description of the panorama laid out before her from the windows and balconies during the 'Tall Sailing Ships Race' held each January."*
—Jennie Fairlie, Broadbeach, Queensland, Australia.

This is the most centrally located hostel in town and quite appealing. It's run by the ever-helpful Brita and Heinz Marti, who arrange sailing, horseback riding, sea kayaking, fishing, and overnight camping trips to Cape Reinga. In addition to dormitories with two to six beds, there are three studio units with toilet and shower, toaster, tea- and coffeemaking facilities, and a balcony. There are no chores, and the place is very clean. Two units have a TV, and there are kitchens, a games room, and bike rentals. The booking office can also arrange sightseeing cruises and trips, sometimes with discounted fares.

Moderately Priced Options
Bay of Islands Motel

6 Tohitapu Rd., Te Haumi Bay (P.O. Box 131), Paihia. ☎ **09/402-7348.** Fax 09/402-8257. 19 cottages (all with bathrm). TV TEL. NZ$84–$145 (US$58.80–$101.50) one-bedroom cottage for 2, NZ$98–$175 (US$68.60–$122.50) two-bedroom cottage for 2. AE, MC, V.

Set in spacious grounds off Seaview Road, these self-contained colonial-style cottages have a lounge, separate bedrooms, a bath, and a full kitchen. To ensure privacy, the units are placed at angles so the windows of one don't face those of another—the configuration creates the feel of a charming village. Other facilities include a swimming pool, a spa pool, a laundry, and a playground for kids, who will also enjoy nearby beaches (within walking distance). There's also a licensed restaurant. The managers can supply cooked or continental breakfasts on request and are happy to book tours, cruises, and fishing trips right from their office. Many readers have commented on the "spotless" accommodations.

✪ Best Western Casa-Bella Motel

McMurray Rd., Paihia. ☎ **09/402-7387.** Fax 09/402-7166. E-mail casa.bel@xtra.co.nz. 21 units (all with bathrm), 1 suite. TV TEL. NZ$85 (US$59.50) unit for 2; NZ$95 (US$67) suite. Best Western discounts available. AE, DC, MC, V.

This charming red-tile-roofed sparkling-white Spanish-style complex is close to shops, restaurants, and the beach. There's a variety of nicely furnished units, each with full kitchen facilities, in-house video, and electric blankets. Some of the superior units have water beds, others have *firm* queen-size beds, and one is a special honeymoon suite with a softer, more attractive decor and queen-size beds. On the premises are both a heated swimming and a hot-spa pool, as well as full laundry facilities. Umbrella-shaded picnic tables and benches are set about on the landscaped grounds. Hosts Stefan and Darryl Vohan are very helpful. The motel is located on the first street on the left after the Beachcomber.

Wairoa Homestays

Bayly Rd. (P.O. Box 36), Paihia. ☎ **09/402-7379.** 2 rms (neither with bathrm). NZ$84 (US$58.80) double bed and breakfast; NZ$28 (US$19.60) per person, bed only. No credit cards.

Dorothy Bayly welcomes visitors to her seaside two-story country home that's 5 minutes from central Paihia and set in gardens overlooking Russell. She'll even take you for a drive around the farm; or for a small additional charge she'll arrange for you to be picked up in Paihia. All rooms have sea views and electric blankets; TV, tea- and coffeemaking facilities, and laundry are available to guests. There's a spa bath and tennis court on the property, with good beach walks and a golf course nearby.

IN KERIKERI
Super-Cheap Sleeps
Kerikeri YHA Hostel

Kerikeri Rd. (P.O. Box 62), Kerikeri. ☎ **09/407-9391.** Fax 09/407-9328. 8 rms (none with bathrm), 26 dormitory beds, 4 tent sites. NZ$32 (US$22.40) for 2 in twin room; NZ$14

(US$9.80) per person dorm bed, NZ$9 (US$6.30) per person in tent site. MC, V. Bus: Ask bus driver to drop you at the door.

Set on 2¹/₂ acres, this hostel consists of eight dormitory rooms—some with five beds, some with four—plus two twin rooms. Other facilities include a communal kitchen and laundry, a lounge and recreation/games room, and a volleyball court. There's river swimming just a 5-minute walk from the hostel, and many of the area's historic sites are within easy walking distance. The hostel is located on the main road just north of the town center.

For a Few Extra Bucks

Orchard Motel

Corner of Kerikeri and Hall rds. (P.O. Box 132), Kerikeri. ☎ **0508/808-869** toll-free in New Zealand. ☎ and fax 09/407-8869. 9 units (all with bathrm). TV, TEL. NZ$85–$100 (US$59.50–$70) double summer; NZ$65–$75 (US$45.50–$52.50) double mid-March to mid-December; extra person NZ$12 (US$8.40). Lower weekly rates. AE, DC, MC, V.

The units here are clean, spacious, and well-equipped, although the interiors are slightly dated. The motel is built on a citrus orchard, and guests can help themselves to fruit. All of the units have fully equipped kitchens; the one-bedroom units sleep five. There's parking right in front of each door. Congenial hosts Peter and Heather West provide a pool, spa, gas barbecue, and free washing machine. A dryer is available for NZ$2 (US$1.40) per load.

Moderately Priced Options

Villa Maria Residence

Inlet Road, P.O. Box 230, Kerikeri, Bay of Islands. ☎ and fax **09/407-9311.** 1 bungalow, 3 villas (all with bathrm). TV. Bungalow NZ$100 (US$70) double B&B; villas NZ$135 (US$95) double, NZ$210 (US$147) for 4 people (without breakfast). MC, V.

Owner Mieke Van Dyck and her sisters Catharina and Jackie are from Belgium. Mieke is the hostess at Villa Maria Residence (where Catharina makes a great breakfast) and Jackie runs the local Stone Store Restaurant. The villas each have two bedrooms (one with king or queen bed, the other with two twins), a lounge, and a full kitchen. Two villas are split-level—if stairs are a problem you can request the one that doesn't have them. While the villas are great for a group that wants to do its own cooking, I think for most travelers the bungalow is the best deal. This smaller unit has two double beds, but lacks a full kitchen. The friendly sisters keep a few Alpine goats and Fresian cattle on their pastoral 13-acre property. There's a view of the inlet, and there's also an estuary, just a 5-minute walk away, where you can see lots of native birds. The big windmill near the saltwater swimming pool supplies water for the property. Guests can pick oranges November through March. This is a good place for families with well-behaved children. The property is off the beaten path, so if you want to stay here, you'll need a car.

IN NORTHLAND

Siesta Homestay

Tasman Heights Rd. (P.O. Box 30), Ahipara. ☎ and fax **09/409-2011.** 2 rms (both with bathrm). TV. NZ$110 (US$77) double. Rates include breakfast. Dinner with wine NZ$30 (US$21) extra. MC, V. Courtesy pick-up from bus depot or local airport.

Siesta is an out-of-the-ordinary homestay, so even if you don't normally like B&Bs, I think you should consider this place. The house was built in 1988 specifically to accommodate visitors. The two guest bedrooms are in a separate wing, and each has a bathroom, a TV, a balcony, a writing desk, a sitting area, tea- and coffeemaking facilities, and a heater. The house sits high on a hill overlooking the Tasman Sea and

Ninety-Mile Beach, with views from every window. Hosts Alan and Carole Harding are full of information on the area. Ahipara is 15km (9 miles) west of Kaitaia and makes a convenient overnight stop after a day trip to Cape Reinga. Individual and organized tours can be easily arranged here.

GREAT DEALS ON DINING

As you'd expect in such a popular resort area, the Bay of Islands has many good places to eat. Seafood tops the list of menu offerings, with fish coming to your table just hours after it's been caught in the waters offshore.

IN RUSSELL
Super-Cheap Eats
✪ Strand Cafe

The Esplanade, Russell. ☎ **09/403-7589.** Reservations not accepted. Breakfast, light meals from NZ$6 (US$4.20). No credit cards. Summer, daily 8am–6pm. Winter, Tues–Sun 9am–4pm. CAFE.

I could sit here all day and admire the water views, drink tea, and read the newspaper, which is provided. Barbara Tunbridge bakes wonderful scones, and the atmosphere she and her husband, Chris, create is beyond welcoming. There's inside and outside seating, checkers and dominos, plus eight kinds of coffee and five kinds of tea. Lunch or dinner choices include blackened squid and green leaf salad, warm chicken salad, "real man's vegetable quiche," and farmhouse pâté. It's not licensed for alcohol, and you can't bring your own either. Their ice-cream parlor sits adjacent to the cafe.

Worth a Splurge
✪ The Gables

The Strand, Russell. ☎ **09/403-7618.** Fax 09/403-7278. E-mail peterj@voyager.co.nz. Reservations required. Main courses NZ$19.50–$27.50 (US$13.70–$19.30). AE, BC, DC, MC, V. Daily 7–11pm. Closed Mon–Tues in winter. SEAFOOD/NEW ZEALAND.

This was one of the first buildings on the waterfront, built in 1847, and was a riotous brothel in the days of the whalers. Its construction is pit-sawn kauri on whalebone foundations (in fact, there's a huge piece of whale vertebra, discovered during the renovation, now on display in the bar). The decor is early colonial, with a kauri-paneled ceiling in the bar, kauri tables, and in winter, the cheerful warmth of open fires. The restaurant enjoys beautiful sunsets and a bay view. The menu changes regularly, but seafood, beef, lamb, game, and fresh seasonal produce are staples. The Gables is fully licensed, with a respectable wine list. Peter and Hilary Johnson are gracious hosts, and The Gables has won several culinary awards, not too mention widespread praise—book early.

In or Near Paihia
✪ Bistro 40 Restaurant and Bar

40 Marsden Rd. ☎ **09/402-7444.** Fax 09/402-7908. Reservations required. Main courses NZ$17–$25 (US$11.90–$17.50). AE, BC, DC, MC, V. Daily 6–11pm. PACIFIC RIM.

This charming 1884 white frame house overlooks the bay. Meals are served in a bright, sunny front room, and from mid-December through March there's also service on a small terrace shaded by a passionfruit-vine-laden trellis. Specialties are fresh local seafood, poultry, meat, and game. You might be blessed by red snapper, simply pan-fried and served with lemon butter; or succulent osso buco with potato gnocchi; or even a grilled heart of lamb rump on fried parsnip ribbons with hazelnut jus. Go early and enjoy a before-dinner drink in their garden. It's fully licensed.

✪ Esmae's

41 Williams Rd. ☎ 09/402-8400. Reservations recommended. Main courses NZ$19.20–$22 (US$13.44–$15.40). AE, BC, DC, MC, V. Daily 5:30pm–"late." Closed Sun in winter. NEW ZEALAND.

Named after its consummate hostess, this restaurant in the center of town features home-style New Zealand cooking, and the menu even tells you where the fish or meat comes from. Esmae Dally will meet, greet, and seat you. There are fresh Kerikeri oysters, scallops, local fish, crayfish, and mussels. Non-seafood lovers are accommodated too; I'm actually quite fond of the marinated lamb steak, grilled and served with emerald sauce. Vegetarians will find at least one offering, such as the vegeroni crêpe, a combination of local vegetables and pasta with a mustard-cream sauce. It's fully licensed, too.

Only Seafood

40 Marsden Rd. ☎ 09/402-6066. Fax 09/402-7908. Reservations not accepted. Main courses NZ$15–$25 (US$10.50–$17.50). AE, BC, DC, MC, V. Daily from 5pm. SEAFOOD.

Located upstairs from the Bistro 40 Restaurant and Bar (see above), this attractive dining spot has a casual atmosphere and serves, as the name suggests, only fresh local seafood. You might like the phyllo parcels (encasing salmon, brie, crab, and spinach served on a fresh tomato and herb sauce), fettuccine, or fresh pan-fried fish with Cajun spices. For my tastes, there were too many sauces, so if you don't want your fish swimming in sauce, let your server know. The interior is plain—wooden floor, white walls, and white tables; outside, you can eat on the veranda overlooking the water. It's fully licensed.

IN OR NEAR KERIKERI

Super-Cheap Eats

✪ Redwoods Cafe

State Hwy. 10 (just north of the Kerikeri turnoff), R.D.3, Kerikeri. ☎ 09/407-6681. Fax 09/407-6691. Reservations accepted. Lunch NZ$3.50–$9.95 (US$2.50–$6.97). AE, DC, MC, V. Daily 7am–5pm (during summer Fri–Sun to 10pm). CAFE.

I have to thank my friends Francis and Cherie Fielding for introducing me to this charming spot. It's located in a garden nursery, and after our meal I enjoyed walking around, learning the names of the plants I'd been seeing in the area. A charming patio overlooks the nursery, and there are also some inside tables. Orders are placed at the counter, and meals brought to the table. They serve the biggest breakfast I've ever seen; it's called a "Jumbo" and consists of two fried eggs, tomatoes, several slices of bacon, and a half dozen sausages. In addition to breakfast, which is served all day, there are lovely cakes and croissants, interesting salads, quiche, pasta, nachos, and sandwiches. Daily specials include items such as chickpea curry, quiche, and kingfish pie. The milk shakes, thick shakes, and fresh fruit smoothies are also good. Cheryl McFarland is the hostess/proprietor.

Rocket Cafe and Robbs Fruit Winery

Kerikeri Rd. (second on the left after turning off Hwy. 10), Kerikeri. ☎ and 09/407-8688. Reservations not accepted. Lunch NZ$7–$12 (US$4.90–$8.40). MC, V. Daily 8:30am–5pm. CAFE.

This cafe and fruit winery is in a parklike setting. It's very light and bright with floor-to-ceiling glass doors that fold open to let in fresh air. Breakfast, cafe lunches, teas, and fruit wines are served. In addition, jars of local honey, jam, and mustard are for sale. Menu items include frittata, calzone, and phyllo parcels with salad. The fruit wines include feijoa (pineapple guava), apple, and kiwi. This is a good place for families—there's a playground and an orchard on the grounds. Guests are welcome to pick a kiwifruit or two March through May.

Stone Store Cafe and Restaurant

Kerikeri Rd., Kerikeri. ☎ **09/407-8479.** Reservations accepted, but not necessary. Lunch NZ$4.50–$9.50 (US$3.15–$6.70); dinner NZ$8.50–$22.50 (US$6–$15.80). AE, DC, MC, V. Daily 9am–9pm in summer, 9am–4pm in winter. CAFE/INTERNATIONAL.

Located across from the landmark Stone Store, this cafe/restaurant feels like a European hunting lodge, right down to "Charlie" (the stuffed deer head hanging over the fireplace). This place, run by Jackie Van Dyck (her sister, Mieke, runs Villa Maria Residence, above), is a cafe during the day and a restaurant at night. Seating is either inside or outside on a nice wooden porch that overlooks the basin of the Kerikeri Inlet. The cafe fare includes the usual sandwiches, salads, and cakes. The house specialty for dinner is curry, but lamb's kidneys are also a very popular dish. Dinner is served from 5:30pm on. It's fully licensed, but you can bring your own if you wish.

Worth a Splurge

Gourmandise Restaurant

Kerikeri Rd. (P.O. Box 482), Kerikeri. ☎ **09/407-6606.** Reservations advisable on weekends. Main courses NZ$17.50–$23.50 (US$12.30–$16.50). AE, MC, V. Wed–Mon 6pm–midnight. ECLECTIC.

Most locals say that Gourmandise is the best restaurant in Kerikeri, and I have to agree. It's located in a house with modern furnishings, hardwood floors, an open fire, and a view of the swimming pool through floor-to-ceiling windows. Main courses include grilled fillet of lamb flavored with rosemary, garlic, and cognac on a bed of rice with pumpkin chutney; vegetarian strudel filled with spinach, mushrooms, and feta cheese and topped with an herb and cream sauce; and fresh fish of the day—it was kingfish caught near Opua when I last ate there—served with a sauce of your choice "or just leave it to the chef."

BAY OF ISLANDS AFTER DARK

Pub pickings are limited to the **Duke** in the Duke of Marlborough Hotel on the Strand in Russell, where conversation is likely to center around fishing. Other possibilities include the **Lighthouse Tavern,** upstairs in the Selwyn Mall in Paihia; and the **Roadrunner Tavern,** 2¹/₂ miles south of town. The **Twin Pines Brew House and Tourist Park** (☎ **09/402-7195,** fax 09/402-7322), in Haruru Falls (between Paihia and Kerikeri), is an old English-style pub that brews ales on the premises. Here you'll also find a park, restaurant, and accommodation.

EN ROUTE TO AUCKLAND, BY WAY OF THE WEST COAST

If you came up to the Bay of Islands from Auckland on Highway 1, you may want to return on a longer, less direct route that takes in the **Waipoua Kauri Forest,** the **Trounson Kauri Park,** and the town of **Dargaville.** If you do this, be sure to plan a picnic or rest stop at one of the view points overlooking the beautiful Hokianga Harbour.

The kauri is the giant of the New Zealand native forest, and at Waipoua the largest trees are over 1,000 years old. Look for *Tane Mahuta* (God of the Forest), the largest known kauri in the country and *Te Matua Ngahere* (Father of the Forest), by volume the second-biggest known tree in New Zealand. These and other special trees are signposted on the tourist drive through the forest.

As you pass through Dargaville, you may want to stop at the **Dargaville Maritime Museum,** Harding Park (☎ 09/439-7555). Here you'll find the relics salvaged from numerous wrecks around the west coast and the mast from the Greenpeace flagship *Rainbow Warrior,* which was blown up by the French in Auckland Harbour in 1985. The museum is open daily from 9am to 4pm; admission is NZ$3 (US$2.10). The **Dargaville Information Centre,** 65 Normanby St., Dargaville (☎ and fax 09/ 439-8360, e-mail dgrvin@nzhost.co.nz), can answer questions.

Another good stop is the **Matakohe Kauri Museum,** Church Road, Matakohe (☎ 09/431-7417, fax 09/431-6969). This is the place to learn all about the big trees and the early years of New Zealand's settlement when so many of the giants were cut down. It's open daily from 9am to 5pm Easter to October 31 and from 9am to 5:30pm from November 1 to Easter; admission is NZ$6 (US$4.20) for adults and NZ$2 (US$1.40) for children 5 to 15; children under 5 are free.

Where to Stay

If you want to stop overnight en route, try one of these two B&Bs.

Awakino Point Lodge

State Hwy. 14 (P.O. Box 168), Dargaville. ☎ and fax **09/439-7870.** 3 units. TV. NZ$70 (US$49) double. Additional person NZ$15 (US$10.50) extra. Rates include continental breakfast. Three-course dinner with wine NZ$25 (US$17.50) per person, advance booking required. AE, BC, DC, MC, V. Courtesy pick-up from Dargaville bus station.

June Birch welcomes guests to her 5-acre farmlet surrounded by attractive gardens and orchard. She offers three self-contained units: One has a small kitchen, a separate lounge, log fire, and two bedrooms; the second also has two bedrooms; the third has one bedroom and a separate lounge.

Solitaire Homestay

State Hwy. 12, Waimamaku, South Hokianga. ☎ and fax **09/405-4891.** 4 rms (none with bathrm). NZ$125 (US$88) double. Rates include breakfast and dinner. MC, V.

Jenny and Les Read welcome guests to their 30-acre property, which is bordered by two rivers and surrounded by scenic farmland. Their lovely 1912 kauri house has high ceilings and the other earmarks of colonial villas. The four guest rooms share two bathrooms. No smoking is permitted in the house. Solitaire Homestay is 6 kilometers (less than 4 miles) north of the Waipoua Kauri Forest and close to the beautiful Hokianga Harbour.

2 The Coromandel Peninsula

119km (74 miles) E of Auckland

This peninsula is one of the most beloved holiday spots for Aucklanders, and that's easy to understand. For city dwellers, it's a haven of natural beauty that's far away from urban hassles. For visitors, it's the perfect taste of the North Island's rich heritage and glorious scenery.

The 1¹/₂-hour drive from Auckland is rewarded by dramatic land- and seascapes; wide sandy beaches; wild and rugged mountain peaks; quaint villages hugging both coastlines; relics of logging, gold mining, and gum fields; and the crafts of many talented artisans who have found an idyllic lifestyle on the peninsula.

While it's certainly possible to make a day trip to the Coromandel Peninsula from Auckland, let me urge you to spend at least one overnight in order to more fully appreciate the area. At the end of your Auckland stay, try to plan 2 days on the peninsula before pressing on—you'll have explored a very special, little-known-to-outsiders part of New Zealand.

ESSENTIALS
GETTING THERE
BY FERRY   Coromandel Ferry Services (☎ **09/379-9072** in Auckland, or **07/866-7084** in Coromandel township) operates between Auckland and Coromandel township. The trip takes 2 hours and costs NZ$49 (US$34.30) round trip.

BY COACH (Bus)   InterCity runs regular schedules from Auckland to the entry town of Thames. These connect with the local bus service (see "Getting Around," below).

BY CAR   Drive south from Auckland on State Highway 1 for about 50km (31 miles), then turn east on State Highway 2. About 34km (22 miles) later you'll pick up Highway 25 to Thames. The other option is to follow the Pacific Coast Highway from Auckland to Thames (see "En Route to the Coromandel Peninsula" at the end of chapter 5).

GETTING AROUND
BY CAR   This is a rugged, wild region you've come to, and you should know that the only easy driving you can count on is the paved road that runs some 56km (35 miles) from Thames to Coromandel township. It skirts the waterfront and waves sometimes spill over onto the highway, but the view is spectacular. Coromandel township is the last bastion of civilization before you hit the really rough, nearly uninhabited part of the peninsula. Before you think about driving in this area, check with the car-rental company—most won't permit their vehicles beyond Coromandel township. North of Coromandel, and on routes crossing the width of the peninsula, you'll find everything from partially paved to gravel roads—they aren't hard to drive on though, if you keep the speed down.

Cautious drivers will be rewarded by spectacular forest and mountain scenery. If you aren't keen on the conditions I've described, consider letting **Coromandel Bus Plan** (☎ **07/868-9088**) act as your personal chauffeur for this portion of your holiday. Their peninsula loop service runs daily. The cost is NZ$40 (US$28) for adults from Thames, NZ$60 (US$42) from Auckland, half-price for children.

Author's note: If you opt for the unpaved but very scenic "309 Road" between Coromandel township and Whitianga, stop at the information center in Coromandel township and pick up the brochure that describes things to do and places to stop along the way.

VISITOR INFORMATION
Thames (pronounced "Tems") is the first town of any size as you reach the peninsula from Auckland. The **Thames Information Centre** is on Queen Street (P.O. Box 545) (☎ **07/868-7284,** fax 07/868-7584, e-mail tmzvin@nzhost.co.nz); other area information offices are located at 66 Albert Street, Whitianga (☎ **07/866-5555,** fax 07/866-2205, e-mail wtzvin@nzhost.co.nz); Whitaker Street, Te Aroha (☎ **07/884-8052**), and the **Coromandel Information Centre,** 355 Kapanga Rd., Coromandel (☎ **07/866-8598**). They can furnish a wealth of information on the area, along with such helpful guides as "The Coromandel Craft Trail," "The Coromandel Directory," and "Coromandel Walks." Coromandel Peninsula phone numbers are in the **07 telephone area code** (STD).

EXPLORING THE PENINSULA: WHAT TO SEE & DO

"Spectacular" isn't quite glorious enough to describe the peninsula's landscape—there's something elemental about this old and historic point of land that makes a visit here so memorable. I think you'll be impressed by the vistas of curving beaches and beautiful old pohutukawa trees, New Zealand's famed "Christmas tree," clinging to cliff faces and lining those beaches, especially during December and January when there's a riot of crimson blooms.

In ancient times, Maori tribes recognized the spirituality of the place and declared the Mount Moehau area tapu, a sacred place. Modern man has been touched by the same spirit and continues to respect and protect those traditions.

You'll find good **walks** around Paeroa (near the Karangahake Gorge), Waihi, Whangamata, Tairua, Whitianga, Colville, Coromandel, and Thames. Information on the **Coromandel Forest Park** is available at the Department of Conservation Office in Kauaeranga (☎ 07/868-6381) just southeast of Thames. They can provide walking guides, help for rockhounds (the peninsula is rich in gemstones), and information on camping in the park. There's also a DOC office in Coromandel township at 355 Kapanga Rd., Coromandel (☎ 07/866-8598). The staff here is very helpful.

In Thames, you'll find historic **mining areas** well signposted, and there's the **School of Mines Museum** on the corner of Brown and Cochrane streets (☎ 07/868-6227). You may also want to tour the Gold Mine and Stamper Battery at the north end of town (☎ 07/868-7448).

As you head north, just beyond Tapu township, turn east off Hwy. 25 and go 6.5km (4 miles)—careful, the road isn't paved all the way—and you'll find yourself at **Rapaura Watergardens,** Tapu P.D.C., Thames Coast (☎ and fax 07/868-4821). The garden was begun 30 years ago by a German couple, Fritz Loenning and his partner Josephine, who developed 14 ponds that feed each other from 3 creeks which cross the property. Today, the gardens cover 64 acres—most of which is native bush. Be sure to take the 10 to 15-minute walk through to the cascading waterfall known as "The Seven Steps to Heaven." The walk is pleasant and it gives people who won't be doing DOC bushwalks a chance to sample something similar. There's a great picnic spot on a lawn by the lily pond. I like this place, but I thought the manicured lower gardens seemed out of place in this rough-and-ready part of New Zealand. There is also a craft shop and tea room on the premises. Rapaura, which means "running spring water," is open daily from 10am to 5pm. Admission is NZ$6 (US$4.20) for adults, and NZ$1.50 (US$1.05) for children.

About 2.5km (1.55 miles) past the Rapaura Gardens, approximately halfway between Thames and Coromandel, stop at the little village of Tapu and ask directions to one of nature's oddities, the **"square kauri,"** a 2,500-year-old kauri whose trunk is a perfect square. When you get there, you'll have a choice of a very steep walk of 175m/190 yds. to the top where there's a great view, or you can avoid the climb by driving a few yards beyond the tree across a little bridge and looking up to your right. **Te Mata Beach**, also at Tapu, is a good hunting ground for specimens of carnelian-agate gemstones.

There are good **coast and bushwalks** all along the road from Thames to Coromandel, and a short detour to Te Kouma leads to a Maori **pa site** enclosed by stone walls. Get the "Walking In Coromandel" brochure from any area DOC office or information center.

Coromandel township is where gold was first discovered in New Zealand, in 1852, and the **School of Mines Museum** (☎ 07/866-8987) here contains many relics of those early gold-fever days. It's open daily from 10am to 4pm and free to those under 15, with NZ$2 (US$1.30) admission for adults. Take time to visit the **True Colours Craft Co-op** near the post office, a space shared by several craftspeople. Coromandel township feels like a cross between an Old West town and very '60s Santa Cruz, California. Incidentally, the town, peninsula, and mountain range take their names from the timber-trading ship HMS *Coromandel*, which called into this harbor for kauri spars (for the Battle of Trafalgar) in 1820.

Also in Coromandel township, the ✪ **Driving Creek Railway** (☎ 07/866-8703) is another popular attraction. Barry Brickell owns New Zealand's only narrow-gauge mountain railway, which passes through replanted native forest. There are usually *at least* two departures daily (at 10am and 2pm), and more from Labour weekend through Easter; call to confirm schedule. Reservations are recommended. Tickets cost NZ$10 (US$7) for adults, NZ$5 (US$3.50) for kids 15 and under, and NZ$22 (US$15.40) for a family (two adults and up to three children); NZ$1 discount to seniors, and YHA and VIP cardholders. The train station is 2.5km (1.55 miles) from Coromandel township. The 1-hour trip covers 3km (1.86 miles) of track. Winter trains may be canceled in inclement weather. Allow time to browse the pottery shop on the premises.

If you plan to drive to the northern tip of the peninsula, you'll find the last gasoline ("petrol") pumps at Colville, along with a good collection of arts-and-crafts studios. Be sure your rental-car agreement permits driving beyond Colville—most don't.

On the peninsula's east coast, Whitianga has blossomed into a wonderful seaside resort with lots of dining, accommodation, and recreation options. The area is a popular spot for surfing, diving, fishing, and boating. If you'd rather keep your feet dry, ask at the visitor information center for the brochure "Mercury Bay Walks." Whitianga also has an excellent **historical museum** and many **arts-and-crafts studios.**

A fun, inexpensive thing to do in Whitianga is to take the **Whitianga Water Transport** (☎ 07/866-5555) passenger ferry to the Ferry Landing. It operates daily from 7:30am to noon and from 1 to 6:30pm. Return fares are NZ$1.50 (US$1.05) for adults and NZ80¢ (US46¢) for children. Once at the Ferry Landing you could either poke around the few shops nearby (best choice is the Ferry Landing Pottery Shop and Tea Garden, Ferry Landing, Purongi Rd., R.D.1, Whitianga; ☎ 07/866-2820) or catch a **Hot Water Beach ConXtions** (☎ 07/866-2478) minibus to Hahei, Hot Water Beach, Cathedral Cove and other area attractions. The best view in the area is the one from Shakespeare's Cliff. The bus costs NZ$15 (US$10.50) per person for all day.

At ✪ **Hot Water Beach,** ask the time of the next low tide—that's when you can dig a hole in the beach, settle in, and soon find yourself immersed in hot sea water—your own private spa pool.

While playing golf at the **Purangi Golf Course & Country Club,** Purangi Road, Cooks Beach (☎ 07/866-3541 or 07/866-3726), if you hit a sheep you get another shot, according to local rules. Greens fees here are NZ$10 (US$7) for nine holes and NZ$15 (US$10.50) for 18 holes. There's an honesty box for payment if there's no one in the clubhouse; clubs are available for hire.

If you're heading south on the highway from Hot Water Beach, you might like to stop at the ✪ **Colenso Orchard and Herb Garden,** R.D. 1, Whitianga (☎ 07/866-3725), on Highway 25 just 2km (1.24 miles) south of Whenuakite and a 5- to 10-minute drive from Hot Water Beach. Orchard owners Ruth and Andy Pettit serve Devonshire tea, fresh juice, homemade scones and muffins with cream and jam, or soup and toast. You can eat on the porch or inside, where strains of classical music set just the right tone. Wonderful local flowers and cute tea cozies accompany the great food. The tearoom and the darling craft shop, which is adjacent, are open daily from 10am to 5pm (closed during August). Lunch for two costs about NZ$14 (US$9.80). American Express, MasterCard, and Visa are accepted.

AFFORDABLE ACCOMMODATIONS

North Islanders flock to the Coromandel Peninsula during December and January, so if you're coming then, be sure to reserve ahead. If you arrive during other months, you'll usually be able to find accommodations through the local information centers. Motel rates on the Coromandel Peninsula are "soft" outside of the peak period—don't be afraid to negotiate a good one. The rates given below include the 12.5% Goods and Services Tax.

Van and **caravan sites** are available on a first-come, first-served basis in **Conservation Lands and Farms Parks** around the peninsula. Camping fees are NZ$5 (US$3.50) per adult, NZ$2 (US$1.40) for school-age children, free for preschoolers; the maximum family charge is NZ$12 (US$8.40). For details, contact the Department of Conservation, P.O. Box 78, Thames (☎ **07/868-6381,** fax 07/868-9734).

IN OR NEAR THAMES
Super-Cheap Sleeps
Glenys and Russell Rutherford

110 Hape Rd., Thames. ☎ and fax **07/868-7788.** 2 rms (1 with bathrm). NZ$35 (US$24.50) single without bath; NZ$60 (US$42) double with bath. Rates include breakfast. No credit cards.

Glenys and Russell Rutherford's comfortable home overlooks the lovely Firth of Thames. They have a double room with a private bathroom and a single room without. There's a game room and a lounge as well as a pool. This engaging couple really know their area and some of the potters and painters who live here, and they're always glad to direct their guests to nearby art studios, as well as to any historic and scenic points of interest.

For a Few Extra Bucks
Brian Boru Hotel

Pollen and Richmond sts., Thames. ☎ **07/868-6523.** Fax 07/868-9760. 47 rms (37 with bathrm). NZ$66 (US$46.20) double without bathrm, NZ$88 (US$61.60) double with bathrm, NZ$125 (US$88) double with spa bath. All-inclusive Agatha Christie weekends NZ$355 (US$249) per person. Off-season, budget rooms are charged from NZ$25 (US$17.50). Continental breakfast NZ$8 (US$5.60), cooked breakfast NZ$12 (US$8.40). AE, BC, DC, MC, V.

In the center of town, this two-story kauri building with a veranda dates back to 1874. Locals love the bar and the fine dining room, which serves great seafood and pub meals at reasonable prices. Barbara Doyle, the managing director here, runs some lively Agatha Christie–style weekends twice a month, and if you're in a sleuthing mood, you might check to see if one is scheduled during your visit—they're great fun and value, since the fee covers accommodation, meals, and sleuthing from Friday night to Sunday lunch. Rooms in the Richmond Court wing have TV, telephone, and spa baths. There's some deferred maintenance throughout the hotel, but if you stay here over one of the mystery weekends, you'll be too busy figuring out "who done it" to notice.

Puru Park Motel

West Crescent and Thames Coast Rd (Hwy. 25), Te Puru (P.O. Box 439, Thames). ☎ and fax **07/868-2686.** 6 units (all with bathrm) TV. NZ$78 (US$54.60) double. Lower winter rates. Continental breakfast NZ$8 (US$5.60), cooked breakfast NZ$12 (US$8.40). AE, BC, DC, MC, V. Take Hwy. 25 11km (6¹/₂ miles) north of Thames. Courtesy pick-up from bus or plane in Thames.

With a nicely landscaped garden in front, these refurbished motel units are spacious and comfortably furnished. Each of the one- and two-bedroom units sleeps two to four and has a fully equipped kitchen. There's a self-service laundry, a children's play area, and tennis courts next door. The beach and a boat ramp are also nearby. Readers report that hosts June and Peter Fullerton are friendly and most helpful. Although there is some traffic noise, this place is still a good deal.

Santa Monica Motel

Thames Coast Rd. (Hwy. 25), (P.O. Box 158), Thames. ☎ **0800/802-429** in New Zealand. ☎ and fax 07/868-2489. 7 units (all with bathrm). TV. NZ$78 (US$54.60) double in winter (Apr 30–Sept 1), NZ$108 (US$75.60) double in summer. Extra person NZ$15 (US$10.50). 10% discount to Frommer's readers; stays of 3 days or more receive an additional 10% discount. Breakfast delivered to units: continental NZ$7 (US$4.90), cooked NZ$14 (US$9.80). AE, DC, MC, V.

If you stay here, be sure to arrive in time to watch the sun set across the Firth of Thames. The Santa Monica's elevated position ensures that you have a great view and that there is no traffic noise. Rooms in this motel have dated interiors but are spacious, and my husband was delighted to find recliner chairs similar to his favorite at home in front of the television. (I, however, didn't like the soft mattress.) The motel is in a good location for those who like bushwalking—several walking tracks start on the property. Host Don Jamieson is a font of information on the area. The large one-bedroom units sleep two to four. Another advantage here is that dinner is offered for NZ$22 (US$15.40). This is important because there aren't any restaurants nearby. Remember to bring your own alcohol, though.

✪ Seaspray Motel

613 Thames Coast Rd. (Hwy 25), Waiomu Bay (P.O. Box 203), Thames. ☎ and fax **07/868-2863.** 6 units (all with bathrm). TV TEL. NZ$88 (US$54.60) double, extra person NZ$15 (US$10.50). Lower weekly rates. Continental breakfast NZ$3.50 (US$2.50), cooked breakfast NZ$7.50 (US$5.30). AE, BC, DC, MC, V. Go 14km (8¹/2 miles) north of Thames on the coast road. Courtesy pick-up from Thames.

At the Seaspray, Waiomu Bay is so close you feel like you're sleeping on an ocean liner. In fact, benches on the front lawn are right at the sea wall. There are attractive one- and two-bedroom units (all with kitchens), self-service laundry facilities on the premises, and out back a stately Norfolk pine, an aviary, and a picnic area. Because it's right on the highway, there is some traffic noise here but the seafront location more than makes up for it. Hosts are Paul and Joanna Whiteman.

IN OR NEAR COROMANDEL TOWNSHIP

Coromandel Colonial Cottages

Ring Rd., Coromandel. ☎ and fax **07/866-8857.** 20 units (all with bathrm). TV TEL. NZ$85 (US$59.50) double. Additional person NZ$15 (US$10.50) extra. AE, BC, DC, MC, V. Courtesy pick-up from Coromandel airport and bus station.

The units here have one or two bedrooms and sleep up to six; each of the self-contained cottages has a fully equipped kitchen, its own carport, and a bathroom with shower only. Radios and electric blankets are provided upon request. Right on the rural premises are a swimming pool, spa pool, children's playground, and barbecue area. Their rental four-wheel-drive bush vehicle is a great way to go exploring, and beaches, golf courses, and shops are close by. A good restaurant is just 2 minutes away and a courtesy car is provided.

Worth a Splurge
✪ Buffalo Lodge

Buffalo Rd., Coromandel 2851. ☎ and fax **07/866-8960.** 3 rms (all with bath). NZ$150 (US$105) double. Rates include continental breakfast. Three-course gourmet dinner NZ$50 (US$35). MC, V.

Isolation and an absolutely breathtaking view are only two of the attractions here. This unique inn is located in lush bush on a secluded 10-acre hill site 2.5km (1.55 miles) north of Coromandel township. Each of the attractive rooms has firm Swiss beds, en suite (attached) bathrooms, and Douglas fir furniture and ceilings. Two have private sundecks with fantastic views of native bush in the foreground and the Hauraki Gulf and Waiheke Island in the distance. It isn't surprising that Raouf and Evelyne Siegrist-Huang's property was named "Best Hosted Accommodation" in 1996 by the New Zealand Tourism Board. In 1994 they commissioned an architect to design this purpose-built pole lodge. Raouf is from Switzerland; she's from Taiwan. Both are artists and world travelers. On display are wooden carvings of the Bataks of Sumatra, Balinese sculpture and masks, as well as their own artistic creations (paintings and terra-cotta sculptures). Persian and Morrocan rugs accent the beautiful miro wood floors and kauri furniture. There is no radio, newspapers, or television, just Evelyne's fantastic gourmet meals, the view, and the beauty and peace and quiet. Her dinners are available to house guests daily, to the public Wednesday through Sunday from 6pm to 10:30pm; reservations are essential.

IN OR NEAR WHITIANGA
✪ Mercury Bay Beachfront Resort

111 Buffalo Beach Rd. N. (P.O. Box 9), Whitianga. ☎ **07/866-5637.** Fax 07/866-4524. 8 two-room units (sleep 2–4) (all with bathrm). TV TEL. NZ$90 (US$63) double May–Aug; NZ$110 (US$77) double April and Sept–Nov; NZ$175 for 4 people Christmas–late Jan; NZ$140 (US$98) double Feb; NZ$130 (US$91) double March. Rate depends on season and unit. AE, BC, DC, MC, V. Courtesy car to bus depot and Whitianga Airfield.

Staying here is like having your own little beachfront apartment. Each unit has cooking facilities and a bedroom separate from the lounge, plus its own private patio or balcony; seven have sea views. This modern, immaculate place sits right on the edge of Buffalo Beach; a laundry with dryers and a car wash are on the premises. There's also a spa pool, plus a windsurfer, sea kayaks, boogie boards, bikes, and fishing equipment for your use. The folks here, Max and Carrol Booker, are especially helpful in arranging boat trips, fishing expeditions, and bushwalks, and their place is a personal favorite of mine.

Spellbound Homestay

77 Grange Rd., Hahei Beach (R.D. 1), Whitianga. ☎ **07/866-3543.** Fax 07/866-3003. 4 rms (all with bathrm). NZ$100–$125 (US$70–$88) double. Rate includes continental breakfast. A 3-course dinner with wine is available for NZ$25 (US$17.50) per person by arrangement. MC, V.

I have reader John W. Behle of Cincinnati, Ohio, to thank for pointing me towards this homestay. Hosts Alan and Barbara Lucas have been hosting guests in their modern home since 1987, and their guestbook is full of positive comments. It's a 40-minute drive from Whitianga (1 1/2 hours from Auckland). Tea- and coffeemaking facilities and a fridge are shared in the hallway near the guest bedrooms, and the family lounge is open to all. Breakfast is usually served on the deck with a panoramic view from the Alderman Islands to the Mercury Islands. Three of the guest rooms have sea views. Hahei Beach is only 5 minutes away and Hot Water Beach is also close by. The area offers bushwalks, surfing, fishing, and spectacular photo opportunities. Smoking is not allowed in the house.

Buffalo Beach Resort, Eyre Street (P.O. Box 19), Whitianga (☎ **07/866-5854,** fax 07/866-5854), is adjacent to the beachfront, within easy walking distance of six beaches, the wharf, and the shopping center. There are powered caravan sites, as well as tent sites, and a lodge for international backpackers. Owners Trudi and Alan Hopping are very helpful. Rates run NZ$9 (US$6.30) per adult for tent and caravan sites, NZ$44 (US$30.80) double for backpackers. Hot pools in a garden setting are under construction. MasterCard and Visa are accepted.

IN TE AROHA

There's a delightful small **YHA Hostel** on Miro Street (P.O. Box 72), Te Aroha (☎ **07/884-8739**). Some folks consider Te Aroha to be in the Waikato District, but technically it's on the southern edge of the Coromandel. The hostel is nestled in the foothills of Mount Te Aroha—only 5 minutes away from the famous hot-spring baths of Te Aroha. Rates are NZ$10 (US$7) per person per night or 3 nights for NZ$25 (US$17.50).

GREAT DEALS ON DINING
IN OR NEAR THAMES

Brian Boru Hotel

Pollen and Richmond sts., Thames. ☎ **07/868-6523.** Reservations not required. Breakfast NZ$5–$15 (US$3.50–$10.50); bistro lunches NZ$10–$15 (US$7–$10.50); dinner NZ$15–$25 (US$10.50–$17.50). AE, DC, MC, V. Daily 7:30–10am, noon–2:30pm, and 6–9pm. NEW ZEALAND/SEAFOOD.

An evening spent at this marvelous old hotel in the center of Thames is like taking a trip back in time to the gold-mining era. The small bar is one of the most attractive on the peninsula. Breakfast, lunch, and dinner are served daily in the dining room, and the à la carte menu features fresh local seafood at modest prices. Mussel soup is the house specialty. Late-night meals are also served in the bar. It's fully licensed, but there's no smoking.

IN OR NEAR COROMANDEL TOWNSHIP

In addition to the places listed, remember you can eat at Buffalo Lodge even if you aren't staying there (see "Affordable Accommodations," above).

Super-Cheap Eats

✪ Karmic Enchilada

24 Wharf Rd., Coromandel. ☎ **07/866-7157.** Reservations not accepted. Menu items NZ$3.50–$10 (US$2.45–$7). No credit cards. Summer daily 9am–6pm, later Fri–Sun; winter daily 9am–4pm. CAFE.

Popular with the locals, this place is right out of the late '60s. Fruit smoothies, which arrive in quart-size Mason jars, can be made with regular or soy milk. The menu includes items like chili chicken enchiladas, veggie and cumin pie, vegetable quiche, calzone, nachos, and pizza. It's not licensed, and you can't bring your own alcohol either.

For a Few Extra Bucks

Pepper Tree Restaurant and Bar

31 Kapanga Rd., Coromandel. ☎ and fax **07/866-8211.** Reservations advisable in summer, not accepted after 7pm. Main courses NZ$18–$24 (US$12.60–16.80). AE, DC, MC, V. Daily 11am–midnight during winter, 8am–1:30am during summer. SEAFOOD.

Fresh local ingredients are the emphasis here, so the menu changes daily based on what's available. They use organically grown local beef and fresh seasonal veggies and seafood. If the weather is nice, you might like to enjoy your lunch outside on the patio; there's a roaring fire in the bar fireplace during the winter. Located on the main road, this friendly spot starts dinner service at 6pm. Main courses may include fresh hapuka steaks pan-fried in a scallion and cream sauce or Thai-style fresh snapper cooked in a light, crispy batter served on a bed of coconut creamed rice, topped with spiced sauce; main courses are served with a choice of vegetables or green salad. The bar is a good place to savor a Lion Red or Steinlager beer. On weekends there's entertainment on the outside patio.

IN OR NEAR WHITIANGA
Super-Cheap Eats
Smitty's Bar and Grill
37 Albert St., Whitianga. ☎ 07/866-4647. Reservations accepted, only necessary midsummer. Main courses NZ$6.50–$16 (US$4.60–$11.20). AE, MC, V. Daily 11am–1am (closed on Monday, Easter–early Nov). STEAK/BURGERS/SEAFOOD.

Canadian Leona Neil Smith is the proprietress of this country-western restaurant. Menu items include a Texas pork riblet burger with barbecue sauce and "fries" (not chips), and grilled orange roughy with parsley sauce, salad, and fries. Lunch is served from 11am to 2:30pm and dinner from 5:30 to 10pm. A snack menu is always available; it includes sandwiches, burgers, and tandoori chicken satay with rice. Lion Red, their most popular beer, will set you back NZ$3 (US$2.10) for a 380ml glass. You could also just come to this lively spot for drinks and/or a chat with the locals. Seating is inside and out.

Worth a Splurge
✪ Doyles Restaurant
21 The Esplanade, Whitianga. ☎ 07/866-5209. Reservations recommended. Main courses NZ$18–NZ$35 (US$12.60–$24.50). AE, BC, DC, MC, V. Daily 5pm–midnight. SEAFOOD/ GRILLS.

Overlooking Buffalo Beach and Mercury Bay, this place offers a wide range of fresh seafood, steaks, a roast of the day, and pasta dishes. You might go with mussel soup (which is terrific), rock oysters, or scallops. The proprietors are Barbara Doyle, who also owns the Brian Boru Hotel in Thames, and Stjepan Hrestak, a well-trained chef/ butcher from Croatia. The seaside building housing the restaurant was built by Barbara's father in 1946. If the weather's good, ask to sit on the balcony. It's fully licensed, but you can't smoke here.

COROMANDEL AFTER DARK
Be sure to notice the kauri bar at the **Brian Boru Hotel,** Pollen and Richmond streets, Thames (☎ **07/868-6523**). Historic photos cover the walls here, and there's a TV for watching sporting events, as well as a pool table. A handle of beer will set you back NZ$4 (US$2.80); light bar meals are available. The bar is open Monday

Readers Recommend

Harbour View Continental Cafe, Whitianga. *"This is a nice restaurant with good food. Similar price range and quality with Doyles."*
—Jan and Christine Mallard Sokol, Portland, OR, USA.

Readers Recommend

Jacaranda Cottage, Thompson's Track, RD 2, Katikati (☎ **07/549-0616**). *"Jacaranda Cottage is certainly in an excellent location with great natural beauty, wonderful accommodations, and exceptional hosts. I rank it as one of the highlights of our trip. I can assure you that a stay with Lynlie and Rick Watson would enhance anyone's trip to New Zealand."*
　　　　　　　　　　　　　　　　　　　　　　　—John A. Rife, Cedar Rapids, IA, USA.

"Lynlie met us with her marvelous friendliness. . . the cottage was wonderfully light and airy yet exuded warmth and charm—a welcome haven with rolling green vistas to the sea."
　　　　　　　　　　　　　　　　　—James and Karen McElroy, Des Moines, WA, USA.

through Saturday from 9am to 10pm. The **Coromandel Hotel,** Kapanga Rd., Coromandel (☎ **07/866-8760**), is also a good choice for a drink.

The bar at the **Pepper Tree Restaurant and Bar,** 31 Kapanga Rd., Coromandel (☎ and fax **07/866-8211**), is perfect for a Lion Red or Steinlager. On weekends you'll find entertainment on the outside patio.

EN ROUTE TO TAURANGA

Katikati, known locally as "Mural Town," is located south of Waihi on Highway 2. In 1996 a festival was held to commemorate the painting of its 20th outdoor mural since 1991 and to reinforce its image as the mural town of New Zealand. Thousands of people each year come to this little town to admire the murals. Katikati has been awarded "The Most Beautiful Town in New Zealand" title four times. If it's time for lunch or tea while you're here, I suggest the **Twickenham Homestead** (☎ **07/549-1383**). This is an English conservatory where hostess Brenda Knight also welcomes you to browse through her antiques and collectibles.

For visitor information and maps while you're in this area, contact the **Mural Town Visitors Centre,** 36 Main Rd., Katikati (☎ **06/549-1658,** fax 06/549-0935).

3　The Waikato: Waitomo and Cambridge

The Waikato, a rich farming area along the central and lower reaches of the Waikato River, offers some of the best scenery in New Zealand. It is one of the most productive grass-growing regions in the world and the home of many successful horse studs. Dairy farms here also benefit from the region's lush terrain. The Waikato is New Zealand's longest river. It stretches for 425 kilometers (about 265 miles).

Hamilton is New Zealand's largest inland city and the commercial and industrial center of this agricultural area, as well as the site of the University of Waikato. Several major religions are centered here: It's the see city for the Anglican Diocese of Waikato; the Mormons have their magnificent South Pacific temple headquarters at Temple View, high on a hill at Tuhikaramea, southwest of the city center; and there's a Sikh temple on the northern outskirts of town at Horotiu. Throughout the city, you'll see lovely gardens in both city parks and private lawns.

WAITOMO

204km (126 miles) S of Auckland; 70km (43 miles) S of Hamilton

Waitomo Village owes its existence to the more than 200,000 visitors who come annually to visit three remarkable limestone caves, and its main street holds a general store, post office, and tavern (which sells tickets to the caves as well as souvenirs and has the usual bottle store, public bar, and bistro restaurant). At the top of a grace-fully winding driveway stands the Waitomo Caves Hotel. Waitomo Cave, with its splendid Glowworm Grotto, is some 400 yards beyond the tavern, and about 2¹/₂ miles away are Ruakuri and Aranui caves, both of which rival Wiatomo as sightseeing attractions.

ESSENTIALS

GETTING THERE & GETTING AROUND   **InterCity** and **Newmans Coach** service connect Auckland and Otorohanga. The **Waitomo Shuttle Bus** (☎ **0800/ 808 279** in New Zealand, or 07/873-8279) will transfer you to the Waitomo caves. Reservations are essential, and the fare is NZ$7 (US$4.90) one way. You could also take *The Overlander* **train** from Auckland to Otorohanga or the 1-day package of-fered by Tranz Scenic, which includes the shuttle to the Waitomo caves. To make reservations for the train call ☎ **0800/802-802** in New Zealand, or 04/498-3301; fax 04/498-3089.

If you're coming from Auckland by car, take Hwy. 1 south to Hwy. 3, just south of Otorohanga, and turn west at the signpost for Waitomo Caves.

VISITOR INFORMATION   The **Museum of Caves Information Centre** is on Main Street (P.O. Box 12), Waitomo (☎ **07/878-7640,** fax 07/878-6184, e-mail waitomomuseum@xtra.co.nz). It's open daily from 8:30am to 5pm; there's a NZ$3.50 (US$2.45) admission charge to the museum on the premises. The **tele-phone area code** (STD) for Waitomo is **07**.

The **Ngaruawahia River Regatta,** Turangawoewoe Marao, Ngaruawahia, is held on the Waikato River near Hamilton. It includes waka (canoe) races and Maori cul-tural performances. Early March. ☎ **07/839-3580.**

EXPLORING THE CAVES

The caves are *the* attraction at Waitomo, chief among them the Waitomo Cave with its Glowworm Grotto. If you have the time, you may also want to include the Aranui Cave on your sightseeing itinerary. Forty-five–minute guided tours are run on regular schedules at two caves—tickets are available at the **Glowworm Cave Ticket Office** (☎ **07/878-8227**). There's a two-cave combination ticket at NZ$25 (US$17.50) for adults; one cave costs NZ$16.50 (US$11.60). Children are charged half price. Be sure to wear good walking shoes and carry a sweater if the weather is a bit cool—it'll be cooler underground.

The best time to visit the ✪ **Glowworm Grotto in Waitomo Cave** is in the mid-to late afternoon—crowds are smaller than at midday. Tours run from 9am to 4:30pm (5:30pm in summer). About 400 yards from the Waitomo Caves Hotel, a guide greets you at Waitomo's entrance to escort you through large antechambers, pointing out limestone formations with names like "The Organ," 8 feet high with a 24-foot base.

The largest cavern in any of the caves is "The Cathedral," which rises 47 feet and is an acoustically perfect auditorium that has seen performances by such recording artists as the Vienna Boys' Choir and Dame Nellie Melba. Then it's on to a small grotto festooned with glowworms, where your guide fills you in on the glowworm's life and death cycle. A very short cycle it is, for the adult fly lives exactly 4 days, just long enough to produce the next generation. Having done that, it simply dies and becomes food for the next batch of glowworms.

The whole process begins with a tiny egg, which has a 21-day incubation period, then hatches into an inch-long grub. The grub then cloaks itself in a hollow mucous tubelike nest, which is attached to the grotto roof with a multitude of slender threads, each holding minute drops of acid and suspended like fishing lines down from the roof. The bait for those lines is the hypnotic blue-green light that comes from the larva's light organs (and that, of course, is what you see as you pass through the grotto) to attract a night-flying midge, which is "caught" by the threads, paralyzed by the acid, and reeled up and eaten by the larva. After about 6 months, the larva pupates for about 2 weeks in a hard, brown cocoon about half an inch long and suspended by a circle of those slender threads. The pupa's flirtatious light show attracts several males, which proceed to help the fly escape her cocoon. Four days of egg laying, then it's time to end it all by diving into the lines cast by new larvae as a main course along with the midges.

Now that you understand how and why the glowworms glow, your guide is ready to take you on an unforgettable boat ride down the underground river, which flows through the 100-foot-long, 40-foot-high, 50-foot-wide Glowworm Grotto. As you board the large, flat-bottomed boat, he will caution you that absolute silence is required, since the glowworms will extinguish their lights at the slightest noise. I must say that the warning is probably unnecessary, since the spectacle of more than 10,000 of those tiny pinpricks of light tends to leave one speechless. The boat glides slowly along what is called the "Milky Way," then returns to the dock, where you climb back up through the cave and are given an opportunity to ask questions. It's truly a memorable experience.

OTHER THINGS TO SEE & DO IN WAITOMO

For the adventurous, **Waitomo Adventures Ltd.,** P.O. Box 29, Waitomo Caves (☎ 07/878-7788, fax 07/878-6184) offers an exciting **black-water rafting** experience on an underground river for NZ$65 (US$45.50), an abseiling/rock-climbing thrill called **Lost World Adventures** (NZ$195/US$137), and an abseiling/canoeing combination called **Cave Canoeing** (NZ$95/US$67). **Horse trekking** and **white-water rafting** can also be arranged with this outfitter.

A scant 16km (10 miles) before you reach Waitomo and the caves, **Kiwi House and Native Bird Centre** is located at Otorohanga. It's open daily from 9:30am to 4pm (to 5pm in summer). Admission is NZ$7.50 (US$5.25). The remaining distance to Waitomo runs through more rolling farmland.

WHERE TO STAY & EAT

The Information Centre mentioned above can tell you about farm and homestays in the area. The rates quoted below include the 12.5% GST.

Waitomo Caves Hotel

Waitomo Village. ☎ **0800/801-111** in New Zealand, or 07/878-8204. Fax 07/878-8858. 21 rms (all with bathrm), plus backpacker hostel rooms. NZ$140 (US$98) double; NZ$18 (US$12.60) hostel bed for YHA members, NZ$20 (US$14) hostel bed for non-YHA member. AE, BC, DC, JCB, MC, V.

This charming 1910 hotel retains much of its stately character. It's nestled in the hills above the village, convenient to the caves. Notable visitors have included Queen Elizabeth II and Prince Philip in 1953, George Bernard Shaw, Zane Grey, and General MacArthur. Premium rooms have telephones and TVs. The economy lodging is an associated YHA hostel—some rooms are in the hotel and some in the adjacent hostel. Lunch is served in the Garden Room; dinner is offered in the Fred Mace licensed restaurant. The Waitomo Caves Tavern is a great spot for a drink.

A Farmstay for Campervans

On State Highway 3, about halfway between Hamilton and Waitomo, the **Parklands Dairy Farm,** Kio Kio, R.D. 4, Otorohanga (☎ **07/871-1818**), is run by Owen

Readers Recommend

Matawha, R.D. 2, Raglan (☎ **07/825-6709**). *"We had a wonderful, restful farm stay in Raglan. It's off the beaten path—the last half hour of travel is on a gravel road, but it's well worth it. Jenny and Peter Thomson have a cattle and sheep farm that overlooks the Tasman Sea and a peaceful black-sand beach. Our girls loved being able to run around on the farm without supervision and play with the cats, see the hens, and try to pet the sheep."*
—Meg Barth Gammon, Kailua, Hawaii, USA.

Author's Note: rates here are NZ$40 (US$28) double bed and breakfast; dinner NZ$15 (US$10.50) per person; lunch NZ$10 (US$7) per person; camper vans NZ$20 (US$14); laundry and bathroom facilities available.

Rountree and family, whose hospitality goes far beyond that of most owners. That is undoubtedly because this is their home, and what they're offering—in addition to power outlets at campervan sites, showers, toilets, and a barbecue—is a real "down home" farm welcome. Guests are invited in for a "cuppa" in the evening, and when it's farm-chore time, guests often go right along. This really is a motor camp with a difference, and it's a convenient base for Waitomo caves sightseeing. Rates, which include GST, are NZ$18 (US$12.60) per person, bed-and-breakfast.

CAMBRIDGE

153km (95 miles) SE of Auckland

Cambridge (pop. 10,533) is a pretty little town on the Waikato River. Its village green, stately trees, and old churches give it an English feel.

ESSENTIALS

GETTING THERE & GETTING AROUND   Cambridge makes an ideal stop when traveling from Auckland to Rotorua. It's on the bus routes run by Newmans, Mount Cook, and InterCity coaches.

VISITOR INFORMATION   The **Cambridge Information Office,** at the corner of Queen and Victoria streets (☎ **07/827-6033,** fax 07/827-3505), is open Monday through Friday from 8am to 4:30pm. The **STD (area code)** for Cambridge is **07.**

EXPLORING CAMBRIDGE: WHAT TO SEE & DO

I'd like to say it was the historic buildings that attracted me to Cambridge, but in truth it was the **Cambridge Country Store,** 92 Victoria St. (☎ 07/827-8715). A wide selection of New Zealand crafts is sold here, and there's a good cafe upstairs. It's housed in a 100-year-old church and open daily from 8:30am to 5pm. Nearby on Empire Street, boutiques and antiques stores await. Serious shoppers should plan to be here in September or April when there are **antiques fairs**.

The **Cambridge Museum,** in the Old Courthouse, Victoria Street (☎ 07/827-3319), is open Tuesday through Saturday from 10am to 4pm and Sunday and holidays from 2 to 4pm. Be sure to notice St. Andrews Church; it's the pretty white one on the corner of Victoria Street and State Highway 1.

Some of New Zealand's best racehorses are bred in Cambridge, and the area is well known for its studs. This is also a popular area for jet boating. Contact the Visitor Information Office for details.

WHERE TO STAY

Birches

Maungatautari Rd. (P.O. Box 194), Cambridge. ☎ **07/827-6556.** E-mail hugh@plade.co.nz. 2 rms (both with bathrm). NZ$85 (US$59.50) double. Three-course evening meal with wine NZ$28 (US$19.60) extra by arrangement. Rates include breakfast. BC, MC, V.

Hosts Sheri Mitchell and Hugh Jellie welcome guests to their 30-acre farm a short distance out of Cambridge and take them on walks to see cows and sheep. Their property has two guest rooms: one in the house with its bathroom across the hall and the other in a tiny adjacent cottage. Both contain heaters, tea- and coffeemaking facilities, and electric blankets. Everyone shares the sitting room, tennis court, and pool. Hugh's a veterinarian, so this is the place to get your farming questions answered. Olivia is their cute young daughter.

WHERE TO EAT

In addition to the Grapevine (see below) you might enjoy **Country Lane Cafe and Gardens,** Pukerimu Lane, Cambridge (☎ 07/827-8839). It's open Wednesday to Sunday 10am to 4pm from mid-October until autumn when leaves fall off the trees.

The Grapevine Winebar

72 Alpha St. ☎ **07/827-6699.** Reservations recommended. Main courses NZ$16.80–$21.50 (US$11.76–$15.10); lunch NZ$6.50–$13.50 (US$4.60–$9.50). AE, DC, MC, V. Daily 10:30am–3pm and 5:30–9pm. MODERN NEW ZEALAND.

In the Old Power Board Building, the Grapevine has a convivial, casual atmosphere. There's live music on weekends, and the bar stays open until the wee hours. For lunch you could have pizza and salad or mushroom-and-parmesan fettuccine. Dinner main courses include boneless lamb loins served with tamarillo sauce, venison steaks with plum sauce, and vegetable parcels with fruit coulis. It's fully licensed too.

Rotorua & The Bay of Plenty

Located in the heart of the North Island, Rotorua is also in the center of the most intense thermal field in New Zealand: the 242km-long, 32km-wide (150-mile-long, 20-mile-wide) Taupo Volcanic Plateau. The city and its environs are rife with bubbling mud, silica terraces, and towering geysers. You'll also notice a rather faint, sulfuric odor that comes along with this thermal activity.

This is also the very heart of New Zealand's Maori culture, and the city's population of 67,000 includes a high percentage of Maori. The city and surrounding area are quite literally soaked with attractions, almost all tied by legend to the Maori culture.

Rotorua is less than an hour's drive from the Bay of Plenty coastline, where the main cities are Tauranga, Te Puke, and Whakatane. The region was named by Captain Cook as he sailed up the coast in 1769, noticing abundant food at numerous Maori villages, which enabled him to replenish his own supplies. Today the Bay of Plenty is known for its fruit orchards and beautiful beaches, which attract New Zealanders—and an increasing number of overseas visitors—on holiday.

1 Tauranga: Beaches & Boats

206km (128 miles) SE of Auckland

If you come from Auckland or the Coromandel, your introduction to the Bay of Plenty will be at Tauranga, an active port city that is home to a commercial fishing fleet and popular with big-game fishers. Many of New Zealand's forestry exports leave from the harbor here, and Tauranga has also become a popular stopping point for cruise ships. Because of its good climate, many New Zealanders retire in the Tauranga area.

The city, and its adjacent beach resort/port of Mount Maunganui, is also a peaceful center of citrus-fruit farming. Tauranga has 71,000 inhabitants; Mount Maunganui, only 11,000. This area is second only to Auckland in popularity among vacationing Kiwis. The majority of overseas visitors have yet to discover this area, which makes it a great destination for those of you who enjoy exploring off the beaten path.

ESSENTIALS
GETTING THERE

BY PLANE   Air New Zealand Link operates flights to Tauranga.

BY TRAIN & BUS   The *Geyserland* train makes daily runs from Auckland. InterCity and Newmans both have bus service to Tauranga from Auckland, Napier, Rotorua, Taupo, Thames, and Wellington. The Magic Travellers Network, an alternative bus service, also stops in Tauranga en route to Rotorua.

BY CAR   Drive south from Auckland on Highway 1, then go east on Highway 2. From the Coromandel Peninsula take Highway 25 or 26 to Waihi and pick up Highway 2. If you're coming from Thames, the trip will be about 114km (71 miles).

GETTING AROUND

Public transportation is limited in Tauranga. Be aware that the toll bridge to Mount Maunganui costs NZ$1 (US 70¢) per car.

VISITOR INFORMATION

The **Visitors Information Centre,** 80 Dive Crescent (☎ **07/578-8103,** fax 07/ 578-1090, e-mail trgvin@nzhost.co.nz), can direct you to interesting historical spots and make accommodations bookings and onward travel arrangements. It's open Monday through Friday 7am to 5:30pm and Saturday through Sunday 8am to 4pm. There's also a Visitor Information Centre in nearby Mount Maunganui on Salisbury Avenue (P.O. Box 1070), (☎ **07/575-5099,** fax 07/578-1090, e-mail mtmvin@nzhost.co.nz). Fishing trips can be organized easily from the wharf on the Strand in Tauranga. The **telephone area code** (STD) for Tauranga is **07.**

ORIENTATION

In recent years, Tauranga has "gone ahead" as the Kiwis say, and the city now offers some cute cafes and nice places to stay. The biggest draw, however, is access to nearby "Mount Maunganui," which refers to both the actual landmark and the beach below it. This is a popular holiday destination for Kiwis who love the more than 60km (37 miles) of continuous white-sand beach that runs from the Mount to Whakatane. This is also one of New Zealand's top areas for surfing. Tauranga's railway station is right at the waterfront, close to Devonport Road cafes and shops.

EXPLORING TAURANGA: WHAT TO SEE & DO
MOUNT MAUNGANUI

✪ **Mount Maunganui** (**Mauao** to the Maori), 5km (3 miles) from Tauranga, is best known and loved by thousands of Kiwis for its **Ocean Beach,** a stretch of sand along the best surfing waves in New Zealand. The 3.5km (2.17-mile) **walking track** around the mount takes about an hour. You can also climb to the top (it's 252 m/819 ft. high), for which you should allow a couple of hours. At the base of the mount, on Adams Avenue, the **Mount Hot Pools** (☎ **07/575-0868**) are hot saltwater pools for swimming or soaking. For a small admission fee (NZ$2.50/US$1.75 adult, NZ$1.50/US$1.05 child, NZ$2/US$1.40 over 60), you can ease your aches away; there's swimsuit and towel rental for those who arrive unprepared. A fresh water supply fills the pools every 3 hours; they're open from 6am to 10pm Monday through Saturday, 8am to 10pm Sunday and holidays year round. For a massage and a private pool there's an additional charge of NZ$25 (US$17.50) for a half hour or NZ$45 (US$31.50) for a full hour.

OTHER ATTRACTIONS

The gardens of the **Elms Mission House,** on Mission Street, built by an early missionary and one of the finest examples of colonial architecture of its time (1847), are open to the public daily at any time. The library dates from 1837 and is probably the oldest in the country. On the carefully tended grounds, you'll see kauri, rimu, and orange trees, along with kiwifruit orchards. There's no admission charge to the grounds; tours of the Mission House are conducted on Sunday from 2 to 3pm for NZ$2 (US$1.40) per person.

Tauranga Historic Village, 155 17th Ave. near Cameron (☎ **07/578-1302,** fax 07/578-1822, e-mail tgamus@enternet.co.nz), bows to the past with 14 acres of a re-created colonial village, with cobblestone streets, a blacksmith's shop, a military barracks, a Maori village, and much more. Rides by train, double-decker bus, or horse-drawn cart are a good idea if you're traveling with young ones. You'll find a tearoom and gift shops in the village. It's open daily year round from 9am to 5pm, with an admission of NZ$6 (US$4.20) adults, NZ$2.50 (US$1.75) children. The Wool Shop here offers local products at good prices. MasterCard and Visa are accepted.

If you'd like to watch the locals playing **cricket,** there's a pitch (cricket grounds) between 14th and 15th avenues at Devonport Rd. You could easily spend an entire afternoon here hanging out and trying to comprehend the complex rules of this popular sport. Chances are you'll leave without fully grasping the game, but I bet you'll have a good time anyway.

AFFORDABLE ACCOMMODATIONS

Don't forget that in addition to the places listed below, you could also stop in **Katikati,** northwest of Tauranga, and stay at **Jacaranda Cottage** (see "En Route to Tauranga" in chapter 6).

IN TAURANGA

Moderately Priced Options

Academy Motor Inn

Corner 15th Ave. and Cameron Rd. (P.O. Box 586), Tauranga. ☎ **0800/782-922** in New Zealand, or 07/578-9103. Fax 07/578-9133. 20 units (all with bathrm). TV TEL. NZ$95–$135 (US$67–$95). Additional person NZ$15 (US$10.50) adult, NZ$10 (US$7) child.

This modernly furnished motor inn opened in late 1996. All units have ceiling fans, kitchens, and hair dryers. The eight studios have spa tubs and separate showers and sleep two people; the 11 one-bedroom units sleep four; and the two-bedroom unit sleeps six. Available are a swimming pool, outdoor spa, and free laundry facilities. The park across the street is a favorite local recreation area. Request a rear unit to avoid traffic noise.

✪ Ambassador 15th Avenue Motel

9 15th Ave. (at Mayfair St.), Tauranga. ☎ **0800/735-294** in New Zealand, or 07/578-5665. Fax 07/578-5226. 20 units (all with bathrm). TV TEL. Special rate for Frommer's readers: NZ$75–$90 (US$52.50–$63) double, NZ$10 (US$7.50) extra person. AE, DC, MC, V.

This motel, with its terra-cotta exterior, is easy to spot, and you won't get a more pleasant welcome anywhere in Tauranga. Owners Brian and Maureen Dudley are great hosts. Facilities here include plenty of flowers and gardens, an outdoor pool, a trampoline, a free laundry, and a portable barbecue. There are 11 studios and 9 larger units, all quite comfortable, with kitchen facilities and nice, firm mattresses. Fifteen units have spa baths. Breakfast is available daily. The Ambassador is 3¹/₂km (2 miles) south of downtown and 1 block from the water. Some upstairs units have limited water views. Request a rear unit to avoid traffic noise.

Worth a Splurge

✪ Cassimir

Williams Rd. (R.D. 3), Tauranga. ☎ **07/543-2000.** Fax 07/543-1999. 6 rms (all with bathrm). TEL. Special rate for Frommer's readers: NZ$150 (US$105) per person per night including dinner, breakfast, and on-site activities; NZ$100 (US$70) per person per night bed and breakfast. AE, DC, MC, V. From Auckland take State Hwy. 2 to Tauranga, turn right onto Cameron Rd. (at McDonald's), which becomes Pyes Pa Rd. After 17km, turn right onto Williams Rd.

If you've ever wondered what it would be like to stay in a great country house, this is your chance. Cassimir is set on nearly 23 hectares (55 acres) of lush green terrain. The historic house dates from 1890 and boasts floors of polished matai and furniture of native rimu. The striking dining room, where a fire warms in winter, has a table that seats up to 14; breakfast is served in the glass conservatory. Consummate host Reg Turner opened Cassimir in 1995; since then his hospitality has been enjoyed by everyone from New Zealand politicians to Joan Collins. Reg has been a professional fishing guide for over 25 years, and he stood (ran) for Parliament in 1996—needless to say dinner-table conversations are lively. If you stay here, you'll wake up to the sound of cows mooing and a view across the paddocks and bush as far as the eye can see. All rooms have king or twin beds and modern bathrooms with large showers, tubs, and marble floors. Big windows throughout the house capture the vistas and let in light, so the rooms are pleasantly bright. Facilities include a great spa pool, an honor bar in the lounge, and open fires throughout. In spite of the grand surroundings, the atmosphere is very homey—sort of like a big house party. On-site activities include archery, tennis, croquet, petanque, and more. I've known Reg for a dozen years and the rates quoted above are a special deal only for Frommer's readers. Note that the dinner/bed and breakfast price does not include wine.

IN NEARBY PAPAMOA

✪ Papamoa Beach Holiday Park

535 Papamoa Beach Rd., Papamoa (about 10km/6 miles from Mt. Maunganui). ☎ and fax **07/572-0816.** 220 powered sites, 45 nonpowered sites, 1 tourist cabin (without bathrm), 6 cabins (without bathrm) 3 deluxe cabins (without bathrm) 3 tourist flats (all with bathrm), 4 motel units (all with bathrm). NZ$10.50–$14 (US$7.40–9.80) per adult, NZ$5.25–$7 (US$3.68–$4.90) per child in powered and nonpowered sites; NZ$45 (US$31.50) double tourist cabin, NZ$38 (US$26.60) double cabin, NZ$48 (US$33.60) double deluxe cabin, NZ$60 (US$42) double tourist flat, extra adult NZ$12 (US$8.40), extra child NZ$9 (US$6.30); NZ$90 (US$63) double motel unit, extra adult NZ$15 (US$10.50), extra child NZ$10 (US$7). MC, V.

I was delighted to discover this spot, because I really wanted to be able to tell you about affordable beachfront lodgings in this area. Here you'll find a safe, surf-patrolled beach, which is an ideal spot for families or anyone who wants to swim, surf, windsurf, fish, or simply relax. Camping and caravan sites here have a view that would cost millions in other parts of the world. The tourist cabin sleeps up to four people and has a kitchen but no en suite bathroom (communal showers and toilets are adjacent). The six cabins (which sleep 4 to 6) and three deluxe cabins (sleep 2) come with toaster, kettle, fridge, and dishes, but no bathroom. The difference between the cabin and the deluxe cabin is linens—included in the deluxe cabins. Tourist flats and motel units both sleep up to six, and have fully equipped kitchens and en suite bathrooms. Only the attractive motel units come with linens, although you can obtain them for the other units for NZ$5/US$3.50 per person, per night. Campers use the communal showers, toilets, and cooking facilities, which are all very nice. When you've had enough beach entertainment, facilities include mini-tennis and a recreation room with table tennis, video games (during peak season), and a color TV; private spa pools are available for hire by the half hour from 4 to 10pm for NZ$3.50 (US$2.45) adult and NZ$2 (US$1.40) child. Boogie boards can be rented for NZ$3 (US$2.10) per hour. A restaurant and shopping center are adjacent. This place is a real find!

GREAT DEALS ON DINING
IN TAURANGA

Many cute cafes line Devonport Road between Spring and Elizabeth streets. In this area, the council has installed used brick in the sidewalk, and it helps to create a trendy atmosphere. In addition to those places below, you might like to try **Muffin Boutique,** 22 Devonport Rd. (☎ 07/578-9285), or **Zuccotti Italian Deli Bakery,** 28 Devonport Rd. (☎ 07/578-8552). Both cafes are open during the day only; neither accepts credit cards. **Memorial Park** (on the waterfront) is a great picnic spot.

The Rock Pool

64 Devonport Rd., Tauranga. ☎ **07/578-6400.** Reservations accepted for dinner. Lunch main courses: NZ$7–$10 (US$4.90–$7); dinner main courses NZ$14.50 (US$10.20). AE, MC, V. 7:30am–4:30pm Sun–Wed, 7:30am–midnight Thur–Sat. ECLECTIC.

This is a casual cafe where locals sit and read or chat while they enjoy coffee or a light meal. Baskets of dried flowers and handcrafted fish hang from the ceiling over the cash register. Diners make their choices from a blackboard menu and order at the counter. Typical main courses include Moroccan lamb with hummus, tabbouleh and sumac yoghurt with warm pita; and penne pasta with smoked salmon, Mediterranean vegetables, and basil. There are a few tables on the sidewalk in addition to those inside. The day starts with breakfast, followed by morning tea and lunch. Coffee and cakes dominate from 2 to 6pm; then dinner service starts. I can personally recommend the chocolate fudge brownie.

Valentine's

Corner Devonport Rd. and Elizabeth St. (P.O. Box 13265), Tauranga. ☎ **07/578-8222.** Fax 07/578-7528. Reservations recommended, essential on weekends. Buffet lunch NZ$15.95 (US$11.17) adults; buffet dinner NZ$24.50 (US$17.20) adults; children lunch and dinner buffet NZ$1.10 (US77¢) per year of age; Sunday brunch NZ$13.95 (US$9.77) adults, NZ$6.50 (US$4.60) children 5–12, under 5 free. AE, DC, MC, V. Sun brunch 8–10:30am, daily noon–2:30pm, 5:30–6pm early dinner seating, 7:45–8:15pm second seating. BUFFET.

This is a great deal for big eaters on tight budgets—an all-you-can-eat buffet that typically includes several soups, breads, pizza, over 20 freshly-prepared salads, cold meats, a wide selection of seafood, ham, chicken, fish, meats, vegetables, cheeses, tea, coffee, and over 20 desserts including pavlova, chocolate mousse, fresh fruit salad, and cheesecake. You can keep refilling your plate over and over again, but you can only stay 1³/₄ hours at a time. The food is all fresh and the attractive dining room is light and bright. Adjacent to the dining room is a soundproof children's video room where Disney reigns supreme. If someone in your party is having a birthday, prearrange for a complimentary cake and balloons. Valentine's is a very accommodating place; you don't even have to eat here to take advantage of their complimentary tea or coffee in the bar or to use the toilets (rest rooms). Fully licensed and nonsmoking.

EN ROUTE TO ROTORUA

About 30km (19 miles) southeast of Tauranga lies the town of **Te Puke,** the "Kiwifruit Capital of the World," and **Kiwifruit Country** (P.O. Box 541), Te Puke (☎ 07/573-6340, fax 07/573-6345), a popular attraction that you'll recognize by the giant slice of fruit (a camouflaged observation tower) out front. Stop by—there's no admission charge to look around the shop and restaurant or watch a short video on kiwi cultivation. For NZ$8.50 (US$6), NZ$4 (US$2.80) for children, you can take a half-hour tour of the working orchard and listen to a taped commentary in the Kiwi Kart (a kiwifruit-shaped tram). The tour goes through the grounds and theme orchard, which features 60 different fruits and nuts, from macadamias to feijoas (try this local fruit if you can) to pomegranates. Their kiwifruit is harvested in May and June. Kiwifruit Country offers complimentary tasting of kiwifruit wines, liqueurs, and apéritifs. There is a children's playground called Magic World, which has an admission charge. The cafe features kiwi burgers and kiwifruit parfait. It's open daily 9am to 5pm, and tours are at 9:15, 10:15, and 11am; and 12:15, 1:15, 2, 3, and 3:45pm. *Author's note:* I suggest you do the free stuff, but don't take the tour unless you have a particular interest in horticulture.

While we were at Kiwifruit Country, my husband, who is an automotive buff (aka "car guy"), went next door to **Te Puke Vintage Auto Barn,** R.D.9, Te Puke (☎ **07/573-6547**), where over 70 vintage and classic vehicles are on display. He said "it was interesting, but not a 'must see'." It's open daily 9am to 5pm. Admission is NZ$5 (US$3.50) for adults, NZ$12 (US$8.40) for a family.

2 Rotorua

221km (137 miles) SE of Auckland; 86 km (53 miles) S of Tauranga

If Maori culture and thermal activity interest you, Rotorua should be included on your North Island itinerary. Be aware, however, that Rotorua is on the agenda of seemingly every bus tour in the country. On Fenton Street, the "Motel Mile," you may well see more than a dozen big coaches lined up head to tail. You can avoid witnessing this scene by staying slightly out of town (see "Affordable Accommodations," below). Obviously the readers of *Travel & Leisure* don't share my skepticism about Rotorua. In 1996 they voted it number 10 in a poll of the Top 10 Cities in the World.

The first visitors to Rotorua were Maori, members of the Arawa tribe whose seagoing canoe reached the shores of the Bay of Plenty sometime during the 14th century. Pushing inland to Lake Rotorua, they stayed on as settlers. Today's visitors will find some 5,000 of their descendants happily following much of the traditional tribal lifestyle.

Because Rotorua sits right in the middle of the most intense thermal activity (that explains the strong smell of sulfur here), overheated water will bubble up all around you in the form of geysers, mud pools, or steam bores. You'll bathe in it, see the locals cooking with it, stay in lodgings that are heated with it, or simply walk carefully around the boiling mud pools, watching them gurgle and sputter.

Wandering through Rotorua is like wandering through a gallery of Maori culture. You'll hear songs that tell of old Maori legends; you'll taste the food at a hangi feast; and you'll even spot young Maori learning how to carve and weave.

ESSENTIALS
GETTING THERE
BY PLANE Ansett New Zealand, Air New Zealand, and Eagle Airways operate daily flights between Auckland and Rotorua, and Ansett flies up from Wellington and Christchurch.

BY TRAIN & BUS The *Geyserland* train makes regular runs from Auckland. InterCity, Mount Cook Landline, and Newmans all operate daily bus schedules

Rotorua & Environs

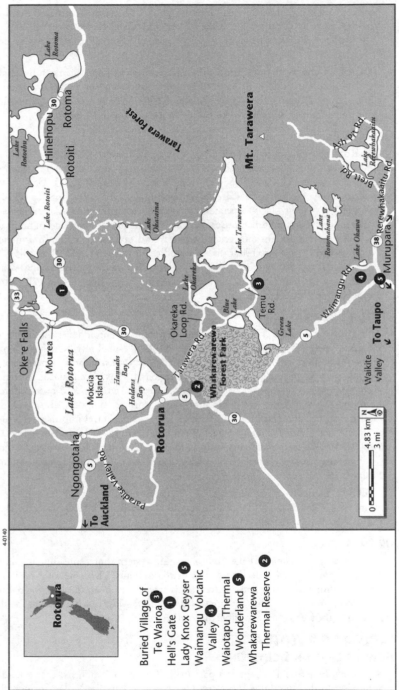

Buried Village of Te Wairoa 3
Hell's Gate 1
Lady Knox Geyser 5
Waimangu Volcanic Valley 4
Waiotapu Thermal Wonderland 5
Whakarewarewa Thermal Reserve 2

Rotorua

Lake Rotoma
Hinehopu 30 Rotoma
Lake Rotoehu
Rotoiti
Lake Rotoiti
Tarawera Forest
Mt. Tarawera
Ash Pit Rd.
Brett Rd.
Lake Rerewhakaaitu
Rerewhakaaitu Rd.
33
Okere Falls
Mourea
Lake Okahu
Lake Rotomahana
Lake Okareka
Lake Tarawera
Waimangu Rd.
To Taupo
38 Murupara
Lake Okataina
Lake Rotorua
Hannahs Bay
Holdens Bay
Mokoia Island
Okareka Loop Rd.
Blue Lake
Green Lake
Temu Rd.
Tarawera Rd.
Whakarewarewa Forest Park
Waikite Valley
Rotorua
Ngongotaha
Paradise Valley Rd.
To Auckland

N

4.83 km
3 mi
0

4-0140

173

between Auckland and Rotorua, arriving at the **Tourism Rotorua Travel & Visitor Centre** at 67 Fenton St., at the corner of Haupapa Street.

Magic Travellers Network and Kiwi Experience, two alternative bus lines, also stop in Rotorua.

BY CAR   Drive south from Auckland on Highway 1 to Tirau, then east on Highway 5 to Rotorua; consider stopping in Cambridge for lunch (see chapter 6). If you're coming from Waitomo, the trip will be about 150km (93 miles). If you're coming from Tauranga, the "back way" along Pyes Pa Road is the most scenic.

GETTING AROUND

The **Rotorua Sightseeing Shuttle** (P.O. Box 67), Rotorua (☎ **0800/927-399** in New Zealand, after hours and fax 07/347-7555), will get you to the major attractions. A half-day pass costs NZ$18 (US$12.60) and a full-day pass is NZ$25 (US$17.50); children are charged half price. **Carey's Sightseeing,** P.O. Box 402, Rotorua (☎ **07/ 347-1197,** fax 07/347-1199), operates a wide variety of half- and full-day excursions.

There are city and suburban **buses,** but they're infrequent (about one an hour) on weekdays and nonexistent on weekends. You'll find **taxi** stands at the Information Centre and on Fenton Street near the Ansett office, or you can call ☎ **07/348-5079.**

If you arrive by plane, train, or bus and decide to rent a car for sightseeing, you'll probably get the best rates and service from **Avon/Percy Rent A Car** (☎ **0800/ 7368-2866** in New Zealand).

VISITOR INFORMATION

The **Tourism Rotorua Travel & Visitor Centre,** 67 Fenton St. at the corner of Haupapa Street (☎ **07/348-5179,** fax 07/348-6044, e-mail rotvin@nzhost.co.nz), is open daily from 8am to 5:30pm. It's loaded with tourist information and has a helpful staff who will make reservations. The center also has a licensed cafe, currency exchange, baggage storage, Department of Conservation office, and postal center. Look for *Thermal Air,* a free publication listing current goings-on; also check the local newspaper, the *Daily Post,* for day-to-day events. Travel information is also available at the **AA Travel Centre,** 59 Amohau St. (☎ **07/348-3069,** fax 07/ 346-2034). The **telephone area code** (STD) for Rotorua is **07.** The post office, on Hinemoa Street at Tutanekai St. (☎ **07/347-7851**), is open Monday through Friday from 8:30am to 4:30pm.

SPECIAL EVENTS   The **Fletcher Challenge Marathon** is a full marathon run around Lake Rotorua. This serious competition takes place annually in early May. (☎ and fax **07/348-8448**).

ORIENTATION

Rotorua sits in the curve of Lake Rotorua's southwestern shore, spreading inland in a neat pattern, so you'll be acclimated in a matter of hours. The center of town is not large: **Fenton Street** is the main drag. This street runs from the lake for 3.4km (2 miles) south to the Whakarewarewa (never mind—just call it "Whaka," as the locals do), the area's most accessible thermal reserve.

EXPLORING ROTOTUA
HOW TO SAVE ON SIGHTSEEING

Rotorua's Five Star Package is a pass (valid for up to 3 months) that provides admission to the Agrodome, *Lakeland Queen* cruise, Paradise Valley Springs, the New Zealand Maori Arts and Crafts Institute, Polynesian Spa, and Skyline Skyrides. In addition, if you buy it at the **Tourism Rotorua** office at 67 Fenton St.

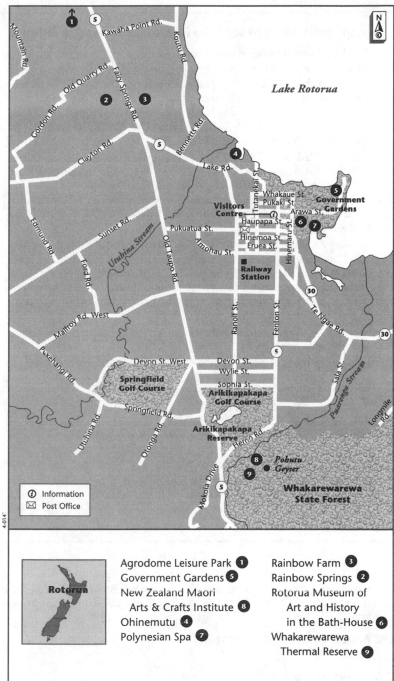

N

Lake Rotorua

Mountain Rd.

Kawaha Point Rd.

Kaitu Rd.

Old Quarry Rd.

Fairy Springs Rd.

Gordon Rd.

Bennetts Rd.

Clayton Rd.

Lake Rd.

Edmund Rd.

Sunset Rd.

Pukuatua St.

Whakaue St.
Pukaki St.

Visitors
Centre

Haupapa St.

Arawa St.

Government
Gardens

Utuhina Stream

Old Taupo Rd.

Amohau St.

Hinemoa St.
Eruea St.

Tutanekai St.

Hinemaru St.

Ford Rd.

Railway
Station

Te Ngae Rd.

Malfroy Rd. West

Ranolf St.

Fenton St.

Pukehangi Rd.

Devon St. West

Devon St.
Wylie St.

Springfield
Golf Course

Sophia St.
Arikikapakapa
Golf Course

Sala St.

Puarenga Stream

Springfield Rd.

Utuhina Rd.

Otonga Rd.

Arikikapakapa
Reserve

Hemo Rd.

Longmile
Rd.

Mokoia Drive

Pohutu
Geyser

Whakarewarewa
State Forest

ⓘ Information
✉ Post Office

4-014.'

Rotorua

Agrodome Leisure Park ❶
Government Gardens ❺
New Zealand Maori
   Arts & Crafts Institute ❽
Ohinemutu ❹
Polynesian Spa ❼

Rainbow Farm ❸
Rainbow Springs ❷
Rotorua Museum of
   Art and History
   in the Bath-House ❻
Whakarewarewa
   Thermal Reserve ❾

Cheap Thrills: What to See & Do for Free (or Almost) in Rotorua

- **Watching Lawn Bowling at Government Gardens**   Walk over to this lovely city park and check out the local seniors competing in their "whites."

- **Soaking in the Waikite Valley Thermal Pools**   Located about 20 minutes south of Rotorua, these pools aren't as glamorous as those at the famous Polynesian Spa, but a soak only costs NZ$4 (US$2.80) for adults, NZ$2 (US$1.40) for children, and NZ$10 (US$7) for a family. They're open 10am to 5pm; call ☎ 07/333-1861 for directions.

- **Hiking the Redwood Grove**   Head to one of the tracks in the Redwood Grove in the Whakarewarewa State Forest Park south of town. Dedicated to the men of New Zealand's Forest Service who gave their lives in both world wars, the Grove, just off Long Mile Road, has trails of varying lengths. Pick up a color-coded tramping map at the Park Information Centre (☎ 07/346-2082) on Long Mile Rd.

- **Strolling Around Ohinemutu**   It's fun to wander around this suburb where Maori families still incorporate cultural traditions in their daily lives. The major attraction is St. Faith's Anglican Church, a remarkable representation of the Pakeha Christian faith as interpreted through Maori art, including intricate carvings and exquisite scrollwork. If you can, catch a concert in the town's Tamatekapua meeting house.

- **Having a Picnic Lunch, Lakeside**   Get your goods, find a spot, and watch the black swans swim by.

- **Touring the Jade Factory**   If you'd like to see how greenstone is transformed into jewelry and carvings, stop by the **Jade Factory and Gift Centre,** 170 Fenton St. at Eruera St. (☎ 07/349-3968) to watch carvers at work.

- **Walking the Okere Falls Track**   Between Kaituna River Bridge and Okere Falls Store, 21km (13 miles) from Rotorua off State Highway 33, you'll find **Okere Falls Track.** This is an easy track—only 1.2km (³/₄ mile) each way. Along the way, you'll catch awesome views of Okere Falls and the Kaituna River; you can fish in the trout pool here year round.

- **Playing in Kuirau Park**   Adjacent to the city center, this park is great for kids and kids at heart. It's got gardens, mud pools, and other thermal action, plus a play area that includes the Toot & Whistle, a miniature steam railway that operates on weekends.

(☎ 07/348-5179, fax 07/348-6044), you'll receive a complimentary lunch on the *Lakeland Queen.* The Five Star Pass costs NZ$65 (US$45.50) for adults. You can use your rental car to get to and from attractions or take the **Rotorua Sightseeing Shuttle.** A full-day pass on Rotorua Sightseeing costs NZ$25 (US$17.50).

THE MAJOR SIGHTS & ATTRACTIONS

In Rotorua

✪ Government Gardens

On the lakefront at the end of Haupapa St. ☎ **07/349-8334.** Fax 07/349-2819. Museum admission NZ$4 (US$2.80) adults, NZ$1 (US70¢) children under 15, NZ$8 (US$5.60) family groups. Gardens, daily dawn–dusk; Bath-House/museum, daily 9:30am–5pm.

Reigning over this downtown city park is the stately **Bath-House,** one of New Zealand's oldest buildings (1908). It was built as a fashionable bathhouse, the largest in the country, much like a European spa. The gardens themselves are a lovely mix of rose gardens (lit at night), croquet and bowling lawns, and steaming thermal pools. The gardens are a delightful in-town resting spot, and the Bath-House is definitely worth a look. Inside, you'll find the **Rotorua Museum of Art and History,** displaying paintings of both local and international artists as well as a significant collection of Maori carvings and artifacts and the unique history of the volcanic plateau. On the eastern side of the Gardens is the **Sulphur Bay Wildlife Refuge** for waterbirds. Many different species of birds use the waters and shores at various times of the year.

Polynesian Spa

In the Government Gardens, on the lakefront at the end of Hinemoa St. ☎ **07/348-1328.** Fax 07/348-9486. Admission from NZ$8.50 (US$6) adults, NZ$3 (US$2.10) children, NZ$17 (US$11.90) family (2 adults and 1–4 children). Lockers are NZ$2 (US$1.40). AE, BC, JCB, MC, V. Daily 6:30am–11pm.

A chief attraction at the Gardens is the Polynesian Spa. Here you can experience the mineral pools at your leisure, for as long as you choose, and you can rent swimmers (swimsuit) and towel, if necessary (NZ$2.50/US$1.80 each plus a NZ$5 deposit). There are outdoor pools, indoor pools, and private pools. The soft alkaline water in the large pool maintains a constant temperature of about 100°F, while the smaller pools contain water high in sulfur and magnesium—very good for sore muscles— at temperatures of 92° to 110°F. Private pools are available for rent by the half hour for NZ$9 (US$6.30) per adult, NZ$3 (US$2.10) accompanied children, and NZ$17 (US$11.90) for a family. The nicest area is the Lake Spa, where you can soak in four natural rock pools of varying temperatures in a garden setting on the edge of the lake. This costs NZ$25 (US$17.50) per adult and NZ$12.50 (US$8.80) for accompanied children (5 to 14), which, frankly, seems a bit pricey to me. A better deal is to sign up for a half-hour AIX (gentle water) massage, which costs NZ$40 (US$28) and includes full use of the Lake Spa facilities (towels, indoor pools, lockers, and changing rooms); prebooking is required. Dollarwise travelers might also postpone their soak until they get to Taupo and the good-value Taupo Hot Springs (see chapter 9). There's a licensed cafe and a souvenir shop on the premises. Remove all silver and copper jewelry before going in the water; the minerals will make it oxidize.

✪ Ohinemutu

Located about a kilometer (half a mile) north of Rotorua, this suburb is home to the largest Arawa subtribe, the Ngatiwhakaue. Although the residences are very much in the Pakeha style—small, everyday bungalows—the lifestyle strictly follows tribal customs. On a *marae* (open courtyard, or clearing) stands the beautifully hand-carved **Tamatekapua meeting house.** This is where most tribal matters are discussed and important decisions made; concerts are also held here every night. Homes are thermally heated, and in every backyard you'll see the steam ovens where much of the family cooking is done.

Perhaps the most outstanding structure in Ohinemutu is ✪ **St. Faith's Anglican Church,** a remarkable representation of the Pakeha Christian faith as interpreted through Maori art. The Tudor-style church building is a revelation of Maori color, intricate carving, exquisite scrollwork, and even an integration of ancient Maori religions, as represented by the figures of mythical demigods and their primitive subjects, which are carved in the base of the pulpit. There's a lovely, truly spiritual blending of the two cultures in a magnificent plate-glass window looking out to the lake; the window shows a full-size figure of Christ haloed and clad in a Maori cloak of kiwi feathers, appearing to be walking on the lake. It was sandblasted by a local Pakeha artist, and in the figure's stance he captured the unmistakable dignity and grace of Maori chieftains. A visit to St. Faith's is a touching, memorable experience. It's open daily beginning at 8am. Sunday services are in Maori at 8am and in Maori and English at 10am.

Tombs of Maori tribal leaders are outside the church, all above ground and safe from the restless rumblings of the thermal activity. Take time to explore the settlement, as there are other examples of Maori carving and decoration in buildings and statues.

Just Outside Rotorua

✪ New Zealand Maori Arts and Crafts Institute

In the Whakarewarewa Thermal Reserve, Hemo Rd. ☎ **07/348-9047.** Fax 07/348-9045. Admission to Institute and Whaka Reserve NZ$11 (US$7.70) adults, NZ$4.30 (US$3.01) children 5–16, children under 5 free, NZ$28.60 (US$20.02) family (2 adults and 4 children) includes tour, which departs on the hour. AE, BC, DC, MC, V. Daily 8am–5pm. Closed Christmas Day. Located 3.4km (about 2 miles) south of town. Bus: Rotorua Sightseeing Shuttle.

On Rotorua's southern edge, at the entrance to the Whakarewarewa thermal area, this institute exists for the sole purpose of preserving the ancient skills of Maori tribes. Youngsters are selected from all over the country to come here as apprentices to master artisans: Boys study carving for a minimum of 3 years, after which they may take their newly acquired skills back to their own tribes or stay on to become teachers at the institute; girls learn to weave traditional cloaks and make distinctive flax skirts and intricately patterned bodices. As a visitor, you're welcome to observe, and it's interesting to watch this blending of beauty, myth, and spiritual symbolism as one generation passes its heritage on to the next. Products made here are for sale in the attached shop.

✪ Whakarewarewa Thermal Reserve

Hemo Rd., Rotorua. ☎ **07/348-9047.** Admission to Institute and Whaka Reserve NZ$11 (US$7.70) adults, NZ$4.30 (US$3) children 5–16, children under 5 free, NZ$28.60 (US$20) family (2 adults plus 4 children); Institute, Whaka Reserve, and concert, NZ$19.90 (US$13.93), adult, NZ$7.85 (US$5.50) children 5–16, NZ$55.50 (US$38.90) family. AE, BC, DC, MC, V. Daily 8am–5pm (to 6pm in summer). Concerts daily at 12:15pm. Closed Christmas Day. Bus: Rotorua Sightseeing Shuttle.

To walk through the Whaka Thermal Reserve is to view the most dramatic concentration of Rotorua's thermal wonders. There's a Maori guide to show you through, on the hour from 9am to 4pm, or you're free to wander on your own. The Maori—who know, understand, and respect this unique landscape—can tell you the legends that interpret its many moods. If you go alone, be sure to stay on the marked paths.

Inside the reserve is a model village patterned after Rotowhio, a pre-European village whose layout and construction have been faithfully reproduced. There are eight active geysers, which may perform for you if your timing is right. The **Prince of Wales Feathers Geyser** and the **Pohutu Geyser** are particularly impressive. The Prince gets things started with a jet that works up to 30 feet, at which time Pohutu goes into action, erupting up to 70 feet, blowing out up to 300,000 liters of water, with little offshoot eruptions that sometimes more than double that height. They're unpredictable—it's publicized that eruptions, on the average, occur one to two times per hour, but can become as frequent as three to four times per hour; but recorded eruptions have been as few as two and as many as nine in a 24-hour period, sometimes lasting 20 minutes, sometimes only five.

✪ Agrodome Leisure Park

In Riverdale Park, Western Rd., Ngongotaha. ☎ **07/357-4350.** Fax 07/357-5307. Admission NZ$10 (US$7) adults, NZ$5 (US$3.50) children 5–15, under 5 free; 10% family discount for adults with school-age children. Horse rides, NZ$15 (US$9.75) for 30 minutes; farm tours NZ$8 (US$5.20). AE, MC, V. Shows daily at 9:30 and 11am, and 2:30pm (additional shows during heavy tourist seasons). Open daily 8:30am–5pm. Located on Hwy. 5, about 10km (6.2 miles) north of town. Bus: Rotorua Sightseeing Shuttle.

The award-winning show here is an interesting addition to any Rotorua visit. The Agrodome is a huge (12,000-sq.-ft.) octagonal natural-timber building set in 350 acres of farmland. Rams of 19 breeds of sheep are the focus of a 60-minute show that packs in more information on the creatures than you probably thought existed. Each ram walks on stage to a live commentary by a professional shearer explaining the origins of the breed, the primary uses of its wool or meat, and its importance to New Zealand's sheep industry. When all 19 are on stage, the master shearer explains the tricks of his trade and proceeds to demonstrate his skill. The sheep dogs are then whistled in and put through their paces, and the audience is invited to meet the dogs and rams and pose for photos with the stars.

Facilities include a farmyard nursery and licensed restaurant. Also available are horse rides and farm tours to a kiwifruit orchard and deer paddock. There's a large shop here, selling sheepskins, souvenirs, and all kinds of wool clothing.

Rainbow Springs

On Hwy. 5 (P.O. Box 25), Rotorua. ☎ **0800/724-626** in New Zealand, or 07/347-9301. Fax 07/346-0641. Admission NZ$10 (US$7) adults, NZ$4 (US$2.80) children 5–15, under 5 free; family ticket NZ$26 (US$18.20). Combination ticket with Rainbow Farm NZ$14.50 (US$10.20) adults, NZ$7.50 (US$5.25) children; children under 5 free; family ticket NZ$33 (US$23.10). Daily 8am–5pm. Take Hwy. 5 about 5km (about 3 miles) north of Rotorua. Bus: Rotorua Sightseeing Shuttle.

Here's what you'll find at Rainbow Springs, north of town: World-famous rainbow trout, which grow to gigantic proportions safely away from the angler's hook in these protected waters; birds, including several rare species; and trees and plants, some 135 varieties of fern alone. Follow the 350-yard path—meandering through bush thick with dark greenery and alive with birdsong; you can stop to watch the antics of brown and rainbow trout—which push and butt one another in their haste to gobble up food pellets thrown by visitors—and gaze at deer grazing peacefully in their paddock. If you haven't seen a kiwi yet, this is as good a place as any. Along the Fairy Springs walk, Maori myth takes on a little more reality when you see the spring from which more than five million gallons of water per day well up through the black and white sands. It isn't hard at all to credit the Maori belief that this spot is the home of the legendary Patupaiarehe, the fairy folk.

There's a large souvenir shop, a cafeteria for light snacks, and a licensed restaurant.

Rainbow Farm

On Hwy. 5 (P.O. Box 25), Rotorua ☎ **0800/724-626** in New Zealand, or 07/347-8104. Fax 07/347-8107. Admission NZ$9.50 (US$6.70) adults, NZ$4 (US$2.80) children 5–15, children under 5 free; NZ$25 (US$17.50) family; also included on combination ticket to Rainbow Springs (see above). Open daily 8am–5pm. Shows at 10:30 and 11:45am and 1 and 2:30pm (extra shows during summer at 9am and 4pm), but you're welcome to stroll around the farm anytime before or after shows. Bus: Rotorua Sightseeing Shuttle.

Directly across the highway from Rainbow Springs, Rainbow Farm features the entire range of farm animals—horses, cows, goats, sheep, pigs, ducks, and dogs—and genuine gumboot farmers. Shows take place in a barn with comfortable seating. The showmen give a lively commentary of a busy day on a farm and combine working animals with an entertaining and educational view of Kiwi farm life.

Skyline Skyrides

Fairy Spring Rd. (☎ **07/347-0027**). NZ$11 (US$7.70) for adults, NZ$4 (US$2.80) for children. Located 4.6km (almost 3 miles) north of town on Hwy. 5.

For a lofty view of Rotorua, the lakes, and the steamy landscape surrounding them, take the glass-enclosed gondola, which ascends some 900 meters (2,970 ft.) up the side of Mt. Ngongotaha. The Luge and Super X Simulator are other thrilling rides here.

MORE THERMAL AREAS

You have a couple of options for visiting the thermal areas in the vicinity of Rotorua: All are accessible by rental car or you can visit them on a tour bus. Of the tours, I like Carey's the best, and they've agreed to give Frommer's readers a 10% discount for direct bookings. For more information on Carey's, see "Organized Tours & Cruises," below. If you drive, you can wander through each area at your own pace. The ✪ **Waimangu Volcanic Valley** (P.O. Box 6141, Rotorua; ☎07/366-6137) is 26km (16 miles) south of Rotorua off Highway 5. Turn east at the sign on the highway 19km (about 12 miles) south of town. This is the southern end of the 1886 Tarawera eruption, and the ongoing thermal activity includes the Inferno Crater Lake, which rises and falls about 10 meters a month. You'll also see the Waimangi caldron—the world's largest boiling lake. There are steaming cliffs, boiling springs, and fumaroles, too. You may also want to take an optional cruise on Lake Rotomahana. Allow 1 to 2 hours for the valley walk, depending on how much gazing you do. If you take the cruise, allow up to another hour. Entrance to the valley costs NZ$10.50 (US$7.35) for adults, NZ$4 (US$2.80) for children, and NZ$25 (US$17.50) for a family. The valley/cruise package is NZ$28.50 for an adult, NZ$7 per child, and NZ$62 for a family. The valley is open 8:30am to 5pm. The first cruise departs at 9:25am; the last one leaves at 3:40pm.

Not as well known perhaps as Waimangu, the **Waiotapu Thermal Wonderland** (P.O. Box 1992, Rotorua; ☎ 07/366-6333), is 29km (18 miles) south of Rotorua and about 10km (6.2 miles) beyond the turn-off for Waimangu on Highway 5. This is a colorful thermal area, sporting hues of yellow, gold, ochre, salmon, orange, and green. It also boasts the largest mud pool in the Southern Hemisphere (you only see about a third of it) and the **Lady Knox Geyser,** which spouts off at 10:15am every day when it's "fed" soap. Some of the highlights include the Champagne Pool, complete with bubbles and fizz; the Artist's Palette, which changes constantly; the Opal Pool, which has a vibrant color; the Terraces, where you'll feel as if you're walking on water; and the Maori Sacred Track—all well marked on the map you're given upon arrival. This is a special place—allow time to enjoy it—at least an hour. It's open daily from 8:30am to 4:30pm (longer in summer); admission is NZ$9.50 (US$6.65) for adults, NZ$3.50 (US$2.45) for children, and NZ$24 (US$18.80) for a family. A snack bar and souvenir shop are on the premises.

Hell's Gate (P.O. Box 2152, Rotorua; ☎ 07/345-3151) is situated 15km (9.3 miles) east of Rotorua on Highway 30. If you're driving from Rotorua to Whakatane, stop here en route and allow an hour to look at the boiling springs, mud holes, and sulphur vents. Admission is NZ$10 (US$7) for adults, NZ$5 (US$3.50) for children, and NZ$25 (US$17.50) for a family. It's open 8:30am to 5pm daily.

ORGANIZED TOURS & CRUISES

Carey's Sightseeing, P.O. Box 402, Rotorua (☎ 07/347-1197, fax 07/347-1199), operates a wide variety of half- and full-day excursions. Coaches depart from all accommodations and the Visitors Information Centre. The 4-hour **Geothermal Wonderland Tour** includes Waiotapu and Waimangu (described above) and costs NZ$55

(US$38.50) for adults, NZ$28 (US$19.60) for a child, and NZ$150 (US$105) for a family and includes admissions. The full-day **Waimangu Round Trip** is the best known and most comprehensive—you'll be exhausted at the end of the day, but it's worth it. The trip includes the Waimangu Volcanic Valley, a cruise on Lake Rotomahana, a bushwalk to Lake Tarawera, a cruise on Lake Tarawera, a visit to the Buried Village, a scenic drive through the Green and Blue lakes, a walk in the Redwood Grove, and a soak at the Polynesian Spa. Needless to say, you'll want to wear comfortable walking shoes. Buses leave from various hotels at various times or from the Visitors Information Centre at 8:30am; you'll return at 5:15pm. The fare is NZ$140 (US$98) for adults and NZ$80 (US$56) for children, which includes all admissions, two cruises, and lunch. These tours and a dozen or so others operate daily. Remember, Frommer's readers receive a 10% discount for "direct bookings" on all Carey's tours.

Mt. Tarawera 4WD Tours (P.O. Box 5157, Rotorua, ☎ **07/348-2814,** fax 07/348-6470), offers a half-day guided tour to the summit of Mt. Tarawera, where you spend 2 hours on the mountain, walk down into the crater, and enjoy magnificent views. The cost is NZ$65 (US$45.50) for adults, NZ$35 (US$24.50) per child, and NZ$180 (US$126)for a family.

The *Lakeland Queen* is a paddle steamer that cruises around Lake Rotorua. A ride will give you a different perspective of the city and a chance to see Mokoia Island, famous for the oft-told story of legendary Maori lovers Hinemoa and Tutanekai. Various trips offer morning or afternoon tea, lunch, and dinner. The boat is fully licensed. The morning tea cruise departs at 9:50am. The luncheon buffet cruise (NZ$25/US$16.25) leaves at 12:30pm, and the dinner buffet cruise (NZ$42.50/US$27.65), including live entertainment, starts at 6 and 8pm. Book at the office on the lakefront (☎ **07/348-6634**). American Express, Diners Club, MasterCard, and Visa are accepted.

OUTDOOR ACTIVITIES

BOATING   In addition to cruises on the *Lakeland Queen*, Rotorua offers jetboating. If this interests you, contact **Aorangi Jet** (☎ **07/347-0100**). Thrill rides cost NZ$20 (US$14) for 15 minutes. On the lakefront, you can also hire kayaks, paddle boats, speed boats, and bumper boats. Call **Lakefront Boat Hire** (☎ **025/813-209**). A half-dozen operators in the area offer rafting on the Kaituna River and other rivers. The 7-meter waterfall on the Kaituna is supposedly the world's highest commercially rafted waterfall. Call **River Rats** (☎ **07/347-6049**) for a run-down on the prices of their various trips.

FISHING   The Rotorua District is one of the best places in the country for trout fishing—in all, the area boasts 11 fishable lakes. Lakes Rotorua and Okareka are open year round. You can fish in the others only from October 1 through June 30. Keep in mind that this district sells their own licenses. The one you buy for the rest of the country won't permit you to fish here. The visitor center can recommend guides, which cost an average of NZ$70 (US$49) per hour. (Maybe you'd rather just look at the trout at Rainbow Springs or Paradise Valley Springs.)

This is hardly a budget activity, but if you've been waiting to splurge on fishing, you might like to go on a fishing/hunting excursion via helicopter. KiwiKopters (☎ **07/345-5459,** fax 07/345-5460), is run by a very nice Maori man Glen Hemopo and his son Clive.

GOLF   There's a nine-hole course in **Government Gardens,** right in the middle of Rotorua. It costs NZ$6.50 (US$4.55) to play. Serious golfers, however, will probably prefer the **Arikikapakapa Course** at the Rotorua Golf Club

(☎ **07/348-4051**), which costs NZ$40 (US$28). The **Springfield Golf Club** (☎ **07/348-2748**) is also popular.

SWIMMING   There's a 50-meter outdoor pool and two indoor pools adjacent to Kuirau Park near the city center. The **Aquatic Centre** (☎ **07/348-4199**) is open daily 6am to 9pm. Adults pay NZ$2.50 (US$1.75); children are charged NZ$1.20 (US$.84).

WALKING   The Department of Conservation operates a **Map & Track Shop** in the Tourism Rotorua Centre on Fenton Street (☎ and fax **07/349-1845**). This is the best source of information on area walks.

Among the favorite rambles in this area are the **Motutara Walkway,** a nature walk along the lakefront with great views and an opportunity to watch the black swans skim across the lake.

My personal favorites are the various treks in **Whakarewarewa State Forest Park** on the southeastern edge of the city. The Redwood Grove (dedicated to the men of New Zealand's Forest Service who gave their lives in both world wars), off Long Mile Road, has trails of varying lengths. Pick up a color-coded tramping map at the Park Information Centre (☎ **07/346-2082**) on Long Mile Road. The center has a helpful staff and interesting displays, and sells a variety of woodcrafts for gifts and souvenirs. It's open Monday through Friday from 8:30am to 5pm; Saturday, Sunday, and holidays from 10am to 4pm. Admission is free, of course, but I've actually heard of slick tour guides charging people to roam here. There are also mountain-biking and horse-riding tracks in the park.

Between Kaituna River Bridge and Okere Falls Store, 21km (13 miles) from Rotorua off State Highway 33, you'll find **Okere Falls Track.** This is an easy track—only 1.2km (³/₄ mile) each way. Along the way, you can view Okere Falls and the Kaituna River. You can fish in the Trout Pool here year round. If you do this walk, leave nothing in your car, for safety reasons.

WINDSURFING   Lake Rotorua is one of the best places in the country to windsurf and **Rotorua Windsurf School,** 12 Willow Ave., Hannah's Bay, Rotorua (☎ **07/345-5327**), can get you started. They offer a "Basic Beginners Course" for NZ$190 (US$133); or if you know what you're doing, you can rent a board for NZ$25 (US$17.50) an hour.

SHOPPING

I've already mentioned the shop out at the Agrodome, and you'll find other good shops at Rainbow Springs and Rainbow Farm—in addition to the shopping at the Maori Arts and Crafts Institute. The shop in the Tourism Rotorua complex is another good area.

You might also want to browse through **Penny's Souvenirs,** at the corner of Hinemoa and Hinemaru streets (☎ **07/348-5787**), opposite the Millenium Hotel, for a selection of carvings, greenstone and paua items, sheepskins, and general souvenirs, as well as T-shirts. Open daily from 8:30am to 6:30pm.

If you'd like to see how greenstone is transformed into jewelry and carvings, stop by the **Jade Factory and Gift Centre,** 170 Fenton St. at Eruera St. (☎ **07/349-3968**, fax 07/349-0668). Visitors are welcome to watch—ask for a free tour if you're really interested. Expatriate Yank John Sheehan won't pay a commission to tour guides, so the prices are fair and a good value. Open daily from 9am to 11pm. American Express, MasterCard, and Visa are accepted.

McLeods Booksellers, 91 Hinemoa St. (☎ **07/348-5388**), is the area's best bookshop. They are open Monday through Friday from 9am to 5pm and Saturday from 9am to 3pm, and accept American Express, MasterCard, and Visa.

AFFORDABLE ACCOMMODATIONS

Rotorua is replete with accommodations in all shapes, sizes, and prices, so it's safe to arrive without prior bookings and drive along Fenton Street, where moteliers post their rates outside. The only time you won't find a bed is during the popular school holidays and at Easter.

The prices listed below include the 12.5% GST.

IN ROTORUA

Campgrounds & Cabins

The **Holdens Bay Holiday Park,** 21 Robinson Ave., Holdens Bay (P.O. Box 9), Rotorua (☎ and fax **07/345-9925**), only 6km (3¹/₂ miles) from Rotorua, has extensive grounds with tent and caravan sites, tourist cabins (bring your own linens and blankets), and modern tourist apartments and motel rooms (just bring yourself), as well as a swimming pool, volleyball court, hot spa pools, a store, children's play area, laundry facilities, TVs for rent, a barbecue, car wash, and games room. Rates are NZ$10 (US$7) per person for tent and caravan sites, NZ$25 (US$17.50) double for standard cabins, NZ$36 (US$25.20) double for tourist cabins, NZ$55 to $60 (US$38.50 to $42) for tourist flats for two people, and NZ$70 to $75 (US$49 to $52.50) motel units for two people, all including the 12.5% GST.

Besides being secluded, right on the lake, and only a little over a mile from downtown Rotorua, the **Lakeside Thermal Holiday Park,** 54 Whittaker Rd., Rotorua (☎ and fax **07/348-1693**), has an abundance of trees, swings and a trampoline; a games and TV room; mineral spas, baths, and pool; showers; laundry; communal kitchen; natural steam cooker, canoes; and store. Swimming, boating, fishing, and water-skiing are all at your doorstep. All units have cooking facilities, and you supply linen and blankets. Tent and van sites are NZ$10 (US$7) per person; cabins, NZ$40 (US$28) for two; tourist flats NZ$50 (US$35) for two; and lakeside tourist flats NZ$60 (US$42) for two. MasterCard and Visa are accepted. The gate to the property closes at 11pm for security reasons.

Super-Cheap Sleeps

Bel Aire Motel

257 Fenton St., Rotorua. ☎ and fax **07/348-6076**. 8 units (all with bathrm). TV TEL. NZ$60 (US$42) unit for 2, NZ$12 (US$8.40) extra person. AE, DC, MC, V. The owners will pick up and deliver guests to the airport or bus terminal.

A reader from Australia wrote to tell me about the Bel Aire, and his recommendation certainly stood the test of close inspection. This centrally located small motel offers spotless, recently renovated one- and two-bedroom units that sleep two to seven people, each with a full kitchen, geothermal heating, a radio, and video. There's a hot mineral pool, as well as a guest laundry and drying room, and owner/operators Selwyn and Lynne Mounsey can provide breakfast on request.

Boulevard Motel

Fenton and Seddon sts., Rotorua. ☎ **07/348-2074**. Fax 07/348-2072. 30 rms (all with bathrm). TV TEL. NZ$65 (US$45.50) standard unit for 2; NZ$84 (US$58.80) unit with spa pool for 2. AE, BC, DC, JCB, MC, V.

The Boulevard is set on 2 acres of landscaped grounds and is family-owned and -operated by the Bradshaws. The two-story, balconied white motel in the town center also has a restaurant on the premises. The units—accommodating one to nine people—have a separate sitting area and one to three bedrooms; they're beautifully furnished and have complete kitchens and central heating. There are serviced units (sleeping two), which are smaller and have tea-making facilities and a fridge. Some units have water beds; others have spa pools. The lovely grounds are set about with garden furniture and hold a multitude of recreational facilities: a putting green, a swimming pool, four spa baths, swirl pools, sauna, and games room. There's a laundry, dryer, and steam iron for guest use. Readers have commented on the good restaurant.

Cactus Jack

54 Haupapa St. (just off Tutanekai St.), Rotorua. ☎ and fax **07/348-3121.** 80 beds in 37 rms (no rooms with bathrm). NZ$16.50–$18.50 (US$11.60–$13) per person double; NZ$14.50–$15.50 (US$10.20–$10.90) dorm bed. MC, V.

This lodge in the center of town offers budget, hostel-type accommodations. There are single, twin, and double cabins, all heated, plus single, twin, and double rooms. Linen and blankets are available for a small fee. All cabins and rooms are carpeted, with mirrors and dressers. The facilities are all communal: a fully equipped modern kitchen, large dining or common room (with a brilliant mural of the area), hot thermal pool, TV lounge, and games room.

YHA Hostel

Eruera and Hinemaru sts., Rotorua. ☎ **07/347-6810.** Fax 07/349-1426. 68 beds (1 with bathrm). NZ$19 (US$13.30) per person double; NZ$15 (US$10.50) dorm bed; NZ$60 (US$42) family room with bathrm. NZ$4 (US$2.60) extra for nonmembers. BC, JCB, MC, V.

This hostel is right in town and just about the best buy in Rotorua. It's a large, comfortable building, accommodating 68 people in 19 rooms, and there are family rooms too. There's a well-equipped kitchen, a provisions shop, laundry facilities and irons, a TV lounge, a recreation room, and a thermal pool.

For a Few Extra Bucks

Acacia Lodge Motel

40 Victoria St., Rotorua. ☎ **07/348-7089.** Fax 07/346-1104. 18 rms (all with bathrm), 8 suites. TV TEL. NZ$75 (US$52.50) double; NZ$82 (US$57.40) suite. Discount of 10% on stays of 3 nights or more. AE, BC, DC, MC, V. Courtesy-car service to/from the airport and bus station.

At this pretty motel, Lynley Turnbull offers brick rooms with large picture windows and colorful flower boxes. Each has full kitchen facilities, Sky TV, a radio, and central heat; some have water beds, and there are some family units. Other amenities include a sauna, mineral pools, a nice play area, and laundry facilities. The motel is located near the city center and all of the big attractions, and the host is happy to arrange tours for her guests.

Eaton Hall

39 Hinemaru St., Rotorua. ☎ and fax **07/347-0366.** 8 rms (1 with bathrm). NZ$72 (US$50.40) double without bathrm; NZ$80 (US$56) double with bathrm; NZ$105 (US$74) triple. Rates include cooked breakfast. AE, JCB, MC, V.

Colin and Maureen Brown have filled this two-story guest house in the center of town with comfortable furnishings (some antiques), old china, and lots of bric-a-brac. All the bedrooms have sinks. There's a cozy TV lounge, with coffee and tea available. An added bonus: The hosts, as ticket agents, can organize and sell tickets for sightseeing attractions, fishing trips, concerts, and sightseeing flights. Colin will take guests on tours at reasonable rates.

Tresco International Guest House

3 Toko St., Rotorua. ☎ and fax **07/348-9611.** 7 rms (none with bathrm). NZ$75 (US$52.50) double; NZ$95 (US$67) triple. Rates include breakfast. MC, V. Courtesy car available.

Barrie Fenton and Gay Scott-Fenton own and operate this guest house with attractive, sparkling-clean rooms that feature hot and cold running water and tea- and coffeemaking facilities. The guest house is only 1 block from the city center, and there's a homey, happy air about the place. In addition to off-street parking, there's a guest laundry, a TV lounge, and a mineral plunge pool. If you stay here, your day will start with a substantial continental or cooked breakfast.

Ledwich Lodge

12–14 Lake Rd. (P.O. Box 2370), Rotorua. ☎ **0800/730-049** in New Zealand, or 07/347-0049. Fax 07/347-0048. E-mail bjhughes@iconz.co.nz. 14 units (all with bathrm). TV TEL. NZ$100 (US$70) double. Additional person NZ$15 (US$10.50) extra. AE, BC, DC, JCB, MC, V.

This motel is small, with a facade that doesn't draw much attention to itself. It's within walking distance of everything in town and has exceptionally pretty units with bay windows, bright tropical-print curtains, large bathrooms with spa pools, queen-size beds covered with feather duvets, full kitchens, thermal heating, and lots of wood trim. In addition, there's a small thermally heated pool and a picnic area, and guests have access to a steam box for hangi-style cooking; breakfast is available. There are also two-bedroom units, as well as two units for the disabled.

Worth a Splurge

✪ Princes Gate Hotel

1 Arawa St. (P.O. Box 112), Rotorua. ☎ **07/348-1179.** Fax 07/348-6215. 52 rms and apartments (all with bathrm). MINIBAR TV TEL. NZ$135 (US$95) room; NZ$200 (US$140) apartment. Complimentary continental breakfast for guests paying the quoted rates who have *Frommer's New Zealand from $50 a Day.* AE, BC, DC, MC, V.

This hotel was constructed in Waihi (95 miles to the north) in 1897 and was a popular spot there until 1909, when the townspeople voted for prohibition and shut down all the pubs. The building sat idle until 1919, when it was dismantled and transported by bullock cart to its present location. Today it's an attractive boutique hotel offering an old-world atmosphere, comfortable accommodations, friendly service, and a central location adjacent to the Government Gardens. Facilities include a guest laundry, health complex, thermal baths, tennis court, sauna, plunge pool, bike rental, and a restaurant, bar, and cafe with indoor/outdoor seating. A convention center is under construction across the street. No-smoking rooms are available, and all rooms have tea- and coffeemaking facilities and hair dryers. Room service is available 18 hours a day. Brett Marvelly is a great host.

✪ Wylie Court Motor Lodge

345 Fenton St., Rotorua. ☎ **0800/100-879** in New Zealand, or 07/347-7879. Fax 07/346-1494. 36 units (all with bathrm). MINIBAR TV TEL. NZ$141 (US$98.70) double. Flag international discounts available. AE, BC, CB, DC, MC, V. Courtesy car to/from the airport.

One of Rotorua's most attractive motels, Wylie Court is set in 2 1/2 landscaped acres on the outskirts of town. The two-story units are decorated in soft colors and have modern, comfortable furnishings. Each unit has a full living room with two convertible sofa beds, full kitchen, and bath on the ground floor; upstairs there's a mezzanine bedroom with a double bed (some have water beds). Each will sleep as many as four in comfort. What wins my heart completely, however, is the pretty roofed and fenced-in patio out back of each unit, with its own private heated plunge pool where you can soak to your heart's content whether or not there's a bathing suit in your luggage—sheer luxury!

Barry and Glen Johnston, their son, Tony, and his wife, Sharon, have provided loads of amenities: a heated swimming pool, a children's playground, a thermal pool, a guest laundry, in-room video, the daily newspaper delivery, and a cooked or continental breakfast at a small additional charge. The property is highly recommended by readers both for its facilities and its genial hosts, but some folks have written to

Readers Recommend

Pohuto Lodge, 3 Meade St., Rotorua. ☎ **07/346-1499.** Fax 07/346-1451. *"Allison and Terry Lawton are a delightful couple, very helpful and friendly. We had a beautiful 6-week-old unit, 2 floors, 2 bathrooms, 2 TVs, absolutely spotless, in a lovely location opposite the golf course. Their rate is NZ$85 (US$59.50) double. I really can't speak highly enough of it."*

—Mr. & Mrs. R. Griffiths, Sarnia, Ontario, Canada.

say it's not appropriate for seniors because the bathroom and bedroom are on different levels.

JUST OUTSIDE ROTORUA

✪ Namaste Point

187 Te Akau Road (R.D.4), Rotorua 3221. ☎ **07/362-4804** or 025/971-092. Fax 07/362-4060. 3 units (all with bathrm). TV. NZ$110 (US$77) double, NZ$140 (US$98) for 4. Rates include continental breakfast ingredients. MC, V.

Host Gillian Marks looked back to her days as a volunteer in a refugee camp in Nepal when naming this slice of heaven. *Namaste* literally means "I salute the light within you." Her home and three guest quarters are located 20 minutes outside of Rotorua in a residential neighborhood right on the edge of Lake Rotoiti. Everything here is modern; each self-contained unit has a lounge with two loveseats (that convert into single beds), table and chairs, TV, fully-equipped kitchenette (breakfast ingredients are provided), and skylight. Each bedroom has a lovely firm king or queen bed, TV, heater, and nice bathroom with toiletries and assorted helpful items. (I particularly appreciated the anti-itch wipes, which I needed for my mosquito bites.) A Canadian canoe, rowing dinghy, paddle boat, and spa pool are available for guests' use. The black swans that live on the lake often swim by Namaste's private dock, and fishing vessels will pick you up here if you'd like to try your luck catching a trout. Gillian is a fascinating person—in addition to running this wonderful place, she breeds and trains Lhasa Apso dogs. Her champions have been shown all over the U.S. and New Zealand. Namaste Point is a great honeymoon spot.

✪ Te Ana Farm

Poutakataka Rd., Ngakuru (R.D. 1), Rotorua. ☎ and fax **07/333-2720.** Web site nz.com/webnz/bbnz/teana.htm. 3 rms (2 with bathrm). NZ$90 (US$63) double. 3-course dinner with glass of wine NZ$30 (US$21). Rates include cooked breakfast. No credit cards.

After more than a dozen trips to new Zealand, a few places stand out in my mind as being really exemplary, and Te Ana is one of them. Heather and Brian Oberer have been welcoming guests to their 569-acre dairy, beef, sheep, goat, and deer farm for more than 13 years, and yet they meet each new face with enthusiasm and genuine warmth. There are two guest bedrooms in the house, adjacent to the guest lounge where there are coffee- and tea-making facilities, a TV, and plenty of reading material. The room with twin beds has a large bathroom; the queen-size room shares the hosts' bathroom. A cottage in the garden offers another two bedrooms and a bathroom. Heather's gourmet meals are legendary: Dinner might start with an appetizer of salmon mousse, followed by a main course of chicken and apricots in puff pastry accompanied by fresh veggies from the garden. If you're lucky, she'll make pavlova for dessert. Te Ana is situated in a picturesque valley 32km (20 miles) south of Rotorua. It's bounded by Lake Ohakuri, and the Oberers make a canoe and fishing rod available for those who want them. Brian takes folks on four-wheel-drive farm tours and for walks across the property. Guests are also welcome to watch their 145 cows being milked. There's no smoking in the house. When fully booked, Heather refers guests to friends in the area. Reader Patricia Downing of Los Angeles, California, says "I was a bit apprehensive driving out there (kind of like a blind date), but was immediately put at ease upon arrival. Thank you for this suggestion."

GREAT DEALS ON DINING

For those times when "eating in" is a good idea either for budget or energy's sake (at the end of a long sightseeing day), you have two good Rotorua alternatives. If you've a yen for fresh New Zealand specialties like marinated mussels, oysters, clams, or cooked lamb, take yourself over to **Fenwick's Delicatessen** (☎ 07/347-0777), next to the post office in Hinemoa Street. It's chock-full of ready-to-eat goodies, as well as a wide selection of cheeses, hot barbecued rotisserie chicken, salads, sweets, and a host of specialty goods, all at very good prices. Hours are 8am to 5:30pm Monday through Thursday, until 6pm on Friday, until 1pm on Saturday; closed Sunday. MasterCard and Visa are accepted.

Chez Suzanne Coffee Shop, 61 Hinemoa St. (☎ 07/348-6495), next to the *Daily Post* building, is a good choice for a quick, cheap lunch. The selection of pastries and sandwiches is good. Beverages include cappuccino, espresso, and hot chocolate. This is a small place, with a few booths, a counter, and a few wooden tables. Filled croissants are NZ$2.50 (US$1.75) and sandwiches run NZ$1.30 to NZ$3 (US 91¢ to $2.10). It's open Monday through Friday from 8am to 5pm and Saturday from 9am to 2pm; closed some Saturdays. No credit cards.

On the theory that you can drop in for a Big Mac almost anywhere in the world, I don't normally send readers to **McDonald's.** In Rotorua, however, I recommend that you go by the one on the corner of Fenton and Amohau streets to view the exquisite wall-size carvings done by the Maori Arts and Crafts Institute. Kudos to McDonald's for this recognition of indigenous culture.

MODERATELY PRICED OPTIONS

✪ Freos
At the lake end of Tutanekai St. ☎ **07/346-0976.** Fax 07/346-0976. Reservations recommended. Main courses NZ$9.90–$22 (US$6.93–$15.40). AE, BC, DC, MC, V. Daily 10am–11pm. MODERN NEW ZEALAND.

The ultra-plain decor of this modern cafe clashes with the lively and delicious food served here. You might like a Greek or Caesar salad, a venison or satay burger, paella, lamb or vegetable curry, or a hearty focaccia sandwich. They also offer three kinds of pasta and three steaks. A children's menu is available. It's fully licensed or you can BYO. If you'd like to bring your own, Arawa Wines and Spirits is right across the street.

✪ Sirocco
86 Eruera St., across from the multiplex cinema. ☎ **07/347-3388.** Reservations not accepted. Main courses NZ$11.50–$13.95 (US$8.10–$9.77). AE, BC, DC, MC, V. Daily 11am–12:30am (later Fri–Sat). MEDITERRANEAN.

Sirocco means a hot, dry wind—the kind found in the Mediterranean, where most of the dishes served in this cozy coffee bar/cafe originate. This is really an old house that's been "done up" by the current owners. The bar is made of used brick, and there's a wooden mantel over the fireplace. Sample "entrees" (which I hope you realize by now are what Americans call appetizers) include warm smoked mussels with sun-dried tomato, or focaccia bread with ham, cheese, avocado, and tomato. Sample main courses include vegetarian ravioli, thin-cut scotch filet, and cotoleta Milano (lamb cutlet, tomato, and olive tapenade). It's fully licensed or you can bring your own.

✪ Zanelli's Italian Cafe

23 Amohia St. ☎ **07/348-4908.** Reservations recommended. Main courses NZ$15–$20 (US$10.50–$14). AE, BC, DC, MC, V. Winter Mon–Fri 11:30am–2pm and Mon–Sat 6–10pm; summer Mon–Fri 11:30am–2pm and daily 6pm–midnight. ITALIAN.

Located in town, Zanelli's serves generous portions, and you can easily make do with an appetizer and salad. There's a whole chalkboard devoted to desserts. The atmosphere is lively, and three-quarters of the tables in this fully licensed restaurant are no-smoking. This is Rotorua's most authentic Italian fare.

WORTH A SPLURGE

Poppy's Villa Restaurant

4 Marguerita St., Rotorua. ☎ **07/347-1700.** Fax 07/347-1700. Reservations recommended. Main courses NZ$17–$27 (US$11.90–$18.90). AE, DC, MC, V. Daily 6–10pm. NEW ZEALAND.

Located in an Edwardian villa at the south end of the city, Poppy's has won several awards from the New Zealand Beef and Lamb Marketing Bureau in recent years. The savvy diner will pick one of these award-winning dishes, which include beef tournedos (grain-fed filet served with a wild mushroom sauce and a fig and port juslie) and lamb racks Canterbury (baby racks of lamb, honey, mustard, and rosemary glazed, roasted pink and laid on a mosaic of minted kiwifruit and Cumberland sauce). In addition to beef and lamb they offer chicken and vegetarian dishes. The sophisticated ambience includes terra-cotta walls, green carpet, and green table cloths. It's fully licensed but you can bring your own. Thanks to Nancy H. Bennett of Moraga, California, for bringing Poppy's to my attention.

ROTORUA AFTER DARK

Check *Thermal Air* for dine-and-dance venues or special events, or plan on a Maori concert with or without a hangi dinner.

MAORI CONCERTS & HANGI FEASTS

Hangi (earth oven) cooking is traditional with the Maori in preparing their communal meal. A large pit is filled with a wood fire topped by stones; then when the stones are heated through, baskets of food are placed on top and covered with damp cloths. Earth is then shoveled over all to create a natural steam oven. After about 3 hours, dinner is unveiled, with intermingling flavors of the various foods lightly touched by wood smoke.

I shudder when I think that in previous editions of this book I suggested that readers attend one of the hangi dinners and concerts held in Rotorua hotels. These are still available, but they just don't compare with the experience of attending a hangi on a real marae (courtyard surrounding a Maori meetinghouse). If you want the most authentic evening, I recommend **Rotoiti Tours** (P.O. Box 862, Rotorua ☎ 07/ **348-8969,** fax 07/362-7187). They transfer guests to their marae on the shore of Lake Rotoiti. During the scenic 15-minute ride, passengers hear commentary and instructions on protocol for entering the sacred ground. Upon arrival, there's a spine-chilling *wero* (challenge). After the *powhiri* (formal welcome) and *hongi* (touching of noses), you're part of the family for the rest of the evening. You are then treated to a *haka* (war dance), singing of traditional songs, and poi ball twirling. Then it's on to the *wharekai* (dining area) to enjoy the hangi dinner. At the end of the evening you will have felt the warmth of the *whanau* (family) and gained an insight into the world of the Maori. The whole experience is like being at a family gathering—it's very real—not the least bit slick. The evening costs NZ$49 (US$34.30) for adults, children 6 to 12 are half price, and children under 5 are free.

Another option is **Tamaki Tours** (P.O. Box 1492, Rotorua; ☎ **07/346-2823,** fax 07/346-2823), also a Maori-run business. They collect their guests from hotels and motels and transfer them to Te Tawa Ngahiri Pa, a purpose-built re-creation of a Maori village located in a native tawa forest. Guests are free to walk around the village and see musical instruments being played, weaving, carving, food source demonstrations and cooking, a *wharenui* (meeting house), Maori medicines being mixed, a *hongi* (greeting), and a *haka* (war dance) being performed. A traditional hangi dinner of native foods is served before the guests are driven back to their lodgings. The cost is NZ$52 (US$36.40) for adults, half price for children 5 to 12. In my opinion, this is a compromise between a truly authentic hangi on a real marae and a totally phony one in a hotel. It all depends on what you want. Tamaki Tours has won several awards for this hangi/concert experience.

The ✪ **Tamatekapua meetinghouse** in Ohinemutu (☎ **07/349-3949**) offers Maori concerts in an authentic setting nightly at 8pm. The singing group was founded by the elders of the tribe to help their young people learn to sing and perform the traditional songs. The performers are mostly 13 to 18 years old; the younger ones stand at the back and work their way forward over the years. Tickets are NZ$15 (US$10.50) for adults, NZ$5 (US$3.50) for children 14 and under, and the money goes for the upkeep of the meetinghouse and to transport the youth abroad for singing engagements and festivals. If you don't have a car, call and ask about the courtesy van. Arrive early and sit down in front or you may have trouble hearing.

EN ROUTE TO TAUPO

The drive to Taupo is a short 84km (52 miles) over excellent roads.

On the shores of Lake Ohakui lies **Orakei Korako Geyserland** (between Rotorua and Taupo—45 minutes south of Rotorua, 25 minutes north of Taupo—take Tutukau Rd. from State Highway 1). The natural beauty of this thermal area—which includes geysers, boiling mud pools, hot springs, and three colored silica terraces—is remarkable. Access is by jetboat, which runs continuously between 8am and 4:30pm during daylight savings (to 4pm in winter). The cost is NZ$12.50/ US$8.80, which includes the boat ride.

Eight kilometers (5 miles) before you reach Taupo, look for the steamy **Wairakei Geothermal Power Station,** which harnesses all that underground energy to furnish electrical power (see chapter 9 for more information).

EN ROUTE TO GISBORNE

There are two ways of getting to Gisborne from Rotorua. You can either drive along the Bay of Plenty past Whakatane to Opotiki and then cut through the Waioweka Gorge (on Highway 2) or you can allow more time and follow the East Cape Road (Highway 35), which takes in the beautiful scenery on the easternmost point of New Zealand.

WHAKATANE

Highway 2 bypasses Whakatane's town center, so if you want to stop at the **Visitors Information Centre** on Boon Street (P.O. Box 307; ☎ and fax **07/308-6058;** e-mail whavin@nzhost.co.nz), you'll have to take a detour. Here, you can get details on some of the more interesting sights in the town and nearby. This is the legendary settling place of Toi (see "A Look Back," in chapter 2) on his search for his grandson, Whatonga, and the earthworks out on the road to Ohope are traditionally held to be those of this *pa*. It is also the landing place of the great Mataatua canoe, part of the Hawaiki migration fleet. A model of that canoe can be seen next to the imposing rock arch known as **Pohaturoa Rock** (once part of a sacred Maori cave and now a memorial to those who died in World War I). On Mataatua Street, right in the center of town, you'll see the beautiful **Wairere Waterfall.** Don't miss seeing the beach at **Ohope,** and consider a closer look at ✪ **White Island,** the active volcano 32 miles offshore.

OPOTIKI

Some 60 km (37 miles) east of Whakatane, Highway 2 brings you to Opotiki and State Highway 35, known as the East Cape Road.

At the **Opotiki Visitor Information Centre,** corner of St. Johns and Elliott streets (P.O. Box 44, Opotiki; ☎ **07/315-8484,** fax 07/315-6102, e-mail opovin@nzhost. co.nz), you can pick up a copy of their free holiday guide "Opotiki and East Cape" and other informative brochures.

Opotiki was once a large Maori settlement, but today it's best known for its **Church of St. Stephen the Martyr,** scene of the particularly brutal murder of German Lutheran missionary Carl Sylvius Volkner in 1865. Bloodstained relics of that grim event are on exhibit in the church.

At this point, you must decide whether to continue on Highway 2 via the Waioweka Gorge or to travel the East Cape Road (State Highway 35) to Gisborne. The following sections "The East Cape Road" and "The Short Route from Opotiki to Gisborne" may help you decide which route to take.

THE EAST CAPE ROAD

The ✪ **East Cape Road** hugs the coastline for most of its 343km (213-mile) route up around New Zealand's most easterly point and down to Gisborne on Poverty Bay. The drive—breathtaking in any season—is a heart-stopper during Christmas, when hundreds of pohutukawa trees burst into brilliant scarlet blooms along the cliffs overlooking the sea. All along, you'll find deserted beaches, sea views, and native bush, which combine to make this one of New Zealand's finest scenic drives. This is an area with a predominantly Maori population, and most of the small villages and towns you'll pass through either still are, or once were, Maori centers. Sadly, some of the most exquisite Maori carvings from the area have been removed: The Auckland Museum's Te Toki-a-Tapiri war canoe and the Museum of New Zealand's Te Hau-ki-Turanga meetinghouse and Nuku te Whatewha storehouse all came from this region. There are, however, still outstanding examples of the art to be seen along the drive.

You should be aware while you're in this area that in recent years the East Cape has become a popular spot for motorcycle gangs. Should you happen upon them, just use common sense and steer clear.

At **Te Kaha,** the Tu Kaihi meetinghouse in the marae has an elaborately carved lintel you'll be welcome to view *if you ask permission before entering the marae.* A little farther along, **Waihau Bay** has good views across Cape Runaway (so named by Captain Cook as he watched Maori canoes "run away" when shots were fired over their heads), as well as very good beaches. **Whangaparaoa** is where the great migration canoe *Tainui* landed—its captain's wife is credited with bringing the kumara to New Zealand.

Hicks Bay—not quite midway—has marvelous views and one of the finest carved meetinghouses on the East Cape. The community's name comes from one of Captain Cook's officers, who first sighted it, and it was the site of a tragic Maori massacre in which one European was killed and eaten on his wedding night (after which complaints were registered that he was too tough and stringy to be tasty!). Turn left at the general store to reach the **Tuwhakairiora meetinghouse,** whose carvings were done in 1872. It is dedicated to local members of the Ngati Porou tribe who died in overseas wars, and its unique rafter design (found only in this region) is symbolic of the honor of death in battle for the warrior.

A little farther along, the road descends to sea level to follow the narrow bay to where the little town of **Te Araroa** nestles under the cliffs. Thirteen miles east of Te Araroa, along an all-weather road, stands the **East Cape Lighthouse,** in an isolated location. There has been a light here since 1906. The track to the lighthouse must be covered by foot, and it leads up some 600 steps—perhaps a look from afar will suffice. Sunrise is lovely here, but you won't be alone if you choose this spot to see the sun rise on the new millenium. Because of New Zealand's proximity to the International Date Line, the East Cape will be the first spot on the North Island to see the dawn on January 1, 2000.

One of New Zealand's most ornate Maori churches is the ❂ **Tikitiki Church,** a memorial to Maori soldiers who died in World War I. The carved panels and rafter patterns depict Ngati Porou tribal history, and two war-hero brothers are featured in the east window. Closer to Gisborne, you can view another beautifully carved modern meetinghouse near the wharf at **Tokomaru Bay.** This is where a brave band of women, two warriors, and three whalers successfully defended a headland *pa* from attack by a large enemy force. **Anaura Bay,** just 69km (43 miles) from Gisborne, was Captain Cook's landing place on his second New Zealand voyage. The *Endeavour* hung around for 2 days trying to get water casks beyond the surf before heading south for a better watering place. **Waioeka,** 28km (17 miles) away from Gisborne, is a good spot to fill up the gas tank (petrol stations are few and far between in these parts). And Gisborne, of course, was the place Captain Cook *first* sighted the New Zealand mainland (for more information, see chapter 8).

THE SHORT ROUTE FROM OPOTIKI TO GISBORNE

For those who simply wish to reach Gisborne from the Bay of Plenty in the least amount of time, there's a shorter, faster way to get there than around the East Cape. Highway 2 is a pleasant, 3-hour drive on a winding road through green farmlands, native bush, along rushing mountain rivers, and through the **Waioeka Gorge**— not a bad drive, mind you, but nothing to compare with the East Cape. **Matawai,** 76km (47 miles) from Opotiki, is a good place to break the trip. The rural settlement has an historic pub, a petrol station, and a cafe.

8 Gisborne & Hawkes Bay

The most isolated city in the country, Gisborne is located on the east coast of the North Island. It lies just south of the sparsely populated East Cape, and is separated by mountain ranges from both the Bay of Plenty and Hawkes Bay. Gisborne is the center of a rich hill-country farming area and enjoys a mild, sunny climate. It is also the port city of Poverty Bay and in recent years has become known for producing great white wines.

Because of its closeness to the International Date Line, Gisborne (pop. 31,000) is judged to be the most easterly city in the world (the Chatham Islands are actually the most easterly place) and the first to see the sun's rays each morning. It will be the birthplace of the Third Millennium, and the city is gearing up for the influx of people wanting to share this experience.

It's also the place where New Zealand's European history began. Capt. James Cook's *Endeavour* entered these waters in early October 1769, and it fell the lot of the surgeon's 12-year-old boy, Nicholas Young, to be the first to sight land—a fact that must have caused some consternation among the rest of the crew, since the good captain had promised a gallon of rum as a reward, two if the sighting should be at night. True to another promise, Captain Cook named the white bluffs at the southern end of the bay's wide entrance "Young Nick's Head." As for Young Nick, he is also celebrated by a statue at the mouth of the Turanganui River at Waikanae Beach. It was 2 days later, on October 9, 1769, that a party ventured forth from the ship, and after a series of misunderstandings with Maori over the next 2 days (during which one Maori was killed when the English thought he was trying to steal a beached longboat, another when he reached toward a sword, and four more when they resisted being taken aboard the *Endeavour* from their canoe), Cook found it impossible to gain Maori cooperation in gathering the fresh water and provisions he needed. He left in despair, writing in his journal that he was sailing "out of the bay, which I have named Poverty Bay because it afforded us not one thing we wanted."

One thing's for certain: Had Captain Cook gotten off on the right foot with the indigenous people, a name incorporating the word "*poverty*" would never have occurred to him. Gisborne is in fact the very center of one of New Zealand's most fertile areas. It's a garden land of vegetable farms and orchards bearing citrus fruits, grapes, and kiwifruit. Cattle, deer, and sheep farms prosper. The sunny climate, combined with beaches that offer ideal swimming, surfing, and fishing conditions, also make it a holiday resort that's becoming increasingly popular with Kiwis from all over the North Island.

Like Gisborne, the Hawkes Bay region—215km (133 miles) to the southwest— is known for fruit and wine. Captain Cook named the bay after Sir Edward Hawke, First Lord of the Admiralty at the time of Cook's 1769 voyage. This name has been retained for the region, but the bay itself, curving from the inner coast of the Mahia Peninsula, is Hawke Bay. Three adjacent communities comprise the Hawkes Bay region. Of these, Napier—the Art Deco Capital—is the largest; Havelock North, an easy 20-minute drive from Napier, is the most affluent; and Hastings is the least interesting.

1 Gisborne

293km (182 miles) SE of Rotorua; 298km (184 miles) SE of Tauranga

Gisborne retains its small-town atmosphere, in spite of being the commercial center for the surrounding farming areas. For visitors, the community offers great beaches, some significant historic sites, and a chance to taste great wines right where they're made. You won't find Gisborne on anyone's list of "must-see" places, but I definitely think it's worth a day or two if you've got the time.

ESSENTIALS
GETTING THERE & GETTING AROUND
BY PLANE   There are scheduled flights from all major New Zealand cities on both Air New Zealand and Ansett.

Note: Don't worry if you look out the window of the plane as you're about to land and see a railway line across the runway. It's a little out of the ordinary, but doesn't pose a problem—planes give way to the freight trains.

BY COACH (BUS)   InterCity offers daily bus service to Gisborne from Auckland and Rotorua.

City buses operate weekdays only, but they're more for commuters than travelers. Gisborne is better explored by car or taxi, not by foot or public transportation.

BY TAXI   For taxi service, call the **Gisborne Taxi Society** (☎ 06/867-2222).

VISITOR INFORMATION
The **Eastland and Gisborne District Information Centre** is located at 209 Grey St., across from the Pizza Hut (☎ 06/868-6139, fax 06/868-6138, Web site eastland.tourism.co.nz), e-mail gisvin@ nzhost.co.nz, where the friendly staff offers assistance to visitors. If you're lucky, expatriate Yank Margaret Mettner will be here when you are. The center is open in summer, daily from 7:30am to 7pm or later; in winter, daily from 7:30am to 5pm. Before you leave this area, check out the giant totem pole next door in **Alfred Cox Park.** The Canadian government presented it to New Zealand in 1969 to mark the Cook Bicentenary and to acknowledge the debt both countries owe that great explorer.

The **telephone area code** (STD) for Gisborne is **06**. *Note:* There's no place to cash travelers checks or foreign currency on weekends or holidays in Gisborne.

ORIENTATION
Gisborne is situated on the northern shore of Poverty Bay where the Waimata and Taruheru rivers come together to form the Turanganui. Riverside park areas abound.

The city center is compact, with Gladstone Road the main thoroughfare. The post office is at 74 Grey St. (☎ **06/867-8867**).

SPECIAL EVENTS

If early inquiries are any indication, **New Year's Eve, 1999** will see tens of thousands of people pouring into Gisborne. Folks from all over the world, it seems, want to be among the first to see the dawning of the new millennium. The ✪ **Gisborne 2000** festival will include concerts, fireworks, and a huge street party. There is even talk of bringing in cruise ships to house people; others talk of tent cities and tall ships in the harbor. Already, on Gladstone Road at Grey Street there is an electronic clock that is counting down the 1,000 days to midnight, December 31, 1999. You can get a printout that says "(your name) was here X-number of days before the dawning of the new millennium." For information on Gisborne 2000, contact **Events Gisborne,** P.O. Box 747, Gisborne (☎ **06/868-1568,** fax 06/868-1368).

The **Gisborne Opera Festival** is held every 3 years; the next one will be in 2000 and will include a week of opera and arts, together with Maori culture, wine trails, and garden visits. Contact Events Gisborne, P.O. Box 747, Gisborne (☎ **06/ 868-1568,** fax 06/868-1368) for more information.

EXPLORING GISBORNE: WHAT TO SEE & DO

To get a panoramic view of Poverty Bay, the city and its harbors and rivers, head for ✪ **Kaiti Hill Lookout.** It's signposted at the northern end of Gladstone Bridge, and you can drive all the way to a brick semicircular lookout point at the very edge of the hill. There's a statue of Captain Cook there that looks suspiciously like Napoleon (notice the hand in the jacket, so characteristic of "The Little Emperor") or a character from an Italian comic opera—for a better likeness of Cook go to the museum—looking out toward Young Nick's Head on the opposite side of the bay.

Author's note: In spite of the poor likeness of Captain Cook, I think this view point is a very special place. The last time I was here the sky and the water were bright blue and the statue of the English seaman seemed almost surreal against them. As I stood there I couldn't help wondering what he was thinking when he went ashore near here for the first time. Did he have a sense of his place in history? Did he know that one day nearly every schoolchild in the world would recognize his name? We all know what Neil Armstrong said when he stepped on the moon. What did James Cook say when he put his foot on this new world?

At the foot of Kaiti Hill, you'll pass one of New Zealand's largest Maori meeting-houses, ✪ **Poho-o-rawiri.** It's so large that the traditional construction of a single ridgepole supported by pillars had to be abandoned in favor of more modern methods. All its carvings (which are splendid) were done in Rotorua. You'll usually find the side door open; if not, look up the caretaker, who lives just next door.

Also at the bottom of Kaiti Hill, on Kaiti Beach Road, there's a memorial on the spot on which Captain Cook landed. This area is filled with historic *pa* sites in the hills behind Poverty Bay Flats—ask at the information center if any meetinghouses are open to the public.

The **Gisborne Museum & Arts Centre,** 18–22 Stout St. (☎ **06/867-3832**), has displays depicting Maori and European history along the East Coast, as well as geological and natural history, decorative arts, and maritime history exhibits. The Art Gallery has an ongoing program of changing art and craft exhibitions (local, national, and international). **Wyllie Cottage,** the oldest house still standing in Gisborne, built in 1872 and the **Star of Canada Maritime Museum** (the ill-fated *Star of Canada* struck rocks at Kaiti Beach in 1912) are on the museum grounds. The Museum

Complex is open from 10am to 4:30pm Monday through Friday, and 1:30 to 4pm Saturday, Sunday, and holidays; longer weekend hours during December and January; closed Christmas Day and Good Friday. Adults pay NZ$3.50 (US$2.45); children and students, NZ$1.50 (US$1.15); a family of 2 adults and up to 4 kids pays NZ$10 (US$7). Near the museum there's a good picnic spot and a rose garden—on the riverfront between Fitzherbert Street and the Gisborne Marina.

The **Eastwoodhill Arboretum,** 35km (22 miles) due west of Gisborne (☎ 06/863-9817, fax 06/863-9081), is the largest collection in Australasia of trees and plants native to the Northern Hemisphere. In spring/summer, daffodils mass yellow, magnolias bloom clouds of pink and white; there is spectacular new foliage, flowering cherries, crab apples, and azaleas. In fall/winter the colors are vivid scarlet, rust, yellow, and gold. Oaks, maples, ash, and nyssa spread colored drifts in May and early June. Open daily from 9am to 5pm. Admission is NZ$5 (US$3.50) per person.

Gisborne is the Chardonnay capital of New Zealand, and if you're interested in tasting some of the local wines, ask the Visitors Information Centre for directions to a couple of outstanding **wineries** just outside of town. One of them, **Millton Vineyard,** on Papatu Road, Manutuke, Gisborne (☎ 06/862-8680), is open Monday through Saturday 9am to 5pm and closed Easter to the end of October.

If you're interested in beer, the **Sunshine Microbrewery,** 109 Disraeli St., Gisborne (☎ 06/867-7777) is the place for you. They make five beers, and their Gisborne Gold Pilsner and Black Magic Stout have both won numerous awards. The brewery is open Monday through Saturday from 9am to 6pm and offers free tastings and an explanation of the process. This unpasteurized beer has a short shelf life and needs to be consumed when it's fresh. If you want more than a taste, head to Smash Palace (see "Gisborne After Dark," below), where it is on tap.

OUTDOOR ACTIVITIES

There are some excellent **walkways** in the area, and the information center can furnish detailed trail booklets. Two of the favorites are "Gray's Bush Scenic Reserve" (which is flat) and "Te Kuri Farm Walkway" (on land donated by Murray Ball, creator of the popular *Footrot Flats* comic strip).

Swimmers will enjoy both **Waikanae** and **Midway beaches.** Body surfers prefer **Wainui Beach,** while board surfing is best at **Makarori Beach.** The ✪ **Olympic Pool Complex** on Centennial Marine Dr. (☎ 06/867-6220, fax 06/867-4953) is also a great place for swimming; there's one pool for working out, one for diving, and another for kids; there are also a huge water slide and a toddler's pool with a mini-hydro slide. Open daily from 6am to 8pm during summer. Small-fry will enjoy the **Adventure Park** and Young Nick's Playground here.

There is excellent **fishing** in these waters, both offshore and in the rivers. You can arrange charters and guides through the information center. Anglers will want to ask for the *Guide to Trout Fishing in the Gisborne Area,* compiled by the Gisborne Anglers Club.

AFFORDABLE ACCOMMODATIONS

The rates given below include the 12.5% GST. All properties offer free parking.

CAMPGROUNDS & CABINS

The ✪ **Waikanae Beach Holiday Park,** at the beach end of Grey Street, Gisborne (☎ 06/867-5634, fax 06/867-9765), has brown-wood blocks of cabins arranged in a U-shape around a grassy courtyard with attractive plantings. There are tourist flats (cabins), which sleep four in two twin-bedded rooms and have private toilet and shower, refrigerator, gas range, crockery, cutlery, and cooking utensils; you supply or hire (rent) linen and blankets. Charges are NZ$12 to NZ$16 (US$8.40 to US$11.20) for two people for tent sites; NZ$16 to NZ$18 (US$11.20 to US$12.60) for two for power sites; NZ$22 to NZ$26 (US$15.40 to US$18.20) for two for cabins; NZ$48 to NZ$50 (US$33.60 to US$35) for two for tourist flats. Bankcard, MasterCard, and Visa are accepted. On the premises are a large laundry, kitchen, showers, children's play area, and tennis courts. It's handy to good swimming and surfing beaches (beautiful and safe Waikanae Beach is just across the road), spotless, and provides above-average facilities. The city center is an easy walk away and the Olympic Pool complex and miniature golf are nearby. This excellent motor camp is run by the City Council. During high season (summer months), advance reservations are absolutely necessary, as it is extremely popular with Kiwis.

SUPER-CHEAP SLEEPS

Gisborne YHA Hostel

32 Harris St. (at Wainui Rd.), Gisborne. ☎ **06/867-3269.** 29 beds (none with bathrm). NZ$14 (US$9.10) per person. MC, V.

This hostel is in a relaxed urban setting close to the city center, beaches, and major sightseeing. There are 29 beds in nine rooms, communal showers, a full laundry facility, and a communal kitchen. A basic food shop is in the hostel, as well as equipment for badminton and volleyball.

Thompson Homestay

159 Esplanade, Gisborne. ☎ and fax **06/868-9675.** 2 rms (none with bath). NZ$70 (US$49) double. Rate includes breakfast. No credit cards. Courtesy pickup from airport and bus station.

Located right on the river, guests of Barbara and Alec Thomson can sit in their lounge and enjoy the river view. This homestay is very clean and homey; the bathroom is shared with hosts. One room has a double bed; the other has twins—neither is overly large. Alec is a taxi driver and knows a lot about the area. Both are really friendly. There's a kayak for guest use and lots of places to eat nearby.

FOR A FEW EXTRA BUCKS

Champers Motor Lodge

811 Gladstone Rd., Gisborne. ☎ **06/863-1515.** Fax 06/863-1520. 14 units (all with bathrm). MINIBAR TV TEL. NZ$80 (US$56) double small studio, NZ$90 (US$63) double large studio, NZ$100 (US$70) double one-bedroom, NZ$120 (US$84) double two-bedroom. Extra person NZ$15 (US$10.50) adult, NZ$10 (US$7) child. Rates include breakfast. AE, DC, MC, V.

Champers—as in champagne—is easy to find. It's the first motel on the left as you come into town on Highway 2; look for the champagne-glass-shaped fountain under a pink sign. Hosts Ross and Julie Candy built this motel in late 1996. The exterior is red brick; the interiors are modern. All rooms have queen beds; five have spa baths and seven have cooking facilities. Laundry facilities are provided free of charge, as are cots (cribs) and highchairs. In addition to the heated outdoor saltwater pool and attached kiddies' pool, there's a children's playground. This is the best choice in Gisborne for individuals in wheelchairs—there are two units for people with disabilities with low light switches and accessible wheel-in showers.

✪ Teal Motor Lodge

479 Gladstone Rd., Gisborne. ☎ **06/868-4019.** Fax 06/867-7157. E-mail motel@teal.co.nz. 20 units (all with bathrm). TV TEL. NZ$89–$113 (US$62.30–$79.10) single or double. AE, BC, DC, JCB, MC, V.

This is something a little different—a New Zealand motel with a decidedly Asian flavor, run by Stewart and Lynda Haynes. Set on almost 2 acres of shaded and landscaped lawns, only a short walk to the city center, the spacious quarters have an airy look, with exposed beams and stained timber exteriors, plus restful color schemes throughout. There's a quiet air about the place, not to mention a saltwater swimming pool. The units have one or two bedrooms and full kitchens, a bonus for budget travelers who want to cook in. Continental and cooked breakfasts are available too.

WORTH A SPLURGE

Repongaere

Lavenham Rd. (P.O. Box 116), Patutahi, Gisborne. ☎ and fax **06/862-7717.** 4 rms (1 with bathrm). NZ$140 (US$98) double without bathrm, NZ$180 (US$126) double with bathrm. Rates include breakfast. Four-course dinner NZ$45 (US$31.50) per person. MC, V. Located 20km (12 miles) from Gisborne.

Repongaere, which means "lake of rippling water," is a 65-hectare (163-acre) farm property with a big, historic kauri homestead that dates from 1909. Hosts Michael and Midge Dods welcome guests to their home, which has large rooms with high ceilings, native timber paneling, wide verandas, and a magnificent staircase. The beautiful interiors include lots of English antique furniture and silver, with handsome upholstery and drapery fabrics. One guest room has an en suite bathroom; the other three share facilities. Guests are welcome to join in farm activities (they grow citrus, grapes, feed corn, zucchini, broccoli, and squash) or enjoy the swimming pool, grass tennis court, petanque, and croquet. The house is surrounded by old English trees that help shade the lawns. If this house seems large to you, consider this: When Michael's father took over the property in 1940, he felt the homestead was too big and had 14 rooms removed!

GREAT DEALS ON DINING

For eating on the fly, **Captain Morgan's,** at 285 Grey St. (☎ **06/867-7821**), is a good choice; this BYO restaurant also has take-away meals and an ice-cream parlor. You might also like to try **Smash Palace** (see "Gisborne After Dark," below).

And be forewarned: Many restaurants in Gisborne are closed on Monday night.

SUPER-CHEAP EATS

Wharf Cafe

No. 1 Wharf Shed, 60 The Esplanade, Gisborne. ☎ and fax **06/867-2039.** Reservations not accepted. Main courses NZ$5–$12 (US$3.50–$8.40). AE, DC, MC, V. Daily 10am–late (closed Monday evenings in winter). CAFE.

As the name implies, The Wharf Cafe is located right on the harbor with fishing boats and yachts moored nearby. Diners place their order at the counter and choose a table inside or out. Lunch items include pizza, filled rolls, bagels, quiche, and salads; dinner is pizza only. The Wharf Cafe has an extensive range of wines available.

FOR A FEW EXTRA BUCKS

Verve Cafe

121 Gladstone Rd., Gisborne. ☎ **06/868-9095.** E-mail verve@bpc.co.nz. Reservations accepted evenings only. Dinner main courses NZ$10.50–$20 (US$7.40–$14). BC, MC, V. Daily 8am–10pm. ECLECTIC.

Talk about a '90s joint—this place has a computer on-site so you can check your e-mail, send e-mail (NZ$3/US$2.10 per half hour plus NZ$1/US70¢ per message), or access the Internet (NZ$7/US$4.90 per half hour). It has a comfortable coffeehouse atmosphere and so is a good place to just hang out. The Wharf Cafe (see above) has a better view, but the food here is more interesting. Dinner service starts at 6pm, and main dishes include Moroccan vegetable tagine, a vegetarian stew with seasonal vegetables, figs, and almonds served on couscous and garnished with yoghurt; fettuccine con calamari; and chicken curry served on basmati rice. It's bring your own alcohol here.

WORTH A SPLURGE

If you feel like splurging and the Marina Restaurant below is booked out, **Pete's on the Beach,** Marine Parade, across from the Olympic Pool Complex (☎ **06/ 867-5861**) is another good choice. Pete's overlooks the water.

✪ Three Rivers Marina Restaurant

Marina Park, Vogel St. ☎ **06/868-5919.** Fax 06/868-5613. Reservations recommended. Main courses NZ$18–$24 (US$12.60–$16.80). AE, BC, DC, MC, V. Tues–Fri noon–2pm; Mon–Sat 6:30–10pm. MODERN NEW ZEALAND.

Housed in a three-story white frame building on the riverfront, "The Marina" offers excellent fresh local seafood, veal, chicken, and steak. Sample dishes include spiced roast duck confit; rare venison in a roasted red pepper sauce; beef carpaccio with mushrooms and Parmesan; and smoked hapuka mousse in a slice of puff pastry. There's more than a little style in both the setting and the food presentation by the friendly, competent staff. It's a favorite with locals, so reserve early. It's fully licensed, with a good wine list.

GISBORNE AFTER DARK

Pete's on the Beach, Marine Parade, across from the Olympic Pool Complex (☎ 06/867-5861) offers a great view of the beach and has a wonderful outdoor area for drinks.

✪ **Smash Palace,** 24 Banks St., Gisborne (☎ **06/867-6967**), is another good watering hole. Michael Dods, host of Repongaere (see "Affordable Accommodations," above), described this spot as "a real ripper of a place" and he wasn't kidding. Located in an industrial area between the town center and the airport, Smash Palace consists of an oversized, glorified tin shed that was originally the tasting room for the Parker Methode Champenoise winery. Today it has evolved into a colorful publike nightspot. It gets its name from the car yards "over the road" and the popular '80s New Zealand film of the same name. A gigantic papier-mâché dinosaur lives in the rafters and bicycles hang from the translucent corrugated plastic ceiling. Hubcaps, license plates, and farm implements line the corrugated tin walls. The DC-3—yes, a real plane—sticking up out of the roof has been turned into a bar. Owner Phil Parker will happily pour complimentary tastes of his Classical Brut or First Light Reds ("bright, fruity, and full of promise of the good things to come"), but it's hard to take anything seriously here (it's like tasting wine in someone's messy garage). This popular spot has Sunshine Brewery's "Gisborne Gold" on tap. Food service lasts as long as they're open and includes cheese-and-fruit boards, pizza (with cheese melted by blowtorch), garlic and herb bread, and nachos. It opens daily at 11am and stays open late.

EN ROUTE TO NAPIER

The 216km (134-mile) drive along Highway 2 from Gisborne to Napier passes through some of the most picturesque natural scenery in the country: rugged hill-country sheep stations, lush native bush, Lake Tutira, and a breathtaking view of Poverty Bay Flats from the top of the Wharerata Hills some 37km (23 miles) outside the city. **Morere Springs Scenic Reserve** (☎ and fax **06/837-8856**), between Poverty and Hawke bays (you'll see the sign along the highway), is a nice stop-off point for bushwalks (there are six tracks, from 10-minutes to 2¹/₂ hours return, from which to choose), picnicking, or soaking in pools (both thermal and cold).

Admission is NZ$4 (US$2.80) for adults and NZ$2.50 (US$1.75) for children and seniors (over 60).

2 Hawkes Bay

216km (134 miles) SW of Gisborne; 423km (262 miles) SE of Auckland; 228km (141 miles) SE of Rotorua

Three adjacent communities comprise the Hawkes Bay region. Of these, **Napier,** the Art Deco Capital, is the largest; **Havelock North,** an easy 20-minute drive from Napier, is the most affluent; and **Hastings** is the least interesting.

Spread around the wedge of Bluff Hill (which was virtually an island when Captain Cook described it on his voyage south from Poverty Bay), Napier was founded by whalers in the mid-1800s. You won't find any trace of those early settlers in today's city, however: In 1931 an earthquake demolished the entire city and nearby Hastings, killing hundreds of people. In its aftermath, not only did a completely new city arise, but it arose on new ground, for the quake had lifted the inner harbor floor, creating 10,000 acres of dry land—the site of the present airport, for instance, was under water prior to 1931.

Rebuilt during the Depression, the town opted for the art deco and Spanish Mission architecture so popular in the 1930s. As a result, Napier claims it has the world's largest collection of buildings in these styles (see "Doing the Art Deco Thing," under "Exploring Hawkes Bay," below).

Havelock North is a genteel community surrounded by wineries and fruit orchards; it's not surprising that it's a favorite retirement area for affluent Kiwis. Upmarket boutiques line the streets in the village—a great place for browsing.

ESSENTIALS

GETTING THERE & GETTING AROUND

BY PLANE   Air New Zealand, in the Travel Centre at Hastings and Station streets, Napier (☎ **06/835-1171**), provides daily service between the Hawkes Bay Airport and most New Zealand cities. The airport shuttle service into town (☎ **06/ 879-9766**) costs about NZ$8 (US$5.20).

BY TRAIN   There is daily rail service between Napier and Wellington via the *Bay Express.* There is no train service from the north.

BY COACH (BUS)   There is daily bus service between Napier/Hastings and Auckland, Gisborne, Rotorua, Taupo, Tauranga, and Wellington via **InterCity** and **Newmans** coach lines. The **Magic Traveller Network** (☎ **09/358-5600**), an alternative bus service, includes Napier on several of its routes. Call for schedules.

There is regular (but not frequent) bus service Monday through Friday between the towns in Hawkes Bay. Call the **Visitors Information Centre** at 100 Marine Parade, the Marine Parade end of Emerson St. (☎ **06/834-1911**) for schedule and fare information.

BY CAR   Both Napier and Hastings are on the north–south Highway 2; Highway 5 reaches Napier from the northwest and State Highway 50 from the southwest. It's best to explore this entire region by car as bus service is infrequent.

BY TAXI   A taxi stand is located at Clive Square; call ☎ **06/835-7777.**

VISITOR INFORMATION

In Napier you'll find the **Visitors Information Centre** at 100 Marine Parade (the Marine Parade end of Emerson St.; ☎ **06/834-1911,** fax 06/835-7219, e-mail npevin@nzhost.co.nz). Hours are 8:30am to 5pm Monday through Friday, 9am to

5pm on Saturday and Sunday and public holidays; extended hours from December 26 through February 28; closed only on Christmas Day. Racks are filled with helpful brochures, maps, and visitor guides. Dianne Chester and her staff can help with accommodations and information on art deco walks, winery tours, and Cape Kidnappers.

The **Hastings Visitor Information Centre** is on Russell Street North (Private Bag 9002), Hastings (☎ 06/878-0510, fax 06/878-0512, e-mail hstvin@nzhost.co.nz). The **telephone area code** (STD) for Hawkes Bay is **06.**

ORIENTATION

The pride—and showplace—of Napier is its **Marine Parade,** a beautiful stretch of waterfront lined with stately Norfolk pines. Many visitor activities center around the Marine Parade, which holds a wide variety of attractions. **Kennedy Road,** the principal thoroughfare, diagonally bisects the town. The best beach in the area is **Westshore Beach,** located in Westshore Domain, part of the new-land legacy of the 1931 disaster. There are no sand beaches along Marine Parade. The Chief Post Office (C.P.O.) is on Dickens Street. **Onekawa Park** at Maadi Road and Flanders Avenue has an outdoor Olympic-size pool (small fee).

SPECIAL EVENTS

The **Harvest Hawkes Bay Wine and Food Festival,** held late January to early February, provides an opportunity to sample local wines and food in one location (☎ and fax **06/879-7603**). The **Ford Art Deco Weekend** is a "not-too-serious celebration," which includes wining, dining, dancing, jazz, vintage cars, special walks and tours, and much more. Most participants dress in 1920s and 1930s fashions. Third weekend in February. For more information contact the **Art Deco Trust,** P.O. Box 133, Napier (☎ **06/835-0022**, fax 06/835-1912).

EXPLORING HAWKES BAY: WHAT TO SEE & DO
THE WINERIES

There are 25 wineries in the Napier area, most open daily for free-of-charge tasting and bottle sales. **Mission Estate Winery,** Church Rd., Taradale, Napier (☎ **06/ 844-2259,** fax 06/844-6023) and **The McDonald Winery,** Church Road, Taradale, Napier (☎ **06/844-2053**), both offer tours. Several wineries serve lunch, and a few have picnic areas. Ask at the information center for brochures about tours and directions for reaching them.

The most interesting wineries are: **Te Mata Estate Winery,** Te Mata Rd., P.O. Box 8335, Havelock North (☎ **06/877-4399,** fax 06/877-4397), a small, privately owned winery that produces a range of wines; **Esk Valley Estate,** Main Rd., SH2, P.O. Box 111, Bay View (☎ **06/836-6411,** fax 06/836-6413), one of the top red wine producers in New Zealand; **Clearview Estate Winery,** Clifton Rd., Te Awanga, R.D. 2, Hastings (☎ **06/875-0150,** fax 06/875-1258), which has won one gold, five silver, and six bronze medals, and a trophy for the best white wine in the region since opening in 1992; **Sacred Hill Winery,** Dartmoor Rd., Puketapu, Napier (☎ **06/844-0138,** fax 06/844-3271), which is set among large stands of trees and is a great place to enjoy a picnic; **Mission Estate Winery,** Church Rd., P.O. Box 7043, Taradale, Napier (☎ **06/844-2259,** fax 06/844-6023), New Zealand's oldest winery; and **Vidal of Hawkes Bay,** 913 Aubyns St. East, P.O. Box 48, Hastings (☎ **06/876-8105,** fax 06/876-5312), a winery that's been around since 1905 and is popular with locals. All offer free tastings; check for hours and days.

Two companies in the area offer wine tours: **Vince's Vineyard Tour,** 9 Thurley Place, Bay View, Napier (☎ **06/836-6705,** mobile 025/506-658, fax 06/844-4940), will introduce you to four of the region's top wineries; the half-day tour costs NZ$30 (US$21) per person. **Bay Tours Mini Coachlines,** P.O. Box 3052, Onekawa, Napier (☎ **06/843-6953,** mobile 025/490-778, fax 06/843-2046), offers "Jenne's Wine Tour" where you have two options: tour four wineries of your choice or five wineries with time for lunch at one of them. The wine tour alone is NZ$32.50 (US$22.80) per person; the wine/lunch tour is NZ$40 (US$28) per person plus lunch at your own expense.

IN NAPIER

Doing the Art Deco Thing

The city of Napier itself is virtually an open-air museum of **art deco and Spanish architecture** as a result of massive reconstruction between 1931 and 1933. More than 60 years later, the buildings are remarkably unchanged and no doubt represent one of the world's most concentrated collections of buildings from this period.

A map outlining a ☺ **self-guided walk** through the downtown area and another showing a more extensive scenic drive are available from the Art Deco Shop and from the Napier Information Centre for NZ$1.50 and NZ$2.50 (US$1.05 and $1.75), respectively. **Guided walks** leave the **Art Deco Shop,** 163 Tennyson Street (opposite Clive Square) every Wednesday, Saturday, and Sunday at 2pm (daily from December 26 to March 31) and include slide and video presentations, a walk leaflet, and refreshments. Winter walks (June to August) are adapted to include more time inside the buildings. They cost NZ$10 (US$7) for adults (children are free) and are conducted by the Art Deco Trust, P.O. Box 133, Napier (☎ **06/835-0022,** fax 06/835-1912), which promotes the city's architecture.

Marine Parade Attractions

The Aquarium

Marine Parade. ☎ **06/834-1404.** Admission NZ$7 (US$4.90) adults, NZ$3.50 (US$2.50) children, NZ$18 (US$12.60) family (2 adults and 2 children under 14; each additional child is NZ$2.25/US$1.60). Daily 9am–5pm (until 9pm Dec 26–Jan). Closed Christmas.

This aquarium's central feature is a huge saltwater oceanarium, which holds over 25 species of ocean-dwelling fish, ranging in size from crayfish to sharks. Feeding time is 3:15pm, when a scuba diver hand-feeds the fish. You'll also get to see a crocodile, turtles, vividly colored tropical fish, sea horses, the lethal piranha, and octopi. The Vivarium, on the top floor, holds the tuatara, a living fossil unique to New Zealand, and also aquatic reptiles like water dragons, turtles, and frogs.

☺ Marineland

Marine Parade. ☎ **06/834-4027.** Admission to Marineland show and Lilliput, NZ$8 (US$5.60) adults, NZ$4 (US$2.80) children, family tickets are available. Daily 10am–4:30pm. Shows are at 10:30am and 2:30pm, with an additional 4pm performance Dec 26 to mid-Jan.

Here, a 45-minute show features dolphins, leopard seals, sea lions, and penguins. Also on hand are cormorants and gannets. Marineland, in the same building as the Aquarium, also houses Lilliput, an animated village and model railway with authentic New Zealand rolling stock and locomotives, and offers a "swim with dolphins" experience.

The Stables Colonial Museum and Waxworks

Marine Parade. ☎ **06/835-1937.** Admission to museum only, NZ$4.50 (US$3.20); film only, NZ$4.50 (US$3.20); combination museum and film, NZ$6 (US$4.20). Daily 9am–5pm.

Getting to Know the Gannets

There's a colony of some 6,000 gannets out at ✪ **Cape Kidnappers,** that dramatic line of cliffs that forms Hawke Bay's southern end some 27km (17 miles) south of Napier. It's one of only two places in New Zealand where these large, rare birds are known to nest on the mainland—they're commonly found on offshore islands. The gannet sanctuary is open to the public from late October to April, and the graceful birds are well worth a visit. To reach them, drive 21km (13 miles) south to Clifton Domain; then it's a 2-hour walk along 6.4 to 8km (4 to 5 miles) of sandy beach. That walk *must* be made at low tide, since high tides come right up to the base of the steep cliffs, which is why private vehicles may not be taken out to the sanctuary. Be sure to check with the Visitors Information Centre in Napier (☎ 06/834-1911) or Hastings (☎ 06/876-0205), or the Department of Conservation in Napier (☎ 06/835-0415), about the time of the tides (or perhaps taking a tour there). The best time to view the birds is from early November to late February.

There are several organized options to going on your own: the half-day tours offered by **Gannet Safaris** (☎ 06/875-0511), which cost about NZ$38 (US$26.60) for adults and NZ$19 (US$13.30) for children 5 to 18, are best for people with limited time and energy—no walking is required. They use an air-conditioned coach for transport; the trip departs at 1:30pm daily and takes 3 to 3¹/₂ hours. If you are a bit more adventurous, **Gannet Beach Adventures** (☎ 06/875-0898) transports you by tractor and trailer (the trailer has been fitted with comfortable seats) along the base of the cliffs to the gannet colonies daily from October to late April. This costs NZ$18 (US$12.60) for adults and NZ$12 (US$8.40) for children 5 to 15. This trip (which includes 20 to 30 minutes of walking) lasts about 4 hours; departure time depends on the tide.

The pièce de résistance of the museum is *Earthquake 31,* a documentary about the infamous earthquake; try to see it before you do your major sightseeing in Napier—you'll get a better understanding of the city's unique history. The 23-minute film includes actual footage of Napier before and after the earthquake and an interview with older citizens who lived through it. Outside the movie theater, which has a floor that actually moves during footage of the quake, there is a dramatic replica of the collapse of the local nurses' home and the rescue performed by sailors and firefighters. (If you have to choose one, pick the film.) The museum is opposite Marineland.

Hawkes Bay Museum

Marine Parade. ☎ **06/835-7781.** Fax 06/835-3984. E-mail hbct@inhb.co.nz. Admission NZ$3 (US$2.10). MC, V. Daily 10am–4:30pm.

The museum and gallery offer a wide range of exhibits, many of which are related to the art and history of the region. A Tourism Design Award–winning exhibition, *Nga Tukemata—The Awakening,* presents the art of the local Ngati Kahungunu people. A dinosaur exhibit features the fossil discoveries from northern Hawkes Bay, the only dinosaur site in New Zealand. An audiovisual presentation tells the story of the disastrous Hawkes Bay earthquake of 1931. The *Newest City on the Globe* exhibition shows the rebuilding of Napier in the early 1930s in its famed art deco style; decorative arts from this period are also featured.

✪ Kiwi House

Marine Parade. ☎ **06/834-1336.** Fax 06/834-0299. Admission NZ$3 (US$2.10) adults, NZ$1.50 (US$1.05) children. AE, DC, MC, V. Daily 11am–3pm.

This is where you're guaranteed to see kiwis. Also on view are owls, night herons, sugar gliders, whistling frogs, and many others. There's a live show at 1pm, and the birds are fed at 2pm. There's also a sheepskin shop in the main entrance. Kiwi House is located at the northern end of the Marine Parade.

A Scenic Driving Tour

The **Waterfront Heritage Trail** is a 60-minute driving tour that follows the shore from Marine Parade to Bay View township—a distance of 22kms (about 14 miles). Stop at the visitor center or Art Deco Trust and pick up a copy of the brochure describing the route and points of interest along the way, including the Marine Parade itself, the historic Old Napier Courthouse, and the Napier Club.

A Couple of Short Walks

If you want to do some walking around while in Napier, you should head to the visitor center or the Art Deco Shop (see above) and ask for the two brochures that describe walking tours that start at different points on the Heritage Trail. **"Napier Hill Walks"** describes two walks over Napier's interesting and beautiful Hill residential area; the **Bluff Hill Walk** affords some beautiful views along with historic homes and takes between 1³/₄ to 2¹/₂ hours; the **Middle Hill Walk** takes 1¹/₂ to 2 hours. The **Ahuriri Walk** is broken down into two stages and takes about 1¹/₂ hours total; visitors will see some examples of very early cottages, plus some large native trees and a look at the Rothmans Building, an architecturally interesting mix of Art Nouveau and the Chicago School.

A Lesson in Fleece

Watch and learn how a fleece gets transformed into car-seat covers, rugs, and more at **Classic Sheepskin Tannery,** 22 Thames St., off Pandora Road (☎ **06/835-9662,** fax 06/835-9662). They offer free 25-minute tours through the factory daily at 11am and 2pm. The shop here sells sheepskin products at factory prices, and they have a fully insured worldwide mailing service. If you don't have wheels, there's a courtesy car available daily. The shop is open Monday to Friday from 7:30am to 5pm and weekends from 9am to 4pm.

IN HAVELOCK NORTH

Climbing Te Mata Peak

I hope you'll take the time to drive to the top of ✪ **Te Mata Peak,** about 11km (7 miles) from Hastings. The 360° panoramic view from here is stunning. Take Havelock Road to Te Mata Road to Simla Avenue to Te Mata Peak Road and ascend the 1,310-foot-high peak. According to Maori legend, a giant named Te Mata was a troublemaker and local chiefs used a beautiful maiden to get rid of him. The giant fell for the girl, but before she would marry him she gave him a series of impossible tasks, which he somehow accomplished. Upon reaching his final challenge—to eat through the mountain range behind Havelock North—he was impatient and took one large, greedy bite, choked, and fell dead. One particular gap is said to be the place from which he took his mouthful. When looking straight down Heretaunga Street, some see the outline of a giant lying on his back in the silhouette of the ranges.

In Hastings

The **Hawkes Bay Exhibition Centre,** Civic Square, Hastings (☎ **06/876-2077,** fax 06/876-2077), is the region's top spot for touring exhibitions of painting, sculpture, craft, and historical material. There's a shop specializing in local craft souvenirs and a fine cafe too. Admission is NZ$3 (US$2.10), with an additional charge for special exhibitions. It's open Monday through Friday from 10am to 4:30pm and Saturday and Sunday from noon to 4:30pm; closed Christmas Day.

AFFORDABLE ACCOMMODATIONS
NAPIER

The rates listed below include the 12.5% GST. All properties listed here offer free parking.

Campgrounds & Cabins

It's hard to find superlatives strong enough for Napier's ✪ **Kennedy Park Holiday Complex** on Storkey Street, off Kennedy Road, Napier (☎ **06/843-9126;** fax 06/843-6113). If you've been impressed with Kiwi motor camps in general, just wait until you see this one! Set in 17 acres of trees, grass, and colorful flowers (including 1¹/₂ acres of roses!), with top-grade accommodations, this has to be the "Ritz" among New Zealand camps. Those accommodations run the gamut from tent sites to ungraded cabins to graded (two-star) cabins to tourist flats and motel units. The 110 sites with powered caravan sites run NZ$20 (US$14) for two adults.

Ungraded cabins come with beds, tables, and chairs, and you supply cooking and eating utensils, linen and blankets, and use the communal toilet and shower facilities. Rates are NZ$25 (US$17.50) for two. The 16 graded cabins sleep four (plus a rollaway bed if needed), have easy chairs, and are furnished with hot- and cold-water sinks, fridge, range, coffee/tea maker, toaster, crockery, cutlery, frying pan, pots, and utensils. You supply linen and blanket, and use the communal toilet and shower facilities. Two people pay NZ$40 (US$28). Tourist flats fill that gap between cabins and motel units—they're like motels, but they're not serviced. These 20 units cost NZ$67 (US$46.90) for two people. Finally, motel units come in varying sizes: bed-sitters (studios) and one- and two-bedroom units. Many have peaked, pine-beamed ceilings, a window wall, and stucco and wood-paneled walls. All are of superior quality, have well-chosen furnishings, look out over lawn and gardens, and are NZ$60 to NZ$74 (US$42 to US$51.80) for two. American Express, Bankcard, Diners Club, MasterCard, and Visa cards accepted.

Super-Cheap Sleeps
YHA Hostel

277 Marine Parade, Napier. ☎ and fax **06/835-7039.** 39 beds (no rooms with bath). NZ$15 (US$10.50) per person dorm, NZ$16 (US$11.20) per person twin, NZ$17 (US$11.90) per person double. BC, MC, V.

This hostel couldn't have a better location—it's right on the beachfront, across from Marineland. The former guest house has 39 beds in 18 rooms. Front rooms overlook the bay, and facilities include a TV and video room, a pleasant kitchen and dining room, an outdoor barbecue and dining area, a smoking lounge, laundry facilities, and bike rental.

In addition to this hostel, **The Stables Backpackers,** 321 Marine Parade, Napier (☎ **06/835-1937**), on Marine Parade is also popular.

For a Few Extra Bucks

Pinehaven Travel Hotel

259 Marine Parade, Napier. ☎ and fax **06/835-5575.** 6 rms (none with bathrm). TV. NZ$66 (US$46.20) double. Rates include continental breakfast. AE, BC, DC, MC, V.

The Pinehaven is down the street from the YHA Hostel and across from Marineland. It's a quaint guest house that enjoys a wonderful sea view. June and Ray Riley have hosted guests from all over the world. The Pinehaven has six comfortably furnished rooms, all with hot and cold running water. The bedrooms are heated and have electric blankets. Downstairs is a TV lounge with tea- and coffeemaking facilities. The optional cooked breakfast is extra.

Reef Motel

33 Meeanee Quay, Westshore, Napier. ☎ **06/835-4108.** Fax 06/835-4789. 7 one-bedroom units (all with bathrm). TV TEL. From NZ$65 (US$45.50) double. AE, BC, CB, DC, JCB, MC, V. Courtesy car from/to the rail, bus, and air terminals.

Each one-bedroom unit here sleeps two to six people, with separate bedrooms and a living area that opens into a fully equipped kitchen. The upstairs units have great views. A spa pool and laundry facilities are on the premises, and both cooked and continental breakfasts are available. The Reef Motel is located in the Westshore area near the beach.

✪ Snowgoose Lodge

376 Kennedy Rd., Napier. ☎ **06/843-6083.** Fax 06/843-6107. 11 units, 7 suites (all with bathrm). TV TEL. NZ$80 (US$52) single; NZ$90 (US$58.50) double; NZ$90–$100 (US$58.50–$65) suite. Best Western discounts available. AE, BC, DC, JCB, MC, V.

You park outside your own unit at the Snowgoose, where Ray and Pierrine Cooper keep things shining, inside and out. The front lawn has even won an award for the best motel garden in Napier. The one- and two-bedroom units are all nicely furnished and have full kitchens, radios, and electric blankets. Most also are brightened with one or two of Pierrine's growing plants. There's a block of executive suites that have their own spa bath (sheer luxury!). On-premises facilities include a laundry, car wash, children's play area, game room, outdoor swimming pool, and private spa pool—all free to guests. Shops are nearby, and the Coopers can arrange baby-sitting. The motel is on the main road 2 miles from the town center.

Spanish Lady Motel

348 Kennedy Rd., Napier. ☎ **06/843-9188.** Fax 06/843-6064. 11 units (all with bathrm). TV TEL. NZ$82 (US$57.40) unit for 2. Best Western discounts available. AE, BC, DC, JCB, MC, V.

The unassuming exterior of this small place, hosted by Dorothy and Ian Finlayson, hides the amenities hard to find in most New Zealand lodgings: washcloths in the bathroom and a sink with one mixer faucet for both hot and cold water. Add to that good lighting and a firm mattress, and you'll feel like you're in heaven! The one- and two-bedroom units are all on the ground floor, eight with wheelchair access. There are also fully equipped kitchens, a pool, a spa pool, a playground, an ice machine, and a cactus garden. The Spanish Lady is on the main road about 3¹/₂km (2 miles) from the center of town.

IN HAVELOCK NORTH

✪ Peak View Farm

Middle Rd., Havelock North. ☎ **06/877-7408.** Fax 06/877-7410. 2 rms (none with bathrm). NZ$60 (US$42) double. Rate includes breakfast. Dinner NZ$20 (US$14) per person. BC, MC, V.

Named for the view it affords of Te Mata Peak, this 90-year-old homestead is situated on 10.25 hectares (25 acres) of land. Friendly hosts Keith and Dianne Taylor are the fourth generation to live in this house, which Keith's grandparents built. They have a few sheep and also grow peas, beans, and tomatoes commercially. The rooms aren't large but are homey, and the beds are firm (one has a double bed, the other twins; a cot is also available). The bathroom is shared with the hosts. Dianne, who bottles her own fruit and makes her own jam, is very sweet and accommodating. You're greeted with a cup of tea and homemade bickies (cookies), and she really bends over backwards to ensure that you feel welcome. They offer home-cooked dinners (corned beef, roast lamb, chicken, or fish), and it's not surprising that about 80% of their guests take advantage of this dollarwise option. Many folks return here again and again, mostly for the great Kiwi hospitality. There's no smoking in the house.

Worth a Splurge
Providencia

Middle Rd. (R.D. 2, Hastings), Havelock North. ☎ and fax **06/877-2300.** Web sites nz.com/ HeritageInns/Providencia, nz.com/webnz/tpac/nz/Providencia.html, and nz.com/webnz/tpac/ gaynz/Providencia.html. 4 rms (2 with bathrm). NZ$150 (US$105) double "Chauffer's Room" with bathrm, NZ$160 (US$112) double without bathrm, NZ$185 (US$130) double with bathrm. Rates include breakfast. AE, MC, V.

Hosts Janet and Raul Maddison-Mejias (she's Australian, he's Chilean) fell in love with this circa-1903 house and in 1994 they had it moved from Hastings to its present location. The property is easy to find; it's just a few minutes out of the village of Havelock North. The leadlight windows in this house are lovely, but my favorite things are the lofty kauri and rimu ceilings and the interesting light fixtures that hang from them. Other features include central heating, open fires, and a huge dining room. Scrambled eggs with smoked salmon is the breakfast specialty. Janet makes the bread, as well as the soap used in the house. The landscaping has yet to mature, but there is a croquet lawn and a patch of garden around a used-brick patio. Janet is a great hostess: She helped my husband, the car buff, locate a local who restores Jaguars and a physiologist who fixed his sore back. Lunch and dinners can be arranged. *Se habla Español.* There is no smoking inside.

GREAT DEALS ON DINING

If you're staying in motels or hostels and cooking for yourself, or if you just prefer picnicking, I think you should know about ✪ **Chantal Wholefoods,** 29 Hastings St., Napier (☎ **06/835-8036**). Even if you're not a strict vegetarian, I think you'll love this store—all sorts of natural foods, dried fruits, nuts, tofu, and, in addition, marvelous whole-grain breads for sandwiches. Chantal's is very much like an old-fashioned grocery store. The foods are all in open drums and you package them yourself—it's lots of fun, and prices come out lower than those in supermarkets.

IN NAPIER
Super-Cheap Eats
Mabel's Restaurant

204 Hastings St., Napier. ☎ **06/835-5655.** Reservations not required. Breakfast under NZ$8 (US$5.60); lunch under NZ$10 (US$7). No credit cards. Mon–Fri 6:30am–3pm. BREAKFAST/ LIGHT LUNCH.

Early risers will appreciate Mabel's, a coffee shop where breakfast is featured weekdays from 6:30am to 9:30am. You can also get a light, reasonably priced meal of soup, quiche, or salad. Just check the blackboard selections. Mabel's is right in the center of town.

For a Few Extra Bucks

○ The Old Flame

112 Tennyson St., Napier. ☎ **06/835-6848.** Reservations recommended, especially on weekends. Lunch NZ$14 (US$9.80); dinner NZ$21 (US$14.70); seniors NZ$18 (US$12.60) for dinner, NZ$11 (US$7.70), for lunch. MC, V. Daily 11:30am–2:30pm and 5:30–9pm or later. NEW ZEALAND SMÖRGÅSBORD.

Terry and Pat O'Reilly will give you a warm welcome at this cozy restaurant, which occupies a single-story house across from the Municipal Theatre. It's strictly smörgåsbord—tables heaped high with tempting New Zealand dishes like sweet and sour pork, lamb in a port sauce, and fried rice. There's also a seafood bar, salad bar, desserts, coffee, and tea. The place has an art deco look. It's fully licensed or you can bring your own wine, and while it's not advertised as an all-you-can-eat place, The Old Flame does allow seconds.

Ujazi

28 Tennyson St. (at Hastings St., 1 block from Marine Parade), Napier. ☎ and fax **06/835-1490.** Reservations accepted. Lunch main courses NZ$10–$15 (US$7–$10.50). MC, V. Daily 8:30am–5pm (varies seasonally). ECLECTIC/CAFE.

Ujazi is a Swahili word that means "a vessel to be filled." And that's what they do at this hole-in-the-wall cafe. Imagine filling your own vessel with pan-fried calamari on salad greens with a sweet basil and garlic mayonnaise, or smoked chicken salad with peaches and herbs. Brunch is served from 8:30am to noon, when lunch kicks in and lasts until 3:30pm; espresso and other fancy coffees, fresh fruit juices, and sandwiches are served until closing. It's BYO here.

HAVELOCK NORTH & BEYOND

If the Rose & Shamrock (see below) is too lively for you, another dining option is **Diva** (☎ **06/877-5149**), across the street, which is a more modern, upscale cafe.

Super-Cheap Eats

○ Rose & Shamrock

Corner Napier Rd. and Porter Dr., North Havelock. ☎ **06/877-2999.** Fax 06/877-2959. Reservations not accepted. Main courses NZ$5.50–$9.50 (US$3.90–$6.70). AE, DC, MC, V. Daily 10:30am–late. PUB.

Publican Paul Ralph was born in England but discovered a pub in Waterford, Ireland, that he really liked. He took photos, but his Kiwi architect couldn't get it right so he flew him to Ireland to see it for himself. The result is this really fun Irish pub in the center of Havelock North. The extremely handsome decor includes an open fire with a beautiful mahogany mantel, a dozen posters depicting scenes of Ireland, and seating in upholstered booths as well as at mahogany tables. Live entertainment is frequent—we enjoyed an evening of Morris dancing. You can drink here six days of the week without eating; Sunday the licensing laws require you to have a meal. Meals include Irish lamb stew, ham steak, crumbed hoki, seafood platter, and a ploughman's plate. Highly recommended.

FOR A FEW EXTRA BUCKS

○ Clearview Winery

Clifton Rd. Te Awanga. ☎ **06/875-0150.** Fax 06/875-1258. Reserve well in advance for weekends. Light lunch NZ$6–12 (US$4.20–8.40); lunch main courses NZ$16–$17 (US$11.20–$11.90). AE, MC, V. Noon–3pm (summer, Thurs–Mon; winter, Sat, Sun, and holidays). MODERN NEW ZEALAND.

Clearview advertises "Mediterranean lunches," and the sea breeze and view of the vineyard do create that feeling. Outdoor seating is at umbrella tables—don't be concerned about the intermittent popping noises—it's not gunfire, but a butane device that scares the birds off the fruit. Light fare here includes soup of the day, cheeseboards, and crépage (layered mini crepes with smoked salmon and cream sauce), all of which are really delicious. The mains are also good, but hardly budget-priced. A thrifty alternative would be to buy cheese and bread at a supermarket, taste some wines here at no charge, and then drive to a scenic spot for a picnic. There's free wine tasting Thursday to Monday during the summer from 10am to 5pm, and Saturday, Sunday and holidays during winter from 11am to 4pm. This winery is best known for its excellent Reserve Chardonnay (a bottle of the 1995 costs NZ$29/US$20.30).

EN ROUTE TO TAUPO

Your drive from Napier to Taupo via Highway 5 will take less than 2 hours, but there was a time when it took 2 days. That was when stagecoach service was first initiated over a route that had been used by Maori in pre-European days on forays to collect seafood from Hawke Bay.

The landscape you'll be passing through changes from lush vineyards to cultivated farm fields to rugged mountain ranges. You'll also see huge stands of pine trees—one of the country's most profitable cash crops. To find more points of interest en route, pick up the "Heritage Trail: Taupo–Napier" brochure in either city's visitor information center. About 3¹/₂ miles before you reach Taupo, look for the lonely peak of **Mount Tauhara,** an extinct volcanic cone rising from the plains.

Lake Taupo & Beyond

Whether you come into Taupo from Rotorua, past Wairakei's steamy thermal power complex, or from Napier, under the lonely eye of Mount Tauhara, it's the lake on whose shores the town sits that will draw you here. Lake Taupo, New Zealand's largest, opens before you in a broad, shimmering expanse, with its far shores a misty suggestion of cliffs, coves, and wooded hills.

The lake was formed in A.D. 186 by an enormous volcanic eruption—estimated to have been 100 times greater than that of Mount St. Helens in 1980. The eruption left a hole more than 32km (20 miles) wide, 40km (25 miles) across, and 600 feet deep in some places. Today, that crater contains the sparkling blue water of Lake Taupo.

To the south lies Tongariro National Park, home to three active volcanoes. Tongariro was New Zealand's first national park (the world's second, after Yellowstone), and the original 1887 deed from Te Heuheu Tukino IV and other Tuwharetoa tribal chiefs transferred only some 6,500 acres (all the land within a 2km (1-mile) radius of the volcanic peaks), an area that has now been expanded to 30,453 acres.

Wanganui, one of New Zealand's oldest cities, was settled amid much controversy over just how title to the land was obtained by Col. William Wakefield on behalf of the New Zealand Company in 1840. Since those early days, the town has grown and over the years developed into a popular holiday spot.

New Plymouth is an active port city in the lush Taranaki district. It's known for the rhododendron festival held annually in late October or early November. The area is dominated by snowcapped Mount Egmont, also known as Mount Taranaki.

1 Taupo

287km (178 miles) SE of Auckland; 84km (52 miles) S of Rotorua; 155km (96 miles) NW of Napier

There's a bit of magic at work in Taupo—and it's easy to see how attractive it must have been to descendants of the *Arawa* canoe. Present-day Maori will tell you that the lake was created by the magic of Ngatoroirangi, the legendary navigator of that migrating canoe. According to the legend, he stood on the summit of Mount Tauhara and flung down a gigantic tree, which landed here, leaving a vast trough as it plowed through the earth. When water welled up to fill the trough, Lake Taupo was born. Its very name is linked to legend—the Maori called it Taupo-nui-a-Tia (the "Great Cloak of Tia") after one of the Awara chiefs who explored much of this region, naming and claiming choice spots for his tribe. If you don't believe in folklore, you'll accept the Pakeha explanation of its origin: that the lake's crater is the result of an enormous volcanic eruption in A.D. 186 (the resultant orange sky was observed as far away as Rome and China).

Taupo's most appealing aspect to many is the fact that this pleasant, medium-sized town of 19,000 people is a *real* place, not just a tourist attraction—probably because travelers often rush past it on their way from Auckland to points south. Taupo certainly welcomes visitors, but you'll also see plenty of people just going about their daily lives, going to work or school, congregating in local cafes, or indulging in an ice-cream cone.

For locals and visitors alike, the lake is as much the center of life today as it was in those far-off times. Fishing is still important; the only difference is that two imported trout species have been added to the lake's fish population. In 1868 brown trout eggs were brought from Tasmania, followed by California rainbow trout in 1884. Lake Taupo rainbows are now considered a totally self-supporting wild population. It's the trout that draw anglers here in such numbers; in fact, they often appear as a human picket fence, packed together so tightly along the shoreline. And there's seldom a time when the lake's surface is not alive with boats trolling lines in their wake. Recreational boating is also a never-ending diversion in these parts, and water skiing has gained such popularity that there are now specified ski lanes along the shoreline.

But landlubbers have also been coming in huge numbers since the late 1870s to visit the thermal pools and view the natural wonders of the lake's environs. The Lake Taupo region offers a full range of adventure activities at reasonable prices, mostly because most visitors are New Zealanders who love to go bungy jumping, jet boating, and rafting but don't want to go broke doing it. In some ways, Taupo is a cross between Rotorua and Queenstown—minus the crowds and inflated prices. It may be a good idea to base yourself here and not in these other places. Taupo has most of the adventure activities associated with Queenstown without the touristy atmosphere, plus the thermal pools are cheaper here than in Rotorua.

ESSENTIALS
GETTING THERE & GETTING AROUND

BY PLANE   **Air New Zealand** (☎ 0800/737-000) provides regular service into Taupo Airport on the edge of town; the best way to get into town from the airport is to take a taxi.

BY COACH (BUS)   There is regular service via Mount Cook Landline, InterCity, and Newmans. The Magic Traveler Network and Kiwi Experience both include Taupo on their routes.

There's **no local bus service,** but Paradise Tours offers minibus excursions (see "Organized Tours," below).

BY CAR   Highways 1 and 5 pass through Taupo. For sorties around the area, try **Rent-a-Dent** (☎ 07/378-2740).

BY TAXI   For taxi service in and around Taupo, call **Taupo Taxis** (☎ 07/378-5100).

BY BIKE   For getting around Taupo by bicycle, contact **Cycle World** on Ruapehu Street (☎ 07/378-6117), where you can rent bikes.

Lake Taupo Region

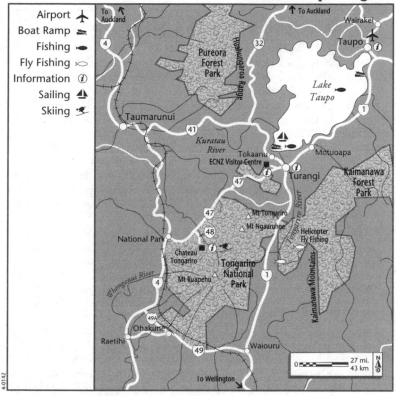

Legend:
- Airport ✈
- Boat Ramp ⇌
- Fishing ►
- Fly Fishing ⌇
- Information ⓘ
- Sailing ⛵
- Skiing ⛷

VISITOR INFORMATION

The **Visitors Information Centre,** in the Great Lake Centre on Tongariro Street (☎ **07/378-9000,** fax 07/378-9003), can book accommodations, tours, and other activities, as well as provide a wide range of informative brochures on area attractions, reserve fishing guides, and sell fishing licenses. It also sells stamps, PhoneCards, and souvenirs. The center is open daily from 8:30am to 5pm.

Note: Readers Sue and Frank Thorn of Fallbrook, California, alerted me to **The Super Loo** in the park next to the information center. They said "This is the most elegant state-of-the-art ladies and gents conveniences we've ever seen." And they're right, this award-winning loo has Asian-style toilets and a bidet, as well as conventional western plumbing fixtures. It costs NZ20¢/US14¢ to use a toilet and NZ$1/US70¢ each for shower and locker use. Another plus here is the adjacent park, which has a very nice children's playground.

The **telephone area code** (STD) for the Lake Taupo region is **07.**

ORIENTATION

Taupo is spread along the northeastern tip of the lake, just where the Waikato River, New Zealand's longest, flows out of Lake Taupo's Tapuaeharuru Bay. The main drag is **Tongariro Street,** named after the largest river flowing into the lake. Perpendicular to Tongariro is another important street, named **Heu Heu** (pronounced "hue-hue"). The post office at the corner of Ruapehu and Horomatangi streets is open Monday through Friday from 8:30am to 5pm.

Cheap Thrills: What to See & Do for Free in Taupo

- **Hanging Out at Huka Falls**   It's not the size of the falls that's impressive, rather the speed at which the foaming blue-green waters of the Waikato River move—234,918 litres/62,000 gallons per second. Be sure to check out the view from the lookout on the road above.
- **Walking Around the Craters of the Moon**   The bubbling, boiling mud pools at this thermal area make strange, gurgling noises. The place looks like the aftermath of a huge fire—it's quite eerie, but fascinating at the same time. Get out of your car to experience it fully, but be sure to stay on the marked paths as the earth's crust is very thin and the surface of the ground is hot.
- **Going for a Walk**   Take one of the many great walks described in the **Taupo Walkways** brochure, which you can pick up, free of charge, at the Visitors Information Centre, in the Great Lake Centre on Tongariro Street (☎ 07/ 378-9000).
- **Touring Wairakei Geothermal Power Station**   If you want to witness the awesome power of steam, you've come to the right place. Stop by the Information Centre for a compelling overview of local geothermal activity and how it's harnessed to create electricity; then follow the marked road, which crosses the borefield itself, to a lookout from which you can view the entire site.
- **Tasting Honey**   You shouldn't leave Taupo without sampling the honey or the fruit wine at the **Honey Hive** in Wairakei Tourist Park (☎ 07/374-8553, fax 07/374-8448). While you're here, you can also take a look into the life of the busy honeybees through glass-enclosed live hives.
- **Witnessing the Aratiatia Rapids**   Four times a day October through March (twice a day the rest of the year) water from the Waikato River, which is usually held behind a dam, is released through the gates here and allowed to foam forward. In less than 10 minutes a dry riverbed goes from being an empty basin of boulders to a raging river. After about a half hour, the gates are closed, the released water flows downstream, and the basin of boulders reappears. It's really fascinating to watch.

The small settlements of **Acacia Bay** and **Jerusalem Bay** are just across on the western shore of the lake.

EXPLORING TAUPO
WAIRAKEI TOURIST PARK: EXPERIENCE THE POWER OF STEAM
Located 8km (5 miles) north of Taupo, Wairakei Tourist Park is home to several worthwhile attractions. In addition to those described below, you'll find details on Huka Jet and Wairakei International Golf Course under "For Serious Thrill-Seekers" and "Outdoor Activities," below. State Highway 1 runs through the middle of this area.

If you want to witness the awesome power of steam, visit the ✪ **Wairakei Geothermal Power Station.** When work began in 1950 to harness all that power, this was the second largest such project in the world and the first to use wet steam. Scientists from around the globe came to observe. Using some 60 bores and over 19km (12 miles) of pipeline, the project now supplies a great deal of the North Island's electricity requirements. Stop by the **ECNZ Geothermal Information Centre** (☎ 07/ 374-8216, ext. 8189), which is open daily from 9:30am to 4:30pm. The display and audiovisual show give a compelling overview of local geothermal activity and furnish answers to all the obvious questions (ask for the sheet titled "Questions Often Asked"). Study the excellent borefield model and drilling-process diagram, then leave the center and follow the marked road, which crosses the borefield itself, to a lookout from which you can view the entire site.

The ✪ **Huka Falls** themselves aren't huge but are impressive for the speed at which the blue-green water of the Waikato River moves over the 24-meter/78-foot drop—234,918 litres/62,000 gallons per second. The word *huka* means "foaming" in Maori, and the water does resemble the agitation cycle of a washing machine. Be sure to check out the view from the lookout on the road above. More adventurous souls might consider taking the path alongside the gorge and across the rushing water on a footbridge, which provides a safe but thrilling way to enjoy the falls. Huka Falls can be reached on foot, so if you're in the mood to walk, follow the track from town (see "Readers Recommend," below); it should take about an hour. If you feel like walking farther, from here you can walk to ✪ **Aratiatia Rapids** (allow 2 hours to get there). Time your arrival for 10am, noon, 2pm, or 4pm October through March, and 10am, noon and 2pm April through September, when water, which is usually held behind a dam, is released through the gates and allowed to foam forward. In less than 10 minutes the dry riverbed goes from being an empty basin of boulders to a raging river. After about a half hour, the gates are closed, the released water flows downstream, and the basin of boulders reappears. It's really fascinating to watch. If you don't have time or don't want to take the trek, you can drive right up to the dam and watch from there, but the best view is about 5 minutes' walk downstream.

Learn about the explosive past and present of the Taupo Volcanic Region at the **Volcanic Activity Centre,** Wairakei Research Centre, Huka Falls Loop Road, Wairakei (☎ 07/374-8375). This is the best place in the country to gain an understanding of volcanoes and geothermal activity. A large 3-D map shows the region, which includes the snowcapped volcanoes of Ruapehu, Tongariro, and Ngauruhoe in the south and the Bay of Plenty to the north. Several films are shown—including one on the 1996 eruption of Ruapehu—and exhibits provide general information on geothermal activity, while touch-screen computers can be used to access information on volcanoes and earthquakes. Planned additions include a working model of a geyser, a tornado machine, an earthquake simulator, and interactive volcanoes. The center is open Monday through Friday from 9am to 5pm, Saturday to Sunday from 10am to 4pm. Admission is NZ$5 (US$3.50) for adults, half price for kids.

I really like ✪ **Craters of the Moon** thermal area, which looks like the aftermath of a huge fire—quite eerie, really, especially with the gurgling sounds, the bubbling and boiling mud, and the hissing of the steam tomos (thermal holes). Get out of your car to experience it fully, but be sure to stay on the marked paths as the earth's crust is very thin and the surface of the ground is hot. There's no admission charge, unlike all the thermal sites around Rotorua. **Orakei Korako Geyserland,** located 25 minutes north of Taupo, charges NZ$12.50 (US$8.80), which includes a boat ride. For more information on this special place see "En Route to Taupo" at the end of chapter 7.

SOAKING IN TAUPO HOT SPRINGS

The **Taupo Hot Springs,** behind the De Brett Thermal Hotel, State Highway 5 (the Napier–Taupo highway), Taupo (☎ 07/377-6502; fax 07/377-6501, e-mail debretts@voyager.co.nz), are part of the Onekeneke Valley of Hot Pools and present a relatively inexpensive alternative to the Polynesian Spa in Rotorua. You could easily spend the better part of a day here—bring something to barbecue for lunch or dinner and use most of the other facilities for only NZ$7 (US$4.90). Areas of the main pool vary from 35° to 40°C (95° to 104°F); the 12 private pools range from 37° to 43°C (98.6° to 109.4°F). There's also a children's pool, two spa pools, a hydro slide, a volleyball court, a 7-hole pitch-and-putt course, and a barbecue area. The pools are drained, cleaned, and refilled every night. Admission to the public pool costs NZ$6 (US$4.20) for adults and NZ$2.50 to NZ$3.50 (US$1.75 to US$2.45) for children 5 to 17; kids under 5 are free; private pools cost NZ$7 (US$4.90), which includes use of public pools; the water slide costs an additional NZ$4 (US$2.80) per person for unlimited use, and you can rent towels and togs (swimsuits). The springs are open daily from 7am to 9:30pm (last entrance 9pm).

If you don't have time for a soak in Taupo, you can stop at the **Tokaanu Pools** at the south end of Lake Taupo (see "En Route to Tongariro," below).

OUTDOOR ACTIVITIES

BIKING   Bicycle tours and rentals can be arranged through **Rapid Sensations,** Wairakei Tourist Park, Taupo (☎ 07/378-7902). Their tours go to the Craters of the Moon thermal area. This half-day (2¹/₂-hour) bicycle tour costs NZ$45 (US$31.50) per person. Bicycle rentals cost NZ$15 (US$10.50) per hour or NZ$25 (US$17.50) for a half day.

FISHING   The top draw in this area is ✪ **trout fishing.** Even if you've never cast a line, this may be the very time to join that proverbial "picket fence" of shoreline anglers and experience the singular thrill of feeling a nibble and pulling in a big one. And they do grow *big* in Lake Taupo—the average trout size is 3¹/₂ pounds, with some 8- and 10-pound catches. Just remember that there's a limit of three trout per person per day (you can catch and release as many as you want). The visitors center can fix you up with a license (you can get one for just 1 day, if you'd like) and fill you in on rules and regulations, as well as help you find a guide. (Be careful, though; hiring a guide is not exactly a budget activity.) Two of the recommended **guides** in the area are Gus Moana (☎ 07/378-4839, mobile 025/977-379) and Richard Staines, 6A Harvey St., Taupo (☎ 07/378-2736, fax 07/378-2734). Most restaurants are happy to cook up your catch of the day, but they aren't allowed to offer it on their menu (a New Zealand law designed to keep the sport in the catching).

GOLF   The 18-hole **Wairakei International Golf Course,** Wairakei Tourist Park, P.O. Box 377, Taupo (☎ 07/374-8152), is challenging, not to mention dramatic, with thermal vapors rising in the background. *Golf Digest* rated this course one of the 10 best in the world. Visitors are welcome and rental equipment is available; book well ahead. Greens fees are NZ$30 (US$21) for 9 holes and NZ$55 (US$38.50) for 18 holes. The adjacent 9-hole **Wairakei Resort Course,** State Highway 1, Wairakei Tourist Park (☎ 07/377-8652), charges only NZ$8.50 (US$6) for 9 holes (NZ$7/US$4.90 for students up to 18 and seniors over 60; NZ$4.50/US$3.15 for children 12 and under). Club and trolley hire is available. The difference between the two courses? This should give you the idea: At the Resort Course there's a sign that says "No gum boots allowed on the greens."

HORSE TREKKING   Taupo Horse Treks, Karapiti Road, Craters of the Moon, Wairakei Tourist Park, Wairakei (☎ 07/378-0356), conducts 1- and 2-hour horse treks in the area. The 1-hour tours are NZ$20 (US$14) per person and the 2-hour tours are NZ$35 (US$24.50) per person.

WALKING   The visitors center puts out an excellent "Taupo Walkways" brochure, which outlines the area's ten most popular tracks. These range from 15 minutes to 1¹/₂ hours. Of these, my favorites are the "Great Lake Walk" and the trek out to Huka Falls from Spa Thermal Park with a possible extension to the Aratiatia Rapids. If you have questions, call the **Taupo District Council** (☎ 07/377-9899) or **Information Taupo** (☎ 07/378-9000).

FOR SERIOUS THRILL-SEEKERS

BUNGY JUMPING   You may also want to experience bungy jumping over the beautiful Waikato River on the world's first purpose-built bungy platform. **Taupo Bungy,** 202 Spa Rd. (P.O. Box 919), Taupo (☎ 07/377-1135, fax 07/377-1136), charges NZ$90 (US$63) per jump. *Budget tip:* It's only NZ$80 (US$56) if booked through the Taupo Visitor Information Centre.

FLIGHTSEEING   Scenic float-plane flights leave from the lakefront near the Taupo Boat Harbour; these range from a 10-minute flight over Wairakei's steaming valley, Huka Falls, and Taupo, to 1-hour forays as far away as Tongariro National Park and a 2-hour excursion that takes you even farther afield. Prices range from NZ$30 to NZ$120 (US$19.50 to $78); children are charged half price. You'll find **ARK Aviation Ltd.** (P.O. Box 238, Taupo) at the Boat Harbour (☎ 07/378-7500 or 07/378-9441, fax 07/377-0843). Ark Aviation also offers flights in conventional planes.

JET BOATING   For the ride of your life, try jet boating on the Waikato River. Contact **Huka Jet,** Wairakei Tourist Park (P.O. Box 563), Taupo (☎ 07/374-8572 or 07/374-8016, fax 07/374-8573). They charge NZ$49 (US$34.30) per adult and NZ$25 (US$17.50) for children 5 to 15 for a half-hour adventure from Huka Falls to Aratiatia Falls. Huka Jet and Shotover Jet in Queenstown are operated by the same company, but Huka's ride costs NZ$20 (US$14) less.

WHITE-WATER RAFTING   To arrange a rafting trip on the Rangitaiki River, contact **Rapid Descents Rafting Co.,** P.O. Box 1189, Taupo (☎ 0800/TO RAFT in New Zealand, ☎ and fax 07/377-0419, or mobile 025/533-438). They charge NZ$75 (US$52.50) and also offer trips on the Wairoa and Mohaka rivers. **Rapid Sensations,** Wairakei Tourist Park (☎ 07/378-7902) also conducts river rafting experiences.

LAKE CRUISES

This is a great way to experience the lake and get a different look at its shoreline. Plus, most cruises pass the Maori rock carvings, which are accessible only by boat. **Ernest Kemp Scenic Tours,** at the Taupo Boat Harbour (☎ 07/378-3444, fax 07/378-6136), runs enjoyable trips aboard their steamer, *Ernest Kemp,* every day, year round at 2pm. This 2-hour cruise will set you back NZ$20 (US$14) adults, and NZ$10 (US$7) children (there are special family prices on holidays, too). You can also take a 1-hour evening cruise from November to February; the boat leaves the Boat Harbour at 7pm. The fare of NZ$40 (US$28) adults, NZ$20 (US$14) children under 16, includes dinner. It's essential to book, through the visitors center or at the Boat Harbour.

Golfing for Dollars

Along the shore of Lake Taupo some local entrepreneurs are running a gambit they call the **Hole-In-One Challenge.** They supply the clubs and you attempt to hit a golf ball 115 meters (125 yards) into a hole on a pontoon in the lake. It costs NZ$1 (US 70¢) per ball, NZ$10 (US$7) for 12 balls, and NZ$20 (US$14) for 25 balls. A red hole-in-one wins a holiday for two to Europe; the 12-inch-wide blue and white holes will earn you local lodgings, attractions, products, adventure packages, or dinners. There's about one winner (in any hole) a week. While this may be amusing to watch, it's definitely not a smart activity for the budget traveler. Unless you're Tiger Woods, you might as well stand on the shore and throw your one- and two-dollar New Zealand coins straight into the lake.

Other lake cruise operators include ***Spirit of Musick,*** Adventure Cruises, P.O. Box 1386, Taupo (☎ **025/924-191,** fax 07/377-2926), and **Barbary Cruise,** P.O. Box 294, Taupo (☎ **07/378-3444**).

ORGANIZED TOURS

Minibus tours of the region around Lake Taupo are given daily by ✪ **Paradise Tours,** led by knowledgeable and affable guide Sue King. Book with Sue (☎ **07/ 378-9955** or 025/904-944, fax 07/378-8899). Local tours, given every morning and afternoon, last 2¹/₂ hours and cost NZ$28 (US$19.60). She also offers half- and full-day tours to Orakei–Korako, Rotorua, and the Waitomo caves.

Tuwharetoa Tourism, top end of Tongariro Street, Taupo (☎ **07/378-0254,** fax 07/378-3714), offers an opportunity to experience fishing, horse trekking, hunting, camping, staying in wilderness lodges, and other outdoor pursuits with a local Maori as your guide. The Ngati (tribe) Tuwharetoa have exclusive access to some of the best wilderness areas in the Taupo district. They also offer marae stays and authentic concerts and hangi dinners.

SHOPPING

Try not to leave Taupo until you've checked out the wool and sheepskin products at **The Woolshed,** Ruapehu Street (P.O. Box 1165), Taupo (☎ and fax **07/ 378-9513**). It sells wonderful sweaters, spencers, slippers, sheepskins, and knitting wool (yarn). This is also the place to look for wool bush shirts, gloves, and car-seat covers. The handknits are all crafted in New Zealand. They are open Monday through Saturday from 9am to 5pm and Sunday from 10am to 4pm (later in summer; closed on Christmas Day). American Express, Diners Club, Japan Credit Bank, MasterCard, and Visa are accepted.

New Zealand Corner, Tongariro St., Taupo (☎ **07/377-0303**), carries a wide selection of souvenirs, including videos in both NTSC (for U.S., Canada, and Japan) and PAL (for NZ, Australia, Europe, and the U.K.), T-shirts, table mats (placemats), coasters, Maori carvings, jewelry, honey, and jams. They're open Monday through Saturday from 9am to 6pm and Sunday from 10am to 5pm (longer during summer) and accept all major credit cards.

The **Honey Hive,** Huka Falls Rd. Tourist Loop, Wairakei Tourist Park, Taupo (☎ **07/374-8553,** fax 07/374-8448), carries a huge range of honey and bee products, fruit wine, and souvenirs. If bees make it, they've got it. You can take a look into the life of the busy honeybee with this attraction's glass-enclosed live hives and free video screening. The Bees Knees Cafe here sells delicious honey ice cream; a double cone is NZ$2.80 (US$1.95), and it's the best I've ever tasted. It's open daily from 9am to 5pm. This is a great place to try the different kinds of honey, but I suggest you purchase the more popular ones at supermarket where prices are much lower. (See "Manuka Honey: An Affordable & Delectable Souvenir" in chapter 3.)

At **New Zealand Woodcraft,** also in Wairakei Tourist Park (☎ and fax **07/ 374-8555**), you can watch talented artisans work, turning native timber into useful and decorative items. Be sure to notice the bottles made from old fence posts. The prices are high here, but watching is free.

AFFORDABLE ACCOMMODATIONS

You'll need to reserve far in advance only if you're planning on staying in Taupo during the holiday season. There are more than 3,000 beds available in the area.

The rates given below include the 12.5% GST and free parking.

CAMPGROUNDS & CABINS

In a quiet rural setting overlooking the lake, the **Great Lake Holiday Park,** Acacia Bay Road (P.O. Box 171), Taupo (☎ **07/378-5159,** fax 07/377-2541), offers tent and caravan sites, cabins, and self-contained tourist flats. On the premises are a hot spa pool and recreation room with a pool table, as well as ample picnic tables and barbecues. Best of all, the friendly owners, Keith Ericksen and Glyn and Carolyn Rushby, take much pleasure in providing visitors with information, maps, and brochures on local attractions. The rates for tent and caravan sites are NZ$9 (US$6.30) for adults and NZ$4.50 (US$3.15) for children; for cabins, NZ$26 (US$18.20) double; for tourist flats, NZ$49 (US$34.30) for two people. MasterCard and Visa are accepted. Located about 1km (one half mile) south of the Napier/Taupo turnoff.

SUPER-CHEAP SLEEPS

Bradshaw's Guest House

130 Heu Heu St., Taupo. ☎ **07/378-8288.** 12 rms (7 with bathrm). NZ$57 (US$39.90) double without bathrm, NZ$62 (US$43.40) double with bathrm. Rates include breakfast. Dinners Mon–Fri by prior arrangement NZ$15 (US$10.50) per person. MC, V.

The friendliness of hosts Karen and Daryl Morris makes this a popular place. Bradshaw's is a homey white house set on a quiet residential street near the center of town. The rooms are nicely done up, with attractive furnishings and lots of wood paneling. There's a cozy TV lounge (with books for non-tube addicts), a tea-and coffee room, a laundry, a dining room that faces the lake, and 12 bedrooms, three of which are singles. While the lodgings here are perfectly acceptable and certainly inexpensive, the atmosphere is impacted by the fact that they often have long-term residents staying here.

☺ Rainbow Lodge

99 Titraupenga St., Taupo. ☎ **07/378-5754.** Fax 07/377-1568. E-mail bakpak@reap.org.nz. 15 rms (none with bathrm). NZ$34 (US$23.80) double; NZ$14 (US$9.80) dorm bed. MC, V. Courtesy pickup from the bus station.

Rainbow Lodge, near the town center just off Spa Road, is only a short distance from main highways, shops, the bus depot, and the lake. Sue and Mark Dumble provide a good, cozy atmosphere and offer dormitory rooms and double rooms. Most guests supply their own linens, but they're also available for rent. Communal facilities include toilets, bathrooms, kitchen, dining room, lounge, laundry, game area, and sauna. Underfloor heating keeps things comfortable in winter. The Dumbles will help you arrange all sorts of activities (fishing, tramping, canoe trips), some at special

Waitahanui Lodge, State Highway 1 (R.D. 2), Taupo (☎ **0800/104-321** in New Zealand, or 07/378-7183). *"I'm enclosing a brochure from the cute lodge my husband and I stayed in at Lake Taupo on our honeymoon in New Zealand. Great fishing and nice family."*

—Karen Rydstrom, Evanston, Illinois, USA.

Author's Note: These self-contained cabins are located 8km (5 miles) south of Taupo. There's a tackle store on the premises. The rates are NZ$60 to NZ$70 (US$42 to US$49) double. American Express, Diners Club, MasterCard, and Visa are accepted.

discounts available only to guests. Mountain bikes and fishing rods can be rented here too.

FOR A FEW EXTRA BUCKS

Cedar Park Motor Lodge

State Hwy. 1 at Two Mile Bay (P.O. Box 852), Taupo. ☎ **07/378-6325.** Fax 07/377-0641. 24 units (all with bathrm). TV TEL. NZ$88 (US$61.60) double, NZ$77 (US$53.90) for AAA members. Rates higher during holidays. AE, BC, DC, MC, V. Located across Hwy. 1 from the lakefront, 4km (2¹/₂ miles) south of the center of town.

Cedar Park offers basic accommodations in Taupo, with some two-story units that feature peaked ceilings and picture windows looking out over the lake. Each unit has a separate sitting area, two bedrooms, and a complete kitchen. The grounds offer a heated swimming pool, hot spa pools, a children's play area, barbecue, laundry, and car-wash facilities. The furnishings are dated and there is some deferred maintenance, but the location near the lakefront is convenient.

✪ Cottage Mews Motel

Lake Terrace (P.O. Box 97), Taupo. ☎ **07/378-3004.** Fax 07/378-3005. 5 studios, 6 units. TV TEL. NZ$85 (US$59.50) double small studio; NZ$110 (US$77) double standard studio and unit; NZ$125 (US$88) double unit with lake view. AE, BC, DC, MC, V.

Some of the prettiest lodging in town is right beside the lake in a colonial-style motel with black wood siding and white trim (a bit of New England in the South Pacific). A wheelbarrow filled with bright posies sits at the entrance. The six impressive split-level one-bedroom units have a kitchen, a balcony, toilets both upstairs and down, a king- or queen-size bed, and striking wood trim throughout; two have lake views. All rooms have large spa baths and either a private garden or balcony. My favorite is the one with the lake view, a bit more expensive than the others but worth it. Breakfast is available at an additional charge.

Delmont Lodge

115 Shepherd Rd., Taupo. ☎ **07/378-3304.** Fax 07/378-3322. 3 rms (all with bathrm). NZ$99–$130 (US$69.30–$91) double. Rates include breakfast. Dinner is available by arrangement for NZ$35 (US$24.50). AE, MC, V.

Delmont Lodge is located very close to the Botanical Reserve, which is a great spot to stretch one's legs. The simply-furnished rooms, one twin with private bathroom and two doubles with en suite bathrooms, aren't large but are very clean. Guests are welcome to use the attractive lounge where there are comfortable places to sit and a view of the lake. The living area of the house is up a flight of stairs from the street level, so the luggage lift is a great convenience. Hostess Jenny Delmont had a long career working for Hyatt and Sheraton, and she runs this business very professionally.

Afternoon tea is served upon arrival, and a predinner wine or beer is also included in the rate.

WORTH A SPLURGE

✪ Clearwater Motor Lodge

229 Lake Terrace (P.O. Box 1127), Taupo. ☎ and fax **07/377-2071.** Fax 07/377-0020. 10 units (all with bathrm). TV TEL. NZ$125 (US$88) double. AE, BC, DC, MC, V. Located just south of the intersection of hwys. 1 and 5.

Thanks to readers Edward and Sandra Adler of Painsville, Ohio, for bringing this modern motor lodge to my attention. All rooms have a spa tub, shower, kitchenette, and a small balcony or patio. One downstairs beachfront unit can be configured as a U.S. king-size bed or twins; the rest are New Zealand kings (a little bigger than a U.S. queen); six of the units are beachfront, with awesome lake and mountain views. My favorites are the three bottom units with their own patios. The exterior is salmon-colored stucco with blue trim. Facilities include free laundry, barbecue, and thermal pool. There are two restaurants within walking distance (one of these is Pepper's Brasserie, described below).

GREAT DEALS ON DINING

If you're really watching your pennies, Taupo has KFC, Pizza Hut, McDonald's, Burger King, and Subway. Woolworth's on the corner of Tongariro and Spa Road is open daily from 8am to 8pm (to 9pm on Thursday and Friday) and is the best place to buy groceries. They also have a good selection of wines, a nice salad bar, and a bakery on the premises, but they don't accept credit cards.

Author's note: Be forewarned that many enthusiastic businesspeople open restaurants in this area during the busy summer period, after which they go out of business, so I can't guarantee that all of these places described below will be there when you are.

SUPER-CHEAP EATS

Mountain Kebabs

17 Tongariro St., Taupo. ☎ **0800/KEBABS** in New Zealand. Reservations not accepted. Main courses NZ$6.50–$9 (US$4.55–$6.30). No credit cards. KEBABS.

On the main drag opposite the lake, this decor-less place serves beef, chicken, seafood, and vegetarian kebabs with toasted pita bread on paper plates. Sauces range from yogurt, tahini, and satay to chili, horseradish, and mustard. This is certainly not a glamorous choice—just a tasty, cheap alternative to the fast-food emporiums nearby. This dine-in or takeaway option is not licensed, and you can't bring your own.

Readers Recommend

Colonial Lodge Motel, 134 Lake Terrace, Taupo (☎ 07/378-9846). *"This motel has to be the best I've ever stayed at in New Zealand. It is run by an English couple, Pauline and Phil, who just couldn't do enough for you. The motel opened in August of 1995 and is of an international standard for decor, fittings, etc. The place is themed as a colonial style. Each unit has a full kitchen plus spa bath etc. I cannot fault the place and the cost of NZ$90 to NZ$105 (US$63 to US$74) made me feel that I had received value for money considering what you can pay for a motel and the standard of some units."*
—Paul Raffray, Barnsley, South Yorkshire, U.K.

Author's Note: This property is located across the road from the lake.

Readers Recommend

Robert Harris Tea and Coffee, Lake Taupo. *"While at Lake Taupo we had a lovely, casual self-service lunch at this cafe. It is located on the street facing the lake on the opposite corner to McDonald's."*

—Christine Jenkinson, Sunbury, Victoria, Australia.

✪ Replete Food Company Delicatessen and Cafe

45 Heu Heu St. (corner of Ruapehu St.), Taupo. ☎ 07/378-0606. Reservations not accepted. Lunch main courses NZ$3–$7 (US$2.10–$4.90). AE, MC, V. Daily 8:45–5pm. MODERN NEW ZEALAND.

Replete was the best cheap-eats discovery of my last trip to New Zealand. I couldn't believe the quality of the food and the low prices. You can have a multicourse lunch here for less than NZ$10 (US$7). I was so impressed that I did a bit of snooping around and learned that owner Greg Hefferman was formerly the head chef at exclusive Huka Lodge just out of town. Now he's creating wonderful food here, as well as running a cooking school and culinary shop and writing a cookbook. Everything is prepared with only the freshest seasonal ingredients. There's no preprinted menu; when I ate there, mains included smoked chicken pasta with creamy tomato sauce, beef curry on rice, and baked potato stuffed with salmon and brie. Quiche, sandwiches, salads, and cakes are also available. Breakfast, which includes a "Complete Replete"—crisp honey-cured bacon, wedges of grilled foccacia, huge field mushrooms, poached eggs, and tomato chutney—is available from 8:45 to 10:30am; lunch is available all day. The sidewalk tables are a wonderful place to hang out, watch the world go by, and have a latté, cappuccino, or espresso. The interior is peaceful, done in shades of pumpkin, terra-cotta, and wood with a scattering of local river stones. It's not licensed and you can't bring your own either. Whether you dine in or take away, this is still one of the best budget deals around.

FOR A FEW EXTRA BUCKS

Pepper's Brasserie

In Manuels Beach Resort Hotel, Lake Terrace, Taupo. ☎ 07/378-5110. Reservations accepted to 7:30pm. Main courses NZ$11–$23 (US$7.70–16.10). AE, DC, MC, V. Daily 7:30am–10am and 6:30–9:30pm. INTERNATIONAL.

I used to list the adjacent Edgewater Restaurant at Manuels as a "Worth a Splurge" restaurant in this book, but on my last trip I decided that Pepper's, a more casual dining option, really makes more sense. The Edgewater's mains now range from NZ$26 to $30, just way too expensive for this part of New Zealand. Pepper's Brasserie and Edgewater share the same chef and the dynamite water's-edge view—so close you feel like you're on a boat. The only difference is the lack of white tablecloths, gourmet menu items, and plush seating. At Pepper's, a trip to the salad bar can sometimes be a meal in itself, or at least an accompaniment to a main course of Thai chicken curry with lemon grass, coconut cream, and steamed jasmine rice; S.O.T.B.B., a beefburger on cornbread with avocado and spicy salsa, served with nachos; or Pepper's roast with the potato of the day and other fixings. It's fully licensed too.

WORTH A SPLURGE

Walnut Keep Restaurant

Spa Rd., Taupo. ☎ 07/378-0777. Reservations recommended. Main courses NZ$21–$25.50 (US$14.70–$17.90). AE, DC, MC, V. Daily 6–9:30pm. PACIFIC RIM.

Located on a rise away from the main street, this is a cozy dining spot with dark green walls and plaid draperies. It feels like an old house, but is rumored to have been a "car yard" and has views of surrounding car yards. Main courses include Asian seafood hot pot served with black mushrooms and nama dashi; roasted herb-coated lamb rack served with a garlic and rosemary kumara mash and a licorice-scented marsala jus; and marinated roast duck restin on a pear and parsnip rosti, served with sweet and sour capsicum. It's fully licensed.

TAUPO AFTER DARK

Nightlife is low-key at best in Taupo. There are sometimes disco nights at various places around town, but if you've been fishing for trout on Lake Taupo all day or engaging in any of the wonderful outdoor activities in this area, you'll be more than ready for bed by nightfall anyway. Here are a few nightspots if you're up to it:

Stop by **Mate's Malt House,** 24 Tuwharetoa St. (☎ 07/378-8213), for a beer. Mate's draught, gold lager, and dark are made in a Napier microbrewery and shipped here. This place has loud music, a pool table, and TVs for watching sporting events. A handle costs NZ$2.50 (US$1.80) and they have NZ$1 (US 70¢) drink specials between 7 and 8pm. The bar is open daily from 11:45am to late night; the kitchen serves lunch from noon to 2:30pm and dinner from 6 to 10:30pm.

Holy Cow, Tongariro St., upstairs, Taupo (☎ 07/378-0040) is a popular spot catering to backpackers under 25. Fun and games prevail with pool tables and horizontal bungy, and live bands perform about once a month. A DJ provides music for the dance floor the rest of the time, and dancing on the tables is encouraged here. A handle will set you back NZ$3.50 (US$2.45). Open daily from 5pm to late; happy hour is from 5 to 7pm and 9 to 10pm.

EN ROUTE TO TONGARIRO

The 94km (58-mile) drive from Taupo to Tongariro National Park is an easy one—good roads with fluctuating scenery as you follow Highway 1 along the eastern shore of Lake Taupo through small towns and fishing settlements, around charming bays, with Lake Taupo always on your right. Look for **Motutaiko Island** (the only one in the lake) as you approach Hatepe. As you near the southern end of the lake, you'll begin to catch glimpses of volcanic cones, which are at the heart of the park. Consider stopping in **Turangi** if trout are your passion. The nice people at the Creel Tackle Shop or the Turangi Fly Shop rent equipment and might even give you some free advice, which you'll need, because fishing techniques in New Zealand are very different from those used in other parts of the world. The **Tongariro River** is one of the best-known trout-fishing places in the world. (There's info on fishing here in chapter 4, "The Active Vacation Planner.")

I also recommend a detour to the nice thermal pools at **Tokaanu.** Even if you don't soak, there's a great nature walk here. Highway 47 cuts off from Highway 1 to lead you through plateau-like tussocklands across to Highway 48 and the entrance to park headquarters and the elegant Grand Château hotel. It's clearly signposted, and as you leave Lake Taupo behind, the volcanic nature of this terrain begins to dominate the landscape. By the time you reach the Château, you will have entered a world completely different from the one you've left behind.

WHERE TO STAY & EAT ALONG THE WAY

✪ Bridge Fishing Lodge

State Hwy. 1, Turangi. ☎ 0800/509-995 in New Zealand, or 07/386-8804. Fax 07/386-8803. 32 rms (all with bathrmrm), 2 suites. MINIBAR TV TEL. NZ$101 (US$70.70) double; family suites from NZ$145 (US$102). AE, DC, MC, V.

Joy Wardell, Omori Road (R.D. 1), Turangi (☎ **07/386-7386**). *"Joy lives in a home adjoining her daughter and son-in-law's property. Joy was our principal host, but the entire family enjoys meeting people, and they dropped by frequently for dinner or drinks. Both homes have magnificent views of Lake Taupo, the mountains, and farmlands and are located near the mighty Tongariro River (fishing, jet boating, and rafting) and Mount Ruapehu (skiing and walking). Joy offers one bedroom (twin beds) with a private bath. She's a fun, energetic, and kind woman who enjoys life. She made us feel most welcome."*
　　　　　　　　　　　　　　　　—Carolann H. Natemeyer, Houston, Texas, USA.

Author's Note: B&B is NZ$30 (US$21) per person; a three-course dinner is available for NZ$20 (US$14) per person; credit cards are not accepted.

Jack and Betty Anderson, 1 Poto St., Turangi (☎ and fax **07/386-8272**). *"I stayed at seven B&Bs in New Zealand, and these were the most fun hosts. They are relaxed, happy people. I went fishing and caught some trout, and Jack did a super Cajun-style dinner with the fish. I ended up staying 3 nights rather than 1. They offer two self-contained cottages, as well as three en-suite rooms in their home."*
　　　　　　　　　　　　　　　　—John W. Behle, Cincinnati, Ohio, USA.

Author's Note: B&B is NZ$70 (US$49) double; no credit cards accepted.

The Bridge Fishing Lodge, at the southern end of Lake Taupo, has rooms for single or double occupancy, seven with fully equipped kitchens. The rooms have tea and coffee facilities, fridges, videos, radios, and heaters. There's a licensed restaurant, a bar, a guest lounge, a sauna, a barbecue, a laundry, and a tour desk. They'll also rent you fishing tackle and waders if the fish in the lake and adjacent Tongariro River prove too great a temptation. Family units sleep six.

The Settlers Motel

State Hwy. 1 and Arahori St. (P.O. Box 30), Turangi. ☎ **07/386-7745.** Fax 07/386-6354. 5 studios and 3 units. TV TEL. NZ$75 (US$52.50) studio for 2; NZ$81 (US$56.70) unit for 2. AE, MC, V.

At the southern end of Lake Taupo, the Settlers offers eight serviced units with kitchens, radios, and heaters, and there's a guest laundry. They can provide fishing guides, and they've even included fish-cleaning facilities, so when you catch your dinner you can cook it up in your unit. Licensed restaurants and shops are a short walk away. There are also two-bedroom units, and one with a water bed. The hosts here are Bryan and Karen Cox.

2　Tongariro National Park

99km (61 miles) SW of Taupo; 141km (87 miles) NE of Wanganui

The landscape, dominated by three volcanoes that rise with stark beauty from heath-like plains, is dramatic. The Maori consider the volcanoes sacred (*tapu*) and have mythical explanations for their origins. In the past, they buried their chiefs in caves along the slopes.

　　Ruapehu, with its 2,796-meter (9,227-foot) snowcapped summit, is the highest mountain on the North Island and provides its principal skiing facilities while holding in its basin the simmering, ice-ringed Crater Lake. This active volcano erupted in June, 1996, catching scientists monitoring the volcano by surprise—a few days

---

For the Love of Pihanga

There were once, so the story goes, many mountains in the North Island's center, all male with the exception of Pihanga. This lovely maiden mountain lived just above Turangi on the edge of Lake Taupo. All the male mountains loved Pihanga, and each wanted her for his wife, but she loved only Tongariro, who defeated each of the others in battle and sent them packing. Taranaki (Mt. Egmont) slunk off to the west where he stands in solitary splendor today. His trail became the Whanganui River, and you can still see the enormous depression under his Fantham's Peak put there by Tongariro's kick. When mists surround Taranaki/Mt. Egmont today, the Maori will tell you he is weeping for his lost love. The defeated Putauaki went to the Bay of Plenty where he is now called Mt. Edgecumbe. Tauhara moved slowly, stopping to glance back at the lovely Pihanga, and only reached the northeastern shore of Lake Taupo, where he still stands today. In Maori, Tauhara means "the lonely mountain."

---

before the eruption they had downgraded the mountain's danger rating after 8 months of relative inactivity following the spectacular eruptions of September and October 1995. Prior to this, Ruapehu had been quiet for 8 years. In-depth information on Ruapehu and up-to-date news can be found at www.geo.mtu.edu/volcanoes/new.zealand/ruapehu and www.nzgeographic.co.nz/ruapehu.

Ngauruhoe, rising 2,290 meters (7,557 ft.), smolders constantly and from time to time sends showers of ash and lava spilling from its crater (the last in 1975) to alter its shape once again. For more information on Ngauruhoe check out the Wairakei Research Centre Web site at www-tpo.gns.cri.nz/wairakei.html. **Tongariro,** lowest of the three (1,968 meters/6,494 ft.), is also the most northerly and the center of Maori legend. The peaks are at the end of a volcanic chain that extends all the way to the islands of Tonga, 1,000 miles away. Their origin is fairly recent, as these things go, dating back only about 2 million years.

Tongariro National Park is now a World Heritage Site, but long before this was declared, a Maori chief had the wisdom and foresight to preserve it. In 1887, Te Heuheu Tukino, a paramount chief of the Tuwharetoa tribe, in an effort to shield the tapu nature of the Tongariro Mountains, gifted the land to the people of New Zealand. By this act, he guaranteed that it would be protected for all people, for all time. The park became the first national park in New Zealand and the second in the world.

ESSENTIALS

GETTING THERE & GETTING AROUND

BY TRAIN   The *Overlander* and the *Northerner* express trains stop at National Park, the community on the west side of Tongariro National Park.

BY BUS   InterCity provides bus service to National Park.

BY CAR   Highway 1 runs along the eastern side of the park; Highway 4 goes through National Park on the west side; highways 47 and 48 bring travelers from the south shore of Lake Taupo into the heart of the park.

VISITOR INFORMATION

The Whakapapa Visitor Centre is in the village of **Whakapapa,** at the end of State Highway 48. The Visitor Centre (☎ **07/892-3729,** fax 07/892-3814) offers information and assistance in planning hikes and tramps within Tongariro National Park.

It is open daily from 8am to 5pm and provides up-to-date volcanic, weather, and track information. Hut and camping passes, detailed maps and brochures, hunting permits, and other items are available here. The center has displays on the natural and human history of the park along with two excellent audiovisual presentations—*The Sacred Gift of Tongariro* and *The Ring of Fire.* Information about the local ski fields 7km (4¹/₂ miles) above the village is also available.

The **telephone area code** (STD) for the national park area is **07.**

EXPLORING THE PARK
SKIING

Skiing is *the* activity during the season, which normally lasts from June to October or November, with three well-developed fields inside the park. The most popular is the **Whakapapa Ski Area,** on the northwestern side of Mount Ruapehu, just 7km (4¹/₂ miles) beyond the village. Whakapapa's "sister resort" is Copper Mountain in Colorado, and there are some reciprocal privileges. When you get here, call ☎ **07/892-3833** or 07/892-3738 for snow and ski information. For more details on skiing, see chapter 4, "The Active Vacation Planner."

WALKING

There are plenty of fascinating walks within the park's boundaries. You can view more than 500 plant species, the giant rimu trees (some well over 600 years old), and 30 bird species. Then there's that hot ✪ **Crater Lake** on Mount Ruapehu, the **Ketetahi Hot Springs,** and a pleasant 20-minute **Ridge Track.** Ambitious trekkers can take a whack at climbing all three volcanoes in 1 day—but believe me, it takes a lot of ambition, with a healthy dose of stamina thrown in! It's much easier to ride the two chairlifts that operate during summer. Check with the park headquarters for details on all possibilities.

AFFORDABLE ACCOMMODATIONS

There aren't a lot of choices if you want to stay in the park; there are more choices in nearby Turangi (see "En Route to Tongariro," at the end of the Taupo section, earlier in this chapter). You might consider a night or two at the elegant Grand Château, but it's hardly budget-friendly. If you do stay in this area, remember that early reservations are absolutely necessary during the ski season.

CAMPGROUNDS & CABINS

The **Whakapapa Holiday Park,** Mount Ruapehu (☎ and fax **07/892-3897**), is down the first right turn after you pass park headquarters. This member of the Top 10 Holiday Parks is set on the banks of Whakapapanui Stream and is surrounded by lush bushland. There are tent and caravan sites (all nicely screened by foliage), four six-berth cabins, and two four-berth cabins. Cabins come with two-tier bunks, table and chairs, and electric heating. On the premises are toilets and showers, electric stoves, a laundry with a drying room, and a camp store. Rates for caravan sites are NZ$10 (US$7) per adult, half price for children; tent sites are NZ$8 (US$5.60) per adult, half price for children; cabins run NZ$33 (US$23.10) for two people. Tourist flats are available for NZ$50 (US$35) for two. Bunk-bed accommodations are available from November to April for NZ$12.50 (US$8.80) per person per night. Bankcard, MasterCard, and Visa are accepted.

Trampers on the mountain slopes can arrange, for a small fee, through the park headquarters to use strategically placed rustic huts, which are equipped with bunks and coal stoves.

Ruapehu Skotel

c/o Mount Ruapehu Post Office. ☎ **07/892-3719.** Fax 07/892-3777. 31 rms (22 with bathrm), 12 hostel rms, 5 chalets. NZ$36 (US$25.20) double hostel rm without bath, NZ$82 (US$57.40) double without bath; NZ$115 (US$81) double with bath; NZ$110 (US$77) deluxe chalet. Rates higher in ski season, lower for solo travelers. AE, DC, MC, V.

This rustic lodge on the lower slopes of Mount Ruapehu, above the Grand Château, offers both self-contained chalets and lodge accommodations. The attractive slant-roofed lodge rooms can accommodate two, three, or four people; most have hot and cold running water, and many have shower and toilet. There's a large, bright guest kitchen with individual food lockers, stoves, and fridge. Also on the premises are a laundry, a sauna, private spas, a gym, and a large games room. The lounge invites conviviality, and there's a restaurant/bar. The chalets sleep six (four bunks and two single beds); the kitchens are completely equipped, and there's a TV. Outside, views of Ngauruhoe's cone are spectacular. All buildings are centrally heated and have piped-in music. This is a lively place, with movies, hikes, fishing, and botany expeditions. A reader wrote to say that she was "very impressed with the food" here.

WORTH a SPLURGE

✪ The Grand Château

Mount Ruapehu, Tongariro National Park. ☎ **07/892-3809.** Fax 07/892-3704. 64 rms (all with bathrm). MINIBAR TV TEL. Summer, NZ$118.15–$174.40 (US$82.70–$122.05) double. Winter, NZ$136.70–$262.15 (US$95.70–$183.50) single or double. AE, BC, DC, JCB, MC, V.

The Grand Château, at the end of State Highway 48, looks out of place in this rugged environment. The huge tricolor chateau-style building stands alone on a wide expanse of barren terrain. It would look more at home in a gentle European setting than it does here in New Zealand. The hotel was built in 1929 and has a 1930s deco-style lounge with plush carpeting, crystal chandeliers, and a grand piano in the public spaces. It is rumored that the design was copied from the Banff Springs Hotel in Canada. The Grand Château is a hotel in the manner of years gone by. The rooms are elegant, and there are such additional comforts as a heated pool and sauna. Other facilities include a 9-hole golf course, tennis courts, a gym, and a bowling green. There is a lovely formal dining room on the lobby level and a casual bistro downstairs. The Château justifies its listing in a budget travel guide on several counts: It's an outstanding hotel, it's internationally famous, and it's one of the only places to stay in this area.

GREAT DEALS ON DINING

You can eat at any price range at ✪ **The Grand Château,** Mount Ruapehu, Tongariro National Park (☎ 07/892-3809).

For the truly budget-minded, there's the paneled, no-frills **Cafeteria,** open every day from 8am to 5pm, where you'll find meat pies, sandwiches, salads, and such at low prices. The cozy, pub-like **Carvery** serves a nice evening meal with a choice of roasts, fish, grills, and salads. For an elegant—and expensive—dinner, it's the high-ceilinged, chandeliered **Ruapehu Room,** from 6:30 to 9pm. The à la carte menu features New Zealand specialties, as well as many exotic dishes, which are prepared or flamed at your table.

The Château can also supply you with **box lunches** for a day on the slopes, and during ski season there are kiosks and snack bars open at the ski fields. Try the **Knoll Ridge Chalet,** a snack bar on the ski field.

EN ROUTE TO WANGANUI

The 141km (87 miles) from Tongariro National Park to Wanganui pass through some of the most scenic countryside in the North Island. Indeed, the winding road between Raetihi and Wanganui passes through what has been labeled the "Valley of a Thousand Hills." These are the **Parapara Hills,** formed from volcanic ash, with shell-rock seams and great walls of "papa" rock (a blue clay), which can, incidentally, be quite slippery when landslides put it across the highway. This entire drive, however, is one to be done at a leisurely pace (with an eye out, especially in winter, for patches of that clay across the road) so as to enjoy the spectacular scenery. Sheep farms appear along the way and deer farms are also visible from the highway. There are numerous rest areas en route, offering delightful panoramic views, and in autumn, silver birches dot the landscape with brilliant golds and oranges.

You'll pass the beautiful **Raukawa Falls,** skirt three small lakes whose waters shade from green into red into black during the course of the year and are held sacred by the Maori, then cross the Whanganui River over the Dublin Street Bridge to enter Wanganui.

3 Wanganui

141km (87 miles) SW of Tongariro National Park; 160km (99 miles) SE of New Plymouth; 193km (120 miles) N of Wellington

Wanganui (the river and park are spelled "Whanganui") was born amid fierce controversy over the way in which Col. William Wakefield, acting for the New Zealand Company in 1840, took title to the land. It seems he came ashore with an assortment of mirrors, blankets, pipes, and other trinkets and piled them on the site of the present-day Moutoa Gardens. With this offering, he "bought" some 40,000 acres of Maori land. The Maori, however, replaced Wakefield's gifts with 30 pigs and nearly 10 tons of potatoes—their customary "gift for gift"—and had no idea they had transferred title to their lands.

Despite the dispute, settlers began arriving and the town prospered, though constantly caught up in Maori-Pakeha conflicts, some of which were quite violent. It wasn't until 1848 that land problems were laid to rest with the payment of £1,000 for about 80,000 acres clearly defined in a bill of sale from the Maori, which ended with the words "Now all the land contained within these boundaries . . . we have wept and sighed over, bid farewell to and delivered up forever to the Europeans."

It was the Whanganui River (whose riverbed was carved out by Taranaki in his wild flight from Tongariro's wrath) that made this site such a desirable one for the Europeans. It had long served as an important waterway to the interior, as well as affording an excellent coastal harbor. It was said by the Maori that the great explorer Kupe sailed the river. Pakehas soon established regular steamer service between the town and Taumarunui, and because of the magnificent scenery along the riverbank, the 3-day journey quickly became an important sightseeing trip for tourists from all over the world. The steamer plied the river until 1934, and it's a pity that fire destroyed the wonderful old hotel and houseboat that provided overnight accommodations to those travelers.

A large portion of the Whanganui River is now part of a national park, with an entrance to its wonderfully wild mix of virgin forest and secondary-growth bush at the historic little settlement of Pipiriki. Set right on the river, this was once the terminus for riverboats, and it nestles among wooded hills, with picnic spots and easily accessible bush reserves. Most of Whanganui National Park is accessible only by boat or on foot.

ESSENTIALS
GETTING THERE & GETTING AROUND

BY BUS **InterCity** and **Newmans** provide service between Wanganui and Auckland, New Plymouth, National Park, and Wellington.

BY CAR Wanganui can be reached via Highways 3 and 4.

VISITOR INFORMATION

The **Wanganui Visitors Information Centre** is located at 101 Guyton St. (P.O. Box 637), Wanganui (☎ and fax **06/345-3286**). Pick up a copy of their handy "Wanganui, The River City" brochure. The center can also furnish you with other useful brochures, book river tours, and provide maps. Be sure to notice the topographical table map on which you can trace your route through this scenic region. Visitors are sure to get a warm welcome here from Vivian Morris and her staff. They're on hand Monday through Friday from 8:30am to 5pm and Saturday and Sunday from 10am to 2pm (extended hours during January and February).

The General **Post Office** is on Ridgeway Street.

The **telephone area code** (STD) for Wanganui is **06.**

SPECIAL EVENTS

Whangamomona Republic Day takes place on the Saturday nearest to November 1. This is a big spoof, which got started when boundary changes moved the town of Whangamomona (located east of New Plymouth and north of Wanganui) from the Taranaki region to that of Wanganui-Manawatu. "Passports" are issued and entry visas sold to visitors when borders are closed around this self-styled republic. There are all sorts of street entertainment and food stalls, with proceeds going to charity. Call ☎ **06/759-6080** for more details.

EXPLORING WANGANUI: WHAT TO SEE & DO
OUTDOOR ACTIVITIES

For a good look at Wanganui and its environs, head to ✪ **Durie Hill,** at the south end of the Wanganui Bridge at Victoria Avenue. Pick up the souvenir booklet that tells you the history of this place, then go through a 672-foot tunnel to reach a unique elevator, which takes you to the summit, 216 feet up. The fare is NZ$1 (US 70¢), and you'll count it money well spent. From the platform at the top, Wanganui is spread before you: The historic river's winding path is clear; to the west stretches the Tasman Sea; and to the north rises Mount Egmont (that unlucky lover, Taranaki). If you're game to walk up 176 steps, the top of the nearby **War Memorial** will give you a view that extends from Mount Ruapehu all the way to the South Island. Even from the ground, the War Memorial Tower is worth a few minutes of your time. It's constructed of shell rock from the riverbanks, which holds two-million-year-old fossils that prove conclusively that Wanganui was once a part of the sea.

There are delightful **walks** in and around Wanganui. Look for the brochure "A Heritage Walk Around Wanganui City" at the information center. Another, the **Atene Skyline Walk,** takes a full day (about 8 hours) but rewards you with stunning views of the area and a "meander" around what was once seabed. Trampers who hanker for a several-days trek through **Whanganui National Park** should ask for requirements and other details at the Visitors Information Centre.

Be sure to stroll down **Victoria Avenue,** Wanganui's main drag. A 4-block area in the city center has been renovated and sports Victorian-style street lights, park benches, brick paving, and pocket gardens—all very attractive.

If you like raspberries (as I do) and you're in Wanganui between November and January, ask the visitor center for directions to a **pick-your-own berry farm.** It's a real treat!

Children will enjoy the romp, grownups the respite, at the **Kowhai Park Playground** on Anzac Parade near the Dublin Street Bridge. The Jaycees of Wanganui built it, and its 4 acres now hold a Tot Town Railway, a huge whale, brontosaurus, a clock tower, sea-serpent swings, all sorts of storybook characters, and even a mini-volcano to explore. And speaking of parks, save time for a leisurely stroll through the one at **Virginia Lake** (adjacent to Great North Road and St. John's Hill), whose grounds are a haven of trees, flowers, water lilies, ducks, swans, an aviary, and beautiful winter gardens.

The riverside ✪ **Moutoa Gardens** historic reserve is where Maori-Pakeha contact was first made and the first controversial "purchase" of Maori land was transacted. There are memorials to Maori war dead, statues, and the city courthouse there now. It's down at Taupo Quay, off Victoria Quay (beside the huge computer center, a vivid contrast between yesterday and today).

Golfers will find the attractive, centrally located 9-hole Gonville Domain Municipal Golf Course on York Street (☎ 06/344-5808). The Castlecliff course (☎ 06/344-4554) has 18-holes. **Swimmers** can head for the family fun center, which has an outdoor pool plus learners' and toddlers' pools, and there are picnic and barbecue areas. The Gonville Complex is on Tawa Street (☎ 06/345-5990).

OTHER INTERESTING SIGHTS

Whanganui Regional Museum
In the Civic Centre, Watt St. ☎ **06/345-7443.** Admission NZ$2 (US$1.40) for adults, NZ60¢ (US42¢) for children over 5, free for children under 5. Mon–Sat 10am–4:30pm, Sun and public holidays 1–4:30pm. Closed Good Friday and Christmas Day. Walk 1 block east of Victoria Ave. toward the end of Maria Place.

You won't want to miss the Whanganui Regional Museum—it's the largest regional museum in the country, and includes a large Maori collection, a gallery showing Maori portraits by Lindauer, a settler's cottage, natural-history exhibits, and a 75-foot war canoe built in 1810, which is one of the largest in the country and still has bullets from the Maori wars imbedded in its hull.

St. Paul's Anglican Memorial Church
In the suburb of Putiki. Free admission. Daily 9am–6pm (if the church is locked, inquire at the house next to the church hall).

St. Paul's was built in 1936 by Maori and Pakehas working together. The stained-glass Williams Memorial Window features the figure of Christ wearing robes with a Maori-design border, and there's fine carving in the church's interior.

✪ Holly Lodge Estate Winery
Papaiti Rd., Upper Aramoho, Wanganui. ☎ and fax **06/343-9344.** Free admission. Paddlewheeler fare NZ$14 (US$9.10) adults, NZ$8 (US$5.20) children under 16. Daily 9am–6pm. Take the Wine Trip aboard the paddlewheeler *Otunui* (☎ 06/345-0344 or 025/432-997) from the city marina at the foot of Victoria Avenue or drive out Somme Parade.

Plan to spend an hour or two at the Holly Lodge Estate Winery. You can drive out Somme Parade to the winery, but the approach by river via the historic paddlewheeler *Otunui* is much more fun. The Wine Shop and Tasting Bar give you a chance to test several of the wines, liqueurs, sherries, and ports and buy at wholesale prices. Papaiti also has several orchard and camellia gardens open to the public. The Estate offers visitors a fully licensed bar and serves light meals and morning and afternoon teas throughout the day.

Bushy Park

Hwy. 3, 24km (16 miles) northwest of Wanganui (Kai Iwi, R.D. 8, Wanganui). ☎ and fax **06/ 342-9879.** Admission for day visitors, NZ$3 (US$2.10) adults, NZ$1 (US70¢) children 7–15; children under 7 free; NZ$7 (US$4.90) family. MC, V. Daily 10am–5pm. Turn off State Hwy. 3 at Kai Iwi and drive 8km (5 miles) to the park.

Bushy Park was originally the homestead of G. F. Moore, who came to Wanganui in the mid-1860s. The fine old home built in 1906 was occupied by his descendants until 1962, when the house and grounds, plus 211 acres of native forest, were bequeathed to the Royal Forest and Bird Protection Society. The large wooden homestead stands in spacious lawns and gardens planted with a large variety of native plants, with a backdrop of some 220 acres of native bush. Located in the native bush is New Zealand's largest flowering Northern Rata, the circumference of which is over 14 meters (45^1/2 feet); it's approximately 1,200 years old. An Interpretation Centre houses displays devoted to forest ecology, and visitors are free to walk the forest trails and picnic on the extensive grounds. Devonshire teas are available.

There is accommodation in a self-catering bunkhouse for NZ$15 (US$10.50) per person, and bed and breakfast accommodation in the homestead for NZ$80 to $100 (US$56 to $70) double.

Bason Botanical Reserve

Rapanui Rd. Free admission. Reserve, daily 8am–dusk; conservatory, Mon–Fri 9am–4:30pm, Sat–Sun and holidays 2–4pm. Take State Hwy. 3 about 5^1/2km (3^1/2 miles) west to Rapanui Rd., turn left, and continue to Mowhanau Beach.

The Botanical Reserve's Homestead Garden is a delightful place for a stroll among more than 100 camellias and a wide assortment of shrubs, vines, annuals, bulbs, and perennials. The ultramodern conservatory holds the interesting display center and tropical plant house. The reserve encompasses 25.6 hectares (64 acres) and includes a deer enclosure, arboretum, lookout point, and picnic flat (where there are three gas barbecues for visitor use).

RIVER TOURS

Exploring the river by ❂ **jet boat** takes top priority for most visitors to Wanganui, and there are several options for doing it. But let me suggest that before you set out, drop by the information center and purchase the excellent Whanganui River map published by the Department of Lands & Survey—it's an excellent investment, showing the river and its banks in detail, with historical notes on each point of interest. I further suggest that you study the map before you book your river trip—while there is certainly no *un*interesting part of the river, there may be some portion you'd particularly like to see, and you'll want to be certain you choose a jet boat that will take you there. The information center can also give you current details on which jet-boat tours are operating, departure and return times, and prices in effect at the time of your visit (I try, but you know what can happen to prices).

Rivercity Tours, P.O. Box 4224, Wanganui (☎ **06/344-2554,** mobile 025/ 443-421, fax 06/344-7462), has a lovely 2-hour jet-boat tour that leaves from the terminal in the city and takes you out to Hipango Park. The guide is not only informative but entertaining as well, giving interesting anecdotes about the river and the country through which you're passing.

Rivercity Tours also offers jet-boat trips on the river, as well as 2- to 5-day canoe adventures, suitable for people of all ages and experience. Their minibus road tours are highly recommended. The **mail run** leaves the post office at 7:15am on Monday through Friday and returns in mid-afternoon; the cost is NZ$25 (US$17.50) and includes tea and coffee (bring your own lunch); reservations are essential. Best of all, friendly Don and Maree Adams and their staff will design a tour tailor-made to your special interests. Call for schedules and prices.

AFFORDABLE ACCOMMODATIONS

That famed Wanganui hospitality extends to virtually every accommodations owner or manager I've met, and you can be sure of a friendly reception no matter where you end up staying. There are good digs both in town and in the suburbs.

The 12.5% GST is included in the rates listed below.

CAMPGROUNDS & CABINS

Four miles east of town, on the city side of the river, the **Aramoho Holiday Park,** 460 Somme Parade, Aramoho, Wanganui (☎ 06/343-8402), has spacious, shady grounds on the riverbank. There are cabins, some with four bunks, some with a double bed and two bunks; graded cabins that sleep two to six, with hot and cold running water, small electric stoves, refrigerators, cooking utensils, and heaters; and tourist apartments and motel units that sleep up to seven, with a complete kitchen, china, cutlery, pots and pans, a toaster, an electric coffee pot, and a private toilet and shower. One motel room sleeps nine and is accessible to wheelchairs. You can rent linen, blankets, and irons. The communal kitchen has gas stoves and a fridge, the laundry includes dryers and an ironing board, and the toilets and showers are tile and Formica. In addition to the barbecue, games room, and children's play area, there's a 7-day grocery store just across the road. Tent and caravan sites are also available in tree-shaded spots. Rates run NZ$8.50 (US$6) per person for tent sites, NZ$23 (US$16.10) for standard cabins, NZ$32 (US$22.40) for a cabin for two, and NZ$60 (US$42) for a motel room for two. Bankcard, MasterCard, and Visa are accepted.

The **Avro Motel** also has caravan and camping facilities (see "Super-Cheap Sleeps," below).

SUPER-CHEAP SLEEPS

Avro Motel and Caravan Court

36 Alma Rd., Wanganui. ☎ **06/345-5279.** Fax 06/345-2104. 18 studios and units, 2 tourist flats, 10 caravan sites. TV TEL. NZ$60 (US$42) studio for 1; NZ$70 (US$49) apt for 2; NZ$50 (US$35) tourist flat for 2, extra person NZ$10 (US$7); NZ$18 (US$12.60) caravan site for 2. Auto club discounts. Weekly rates available. AE, BC, DC, MC, V.

There's much to choose from at the Avro. The gardenlike grounds hold bed-sitters (studios) and one-, two-, and three-bedroom units, all with kitchens and wide windows overlooking the lawns. There's an outdoor swimming pool, two indoor spa pools, a children's play area, and a laundry. Mary and Harvey Nixon are the hosts at this nice motel about a mile from the town center. There's a licensed restaurant just 100 yards from the motel, with a 9-hole golf course nearby.

Incidentally, the Avro has very good caravan facilities: 10 hookups, each with a small cabin enclosing a shower, toilet, and dressing room. Caravan guests may also use the laundry.

The Riverside Inn and YHA Hostel

2 Plymouth St., Wanganui. ☎ and fax **06/347-2529.** 8 rms (none with bathrm), 22 backpacker beds in 6 rms. NZ$65 (US$45.50) double bed and breakfast; NZ$16 (US$11.20) per person dorm (without breakfast); NZ$17 (US$11.90) per person double/twin (without breakfast). BC, MC, V.

Set back from the street in a flower garden, this rambling 1895 wooden house has been lovingly brought up to date through renovation, with due respect for its age and character. The guest house accommodations are decorated with lace curtains, fringed lampshades, and potted plants. The parlor is furnished in wicker and cane, and there's a TV lounge and breakfast room with tea and coffee facilities. The backpacker lodgings are in the rear of the building. Cooked breakfast and dinner are available for an extra charge. Patricia Moore is a helpful host.

FOR A FEW EXTRA BUCKS

✪ Acacia Park Motel

140 Anzac Parade, Wanganui East. ☎ and fax **06/343-9093**. 13 units (all with bathrm). TV TEL. NZ$65 (US$45.50) double in studio; NZ$70–$75 (US$49–$52.50) double in family unit. AE, BC, DC, MC, V.

One of Wanganui's prettiest motels, the Acacia is set in 2 acres of parkland overlooking the river, with units spread among magnificent old trees. The attractive units have radios, electric blankets, and electric heating. Eight are fully self-contained, sleeping four to six, with shower, toilet, fridge, electric range, and full kitchen. Five serviced units sleep up to three and have a fridge, tea and coffee facilities, toaster, and electric frying pan. There's a guest laundry, a spa pool, a games room with a pool table, a children's play area, and a trampoline. The more expensive units have a kitchen. The Acacia is 1.5km (1 mile) from the center of town.

Grand Hotel

Guyton and St. Hill sts., Wanganui. ☎ **06/345-0955**. Fax 06/345-0953. 57 rms (all with bathrm), 1 suite. TV TEL. NZ$55–$65 (US$38.50–$45.50) double; extra person NZ$10 (US$7); NZ$95 (US$67) double two-bedroom suite. AE, BC, DC, MC, V.

Modernization in this older hotel is limited to facilities and furnishings, with holdovers from its beginnings like dark-wood paneling and fireplaces in the spacious public rooms, oil paintings in gold-leafed frames, the old carved-wood staircase, and a bar crammed full of excellent carvings by local Maori. The furniture is modern (huge, comfortable chairs grouped around low tables in the lounge), yet the decor (upholstering, draperies, and so on) retains a period look.

The guest rooms range from those accommodating just one to those sleeping up to five comfortably. Each is individually decorated, a nice departure from the standardized look of most present-day hotel rooms. A two-family suite features two bedrooms, one on each side of the central lounge. There's a Cobb & Co. restaurant on the premises.

GREAT DEALS ON DINING
SUPER-CHEAP EATS

Capers

Victoria Arcade, Victoria Ave ☎ **06/345 8119**. Reservations recommended. Lunch main courses NZ$4–$6.50 (US$2.80–$4.55). No credit cards. Mon–Fri 7:30am–5pm, Sat 8am–3pm. NEW ZEALAND.

At the rear of Victoria Arcade, Capers offers wholesome fare and very good value prices. The high ceiling and large number of green plants contribute to the pleasant atmosphere. Daily specials are described on a chalkboard menu. The best bet is the NZ$5 (US$3.50) luncheon plate served from noon to 2pm. Locals congregate here to enjoy the homemade cakes—especially the Chelsea buns. The hosts are Judith and Peter. (I forgot to ask their last name, but I remember she told me she does all the baking.) Licensed.

Cobb & Co.

In the Grand Hotel, Guyton and St. Hill sts. ☎ **06/345-0955**. Fax 06/345-0953. Reservations recommended Fri–Sat for dinner. Light meals NZ$6–$15 (US$4.20–$10.50). AE, BC, DC, MC, V. Daily 7am–5pm and 5:30–10pm. NEW ZEALAND/BISTRO.

No matter what your price or appetite range, this Cobb & Co. in the town center comes up with just the right dish. The coffee shop has an attractive light, bright decor and offers both booths and tables. (Be sure to notice the plaster detailing on the ceiling.) The same family-friendly menu is served for lunch and dinner and features steaks, fish, chicken, and roasts prepared with basic, unimaginative sauces. Fully licensed.

Top-o-Town's Coffee Shop

198 Victoria Ave. ☎ **06/345-7615.** Reservations not required. Light meals NZ$3–$11 (US$2.10–$7.70). No credit cards. Mon–Fri 6:30am–4pm, Sat 8am–2pm, Sun 10am–2pm. KIWI.

My favorite small, inexpensive restaurant in the center of Wanganui is a cozy place with friendly people behind the self-service counter. Everything served is fresh and homemade, and the menu includes morning and afternoon teas and light meals. There are savories, meat pies, bacon and eggs, steak, salad and chips, ham steak, fish, sandwiches, pies, and some of the best homemade cakes and pastries you're likely to find anywhere.

FOR A FEW EXTRA BUCKS

✪ Rutland Arms Inn

Victoria Ave. and Ridgeway St. ☎ **06/347-7677.** Reservations recommended Thurs–Sat for dinner. Main courses NZ$12.50–$23 (US$8.80–$16.10); lunch NZ$3–$8 (US$2.10–$5.60). AE, BC, DC, MC, V. Mon–Fri 8:30am–10pm; Sat–Sun 8am–10pm; brunch Sun 10am–2pm. ENGLISH.

This atmospheric upmarket pub has an open-beam ceiling, and the walls are decorated with farm implements and horse brasses. Old bottles line the plate rail above the window, and a large open fireplace keeps things cozy in winter. Built in 1846, the Rutland Arms is only one of the restored 19th-century buildings in this neighborhood. In addition to roast beef and Yorkshire pudding, fish and chips, and a ploughman's platter, there's a wide selection of English beers. If you hail from England and you're homesick, you can even order pea, pie, and pud (steak-and-kidney pie served with mashed potatoes and peas). The hours quoted above are for meal service. The bar is open daily until 11pm. Licensed.

WORTH A SPLURGE

Michael's Restaurant

281 Wicksteed St. ☎ **06/345-2690.** Reservations recommended. Lunch main courses NZ$13 (US$9.10); dinner main courses NZ$19–$25 (US$13.30–$17.50). AE, DC, MC, V. Mon–Fri noon–2pm; Mon–Sat 6–9pm. NEW ZEALAND.

This lovely award-winning restaurant is set in a 1911 Victorian villa surrounded by gardens. The house retains its original character, with kauri furniture and soft tones of dusty rose and green. All meals are à la carte; however, Michael's isn't stuffy—they strive for a casual, relaxed atmosphere. Favorites among its specialties are noisette of venison, lamb rump, and filet of salmon. Michael's is located right in town and is fully licensed.

EN ROUTE TO WELLINGTON

Following Highway 3 south from Wanganui until it joins Highway 1, you're in for an easy 3-hour, 193km (120-mile) drive along excellent roads: pastoral scenes of grazing sheep and cultivated fields at first, smashing sea views later, then a four-lane expressway leading into the beautiful harbor and splendid hills of wonderful, windy Wellington.

If you've got the time and the inclination, you might like to stop for tea at the **Bridge Inn Tea Rooms** (☎ 06/322-1594) in Bulls—this tearoom has long been a favorite spot of mine. Look for it outside town at the north end of the bridge adjacent to the Bridge Motor Lodge.

After Bulls, you can decide if you want to turn south on Highway 1 or continue on Highway 3 to **Palmerston North.** This city isn't on most visitors' itinerary unless they have a need to visit Massey University or a penchant for rugby. The **New Zealand Rugby Museum,** at 87 Cuba St. (P.O. Box 36, Palmerston North) (☎ 06/358-6947, fax 06/358-6947), is open Monday through Saturday from 10am to noon and 1:30 to 4pm, and Sunday from 1:30 to 4pm. Admission NZ$3 (US$2.10) adults, NZ$1 (US70¢) for children. You might also like to check with the **Palmerston North Information Centre,** The Square (☎ 06/358-5003, fax 06/356-9841), about other sights and activities in this city. It's open Monday to Friday from 8:30am to 5pm, Saturday, Sunday, and public holidays from 9am to 5pm.

Back on Highway 1, my auto-phile spouse would never forgive me if I didn't tell you about the **Southward Car Museum** in Paraparaumu (☎ 04/297-1221, fax 04/297-0503). Here you'll find the largest and most varied collection of motor vehicles in the Southern Hemisphere, including vintage and veteran cars dating from 1895, as well as motorcycles, stationary engines, and a model railway. It's the private collection of Len—make that Sir Len—Southward, who started working as a messenger in a Wellington motor house in 1919 and now owns 250 vehicles. He began collecting cars in 1956 when he purchased a Model T for £40 and was knighted in 1986 "for services to community." There's a large cafeteria on the premises for lunch and teas. The museum is open daily from 9am to 4:30pm; closed Good Friday, ANZAC morning (April 25), and Christmas Day. The admission is NZ$5 (US$3.50) for adults and NZ$2 (US$1.40) for children.

The Southward Car Museum is only one of the attractions in the area known as the **Kapiti Coast,** a stretch along Highway 1 about 58km (36 miles) northeast of Wellington. Waikanae is the principal township. If you're particularly interested in bird life and/or Maori culture, you might want to make arrangements with the Department of Conservation (☎ 04/472-7356, fax 04/499-0077 for information; for booking call 0900/52748 in New Zealand) to go out to **Kapiti Island,** where there's a nature reserve and a marine reserve. Three boat operators offer transport. The Kapiti Coast also offers scenic helicopter flights, golf, bushwalks, rafting, fishing, and a flora and fauna reserve called the **Nga Manu Sanctuary.** The latest attraction is the thrilling Fly-by-Wire adventure.

Affordable Accommodations Along the Way

Waikanae Beach Homestay

115 Tutere St., Waikanae. ☎ **04/293-6532** Mobile 025/300-785 Fax 04/293-6543. 3 rms (none with bathrm). NZ$70–$75 (US$49–$52.50) double. Three-course dinner NZ$20–$25 (US$14–$17.50) extra. Rates include breakfast. BC, MC, V.

If it's genuine Kiwi hospitality you're after, this is the place. Alan and Pauline Jones have a comfortable family home on the beach. Their two-story house has two spare bedrooms downstairs (these share a bathroom) and one room upstairs with its own toilet and sink (occupants use the shower downstairs). There's no smoking, and children are welcome. Try to be here from November to March when it's warm enough to swim at the beach.

Waimoana

63 Kakariki Grove, Waikanae. ☎ **04/293-7158.** Fax 04/293-7156. Web site nz.com/webnz/bbnz/waimoana.htm. 3 rms (all with bathrm). NZ$110–$170 (US$77–$119) double. Multicourse dinner with wine NZ$45 (US$31.50) extra. Rates include breakfast. AE, BC, DC, MC, V.

This contemporary custom-designed house has three guest bedrooms, two with a queen-size and a single bed, one with two single beds. An unusual aspect is the indoor swimming pool that's the focus of the living area. Whether eating dinner at the glass-top table in the starkly modern dining room or enjoying a before-dinner drink in the living room, you get a view of the pool. Ian Stewart is a retired life insurance executive; his wife, Phyllis, is an outstanding cook and hostess. Their home is adjacent to a reserve where there are bushwalks, and the large windows afford views of Kapiti Island and the South Island. The hosts have a brochure rack in their front hall and a supply of souvenirs for sale. Guests can take the train into Wellington or do local activities. There's no smoking here, and children are not accepted.

4 New Plymouth: Gateway to Egmont National Park

164km (102 miles) NW of Wanganui; 369km (229 miles) SW of Auckland

New Plymouth is New Zealand's energy center, with major reserves of natural gas—both onshore and offshore—as well as an oil and natural gas–fueled electric power station. It also has a busy port from which cheese and oil are shipped. In contrast to its energy-based industries, the city boasts several beautiful parks and gardens and is the gateway to Egmont National Park, where conical Mount Egmont/Taranaki dominates. The Taranaki region is also known for its lush farmlands and as a major dairy center.

The city gets its name from Plymouth in Devon, England—former home of the first to settle here.

ESSENTIALS
GETTING THERE
BY PLANE   Air New Zealand Link provides daily service from Auckland, Wanganui, and Wellington, with connecting service to other New Zealand cities.

BY BUS   InterCity and **Newmans** provide daily coach service.

BY CAR   New Plymouth can be reached by State Highway 3 and State Highway 45.

VISITOR INFORMATION
Take your questions to the **New Plymouth Information Centre,** at Liardet and Leach streets (☎ **06/759-6080,** fax 06/759-6073), open Monday through Friday from 8:30am to 5pm and Saturday, Sunday, and holidays from 10am to 3pm. It also sells postage stamps, phone cards, maps, and so on.

The **telephone area code** (STD) for New Plymouth is **06.**

ORIENTATION
New Plymouth (pop. 49,000) is sited on the west coast of the North Island, in the shadow of Mount Egmont/Taranaki. It's a good base from which to explore the beautiful Taranaki district. Devon Street East and Devon Street West are the main thoroughfares. The post office, on Currie Street (☎ **758-2110**), is open Monday through Friday from 8:30am to 5pm.

EXPLORING THE AREA
New Plymouth has numerous near-perfect swimming and surfing **beaches** in close proximity and is well known for its excellent **Govett-Brewster Art Gallery,** on Queen Street, and the **Taranaki Museum,** on Ariki Street. The dazzling array of

rhododendrons and azaleas at ✪ **Pukeiti Rhododendron Trust,** on Carrington Road, a 30-minute drive south of the city, draws visitors from all over the country. **Pukekura Park,** only 3 blocks from the Visitor Centre, also has lovely gardens as well as two lakes. The New Plymouth Information Centre can furnish directions and open hours for these and many other local attractions. You might want to ask for the "Heritage Walkway" brochure.

Some 7km (4 miles) south of New Plymouth, the **Tupare Garden,** 487 Mangorei Rd., has 9 acres of English-style gardens that are some of the finest in the country. The most spectacular season in the gardens is September to November, and if you arrive here in late October to early November, a highlight of your visit will be the annual Rhododendron Festival.

In Hawera, the **Tawhiti Museum,** 47 Ohangai Rd. (☎ and fax **06/278-6837**), is run by local potter Nigel Ogle and his wife, Teresa. Housed in an old dairy factory, this unique museum includes a model of a Maori bush village, a one-twelfth-scale war canoe, and many exhibits tracing Maori and Pakeha histories in this region. Many have lifelike animated figures illustrating everyday activities over the years. Open 10am to 4pm Friday through Monday (open Sunday only June through August).

The Taranaki landscape is dominated by the cone-shaped ✪ **Mount Egmont/ Taranaki,** a volcano that has been dormant for over 400 years. This is one of the few mountains you can drive completely around, and there are over 300km (180 miles) of walking tracks within **Egmont National Park,** ranging from 10 minutes to 5 days, with a selection for both inexperienced and veteran walkers. There are inexpensive huts for walkers within the park, maintained by the Department of Conservation (details from the Visitor Information Centre).

AFFORDABLE ACCOMMODATIONS

In addition to the places described below, there's a Department of Conservation back-packer hostel at Dawson Falls. For information on **Konini Lodge,** contact the DOC, on Pembroke Road in Stratford (☎ **06/765-5144** or mobile 025/430-248). The cost is NZ$12 (US$8.40) for each adult and NZ$6 (US$4.20) per child; credit cards not accepted.

✪ Dawson Falls Tourist Lodge

Manaia Rd. (P.O. Box 91), Stratford. ☎ **0800/651-800** in New Zealand, or 06/765-5457. Fax 06/765-5457. 11 rms (all with bathrm). TEL. NZ$110 (US$77) double, NZ$120 (US$84) double room with conservatory; NZ$130 (US$91) honeymoon room. AE, BC, DC, MC, V.

This is one of my favorite places in New Zealand. I love the feeling of being isolated and cozy amid the Swiss decor and the wonderful print comforters and matching shams. The lodge is 45 minutes south of New Plymouth and 20 minutes west of Stratford, one-third of the way up the forested slopes of Mount Egmont/Taranaki in Egmont National Park; walking trails start right outside the front door, and the national park visitor/display center is steps away. Those who aren't energetic enjoy lounging in front of the log fire or just staring out the window at the alpine scenery. There are also a sauna and plunge pool on the premises. I can recommend the honeymoon room—whether this is your first, second, or a trial. You might also want to consider Room 8, which has "a loo [toilet] with a view," or Room 7, which has a huge bathtub and a great view of the mountain. Number 4 is a cozy single. There's no smoking in the bedrooms. Hosts Nell and Tom Lilford are super-friendly. The lodge is licensed and offers all meals. Reserve well ahead if you want to stay on a weekend.

Mountain House Motor Lodge

Pembroke Rd. (P.O. Box 303), Stratford. ☎ **0800/657-100** in New Zealand. ☎ and fax 06/765-6100. 10 rms (all with bathrm). A/C TV TEL. NZ$90–$110 (US$63–$77) double. AE, BC, DC, JCB, MC, V.

Here are more rooms within Egmont National Park, 10 minutes west of Stratford on the east side of Mt. Egmont/Taranaki, surrounded by natural beauty and close to hiking trails. Six chalets have kitchens, and all the spacious quarters are attractive and have tea- and coffeemaking facilities, small refrigerators, and radios. You will find a piano and an open fire in the lounge and a sauna. Keith Anderson and his Swiss wife, Berta (they're responsible for the decor of Dawson Falls Lodge; see above), are the hosts here. She's the chef who's earned the dining room several awards and a loyal following. As we go to press, Keith is developing another five-bedroom property. (If you're going to Taranaki, ask him about it; it will finished by the time you get there.)

Patuha Farm Lodge

Upper Pitone Rd. (R.D. 4, New Plymouth), Okato. ☎ and fax **06/752-4469.** 10 rms (all with bathrm). TEL. NZ$70 (US$49) per person. Rates include all meals. BC, MC, V.

Compared to the two lodges described above, this spot lacks atmosphere, but it's a great location for those visiting the gardens at the adjacent Pukeiti Rhododendron Trust, 30km (18 miles) from New Plymouth. The 2km (1 1/2-mile) driveway passes some of the 1,000 ewes that graze on these 600 acres. Peter Henderson, with his parents, Morris and Janet, are the hosts here. All rooms have heaters and clock radios; some have TVs, tea and coffee facilities are in the hall, and there's a spa tub. The rates are good value. Licensed.

"**W**onderful, windy Wellington" this city is called—with derision by Kiwis who don't live here, with affection by those who do. Well, there's no denying that it *is* windy: 60-mile-per-hour winds sweep through here—through the only substantial gap in New Zealand's mountain chain—on an average of 40 days each year. Winds notwithstanding, however, Wellington is easily New Zealand's cultural center and one of its most beautiful cities. Indeed, its magnificent harbor rivals any in the world. Your first view of that harbor, with the city curved around its western and southwestern shoreline and the surrounding hills abloom with what appear to be tiny dollhouses spilling down its sides, is breathtaking, even if that view should happen to be in the rain (which is a distinct possibility). On a fine day, there are few city views that can beat it.

Wellington was discovered in A.D. 950 by Kupe, the great Polynesian explorer, and by the time Captain Cook stopped by (but didn't land) in 1773, the harbor was lined with Maori settlements. When New Zealand Company representative Col. William Wakefield's good ship *Tory* arrived on the scene in September 1839, warring between the Maori tribes had become so fierce, and the local tribes were so fearful of their more powerful enemies, that (after a bit of negotiating back and forth, and a few of the usual misunderstandings about land transfers and so forth), they accepted the Pakeha as the lesser of two evils.

By January 1840 settlers began coming in goodly numbers, and after a rather rowdy beginning (when, according to contemporary reports, meetings were held to try to determine how the citizenry could protect itself from the lawless police force), the town began a growth that has never really stopped. A tug-of-war with Auckland finally resulted in Wellington's being named the colony's capital on the basis of its central location and the belief that the "middle island" (that's the South Island's claim to being the "mainland") might well pull out and establish a separate colony altogether if it were not afforded better access to the capital than faraway Auckland provided.

Wellington today, while peopled mainly by civil servants, diplomats, and corporate home-office staffs, maintains a conservative—but far from stuffy—air. There is, perhaps, more sheer diversity here than in any of New Zealand's other cities: Narrow streets and Edwardian buildings nudge modern edifices of concrete and glass; massive office buildings embrace colonial-style restaurants; fashionable

Wellington

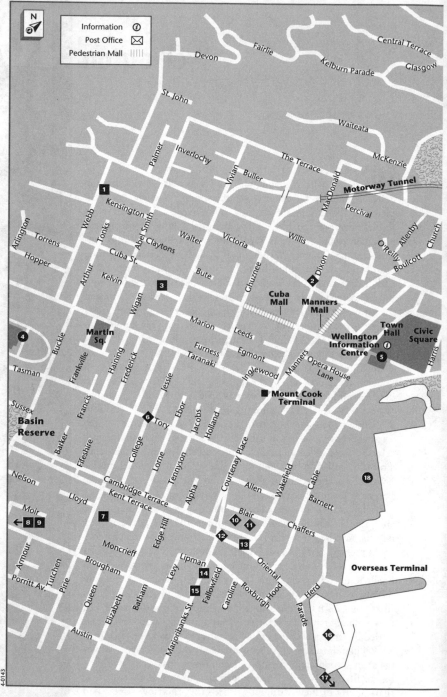

Information ⓘ
Post Office ✉
Pedestrian Mall ‖‖‖‖

N

Central Terrace
Glasgow
Fairlie
Devon
Kelburn Parade
St. John
Waiteata
McKenzie
Palmer
Inverlochy
The Terrace
Motorway Tunnel
MacDonald
Vivian
Buller
Percival
1
Kensington
Victoria
Willis
O'Reilly
Allenby
Church
Boulcott
Arlington
Torrens
Webb
Tonks
Abel Smith
Claytons
Walter
Dixon
Hopper
Arthur
Kelvin
Cuba St.
Bute
Ghuznee
2
3
Cuba Mall
Manners Mall
Wigan
Marion
Leeds
Manners
Opera House Lane
Town Hall
Civic Square
Martin Sq.
Buckle
Haining
Frederick
Furness
Taranaki
Egmont
Inglewood
Wellington Information Centre ⓘ
5
4
Tasman
Frankville
Jessie
Harris
Francis
Ebor
Jacobs
Holland
Mount Cook Terminal
Sussex
Barker
Fifeshire
College
Lorne
Tory
6
Basin Reserve
Nelson
Lloyd
Cambridge Terrace
Kent Terrace
Tennyson
Alpha
Courtenay Place
Allen
Wakefield
Cable
Barnett
18
Moir
8 **9**
7
Edge Hill
Blair
Chaffers
10 **11**
Moncrieff
Brougham
Lipman
Levy
12
13
Oriental
Armour
Tuichen
Pine
Queen
Batham
Elizabeth
Marjoribanks St.
Lipman
Fallowfield
Caroline
Roxburgh
Hood
14
Overseas Terminal
Porritt Av.
15
Herd
Parade
Austin
16
17

4-0143

238

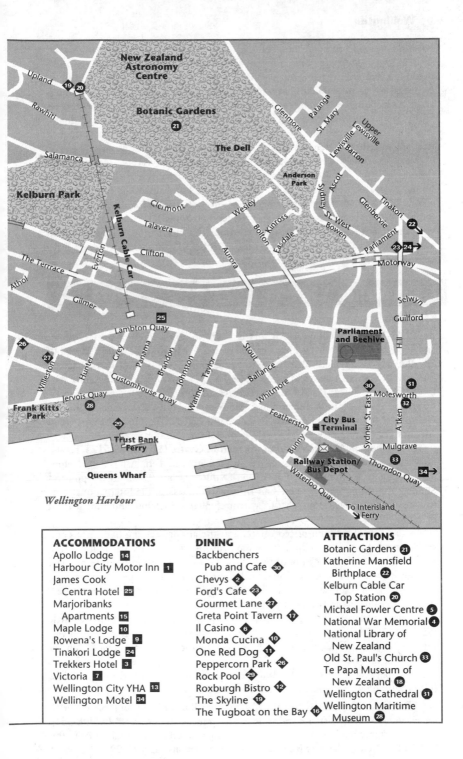

ACCOMMODATIONS
Apollo Lodge ■14
Harbour City Motor Inn ■1
James Cook
  Centra Hotel ■25
Marjoribanks
  Apartments ■15
Maple Lodge ■10
Rowena's Lodge ■9
Tinakori Lodge ■24
Trekkers Hotel ■3
Victoria ■7
Wellington City YHA ■13
Wellington Motel ■34

DINING
Backbenchers
  Pub and Cafe ◆30
Chevys ◆2
Ford's Cafe ◆23
Gourmet Lane ◆27
Greta Point Tavern ◆17
Il Casino ◆6
Monda Cucina ◆10
One Red Dog ◆11
Peppercorn Park ◆26
Rock Pool ◆29
Roxburgh Bistro ◆12
The Skyline ◆19
The Tugboat on the Bay ◆16

ATTRACTIONS
Botanic Gardens ●21
Katherine Mansfield
  Birthplace ●22
Kelburn Cable Car
  Top Station ●20
Michael Fowler Centre ●5
National War Memorial ●4
National Library of
  New Zealand
Old St. Paul's Church ●33
Te Papa Museum of
  New Zealand ●18
Wellington Cathedral ●31
Wellington Maritime
  Museum ●28

boutiques are housed in pseudo–colonial-style complexes while craft shops hold sway in avant-garde structures; and the after-dark scene is one of New Zealand's liveliest. The legislative requirement that all major buildings must be brought up to earthquake-resistant standards has resulted in massive demolition of older buildings and the erection of even more modern high-rise structures. Wellington has also recently completed a redevelopment of the harbor front, providing many more dining and drinking spots with water views and, by the time you get here, will have opened its much talked about, long awaited Te Papa Museum of New Zealand.

What is *not* likely to change—and it's important to us as visitors—is the ebb and flow of the city's population as government workers depart on weekends for visits home, then flood back into town on Monday. That means an abundance of accommodations are available over weekends, and very few during the week (I'll talk more about this later under "Affordable Accommodations").

In short, Wellington has long been a cosmopolitan city, and it's growing more so all the time. It's also your gateway to the South Island's wonders—but don't leave without exploring Wellington's own wonders.

1 Orientation

ARRIVING

BY PLANE   The **Wellington Airport** is 10km (6 miles) south of the city center and served by the following international airlines: **Air New Zealand** (☎ 0800/737-000 in New Zealand), **British Airways** (☎ 04/472-7327), **Lufthansa** (☎ 09/303-1529), **Qantas Airways** (☎ 0800/808-767 in New Zealand), **Singapore Airlines** (☎ 04/473-9749), and **United Airlines** (☎ 04/472-0470). Leading domestic airlines that fly into Wellington are: **Air New Zealand** (☎ 04/388-9900), **Air Nelson** (☎ 04/388-2770), **Ansett New Zealand** (☎ 04/471-1146), **Mount Cook Airlines** (☎ 04/382-2154), and several smaller airlines.

The **Wellington Airport Visitors Information Centre** (☎ **04/385-5123,** fax 04/385-5137, e-mail wlg4vin@nzhost.co.nz), in the Domestic Terminal, is staffed Monday through Friday from 7:30am to 8:30pm, Saturday from 7:30am to 7:30pm, and Sunday from 8am to 8pm. There's an Information Desk in the International Terminal staffed Monday through Saturday from 5:30am to 7:30pm and Sunday from 8am to 7:30pm.

There's a good medium-priced cafeteria at the airport, serving light meals and snacks, open from 6am to 9pm every day. Also, there are bars, car-rental desks, bookshops, and gift shops in both terminals; a duty-free shop in the International Terminal; and a nursery in the Domestic Terminal. The bank is open normal hours, as well as 1 hour before any overseas departure and for 1 hour after each overseas arrival. Ample luggage carts are provided at no charge.

Airport shuttle services are provided Monday through Friday by **Super Shuttle** (☎ **04/387-8787**). The one-way fare from the airport to the railway station (or vice versa) is NZ$5 (US$3.50) per person. A door-to-door service is also provided "on demand," but the fare is higher.

A **taxi** between the city center and the airport will cost approximately NZ$22 (US$15.40) on weekdays, a little more on weekends.

BY TRAIN & COACH (BUS)   The Wellington **Railway Station** is on Waterloo Quay, and most **long-distance trains** depart from that station. Call ☎ **04/498-3413** for long-distance rail information. For coach information call **InterCity** (☎ **0800/731-711** in New Zealand, or 04/472-5111) or **Newmans** (☎ **04/499-3261**). Both of these coach lines operate out of the Railway Station. The **Mount Cook** bus depot is on Courtenay Place.

BY ALTERNATIVE COACH (BUS)   Kiwi Experience (☎ 09/366-1665) and the **Magic Travellers Network (☎ 09/358-5600)** both stop here.

BY CAR   Wellington is reached via Highways 1 and 2. It's 195km (121 miles) from Wanganui, 460km (285 miles) from Rotorua, and 655km (406 miles) from Auckland.

BY FERRY   For information on the **Inter-Island Wellington–Picton Ferry,** call **☎ 0800/658-999.**

VISITOR INFORMATION

The **Wellington Visitor Centre,** Civic Square, Wakefield Street (**☎ 04/801-4000,** fax 04/801-3030), is open from 8:30am to 5:30pm Monday to Friday and from 9:30am to 4:30pm weekends. They will provide you with details of Wellington regional attractions and offer an extensive range of brochures. The free publications, *Capital Times* and *City Voice,* are available from the Visitor Centre and leading hotels; they are published weekly, with information on current activities. The center also has information on the entire country, not just Wellington, and sells souvenirs, postage stamps, and PhoneCards.

SPECIAL EVENTS

You might like to plan your trip to Wellington to coincide with the following festivals. For additional information on special events and festivals, contact **Tourism Wellington (☎ 04/499-9995,** fax 04/499-9996).

- **Summer City Festival**   A wide range of daily cultural, entertainment, and recreational events in the capital city. Including a Mardi Gras, teddy bear's picnic, and Summer City Valentine's night. January and February. Call **☎ 04/ 801-3222** for details.
- **World Dragon Boat Festival**   Dragon boats are modified Chinese long boats that are used for racing with a crew of 20 paddlers, one drummer or caller who sets the stroke speed, and a steerer. Every year teams from all over the world come to compete in these colorful races. February 17–22, 1998. Call or write to World Dragon Boat Festival, P.O. Box 10629, Wellington (**☎ 04/471-0205,** fax 04/ 471-0495) for details.
- **Wellington Cup Racing Meeting**   This is a leading horse-racing event (galloping) that is held in conjunction with the **National Yearling Sales.** Late January. Call **☎ 04/801-4000** for details.
- **۞ Golden Shears,** Masterton   This international shearing contest lasts for 3 days and includes wool handling and lamb and goat shearing. Masterton is located 103km (64 miles) northeast of Wellington. Late February–early March. Call **☎ 06/378-7373** for details.
- **Devotion Festival**   This is New Zealand's second-largest annual gay and lesbian event. Only the Hero Parade in Auckland is bigger. February 14, 1998. Call **☎ 04/801-4000** for details.
- **Martinborough Country Fair,** Martinborough   Popular gathering of crafts artisans from around the country. Martinborough is about an hour's drive east of Wellington. First Saturday in February and first Saturday in March. About 30,000 attend this popular event. Call **☎ 06/306-9043** for details.
- **Toast Martinborough,** Martinborough   Catch a special festival train from Wellington. Shuttle buses run a continuous circuit within a 10km area of the

town square to Martinborough vineyards, where tasting takes place with the winemaker. NZ$40 (US$28) per person includes wine tasting, local transport, a festival glass, and entertainment, which runs the gamut from classical to jazz concerts. November 16, 1997. Always the third Sunday in November. Call ☎ 06/306-9043 for details.

CITY LAYOUT

The main focal point of Wellington is the harbor. The new Te Papa Museum of New Zealand fronts this water, as does the Queen's Wharf dining and shopping complex. Having said that, the best shopping is still along Lambton Quay; Willis Street, Manners Street, and Cuba Street also have their fair share of stores. In the city center, Willis Street and Lambton Quay are where you'll find the headquarters of many of the nation's businesses. Wellington's after-dark scene is centered on Courtenay Place, Wakefield Street, and the lanes running between them (including Blair and Allen streets).

Thorndon is a good suburb in which to stay and dine. The area has several historic buildings, including Katherine Mansfield's birthplace. Thorndon also has the advantage of being handy to the Parliament Buildings. **Mt. Victoria** is another good suburb in which to sleep. Some accommodations in this area offer harbor and city views. A cable car runs from Lambton Quay up a steep hill to **Kelburn,** and there's a great view from the top. This is also where you'll find the Botanic Gardens and Victoria University. **Brooklyn** has a couple of cute cafes. **Oriental Bay,** about 800 meters (about half a mile) from the city center, is a great spot for summertime lunching and swimming. Because of the good harbor views from this area, it has become a popular place to live, and there are many high-rise apartment buildings. The sand on the beach at Oriental Bay arrived as ballast in sailing vessels bringing settlers to the new colony. **Evans Bay** is farther out, but accessible by public transport.

2 Getting Around

It's easy to navigate Wellington on the city buses. You can save money by buying either the **City-10-Trip** or **All-day City Bus Pass** (see below). Allow plenty of time to get where you're going so you won't be tempted to take a taxi—they can get pricey.

BY BUS   There's good city bus service; the main city bus terminal, **Lambton Interchange,** is adjacent to the main railway station at the corner of Bunny and Featherston streets. For NZ$5 (US$3.50) you can buy an **All-day City Bus Pass** (after 9am two children under age 15 can also ride on this pass). The other good deal is the **City-10-Trip** (a 10-trip concession ticket) that costs NZ$8 (US$5.60). Newlands and Eastbourne buses arrive on Featherston Street and depart from the Lambton Interchange. For information on all urban services, call **Ridewell** (☎ 04/801-7000). The Information Centre will give you a comprehensive city map that also shows major bus routes, plus timetables for specific routes. Timetables are also available from newsstands.

BY TRAIN   Ridewell runs commuter trains to the suburbs on fairly frequent schedules; phone ☎ 04/801-7000 for timetable information.

BY CAR   If you're driving, avoid downtown Wellington. Traffic congestion is significant, and parking spaces are scarcer than hen's teeth. **Avon/Percy Rent A Car** (☎ 0800/7368-2866 (RENT AVON) in New Zealand, or 03/379-3822; fax 03/365-5651) has an office in Wellington and offers competitive rates.

BY TAXI   You'll find taxi stands in front of the railway station, in the Lambton Quay shopping area between Grey and Hunter streets; on Bond Street, just off Willis Street; on Dixon Street between Cuba and Victoria streets; and on Cambridge Terrace near Courtenay Place. There's a NZ$1 (US 70¢) surcharge if you telephone for a taxi (☎ 04/384-4444), or use one on weekends and holidays. A so-called "green" (lower) fare applies between 6am and 8pm on weekdays; outside those hours, you'll pay the "red" (higher) fare—you can check the light on the taxi meter to be sure which fare is in effect.

FAST FACTS: Wellington

American Express   The American Express office is located at Shop 4, Sun Alliance Centre, 280–292 Lambton Quay (☎ 04/473-7766, fax 04/473-7765), open Monday through Friday from 8:30am to 5pm.

Area Code   Wellington's telephone area code (STD) is **04.**

Baby-sitters   Most B&Bs and motels can furnish baby-sitters, or you can call **Wellington Nannies Connection** (☎ 04/384-1135).

Cameras & Film   Try the Langwood Photo Centre, 59 Manners Mall, in the Breeze Plaza (☎ 04/473-1557, fax 04/473-1558). Open Monday through Thursday from 8am to 6pm, Friday from 8am to 7pm, Saturday from 9:30am to 4pm, and Sunday from 11am to 2pm.

Crime   **Manners Mall** and **Cuba Street** are areas to avoid after dark—they have a reputation as being the places where a mugging is most likely to occur.

Doctor   For emergency doctor referrals, call ☎ 04/472-2999.

Drugstores   There are late-hour pharmacies at 17 Adelaide Rd., Wellington (☎ 04/385-8810), and 729 High St., Lower Hutt (☎ 04/567-6725).

Embassies/Consulates   The **U.S. Embassy** is at 29 Fitzherbert Terrace, Thorndon (☎ 04/472-2068); the **Canadian Embassy** is at 61 Molesworth St. (☎ 04/473-9577); the **British High Commission** is at 44 Hill St. (☎ 04/472-6049).

Emergencies   Call ☎ 111 for police, fire, and ambulance emergencies.

Hospitals   **Wellington Hospital** is on Riddiford Street, Newtown (☎ 04/385-5999).

Libraries   The **National Library,** Molesworth Street (☎ 04/474-3000, fax 04/474-3035), is open Monday through Friday from 9am to 5pm. The **Wellington Public Library,** 65 Victoria St. (☎ 04/801-4040), is open Monday through Thursday from 9:30am to 8:30pm, Friday from 9:30am to 9pm, and Saturday from 9:30am to 5pm. It's also open on Sunday from 1 to 4pm for reading only.

Newspapers   Wellington's morning newspaper is *The Dominion,* and in the evening there's the *Evening Post,* both published Monday through Saturday. On Sunday morning, look for *The Sunday Star Times.* Overseas newspapers are sometimes available from newsstands and are available in the reading room of the National Library.

Police   See "Emergencies," above.

Post Office   The Visitor Centre sells stamps. Collect *Poste Restante* mail at the railway station.

Radio　Wellington's leading stations are 99 and 100 on the FM dial; Radio Windy Classic Rock is 94.1 and 98.1 on FM.

Transit Info　Ridewell ☎ **04/801-7000.**

3 Affordable Accommodations

Plan to visit Wellington on a weekend (Friday, Saturday, and Sunday nights), when rooms are easier to come by and when many hotels and motels, including the ultraluxurious ones, offer discounted rates to fill up vacancies—Wellington is bustling with business travelers Monday through Friday, but is relatively quiet on the weekends. More and more restaurants, shops, and sightseeing attractions are remaining open for the weekend, too, making it quite possible to take advantage of those special rates without sacrificing weekday activities. You'll also find that rates are lower in winter than they are in the summer months. However, if you're staying here during the summer, it's best to book well in advance.

If you would like to hang your hat with a local family, contact **Harbour City Homestays,** 1 Kilgour Way, Chartwell, Wellington (☎ **04/479-3618**). They have a list of high-standard homes that offer this type of hospitality at reasonable rates.

The rates given below include the 12.5% GST.

IN THE CITY

Super-Cheap Sleeps

○ Wellington City YHA

At Wakefield St. and Cambridge Terrace (P.O. Box 24-033), Wellington. ☎ **04/801-7280.** Fax 04/801-7278. 7 rms (all with bath), 88 dormitory beds in 22 rms. NZ$28 (US$19.60) single; NZ$22 (US$15.40) per person double; NZ$18 (US$12.60) dorm bed. Nonmembers pay NZ$4 (US$2.40) additional. MC, V.

This luxurious modern hostel is considered the flagship of the New Zealand Youth Hostel Association. There are 22 four-bed dormitories and 5 double rooms, all with private bath, plus 2 single rooms with shared facilities. A mattress cover, a quilt, and clean pillows are supplied free, and there is a limited number of free sleeping sheets (bring your own to be on the safe side). Facilities include a self-catering kitchen, dining room, TV/common room, games room, and well-stocked shop for basic food and toiletries. The hostel is across from a supermarket and in the center of a restaurant/theater area. All your reservations for ongoing ferry, bus, and train services (both domestic and international) can be handled right on the premises, and they can also book ahead in other YHA hostels around the country.

For a Few Extra Bucks

Apollo Lodge

49 Majoribanks St., Wellington. ☎ and fax **04/385-1849.** 25 studios, 8 units. TV TEL. NZ$100 (US$70) studio or unit for 1 or 2. AE, DC, MC, V.

This would be a real find even if it weren't conveniently located and reasonably priced. The superb location is really the icing on the cake—it's so close to city-center shopping, entertainment, and sightseeing that you can leave the car and walk (a longish but pleasant stroll) or use the convenient city bus transport, and there are several first-rate restaurants right in the neighborhood. I found the staff here extremely friendly and helpful. The attractive units are set off the street, and eight have separate bedrooms. You have a choice of full kitchen facilities or of serviced units with coffee pot, toaster, and fridge. All are fully carpeted and come with radio, electric blankets, and heaters. Cooked or continental breakfasts are available, and there's a full-service laundry as well as highchairs and a play area for children. If you're traveling with a large party, you might want to book the three-bedroom (sleeps seven) bungalow, also on the grounds, that goes for the same rate as a motel unit—you'll have to negotiate the price, since it depends on the number of people and length of stay. You should note that the Apollo is popular with regular Kiwi visitors to Wellington and that your best bet here is on weekends.

Majoribanks Apartments

38 Majoribanks St., Wellington. ☎ **04/385-7305** or 385-8879. Fax 04/385-1849. 15 apartments. TV TEL. NZ$100 (US$77) apartment for 2. Additional person NZ$15 (US$10.50) extra per adult, NZ$10 (US$7) extra per child. AE, BC, DC, MC, V.

An American guest from Washington, D.C., greeted me here with an unsolicited recommendation—"This place is fantastic, not only for the facilities and comfort, but for the friendliness of the owner." My encounter with owner John Floratos certainly confirmed the traveler's comments. In addition, I was much impressed with the bright, nicely decorated apartments in this hostelry just across from the Apollo. All have fully equipped kitchen and radio. There are one- and two-bedroom units, and there's good off-street parking. Majoribanks is within walking distance of the city center.

Wellington Motel

14 Hobson St., Wellington. ☎ **04/472-0334**. Fax 04/472-6825. 3 studios, 2 units. TV TEL. NZ$90–$105 (US$63–$73.50) studio or unit for 2. Additional person NZ$12 (US$8.40) extra. MC, V. Free off-street parking.

About a 5-minute walk from the railway station, this large house was built back in 1912 and has been renovated to create five nice accommodations with such charming extras as bay windows, beamed ceilings, and small leaded windowpanes. Three of the spacious units are bed-sitters (studios), and two have one bedroom and can sleep up to six. All are attractively furnished and have showers and kitchens. There's limited off-street parking. The motel is near Davis Street at the northern edge of the city center. Continental and cooked breakfasts are available.

Trekkers Hotel

213 Cuba St., Dunlop Terrace (P.O. Box 27-125), Wellington. ☎ **04/385-2153**. Fax 04/382-8873. 107 rms (65 with bathrm), 6 units (all with bathrm). TV. NZ$79 (US$55.30) double with bathrm; NZ$89 (US$62.30) one-bedroom unit for 2; NZ$99 (US$69.30) two-bedroom unit for 2; NZ$17 (US$11.90) per person backpacker's bunk; NZ$19 (US$13.30) per person backpacker's twin. AE, BC, DC, MC, V. Free parking.

This licensed hotel off Vivian Street is centrally located and offers a variety of accommodations, including small dormitories (two or four bunk beds), singles both with and without private facilities (there's hot and cold running water in those without), doubles with facilities, six rooms with facilities for travelers with disabilities, and six motel units in a separate block. They vary in style from new and modern to older and recently renovated. Guest laundry, sauna, and spa pool are available. The attractive restaurant features good meals for around NZ$16 (US$10.40). There's free off-street parking and a travel shop for tours and travel.

Worth a Splurge

Harbour City Motor Inn

92–96 Webb St. (P.O. Box 9248), Wellington. ☎ **04/384-9809**. Fax 04/384-9806. 23 rms (all with bathrm), 2 suites. MINIBAR TV TEL. NZ$140 (US$98) double weekdays, NZ$110 (US$77) double weekends; NZ$160 (US$112) suite. Best Western discounts available. AE, BC, DC, MC, V. Free parking.

The Harbour City could justify its rates solely on location—it's convenient to all city-center attractions, major theaters, shopping, and good restaurants—but its merits certainly don't stop there. The guest rooms are attractively furnished, with comfortable sitting areas and excellent lighting. Suites come with kitchens, and there's a covered garage. Other facilities include a guest laundry, dry-cleaning service, and photocopying and fax service for guests. A moderately priced licensed restaurant is on the premises, and there's a spa pool.

✪ James Cook Centra Hotel

The Terrace, Wellington. ☎ **04/499-9500.** Fax 04/499-9800. 260 rms (all with bathrm). A/C MINIBAR TV TEL. NZ$265 (US$186) double. Weekend discounts available. AE, DC, MC, V. Free valet parking.

This splurge is well worth considering. The hotel is in the very heart of the city center, and its spacious rooms are decorated with modern furnishings and soft tones. All rooms come with tea- and coffee-making facilities, fridges, ironing boards, bathrobes, hair dryers, and pay-per-view in-room movies; half of the rooms have modems; and 30 rooms have harbor views. Request one of these—there's no extra cost. There's same-day laundry and dry-cleaning service (except Sunday), business facilities that include secretarial service, and copy machines. Whitby's Restaurant has both a buffet and an à la carte menu. It's also just steps away from shopping, sightseeing, dining, and entertainment. The normal rate is lowered dramatically for weekend specials. Readers Patricia Downing of Los Angeles, California, and Fred and Edith Terrill of Neskowin, Oregon, have both written recently to say that this is worth the extra money and is a first-class hotel.

IN THORNDON

✪ Tinakori Lodge

182 Tinakori Rd., Thorndon, Wellington. ☎ **04/473-3478.** Fax 04/472-5554. E-mail 10035.3214@compuserve.com. 9 rms (3 with bathrm). TV. NZ$98 (US$68.60) double without bathrm, NZ$125 (US$84) double with bathrm. Rates include breakfast. AC, BC, DC, MC, V.

This charming, century-old home on the northern edge of the city center is presided over by Mel and John Ainsworth. The guest rooms are fresh and bright, each with hot and cold running water, electric blankets, and a heater. The substantial breakfast is served buffet style, and an attractive feature here is the availability of tea, coffee, hot chocolate, soup, cheese, crackers, and cookies all day. Local restaurants are within a 10-minute stroll. Complimentary morning and evening local newspapers are available. There's no smoking in the lodge. Not suitable for children under 12 years old.

IN MT. VICTORIA

Super-Cheap Sleeps

Maple Lodge

52 Ellice St., Mount Victoria, Wellington. ☎ **04/385-3771.** 11 rms (none with bathrm), 2 dormitories. NZ$18 (US$12.60) single; NZ$32–$34 (US$22.40–$23.80) double; NZ$15 (US$10.50) dorm bed. No credit cards.

Near the center of the city, the Maple Lodge is perched on one of Wellington's picturesque hillsides in a row of small colonial houses. Recently renovated, most rooms in this nonsmoking hostel are spacious. There are singles, twins, and doubles, all with hot and cold running water, plus two dormitories. Other facilities include a fully equipped kitchen, dining room, TV lounge, car park (parking lot), and laundry.

Rowena's Lodge

115 Brougham St., Mount Victoria, Wellington. ☎ **0800/801-414** in New Zealand. ☎ and fax 04/385-7872. 50 rms (none with bathrm). NZ$14–$15 (US$9.80–$10.50) per person shareroom, NZ$20–$39.50 (US$14–$27.70) single; NZ$33–$49.50 (US$23.10–$34.70) double. Additional person NZ$10 (US$7) extra. Discount to VIP cardholders. BC, MC, V. Free pickup and dropoff service to trains, buses, and the Inter-Island Ferry.

Rowena's has a variety of accommodations: dormitories, singles, doubles, twins, and triples. In addition to the three guest lounges, facilities include a dining room (cooked or continental breakfasts are available at a small charge), a large guest kitchen, a barbecue, and picnic areas. It's near the city center, on four city bus routes, and drivers will appreciate the off-street parking. The staff can make reservations for ongoing travel.

For a Few Extra Bucks

Victoria Homestay

58 Pirie St., Mount Victoria, Wellington. ☎ **04/385-8512.** 3 rms (1 with bathrm). NZ$60–$70 (US$42–$49) double. Rates include breakfast. No credit cards. Exit from the hwy. onto Ghuznee St. and take Taranaki St. to Vivian St. and Vivian St. across Kent Terrace, and turn up Pirie St. Bus: 2 or 5.

Elizabeth and Robert McGuigan and their three teenagers live upstairs in this two-story home adorned with lacy cast iron. Downstairs are three guest rooms and two baths, a TV lounge, and a dining room with tea and coffee makings. The cooked breakfast has won raves from our readers, who also like the location, which is convenient to the city center and to Mount Victoria. There's no smoking in the house.

IN NEARBY LOWER HUTT

Campgrounds & Cabins

✪ Hutt Park Holiday Village

95 Hutt Park Rd., Moera, Lower Hutt. ☎ **04/568-5913.** Fax 04/568-5914. 53 cabins. NZ$78 (US$54.60) double motel apts; NZ$58 (US$40.60) double tourist apts with kitchen and toilet; NZ$40 (US$28) double tourist cabins with kitchens; NZ$30 (US$21) double standard cabins; NZ$20 (US$14) powered caravan sites double, additional person NZ$10 (US$7); NZ$9 (US$6.30) tent sites per person. BC, MC, V. Public transport into Wellington or Lower Hutt is located nearby.

Some 7 miles northeast of the city, this large camp is abundant in native shade trees. Many of the cabins are equipped for wheelchair access. They range from two-berth standard cabins with basic furnishings to fully equipped motel apartments; all units with kitchens come with a full range of cutlery and crockery. Bedding and linen are required in most cabins and are available for rent from the office, along with TVs. There are two coin-operated laundries and three facility blocks, each with a kitchen, a dining area, a TV room, showers, and toilets.

4 Great Deals on Dining

The greatest cluster of Wellington's moderately priced restaurants are located in and around Courtney Place near Blair and Allen streets. If you don't find something that sounds good below, take a stroll in this area. In addition, **Opera Restaurant and Bar,** Courtney Place (corner of Blair St.; ☎ **04/382-8654**) and **Sandbar** in the Queen's Wharf Retail Complex (☎ **04/499-4505**) both serve meals. (See "Wellington After Dark," below.)

FOOD COURTS   Wellington is full of them and the best one is **Gourmet Lane,** in the BNZ Centre, 1 Willis St. This spot is a dream for dollarwise travelers because most main courses are NZ$5 to NZ$6 (US$3.25 to US$3.90). Some of the vendors here include Wellington's Gourmet Pies, Sizzler's BBQ'D Food, Stars & Stripes, and Chinese Wok. Gourmet Lane is open Monday through Thursday and Saturday from 9am to 3pm and Friday (late-night shopping night) from 9am to 9pm. Some, but not all, places accept credit/charge cards. You can buy beer and wine to accompany your meal, too. This area is particularly popular at lunchtime, when entertainment is often offered. The BNZ (Bank of New Zealand) has a counter adjacent to the food court—handy if you need to make a transaction. There's also a food court in the **Queen's Wharf Retail Complex,** where all meals are under NZ$6 (US$5.40). It's open Saturday and Monday through Thursday from 10am to 6pm, until 7pm on Friday, and Sunday from 10am to 5pm. If the weather's good, you might like to get your meal and find a place to sit outside near the water.

IN THE CITY
Super-Cheap Eats

Peppercorn Park
1st floor in the Grand Arcade, Willis St. ☎ **04/472-2255.** Reservations not accepted. Breakfast NZ$11 (US$7.70); sandwiches with salad and fries NZ$8 (US$5.60); dinner NZ$9–$11 (US$6.30–$7.70). AE, DC, MC, V. Mon–Thurs 7am–4pm, Fri 7am–8:30pm, Sat 9am–1:30pm. BREAKFAST/PASTRIES/SANDWICHES.

This pleasant upstairs self-service restaurant is one of my favorite drop-in eateries in the city center. Its reputation for the best bagels in Wellington certainly gets my endorsement, and the phyllo pastry filled with chicken, smoked salmon, or some other delicacy just melts in your mouth. For heartier eating, there's Indonesian lamb rendang, pork in ginger-and-orange sauce, Mexican beef, lasagna, and on Friday nights, traditional roast meals of pork or beef and vegetables. It's fully licensed.

For a Few Extra Bucks

Backbenchers Pub and Cafe
Molesworth St. and Sydney St. E., opposite Parliament. ☎ **04/472-3065.** Fax 04/499-3937. Reservations not required. Main courses NZ$9–$16 (US$6.30–$11.20). AE, DC, MC, V. Mon–Sat noon–2:30pm; daily 5:30–10:30pm. CAFE.

A Wellington friend steered me to this place. The walls of the old building are lined with political cartoons, and wax caricatures of current political figures hover overhead. The natural brick-and-wood interior creates a sense of history that just can't be reproduced in a more modern edifice. The menu is even better. Take, for example, Rogers "no tax" chicken—roulade of chicken, pesto, and ham in a grain mustard—cream sauce. Or you may opt for the "new Labour loaf" (lefter-leaning slices). The menu changes with each new political event. The ambience in this popular place is lively and convivial. It's fully licensed, of course. The bar is open daily from 11am to late; some food is always available.

Chevys
97 Dixon St. ☎ **04/384-2724.** Reservations not required. Main courses NZ$14–$18 (US$9.80–$12.60). AE, DC, MC, V. Mon–Thurs 11:30am–11pm, Fri–Sat 11:30am–midnight. AMERICAN.

Anyone tempted by the offer of "two meals for the price of one" should head over to Chevys after 5pm on Monday and Tuesday. You'll see the neon cowboy and his wiggling lasso a few blocks before you arrive at the door. The casual, congenial place has decidedly American fare: BLTs, chicken wings, nachos, barbecued spareribs, Philadelphia steak sandwiches, omelets, seven kinds of burgers, potato skins, and even banana splits. Your final bill will depend entirely on your appetite. It's fully licensed.

✪ One Red Dog
9–11 Blair St., Wellington. ☎ **04/384-9777.** Reservations not accepted. Main courses NZ$11–$14.90 (US$7.70–$10.43). AE, DC, MC, V. Sun–Thurs10am–1am, Fri–Sat 10am–3am. ECLECTIC.

I love the Italian country farmhouse decor here, including the wooden tables, worn wooden floor, wicker baskets, and strings of garlic hanging from the ceiling. It helps to create an atmosphere that is very convivial, friendly, and relaxed; they also provide good service. You might like to try the "Elvis was an Alien" calzone filled with chicken marinated in honey, ginger, and orange zest, with mushrooms, onion, and roasted red capsicum; or the smoked chicken Caesar salad. Pizzas come in medium or large sizes and include "One Reptile"—crocodile meat marinated in coconut cream and mild chili, with mangoes, and green peppers; chicken, cranberry, and brie; or a "Greenpiece"—roasted vegetables, goat's-milk cheese, and marinated mushrooms. There are five One Red Dogs in New Zealand. The bar, which is especially lively Friday and Saturday nights, serves Loaded Hog beers.

Rock Pool
Second floor, Queen's Wharf Retail Centre, Jervois Quay near Customhouse Quay. ☎ **04/499-4505.** Reservations accepted, required Fri and Sat. Main courses NZ$13.50–$22.50 (US$9.50–$15.80). AE, BC, DC, MC, V. Sun–Thurs 11:30am–10pm, Fri–Sat to 1am. ECLECTIC.

Located right on the water, the Rock Pool's full-height glass wall affords great views of the harbor to Mt. Victoria. The decor is very plain—the floors are concrete, and chairs are made of modern wood and chrome—as if the aim were not to compete with the view. Main course options include Thai beef salad, fettuccine carbonara, and prime Scotch fillet. The Rock Pool has a good wine list, too. The restaurant is located right above the Sandbar and noise from the bar floats upstairs. Seating is both inside and out.

Worth a Splurge

Il Casino Restaurant & Piano Bar
108 Tory St. ☎ **04/385-7496.** Fax 04/385-9388. Reservations recommended. Dinner main courses NZ$19.50–$32.50 (US$13.70–$22.80). AE, BC, DC, MC, V. Mon–Fri noon–2pm; Mon–Sat 6pm–"late." NORTHERN ITALIAN.

Home to Wellington's first wood-burning pizza oven, this is the place to come for designer versions of that Italian favorite—served at lunch, but not at dinner. Il Casino also offers pasta dishes in two sizes and an extensive menu of fish and meat dishes—all definitely worth a splurge. You might decide to try the vitello al marsala, veal medallions served in a marsala wine sauce; or the gamberoni ai ferri, king prawns grilled over charcoal and flavored with fresh herbs. Frugal travelers can stay within their budget guidelines by ordering the entree-size portions of pasta and a salad. Look for the Italian street scene painted on the outside of the building. It's fully licensed.

Mondo Cucina
15 Blair St., between Courtenay and Wakefield (P.O. Box 6300). ☎ **04/801-6615.** Reservations advisable Thurs–Sat. Main courses NZ$22.50–$26.50 (US$15.80–18.60), risotto or pasta main dishes NZ$16.50 (US$11.60). AE, DC, MC, V. Daily 6pm–late. MODERN MULTICULTURAL/ITALIAN.

The atmosphere here is warm with an interesting postmodern industrial decor. Rosemary roast lamb shank with mustard mash and gravy is the most popular dish. Others include chargrilled eggplant, pesto, tomatoes on potato rosti, and grilled bacon and chicken Caesar salad. Owner Simon Nigtengale worked for vintner Robert Mondavi in Napa, California; as you'd expect, the wine list is good. The bar, which is open until 4am, is lively Thursday through Saturday after 10pm.

Roxburgh Bistro
218 Majoribanks St. ☎ **04/385-7577.** Reservations required. Main courses NZ$25.50–$27.50 (US$17.85–$19.25). AE, DC, MC, V. Tues–Fri noon–2pm; Tues–Sat 6–10pm. INTERNATIONAL.

This pleasant place is in an old, two-story house just off Cambridge Terrace, a short distance from the city center—and its history includes being home to a "knock shop" (brothel) at some point in the past. Entrees (appetizers) include braised ox tongue, tuna sashimi, and Queensland prawn tails. Sample main dishes are beef tartar, rack of lamb, and vegetarian samosas. Friendly service, pink linen napkins, fresh flowers at each table, complimentary sherry, and an open fireplace on cool evenings add the pampered feeling that makes your pricey dinner tab seem well worth the extra money. No smoking is allowed in the bistro. If you want wine with dinner, you'll have to bring your own.

IN ORIENTAL BAY
Worth a Splurge
The Tug Boat on the Bay
Freyberg Lagoon, Oriental Bay. ☎ **04/384-8884.** Reservations recommended on weekends. Main courses NZ$18.50–$24.50 (US$13–$17.20). AE, BC, DC, MC, V. Daily noon–2pm; tea, coffee, drinks from the bar daily 2–10pm. NEW ZEALAND.

This really is an old tugboat—restored, of course. It's believed the tug was part of the fleet taking supplies across to Normandy after the D-Day invasion. Later it was used by the British Royal Navy in Singapore before coming to New Zealand in 1947. The *Tapuhi* worked on Wellington harbor for the next 26 years. Today it's the city's only floating restaurant and affords wonderful water and city views. Diners walk a red gangplank from the parking lot to reach the boat. The attractive decor includes marine artifacts and crisp white tablecloths. Dinner main courses include Canterbury rack of lamb, oven-baked baby salmon, Palliser Bay flounder topped with a tangy bacon-and-onion sauce, and vegetarian phyllo strudel. It's fully licensed.

IN BROOKLYN
✪ Brooklyn Café & Grill
1 Todham St., in Brooklyn. ☎ **04/385-3592.** Reservations not required. Main courses NZ$17–$24 (US$11.90–$16.80). AE, BC, DC, MC, V. Daily 6–11pm. NEW ZEALAND.

One of the city's most popular restaurants, the Brooklyn Café & Grill occupies a corner in this inner-city suburb. Owner Lois Dash, a local food columnist, took over several old shops and created a rather spare but comfortable interior that has won an architectural award. The menu features appetizers that could well serve as a light meal (like the potato cakes with gherkins, sour-cream dressing, and tomato salsa), steaks, lamb, fish, chicken, and vegetarian dishes such as polenta served with charcoal-grilled mushrooms, red-pepper sauce, and arugula. The vegetables are terrific and served with all main courses as well as organically grown leafy salads and steamed baby potatoes. There's limited parking in back of the restaurant, and it's BYO as well as licensed.

IN THORNDON
✪ Ford's Cafe
342 Tinakori Rd., Thorndon. ☎ **04/472-6238.** Reservations not accepted. Small plates NZ$10.50–$12.50 (US$7.40–$8.80); large plates NZ$14.25–$16.75 (US$9.98–$11.73). AE, BC, DC, MC, V. Mon–Fri 7am–"late," Sat–Sun 9am–"late." MODERN NEW ZEALAND.

I like this place both for its good food and for its casual cafe decor. Contemporary paintings hang on pale maize walls. Diners can sit at wooden tables or at a counter.

Small plates, which make an adequate light meal, include vegetable crêpes, chicken kebabs with spicy peanut sauce, and several pasta choices. The *really* hungry can have lamb filets rolled in fresh herbs; a pumpkin, tomato, and feta frittata; or pork with paprika and cream sauce. This two-story restaurant serves all three meals, and smoking is not permitted on the ground floor. Licensed.

IN KELBURN

The Skyline

1 Upland Rd., Kelburn. ☎ **04/475-8727.** Fax 04/475-8518. Reservations recommended for a window table. Full buffet lunch NZ$25 (US$16.25); 1 plate NZ$8.50–$13.50 (US$5.55–$8.80). AE, BC, MC, V. Daily 10am–4pm (buffet lunch noon–2:30pm). BUFFET.

This is a great spot to have morning or afternoon tea or lunch with an expansive view of the city and beyond. It's located steps from the top station of the Kelburn Cable Car, so it's even fun to get to. I don't like midday buffets because I end up feeling like a slug all afternoon, but this place is great because you can opt for a single stroll through the line with either a small or a large plate. It's fully licensed, too.

IN EVANS BAY

Greta Point Tavern

467 Evans Bay Parade. ☎ **04/386-1065.** Reservations not required. Main courses and vegetables or salad NZ$10–$20 (US$7–$14). AE, MC, V. Mon–Sat noon–2:30pm and 5:30–9:30pm, Sun 11:30am–2:30pm and 5:30–9pm. SEAFOOD.

If you're driving or happen to find yourself out in the lovely Evans Bay area, 3km (2 miles) from the city center, Greta Point is a good choice. Actually, the walk from downtown along Oriental Bay, Roseneath, and Evans Bay Parade to the tavern is picturesque and well worth doing. The large black building with rose trim sits right on the waterfront and has windows the entire length of its south side, looking out to sweeping views of the bay (often filled with sailboats) and a nearby marina with its forest of masts. The high-ceilinged room, which once housed a commercial laundry, now has a wooden lifeboat suspended from the overhead pipes. Upstairs is the Promenade Deck bar and downstairs you'll find the Anchorage Lounge Bar, as well as the Galley Restaurant that features fresh seafoods. The restaurant is self-service and fully licensed, and the long counter offers Bluff oysters, roast baron of beef, marinated mussels, baked leg of lamb, and a host of other tempting dishes.

5 Exploring Wellington: What to See & Do

THE TOP ATTRACTIONS

✪ Te Papa Museum of New Zealand

On Cable Street at the harbor front, Wellington. ☎ **04/381-7000.** Free admission. Daily 9am–5pm or later. Closed Christmas Day.

I wore a hard hat and toured this fabulous new museum while it was still under construction so that I could include it in this edition. What a treat you have in store! I was overwhelmed by what I saw. If you can, allow a full day to tackle this museum, but if you're on a tight schedule, you shouldn't spend less than 3 hours here.

When the Museum of New Zealand (known locally as "Te Papa") opens in February 1998, it will be not only the country's first bicultural museum but also its largest museum. For the first time, Maori history will be told side by side with Pakeha history. It will also be a treasure trove of the nation's finest exhibits. You'll learn about New Zealand's social history, its geology and geography, its plants and animals, and

Te Papa Museum of New Zealand

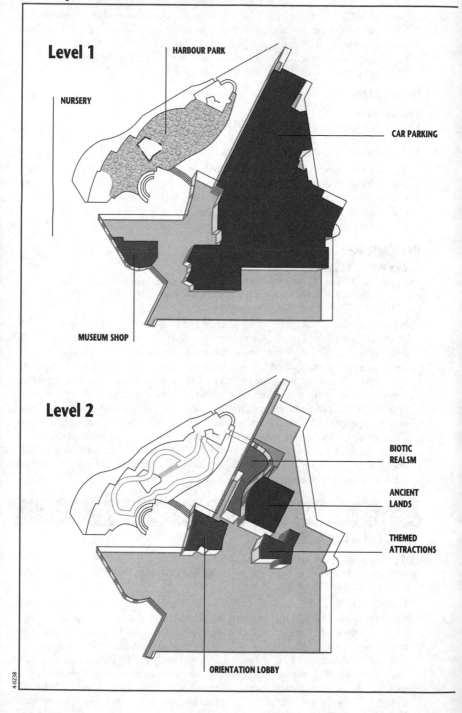

Level 1

NURSERY

HARBOUR PARK

CAR PARKING

MUSEUM SHOP

Level 2

BIOTIC REALSM

ANCIENT LANDS

THEMED ATTRACTIONS

ORIENTATION LOBBY

4-0238

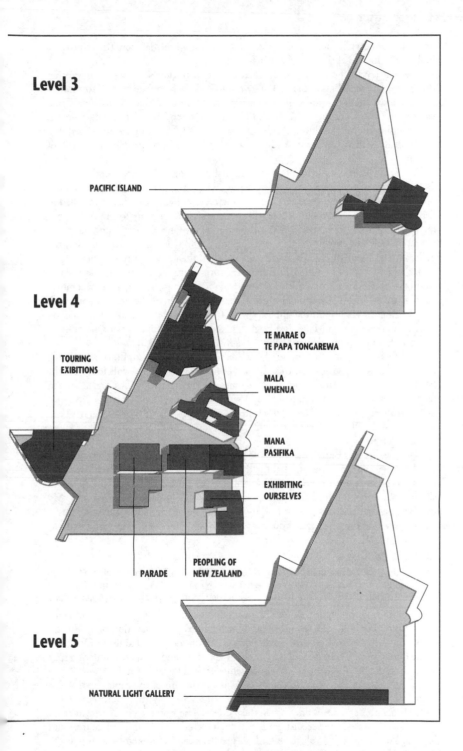

Level 3

PACIFIC ISLAND

Level 4

TOURING
EXIBITIONS

TE MARAE O
TE PAPA TONGAREWA

MALA
WHENUA

MANA
PASIFIKA

EXHIBITING
OURSELVES

PARADE

PEOPLING OF
NEW ZEALAND

Level 5

NATURAL LIGHT GALLERY

253

its contemporary culture. You could easily spend the whole day here (this five-story building is the size of three rugby fields).

The first level is home to the interactive (virtual reality) section—among other things, you can see what it's like to bungy jump. Level two contains the **"Mountains-to-Sea"** area, the focal point of which is the skeleton of a blue pigmy whale that was hit by a container ship in Auckland Harbour. (When I was there, the whale was still dripping oil on the floor.) At the entrance to the **"Awesome Forces"** exhibit, which deals with volcanoes and earthquakes, visitors will be greeted by a blast of hot air.

The Maori exhibits include both traditional and contemporary meetinghouses. The traditional one comes from the Rongowhakaata tribe in Gisborne, and a procession of 600 Rongowhakaata descendants were present when it was installed in September '96—you can only enter without shoes. The doorway to the contemporary meetinghouse was carved by Maori master carver Cliff Whiting, and he supervised polytech students from all over the country who worked on other areas of the marae. An adjacent Resource Centre gives children the opportunity to touch Maori cloaks, skirts, and poi balls. All of these treasures were transferred here by Maori warriors—five busloads of Te Arawa came from Rotorua to participate in the move. The Treaty of Waitangi area will feature a Maori translation of the treaty on one wall, with an English version on the opposite wall. In the court between the two walls are story poles representing Maori and English people (coming together or separating—depending on the point from which they are viewed).

The **"Passports"** area, also on level four, tells the story of British, European, Pacific Islander, and Chinese immigration. The **"Mana Pacifica"** area will focus on the Islander's culture. In the Resource Centre nearest the Mana Pacifica area, Samoan men were building a *fale* (Samoan house) when I was there.

"Exhibiting Ourselves" looks at selected world expos that New Zealand has been involved with, including Seville in 1992, Wellington in 1940, Christchurch in 1904, and London in 1902.

"Off the Sheep's Back" examines the importance of agriculture in New Zealand. Level five will feature a natural-light gallery and library. **"Harbour Park"** will display native plants contributed by Maori tribes from around the country. There will also be an outdoor amphitheater and a restaurant with a bodacious harbor view. My back felt nearly broken at the end of my tour; the floors are hard, and I was carrying a heavy briefcase. I suggest you wear your most comfortable shoes and carry as little as possible.

✪ Kelburn Cable Car

Lambton Quay. ☎ **04/472-2199.** Fare, NZ$1.50 (US$1.05) for adults 1 way, NZ$2.50 (US$1.75) round-trip; NZ70¢ (US49¢) children 1 way; NZ$1.40 (US$1) round-trip. Cable car runs every 10 minutes, Mon–Fri 7am–10pm, Sat 9am–10pm, Sun and public holidays 9am–10pm.

For the fullest appreciation of Wellington's spectacular setting, take a marvelous $4^{1}/_{2}$-minute ride in a sleek red cable car, which climbs to an elevation of 1,980 feet up Mount Victoria to Kelburn, leaving every 10 minutes from Lambton Quay opposite Grey Street. The beautiful harbor lies at your feet, and it's a great loitering spot to drink in the beauty of that curving shoreline backed by jagged hills.

The entrance to the **Botanic Gardens** is also at the top of the cable-car ride; it's open from dawn to dusk with no admission charge. Stop by the Interpretive Centre for brochures and a full briefing on the gardens. The Botanic Gardens feature 26 hectares ($64^{1}/_{4}$ acres) of specialist gardens, which include exotic and ornate trees and flowers. Your downhill stroll through lush greenery can be broken by a stop at the **Begonia House** and its **Tea House** in the **Lady Norwood Rose Gardens** (open from

Cheap Thrills: What to See & Do for Free in Wellington

- **Taking in the Views from Mount Victoria**   The harbor literally sparkles throughout the day, and the city lights twinkle around its perimeter after dark.
- **Strolling through the Botanic Gardens**   On your way through the lush greenery here, stop by the *Begonia House* and its *Tea House* in the **Lady Norwood Rose Gardens** (open 10am to 4pm) for a look at hundreds of begonias, bush foliage, ferns, and of course roses.
- **Exploring Te Papa Museum of New Zealand**   It doesn't open until February 1998, but when it does you're in for a real treat. All six floors will dazzle you with everything from virtual reality bungy jumping to ancient Maori artifacts to the looming skeleton of a blue pigmy whale.
- **Experiencing Old St. Paul's Church**   Located on Mulgrave Street, this lovely old church provides a peaceful interlude for busy sightseers.
- **Touring the Beehive**   This is one of the beautifully restored Parliament Buildings and the symbol of New Zealand government. Inside are some wonderful works of art. If the members of Parliament are in session, be sure to stay and watch the sometimes-raucous debates.
- **Walking the Waterfront**   Start at Queen's Wharf and wind your way along Lambton Harbour, following Oriental Parade until you can look back on the city skyline.

10am to 4pm) for a look at hundreds of begonias, bush foliage, and ferns. From the foot of the gardens, you can get back to the city on a no. 12 bus.

Katherine Mansfield Birthplace

25 Tinakori Rd., Thorndon, Wellington. ☎ and fax **04/473-7268**. Admission NZ$4 (US$2.80) adults, NZ$1 (US70¢) children. Mon 10am–2:30pm, Tues–Sun 10am–4pm.

Katherine Mansfield, New Zealand-born short-story writer, poet, and essayist, first saw the light of day in 1888. One of the country's most prestigious writers—and arguably its most famous worldwide—she inspires such veneration that a nonprofit organization was formed to restore the old house to the decor of the year of her birth. There's a shop with books, cards, posters, and souvenirs, and if you order in advance, you can enjoy a light lunch or morning/afternoon tea on the premises. This Tourism Award winner is the first stop on the Thorndon Heritage Trail.

Wellington Maritime Museum

In the Wellington Harbour Board Building, Queen's Wharf. ☎ **04/472-8904**. Fax 04/471-1373. E-mail maritime@xtra.co.nz. Admission by donation; suggested amounts, NZ$2 (US$1.40) adults, NZ$5 (US$3.50) family group. Mon–Fri 9:30am–4pm, Sat–Sun and public holidays 1–4:30pm. Closed Good Friday and Christmas Day.

Those interested in things of the sea will want to visit this museum, where Wellington's close association with seafarers and their vessels is well documented, with displays of ship models, paintings, flags, bells, photographs, ships' artifacts, and a reconstructed captain's cabin. A major refurbishment is planned to begin in late 1997; specifics have not been finalized, and the museum may move off site during work, with the reopening scheduled sometime in late 1998. Call for details when you get to town.

THE PARLIAMENT BUILDINGS

New Zealand's Parliament Buildings are located on Molesworth Street in the city center and include the distinctive beehive-shaped building that is the administrative headquarters. You can visit Parliament daily free of charge (☎ **04/471-9503** or 04/471-9999). Tours are given Monday through Friday from 10am to 4pm, Saturday from 10am to 3pm, and Sunday from 1 to 3pm. The very informative 1-hour tour includes **Parliament House** and the **Parliamentary Library.** Restoration of both was completed in 1995 and the buildings contain some wonderful works of art. If you're there on a day when there isn't a political brouhaha going on and your group isn't too large, the tour may also include **The Beehive.** If Parliament is sitting, you can go to the Public Gallery before, after, or instead of the tour and watch the sometimes-raucous goings on. Ring to find out if they're sitting (the house sits Tuesday from 2 to 6pm, Wednesday from 2 to 10pm, and Thursday from 10am to 6pm for 30 weeks of the year). If you aren't going to Wellington, you can listen to the House of Representatives on Radio New Zealand.

On the tour, you'll notice in the Debating Chamber of the House of Representatives that some of the seats are covered with sheepskins. This is a matter of preference, not of status. Also notice the bronze camellias to the right and left above the Speaker's chair. These were given by the Women's Welfare League in 1993 to commemorate 100 years of women's suffrage.

Across the road from Parliament, you could spend some time at the **National Library of New Zealand,** 70 Molesworth St. (☎ **04/474-3119,** fax 04/474-3063, e-mail ATL@natlib.govt.nz). Here you can browse in the National Library Gallery, in the shop, and through the collection of New Zealand books—all on the ground floor. The **Alexander Turnbull Library,** in the same building, is the research wing of the National Library, specializing in New Zealand and the Pacific. Books, serials, sound recordings, manuscripts, and archives are researched on the first floor, and newspapers on the lower ground floor. On the second floor, visitors can peruse files of photographs; and drawings, paintings, and maps are available for research by appointment. The Library is open Monday through Friday from 9am to 5pm, and 9am to 1pm on Saturday for nonpictorial materials.

MORE ATTRACTIONS

✪ **Old St. Paul's Church,** on Mulgrave St., in the suburb of Thorndon (☎ **04/473-6722**), is a marvelous Early English Gothic–style wooden church much beloved by Wellingtonians. Using the native timbers of totara, matai, rimu, and kauri, the softly lit church with its dark timbers, soaring wooden arches, and brilliant stained glass radiates peace and calmness, a relaxing stop in your sightseeing itinerary. There's no admission charge (donations are welcome), and it's open to the public Monday through Saturday from 10:30am to 4:30pm and Sunday from 1 to 4:30pm; closed Good Friday and Christmas Day.

Wellington Zoo

Newtown. ☎ **04/389-8130.** Admission NZ$7.50 (US$4.90) adults, NZ$3.50 (US$2.30) children 3 and above, free for children under 3. Daily 9:30am–5pm. Bus: 10 (Newtown Park) from the railway station.

This zoo dates back to 1906 and its collection includes kangaroos, wallabies, monkeys, lions, tigers, chimpanzees, and golden lion tamarin. There's also a nocturnal **Kiwi House** (open daily from 10am to 4pm), featuring kiwi, tuatara, and giant weta.

ORGANIZED TOURS
BUS TOURS

A good way to get an in-depth look at the city itself and its immediate environs is to take the escorted ✪ **Wally Hammond's Wellington City Scenic Tours bus tour**

(☎ **04/472-0869** for information and reservations, fax 04/471-1730), which leaves from the Visitor Information Centre on Wakefield Street every day at 10am and 2pm. For the bargain price of NZ$20 (US$14) for adults (children ride for half price), you'll be driven some 49km (30 miles), with 2¹/₂ hours of informative narrative as you see the financial and commercial center, take a look at government buildings and Parliament's unique Beehive building, visit the lookout on Mount Victoria (with a stop for picture taking), skirt the bays, stop for afternoon tea, then reenter the city via View Road. It's a scenic drive, which does full justice to Wellington's headlands, hills, bays, and beaches. Wally Hammond also offers a Wellington Twilight Tour during daylight savings season (October to March) for (NZ$25/US$17.50 adult) and full-day scenic tours to the Kapiti Gold Coast (NZ$55/US$38.50 adult) and Wairarapa/Palliser Bay (NZ$85/US$59.50 adult). Bankcard, MasterCard, and Visa are accepted.

HARBOR CRUISES

There's no doubt about it—that spectacular harbor exerts an irresistible pull to see Wellington from the water. The bargain way to accomplish this is via the ✪ **Trust Bank Ferry** (☎ **04/499-1273** for timetable information), which crosses the harbor from Queen's Wharf in Wellington to Days Bay. The 25-minute ride on the Trust Bank Ferry costs NZ$7 (US$4.90) for adults each way, and NZ$3.50 (US$2.45) for children, or NZ$35 (US$24.50) for a round-trip family excursion ticket that covers two adults and up to four children. The ferry has a full bar and also serves coffee. At Days Bay, you can enjoy the park, have afternoon tea in the pavilion, or take the 3-minute stroll around to Eastbourne where there are galleries and gift shops.

Another option is an excursion to **Somes Island** with the Trust Bank Ferry. Recently opened to the public after 100 years of restricted access, the island was an early Maori settlement; in more recent times it served as a quarantine station and prisoner of war camp. The island, which has been replanted and developed as a wildlife refuge, offers walking tracks, bird life, native bush, and 360° panoramic views. The round-trip cost of this is NZ$14 (US$9.80) for adults, NZ$7 (US$4.90) for children 5–15, and NZ$35 (US$24.50) for a family of two adults and four children. This is a fun trip on a nice, sunny day.

Incidentally, if the ✪ **Wellington–Picton Inter-Island Ferry** (☎ **0800/802-802** in New Zealand, or 04/498-3000) is not on your travel itinerary, ask about their excursion special that lets you pay one way and return the same day for free. You'll pay NZ$44 (US$30.80) for the standard return fare and NZ$38 (US$26.60) for the economy day return (when it's available). The ship crosses Cook Strait; its South Island destination is Picton in the Marlborough Sounds. It's one of Wellington's special experiences but do it only on a calm, sunny day. You'll see lots of wonderful scenery. For details, see "Getting Around" in chapter 3.

6 Outdoor Activities

CANOEING See "Wairarapa: A Side Trip from Wellington" at the end of this chapter for a canoeing adventure in the nearby Wairarapa region.

GOLF There are a number of courses near Wellington; the following are within 25 minutes of the city center: **Paraparaumu Beach Golf Club,** 376 Kapiti Rd., Paraparauma Beach (☎ **04/298-4561**). This 18-hole, par-71 course was rated one of the top 50 courses in the world by *Golf Digest;* a round of golf here costs NZ$75 (US$52.50); club hire is NZ$25 (US$17.50), and buggy (cart) hire is NZ$28 (US$19.60). Reserve well in advance. **Hutt Golf Club,** Military Rd., Lower Hutt

(☎ 04/567-4722), is an 18-hole, par 70 course; a round of golf costs NZ$35 (US$24.50); club hire is NZ$25 (US$17.50), trundler (pull cart) is NZ$5 (US$3.50), and a buggy costs NZ$25 (US$17.50). **Karori Golf Club,** South Makara Rd., Wellington (☎ 04/476-7337), is an 18-hole, par-70 course; a round of golf costs NZ$15 (US$10.50) during the week and NZ$25 (US$17.50) on weekends; club hire (including a trundler) is NZ$15 (US$10.50).

SWIMMING The **Wellington Regional Aquatic Center,** in the suburb of Kilbirnie (☎ 04/387-8029), has four heated pools: a lap pool, a learners' pool, and adjoining junior and toddlers' pools with an access ramp for people with disabilities. There are also diving facilities, spa pools, saunas, a sundeck, cafe, and YMCA fitness center. You can rent swimsuits and towels; goggles are for sale. The no. 2 bus to Miramar takes you to the door.

TENNIS The **Wellington Renouf Tennis Centre,** 20 Brooklyn Rd. at Central Park (P.O. Box 9818), Wellington (☎ 04/384-6294, fax 04/384-6291, e-mail fitz@ihug.co.nz), has 14 outdoor courts for about NZ$16 (US$11.20) per hour and four indoor courts available for about NZ$36 (US$25.20) per hour. It's open Monday through Friday 6am to 11pm and Saturday and Sunday from 8am to 11pm. Practice or hitting partners can be arranged on short notice, as can coaching, and there's a cafe and bar on the premises.

7 Shopping

Much of Wellington's best shopping is along **Lambton Quay.** Don't miss **Capital on the Quay,** three linked arcades at 250 Lambton Quay, and **Kirkcaldie & Stains** (☎ 04/472-5899), Wellington's famous department store. Both are open 7 days a week.

For window shopping and browsing, you might also like to stroll the ✪ **Manners and Cuba pedestrian malls.** You'll find crafts and secondhand shops on **Cuba Street** near Ghuznee Street. The **Queen's Wharf Retail Centre** is open Monday through Thursday 10am to 6pm, Friday 9am to 7pm, and Sunday 10am to 5pm.

The **Great New Zealand Shop,** 13 Grey St. (☎ and fax 04/472-6817), is a good souvenir shop, open Monday through Thursday 8:30am to 5pm, Friday until 6:30pm, and Saturday 10am to 4pm. For splurge shopping, head to ✪ **Vibrant Handknits,** Lee Andersen's Designer Gallery, Shop 5, Sun Alliance Centre, 280 Lambton Quay (☎ 04/472-8720, fax 04/388-1749); it's next to Cable Car Lane and open Monday through Thursday 9am to 5:30pm, Friday until 7pm, and Saturday 10am to 2pm. **Mainly Tramping,** 39 Mercer St. (☎ 04/473-5353, fax 04/473-5353), will help you get outfitted for the bush, backpacking, mountaineering, and kayaking; it's open Monday through Thursday 9am to 5:30pm, Friday 9am to 8pm, and Saturday 10am to 4pm.

8 Wellington After Dark

Check the current issue of *Capital Times* and *What's On,* available at tourist information centers, for entertainment news. Wellington is home to four professional theaters, the New Zealand Symphony Orchestra, and the Royal New Zealand Ballet.

Budget tip: The Wellington Visitor Information Centre sells discounted day-of-performance tickets for many performing-arts events.

THE PERFORMING ARTS

The **Downstage Theatre,** in the Hannah Playhouse on Courtenay Place at the corner of Cambridge Terrace, Wellington (☎ 04/801-6946, fax 04/801-6948, e-mail downstge@globe.co.nz), presents first-rate theater in an exciting, award-winning structure that provides for flexibility in staging in the main auditorium plus space for bars and a restaurant. Downstage is a year-round enterprise, presenting its own productions and the best of touring shows, including classics, contemporary drama, comedy, and dance, with an emphasis on quality New Zealand works. Check the newspapers for current showings or contact the theater directly. Reserve as far in advance as you possibly can, however, because Downstage productions are very popular. Ticket prices are about NZ$25 (US$17.50) for most shows, and they accept American Express, Discover, MasterCard, and Visa. Students, senior citizens, and groups of 10 receive a discount.

Other theaters include **Circa Theatre,** 1 Taranaki St. (☎ **04/801-7992**); **Taki Rua Theatre,** 12 Alpha St. (☎ **04/384-4531,** fax 04/384-4571), and **Bats Theatre,** 1 Kent Terrace (☎ **04/384-9507,** fax 04/385-9486). Circa is probably the most conservative of the lot; Taki Rua produces new indigenous works, including some in the Maori language; Bats presents new and experimental plays and dance, which attract a young audience, as well as folks who are not traditional theatergoers. Ticket prices vary with each performance.

THE CLUB & BAR SCENE

Wellington is well known for its large variety of bars and cafes set in a concentrated area. The two main areas are **"The Playground,"** which includes Courtenay Place, Blair, and Allen streets, and **Queen's Wharf.** The Playground has possibly the largest concentration of bars, nightclubs, cafes, and restaurants in New Zealand within walking distance of each other. On weekends in this area you can enjoy Wellington's street musicians as you wander between bars. Queen's Wharf is down on the waterfront. These upmarket bars have beautiful day and nighttime views of the harbor. In Wellington the after-work bar scene starts on Queen's Wharf at Chicago, the Sandbar, Rock Pool, etc., and, as the night goes on, moves on to Courtenay Place.

A Note on Safety: If you're a night owl, be aware that upper Cuba Street and Manners Mall are *not safe* after dark.

One of the most popular bars in Wellington is the ✪ **Opera Restaurant and Bar,** Courtney Place on the corner of Blair Street (☎ **04/382-8654**). Popular with yuppies in the twenty-and-thirtysomething crowd, after-work drinkers listen to opera, which is played during the dinner hour. Later the music ranges from rap to '70s disco from 11pm until 3am. This is a full-on party bar Thursday, Friday, and Saturday nights with dancing, plus live bands on Thursday and a DJ on Friday and Saturday. There's no cover, and a handle of Export Gold (their most popular beer) will set you back NZ$4 (US$2.80). Open daily 11am until late, the Opera Bar was named "One of the World's Best Bars" by *Newsweek International* in 1996. **Tatou,** 22 Cambridge Terrace (☎ **04-384-3112**), which is across the street and around the corner, plays techno until 6am.

For a diverse crowd, head to the **Sandbar** in the Queen's Wharf Retail Complex (☎ **04/499-4505**). It draws mid-20s to late-30s Lambton Quay business people and yachties who like to be near the wharf. Cafe by day and bar by night, the Sandbar serves meals until 4pm—after that it's snacks only. Open daily 8am until 10pm, during the week, and until 2:30am on weekends, the club features live bands on Friday night after 9:30pm and CDs the rest of the time. A handle of Export Gold costs NZ$5 (US$3.50); a bottle of Heineken will set you back NZ$4.50 (US$3.20).

The **James Cook Centra Hotel,** on The Terrace (☎ **04/499-9500**), has a piano bar nightly and a classical string quartet on Saturday and Sunday; the **Greta Point Tavern,** Evans Bay Parade (☎ **04/386-1065**), has live entertainment Friday and Saturday nights.

9 Wairarapa: A Side Trip from Wellington

Less than 2 hours' drive northeast of Wellington, the **Wairarapa region** is well worth a day-trip from the city—even better, an overnight stay in order to explore all the riches of the region.

En route to Masterton, the region's chief town, you might want to plan your first stop in Featherston to visit ✪ **Kahutara Canoes,** RD 1, Featherston (☎ **06/ 308-8453**). Owner John McCosh, also known as "Tuatara Ted" (New Zealand's answer to Crocodile Dundee), and his wife, Karen, have put together an interesting taxidermy museum. In a spacious Canadian log structure, the museum houses more than 350 mounted animals from around the globe. John is a friendly, colorful character, always happy to show you around and talk about all the specimens. He's also enthusiastic about their animal park, which houses deer, sheep, wild pigs, and birds. Because it is small and informal, this is a good hands-on experience for children.

The museum, however, is only a small part of what the McCoshes get up to. They and their staff of expert guides operate a variety of **canoe trips** on the scenic Ruamahanga River. The canoes range from large, stable Canadian craft down to fast one- and two-person kayaks, and the river trips are designed to appeal to all ages, from toddlers to grandparents. Some are as short as 2 to 3 hours; others are 3 or more hours. You'll have to call ahead for hours, charges, and reservations. The half-day trip costs NZ$30 (US$21) for adults and NZ$12 (US$8.40) for children. Even if you plan to visit only the museum (NZ$3/US$2.10 for adults, NZ$1/US 70¢ for children, free for canoeists; open daily from 10am to 5pm), be sure to allow extra time here—it's very hard to pop in and right back out. Barbecue and picnic facilities are available.

In Carterton, a stop at the **Paua Shell Factory Shop,** 54 Kent St. (☎ **06/ 379-6777,** fax 06/379-6775), can yield unique gifts, jewelry, and souvenirs, and there are free factory tours. It's open Monday through Friday 8am to 4:30pm and Saturday, Sunday, and public holidays 9am to 5pm; they accept American Express, Bankcard, Diners Club, MasterCard, and Visa. Carterton is also a good place to look for New Zealand leather products—**Jeffrey Chandel Leathers,** 69–73 Nelson Crescent (☎ **06/379-8927**), makes an extensive line of ladies' and men's jackets and coats, as well as a wide range of other leather products—all at competitive prices. It's open Monday through Friday 9am to 5pm, Saturday 9am to 3pm, and most Sundays 10am to 2pm (call in advance to see if it's open).

In Masterton, the **Tourism Wairarapa Visitor Information Centre,** 5 Dixon St. (☎ **06/378-7373,** fax 06/378-7042), is open daily and should be your very first stop. The bright, modern building houses loads of literature on attractions in the region, the many nature walks, and sporting opportunities. The friendly staff can also furnish information on and book accommodations (everything from motels to farmstays) as well as recommend places to eat.

About 17 miles north of Masterson on State Highway 2, the ✪ **Mount Bruce National Wildlife Centre** (☎ **06/375-8004**) is a significant experience. Its 10 different aviaries; a nocturnal complex inhabited by a small population of kiwi, morepork owls, and lizards; and outside paths that wind through native bush are a world apart and one seldom accessible to the likes of you and me. They do a lot of work with New Zealand's rare and endangered species. I also like the fact that paths have been made accessible for wheelchairs. In the Visitor Centre at the entrance there's an audiovisual exhibit, a souvenir shop, and tea rooms overlooking the natural splendors just beyond wide picture windows. It's open daily from 9am to 4pm (closed

Christmas Day), and there's a NZ$6 (US$4.20) admission fee for adults, NZ$1.50 (US$1.10) for children, and NZ$12 (US$8.40) for a family ticket.

About 21km (13 miles) south of Masterton and an hour east of Wellington, the little township of Martinborough is home to Wairarapa's best **wineries.** They include **Te Kairanga,** Martins Rd., Martinborough (☎ **06/306-9122,** fax 06/306-9322); **Muirlea Rise,** Princess Street, Martinborough (☎ and fax **06/306-9332**); **Blue Rock,** Dry River Road, Martinborough (☎ **06/306-9353,** fax 06/306-9353); and **Cifney,** Huangarua Road, Martinborough (☎ and fax **06/306-9495**).

Martinborough hosts several popular special events throughout the year. See "Special Events" earlier in this chapter for details on the **Martinborough Country Fair,** held on the first Saturdays of both February and March, and **Toast Martinborough,** which is always the third Sunday in November. Call the Martinborough Information Centre (☎ **06/306-9043,** fax 06/306-9183) for details.

EN ROUTE TO WANGANUI

For information on the **Kapiti Coast,** a stretch along Highway 1 about 58km (36 miles) north of Wellington, see "En Route to Wellington" in chapter 9. This area is popular with car buffs because it is the home of the **Southward Car Museum.** Kapiti Island is a favorite with birders.

11

Marlborough, Nelson, the West Coast & Wanaka

As soon as you cross Cook Strait, you'll start to notice the differences between New Zealand's two main islands. To begin with, the South Island is much more sparsely populated. It's not that the North Island is crowded; it's just that here there never seems to be anyone around. In fact, two-thirds of the nation's population lives north of Lake Taupo. In all, there are about 2,700,000 North Islanders and just over 900,000 South Islanders—and the South Island is the larger of the two. Because of the low population numbers, there's less traffic on the South Island. If you haven't driven on the left before, it might be a good idea to cut your teeth here before navigating the busier north.

The South Island is also more rugged and more majestic. The Southern Alps form a spine down the length of it and are visible from almost any point. By comparison, the North Island is more gentle. The rolling green hills of Northland and the Waikato District won't be found down here. Instead, the South Island is home to huge sheep stations that operate like cities unto themselves. And you won't see much thermal activity now that you've crossed Cook Strait—you've left the land of volcanoes and bubbling mud pools behind.

You'll also notice that few Maori live here. Historically there've been some—they sought the greenstone on the West Coast for their prized adzes and war clubs, but generally speaking these Polynesians have always preferred the warmth of the North Island.

Another difference—and this is good news for budget travelers— things are generally a little less expensive on the South Island.

If you cross over on the ferry, your introduction to the South Island will be at Picton, which sits at the head of the beautiful Marlborough Sounds. To the west lies Nelson, the home of potters and other artisans, as well as retired folks who love good weather and wide beaches. Beyond Nelson is the West Coast—a remote area of magical beauty and an area now protected by World Heritage status.

1 Picton & Blenheim

Picton: 146km (91 miles) E of Nelson; Blenheim: 117km (72.5 miles) ESE of Nelson

Picton sits at the head of Queen Charlotte Sound, ready to receive the ferryloads of visitors who arrive daily. It's a quiet community that's foolishly overlooked by many who disembark the ferry and head straight through town and onto the southbound highway or onto the Queen Charlotte Drive leading to Havelock and Nelson. In their haste these folks miss one of New Zealand's most wonderful playgrounds, because Picton is the jumping-off point for the glorious Marlborough Sounds.

Savvy New Zealanders have vacation homes on the tree-clad fingers of land that protrude into the green waters of the sound, and on holiday weekends they can be seen in their dinghies or on the water taxi heading out to their little patches of paradise. The area is ideal for sailing, kayaking, and bushwalking, as well as for kicking back on one of the area's hundreds of secluded bays and tiny beaches. Because the island is sparsely populated, pollution is practically unheard of. Dolphins, whales, and occasionally seals are seen here, and the fishing is great.

Picton (pop. 3,300) actually lies *north* of Wellington, so the ferry curiously sails north to reach the South Island. Queen Charlotte Sound was named by Captain Cook in 1770 for George III's wife. He found it "a very safe and convenient cove," and, indeed, used it as an anchorage for much of his later Pacific exploration. He can also be credited for bringing the first sheep to New Zealand because he put ashore a ram and a ewe in 1773—prophetic, even though that particular pair survived only a few days, and thus the good captain cannot lay claim to having furnished the fountainhead of today's millions of woolly creatures.

Blenheim, 29km (18 miles) to the south, is New Zealand's most popular wine region.

ESSENTIALS
GETTING THERE & GETTING AROUND
BY PLANE   Air service to Picton from Wellington is provided by **Soundsair** (☎ 04/388-2594 or 03/573-6184). **Ansett New Zealand** and **Air New Zealand Link** fly into nearby Blenheim.

BY TRAIN   The *Coastal Pacific* provides daily rail service between Picton and Christchurch.

BY COACH (BUS)   Coach service into both Picton and Blenheim is provided by **InterCity** and **Mount Cook Landline.** The trip from Christchurch takes 5 hours; from Nelson, 2 hours.

Picton doesn't have a local bus system, but **water taxis** of the **Cougar Line** (☎ 03/573-7925) will take you to the inlet of your choice.

BY ALTERNATIVE COACH (BUS)   Picton and Kaikoura (see "En Route South" at the end of this section) are both included in the routes of **Magic Traveller** and **Kiwi Experience.**

BY FERRY   See "By Inter-Island Ferry" under "Getting Around," in chapter 3.

BY CAR   Most car-rental companies request that you turn in one car in Wellington and pick up a new one in Picton. However, you can take cars and campers on the ferry, should the need arise.

VISITOR INFORMATION
The **Picton Information Centre** is on the Picton foreshore, located in the same building as the Department of Conservation (☎ 03/573-7477, fax 03/573-8362). The **telephone area code** (STD) for Picton is **03.**

ORIENTATION
Picton faces Queen Charlotte Sound whence cometh ferries and fishing boats—with great regularity. The shopping area is small and centered around **High Street.**

Marlborough, Nelson & Beyond

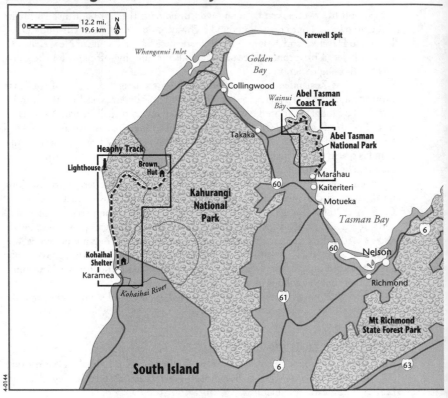

London Quay runs along the foreshore, with the ferry terminal at one end and the town wharf at the other. **Paper World,** 28 High St. (☎ **03/573-6107**), is a handy place to pick up maps, postcards, and reading material.

EXPLORING PICTON & BLENHEIM: WHAT TO SEE & DO
GETTING OUT ON THE WATER IN PICTON

It's not a question of *whether* you'll go out on the water in the Marlborough Sounds, but rather *which* vessel you'll be on. The ferry from Wellington provides a good introductory view as it makes its way toward Picton, though for a closer look you'll need to go out on a smaller, more specialized boat. **The Cougar Line,** P.O. Box 238, Picton (☎ **03/573-7925,** fax 03/573-7926), operates a water taxi and cruise service on Queen Charlotte Sound and offers **3-hour cruises** covering about 80km (50 miles) of coastline (NZ$40/US$28). You can go out on the morning cruise, be dropped off at one of the resorts on the sound, and then return on the afternoon excursion. Another option is to join the **mail run** operated by Beachcomber Cruises (☎ **03/573-6175**) and cruise around the sound on the mail boat. This trip departs at 11:15am on Monday, Tuesday, Thursday, and Friday and, depending on how much mail needs to be delivered, returns between 4:30 and 6pm (NZ$45/US$31.50).

Sea kayaking is another popular activity. **The Marlborough Sounds Adventure Company** (MSAE), P.O. Box 195, Picton (☎ **03/573-6078,** fax 03/573-8827),

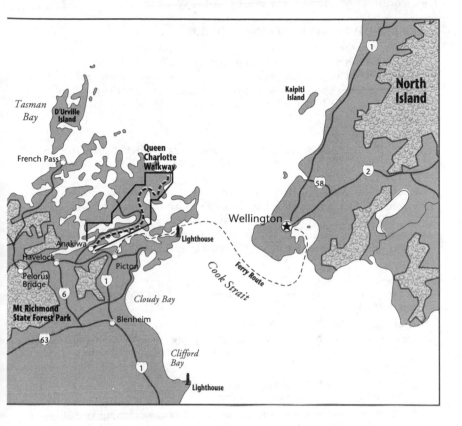

offers 1-day guided trips for NZ$70 (US$49) per person, including morning tea and lunch. These excursions are accompanied by a naturalist interpreter. The MSAC also offers a twilight paddle and barbecue (NZ$55/US$38.50) and fully catered 4-day trips for groups of six (NZ$550/US$385, including meals and camping gear). The 4-day kayaking trip is very popular so be sure to book early. The Marlborough Sounds Adventure Company was awarded the 1993 New Zealand Tourism Award for Best Visitor Activity. For those who like **sailing,** the 16-meter yacht *Te Anau* (☎ 03/573-7726) cruises along the coastline (NZ$25/US$16.25 for 2 hours). While passengers on any of these vessels may see dolphins, **Dolphin Watch Marlborough,** P.O. Box 197, Picton (☎ **03/573-8040,** fax 03/573-7906), makes these lovely creatures the focus of their naturalist tours. Trips of 3¹/₂ to 4 hours cost NZ$55 (US$38.50) for adults and NZ$30 (US$21) for children; those under 6 are free. You might even be able to swim with them for an additional NZ$20 (US$13) per person for the equipment hire.

THE QUEEN CHARLOTTE WALKWAY

The Queen Charlotte Walkway is a wonderful 1- to 4-day experience. The views are amazing, and you don't have to carry a pack because it can be transferred by boat. You don't even have to camp or stay in rustic huts; a variety of different lodgings are available along the way. See "Tramping," in chapter 4, "The Active Vacation Planner," for more information on the Queen Charlotte Walkway.

TOURING THE WINERIES IN NEARBY BLENHEIM

While water is the focus of attention in Picton, wine is the big draw to nearby Blenheim. Here in the heart of the Marlborough District, some of the country's finest **wineries** are open for tours and tastings. Three of my favorites are listed below, but I recommend picking up a copy of the *Wine Trail Guide* from the **Blenheim Information Centre,** The Forum, Queen Street, Blenheim (☎ **03/578-9904,** fax 03/578-6084), before you go.

Hunter's Winery

Rapaura Rd. ☎ **03/572-8489.** Fax 03/572-8457. Web site nz.com/webnz/pelorus/hunters. Free tasting (no tours). Winery, Mon–Sat 9:30am–4:30pm, Sun 10:30am–4pm. Restaurant, daily noon–4pm and 6–9:30pm.

The *London Sunday Times* wine critic called Jane Hunter one of the world's top five women winemakers, and you'll understand why when you taste her wine. The Vintners Restaurant on the premises specializes in Marlborough produce, including seafood, lamb, venison, rabbit, freshwater trout, and salmon. Diners can sit out next to the swimming pool and enjoy the garden; an open fire warms diners in winter.

Cloudy Bay

Jacksons Rd., P.O. Box 376, Blenheim. ☎ **03/572-8914.** Fax 03/572-8065. Free tasting (tours by arrangement). Daily 10am–4:30pm.

One of my favorite Christmas presents this year was a bottle of Cloudy Bay Sauvignon Blanc—a gift from a Kiwi friend who managed to find it for sale in San Diego. The *Wine Spectator* calls it "wild and exotic"—who am I to disagree?

Cellier Le Brun

Terrace Rd., Renwick. ☎ **03/572-8859.** Nominal fee for tasting (tours available most of the time). Winery, daily 9am–5pm. Cafe, daily 9am–4pm.

Cellier Le Brun produces four *méthode champenoise* wines as well as a still chardonnay and a pinot noir. The winery was established more than a decade ago by Champenois Daniel Le Brun, whose brother and father are still making wine in France. The Courtyard Cafe here offers a champagne breakfast and gourmet sandwiches served at wooden umbrella tables on a tile courtyard. Reservations are advisable during summer.

AFFORDABLE ACCOMMODATIONS

Picton is a busy place during January, so reserve your bed early if that's when you'll be here.

PICTON

Campgrounds & Cabins

✪ Blue Anchor Holiday Park

70–78 Waikawa Rd., Picton. ☎ and fax **03/573-7212.** Web site nz.com/webnz/pelorus/blueanchor. 12 tourist flats, 20 cabins, caravan and tent sites. NZ$55 (US$38.50) studio tourist flat for 2, NZ$68 (US$47.60) 2-bedroom tourist flat for 2, NZ$32–$40 (US$22.40–$28) cabin for 2, extra adult NZ$12 (US$8.40), extra child NZ$10 (US$7); NZ$20 (US$14) powered site for 2, extra adult NZ$9 (US$6.30), extra child NZ$6 (US$4.20). AE, BC, DC, MC, V.

I was impressed with how clean everything was when I visited this caravan park. Besides lots of housing, there's a playground with a trampoline, a pool, a barbecue area, and a games room. Eight of the studio tourist flats sleep three; two sleep seven; one of the two-bedroom tourist flats sleeps five, and the other sleeps six; the fifteen standard cabins sleep eight, and five deluxe cabins sleep six.

Super-Cheap Sleeps
The Villa Backpackers Lodge
34 Auckland St., Picton. ☎ and fax **03/573-6598.** 4 rms (none with bathrm), 5 dormitories. NZ$42 (US$29.40) twin or double, extra person NZ$10 (US$7); NZ$16 (US$11.20) dorm bed. Discounts to VIP cardholders on cash-only basis with direct booking. Rates include breakfast. MC, V. Courtesy shuttle to and from the ferry.

Carolyn and Rob Burn own and operate this out-of-the-ordinary hostel in a 100-year-old villa on the main street. They provide—free of charge—blankets and quilts for all beds (if required), the use of mountain bikes and 10-speeds, fishing gear, guitar, herbs and spices for cooking, storage, and tea and coffee. On the premises are a well-equipped kitchen, a coin-op laundry, shower and bathroom facilities for travelers with disabilities, indoor/outdoor living areas, heated spa, a barbecue, fax facilities, and a cardphone. I don't know of another hostel that offers so much at such a great price.

For a Few Extra Bucks
Aldan Lodge Motel
86 Wellington St., Picton. ☎ **03/573-6833.** Fax 03/573-6091. 11 units (all with bathrm). TV TEL. NZ$79 (US$55.30) double. Lower winter rates. AE, BC, DC, MC, V.

All units here have cooking facilities, and one is specially equipped for people with disabilities. There are also laundry facilities, a pool, spa, and playground. Units sleep up to six: All upstairs quarters have a double and a single bed on one level and a spiral staircase leading to three singles. Everything is neat and clean, the beds have electric blankets, and the management is friendly.

✪ Craglee Lodge
Bay of Many Coves, Queen Charlotte Sound (Private Bag 407, Picton). ☎ **03/579-9223.** Fax 03/579-9223. 5 rms (2 with bathrm). NZ$80 (US$56) double without bathrm, NZ$106 (US$74.20) double with bathrm, NZ$130 (US$91) double in honeymoon suite with bathrm. Meal plan (3 meals) NZ$45 (US$31.50) per person. MC, V. From Picton, take a water taxi (NZ$20/US$14 per person 1 way).

Robin and Anne Perret own this modern home in the Marlborough Sounds and do their best to see that all guests have a good time. They're knowledgeable about the area—and even seem to know where the fish are biting. Anne is a keen walker and, if requested, can take folks hiking on the nearby Queen Charlotte Walkway. Guests stay on a separate level of the house, which has its own TV lounge. Anne is an excellent cook and includes fresh Marlborough produce on the menus; fresh salmon, scallops, and green-lip mussels frequently appear for dinner. Guests can be active here or spend their days on the balcony admiring the spectacular view and their nights in the spa tub watching the stars.

✪ The Gables
20 Waikawa Rd., Picton. ☎ **03/573-6772.** Fax 03/573-8860. Web site: nz.com/webnz/bbnz/gables.htm. 3 rms (all with bathrm). NZ$95 (US$66.50) double. Rates include breakfast. BC, MC, V. Courtesy transfers from the ferry, bus, and train.

What a treat you'll receive if Ann and Dick Smith are going to be your hosts. I'm not a random hugger, but I must say I felt compelled to give each of them a squeeze after my last stay. Words like *kind, thoughtful,* and *caring* just don't seem adequate to describe these two. The house that holds their little inn was built in 1924, and they're in the process of restoring it. Already there are fine bed and bath linens, toiletries in the bath, chocolate pillow treats, an open fire in the lounge, and attractive touches everywhere. Complimentary before-dinner drinks and snacks are offered. Ann's breakfasts are legendary: Seafood crêpes, scrambled eggs with Marlborough salmon, fresh fruit, homemade muffins, and freshly brewed coffee are specialties. A

Bridgend Cottage, 36 York Street, Picton. ☎ **03/573-6734.** Fax 03/573-8323. *"We were unable to get reservations at The Gables, but Ann Smith recommended Bridgend Cottage. This should be in your book. Lurleen and Bevan Fowler were exceptional hosts and the two-bedroom cottage we stayed in was quite pleasant."*

—Patricia Downing, Los Angeles, California, USA.

Author's Note: Rates are NZ$65–$70 (US$45.50–$49).

Historic Homestay, 22 Broadway, Picton. ☎ **03/573-6966.** Fax 03/573-7735. *"This B&B was right in Picton yet peaceful and quiet. Neale and Birgite Armstrong make you feel right at home in their quaint and comfortable home from which they also run a weaving school. Highly recommended!"*

—Donya Geagah, Wayne, Pennsylvania, USA.

Author's Note: Rates are NZ$75 (US$52.50) twin, NZ$95 (US$67) double. Rates include breakfast. Not suitable for children.

queen-size room and a single have attached bathrooms, and the other room has a private bathroom across the hall.

IN NEARBY BLENHEIM

Admirals Motor Lodge

2161 Middle Renwick Rd., Blenheim. ☎ **03/577-7711.** Fax 03/577-7712. 4 rms (all with bathrm), 12 units (all with bathrm). TV TEL. NZ$70 (US$49) double room; NZ$89 (US$62.30) apt for 2. AE, BC, DC, MC, V.

Gerald and Helen Talbot started with a large house on a good site and have added 12 motel units. Each of the four attractive, spacious rooms upstairs in the house has coffee- and tea-making facilities, a small fridge, and electric blankets; 4 of the 12 motel units have cooking facilities. Everyone uses the outdoor pool, enclosed spa room, and licensed restaurant. Cooked and continental breakfasts are available.

GREAT DEALS ON DINING

In addition to the places mentioned here, don't overlook the possibility of dining at Hunter's Winery or Cellier Le Brun in Blenheim. See "Exploring Picton & Blenheim: What to See and Do," above.

Toot 'n' Whistle Inn

Auckland St., next to the railway station. ☎ **03/573-6086.** Reservations not required. Lunch NZ$5–$16.50 (US$3.50–$11.60); dinner NZ$16.50 (US$11.60). AE, BC, DC, MC, V. Summer, daily 8am–3am. Winter, Mon–Fri 10am–3am, Sat–Sun 8am–3am. MODERN NEW ZEALAND/PUB.

The chalkboard menu here lists such offerings as tandoori chicken; burritos; steak, egg, and chips; and a stuffed potato with salad. There's usually some pretty good music playing, and the pub atmosphere is lots of fun. A 12-ounce beer will set you

Fifth Bank Restaurant, 33 Wellington Street, Picton. *"This is in a building built in 1903 and, until 1969, housed a Bank of New Zealand. The atmosphere was warm, even without the wonderful fireplace and we had perhaps the best meal and service of the trip— butterfish and gingered pork filets for only NZ$44 (US$30.80)."*

—Patricia Downing, Los Angeles, California, USA.

Readers Recommend

Futuna Rocks, 158 Esplanade, Kaikoura. ☎ 03/319-6333. *"These comfortable, self-contained units are a terrific value at NZ$40/US$28 double in winter and NZ$50/US$35 in summer. Owners Richard Grady and Sue Natuka offer four units."*
—B. and J. Hermann, Point Vernon, QLD, Australia.

Kaikoura: *"In waxing lyrical about whales and dolphins, no one seems to comment on what a truly beautiful town Kaikoura is in its own right. Majestic snowcapped peaks roll towards a sandy beach and the peninsula has large bird life and incredible views. Additionally, the* **Maui YHA,** *270 Esplanade, Kaikoura (☎ and fax 03/319-5931), is a gorgeous hostel, although it is a 30-minute slog on foot out of town. It's peaceful and calm, with no television."*
—Chris Jones, Australia.

Author's Note: Maui YHA charges NZ$12 (US$8.40) per person.

back NZ$2.30 (US$1.61). A separate area for families and seating on a wooden deck outside are available. Breakfast, lunch, and dinner are served all day, and they even offer tea, coffee, and scones. Licensed.

EN ROUTE SOUTH
WHALE WATCHING IN KAIKOURA

If you follow Highway 1 south along the coast for the leisurely 2¹/₂-hour drive to **Kaikoura**—almost midway between Christchurch and Picton—you'll have arrived at a place whose name means "crayfish food," and the only place on New Zealand's east coast where the mountains (the Kaikoura Range) meet the Pacific. It is also fast gaining an international reputation for the animal and marine life that calls it home: seals, dolphins, whales, and numerous seabirds, including albatross, terns, penguins, and petrels. Sperm whales are most often seen between April and August, and dolphins are seen most between August and April. Seals and birds are always on hand.

Whale Watch Kaikoura Ltd., in the Kaikoura Whaleway Station, P.O. Box 89, Kaikoura (☎ 03/319-5045, or 0800/655-121 in New Zealand; fax 03/319-6545), organizes up to six daily 3-hour whale-watching cruises—they must surely be the highlight of any Kaikoura visit, and to avoid disappointment, you should book as far ahead as possible. The fare runs about NZ$95 (US$67) adult, NZ$60 (US$42) child; and they accept American Express, Bankcard, Carte Blanche, Diners Club, Japan Credit Bank, MasterCard, and Visa. Check schedules when booking. Remember that you'll see the most whales between April and August, and the giant sperm whales can be seen year round.

SHORT WALKS

If you plan to wander on your own, just follow the **Shoreline Walk** along the coast to the tip of the peninsula. You should see seals and a variety of birds; the walk is almost 4¹/₂ km (3 miles) long and takes 1¹/₂ hours. Or you could opt for the ✪ **Cliff-Top Walk,** which affords panoramic views; it's 4¹/₂ km (3 miles) long and takes an hour.

WHERE TO STAY & EAT ON THE ROAD

About 6km (4 miles) south of Kaikoura on State Highway 1, **Fyffe Gallery and Restaurant,** R.D. 2, Kaikoura (☎ 03/319-6869, fax 03/319-6865), is a great place to stop for a meal, a snack, or an overnight accommodation. Breakfast is served from 8 to 10am, and lunch is from noon to 3pm. Evening dining is offered daily during summer, and Friday through Sunday during winter. Morning and afternoon tea are offered daily year round. The restaurant serves New Zealand specialties and seafood and is fully licensed. Four pretty rooms upstairs offer fluffy duvets, window boxes, TVs, and bathrooms. They share the restaurant's view of black-and-white dairy cows and pretty gardens against a backdrop of snowcapped mountains. The cost of these quarters ranges from NZ$105 to NZ$200 (US$73.50 to US$140) for two, including continental breakfast. Be sure to say hello to congenial hosts Chris Rye and Colin Ashworth (ask them about their all-natural interior and exterior wall finishes). They accept all major credit/charge cards.

EN ROUTE TO NELSON

The **Queen Charlotte Drive** affords wonderful vistas of the Marlborough Sounds. The narrow road climbs high over the water and forested extensions of land to reveal beautiful beaches and tiny coves. Allow plenty of time for this trip. Even if you're a saturated sightseer, I think you'll want to stop and survey this view. After passing the township of Havelock, you'll come to **Pelorus Bridge** where there are nice tearooms, picnic spots, and walking tracks.

2 Nelson & Beyond

110km (68 miles) W of Picton; 290km (179 miles) NE of Greymouth

Nelson sits on the shores of Nelson Haven, sheltered by the unique 11km (7-mile) natural wall of Boulder Bank. Its 2,500 hours of annual sunshine, its tranquil waters, and its golden sand beaches make it perhaps the South Island's most popular summer resort. That wonderful climate, combined with the fertile land hereabouts, also makes it an important center for growing fruit, grapes, hops, and tobacco (although tobacco is being phased out). And maybe all that sunshine has something to do with an easygoing, tolerant outlook that makes it a haven for those of an artistic bent. Potters are here in abundance, drawn by a plentiful supply of fine clay and the minerals needed for glazing; weavers raise sheep and create natural-wool works of art; artists spend hours on end trying to capture on canvas the splendors of a Nelson sunset or the shifting light on sparkling water.

Colonel William Wakefield hoisted the New Zealand Company flag on Britannia Heights in December 1841 and placed a 9-pound cannon there as a signal gun (it's there today for you to see), and settlers began arriving on February 1, 1842, a day still celebrated annually in Nelson. They named the new town Nelson to honor that great British seafaring hero since the company's first New Zealand settlement, Wellington, had been named for Britain's most famous soldier. Lord Nelson's victories, ships, and fellow admirals are commemorated in street names like Trafalgar, Vanguard, and Collingwood. Graves of some of those early settlers lie under the trees at Fairfield Park (at the corner of Trafalgar Street South and Brougham Street), and many of the gabled wooden houses they built still cling to Nelson's hillsides and nestle among more modern structures on midtown streets. Some have become the homes and studios of the artistic community.

Nelson has two distinctions of which it is equally proud: It's known as the "cradle of rugby" in New Zealand, which was first played here in 1870 (although Christchurch's Football Club is older than Nelson's, it didn't adopt the national sport until some 5 years after its introduction at Nelson's Botanical Reserve); and a native son, Baron Rutherford, has been called the "father of nuclear physics" because it was he who first discovered the secret of splitting the atom, and because of other scientific achievements that brought him international renown. His name is perpetuated in place names like Rutherford Park and Street.

Central Nelson

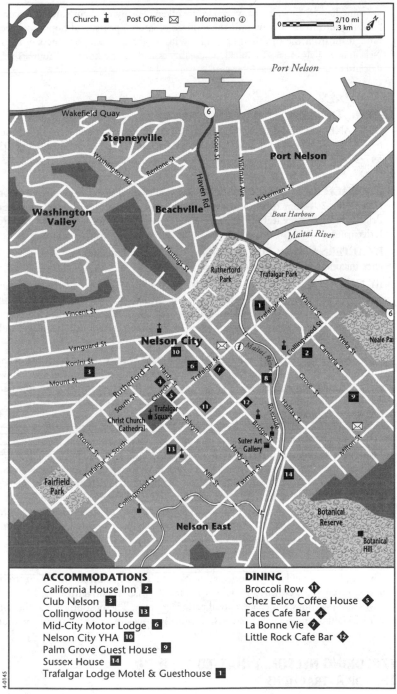

Church ✝ Post Office ⊠ Information ⓘ

0 |▬▬▬▬| 2/10 mi / .3 km

Port Nelson

Wakefield Quay

Stepneyville

Washington Rd

Rentone St

Moore St

Haven Rd

Wildman Ave

Port Nelson

Vickerman St

Boat Harbour

Washington Valley

Beachville

Hastings St

Maitai River

Vincent St

Rutherford Park

Trafalgar Park

Trafalgar Rd

Walnut St

Nelson City

Vanguard St

Konini St

Mount St

Rutherford St

Hardy St

Trafalgar St

Collingwood St

Cambria St

Weka St

Neale Pa

Grove St

Halifax St

Milton St

South St

Church St

Selwyn

Trafalgar Square

Christ Church Cathedral

Bronte St

Trafalgar St South

Collingwood St

Nile St

Tasman St

Riverside

Bridge St

Hardy St

Suter Art Gallery

Fairfield Park

Nelson East

Botanical Reserve

Botanical Hill

ACCOMMODATIONS
California House Inn **2**
Club Nelson **3**
Collingwood House **13**
Mid-City Motor Lodge **6**
Nelson City YHA **10**
Palm Grove Guest House **9**
Sussex House **14**
Trafalgar Lodge Motel & Guesthouse **1**

DINING
Broccoli Row **11**
Chez Eelco Coffee House **5**
Faces Cafe Bar **4**
La Bonne Vie **7**
Little Rock Cafe Bar **12**

4-0145

Come harvest time, as many as 3,000 workers—many of them students—come trooping into town to stay until the millions of apples, pears, and hops have been brought in from the surrounding fields. With its characteristic openness of spirit, Nelson assimilates them as quickly and easily as it does the hordes of tourists who descend on its beaches year after year.

ESSENTIALS
GETTING THERE
BY PLANE   Service between Nelson and all major New Zealand cities is provided by **Air New Zealand Link** and **Ansett New Zealand.** The airport shuttle (☎ **03/ 547-5782**) operates regularly between the airport and the city center for NZ$6 (US$3.90) one way.

BY COACH (BUS)   **InterCity** and **Mount Cook Landline** coaches service Nelson. During the 2¹⁄₄-hour trip from the ferry at Picton, buses stop at the tearoom near Pelorus Bridge—they travel Highways 1 and 6, not on the scenic Queen Charlotte Drive route.

BY ALTERNATIVE COACH (BUS)   Both **Magic Traveller** and **Kiwi Experience** include Nelson on their schedules.

BY CAR   From Picton it's a pretty drive to Nelson—via either the Queen Charlotte Drive or along Route 6—filled with clifftop views, seascapes glimpsed from bush-lined stretches of the road, and rolling farmlands. It's a pleasant, picturesque journey you may want to break with a stop by the giant totara tree in picnic grounds near Pelorus Bridge.

BY TAXI   Taxis pick up riders outside the Majestic Theatre on Trafalgar Street and on Bridge Street opposite the Suburban Bus Company. Contact one of the following companies: **Bluebird Taxis,** 41 A Bridge St. (☎ **03/546-6681**); **Nelson City Taxis,** 200 A Hardy St. (☎ **03/548-8225**); or **Sun City Taxis,** 135 Bridge St. (☎ **03/548-2666**).

VISITOR INFORMATION
You'll find the **Nelson Visitor Information Centre** on the corner of Trafalgar and Halifax streets (☎ **03/548-2304,** fax 03/546-9008). It's open Monday through Friday from 9am to 5:30pm with extended summer hours. The *Nelson Visitors' Guide,* available from the Visitor Information Centre and local hotels and motels, will give you an update on what to see and do. The **Department of Conservation** counter in the Visitor Information Centre is staffed only October to Easter. The **telephone area code** (STD) for Nelson is **03.**

ORIENTATION
Two landmarks will keep you oriented in Nelson: **Trafalgar Street** (the main street) and **Church Hill,** crowned by Christ Church Cathedral and surrounded by lush lawns and plantings, which are a local gathering point. The post office is at the corner of Halifax and Trafalgar streets, diagonally opposite the Visitor Information Centre.

EXPLORING NELSON: WHAT TO SEE & DO
THE TOP ATTRACTIONS
Christ Church Cathedral
365 Trafalgar St. ☎ **03/548-8574.** Free admission. Daily from dawn to dusk.

There's no way you're going to miss seeing this cathedral on a splendid elevation at the end of Trafalgar Street in the center of town. And chances are good that you'll find yourself, at some point during your Nelson stay, stopping for a rest in its beautiful grounds—if you follow the lead of the locals, you'll bypass the handy benches to stretch out on the grass. That site, now known as Church Hill, in the past has held an early Maori *pa*, the New Zealand Company's depot, a small fort, and a tent church. The present Gothic cathedral is made of local Takaka marble; above its west door are the carved heads of five bishops, one archbishop, and George V. The most striking aspects of the interior of the cathedral are its stained glass, particularly the rose window, and its unique freestanding organ. A message from the dean of the cathedral to the readers of this book: "The original Maori name for the hill is 'come higher' and we hope visitors will do that."

Tour guides are available between Christmas and Easter and at all other times by arrangement.

✪ Suter Art Gallery

Bridge St. ☎ **03/548-4699.** Fax 03/548-1236. Admission NZ$2 (US$1.40). Daily 10:30am–4:30pm.

Nelson's affection for the arts is exemplified in this excellent museum in the town center. Works by a bevy of important New Zealand painters are on display, and there's an outstanding collection of works by master painter John Gully, who lived here for a time. If the paintings are not on display, they can be seen by appointment. The gallery also has a craft shop selling cards, reproductions, and a wide variety of local crafts, plus a good restaurant overlooking the Queen's Gardens. Its multifunctional theater seats 160 people and offers an extensive program of film, theater, music, and dance; to find out what's on, check the local newspaper. The restaurant offers lunches, snacks, and dinner. Bring your own liquor.

Founder's Park Historical and Craft Village

87 Atawhai Dr. ☎ **03/548-2649.** Admission NZ$5 (US$3.50) adults, NZ$2 (US$1.40) children, NZ$13 (US$9.10) for a family, NZ$4.50 (US$3.15) for members of the YHA, AA, or AAA. Daily 10am–4:30pm. Closed Good Friday and Christmas Day.

This turn-of-the-century city in miniature is a true celebration of Nelson's commercial and industrial development. Old St. Peter's Church, built in 1874, has been moved here. You can see a 17-minute audiovisual show, and a gift shop with reasonable prices is located on the premises. The unique entry building, a windmill, is a replica of an old mill that used to stand in Nelson where the visitors center is now. Among all the exhibits, my favorites are the Newmans coaches from 1923, 1947, and 1952, which actually saw years of service. The bakery is open daily until midday, and the Leadlight Shoppe, where you can watch leadlight windows and lampshades being made, welcomes visitors at any time. The Maritime Buildings include a huge display of model ships and ships in bottles—the bottles range from barely 2cm (less than an inch) long to very large, with up to 14 ships inside.

IN NEARBY STOKE

One place you should definitely plan to visit is the suburb of **Stoke,** where you'll find the two attractions listed below.

Nelson Provincial Museum

Isel Park, Stoke. ☎ **03/547-9740.** Fax 03/547-9740. E-mail museumnp@central.co.nz. Admission to museum, NZ$2 (US$1.30) adults, NZ$1 (US 70¢) school age children, to a maximum family charge of NZ$5 (US$3.50); Isel House, NZ$1 (US 70¢) adults, NZ50¢ (US 35¢) children. Museum, Tues–Fri 10am–4pm, Sat–Sun and holidays 1–4pm; Isel House, Sat–Sun 2–4pm in Nov–Mar.

Filled with artifacts and displays depicting the area's Maori and European history, the museum also boasts the largest collection of historical photographs in New Zealand, with more than a million images, as well as a large historical reference library. The gardens here, especially the rhododendrons, are lovely.

The museum sits directly behind **Isel House,** an elegant 19th-century stone house with dormer windows and an ornate veranda, which is situated in manicured grounds set back from Main Road. The house, with its collections of early porcelain, pottery, and furniture, is open only on weekends from November to March, but the park itself is well worth a stroll to relax beneath trees that came to New Zealand from world-wide origins as seeds or mere saplings in the 19th century.

Broadgreen House

276 Nayland Rd., Stoke. ☎ **03/546-0283.** Admission NZ$3 (US$2.10) adults, NZ50¢ (US 35¢) children. May–Oct, Tues–Sun, and public holidays 2–4:30pm. Nov–Apr, Tues–Fri 10:30am–4:30pm, Sat–Sun and public holidays 1:30–4:30pm. Closed Good Friday and Christmas Day.

This marvelous old cob house (thick walls made of packed earth) was built in 1855 and has been authentically restored and furnished by dedicated volunteers. Their care and attention to detail are evident all through the house, from the drawing room with its slate mantelpiece and original French wallpaper to the upstairs nursery with wicker carriages and antique dolls. All that work has earned the house a New Zealand Tourism Award. Outside, the rose garden holds more than 2,500 plants, with some 250 varieties represented. The house is in town, near Nayland pool.

OUTDOOR ACTIVITIES

A map detailing **scenic drives** from Nelson, all of which pass points of historical significance as well as natural beauty, is available at the visitor center. There are three national parks within driving distance, sheltered sandy beaches all along the coast (one of the best is ✪ **Tahuna Beach,** 5km [3 miles] to the south, or if it's too crowded, the beach at Rabbit Island), and several **wineries** open to the public (ask at the visitor center for "A Guide to Nelson's Wineries"). If you don't relish being behind the wheel yourself, several bus tours and scenic flights are available.

FISHING   If you've ever cast a line or dropped a hook, the South Island's fishing waters are bound to tempt you to try your luck. The only problem is knowing just where, when, and how to fish all those rivers, lakes, and streams. Fishing guides cost an arm and a leg, but if you want to spend your money this way, go into **Tony Entwistle's Hunting and Fishing,** Montgomery Square, near Trafalgar Street (☎ **03/548-1840,** fax 03/548-2150), and talk to Tony Entwistle and his staff. It's open Monday through Thursday 9am to 5:30pm, Friday 9am to 8:30pm, Saturday 9am until noon. American Express, Diners Club, MasterCard, and Visa are accepted.

Vern Brabant, of **Nelson River Guides,** P.O. Box 469, Nelson (☎ **03/548-5095,** fax 03/544-5561), is also highly regarded locally as a guide. He offers excellent trout-fishing forays, with a maximum of two anglers at a time. He'll take you into remote places—using combinations of helicopters and planes—and camping is in tents. He also offers fly-fishing expeditions to lowland streams. You could also fish with Graeme Marshall of **Motueka River Guides** (☎ **03/526-8800**).

WALKING   Walkers will be in their element in Nelson and the immediate vicinity. Good walks abound, both in the city and in the environs, varying from an hour to a full day's trek. See the box above, plus the "Tramping" section in chapter 4 for information on the wonderful **Abel Tasman Coast Track.** The visitors center has detailed guide pamphlets from which to select those you'll have time to enjoy. Be sure to ask for **"Nelson—The City of Walks,"** for which there's a small charge. My favorite stroll is along **Shakespeare Walk,** which follows the Maitai River and can be

Abel Tasman National Park

Anyone who appreciates natural beauty, especially those who like to hike, should put this park high on their New Zealand agenda. Abel Tasman National Park, named for the 17th-century Dutch explorer, covers 56,333 acres between Tasman Bay and Golden Bay. **Marahau,** the southern gateway, is 67km (42 miles) northwest of Nelson. The park encompasses beautiful beaches and coastal forest. The 51km (32-mile) **Coast Track** (see also "Tramping," in chapter 4) can be walked independently or with a guided group in 3 to 5 days. (Backpacks are transferred by boat from one overnight stop to the next.)

There are also several shorter day-excursion options from 3¹/₂ hours to a full day, for those with less time. One popular alternative is to take a bus from Nelson to **Kaiteriteri,** on Tasman Bay, and then a launch to **Bark Bay.** From here it's an easy 2¹/₂-hour walk to **Torrent Bay,** where the launch collects hikers for the return trip to Kaiteriteri and Nelson for NZ$37 (US$25.90). You can also stay on the launch for the whole 5¹/₂ hours as it cruises from Kaiteriteri to Totaranui and back for NZ$46 (US$32.20) for adults and NZ$16 (US$11.20) for children for the boat, plus the bus fare of NZ$18 (US$12.60) per person. The **Department of Conservation,** King Edward Street, P.O. Box 97, Motueka (☎ **03/528-9117**), provides huts along the way, and there are lodges at Awaroa and Torrent Bay.

Abel Tasman National Park Enterprises, 234 High St., P.O. Box 351, Motueka, Nelson (☎ **03/528-7801,** fax 03/528-6087, e-mail enquiries@ abeltasman.co.nz, Web site nz.com.webnz/abel_tasman), run by the Wilson family who have been associated with the park since the 1870s, operates the buses, launches, beachfront lodges, guided walks, and sea kayaking. While experiencing the guided walks or kayaking, you stay at their Torrent Bay Lodge and the Homestead Lodge at Awaroa Bay; both offer twin rooms. The Homestead Lodge is a replica of the first settlers' home on this site, complete with antiques dating back to the settlement of this area by the Europeans, with the addition of today's conveniences. Skilled guides and chefs provide quality experiences and meals.

The 3-day guided walk costs NZ$625 (US$438) for adults and NZ$370 (US$259) for children 8 to 14. The 5-day guided walk costs NZ$895 (US$626.50) for adults and NZ$580 (US$414.30) for children. The 3-day kayaking and trekking trip costs NZ$580 (US$406) for adults. Rates are higher mid-October through mid-April. Contact them and request their brochure and video.

picked up where Collingwood and Halifax streets intersect at the bridge. You'll see ducks and quaint cottages and cross a pedestrian bridge that will point you back into town.

SHOPPING FOR ARTS & CRAFTS

One of the great pleasures of a stop in Nelson is visiting some of its many resident artists and artisans. The visitor center can give you a brochure of names and addresses of those who welcome visitors to their studios and suggested tour itineraries. It's interesting to talk with painters, weavers, potters, and other craftspeople about the subject dearest to their hearts—and fun to browse their wares for sale.

I suggest you spend an hour or two along ✪ **South Street** with its artistic population. It's lined with small colonial homes, which have been creatively restored, and the street gives you a sense of what early Nelson must have been like. At the corner of Nile and South streets, visit the **South Street Gallery,** 10 Nile St., Nelson

(☎ and fax **03/548-8117**), in an old two-story house, to see some of Nelson's finest pottery. They provide full packaging and overseas posting and accept MasterCard and Visa. It's open from 9am to 5pm daily. **✪ Art of Living** at 20 Nile St. is my favorite. It's next door to **Painted Pots Partnership,** 14 Nile St.

The **Nelson Community Potters,** 136 Rutherford St.(☎ **03/545-1287**), is the hangout of talented amateur potters and offers regular day schools and night courses (just in case you're an aspiring potter yourself). There's usually someone at work there, and many of their finished products are for sale.

Other interesting craft shops are the **Glass Studio,** 276 Hardy St., which also stocks small sculptures, paintings, pottery, and jewelry; and **Jens Hansen,** a cooperative goldsmith and silversmith workshop and sales room at 320 Trafalgar Sq.

You might also want to drop by **Silkwood Fibre Arts and Crafts Centre** (☎ **03/ 544-2730,** fax 03/540-2273), 10 minutes from Richmond on Coastal Highway 60, for exclusive designer handknits; woven, natural wools; specialty fiber yarns; and an abundance of quality local crafts. The shop is open daily 10am to 5pm, and accepts American Express, MasterCard, and Visa.

Still farther south, on the Richmond By-Pass (Salisbury Road), Paul Laird runs **Waimea Pottery Ltd.** (☎ and fax 03/544-7481) as part of the **Craft Habitat,** a collection of nine quality craft workshops and a coffee shop and gallery. His ovenproof stoneware and lusterware are sold in the Richmond showroom and throughout New Zealand, as are the unique hand-printed tiles by Colleen Laird. Open daily 10am to 5pm, the workshops accept American Express, Bankcard, MasterCard, and Visa.

If you like beautiful glass pieces, you won't want to miss **✪ Höglunds Glassblowing Studio** at Korurangi Farm, Landsdowne Road, Richmond (☎ and fax 03/ 544-6500). Ola and Marie Höglund worked at Orrefors and Kosta Boda before emigrating from their native Sweden. On the premises there's a design gallery, which displays the latest in design and art glass, silver jewelry, and bone and greenstone carvings; and a nice cafe. The studio is open 9am to 5pm daily, closed Christmas Day and Good Friday. They accept Bankcard, Discover, MasterCard, and Visa.

AFFORDABLE ACCOMMODATIONS

It is true of Nelson, as of most beach resorts, that accommodations are hard to come by during the summer holidays (December through January), and many Kiwi families book here from year to year. While it's not impossible to arrive roomless and find a place to lay your head, you might be better off booking before arrival. Or plan to come in fall (March and April) or spring (October and November) when things aren't so crowded and the weather is still nice.

As is also true of most resorts, Nelson has a wide variety of accommodations. You'll find them in the city proper and at the beachside suburb of **Tahunanui,** which is 7km (4 miles) away, but served by city buses.

The rates given below include 12.5% GST and free parking.

NELSON

Super-Cheap Sleeps

✪ Club Nelson

18 Mount St., Nelson. ☎ **03/548-3466.** 5 rms (none with bathrm), 20 cubicles and dormitories. NZ$17 (US$11.90) per person in shared room; NZ$19.50 (US$13.70) per person double; NZ$16 (US$11.20) dorm bed. No credit cards. Courtesy transfers to and from the airport and bus station.

Host Peter Richards describes the property as a "boutique" backpackers' hostel—this is an out-of-the-ordinary place. Formerly Kirkpatrick House, a private home and later a girls' boarding house, this hostel is set on 2¹/₂ acres and has a pool and tennis court. The house was built in 1902 by Samuel Kirkpatrick, who made his fortune manufacturing jam. Free tea and coffee are supplied, as is bed linen, and there's a lounge with a TV and a good music system, as well as a large communal kitchen. There's no phone or fax for guest use, but there's a pay phone nearby. There's no smoking in the house, but Samuel's Rest is a little converted garden shed out back where smoking is permitted.

Nelson City YHA

59 Rutherford St., Nelson. ☎ **03/548-8817.** Fax 03/545-9989. E-mail yhanels@ avon.hindin.co.nz. 73 beds in 30 rms (2 with bathrm). NZ$17 (US$11.90) adult in dorm, NZ$12 (US$8.40) youth (15–17) in dorm, NZ$9 (US$6.30) junior (under 15) in dorm; NZ$19 (US$13.30) per person twin, NZ$26 (US$18.20) single; NZ$40 (US$28) double without bathrm, NZ$50 (US$35) double with bathrm. Rates quoted are for members; nonmembers add NZ$4 (US$2.80) per person. MC, V.

This new purpose-built facility is in the center of Nelson. There is a fully enclosed garden and courtyard area, two fully equipped large kitchens, two dining rooms, a lounge, TV room, reading room, fully equipped laundry, and facilities for people with disabilities. There are seven four-bed dorms, and one five-bed dorm; the other 22 rooms are singles, twins, doubles (two with bathroom), and triples.

For a Few Extra Bucks

In addition to the accommodations below, I want you to know about two homestays in Nelson. Charming Ida Hunt offers three rooms at **Sussex House,** 238 Bridge St. (☎ and fax **03/548-9972**), and Emmy and Lane Wessel have three rooms at **Collingwood House,** 174 Collingwood St. (☎ **03/548-4481**).

Mid-City Motor Lodge

218 Trafalgar St., Nelson. ☎ **0800/2643-2489** in New Zealand, or 03/546-9063. Fax 03/ 548-3595. 15 units (all with bathrm). TV TEL. NZ$88 (US61.60) double. NZ$5 (US$3.50) discount to readers who present this book. AE, DC, MC, V.

Hosts Tim and Aileen Rich welcome guests to their city-center property. Restaurants, bars, parks, and shopping are all only minutes away. Some units have full kitchens, others only limited cooking facilities. All quarters have TVs and in-house video. Decors are in soft pastel shades. Cooked and continental breakfasts are a specialty, and lunches and evening meals are available on request.

Palm Grove Guest House

52 Cambria St., Nelson. ☎ **03/548-4645.** 6 rms (none with bathrm). NZ$70 (US$49) double. Rates include breakfast. No credit cards.

There may not be a palm grove on the premises, but two 50-foot palm trees do dominate the landscaped gardens of this guest house. Host Richard Tidmarsh emphasizes service, comfort, and cleanliness and provides a cooked Kiwi breakfast. Most rooms have sinks, and bathrobes are supplied for the trip down the hall to showers and a "ladies' bath." Off-street parking, laundry facilities, tea and coffee facilities, and a TV lounge are other positive points. Palm Grove is a short walk from the town center. Smoking is not permitted in the house.

Trafalgar Lodge Motel and Guesthouse

16 Trafalgar St., Nelson. ☎ and fax **03/548-3980.** 6 B&B rms (none with bathrm), 6 motel units (all with bathrm). TV. NZ$65 (US$45.50) double B&B; NZ$68–$74 (US$47.60–$51.80) double motel, extra person NZ$15 (US$10.50). DC, MC, V.

In addition to bed-and-breakfast accommodations, the Trafalgar offers motel units that are bright, clean, and attractively furnished. Each motel unit sleeps up to four, and all have fully equipped kitchens, radios, and electric blankets. Off-street

Readers Recommend

Cathedral Inn, 369 Trafalgar Street S., Nelson. ☎ **03/548-7369.** *"Excellent B&B/ small hotel. It opened in March 1996, and is located in what used to be the Bishop's house directly behind the cathedral. It has been fully restored and very tastefully decorated with nice extras such as towel warmers and electric blankets. It has seven rooms all with bathroom, there is a nice city view, and the city is less than a 5-minute stroll through the Cathedral Gardens. The hosts, Jim and Susie Tohill, were very warm and helpful. They even offered to baby-sit our children so that we could go out and enjoy the town. The breakfast was excellent, especially Susie's homemade yogurt and muffins. I highly recommend it to your travelers."*

—Jan and Christine Mallard Sokol, Portland, Oregon, USA.

parking and laundry facilities are available. Bert and Shona Barber are the friendly, helpful owners. It's a 2-minute walk to the city center.

Waimarie Motel

45 Collingwood St., Nelson. ☎ and fax **03/548-9418.** 6 units (all with bathrm). TV TEL. NZ$75–$95 (US$52.50–$67) apt for 2. AE, DC, MC, V.

I particularly like this motel's setting on the bank of the Maitai River, 1 block from the bus depot and Visitor Information Centre and a few minutes' walk from downtown. There are only a few units, but each has a separate bedroom (some have two), a fully equipped kitchen, and video. One, called the "executive suite," has a sun balcony with a view of the river.

Worth a Splurge

✪ California House Inn

29 Collingwood St., Nelson. ☎ and fax **03/548-4173.** 5 rms (all with bathrm). NZ$130–$165 (US$91–$116) double. Rates include breakfast. MC, V.

Near the center of town, this charming yellow historic villa has a flower-trimmed walkway, a wraparound porch, leaded-glass trim, a guest sitting room complete with open fire, games, and library, a country kitchen, and delightful rooms. The guest rooms are furnished with antiques, memorabilia, fluffy quilts, and fresh flowers. The home-cooked breakfasts are well known for fresh fruit and berries, juices, and fresh-baked muffins. Owners Shelley and Neil Johnston couldn't be nicer, and their daughter, Grace, is adorable. No smoking in the inn.

IN NEARBY TAHUNANUI

The ✪ **Tahuna Beach Holiday Park,** 70 Beach Rd. (Private Bag 25), Tahunanui, Nelson (☎ **03/548/5159,** fax 03/548-5294), is the largest motor camp in New Zealand, regularly handling several thousand travelers per night during summer months. Spread over 55 acres, the camp is a 3-minute walk to the beach, and local bus service is at the corner. The well-kept grounds hold a large selection of vacation accommodations as well as tent, caravan, and campervan sites. If you're not traveling with your own linens, you may rent them for a small charge. Amenities include good shower-and-toilet blocks, kitchens and laundries, ironing boards, car wash, TV lounge, children's playgrounds, and miniature golf. A large food shop on the grounds is open every day. This is a beautifully maintained place, with all accommodations kept freshly painted, carpeted, and comfortably furnished. The accommodations are priced as follows: Motel units (top-quality, fully self-contained) are NZ$70 to NZ$75 (US$49 to US$52.50), tourist cabins (self-contained) are NZ$38 (US$26.60), and semi–self-contained) are NZ$53 (US$37.10), standard cabins go for NZ$25

(US$17.50), and graded cabins are NZ$30 (US$21). Sites are NZ$18 (US$12.60). All rates are double occupancy, and American Express, Diners Club, MasterCard, and Visa are accepted.

If you're not into roughing it, you may opt for the motel below.

Courtesy Court Motel

30 Gulf Rd., Tahunanui, Nelson. ☎ and fax **03/548-5114.** 15 units. TV TEL. NZ$83–$89 (US$58.10–$62.30) unit for 2. Additional person NZ$15 (US$10.50) extra. Best Western discounts available. AE, DC, MC, V.

Several factors make this a good motel: its proximity to the beach (a short walk), pretty grounds (with well-tended, colorful flower beds), and comfortable accommodations. I also like the arrangements of the units around an inner court away from street noises and facing the attractive heated swimming pool. There are bed-sitters, one-bedroom units that sleep as many as four, and two-bedroom units that will sleep six; all have complete kitchen, soft carpets, electric blankets and heaters, radio, and a complimentary morning paper; one "honeymoon unit has a water bed and spa bath. A guest laundry, spa pool, and children's play area are additional conveniences. Owner Tony Hocking welcomes children and will gladly provide a cot and highchair as well as arrange for baby-sitters. The Courtesy Court Motel is 2^1/$_2$ miles from the town center, near Tahuna Beach. The entrance to Golf Road is at Kentucky Fried Chicken in the Tahunanui shopping area.

IN NEARBY RICHMOND

In addition to the inn detailed below, Deidre and Ashley Marshall provide bed and breakfast at **Kirshaw House,** 10 Wensley Rd., Richmond (☎ **03/544-0957**). Richmond is 15 minutes by car from Nelson.

Mapledurham

8 Edward St., Richmond, Nelson. ☎ and fax **03/544-4210.** Web site nz.com/HeritageInns/ Mapledurham. 3 rms (all with bathrm). NZ$150–$165 (US$105–$116) double. Rates include breakfast. Dinners (by prior arrangement) NZ$30 (US$21) extra. MC, V. Courtesy transfers are provided to and from the airport and bus station.

Gracious is the word that comes to mind when I think of hosts Deborah and Giles Grigg. The house was built in 1910 by "a man with pretensions" and is fronted by a large lawn where guests are welcome to play croquet. Each room is appointed with fresh flowers and fruit, tea- and coffeemaking facilities, and a little tin of delicious almond cookies. Giles is a fourth-generation New Zealander who grew up on a large Canterbury sheep station; Deborah is English (so, of course, the gardens are lovely).

Readers Recommend

Kimi Ora Holiday and Health Resort, Kaiteriteri Beach ☎ 03/527-8027. Fax 03/527-8134. *"This place is great. It's only a short walk from where the boats leave for Abel Tasman National Park, and the chalets have a view of the beach. The restaurant serves vegetarian food, and lots of health treatments—including Kneipp water treatment, therapeutic baths, and Fibrosaun body conditioner—are offered. There are also a pool, a sauna, a gym, a fitness trail, and tennis courts."*

—Viktor Hauke, Lindenberg, Germany.

Author's Note: Jan and Christine Mallard Sokol of Portland, Oregon, say "Kimi Ora is located 1 hour from the airport, not convenient if you plan to explore Nelson. However, very convenient for Abel Tasman National Park. While the accommodations were adequate, you could hear the people next door rolling over in their bed. The vegetarian restaurant was very good."

Todd's Valley: "Free" Room & Board

Well, it isn't exactly "free"—it's room and board in exchange for daily farm and domestic work (about 4 or more hours a day) at **Todd's Valley,** c/o G. R. Roberts, Todd's Valley, R.D. 1, Nelson (☎ and fax **03/545-0553**).

You get three healthy meals, rather basic accommodations, and a lesson or two in conservation. If that has an appealing ring, read on.

This is the home, farm, dream, and ecological laboratory of G. R. (Dick) Roberts, a graduate of Cambridge University, teacher of biology and geography, and documentary photographer. After a few years of teaching, Dick decided in 1969 that the time had come to translate ideas into action, and he bought a beautiful, but uneconomical, 200-acre valley farm 10km (6 miles) north of Nelson. Only about 15 acres are flat land—the rest rise as high as 1,400 feet above the valley floor. Dick does not claim to be 100% "organic" in his farming methods, but he has nurtured the flourishing vegetable garden with none of the dubious benefits of insecticides. On the slopes, he is working out an integrated approach to biological control by mixing many species of fruit and nut trees according to microclimates. Rough hill pastures are grazed by about 200 sheep, and 40 acres have been converted to plantation forestry.

Dick welcomes visitors who are genuinely interested in conservation, willing to work at it, and ready to take instruction and suggestion. Although the farm is not by any means a commune, he believes that the cooperative efforts of like-minded people contributing toward a constructive alternative way of life provide an important contribution to society as a whole. "Dropouts, unproductive people, and those not willing to accept responsibility," he says, "are not part of that plan." Please do not apply unless you can stay a minimum of 2 weeks (brief visits may be arranged, however, for those with an avid interest in ecological land use). At Todd's Valley, conservation is a way of life: You are expected to recycle all wastes and to refrain from smoking in the house or using drugs. You are heartily invited, however, to enjoy the warm, sunny valley, 2 miles from the sea, in all its natural beauty, to gorge yourself on varied fruits, and to become intimately involved with the land and its problems.

If you'd like to stay at Todd's Valley, write or telephone Dick in advance. He can only give beds to a few people at a time although those who wish to camp are also welcome. Be aware, however, that occasionally the farm is closed to visitors.

Both are well traveled. Breakfasts include homemade marmalade and jam, as well as such items as scrambled eggs with smoked venison, and omelets with mushrooms or fresh strawberries.

GREAT DEALS ON DINING IN NELSON
SUPER-CHEAP EATS

✪ Chez Eelco Coffee House
296 Trafalgar St. ☎ **03/548-7595.** Reservations not required. NZ$1.70–$19 (US$1.20–$13.30). MC, V. Mon–Sat 7am–11pm, Sun 7am–9pm. SNACKS/LIGHT MEALS.

Chez Eelco is just about the most popular meeting place in town for students, artists, craftspeople, townspeople, and tourists. In fine weather there are bright umbrella tables on the sidewalk out front. Inside are red-and-white cafe curtains, matching ruffled lampshades, and candles in wine bottles after dark. Eelco Boswijk (a Dutchman who came to New Zealand over 30 years ago) has owned the high-ceilinged, cavernous place since 1961, and it's been a popular coffeehouse the whole time. You'll find the buzz of contented conversation, table-hopping regulars, a back room whose walls are a virtual art gallery, a piano for the occasional pianist, and paper place mats that give names and addresses of local artists. The extensive menu includes toasted sandwiches, hamburgers, scones, omelets, yogurt, salad plates, steaks, chicken, Marlborough mussels, Nelson scallops, native cheeses, and sweets that include fresh cream cakes. In short, it's a place to drop in for coffee or tea and a snack, enjoy a light meal, or order your main meal of the day. Incidentally, my favorite menu item is also quite popular with locals—the truly superb mussel chowder. Most main courses are well under NZ$10 (US$7). Breakfast is available, and the place is fully licensed.

FOR A FEW EXTRA BUCKS

✪ Broccoli Row

5 Buxton Sq. (near Hardy St.). ☎ **03/548-9621.** Reservations recommended. Main courses NZ$15.50–$18 (US$10.90–$12.60). AE, DC, MC, V. Mon–Sat 9:30am–9:30pm (lunch 11:30am–2pm and dinner 7–9:30pm). Closed June and Christmas–New Year's Day. SEAFOOD/VEGETARIAN.

This is an appealing little place with a chalkboard menu that changes daily. You might be offered snapper filets baked with ginger, grapefruit, and spring vegetables or fresh pasta tossed with artichokes, sun-dried tomatoes, olives, and spinach. The service is a little slow, but the food is superb. Focaccia bread is made on the premises, and I could see huge containers of olive oil, a large pepper mill, and big jars of sun-dried tomatoes when I looked into the open kitchen. Lunch is self-serve, and you can eat in the large outdoor courtyard. There's table service for dinner, which is best enjoyed in front of the open fire. Warm colors make the place feel Mediterranean. Mississippi mud pie is a favorite dessert. If you want wine with dinner, you'll have to bring your own.

Faces Cafe Bar

136 Hardy St. ☎ **03/548-8755.** Reservations recommended, especially weekends. Main courses NZ$8.50–$16 (US$6–$11.20). AE, BC, DC, MC, V. Mon–Sat noon–2pm; daily 6–10pm; brunch Sun 11am–1pm. Bar, daily 11am–"late." ITALIAN.

This is a handy spot to know about because of its long hours and flexible menu. The posted all-day snack menu features an antipasto platter, lasagna, cannelloni, or—for your sweet tooth—a slice of fresh-baked gâteau with whipped cream. (No one in New Zealand seems to have heard of cholesterol.) Faces has a light, airy ambience and serves a wide selection of coffees and teas. It's fully licensed.

Little Rock Cafe Bar

165 Bridge St. ☎ **03/546-8800.** Reservations not accepted. Main courses NZ$10–$18.50 (US$7–$13). AE, BC, DC, MC, V. Daily noon–2:30pm and 5:30–10pm. Closes earlier in winter. Bar, daily 11am–"late." MODERN NEW ZEALAND.

I was experiencing a rare moment of homesickness when I stopped in here for lunch, and my heart rejoiced at the sight of a quesadilla on the menu and the place's unusual recycled decor. "Save our rock" is the theme here, and the "little rock" in question is New Zealand. The floors of the dining and bar areas were formerly the cafeteria walls in an old slaughterhouse in Christchurch; the matai bar top was a roof beam supporting the Southland Malting Works. The informal, industrial look works well in this building—once an automotive repair garage. Specials on the chalkboard, "created by the chef in secret and solitude," change every Wednesday. Beefy boulder burgers are popular, as are the focaccia sandwiches. The recorded music was a little loud, but I didn't care. My chicken-and-mushroom quesadilla was great. It's licensed, with 11 beers on tap and a good selection of New Zealand and Australian wine.

NELSON AFTER DARK

Nelson isn't known for its bar scene, but it's worth remembering that music, Hogs Head Ale, Weiss Beer, and lots of other fun stuff are on tap every night at the **Little Rock Cafe Bar,** 165 Bridge St. (☎ **03/546-8800**). You also might want to check out the ✪ **Victorian Rose,** 281 Trafalgar St. (☎ **03/548-7631**). This Old English–style pub is also open "until late" and offers entertainment and filling, inexpensive meals. You'll find 10 different beers on tap here, including Guinness, plus a good selection of local and imported wine. Discounts are offered to backpackers. **Faces** and **Chez Eelco** (see "Great Deals on Dining in Nelson," above) are other good watering holes.

SIDE TRIPS FROM NELSON
GOLDEN BAY

A road trip to Golden Bay affords a good look at some of New Zealand's most spectacular scenery, especially long, wide, empty beaches. This is not a drive for the faint-hearted, however, as the road up and over Takaka Hill, also known as Marble Mountain, is a series of switchbacks. Your journey will take you along Highway 60 to **Motueka** (pop. 4,700), the heart of a major hops- and tobacco-growing region, and past lots of apple and kiwifruit orchards. The area around Motueka is popular with craftspeople and devotees of alternative lifestyles (whatever that means today).

After "Mot," perhaps make a short diversion to **Kaiteriteri** and go up to ✪ **Kakapah Point** for one of the best beach-and-blue-water views in the country. After Kaiteriteri, you go through Riwaka Valley and over **Takaka Hill/Marble Mountain** (you may want to have a soda crackers on hand if you get queasy). **Abel Tasman National Park** will be on your right until you get to **Takaka** (pop. 1,238), the main business-and-shopping center for Golden Bay. You'll see signs along the road directing you to craft shops and people who sell crafts from their homes. Another possible diversion: Beautiful beaches stretch out along the coast from here to Totaranui in the national park, but parts of the road are pretty rough.

COLLINGWOOD & THE HEAPHY TRACK

From Takaka, it's an easy 28km (17 miles) to **Collingwood** and another 26km (16 miles) from Collingwood to the visitor center at the base of ✪ **Farewell Spit.** The sandspit is about 35km (22 miles) long and 800 meters (about half a mile) wide. All along its length are sand dunes as high as seven- or eight-story buildings. The bird life is amazing: Over 90 species have been recorded, including many migratory waders. The spit has been the site of several mass whale strandings, and the rescue attempts have brought caring people from all over the area. The Visitor Centre (☎ and fax **03/524-8454**) can give you information on four-wheel-drive nature tours. It's open daily from Labour Day Weekend in October to the end of the May school holidays.

The ✪ **Heaphy Track,** one of New Zealand's best-known hiking trails, starts southwest of Collingwood and ends at Karamea on the West Coast. It can be walked in 4 days, but it's better to allow 5 or 6. For more information on the Heaphy, contact the Department of Conservation Office in Takaka (☎ **03/525-8026**) and see "Tramping," in chapter 4.

AFFORDABLE ACCOMMODATIONS IN COLLINGWOOD

Northwest Lodge

Totara Ave., Pakawau, Collingwood. ☎ **03/524-8108.** 2 rms (both with bathrm). NZ$120 (US$84) double. Rates include breakfast. MC, V.

This homestay is probably one of New Zealand's most remote and also probably one of its nicest. Angela (an amazing cook) and Philip (a potter) England designed this contemporary timber-and-glass house with the idea of accommodating travelers. It's built on a sandspit overlooking an estuary, and the bird life is amazing. When I was last there, they served whitebait omelets for breakfast with homemade muffins, fresh fruit, and delicious homemade yogurt. The dinner main course of local scallops was accompanied by organic vegetables and salad. The guest rooms have tea- and coffeemaking facilities and wood decks. If you want absolute quiet and privacy, this is the place to stay, 12km (8 miles) north of Collingwood, about 2½ hours' drive from Nelson.

GREAT DEALS ON DINING

In addition to the suggestion below, keep in mind that there's a licensed cafe at the Farewell Spit Visitor Centre (open daily from late October through mid-May).

The Mussel Inn

Hwy. 60, Takaka. ☎ **03/525-9241.** Reservations not accepted. Snacks NZ$2.50–$8 (US$17.50–$5.60); dinner NZ$12–$18 (US$8.40–$12.60). MC, V. Mid-Oct to mid-Apr, daily 11am–"late" (dinner 6–8pm, snacks all day). NEW ZEALAND.

The folks who frequent this place would've been happy at Woodstock. There's nothing mainstream about it, not even the beer, which is from their own microbrewery. Hosts Jane and Andy Dixon welcome all who gather here—mostly locals, including families. The menu includes mussel chowder, quiche, pizza, and fresh steamed mussels. Everyone shares big wooden tables inside and out. Darts, horseshoes, backgammon, cards, and chess are provided, and there's live music most weekends. Licensed.

EN ROUTE SOUTH

The choice is up to you: A day's driving—4½ to 5 hours will get you to **Greymouth** or **Hokitika** via Highway 6; or you can proceed at a more leisurely pace and stop off at **Westport,** which is emerging as a center for outdoor-adventure activities and a place that, though fiercely noncommercial, makes a real effort to make visitors feel welcome. You can stop for lunch in **Murchison** or in Westport if you can hold out that long, where there's a wider choice of eateries.

If you're traveling by InterCity coach, your driver's interesting narrative will fill you in on the history of most of the terrain you'll be covering along a road that's steep and winding at times, drops through heavily wooded mountain gorges at others, touches the sea, and then turns south along a dramatic coastline, which sometimes can be seen from the high bluffs where the road passes. If you're driving, look for the following key landscape notes.

Between Murchison and Westport, you'll be following the **Buller River** much of the way. Those jagged gaps and high scarped bluffs above the wall of the gorge between Murchison and Lyell are the legacy of a disastrous earthquake in June 1929. Passing through the gold-mining ghost town of **Lyell,** you'll see little left to suggest the thriving, bustling town of gold-rush days. Its last surviving building, the Lyell Hotel, burned in 1963, leaving only a few faint vestiges of those turbulent times. Descending to the lower gorge, you'll be driving through flatlands, then under **Hawkes Crag,** where the road has been hewn from a sheer face of solid rock above the river, and on to a stretch of road between bush-clad walls and rocky ravines.

3 Westport: Adventure Center of the West Coast

101km (62 miles) N of Greymouth; 226km (140 miles) SW of Nelson

Far too many people zip past Westport on their way to Greymouth or Hokitika rather than bothering to turn off Highway 6 onto Buller Gorge Road and drive to the coast. Westport is fast becoming known as the "Adventure Capital of the West Coast." Its mild climate and coastal and subtropical mountain scenery provide an ideal setting for such outdoor activities as white-water rafting, jet boating, horse trekking, caving, underworld rafting through caves, and rock climbing. The information center can fill you in on just where to go to indulge in any of these that suit your fancy. Just remember this when you are near the water: West Coast beaches are great to look at, but not so great for swimming. Undertows are a common and ever-present hazard. If you want to surf or windsurf, check locally before getting wet. For the not-so-adventurous, this region offers excellent sea and river fishing, gold panning, and a good variety of scenic and historic walkways.

The town of Westport (pop. 5,800) found relative prosperity as a coal-mining center after weathering the gold bust.

ESSENTIALS
GETTING THERE & GETTING AROUND

BY PLANE Air New Zealand Link flies into Westport from Wellington.

BY COACH (BUS) Westport is served by daily **InterCity** and **Mount Cook Landline** coaches.

BY ALTERNATIVE COACH (BUS) Both **Magic Traveller** and **Kiwi Experience** include Westport on their schedules.

BY CAR Westport can be reached on Highway 6 from Nelson or Greymouth.

VISITOR INFORMATION

The **Westport Information Centre,** 1 Brougham St. (☎ and fax **03/789-6658**), opposite the post office, is open from 9am to 5pm Monday through Friday, and also Saturday and Sunday from October to March. The **telephone area code** (STD) for Westport is **03.**

EXPLORING WESTPORT: WHAT TO SEE & DO

Coaltown, on Queen Street South (☎ 03/789-8204), is a mining museum that provides wheelchair access, with a walk-through coal mine and a multiscreen audiovisual presentation. A new wing holds displays on maritime and pioneering history. It's open daily from 9am to 4pm, with admission of NZ$5 (US$3.50) for adults, NZ$4 (US$2.80) for students, and NZ$2 (US$1.40) for children.

If you'd like to try ✪ **underworld rafting,** literally floating through caves on an inner tube, **Norwest Adventures Ltd.,** 41 Domett St., Westport (☎ 03/789-6686) supplies tubes, wet suits, and lighted helmets; you bring swimwear, a towel, and stout footwear. This 4 to 5-hour trip is not suitable for young children, but it's slightly tamer than the one offered by Wild West Adventures in Greymouth; the cost is NZ$90 (US$63). Norwest also guides **abseiling** and **adventure caving** for serious thrill seekers. The cave rafting takes place at Charleston, between Westport and Greymouth.

AFFORDABLE ACCOMMODATIONS

Westport is a small place, but plenty of decent accommodations options are available. The rates quoted below include the 12.5% GST.

SUPER-CHEAP SLEEPS

Marg's Travellers Rest

Bed and breakfast lodge: 56 Russell St., Westport. Hostel: 129 Palmerston St., Westport. ☎ **0800/808-627** on the South Island, or 03/789-8627. Fax 03/789-8396. B&B lodge 6 rms (none with bath). Hostel: 34 beds in 5 units. NZ$68 (US$47.60) double in B&B lodge includes continental breakfast. NZ$16.50 (US$11.60) per person in hostel. Off-season discount May–Sept. BC, MC, V. Courtesy pickup from the bus stop on request.

This unusual hostel/bed and breakfast combination is actually two adjacent buildings sharing the same lobby. Each of the six B&B rooms has either a double bed or two twins and its own TV. The hostel is comprised of 2 two-bedroom, two-bathroom flats; a one-bedroom, one-bathroom flat; and two studio units. Each unit is fully self-contained with a kitchen. The flats also have a lounge; the two-bedroom units sleep up to 10. Margaret Broderick welcomes guests and provides central heating, an undercover garden, a barbecue area, lock-up bike storage, off-street parking, and bike rental—all in a central location. In addition to the B&B and hostel, Margaret also offers five powered campervan spots at NZ$20 (US$14) for two people.

Tripinns

72 Queen St., Westport. ☎ **03/789-7367.** Fax 03/789-6419. 64 beds in 18 rms (none with bath). NZ$34 (US$23.80) double; NZ$15 (US$10.50) in shared room. AE, MC, V.

Margaret and Jerry Poels' hostel is in a centrally located home built during the gold-rush era. They also offer newer units, all surrounded by spacious lawns and trees. Linen and blankets are provided free. Guests share the fully equipped kitchen, large dining room, TV lounge, barbecue, and laundry. There are also tent sites, luggage storage, bike rental, cycle lock-up, and off-street parking.

FOR A FEW EXTRA BUCKS

Buller Bridge Motel

On the Esplanade (P.O. Box 187), Westport. ☎ **0800/500-209** in New Zealand, or 03/789-7519. Fax 03/789-7165. 11 units (all with bath). TV TEL. NZ$86 (US$60.20) double. Additional person NZ$16 (US$11.20) extra. AE, BC, DC, MC, V. Take the first left turn off the bridge on the outskirts of town.

This genuine retreat, under the friendly management of Pat and Sylvia Bradley, offers self-contained motel apartments in a spacious garden setting close to all town amenities. Each unit has a complete kitchen and video, and some have water beds. I particularly like the large, grassy courtyard; kids like the play area with trampolines and swings. A guest laundry, as well as a luxurious spa pool, are available.

EN ROUTE TO GREYMOUTH

Turning sharply south at Westport to follow the coastline, you'll pass **Mitchell's Gully Gold Mine** only 22km (14 miles) along your way. It's a fascinating place, not a tourist attraction but a real working mine, open from 9am to 4pm daily except Christmas. It has been in the Mitchell family since 1866, and Ian and Helen McKinnon are the friendly miners. Back on the road, you'll soon pass through Charleston, where gold was discovered in 1866, leading to a population boom, with dance halls, stores, and some 92 hotels—few reminders remain today.

About halfway between Westport and Greymouth, you'll come to one of the West Coast's most unusual natural formations, the ✪ **Punakaiki Pancake Rocks** located in Paparoa National Park. (InterCity and Mount Cook Landline coaches stop here so passengers may walk down to see them.) At the top of a steep headland, a simple tearoom, rest room, and shop are on the inland side of the road, along with space for parking to allow you to leave your car. Follow the track across the road through native bush to the sea, where limestone structures, which look like a gigantic stack of pancakes, jut out into the water. When the seas are high and rough, water comes surging into the deep caverns below and is spouted up some 20 to 30 feet into the air, accompanied by a tremendous whoosh of sound. It's really beautiful, but don't take my word for it. Even if you take the train to Greymouth from Christchurch or drive to the West Coast via Arthur's Pass, I think you should make the detour north and see these natural wonders for yourself. The surrounding area offers several marked **walking tracks.** My favorite is the 20-minute Truman Track.

From the Punakaiki Rocks, the road is almost continually within sight of the sea until you turn to cross the **Grey River** and drive into Greymouth.

4 Greymouth & Lake Brunner

290km (180 miles) SW of Nelson; 101km (62 miles) SW of Westport; 45km (28 miles) N of Hokitika

At Greymouth, it's decision-making time: You can stop here, or detour to Lake Brunner, or push on another 45km (28 miles) to Hokitika. Personally, I find Lake Brunner and the little township of Moana, sited on its northern shore, so appealing that it wouldn't be much of a decision for me, especially because it's only 30 minutes east of Greymouth. You'll have to read on and make your own mind. Hokitika offers lots of shopping and things to do; Greymouth's only commercial attraction is Shantytown, a reconstructed gold-mining town.

Whether you stop in Greymouth or push on, you'll soon realize that New Zealand's West Coast is a rugged stretch of country whose incomparable beauty has been molded and shaped by the elements—and its inhabitants are perhaps the most rugged and individualistic of a nation of individuals. Lured by nature's treasures, they have, from the beginning, seemed to revel in its challenges. Along with a resilient toughness, they have developed a rollicking sense of fun, a relaxed acceptance of the vicissitudes of West Coast life, and a brand of hospitality that's recognized—and even touted—by Kiwis in every other part of the country. "Coasters" are a hardy, good-hearted breed who will welcome you warmly to this unique region.

The coast's beauty and hidden wealth were entirely lost on Captain Cook when he sighted it from the sea, remained offshore, and described it in his journal as "wild and desolate and unworthy of observation." Of course, his sea-based observation could not possibly reveal the presence of nuggets of gold strewn about those "unworthy" beaches. That discovery was left for 1864, when it precipitated an influx of prospectors and miners from as far afield as California (along with a goodly number from Australia), many of whom would remain after the goldfields played out in 1867 to form the basis of a permanent population who take fierce pride in their particular part of New Zealand.

Greymouth, with a population of 11,000, keeps busy these days with coal and timber exports and the import of tourists who come to roam the beaches in search of gemstones and greenstone, fish in the clear streams nearby, perhaps pan for gold, and participate in a range of adventure activities.

ESSENTIALS
GETTING THERE
BY PLANE   The closest air service is in nearby Hokitika; there's air service via **Air New Zealand Link** between Hokitika and Christchurch.

BY TRAIN   The *TranzAlpine* runs daily between Christchurch and the Greymouth railroad station on Mackay Street and will stop in Moana (Lake Brunner) on request. This is New Zealand's best train-travel experience (see chapter 15, "Christchurch," for more details).

BY COACH (BUS)   **InterCity** buses reach Greymouth from Christchurch, the Fox and Franz Josef Glaciers, Nelson, and Westport.

BY ALTERNATIVE COACH (BUS)   **Kiwi Experience** and **Magic Traveller** both include Greymouth on their routes.

BY CAR   Greymouth is reached via Highway 6 from the north and south. Highway 7 brings travelers from the east coast via the Lewis Pass, and Highway 73 is the route that goes through Arthur's Pass National Park on its way from Christchurch to the West Coast. If you arrive in Greymouth on the train or via highways 7 or 73, you may want to detour north to see the Punakaki Pancake Rocks before heading down the coast.

VISITOR INFORMATION
The **Visitor Information Network Centre,** in the Regent Theatre Building on the corner of Herbert and Mackay streets (☎ **03/768-5101**), is open in summer daily from 9am to 6pm. They can furnish information about the area and book accommodations at no charge. They are also the Department of Conservation agency for the region. The **telephone area code** (STD) for Greymouth is **03.**

EXPLORING GREYMOUTH: WHAT TO SEE & DO
The star attraction at Greymouth is **Shantytown** (☎ **03/762-6634**), a replica West Coast gold-mining town dating back to the turn of last century. It's set amid native bush, and a steam train operates hourly and threads its way through this picturesque setting. Horse-and-buggy rides are also available, and the stagecoach will rattle you over an old bush road. Visitors can also pan for gold.

Shantytown is open October to March (except Christmas Day), daily from 8:30am to 7pm; April to September, daily from 8:30am to 5pm. Admission (which includes steam-train rides) is NZ$8 (US$56) for adults and NZ$5 (US$3.50) for children. They accept American Express, Diners Club, MasterCard, and Visa. To find

Shantytown, drive 8km (5 miles) south of Greymouth to Paroa, make a left turn, and drive another 3km (2 miles) inland. The route is well signposted. If you're carless, **taxi service** (☎ **03/768-7078**) to Shantytown (which includes admission charge) from Greymouth costs NZ$20 (US$14) per person, round trip. *Author's note:* Reader Patricia Downing of Los Angeles, California, said, "I did not feel it was worth the taxi ride out there." I'd say it's worth a stop if you're traveling with children.

Scenicland Ocean Jets, Mawhera Quay, Greymouth (☎ **0800/929 991** in New Zealand, or 03/768-9770; fax 03/376-7538), offers 1¹/₂-hour dolphin-watch cruises to see the "Mickey Mouse" or Hectors Dolphin, one of the rarest members of the dolphin family. You'll probably also see fur seals and shag-nesting sites. They also offer river excursions, jet boat rides, and ecotours.

OUTDOOR ACTIVITIES
IN GREYMOUTH

CYCLING   Mountain biking is really popular around Greymouth. Pick up maps from the information center. Bikes can be hired from **Mann Security and Cycles,** 173 Tainui St., Greymouth (☎ and fax **03/768-0255**).

RAFTING   Greymouth is one of three places in New Zealand to go cave (blackwater) rafting. (Waitomo and Westport are the other two.) **Wild West Adventure Tours** (☎ **03/768-6649**) offers cave rafting for hardy types. This costs NZ$89 (US$62.30) for 5 hours. For slightly less strenuous rafting see the listing for Norwest Adventures Ltd. in the "Westport" section above or consider Wild West's "float-through" trip (better for families with young children and anyone short of energy and nerve). This is pricier because it requires more staff—NZ$95 (US$66.50) for 3¹/₂ hours. White-water rafting is also available in this area.

SURFING   The main breaks are on the Cobden and Blaketown beaches.

WALKING   The Grey District sports a number of walking tracks, several are suitable for the not-so-able bodied and one has wheelchair access; inquire at the visitor information center for particulars.

The ✪ **Point Elizabeth Walkway** is my favorite trek (and not because of the name). This walkway starts at Rapahoe, and follows the coast south around the headland to the Cobden Beach road end. The track is well graded and surfaced and provides spectacular views north and south. It takes less than 2 hours one way. An alternate return route, if the tide is low, is down the steps and along the beach where you may spot dolphins in the water and seals on the beach.

IN NEARBY LAKE BRUNNER

FISHING   Lake Brunner is a great place to fish for brown trout. Locals say it's "the only lake in the world where the trout die of old age." The rule of thumb here is this: "If it holds water it will probably hold a brown trout." Get free advice from one of the local fly shops. Hostelries in the area offer equipment hire. For a guided expedition, you might call Ray Grubb at **Lake Brunner Guides,** RD 1 Kumara, Westland (☎ **03/738-0163;** e-mail fish@brunner.co.nz). For more information see "Fishing," in chapter 4.

WALKING   There are a number of good walks in the area. My favorite is the **Carew Falls Walk,** which starts just beyond Lake Brunner Lodge in Mitchells Scenic Reserve, and takes about 45 minutes to an hour. The scenery along this track, which winds past a podocarp forest with ferns of all shapes and sizes, moss covered trees, and granite boulders, looks like a page from a child's storybook.

Author's note: I didn't have time, but I hope you'll bring a picnic lunch and enjoy it in the forest where fantails flit between trees.

SHOPPING FOR GREENSTONES

Jade Boulder Gallery

1 Guinness St. (corner of Tainui St.), Greymouth. ☎ **03/768-0700.** Daily 8:30am–9pm summer, 8:30am–5pm winter. AE, DC, MC, V.

While Hokitika has lots of shops selling greenstone jewelry and objects, Greymouth has only one—but it's very comprehensive and offers educational displays as well as items for sale. Owner Ian Boustridge is one of the top five jade carvers in the world according to the September, 1987 issue of *National Geographic*. He carves the bigger pieces (the sculptures) on display here, as well as supervising the production team that makes most of the jewelry. Other craft items are sold here, including wooden bowls, hand-knitted sweaters, and furniture. Light meals and snacks are available at the Jade Rock Cafe.

AFFORDABLE ACCOMMODATION

Greymouth and the nearby Lake Brunner area offer an adequate selection of places to stay.

The rates given below include the 12.5% GST.

IN GREYMOUTH

Campgrounds & Cabins

Greymouth Seaside Holiday Park, Chesterfield Street, Greymouth (☎ **03/ 768-6618,** fax 03/768-5873), as its name implies, is situated by the sea. On level, sheltered sites on the beachfront at the southern edge of town, there are 50 tent sites, 65 powered sites, 10 on-site caravans, 25 standard cabins, 10 tourist cabins, 12 tourist flats, 5 motel units, and a backpackers' bunkhouse with 12 beds. Chesterfield Street is just off the Main South Road, and the camp is signposted. A modern TV lounge, kitchen, washing machines and dryers, hot showers, linen for rent, and a camp store are available. Grounds and all accommodations are well kept, and a courtesy van is available to and from public transport. Double-occupancy rates are NZ$17 (US$11.90) for tent sites, NZ$19 (US$13.30) for powered sites, NZ$32 (US$22.40) for standard cabins, NZ$40 (US$28) for tourist cabins, NZ$59 (US$41.30) for tourist flats, and NZ$72 (US$50.40) for a motel units; backpackers pay NZ$12 (US$8.40) per person.

Super-Cheap Sleeps

Greymouth YHA Hostel

"Kainga-Ra," 15 Alexander St., P.O. Box 299, Greymouth. ☎ and fax **03/768-4951.** 40 beds in 12 rms (1 with bathrm). NZ$30–$34 (US$21–$22.80) single; NZ$17 (US$11.90) per person double or twin; NZ$15 (US$10.50) per person single-sex shared room; NZ$13 (US$9.10) dorm bed in ten-bed dorm. Non-members pay NZ$4 (US$2.80) extra. Rates include linen. MC, V. Call for free pickup from information center and bus/railway station.

This hostel is close to town in a historical building, the ex–Marist Brothers' home, and is surrounded by nice gardens. There are numerous rooms, but the former chapel holding 10 beds is probably the most interesting. Everyone uses the fully equipped kitchen, dining room, living room with open fireplace, and TV/video room. This hostel is wheelchair accessible, and there is one unit for travelers with disabilities that has an attached bathroom. There are also a laundry, bicycle shed, barbecue, and partially covered veranda; all bedrooms have a heaters.

For a Few Extra Bucks
Aachen Place Motel
50 High St., Greymouth. ☎ **0800/663-030** in New Zealand, or 03/768-6901. Fax 03/768-6958. 10 units (all with bathrm). TV TEL. NZ$86 (US$60.20) double. Additional person NZ$12 (US$8.40) extra. Best Western discounts available. AE, DC, JCB, MC, V. Drive about 1km (¹/₂ a mile) south of the town center on Highway 6.

This well-kept Best Western offers 10 units that sleep one to three, all with full kitchen facilities. All have radios, electric blankets, and heating, and some are smoke free; full laundry facilities are available. It's handy to a restaurant and supermarket and about a 10-minute walk from the center of town. Cooked and continental breakfasts are available.

Golden Coast Guest House
10 Smith St., Greymouth. ☎ **03/768-7839.** 5 rms (1 with bathrm). NZ$70 (US$49) double; NZ$99 (US$69.30) triple. Rates include breakfast. MC, V.

Gladys Roche is the hostess at this B&B on Highway 6 above the railroad station, 5 minutes from the town center. The red-roofed house is set in a sloping, flower-bordered lawn. The guest rooms are bright and clean, with heaters and electric blankets. There's a TV lounge with a pretty rock fireplace where you're welcome to make tea and coffee whenever you wish.

✪ South Beach Motel
318 Main South Rd., Greymouth. ☎ **03/762-6768.** Fax 03/762-6748. 11 units (all with bathrm). TV TEL. NZ$75–$82 (US$52.50–$57.40) double. Additional person NZ$14 (US$9.80) extra. Best Western discounts available. AE, BC, DC, MC, V.

Across from the beach, this motel has a quiet location only a 5km (3-mile) drive from town. Each unit comes with complete kitchen, video, a radio, and electric blankets. There's one unit for travelers with disabilities, a waterbed unit, and one "executive suite." Amenities include a guest laundry, children's playground, barbecue area, and spa. Breakfast is available.

Willowbank Pacifica Lodge
Hwy. 6, P.O. Box 260, Greymouth. ☎ **03/768-5339.** Fax 03/768-6022. 7 units and suites. TV TEL. NZ$75 (US$52.50) double; NZ$85 (US$59.50) one-bedroom suite for 1 or 2. AE, BC, DC, JCB, MC, V. Courtesy pickup available.

Located 3km (2 miles) north of town on the Greymouth–Westport highway, this motor lodge offers modern studios and suites, all nicely furnished right down to potted plants. All units have been given old West Coast hotel names like Welcome Nugget, Diggers Home, and Plough Inn by hosts Lois and Ted Gutberlet, one of Greymouth's most gracious couples. They delight in making their guests feel at home—they ask that you let them know you're a Frommer's reader. The suites are spacious and airy, with slanted roofs and paneled walls; bed-sitters (studios) are more modest but have full kitchens and electric blankets. A heated indoor swimming pool and a spa pool, as well as a guest laundry are available. The one-bedroom suite boasts a spa bath, full kitchen, hair dryer, lounge, and tea-and-toast breakfast served in your suite. Cooked or continental breakfast is available at an additional charge. The hosts' son Tony is a professional trout fishing guide.

IN BLACKBALL
This tiny settlement is located just 28km (17 miles) northeast of Greymouth. It is acknowledged as the birthplace of the Labour party but best known for the tasty salami made at the **Blackball Salami Company,** Hilton St., Blackball (☎ and fax **03/732-4111**).

Formerly the Blackball Hilton

Hart St., Blackball. ☎ **03/732-4705.** Fax 03/732-4111. 15 rms (none with bathrm). NZ$20 (US$14) per person double or twin; NZ$15–$17 (US$10.50–$11.90) dorm bed. Dinner, bed, and breakfast NZ$50 (US$35). BC, CB, DC, MC, V. .

Jane Wells and Linda Osborn, owners of this hostel since 1994, offer budget lodging as well as meals and drinks from their bar. You might want to seize this opportunity to try Miner's, a natural West Coast brew. A sample three-course dinner might start with pumpkin soup, followed by beef Stroganoff accompanied by salad and vegetables, followed by Jamaican banana treat with snowflake ice cream for dessert. The kitchen is also freely available for guests to fix their own meals. This no-smoking place isn't posh, but it's homey and cozy.

AROUND LAKE BRUNNER

In addition to the two places described below, hosts Grahame and Jackie Ott at the **Lake Brunner Motor Camp,** Ahau St., Moana (☎ and fax **03/738-0600**), provide cabins, caravan sites, and tent sites for NZ$14 to $16 (US$9.80 to $11.20) per person.

Super-Cheap Sleeps

Moana Hotel

Ahau St., Moana, Westland. ☎ and fax **03/738-0388.** 20 cabins (without bathrm); 5 hotel rms (1 with bathrm); 3 motel units (all with bathrm). NZ$13–$16 (US$9.10–$11.20) per person cabin; NZ$50–$60 (US$35–$42) double hotel rm; NZ$80 (US$56) double motel unit. Extra person NZ$15 (US$10.50). AE, DC, MC, V.

The Moana Hotel, built in 1935, is located on the north shore of Lake Brunner. The three motel units adjacent to the hotel are the best value. They offer a great view of the lake, cooking facilities, ensuite bathrooms, and TVs. One sleeps two, the other four. Only one of the hotel rooms has an ensuite and TV, the others have only sinks. Ten of the cabins sleep 2, while the remaining 10 sleep 8. Cabin dwellers use a communal kitchen and bathroom; rates do not include linen. Publican Brent Beadle offers guided fishing trips and rents equipment if you want to try your luck fishing from the shore. He also recommended that we not eat here—a suggestion I took seriously.

Worth a Splurge

✪ Lake Brunner Lodge

Mitchells, RD 1, Kumara, Westland. ☎ and fax **03/738-0163.** E-mail: fish@brunner.co.nz. 11 rms (all with bathrm). NZ$215–$265 (US$151–$186) per person based on double occupancy. Rates include breakfast and dinner. Frommer's readers making direct bookings receive a 20% discount. Fishing packages are available. AE, DC, MC, V. Located 2^1/2 hours-drive from Christchurch; 30 minutes from Greymouth.

What makes Lake Brunner Lodge worth a splurge? In my opinion, four things. First is the fact that it's located right on a beautiful lake surrounded by equally-beautiful scenery. The view to the water's edge (about 150 meters/162 yards) is completely unobstructed—only a single-lane gravel road and a lush green paddock are in the foreground. It's remote; it's quiet; it's peaceful. The second reason is the food. Suffice it to say that on our last trip to New Zealand our most memorable meals were consumed here. They "source" the best ingredients from far and wide and hire chefs who know how to make the most of them. Still not convinced? Then let me tell you that host Ray Grubb and his staff are all good fishing guides, and they aren't as expensive as others in the country. Don't fish? Well, I bet you'll enjoy their guided environmental experiences into Arthur's Pass National Park and thereabouts.

The house was built in 1935 as a country inn and has retained its historic ambience, in spite of having been expanded and remodeled several times. Ray Grubb and

Marian van der Goes bought it in 1985. Furnishings are modern and very comfortable; there's a nice used-brick fireplace in the dining room, wood paneling in some areas, and hardwood floors throughout the single-story structure. There are three bedrooms on the front, four in the courtyard wing, and four in a separate villa at the rear of the lodge. Guests can also enjoy the library, bar, and lounge. Dinner is included in the rate, but predinner drinks and wine are extra. There are walking tracks in the area, and canoes, mountain bikes, and fishing equipment are provided.

GREAT DEALS ON DINING
IN GREYMOUTH

✪ The Smelting House Cafe

102 Mackay St., (P.O.P.O. Box 464), Greymouth. ☎ **03/768-0012.** Fax 03/731-1821. Reservations not accepted. Main courses NZ$6.50–$7 (US$4.55–4.90). No credit cards. Daily 7:30am–5pm. Dinner served Sat–Sun during summer. CAFE/MODERN NEW ZEALAND.

Once the site of a bank that used to smelt gold in a shed out back—hence the name—this cute little spot is pretty trendy for the West Coast; in fact, locals didn't quite know what to make of it. Eventually overseas visitors introduced the concept of "hanging out" here, and now it's enjoyed by locals and travelers alike. Owners Margaret and Brian Weston, a former dietitian and doctor respectively, turn out wholesome homemade meals like broccoli, mushroom and sausage calzones or roast chicken with a mushroom and wine sauce. Margaret uses only high quality ingredients, and meals are listed daily on a blackboard menu. This licensed cafe is a great place to enjoy a cappuccino and write postcards.

Steamers Cafe and Bar

58 Mackay St. (corner Albert Mall), Greymouth. ☎ **03/768-4193.** Reservations advisable in summer. Main courses NZ$10.50–$16 (US$7.40–$11.20). AE, DC, MC, V. Sun–Thurs 11am–10:30pm, Fri–Sat 11am–2am. NEW ZEALAND.

Until the early '80s, this historic building housed the Union Steamship Company where bookings could be made for the ships that called into Greymouth. The red-brick building still has an historic atmosphere. A bar/snack menu is served all day; lunch items include dishes such as lamb curry and rice pilaf, vegetarian pizza, and fish and chips. For dinner you could choose pork steak, mixed grill, or fettuccine tossed with tomato salsa and garnished with parmesan shavings. A handle of the favorite local beer— Monteith's, a dark beer brewed in Greymouth—will cost you NZ$3.50 (US$2.45).

AROUND LAKE BRUNNER

Stationhouse Cafe

Koe St., Moana. ☎ and fax **03/738-0158.** Reservations accepted, required weekends and holidays. Main courses NZ$15.50–$28 (US$10.980–$19.60). AE, DC, MC, V. Daily 10am–9pm. NEW ZEALAND CAFE.

The setting is what makes the Stationhouse Cafe special. It's located across the train tracks from the tiny little Moana Station and overlooks beautiful Lake Brunner. Lunch items include pasta, sandwiches, and a ploughman's plate. Dinner options include rib eye steak with a salami mushroom sauce, creamy scallop Mornay, roast lamb, and roast or pasta of the day.

EN ROUTE TO HOKITIKA

The 45km (28-mile) drive south follows the coastline closely along mostly flat farmland. But look to your left and the snowcapped tips of the Southern Alps become clearer and clearer, sharply defined against the sky, as though painted on the horizon. This is just a tease of the mountain scenery that awaits in a few days when you turn away from the Tasman Sea. Also, drive carefully along the West Coast, especially when crossing single-lane bridges that are shared by both cars and trains.

About 32km (20 miles) from Greymouth, you'll cross the **Arahura River.** This is where Maori found a huge supply of greenstone, which they used for making weapons, ornaments, and tools. Another 8km (5 miles) and you'll be in Hokitika, where you can see artisans still working that gemstone into various items.

EN ROUTE TO CHRISTCHURCH

If your time on the South Island is limited, you can drive from Greymouth to Christchurch (allow the better part of the day in order to enjoy the drive to its fullest) by way of **Arthur's Pass National Park** and some of New Zealand's most spectacular scenery. Just south of Greymouth, turn left onto Highway 73. Opened in 1866, this road was one of the last in the country to be used by horse-drawn Cobb and Co. coaches. If you come in winter, Mount Temple Basin offers a full range of winter sports; in summer, the wild mountain landscape is a marvel of alpine flowers. Regular coach service is also available from Greymouth to Christchurch and this is the route of New Zealand's best train trip, the *TranzAlpine.*

5 Hokitika: Greenstone, Glowworms & Gold

45km (28 miles) S of Greymouth, 147km (91 miles) N of Franz Josef

As you drive into quiet, peaceful little Hokitika, you'll find it hard to believe that this was once the boisterous, rowdy "Goldfields Capital," where more than 35,000 miners and prospectors kept the dance halls roaring and filled some 102 hotels. And because it was more accessible by sea than overland, ships poured into its harbor. As many as 80 boats would be tied up at Hokitika wharves, many of them waiting to transport the gold that poured out of the area—often at the rate of half a million ounces per year. But the supply wasn't endless, and when the gold was gone, Hokitika's economy took another turn—this time, decidedly downward.

Today, you'll see only remnants of those once-bustling wharves and almost no remnants of all those hotels. Still, Hokitika has more attractions than any other West Coast town, and its present-day prosperity relies on farming, forestry, and tourism—likely to keep the town going longer than gold did. Many visitors come here to shop for greenstone items made from locally quarried stone. Most greenstone jewelry you'll see throughout New Zealand comes from Hokitika. The major airport of the West Coast is located here; there's good coach service; and you'll find it an ideal base for exploring this part of the South Island.

ESSENTIALS
GETTING THERE & GETTING AROUND

BY PLANE   There is air service via **Air New Zealand Link** between Hokitika and Christchurch.

BY TRAIN   The nearest rail service is in Greymouth (see Section 4, in this chapter).

BY COACH (BUS)   **InterCity** serves Hokitika via the Franz Josef–Greymouth route.

BY ALTERNATIVE COACH (BUS)   Both **Magic Travellers** and **Kiwi Experience** pass through Hokitika on their way from Greymouth to the glaciers.

BY CAR   Hokitika can be reached via Highway 6.

BY TAXI   For taxi service, call **Gold Band Taxis** (☎ **03/755-8437**).

VISITOR INFORMATION

The **Westland District Council Information Centre,** on Weld Street, Hokitika (☎ **03/755-8322,** fax 03/755-8026), is open December to March, daily from 8:30am to 6pm; April to November, Monday through Friday from 8:30am to 5pm and Saturday from 10am to 1pm. The center's friendly staff can furnish detailed information on the area's attractions and make reservations for transportation and accommodations. The information center may move to the Carnegie Library on Hamilton Street in 1998.

The **post office,** on Revell Street, is open Monday through Friday from 9am to 5pm. The **telephone area code** (STD) for Hokitika is **03.**

Special Events

If you're in the area in March, try to plan your stop in Hokitika at the time the **ECNZ Wild Foods Festival** is scheduled. You'll be able to taste wild pig, venison, possum pâté, goat, all sorts of wild herbs, honey, and fish from local waters. It's a fantastic 1-day West Coast celebration that's bound to be a memorable travel experience. Call ☎ 03/755-8322 to find out when the festival will take place this year.

EXPLORING HOKITIKA: WHAT TO SEE & DO
IN TOWN

One of the best ways to gain an immediate insight into this interesting little town is to pick up the **Hokitika Heritage Trail** brochure from the information center or the West Coast Historical Museum. In less than a half hour on this self-guided walk, you'll learn about the historical buildings and sites and the part each played in the town's history.

The ✪ **West Coast Historical Museum,** on Tancred Street (☎ and fax **03/755-6898**), features reconstructions and artifacts of the 19th-century "Alluvial placer" gold-mining era on the West Coast. Wood and slab dwellings display cooking utensils and furnishings, with equipment represented by pit-sawing and a blacksmith's forge for servicing the tools needed to open up cemented wash concealing the golden treasure. In direct contrast to this sort of hardship and poverty, there are church fittings and elaborate furniture from a merchant's home, along with a typical hotel bar. There are horse-drawn vehicles on display, and pictorial records of the rich maritime trade of the river harbor. In addition, a mechano-model gold dredge is operated on request, and there's a 20-minute audiovisual presentation of Westland's goldfields history. Early Maori occupation is represented by authentic artifacts and jade workings. Displays also feature decorative jade craft works. Gold panning is an all-weather attraction in the miner's hut built just for panning; the cost is NZ$5 (US$3.50) per person. The museum is open daily from 9:30am to 5pm. Admission is NZ$3 (US$2.10) for adults, NZ$1 (US 70¢) for children, NZ$7 (US$4.90) for a family group. A treasure hunt is available for children at no extra charge. Around March 1998 the entrance to the museum will be moved to the restored Carnegie Free Public Library on Hamilton Street. Scottish-American philanthropist Andrew Carnegie assisted in establishing 18 libraries in New Zealand. This is one of three still standing; it served as Hokitika's library from June 1908 until April 1975.

Hokitika's Rotary Club has provided an excellent orientation base at the **lookout point** just off the road to the airport. From there you can look over valley farmland to the towering peaks of the Southern Alps (each one identified by a revolving bronze pointer, which stands on a stone base) or across the town to the glistening Tasman

Gazing at Glowworms

One of the highlights of any visit to Hokitika is checking out the glowworms that make their home here—it's the largest outdoor group of them in the country. You'll find them after dark in a charming dell at the north edge of town, right on the main road (Highway 6). The 40-foot-and-higher wooded banks are filled with sparkling clusters of thousands of these critters, a really memorable sight. And as interesting as the more touristy Waitomo displays are, there's something about walking down a dirt path under a natural archway of treetops and standing alone in absolute silence that makes for a more enjoyable personal experience. No charge, but there's a donation box at the entrance. Best bring a flashlight for the first part of the path, but remember to turn it off when you begin to see the glowworms or they'll turn their lights off.

Sea on a clear day. It's a good view, within walking distance of the center of town. While you're in the area, also take time to go down to the mouth of the Hokitika River and see the driftwood-strewn beach. The Rotary Club has also built a replica signal tower at the end of Gibson Quay for beach and sunset viewing.

Author's note: I was disappointed in **Westlands Water World,** Sewell Street, Hokitika (☎ **03/755-5251**) and suggest you not spend your travel dollars on the admission here.

✪ A SIDE TRIP TO LAKE KANIERE SCENIC RESERVE

This beautiful nature reserve, centered around one of the South Island's largest lakes, is just 18km (11 miles) from Hokitika—drive inland from the main road to Kaniere township and drive straight ahead instead of turning right to go over the Hokitika River. If you don't have time to stop, there's a lovely 58km (35-mile) circular scenic drive past the lake and back through Kakatahi Valley farmlands. Loitering, however, will be rewarded by beautiful, peaceful vistas of the lake ringed by unspoiled forests with a backdrop of distant mountains. You'll find an information kiosk and toilets at the Landing, where the road first comes to the lake's edge. There are picnic tables, fireplaces, and toilets at Sunny Bight. This is also the starting point for two walks: The **Kahikatea Forest Walk** is a 10-minute stroll through the forest; the **Lake Kaniere Walkway** is a 3¹/₂-hour trek and features beaches, rain forest, and bird life. Pick up advance information on lake and bushwalks at the Information Centre in Hokitika, or contact the **Department of Conservation,** on the corner of Gibson Quay and Sewell Street, Hokitika (☎ **03/755-8301**). It's only 10 minutes to the lake, but if you're interested in doing everything (including the Lake Kaniere Walkway), you might want to spend an extra day in Hokitika.

SHOPPING

Hokitika offers some of the best shopping on the South Island. In addition to greenstone objects, look for assorted craft items.

Westland Greenstone Company Ltd.

Tancred St. between Weld and Hamilton sts. ☎ **03/755-8713.** Fax 03/755-8713. Open daily from 8am–5pm. AE, BC, DC, MC, and V.

This is a good place to see greenstone and paua shell jewelry being made. The workroom is open for you to wander through, watching talented artisans carving tikis and meres, fitting earrings and pins, and shaping a hundred other souvenirs from the gemstone. In the showroom there's an extensive range of greenstone, paua, and pink mussel-shell jewelry from which to choose.

Mountain Jade Complex

41 Weld St. ☎ **03/755-8007.** Fax 03/755-7804. Open daily 8am–8pm. AE, BC, DC, JCB, MC, and V.

Here you can see some intricately carved greenstone and handblown glass pieces. Carving is done on the premises and visitors are welcome to watch. Also in the complex is **Schroder's Handblown Glass Ltd.** (☎ **03/755-8484,** fax 03/755-6681), where you can watch glass blowers at work and purchase perfume bottles, paperweights, goblets, and much more. Cafe 41 is located here too.

The Gold Room

Tancred St. (P.O. Box 261), Hokitika. ☎ and fax **03/755-8362.** Open daily 8am–7pm. DC, JCB, MC, and V.

The staff at The Gold Room have put together a selection of handmade pendants, rings, bracelets, earrings, necklaces, tie tacks, and much more. Many of the items are fashioned from natural gold nuggets that come from the local mines. It's worth a visit even if you don't plan to buy anything. The shop also sells greenstone jewelry.

✪ Hokitika Craft Gallery

25 Tancred St. ☎ **03/755-8802.** Fax 03/755-8803. Open daily 8:30am–5pm, until 8:30pm during summer. AE, MC, and V.

In an attractive gallery lit by skylights, this cooperative displays and sells the work of 19 top West Coast artists and craftspeople. There are lovely contemporary works in fiber, pottery, wood, art, jade, leather, and bone—all very high quality. The gallery also ships worldwide.

✪ Revelations

18 Weld St. ☎ **03/755-7649** or 03/755-5040. Open daily 9am–6pm, Sept–May; Mon–Sat 9am–5pm, Sun 10am–2pm Jun–Aug.

Here you'll find primarily local crafts, native timber products, bone and jade carvings, New Zealand hand-knit garments, knitting wool, and local souvenirs. On a recent visit, I found some of the best greenstone jewelry prices in Hokitika in this shop.

✪ Brent Trolle's Studio

13 Whitcombe Terrace. ☎ **03/755-7250.**

Some of the best paintings of the South Island's West Coast are done right here in Hokitika by Brent Trolle, whose work is known throughout the country. You can visit at his home, which also serves as gallery and studio, *by calling for an appointment.* His work is also on show at the **House of Wood,** Tancred Street (☎ **03/755-6061**).

AFFORDABLE ACCOMMODATIONS

Hokitika offers a nice selection of lodgings. There's no YHA, but backpackers are welcome at the Beach House and the Hokitika Holiday Park (see below); the nearest YHA hostel is in Greymouth. The rates below include the 12.5% GST.

CAMPGROUNDS & CABINS

The **Hokitika Holiday Park,** 242 Stafford St., Hokitika (☎ and fax **03/755-8172**), has accommodations to suit any traveler. Tent sites are NZ$8 (US$5.60) per person; power caravan sites, NZ$9 (US$6.30) per person; backpacker cabins with double or twin beds, NZ$26 (US$18.20) for two; and additional people are NZ$10 (US$7) extra. Tourist cabins with hot and cold running water, kitchen, and toilet cost NZ$40 (US$28) for two. Tourist flats with kitchen and bathroom are NZ$52 (US$36.40) for two; an additional person is NZ$11 (US$7.70) extra for adults, half price for children under 16. They accept MasterCard and Visa.

SUPER-CHEAP SLEEPS

Beach House Cafe, Laundromat, and Backpackers Hostel

137 Revell St., Hokitika. ☎ **03/755-6859.** 4 bunk rms, 2 twin rms, 5 double rms (none with bathrm). NZ$15 (US$10.50) per person in dorm, NZ$35 (US$24.50) double or twin for 2. No credit cards.

Colleen Laywood and Ray Oliver are the proprietors here. The hostel is a little rough around the edges now, but they're fixing it up. There are two shared kitchens, one TV lounge, and a reading lounge—also a coin-op laundry and licensed cafe on the premises. Guests get free use of mountain bikes.

FOR A FEW EXTRA BUCKS

Hokitika Motel

221 Fitzherbert St. (Hwy. 6), Hokitika. ☎ **03/755-8292.** Fax 03/755-8485. 7 studios, 8 units. TV TEL. NZ$70–$80 (US$49–$52.50) double. Additional person NZ$15 (US$10.50) extra. AE, DC, MC, V. Courtesy car available.

The Hokitika is just across from the famous glowworm dell. There are one- and two-bedroom units with full kitchens, as well as three bed-sitters (studios) with only electric tea/coffee pot, toaster, teapot, crockery, and fridge. All units have central and electric heating, electric blankets, and radios. There's a ministore for essential provisions. A car wash, a laundry, and a courtesy car to the airport are available to guests.

✪ Jade Court Motor Lodge

85 Fitzherbert St. (Hwy. 6), Hokitika. ☎ **0800/755-885** in New Zealand, or 03/755-8855. Fax 03/755-8133. 18 units (all with bathrm). TV TEL. NZ$80–$92 (US$56–$64.40) double winter, NZ$85–$95 (US$59.50–$67) double summer. Extra person NZ$15 (US$10.50). AE, BC, DC, MC, V.

Frank and Karen Bradley are the owner/operators of this conveniently located motor lodge. Built in 1993, the units are immaculate and spacious, and the furnishings modern. When I was there, they lacked art on the walls, but maybe this will have been added by the time you arrive. All units have fully equipped kitchens. There are six one-bedroom units that sleep four; seven studios (three have spa baths) that sleep two; and five two-bedroom units that sleep six. A coin-op laundry and a playground are located on the premises.

The Southland Hotel

111 Revell St., Hokitika. ☎ **03/755-8344.** Fax 03/755-8258. 23 rms (all with bathrm). TV TEL. NZ$75–$92 (US$52.50–$64.40) double, NZ$106 (US$74.20) double spa room. AE, DC, MC, V.

This small hotel near the river in the town center has a range of accommodations—all first class. The rooms are nicely appointed, with attractive decor and comfortable furnishings, and there are units designed for travelers with disabilities. Facilities include in-house video, a launderette, and two units with spa baths and king beds. Some readers wrote recently to comment on the good dinner they had here. Check that they don't have a band on the night that you're staying there. Reservations can be made through Flag Inns.

✪ Teichelmann's Central Bed and Breakfast

20 Hamilton St., Hokitika. ☎ **0800/743-742** in New Zealand, or 03/755-8232. Fax 03/755-8239. Web site nz.com/webnz/bbnz/teichel.htm. E-mail teichel@xtra.co.nz. 6 rms (4 with bathrm). NZ$76 (US$53.20) double without bathrm, NZ$86–$96 (US$60.20–$67.20) double with bathrm. Rates include cooked breakfast. AE, BC, DC, MC, V.

As its name implies, this guest house is centrally located, with banks, restaurants, attractions, and the bus station nearby. All of the attractive bedrooms are heated and have electric blankets (some have king beds), and the lounge has a TV and tea- and coffeemaking facilities. Laundry facilities and a telephone are also available. Owners Russell Wenn and Julie Collier are happy to provide information on dining and outdoor activities. They've even written out an itinerary for travelers heading up or down the coast —an invaluable resource they provide to their guests free of charge. A cooked breakfast can be ordered. There's no smoking in the house, and it's really not suitable for children under 10. I highly recommend this one.

GREAT DEALS ON DINING

In addition to the places listed below, **Cafe 41,** in the Mountain Jade Complex at 41 Weld St. (☎ 03/755-5445, fax 03/755-7804) is a good choice. This licensed, self-serve cafe has good food, and if you'd rather bring your own wine, you can.

Bohéme Cinema Café

23 Weld St., Hokitika. ☎ **03/755-7530.** Reservations not required. NZ$5–$10 (US$3.50–$7) light meal. No credit cards. Tues–Thurs 10am–5:30pm, Fri–Mon 10am–10:30pm. PIZZA/SANDWICHES/ICE CREAM.

Located in the Regent Theatre building, the Bohéme offers a variety of light meals, made-to-order sandwiches, pizza, and ice cream. With plenty of seating for foot-weary sightseers, this place offers a comfortable rest stop combined with nutritious food and lots of friendly conversation. There's always a brisk business at the ice-cream bar, but take my advice and sample at least one of their unusual sandwiches. All come on hearty fresh-baked bread; you might like the venison (which, with a bowl of home-made soup, makes a satisfying meal). A local favorite is the honey, walnuts, and raisins combination, with cheese and corn also very popular. Pork, salami, and beef are also available.

Preston's Bakery and Restaurant

105 Revell St., Hokitika. ☎ **03/755-8412.** Reservations not required. Under NZ$10 (US$7). No credit cards. Mon–Fri 8am–5pm, bakery closes at 6pm; Sat 9am–1pm. BREAKFAST/SANDWICHES/STEAKS/PASTRIES.

A breakfast tradition in Hokitika is to congregate at this restaurant, which has a perfect small-town decor. Eggs, toast, and bacon or sausage costs NZ$6.50 (US$4.55); poached eggs and toast, NZ$3.30 (US$2.31); fruit and cereal, NZ$3 (US$2.10). You can also get sandwiches, steaks, roast chicken, stew, fresh vegetables, and sweets. This also is a great place to load up your camper van before driving farther along the West Coast.

FOR A FEW EXTRA BUCKS

✪ PR's Coffee Shop

Tancred St., Hokitika. ☎ **03/755-8379.** Reservations advisable for dinner. Dinner main courses NZ$14.50–$19.50 (US$10.50–$13.70). AE, DC, MC, V. Daily 8am–8:30pm, later in summer. CONTINENTAL.

I chose this spot because I heard they had an extensive display of teapots—I have a soft spot for such things—and I wasn't disappointed. No less than 300 line the shelves that wrap around the room. There are cat-shaped teapots and car-shaped teapots, and you-name-it-shaped teapots. I loved it, and we also enjoyed our meals. I had lamb provençale and my husband had venison in blueberry sauce. During the day, PR's is a coffee shop serving hot dishes as well as sandwiches and a wide range of coffees and teas. The dinner menu changes every 3 months. Location is another plus.

Tasman View Restaurant

In the Southland Hotel, 111 Revell St., Hokitika. ☎ **03/755-8344.** Fax 03/755-8258. Reservations recommended. Main courses NZ$20 (US$14). AE, DC, MC, V. Daily 6–9:30pm. SEAFOOD/NEW ZEALAND.

The Tasman View scores high on its seafood and its view of the Tasman Sea, but it lacks a great atmosphere. Try their lightly sautéed whitebait (only when it's in season, of course). They also have a few dishes you're not likely to encounter elsewhere, such as chili venison balls served with a plum compote or wild pork with port and juniper berries. Crystal and flowers are on the tables and the wood beams are rimu. It's fully licensed.

EN ROUTE TO FRANZ JOSEF & FOX GLACIERS

There's no pharmacy, supermarket, or bank between Hokitika and Wanaka, although you'll find a small country hospital and a doctor in Whataroa. Be sure to stock up in advance.

About 31km (20 miles) south of Hokitika is the historic little town of **Ross,** well worth a drive over from Hokitika or a stop on your way to Franz Josef Glacier. Look for the information center in a restored miner's cabin.

At **Whataroa,** located 35km (21.7 miles) north of Franz Joseph, you'll find New Zealand's only *kotuku* (white heron) colony. ✪ **White Heron Sanctuary Tours,** Box 19, Whataroa (☎ 03/753-4120), makes trips on Okarito Lagoon to see the colony. This 2-hour trip starts in Whataroa where you take a 40-minute jet boat ride to the herons; then there is a short walk along a boardwalk through native bush to a hide for bird viewing. Royal spoonbills and fur seals are often also seen. Nesting season is November to February. This trip, which includes a minibus transfer to the waterfront, costs NZ$75 (US$52.50) per person. The great scenery is a bonus.

Okarito Lagoon is also a good place for **canoeing.** Ian and Debbie at **Okarito Nature Tours** (☎ 03/753-4014) can set you up with the necessary equipment. They can also tell you about the 3-mile **coastal walk.** If golf is more your style, **Whataroa Golf Club** charges NZ$5 (US$3.50) for nine holes; clubs are available for hire.

WHERE TO STAY ALONG THE WAY

✪ Matai Lodge Farmstay

P.O. Box 23, Whataroa. 3.5km (2 miles) out of Whataroa. ☎ and fax **03/753-4156.** 3 rms (2 with bathrm). NZ$50 (US$35) per person. Rate includes breakfast. Three-course dinner with wine NZ$25 (US$17.50) per person. No credit cards.

Located on 350 acres, Glenice and Jim Purcell's contemporary home overlooks sheep and cows grazing in surrounding paddocks. I'm grateful to reader Joseph Seminara of Los Altos, California, for telling me about Matai Lodge. He wrote: "My daughter and I had a great time visiting the Purcells—they embraced us like family from the moment we arrived to our reluctant departure. The accommodations were splendid and the meal that they prepared was the best that we enjoyed. It's perfectly situated to access the glaciers and is very reasonably priced—we plan to return soon."

I couldn't agree more. Staying here is a real treat. People like Glenice and Jim are the heart and soul of New Zealand—warm, open, and hospitable. They raised eight

---

Impressions

Far South Westland is as remote from the settled centres of New Zealand as one can reach; its extent is vast enough to test all the powers of the body and the imagination. Set between sky-propping peaks of the alps and the vast emptiness of the western seas are forests and lakes, rivers and seashores, as beautiful, as mysterious, as rich in elemental spirit as any left on earth.

—West Coast poet Peter Hooper

children and have 17 grandchildren. Glenice is an expert at woolcrafts (spinning, felting, knitting, and weaving) and reminds me of my Aunt Mable (which is a compliment of the greatest magnitude). Jim will take guests out to see the sheep and cows. The views over the farmland are lovely. Two of the bedrooms are upstairs and share a bathroom, but they leave one room empty unless they're both occupied by people traveling together. I was delighted that we were in the downstairs bedroom where there is a spa tub in the bathroom.

Next stop is Franz Josef, 112km (69 miles) down the road. As soon as you get there, pick up a copy of the *World Heritage Highway Guide—South Westland & Haast Pass* published by the Department of Conservation. It provides details of points of interest along the way, including many walking tracks. The guide covers the area from Whataroa to Haast Pass.

6 Franz Josef & Fox Glaciers

Franz Josef: 188km (117 miles) south of Greymouth

Glaciers are pretty impressive regardless of where you happen to experience them. What makes the Fox and Franz Josef glaciers so unforgettable (and this is sure to be one of your most memorable New Zealand experiences) is that they reach such low altitudes: sometimes 1,000 feet above sea level. Plus, they're framed by valley walls of deep-green bush until they terminate near luxuriant rain forests. Nowhere else in the world outside arctic regions do glaciers go so low. Fox is the longer of the two glaciers and has a more gradual slope.

On equal footing with your memories of these giant rivers of ice, however, will be those of the sunsets in this part of the country. Julius von Haast, the first European to explore this region, wrote of the sunsets, "New changes were every moment effected, the shades grew longer and darker, and whilst the lower portion already lay in the deep purple shade, the summits were still shining with an intense rosy hue." If you take the time to walk around Lake Matheson, you'll also have special memories of the reflections of Mt. Tasman and Mt. Cook on the surface of the lake.

The small townships of Franz Josef and Fox Glacier are only 24km (15 miles) apart, about a 30-minute drive.

The two glaciers are only a small part of the 284,000-acre **Westland National Park,** an impressive park of high mountain peaks, glacial lakes, and rushing rivers. The park is popular for tramping, mountain climbing, fishing, canoeing, hunting, and horse trekking. In 1990, the combined Mount Cook/Westland National Parks, Fiordland National Park, Mount Aspiring National Park, and all the significant intervening and adjacent natural areas were incorporated into a single vast **Southwest New Zealand World Heritage Area (Te Wahipounamu)** that contains about 10% of New Zealand's total land area or 2.6 million hectares (6.4 million acres). The World Heritage Highway traverses the northern third of this region and is largely confined to the West Coast side of the Main Divide.

ESSENTIALS
GETTING THERE
BY COACH (BUS) **InterCity** provides transportation to the glaciers.

BY ALTERNATIVE COACH (BUS) Both **Magic Travellers** and **Kiwi Experience** include the glaciers on their itineraries.

BY CAR The **World Heritage Highway** (Highway 6) follows the coast from Whataroa to Franz Josef Glacier to Fox Glacier to Haast and over the Haast Pass. The

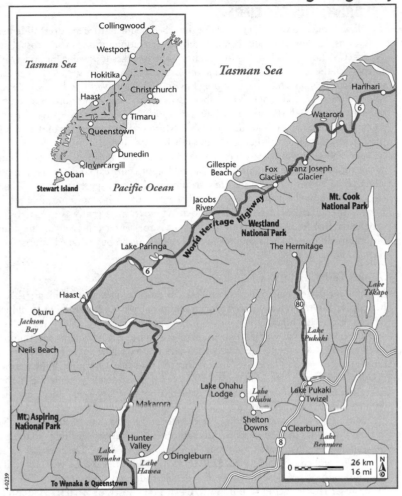

Department of Conservation's *World Heritage Highway Guide* provides ideas for places to stop along the way.

GETTING AROUND

There is sometimes taxi service available (ask locally about telephone numbers). Bike hire is available in both townships. For travel between the two townships, InterCity coaches provide once a day drop-off service year round. Mopeds can be hired at Franz Josef.

VISITOR INFORMATION

There are **visitor centers** at both glacier townships; **Franz Josef Visitor Centre,** Westland National Park, SH6, P.O. Box 14 (☎ 03/752-0796); and **Fox Glacier Visitor Centre,** Westland National Park, SH6, P.O. Box 9 9 (☎ 03/751-0807). Their displays, literature on the park, and visitor activities are essential to a full appreciation of the area. The center at Franz Josef has slightly more extensive displays.

EXPLORING THE GLACIERS

Check with the two visitor centers about the schedule for **nature lectures, slide presentations,** and **guided walks** conducted by conservation officers. These cost about NZ$4 (US$2.60) per adult, less for children, which makes it possible for budgeteers to enjoy all the park has to offer with a minimal effect on the pocketbook. They also administer the alpine huts and tramping huts available for overnight hikers and keep track of trampers and mountain climbers (you must check conditions and register your intentions with the officers before setting out). The center's displays give you a complete rundown on how the glaciers were formed, the movement of the ice, the mountains, the history of the region, and much, much more.

Your sightseeing at the glaciers can be as costly or as inexpensive as your budget dictates. There are, it must be said, several sightseeing experiences that can put a large hole in that budget—and they are among the most spectacular travel experiences in the world, worth every cent of their cost. Yet it's quite possible to enjoy Mother Nature's free display and leave with an equally soul-satisfying experience that has cost you nothing. Either visitor center can give you literature outlining self-guided walks, and for just pennies, you can buy detailed information sheets on each of these.

GLACIER TRIPS

Now, about those glacier experiences. You can do three very special things: Take a **helicopter flight,** go for a guided **glacier walk,** or go for a **heli-hike** (a combined helicopter ride and hike).

The choice of what you do may not turn out to be as agonizing as you think—weather can make it for you. The weather is very unpredictable, and especially if your time is short, my best advice is to take the first trip available. Of course, if the weather is fine, it's agonizing time again (flights are more likely to operate in winter). But even if weather really closes in and neither is available, not to worry—you'll have another opportunity to flightsee at Mount Cook.

There are more operators offering glacier hikes and flights than listed here, but I've selected those with the best safety records and prices. ✪ **Helicopter flights** to the glaciers, including those that make a snow landing, happen daily. The trips last 12 to 40 minutes and cost NZ$80 to NZ$230 (US$56 to $161). Take my word for it, it's a thrilling way to get close to nature. For details and reservations, contact **Fox and Franz Josef Heliservices** (☎ **03/752-0764** in Franz Josef, or ☎ **03/751-0866** in Fox Glacier) or **Glacier Helicopters,** Main Road, Franz Josef (☎ **03/752-0755,** fax 03/752-0778), or Main Road, Fox Glacier (☎ **03/741-0803**).

There's another great way to experience Fox Glacier that's far less expensive than the flights and—in my opinion—actually complements them. That's the **glacier walk,** with an expert guiding you along the surface of the ice. If you're in good shape, you'll be able to do the walk, regardless of age. Guides chip steps in the ice, which, during warm weather, is granular instead of glass-slick. You'll go up into the ice fall, walk among the crevasses, and listen to the deep-throated grumble of the moving glacier. Hobnailed boots, a waterproof parka, heavy socks, and a walking stick are provided. And the walk proceeds regardless of the weather. The cost of the 3 to 4-hour trip offered by Alpine Guides (see below) is NZ$39 (US$27.30) for adults and NZ$26 (US$18.20) for children.

Also at Fox, in addition to a glacier walk, there's a half-day ✪ **heli-hike.** You fly by helicopter to about 1km (½ mile) up the glacier and walk to Victoria Falls before being picked up. All equipment is provided. This requires less fitness than the glacier walk but still isn't for weaklings. The cost of the heli-hike is NZ$165

(US$116) per person. Other tours, including a terminal face walk, a full-day glacier walk, and overnights, are offered.

For details on the heli-hike and glacier walk described above, contact **Alpine Guides (Westland) Ltd.,** P.O. Box 38, Fox Glacier (☎ **03/751-0825,** fax 03/751-0857; e-mail foxguides@minidata.co.nz).

If you're reading this book at home and the glaciers have you hooked, or if you were hooked already and are coming to New Zealand primarily to spend time at the glaciers, you might like to know that Alpine Guides also offers several **mountaineering courses,** varying in length from 1 day to 2 weeks or more. These are the guides who conduct the walks just described (check with them for schedules and prices), and their experience covers mountain and ice climbing from the Himalayas to Antarctica. Write ahead for details on physical requirements, enrollment, and prices.

WHAT TO SEE & DO BEYOND THE GLACIERS
LAKE MATHESON & LAKE MAPOURIKA

Lake Matheson, 5km (3 miles) from Fox Glacier township, shows up on all the postcards, but what the pretty pictures don't show is the wonderful **Lake Matheson Walk,** an easy track around the lake, which takes about 1 1/2 hours. If you've got the time, bring a journal to write in or a book to read and pause on the jetty at the lake's edge, or put lunch in your day pack and eat at one of the sitting places provided along the way. There are great views of Mt. Cook (on the right) and Mt. Tasman (to the left), a wonderful array of ferns and mosses, a podocarp forest (including rimu trees), and the lake itself. When the air is still the lake provides a perfect mirror image of the mountains. If you didn't bring something to eat, you might consider stopping at **Cafe Lake Matheson,** right at the carpark where the walk starts. The cafe is open daily from 7am to 5pm and the view is great.

Lake Mapourika, 9km (5 1/2 miles) north of Franz Josef, the largest lake in Westland National Park, deserves attention for its own arresting reflections and setting. You can swim and fish in the lake as well.

IN FRANZ JOSEF

In Franz Josef township, take a few minutes to visit **St. James Anglican Church,** the Tudor-style church whose east window frames a spectacular alpine view behind the altar. Watch for the sign just south of the visitor center. If you'd like to do an hour-long **hike,** follow the sign opposite St. James Church and you're on your way.

If you managed to miss the **glowworm dells** in Waitomo or Hokitika, you can at least get the idea, on a smaller scale, in Franz Josef. Day or night, follow the sign-and rock-lined path to the helipad (it's across the street from the gas station). The path will tunnel through some trees and lead you down 11 steps to where you see the roots of a tree overhanging the path at a height of about 4 feet. Stoop down and take a peak—it's like looking at a starry night in an underground world.

Author's note: Sand flies and mossies abound in this area, so be sure to bring and use repellent. Also consider bringing hydrocortisone ointment or something else to relieve the itch in the event you are unlucky enough to be bitten.

AFFORDABLE ACCOMMODATIONS

During peak season, accommodations are woefully short in these parts. My best advice is to book well ahead for this popular section of the West Coast or travel outside of the summer months. You can experience the glaciers without staying overnight in Fox or Franz Josef townships, but the advantage of sleeping here is being close enough to jump on flights when there's a break in the weather.

The rates listed below include 12.5% GST and free parking.

IN FRANZ JOSEF
Campgrounds & Cabins

The **⊕ Franz Josef Holiday Park,** on the main road (☎ and fax **03/752-0766**), is set in attractive grounds of bush and hills. There are tent sites, powered sites, and eight basic cabins sleeping two to four people on bunks, all with good, comfortable mattresses. The 24-room lodge has private bedrooms, each with hot and cold running water, central heating, and internal access to shared baths and kitchens. The bedrooms sleep two to five people, and there are family rooms. Four tourist cabins, sleeping two to five, have hot and cold running water, stoves, refrigerators, crockery, cutlery, cookware, blankets, and heaters. Three tourist flats sleep two to four people, all with kitchens, showers, toilets, blankets, and heaters. Other facilities include kitchens with microwaves, showers, an automatic laundry, a TV, a recreation room, a barbecue, and a children's playground. Bedding can be rented, and there's a bus stop near the entrance. Dormitory bunks are NZ$13.50 (US$9.50), cabins are NZ$35 (US$24.50) for two people (additional people are charged NZ$14/US$9.80), and lodge rooms are NZ$17 (US$11.90). Tourist flats run NZ$59 (US$41.30) for two, plus NZ$14 (US$9.80) for each additional person. Tent sites cost NZ$9.50 (US$6.70) per person.

Super-Cheap Sleeps
Franz Josef YHA Hostel

2–4 Cron St. (P.O. Box 12), Franz Josef. ☎ and fax **03/752-0754.** 60 beds in 15 rms (none with bathrm). NZ$18 (US$12.60) per person double or twin; NZ$16 (US$11.20) dorm bed for members. Nonmembers add NZ$4 (US$28). MC, V.

This modern hostel, with a spacious kitchen, new owners, and 60 beds in 15 rooms, is convenient to shops and the bus stop in the town center and close to the rain forest. Double and family rooms are available; all rooms have heaters and quilts. Facilities include TV and video, a laundry and drying room, a hostel shop, bikes, and a pool table. Advance reservations are always advisable, especially November to April and during holiday periods.

For a Few Extra Bucks
⊕ Glacier Gateway Motor Lodge

State Hwy. 6 (P.O. Box 1), Franz Josef. ☎ and fax **03/752-0776.** 23 units (all with bathrm). TV TEL. NZ$98 (US$68.60) double. Additional person NZ$15 (US$10.50) extra. AE, DC, MC, V.

Micky and Hamish Anerson's attractive motel, totally refurbished in 1994, has studios, plus some units that sleep up to six; two have spa baths. The facilities include a spa pool, sauna, guest laundry, and children's playground. There's also off-street parking. It's located on the outskirts of the township, just south of the bridge, opposite Glacier Access Road. Cooked or continental breakfasts are available. No smoking is permitted inside.

Glacier View Motel

State Hwy. 6, (P.O. Box 22), Franz Josef. ☎ **03/752-0705.** Fax 03/752-0761. 14 units (all with bathrm). TV TEL. NZ$85 (US$59.50) one-bedroom unit for 2; NZ$95 (US$67) two-bedroom unit for 2. Additional person NZ$12 (US$8.40) extra. AE, BC, DC, MC, V.

There's a small shop on the premises here, plus a spa pool in a natural setting. The hosts offer courtesy transfers to the bus stop, and breakfasts are available. The neat and tidy motel is 2km (1¼ miles) north of the township.

Worth a Splurge
✪ Westwood Lodge
State Highway 6 (P.O. Box 37), Franz Josef. ☎ and fax **03/752-0111**. 6 rms (all with bathrm). TV. NZ$145 (US$10.20) double. Rate includes cooked or continental breakfast. Lower winter rates April–May and July–Sept. MC, V. Closed mid-May–mid-July.

Staying at Westwood Lodge is like being in a big log cabin, but with all the modern amenities and wall-to-wall carpeting. It is located 1.6km (1 mile) north of the town center and was built in 1994 by helpful hosts Annette and Peter Gardiner to cater to a maximum of 12 guests. All rooms are decorated in colonial style and have wood-paneled walls; half have views of the mountains, and one is outfitted for visitors with disabilities. There's a great view of the mountains from the lounge. A full-size billiard table sits in a separate room. Smoking is not permitted anywhere in this very attractive property.

IN FOX GLACIER
Campgrounds & Cabins
About one-half km (one-quarter mile) from Fox Glacier township, you'll find the **Fox Glacier Motor Park** (☎ **03/751-0821,** fax 03/751-0813), with six motel units, four tourist flats, 20 cabins, 14 lodge cabins, a backpacker's bunkhouse, 65 tent sites, and 65 powered sites. There are two kitchen blocks with dining rooms, three shower blocks, and a coin-operated laundry. Linens may be rented, and canned and frozen goods are available at the camp store. Double-occupancy rates are NZ$17 (US$11.90) for tent sites, NZ$20 (US$14) for caravan sites, NZ$32 (US$22.40) for cabins, NZ$36 (US$25.20) for lodge rooms, and NZ$54 (US$37.80) for tourist flats. A bed in the bunkhouse is NZ$12 (US$8.40). American Express, Bankcard, Diners Club, MasterCard, and Visa are accepted.

Moderately Priced Options
A1 Motel
Lake Matheson Rd. (P.O. Box 29), Fox Glacier. ☎ **03/751-0804**. Fax 03/751-0706. 10 units (all with bathrm). TV TEL. NZ$80 (US$56) double. Additional person NZ$15 (US$10.50) extra. AE, BC, DC, MC, V. Courtesy pickup.

This motel sits in a valley about 2km (1 mile) from the township down Lake Matheson Road. The units, nicely designed and attractively furnished, sleep two to five. Other amenities include a laundry, barbecue facilities, a swimming pool, a nine-hole putting green, a squash court, a spa pool, and a children's playground. A continental breakfast is available.

The Homestead
P.O. Box 25, Fox Glacier. ☎ **03/751-0835**. Fax 03/751-0805. 3 rms (2 with bathrm). NZ$85–$95 (US$59.50–67) double. Rates include continental breakfast; cooked breakfast NZ$2 (US$1.40) extra. No credit cards.

Noeleen and Kevin Williams welcome guests to their 820-hectare (2,000-acre) farm that Kevin's grandfather started in 1890. The house dates from 1896 and is decorated with an odd mix of heirloom and inexpensive pieces. Chances are, however, that you'll be too busy walking on glaciers and hopping on helicopters to pay much attention to the decor. The breakfast here is very good and includes homemade jam, yogurt, marmalade, muesli, and especially tasty tea. Guests enjoy the wonderful views of farmland at breakfast—the property is home to 1,500 sheep and 330 head of beef—and Noeleen keeps binoculars handy for birders. She's very chatty and helpful. Stay here only if you have a rental car; it's located 1km from the town center (.5km off the road and .5km from town).

☺ Rainforest Motel

Cook Flat Rd., Fox Glacier. ☎ **0800/520-000** in New Zealand, or 03/751-0140. Fax 03/751-0141. 8 units (all with bathrm). TV TEL. NZ$80 (US$56) double. Additional person NZ$15 (US$10.50). Breakfast available. AE, DC, MC, V.

Kevin and Rachael Sullivan are the hosts at this modern, new motel. All of the units are clean and spacious, and have sitting areas and twin or queen beds. Full kitchens always provide an opportunity to save money, but they are especially handy here because there aren't many places to eat in the area. This motel is convenient to town and within walking distance of area activities. There are views of both Mt. Cook and Mt. Tasman. The good-value rate quoted above also includes parking right outside your door and laundry facilities on the premises.

GREAT DEALS ON DINING

There aren't a whole lot of places to eat in either Franz Josef or Fox Glacier townships; in fact, this may be where you do the most home cooking on your tour of New Zealand. If you do choose to dine out, the following options are quite good.

IN FRANZ JOSEF

A good place to stock up on groceries is **Fern Grove Food Centre,** Main Rd., Franz Josef (☎ **03/752-0731**). The **Blue Ice Cafe,** Main Rd., Franz Josef (☎ **03/752-0707**) serves pizza and is fully licensed.

Cheeky Kea Cafe

Main Road, Franz Joseph (P.O. Box 56), South Westland. ☎ and fax **03/752-0139.** Reservations not necessary. Main courses NZ$9.50–$16 (US$6.70–$11.20). AE, DC, MC, V. Daily 7am–8:30pm summer, 7:30am–7:30pm winter. NEW ZEALAND.

This cafe's theme is developed around the kea, a native mountain parrot that is notoriously cheeky or bold. Breakfast is served daily from opening until 5:30pm when dinner service starts; lunch is from 11:30am to 2:30pm. Their light menu includes sandwiches, pies, fried chicken, and burgers. For dinner you might like the roast of the day (lamb, pork, or chicken—two of which are prepared daily) served with five vegetables; a porterhouse steak; or pork chops and applesauce. This is a popular spot among families, and it's BYO.

IN FOX GLACIER

The **Fox Glacier General Store,** Main Road, Fox Glacier (☎ **03/751-0829**), sells foodstuffs, hot meat pies, and sandwiches right along with camping supplies, hardware, boots, heavy jackets, and polyester shirts.

Cook Saddle Cafe and Saloon

Main Rd., State Hwy. 6 (Box 29), Fox Glacier. ☎ **03/751-0700.** Fax 03/751-0809. Reservations not accepted. Main courses NZ$12.50–$22.50 (US$8.80–$15.80). AC, MC, V. Daily 11am–9pm winter, 10am–10pm summer. NEW ZEALAND/TEX-MEX.

It's a little weird to find Tex-Mex in South Westland, New Zealand, but here it is. "The owner is Canadian"—that's the answer I got when I asked "why?" It was hardly an explanation, but it was too noisy to keep talking. The bar here is popular with young backpackers and they keep the tempo lively—sometimes even loud. Main courses include pecos pasta, venison burgers, ponderosa pizza, coyote calamari, and saddle bag salmon. This is one of the few places in the area that's open daily for dinner year-round.

Hobnail Café

In the Alpine Guides Bldg., Main Rd. (Hwy. 6), Fox Glacier. ☎ **03/751-0825.** Fax 03/751-0857. Dinner main courses NZ$10.50–$23.50 (US$7.40–$16.50). MC, V. Daily 8am–9:30pm. MODERN NEW ZEALAND.

This is a popular spot because the glacier walks as well as helicopter flights are booked at a counter just steps away. Lunch is cafe fare: soup, muffins, and sandwiches. Dinner items include spinach and ricotta lasagna, chicken breast in cashew crust pan-fried and served with apricot salsa, and venison steak with grilled chili bananas and tomatoes. Like everything else on the West Coast, this is a casual place.

EN ROUTE TO HAAST

During my last trip, I found that the roads on the West Coast have been greatly improved—probably because of the World Heritage designation. Along with the good walking tracks, view points, and signage, they make traveling here a real pleasure.

Between Fox Glacier and Haast there are a couple of cute places to stop for lunch or tea. About an hour out (62km/38 miles) you will come upon **Salmon Farm Cafe,** State Highway 6, South Westland (☎ **03/751-0837**). As you might guess, salmon is the specialty here. They raise it on the premises, and it's available fresh or smoked. The cafe is open daily from 7am to 7pm. Another good place is located 70km (43 miles) south of Fox Glacier. **Lake Paringa Café,** State Highway 6, South Westland (☎ and fax **03/751-0110**), is an appealing eatery with fresh sandwiches and afternoon tea treats. Lake Paringa Café is open daily during the summer from 8am to 8pm, with shorter off-season hours, and closed during June and July.

South of the Lake Paringa Cafe, the bodacious ☼ **Knight's Point View Point** affords a wide view of sandy coves, rocky headlands, and ocean as far as the eye can see. The abrupt hillsides and dense vegetation mean that fur seals and penguins have the coast pretty much to themselves. Anyone who's ever driven along Northern California's beautiful Big Sur coastline is bound to experience a sense of déjà vu here.

HAAST

Haast is 121km (75 miles) south of Fox Glacier. The **South Westland World Heritage Visitor Centre,** situated on the junction of State Highway 6 and Jackson Bay Road, P.O. Box 50, Haast (☎ **03/750-0809,** fax 03/750-0832), is certainly one of the best in the country. Allow no less than 30 minutes to view the exhibits—longer if you can spare the time. The center is open daily from 8:30am; mid-April to early November it closes at 4:30pm, early November to December 25 and February 7 to mid-April it closes at 6pm, and December 26 to February 6 it closes at 7pm.

EN ROUTE TO WANAKA

The Haast Pass used to be one of the most treacherous roads in the country, but now I think it's one of New Zealand's best highways. Completely paved since 1995, the road follows the course of the Haast River as it flows toward the sea. Along the way the Department of Conservation has created bushwalks ranging from 2 minutes to several hours. These walks provide a chance to explore the river, streams, and bushland along the road. At the top of the pass the verdant terrain of Westland changes dramatically to the dry, barren hills and mountains typical of the Otago Region—the driest part of New Zealand. If you drive straight through, the trip from Haast to Wanaka will take about 2 hours, but I *really* recommend stopping to walk or picnic while you soak up the scenery. Remember, however, that sand flies are prevalent throughout this area, so you'll need to keep insect repellent handy.

Before this road was built, the only passage from east to west was an old bridle path, and at the very top of the Haast Pass there's a signpost that will point you to that path, a pretty walk back into the past. The road itself took 40 years to build, and in fact work still goes on in sections as rock slides occur. At 1,847 feet above sea level, the Haast Pass is actually the lowest pass through the Southern Alps, very seldom blocked by snow, but peaks on either side rise as high as 10,000 feet.

7 Wanaka: Gateway to Mt. Aspiring National Park

117km (72.5 miles) N of Queenstown; 145km (90 miles) S of Haast

Pretty Lake Wanaka is surrounded by the dry, barren mountains that are typical of the Otago region and reminiscent of Southern California. The Southern Alps catch the rain and keep it on the consequently green West Coast. Here you've got a good chance of finding sunny skies.

Many people say Wanaka is Queenstown 20 years ago, before it became touristy, as this town of 2,500 is not a stop on package tours and more than 50% of visitors are New Zealanders. You could conceivably stay in Wanaka and do many of the same outdoor activities offered in Queenstown—the difference being that here most businesses are owner-operated, so whether you go rafting or jet boating, you'll be with the boss.

ESSENTIALS
GETTING THERE
BY PLANE   Aspiring Air (☎ 0800/100-943 in New Zealand, or 03/443-7943) has three flights a day from Queenstown.

BY COACH (BUS)   InterCity provides coach service to Wanaka.

BY ALTERNATIVE COACH (BUS)   Kiwi Experience and **Magic Travellers** both include Wanaka on their routes.

BY CAR   Wanaka is reached via the **Haast Pass** from the north. Highway 6 connects the town with Cromwell and Queenstown to the south. Highway 89 is a more direct route from Wanaka to Queenstown, but rental cars are not permitted on this narrow, windy road.

VISITOR INFORMATION
The **Wanaka Visitor Information Centre,** located on Ardmore St., P.O. Box 147, Wanaka ☎ **03/443-1233**, fax 03/443-9238, e-mail wkavin@nzhost.co.nz or wpa@wanaka.co.nz), can provide you with information about local activities. Check out their Web site: www.wanaka.co.nz. **Mount Aspiring National Park** has its park headquarters in Wanaka, although the park is some 45km (27 miles) to the northwest. If you plan to spend time here, drop by the **Mount Aspiring National Park Visitor Centre** on the corner of Ballantyne Road and Highway 89 (☎ **03/443-7660,** fax 03/443-8776) for information on park activities. The **telephone area code** (STD) for Wanaka is **03.**

SPECIAL EVENTS
Warbirds Over Wanaka is a biannual air show, held over Easter weekend, that features airplanes from the New Zealand Fighter Pilots Museum. Contact the museum at ☎ **03/443-7010** for more information.

Wanaka Winter Wonderland takes place in Wanaka and at Treble Cone Ski Field. Events during this winter carnival include the Rip Curl Heli Challenge, the Merrell Classic Telemark Race, the ETA Ripples NZ Extreme Snowboarding

Challenge, the NZFSA Mogul Tour, the Cardrona Snowboard Cup, and the Virgin Vodka NZ Snowboard Masters. The Wonderland runs from late June through early October. Call ☎ **03/443-1233** for details.

EXPLORING WANAKA: WHAT TO SEE & DO

Feel like getting lost and found—and totally bewildered!—in Wanaka? Head for ✪ **Stuart Landsborough's Puzzling World** on Highway 89, 2km (1 mile) from Wanaka (☎ **03/443-7489**). Behind tall fences are pathways that lead somewhere and passageways that lead nowhere. The fun comes in finding your way through without becoming hopelessly lost. But there's *much* more to this unique place that has been some 21 years in the making, including a display of holograms and an exhibition of illusion pictures. Take my word for it, adults and youngsters will be intrigued and entertained. A tilted house is the most recent addition. Admission is NZ$6 (US$4.20) for adults, NZ$3.50 (US$2.50) for children. They accept American Express and Visa. There's no admission charge to two rooms where you can sit and work puzzles—a good rainy-day activity.

If World War I and II fighter planes are your passion, you'll love the **New Zealand Fighter Pilots Museum,** 10km (6.2 miles) southwest of Wanaka, P.O. Box 218, Wanaka (☎ **03/443-7010,** fax 03/443-7011, Web site nzfpm.dcc.govt.nz/nzfpm/ nzfpm.htm, e-mail ibrodie@nzfpm.co.nz). The museum was established in 1993 to honor and record the history of New Zealand Fighter Pilots and their crews and to educate the public about their history. The museum achieves this through static displays, airplanes (from Great Britain, the USA, Germany, Japan, and Russia), wartime film footage (which is shown in the briefing room), models, and personal memorabilia. During summer months restored fighters take to the air. Check out the Web site for a list of planes and restoration projects. Admission is NZ$6 (US$4.20) for adults and NZ$2 (US$1.40) for children; it's open daily from 9:30am to 4pm.

OUTDOOR ACTIVITIES

ECORAFTING This is *not* white-water rafting; the emphasis is more on scenic and environmental pleasure. From September to April, **Pioneer Rafting,** P.O. Box 124, Wanaka (☎ **03/443-1246**), conducts half- and full-day excursions down the Upper Clutha. During your trip a guide explains the local birds, plants, and ecology of the river; you'll pan for gold, swim, and relax. This is a great excursion for less active people. Longer raft-camping trips are available.

HORSE RIDING For half-, full-day, and overnight horse treks contact **Backcountry Saddle Expeditions,** R.D. 1, Cardrona Valley, Wanaka (☎ **03/ 443-8151,** fax 03/443-1712). The half-day trek lasts 2 hours and costs NZ$45 (US$31.50) for adults, NZ$30 (US$21) for children. They're located 25km (15.5 miles) south of Wanaka off Highway 89.

KAYAKING **Alpine River Guides,** 99 Ardmore St., P.O. Box 9, Wanaka (☎ **03/ 443-9422**), offers a number of 1-day adventures with varying degrees of difficulty (from beginner to expert). Trips run daily October through April to Matukituki Valley, Makarora River, Hawea River, and Upper Clutha River. Trips include equipment, lessons, and lunch.

MOUNTAIN BIKING This is a popular activity in the area. If you want to do it alone you can hire a bike from **Lakeland Adventures,** the Main Wharf, Ardmore St., Wanaka (☎ **03/443-7495,** fax 03/443-1323). **Alpine Mountain Biking,** (☎ **03/443-8943** or 025/331-714) conducts guided half- or full-day, overnight, and heli-biking trips.

SKIING   **Cardrona Ski Field** is 40 minutes from Wanaka on Highway 89. The more challenging Treble Cone ski field is also about 40 minutes away. In addition to downhill skiing, cross-country skiing and heli-skiing into the Harris Mountains are available. For information on these two places, see chapter 4, "The Active Vacation Planner."

WALKING   Make the 1-day trek to **Rob Roy Glacier** in Mt. Aspiring National Park, which offers a view of the glacier. This bushwalk takes about 5 hours return (round-trip) and can be done independently at no charge. **Edgewater Adventures** (☎ and fax **03/443-8311,** fax 03/443-8422) offers a guided version for NZ$215 (US$151) per person as well as other half-day to multiday treks.

At **Diamond Lake,** 20 minutes from town, you'll find a number of short walks. It's a 40-minute return to the viewing platform and 2^1/$_2$ hours back to Rocky Hill.

FOR SERIOUS THRILL-SEEKERS

CANYONING   Wanaka is the only place in New Zealand where you can go canyoning. No experience is necessary, just a sense of adventure and a high level of fitness. **Deep Canyoning Experience,** P.O. Box 101, Wanaka (☎ **03/443-7922**), will supply all equipment and take you on a full-day adventure, which includes a canyon descent and exploration, wild toboggan rides, swimming, and abseiling for NZ$145 (US$102) per person.

JET BOATING   For jet boating with an eco-slant, contact **Jet Boat Charters** (☎ **03/443-8408,** fax 03/443-8403). Ernie will take you on the Matukituki River for 3^1/$_2$ hours or the Clutha River for 2^1/$_2$ hours; the cost is NZ$75 and NZ$65 (US$52.50 and US$45.50), respectively, for adults; children 5 to 13 pay NZ$35 (US$24.50); kids under 5 are free. Trips emphasize scenery and points of interest, not just thrills.

ROCK CLIMBING   For rock climbing, contact **Mount Aspiring Guides,** 99 Ardmore St., P.O. Box 345, Wanaka (☎ **03/443-9422,** fax 03/443-8589).

AFFORDABLE ACCOMMODATIONS
SUPER-CHEAP SLEEPS

In addition to the hostel listed below, you might be interested in **Wanaka Bakpaka,** 117 Lakeside Rd., Wanaka (☎ **03/443-7837,** fax 03/443-7837).

YHA Hostel

181 Upton St., Wanaka. ☎ **03/443-7405.** 35 beds in 10 rms. NZ$17 (US$11.90) per person double or twin; NZ$15 (US$10.50) dorm bed for members. Nonmembers add NZ$4 (US$2.80). MC, V.

This hostel is well located for activities on the lake and skiing at Treble Cone or Cardrona or activities in Mount Aspiring National Park. The hostel offers bike-storage and ski-tuning facilities.

FOR A FEW EXTRA BUCKS

Aspiring Lodge

Dunmore and Dungarvon sts. ☎ **0800/BOWENS** in New Zealand, or 03/443-7816. Fax 03/443-8914. E-mail aspiring@voyager.co.nz. 11 studios, 2 family units, 2 suites (all with bath). TV TEL. NZ$95 (US$67) double, extra person NZ$15 (US$10.50). Lower rates April through June. AE, DC, MC, V.

Thanks to reader Deborah Brudno of Washington, D.C., who clued me in on this motel near the lake. Units here have panoramic lake and mountain views. All rooms are very clean and have minikitchens, nice comforters, ski racks, and a queen bed or

Cliffords Hotel, Ardmore St., Wanaka (☎ 03/443-7826). *"I got a discounted rate and enjoyed a very comfortable room. I was practically frightened out of bed by the spectacular scenery I woke up to."*
—Amelia Conrad, Wilkes, Connecticut, USA.

Archway Motels, Hedditch St., Wanaka. ☎ 03/443-7698. Fax 03/443-8642. *"Our unit with bathroom and kitchen was NZ$65 (US$42.25), and the hostess was very pleasant. The bistro next door has tremendous food—and cheap."*
—Valerie, Stanley, and Renata Vicich, Bateman, Western Australia.

Author's Note: The rate is NZ$68 (US$47.60) studio for two, NZ$75 (US$52.50) double in chalet, NZ$78 (US$54.60) family unit, extra person NZ$12–$15 (US$8.40–$10.50). American Express, Bankcard, Diners Club, Japan Credit Band, MasterCard, and Visa accepted.

---

a queen and a single. Upstairs rooms have pine walls, cathedral ceilings, and balconies; room no. 8 has the best view. Studios sleep up to three; the 2 one-bedroom family units are large and sleep up to six, as does the suite that is equipped for travelers with disabilities. There's no laundry facility on the premises, but a 24-hour Laundromat is nearby. Aspiring Lodge is located 100 meters (108 yards) from the beach and 29km (18 miles) from the ski fields. Breakfast is available. This totally nonsmoking lodge is run by Dave and Maureen Bowen.

✪ Best Western Manuka Crescent Motel

51 Manuka Crescent (off Beacon Point Rd.), Wanaka. ☎ 03/443-7773. Fax 03/443-9066. 10 units (all with bathrm). TV TEL. NZ$65–$90 (US$45.50–$63) double. Additional person NZ$15 (US$10.50) extra. AE, DC, JCB, MC, V. Courtesy car from town.

Set in a residential neighborhood about 2km (1 mile) from town, the Manuka Crescent has views of the mountains in the distance. The units have full kitchens, radios, and parking spaces at the door. Guest laundry, barbecue area, trampoline, and children's play area are additional amentities. In addition to cooked and continental breakfast, there are frozen TV meals available.

✪ Te Wanaka Lodge

23 Brownston St., Wanaka. ☎ 0800/WANAKA (926-252) or 03/443-9224. Fax 03/443-9246. Web site nz.com/webnz/bbnz/wlodge.htm. E-mail tewanakalodge@xtra.co.nz. 12 rms (all with bathrm). TEL. NZ$115 (US$81) double. Rates include breakfast. MC, V.

A sophisticated, European ambience prevails at Te Wanaka Lodge. Rowland and Nora Hastings are the hosts; he's Scottish and a keen fisherman; she's Philippino. The eight queen rooms and four twins are all heated and have electric blankets, heated towel rods, hair dryers, and heated bathroom mirrors that don't fog up when you're showering. The bedrooms are attractive, but what really makes this place special is the shared spaces. There are two cozy lounges—one with TV, one for conversation—a breakfast room, which is also used throughout the day, and a cedar hot tub in the garden. The breakfast buffet includes sliced meat and cheese, fresh dark bread, and fresh croissants. Guests can use the kitchen for making sandwiches or heating takeaway meals, but not for cooking.

GREAT DEALS ON DINING

There are good picnic places and a playground on the lakefront adjacent to the visitor center.

Purple Sage Restaurant and Bar

72 Ardmore St., Wanaka. ☎ **03/443-8269.** Reservations accepted. Main courses NZ$16–$23 (US$11.20–$16.10). AE, MC, V. Daily 5–10pm winter, 6–10:30pm summer. ECLECTIC.

The good food here is the creation of Austrian chef Ewald Truner. Appetizers include Austrian sausage salad, Greek salad, and tempura battered vegetables. Main dishes include Cajun chicken salad, warm smoked salmon, Oriental pork, and chicken-apricot strudel. My husband and I both enjoyed the goulash soup with fresh bread. If you dine here, don't be surprised if your cloth napkin is damp. Ours were and we asked for dry ones only to be told that they always use them damp because the fabric "isn't sufficiently absorbent otherwise." I left mine on the table, but my husband, who is more polite than I am, kept his on his lap, where water soaked through his jeans. It's fully licensed, or you can bring your own spirits.

Ripples

Pembroke Village Mall. ☎ **03/443-7413.** Fax 03/443-7255. Reservations not required. Lunch NZ$3–$14 (US$2.10–$9.80); dinner NZ$15–$40 (US$10.50–$28). AE, DC, JCB, MC, V. Summer, daily noon–2pm and 6–10pm. Winter, Mon–Sat 6–10pm. NEW ZEALAND.

It's hard to say if the setting or the food is more agreeable at this cozy little place in town. In summer, you can dine outside on the veranda with those wonderful views of the mountain in the distance; other times, inside is just as pleasant. The menu offers some truly innovative dishes, and it changes from month to month. A sampling includes pan-fried lamb noisettes dipped in egg and rosemary, wild pork and venison combo, smoked chicken and Camembert triangles wrapped in phyllo pastry, and an avocado, crab, and prawn plate. If you want wine, you can bring your own.

✪ The White House Bar Cafe

33 Dunmore St., Wanaka. ☎ and fax **03/443-9595.** Reservations advisable. Main courses NZ$11–$21 (US$7.70–$14.70). Daily 11am–the last person leaves. ECLECTIC.

People in town said "the white house" when I asked about the best dining spots, but we kept driving up and down the street it was supposed to be on and couldn't find it—just a sign that said "cafe-open." Then in a flash of brilliance we both realized that this cafe was located in a *white house*—so much for the thinking capacity of tired travel writers. The whitewashed house with blue window frames would look more at home in Greece than Wanaka. Happily, fresh local produce is used to create dishes with a Mediterranean feel. The menu, which changes frequently, always has several good vegetarian choices. It may also include baked field mushrooms, steamed mussels, spanikopita, hot or cold pasta, lamb kebab, and roast vegetable salad. It's a nice place to have a drink on the outdoor patio, weather permitting, and in Wanaka it usually does. This is not the least expensive place in town, but easily the best.

Readers Recommend

Relishes Café, 99 Ardmore St., Wanaka. ☎ **03/443-9018.** Fax 03/443-7538. *"We had two of the most memorable meals of this or any other trip here. The food was imaginative and reasonable, the setting was casual. When it came time for dessert we were stuffed, but items interested us; the waitress suggested 'half portions.' We took her up on this and out came two of the largest portions we had ever seen. We managed to finish them and return another night for more!"*

—Deborah Brudno, Washington, D.C., USA.

Author's Note: Dinner main courses are NZ$14–$22 (US$9.80–$15.40). American Express, MasterCard, and Visa are accepted. Open daily 9:30am–3pm and 6:30pm–late.

EN ROUTE TO CARDRONA

The **Cardrona Ski Field** is located on Highway 89 between Wanaka and Queenstown. If your next stop is Queenstown, don't continue on Highway 89; return to Wanaka and take Highway 6.

APRÈS SKI: WHERE TO STAY & EAT

✪ Cardrona Hotel Restaurant and Bar

Hwy. 89, 24km (15 miles) south of Wanaka. ☎ **03/443-8153.** Reservations recommended but not required. Snacks under NZ$10 (US$7); lunch NZ$6–$13.50 (US$4.20–$9.50); dinner NZ$13.50–$16.50 (US$9.50–$11.60). MC, V. Daily 9am–"late." NEW ZEALAND.

Sited at the base of two ski fields, this building was born as an inn back in 1865 at the height of the gold-rush era—it's now primarily a restaurant/bar. The decor is one of hardwood floors, antique oak tables and chairs, and patchwork cushions on the chairs. It has long been one of the area's most popular après-ski spots, where slopes-weary skiers relax with mulled wine before a blazing log fire. In summer there's dining in lovely sheltered gardens. The menu features local lamb, game, and seafood. Fully licensed, the Cardrona also offers accommodations if you want to stay overnight.

EN ROUTE TO QUEENSTOWN

Highway 6 is good traveling all the way. You'll drive alongside artificial **Lake Dunstan,** which was formed behind the **Clyde Dam.** When you get near Cromwell, you'll see lots of roadside stalls selling local fruit. The stone fruit (peaches, plums, apricots, and nectarines) is great from about December through March.

You may want to stop in historic **Arrowtown,** although it's just a short drive back from Queenstown if you're ready to push on to dinner and bed after a long day behind the wheel.

12 Queenstown, Fiordland & Mount Cook

The southwest quarter of the South Island holds some of the country's greatest beauty. Fiordland National Park, with good reason, is included in the South-West New Zealand World Heritage Area (Te Wahipounamu). This region offers peaks and valleys, waterfalls and fiords, and magnificent wilderness terrain. Queenstown is nestled at the foot of mountains, called The Remarkables, on the northeastern shore of Lake Wakatipu, the third largest lake in New Zealand. It's a 86km (53-mile) long, 1,280–foot-deep beauty encased in a glacial bed. The community is an international resort which offers myriad adventure activities as well as scenic beauty.

The shape of Lake Wakatipu vaguely resembles that of a reclining figure with its knees drawn up. Maori legend will tell you that's because at the bottom of the lake lies the heart of a great *tipua* (giant) named Matau, who captured a beautiful girl who caught his fancy and took her back to his mountain home. Her valiant lover, however, came to her rescue and set fire to the giant as he lay sleeping on a bed of fern. As the flames flared higher and higher, fed by the fat from his enormous body, he was suffocated by the smoke and sank deep into the earth to form a vast chasm. Only his heart remained. As the rains fell and mountain snows melted with the heat of the fire, the chasm filled with water to form a lake in the shape of the giant, his knees drawn up in agony. His head, they say, is at Glenorchy, his knees at Queenstown, and his feet at Kingston. His heart beats on from far below, and that, they say, explains the fact that the surface of the lake rises and falls three inches every 5 minutes. Of course, scientists have another explanation—they call the phenomenon seiche action.

Sheepherders were the first settlers in this district, and they endured the onslaught of hundreds of gold miners when the Shotover River, which feeds Lake Wakatipu, was proclaimed "the richest river in the world." The claim was well founded, for as much as £4,000 was dredged by the discoverer of gold in his first 2 months. When the gold played out in fairly short order, the sheep men came into their own once more, and today the Wakatipu district is filled with vast high-country sheep stations, a source of less spectacular, but certainly more reliable, riches. Tourism is also extremely important to the local economy.

Mt. Cook, which the Maori named Aorangi (the cloud piercer), is the highest point in the country. It lies close to the West Coast, but the only road access is from the south.

Queensstown & Fiordland

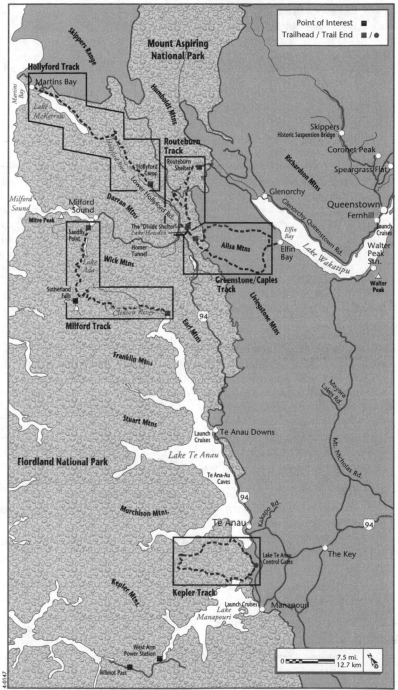

Point of Interest ■
Trailhead / Trail End ■ / ●

Skippers Range

Mount Aspiring
National Park

Hollyford Track

Martins Bay

Lake
McKerrow

Humboldt Mtns

Routeburn
Track

Hollyford Camp

Routeburn
Shelter

Skippers
Historic Suspension Bridge

Coronet Peak

Richardson Mtns

Speargrass Flat

Milford
Sound

Milford
Sound

Darran Mtns

Lower Hollyford Rd.

Glenorchy

Glenorchy Queenstown Rd.

Queenstown

Fernhill

Mitre Peak

Sandfly
Point

The "Divide Shelter
Lake Howden

Homer
Tunnel

Wick Mtns

Lake
Ada

Ailsa Mtns

Elfin
Bay

Elfin
Bay

Lake Wakatipu

Launch
Cruises

Walter
Peak
Stn.

Sutherland
Falls

Clinton River

Greenstone/Caples
Track

Livingstone Mtns

Walter
Peak

Milford Track

Earl Mtns

94

Franklin Mtns

Stuart Mtns

Launch
Cruises

Te Anau Downs

Lake Te Anau

Mavora
Lakes Rd.

Fiordland National Park

Te Ana-Au
Caves

94

Murchison Mtns

Te Anau

Mt. Nicholas Rd.

94

Kakapo Rd.

Lake Te Anau
Control Gates

The Key

Kepler Mtns

Kepler Track

Launch Cruises

Manapouri

Lake
Manapouri

West Arm
Power Station

Wilmot Pass

0   7.5 mi.
     12.7 km

4-0147

315

1 Queenstown

404km (250 miles) SW of Franz Josef; 172km (107 miles) NE of Te Anau; 263km (163 miles) SW of Mount Cook

Chances are your itinerary will include Queenstown. It's on the South Island's "golden triangle" route which also includes Christchurch and Mt. Cook. Personally, I have mixed emotions about this destination. While it's undeniably beautiful, it has also become very touristy and un-Kiwi. The community (population 3,500) has become an international resort—only about 5% of the city's visitors are New Zealanders. Sadly, some of the locals have become a bit jaded, and if you are treated rudely anywhere in New Zealand, it will be here.

If you visit here, you'll find the streets dominated by booking offices for rafting, jet boating, bungy jumping, and the like. In winter this adventurous spirit really gets revved up when skiers, who use the town as a base for the four ski fields in the area, invade the city. But the crowd in ski season is also much more international, giving Queenstown a decidedly cosmopolitan air. The city itself is undeniably beautiful and can still be enjoyable with a little planning. The savvy budget traveler will seek out the quality natural experiences offered here and won't get sucked in by the more pricey thrill seeker's adventures. That must be what the readers of *Travel & Leisure* did: In January 1997, they voted Queenstown No. 3 in the World's Best Cities poll.

The best time to visit, if you want to avoid crowds, is the off season—the period from Easter to the start of ski season (usually early June).

ESSENTIALS
GETTING THERE & GETTING AROUND

BY PLANE There's air service via **Mount Cook Airlines, Air New Zealand Link,** and **Ansett New Zealand** from all major cities in New Zealand. The airport shuttle (☎ **03/442-9803**) runs to and from the airport regularly and will drop you off or pick you up at your hotel for about NZ$5 (US$3.50). A taxi (☎ **03/442-7788**) from the airport to the town center costs about NZ$15 (US$10.50).

BY COACH (BUS) **InterCity** and/or **Mount Cook Landline** run between Queenstown and Christchurch, Dunedin, Fox Glacier, Franz Josef, Invercargill, Milford Sound, Mount Cook, Te Anau, and Wanaka. The InterCity depot is in the Visitor Centre, at the corner of Camp and Shotover streets (☎ **03/442-8238**), and the Mount Cook depot is on Church Street (☎ **03/442-4640**).

The **Shopper Bus** provides transportation to town from outlying lodgings for NZ$2 (US$1.40) each way.

BY ALTERNATIVE COACH (BUS) **Kiwi Experience, Backpackers Express,** and **Magic Traveller** service Queenstown.

BY CAR Queenstown can be reached via Highway 6 and Highway 89, but I don't recommend the latter. It's very narrow and windy; in fact, most rental car companies don't permit their vehicles to travel on this road.

BY TAXI To call a taxi, phone ☎ **03/442-7888** or 03/442-6666.

VISITOR INFORMATION

The **Queenstown Travel & Visitor Centre** in the Clocktower Centre, at Shotover and Camp streets (☎ **03/442-4100**, fax 03/442-8907, e-mail zqnvin@nzhost.co.nz), is open daily from 7am to 7pm during summer and from 7am to 6pm from Easter to the end of October. It sells stamps, sends faxes, operates a currency exchange, and makes reservations for accommodations and activities. The **Mount Cook Line**

Queenstown Travel Centre is at 18A Shotover Street (☎ 03/442-4600, fax 03/442-4605); they are also the agents for Air New Zealand. The **Fiordland Travel Centre** is on the Steamer Wharf, Beach Street, P.O. Box 94, Queenstown (☎ 03/442-7500, fax 03/442-7504). The **Department of Conservation Information Centre,** at 37 Shotover St. (☎ 03/442-7933), is the place to go for information on walking trails, tramping in national parks, and conservation souvenirs.

While at the Travel & Visitor Centre pick up a copy of the **"Queenstown Today and Tonight"** brochure, which lists all current attractions, prices, hours, and reservations details. The free booklet **"Queenstown A to Z"** is also a useful directory for public services, accommodations, restaurants, sightseeing, and a host of other details. It also contains money-saving coupons. Look also for the free tourist newspaper *The Mountain Scene,* available at most accommodations and at the Travel & Visitor Centre. Armed with all that information, your dilemma becomes one of setting priorities.

ON THE WEB   Before you leave home take at look at **Queenstown's** web site at **nz.com/Queenstown**. It contains a wealth of information about the city and links to a number of other good sites. You can also read the brochure mentioned above, "Queenstown A to Z" on the Web at **www.AtoZ-NZ.com/Queenstown**, and print out the discount coupons.

SPECIAL EVENTS   The **Queenstown Winter Festival** is a boisterous, fun-filled celebration of winter, with ski events and street entertainment; it takes place in late June. Call ☎ 03/442-4100 for more details. The **Arrowtown Autumn Festival,** in Arrowtown (20km/12 miles northeast of Queenstown), is a week of market days, miners' band, and street entertainment celebrating the gold-mining era; it takes place the week after Easter. Call ☎ 03/442-4100, or 03/442-1824 for details.

FAST FACTS   The **Thomas Cook Bureau de Change,** in the Mall at Camp Street (☎ 03/442-8600, fax 03/442-9385), is open daily from 8am to 7pm in winter and from 8am to 8pm in summer. The **BNZ Bureau de Change** on Rees Street (☎ 03/442-7325) is open daily from 9am to 8pm.

The **post office** (for Poste Restante mail) is on the corner of Camp and Ballarat streets. The **American Express** representative in Queenstown is located at 59 Beach St. (☎ 03/442-7730).

The **telephone area code** (STD) for Queenstown is **03**.

ORIENTATION

The lakefront is the hub of Queenstown, and the street fronting the sheltered horseshoe bay is **Marine Parade.** On the northern edge, at Beach Street, are the jetty, pier, and wharf. To the south are lovely public gardens. The Mall, reserved for pedestrians only, runs from Rees Street for one bustling block. It's a busy concentration of activity: shops, booking agencies, and restaurants are cheek to jowl.

EXPLORING QUEENSTOWN: WHAT TO SEE & DO

For the best overview of Queenstown, take the ✪ **Skyline Gondola** (☎ 03/442-7860) up to Bob's Peak, and don't forget your camera. The view is breathtaking—especially if you time your trip to coincide with the sun setting on the Remarkables. If you go at lunch or dinner, you can stretch your viewing time by eating at the buffet restaurant or cafe (see "Great Deals on Dining," below). The gondola operates from 10am until the restaurant closes at midnight, with a round-trip fare of NZ$12 (US$8.40). Completely renovated in 1994, the attractive complex now includes several shops and a large viewing platform. If you go up on the half hour, you'll arrive in time to see the thrills-and-spills film *Kiwi Magic,* starring Maori

---

Cheap Thrills: What to See & Do for Free in Queenstown

- **Watching Bungy Jumpers**   If you're not into the real thing, it's fun to see thrill seekers take the plunge off of the Kawarau Gorge Suspension Bridge on Highway 6 north of town. Not only can you share the high vicariously through them, but you can also enjoy the scenic backdrop.
- **Strolling in the Queenstown Gardens**   Take a break from sightseeing or thrill seeking and lollygag through this beautiful 11-acre park, which is right in town. There are also tennis courts, lawn bowls, and a walking track available at no charge, and the park is always open.
- **Driving to Glenorchy**   Get in the car and head out to the Glenorchy Waterfront Reserve on the edge of Lake Wakatipu. It's an ideal place for a picnic, so don't forget to pick up some foodstuffs before you hit the road.
- **Taking in the View from Coronet Peak**   It's worth the drive to this ski area to see the panoramic vista over the Wakatipu Basin. From here, you can sometimes also watch hang gliders descend into the valley below.

---

comedian Billy T. James and American actor Ned Beatty—it's shown on the hour from 10am to 8pm. To feel as if you're in the middle of the action, be it jet boating, tobogganing, or flying in a small plane, sit in the middle of the theater toward the front. Admission is NZ$7 (US$4.90) for adults, NZ$3 (US$2.10) for children 5 to15.

At the base of the gondola ride is the **Kiwi & Birdlife Park** (☎ **03/442-8059**), which several readers have commented isn't worth the NZ$7.50 (US$5.30) admission price.

LAKE CRUISES

A voyage on the 1912 vintage steamship **TSS *Earnslaw,*** Fiordland Travel, Steamer Wharf, P.O. Box 94, Queenstown ☎ **0800/656-503** in New Zealand, or 03/442-7500; fax 03/442-7504), is a perennial favorite. Known affectionately as the "Lady of the Lake," the *Earnslaw,* does a 1-hour midday cruise on Lake Wakatipu, which departs at 12:30pm (NZ$22/US$15.40 for adults, NZ$10/US$7 for children). Moderately priced lunches are available on board. Three-hour morning and afternoon excursions to Walter Peak High Country Farm depart daily at 9am and 2pm, respectively. Once at Walter Peak, you can learn about New Zealand farming life and enjoy complimentary afternoon tea while taking in the wonderful scenery. The cost for adults is NZ$45 (US$31.50) and NZ$10 (US$7) for children. Evening lake cruises depart at 7:30pm and cost NZ$27 (US$18.90) for adults and NZ$10 (US$7) for children. You may also decide to have dinner at Walter Peak. This costs NZ$65 (US$45.50) for adults, half price for children, and includes the lake cruise, a three-course carvery buffet, and a farm tour. If all this isn't confusing enough, there's also a package that combines the lake cruise with a farm tour and horse trek (NZ$95/US$67 for adults and NZ$46/US$32.20 for children).

WINERIES

Three interesting wineries are located in the Queenstown area. They are Gibbston Valley, Chard Farm Vineyard, and Taramea. **Chard Farm** is high above the Kawarau River, on the Cromwell–Queenstown Road which winds through the Kawarau Gorge (the turnup is opposite the bungy jumping area). Keith "Tiger" Thompson, the man in charge, is quite eloquent in his description of their wines. They're open daily from

Central Queenstown

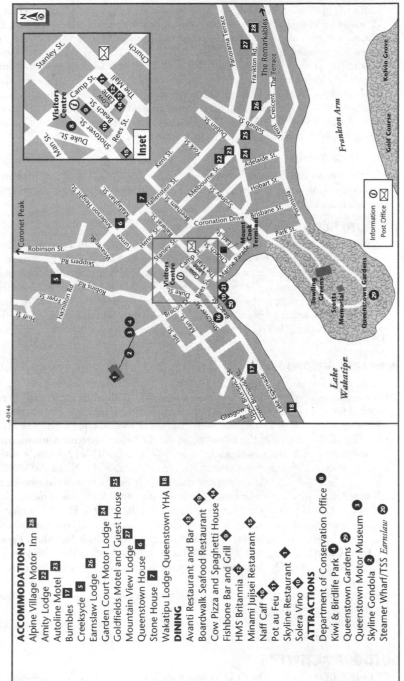

ACCOMMODATIONS

Alpine Village Motor Inn **28**
Amity Lodge **22**
Autoline Motel **23**
Bumbles **17**
Creeksyde **5**
Earnslaw Lodge **26**
Garden Court Motor Lodge **24**
Goldfields Motel and Guest House **25**
Mountain View Lodge **27**
Queenstown House **6**
Stone House **7**
Wakatipu Lodge Queenstown YHA **18**

DINING

Avanti Restaurant and Bar **13**
Boardwalk Seafood Restaurant **19**
Cow Pizza and Spaghetti House **14**
Fishbone Bar and Grill **9**
HMS Britannia **12**
Minami Jujisei Restaurant **15**
Naff Caff **16**
Pot au Feu **11**
Skyline Restaurant **1**
Solera Vino **10**

ATTRACTIONS

Department of Conservation Office **8**
Kiwi & Birdlife Park **4**
Queenstown Gardens **29**
Queenstown Motor Museum **3**
Skyline Gondola **2**
Steamer Wharf/TSS *Earnslaw* **20**

11am to 5pm. A few minutes down the same road is the **Gibbston Valley Winery** (☎ 03/442-6910). The first vines were planted in 1981 and the winery has a large, pleasant, modern restaurant area indoors and in a courtyard surrounded by vines. It is open Monday through Saturday 10am to 5:30pm and Sunday noon to 5:30pm. Wine tasting is daily from 10am to 5:30pm and costs NZ$4 (US$2.80) for four wines. The wine tour includes access to the network of caves and tunnels where the barrels are kept. We found a large cheese platter at NZ$15 (US$10.50) and four glasses of sample wines at NZ$4 most enjoyable. **Great Sights Tours,** 37 Shotover Street, Queenstown (☎ **03/442-9708,** fax 03/442-7038) has a wine tour called "Grape to Glass," departing daily at noon with hotel pickups.

PARKS & GARDENS

Right in town—and free for everyone—is the 11-acre ✪ **Queenstown Gardens,** which offers tennis courts, lawn bowls, and a walking track to use at no charge, and the park is always open.

FOR AUTO BUFFS

If you're a motoring enthusiast, go by the **Queenstown Motor Museum,** on Brecon Street just below the gondola (☎ **03/442-8775**). Opened in 1971, the modern museum houses 35 vehicles in two hangar-like wings, and is managed by John and Glenys Taylor, who are happy to chat away about any of the displays. A 12-horsepower 1903 De Dion and other reminders of automobile travel as it has evolved over the years are displayed. Admission is NZ$7 (US$4.90) for adults, NZ$3 (US$2.40) for kids, and NZ$17 (US$11.90) for a family of four; hours are 9:30am to 5:30pm daily.

IN NEARBY ARROWTOWN

For an enjoyable outing, drive 20km (12 miles) northeast to Arrowtown. It was a boomtown during the gold-mining days back in the 1860s when the Arrow River coughed up a lot of glittery stuff. Many of the original stone buildings remain, along with a stunning avenue of trees that were planted in 1867. To get a better understanding of the history of the town, go to the ✪ **Lakes District Museum** on Buckingham Street, the town's main street (☎ and fax **03/442-1824,** e-mail arrow@inq.co.nz, Web site www.arrowtown.org.nz) Admission is NZ$4 (US$2.10) for adults and NZ$2.50 (US$1.80) for children. Or head to the **Reconstructed Chinese Camp** (don't miss Ah Lum's General Store) on Bush Creek at the northern end of town. Other places to explore include the **Royal Oak Hotel,** the oldest licensed hotel in Central Otago (you can still have a drink there); **Hamilton's General Store,** which has been in business since 1862; the **Old Gaol; St. John's Presbyterian Church,** dating from 1873; and the **post office,** where the staff dress in period costumes. The **Opal & Jade Factory** on Buckingham Street is a great place to buy jewelry.

Plan to have lunch or Devonshire tea at the **Stone Cottage,** Buckingham Street beside the museum (☎ 03/442-1860).

If you're driving from Queenstown, go via Arthur's Point and return via Lake Hayes and Frankton for a different view on the return.

OUTDOOR ACTIVITIES

ECO-JET BOATING   The ✪ **Dart River Jet Safari** (P.O. Box 76, Queenstown (☎ **0800/327 853** in New Zealand, or 03/442-9992; fax 03/442-6728; Web site http://nz.com/Queenstown/DartRiverJetSafari), provided us with some of our best New Zealand memories. I was hesitant, having heard horror stories about wild jet boat experiences, but I have to say that my ride was more fun that I had ever imagined. We skimmed up the Dart River stopping to admire the unbelievably beautiful scenery of Mt. Aspiring National Park—if you've seen the Coor's beer commercial in the US or the Milka Chocolat ad on TV in Europe, you've seen this area, as both were filmed here. We disembarked at one point and took a short walk to a natural trout pool where we could see fish in the clear water. Yes, we did zoom on the river and do some 360s, but our driver, Mick Holtzmann, wasn't a reckless cowboy, and the experience was exhilarating, not frightening. Mick guides heliskiers in winter, but ask for him spring, summer, and fall. This 5¹/₂-hour experience costs NZ$129 (US$90.30) for adults and NZ$65 (US$45.50) for children from Queenstown and NZ$119 (US$83.30) for adults and NZ$55 (US$38.50) for children from Glenorchy.

FISHING   The lake is great for fishing, and the Travel & Visitor Centre can help you get gear and guides together. At **Southern Trout Flyfishing, Guides and Outfitters,** P.O. Box 642, Queenstown (☎ 025/338-187, e-mail infocus@ xtra.co.nz, Web site nz.com/webnz/Queenstown/SouthernTrout.htm), Grant Alley limits expeditions to two persons per guide, with full-day or overnight trips available; they also offer flyfishing clinics. **Jeff Jones** (☎ 03/442-6570) is another good guide.

FUN YAKING   "**Dart River Canoe Adventure,**" P.O. Box 1241, Queenstown (☎ 03/442-7374, fax 03/442-6536, e-mail funyaks@inq.co.nz), is a unique full-day excursion on the Dart River. It includes a 90-minute jet boat ride up river where you disembark, inflate your "Fun Yak" (an inflatable Canadian-style canoe) and then paddle downstream for a picnic lunch. I saw this while we were on our jet boat trip and it looked like fun, but we didn't have time to try it. The cost of this trip is NZ$159 (US$111.30) for adults and NZ$85 (US$59.50) for children under 15, and includes transfers, jetboat ride, use of inflatable canoes, guides, and lunch. The canoeing portion takes about 2¹/₂ hours, and no experience is necessary. Fun Yaks also offers a day trip which includes a 2¹/₂-hour guided walk, 1 hour of canoeing, and lunch for NZ$165 (US$116).

GOLF   Golfers will want to head for the 18-hole **Queenstown Golf Club,** Kelvin Heights (☎ 03/442-9169), or the 9-hole **Frankton Golf Club** (☎ 03/442-3584). Greens fees are NZ$30 (US$19.50) at Queenstown and NZ$9 (US$5.85) at Frankton.

SKIING   From late June through September, an international skiing crowd flocks to the slopes of **Coronet Peak** (the most accessible), **The Remarkables** (the least crowded), **Cardrona** (the best family field), and **Treble Cone** (the most challenging). The dry, powdery snow in this area is said to be the best in Australasia. See "Skiing & Snowboarding" in chapter 4 for more information on these areas.

WALKING   Three well-known multiday walks start in the Queenstown vicinity. See "Tramping" in chapter 4, "Getting Outdoors: The Active Vacation Planner," for information on the **Routeburn Track,** the **Greenstone Valley Track,** and the **Grand Traverse.** Each of these starts near the little township of Glenorchy, which is at the far end of Lake Wakatipu, 47km (29 miles) from Queenstown. It's possible to sample these great walks—you can walk in several hours and turn around and walk back out on the same day.

The **Department of Conservation Information Centre,** 37 Shotover St. (☎ 03/ 442-7933), is the place to go for information on all walking tracks. They can furnish details and brochures on short walks around Queenstown as well as those farther afield. It's open daily from 8am to 8pm.

Factoid

Bungy jumping was actually born in Queenstown, the "thrills" capital of New Zealand. This daredevil activity was pioneered by New Zealanders A.J. Hackett and Henry Van Asch in 1988. Over 100,000 leaps—guided by experienced professionals—have been made from the historic Kawarau Gorge Suspension Bridge since it opened. On the main road into Queenstown, the site is easily accessible to visitors that would rather watch than jump.

There are about a dozen excellent walkways through the **Wakatipu Basin,** some well formed and suitable for the average walker, others that require a bit more physical fitness, and still others that should be attempted only by experienced and well-equipped trampers. Before setting out, consult the Department of Conservation and follow its advice. Ask, also, about the **Otago Goldfields Heritage Trail** that runs throughout Otago.

If you'd rather go on a guided walk, Richard Bryant of **Guided Walks New Zealand,** P.O. Box 347, Queenstown (☎ 03/442-7126, fax 03/442-7128, e-mail walk@ing.co.nz), operates full- and half-day options which include bird watching and nature interpretation. Richard doesn't do all the guiding himself, but limits groups to a maximum of seven people per guide. Trips range from easy to strenuous. Of the half-day walks "Lake Shore Forest and Bird" is the easiest; "Miner's Forest Retreat" (which includes mining history) is a little harder; and "Alpine Rambles" is the hardest. The cost of half-day walks is NZ$85 (US$59.50). The full-day "Routeburn," which covers part of the Routeburn Track, costs NZ$135 (US$95). The "Ultimate Nature Experience" which includes a jet boat ride on the Dart River is NZ$255 (US$179). Half-day trips include morning or afternoon tea; full-day trips include lunch.

FOR SERIOUS THRILL-SEEKERS

BUNGY JUMPING   You won't be in Queenstown for long before learning about or seeing someone bungy jumping, which I'm convinced is more fun to watch than to do. It means taking a 43-meter (143-foot) head-first plunge off the Kawarau Gorge Suspension Bridge, the world's first bungy site, with **A. J. Hackett Bungy (☎ 03/442-7100).** There's a super-strong and long bungy cord attached to your ankles so you actually stop just shy of the water. You then swing back and forth about five times. You'll pay about NZ$99 (US$69.30) for this moment of madness that some people consider "fun." The jump at Skippers Canyon is 70 meters (229 feet) (NZ$110/US$77). Prices include a souvenir T-shirt. Or you can watch the videos for free at the A. J. Hackett station at the corner of Shotover and Camp streets in town.

JET BOATING   In summer, the Shotover River's white-water rapids are the scene of jet-boat trips guaranteed to give you a thrill as expert drivers send you flying between huge boulders amid the rushing waters. They'll point out traces of gold mining along the river as you go along. Several jet-boat operators offer a variety of trips and prices. **Shotover Jet,** P.O. Box 189, Queenstown (☎ 03/442-8570, fax 03/442-7467, Web site nz.com/Queenstown/ShotoverJet), is the best known outfitter. You can drive out to the river (allow half an hour), or there's courtesy-coach service from town. The jet-boat rides cost about NZ$65 (US$45.50) for adults, NZ$30 (US$24) for children.

PARAGLIDING/HANG GLIDING   At the **Flight Park,** at the base of Coronet Peak on Malaghans Rd. (☎ 03/442-1586), you can learn to paraglide or hang glide.

Instruction and tandem flights are available. This area is considered one of the best flying sites in the world. The price of this adventure is about NZ$125 (US$88).

SKYDIVING Skydive tandem with **The Ultimate Jump** (☎ 021/325-961). Harnessed to your tandem instructor you freefall thousands of feet at speeds of up to 200kph (124mph). This rush, however, will set you back about NZ$245 (US$172).

WHITE-WATER RAFTING This is another popular Queenstown activity. The Shotover and Kawarau rivers are the top spots. **Raging Thunder Adventures,** Camp and Shotover streets (☎ 03/442-7318, fax 03/442-6749), offers several options. The **"Awesome Foursome"** is an adventure package which includes rafting, a helicopter flight, bungy jumping, and jet boating; it costs NZ$219 (US$153.50).

SHOPPING

Surely Queenstown has more shops per capita than anywhere else in New Zealand, and it's the only place in the country where shops are open until 11pm every day. Whether you want to buy souvenirs or sweaters, sheepskin rugs or spinning wheels, you can do it here. The **Steamer Wharf,** which opened at the end of 1994, houses Polo, Ralph Lauren, Tiffany, Benetton, and so forth (although business isn't thriving and they may be closed by the time you get here). Personally, I love the beautiful sweaters at ✪ **Sheeps,** 75 Beach St. (☎ 03/442-7064). They're almost all made in New Zealand, and about 60% are handcrafted. Sheeps is open daily from 9am to 10pm and they accept American Express, Diners Club, MasterCard, and Visa. **Aotea Souvenirs,** across from the Steamer Wharf, is also open daily.

You'll find the best value on books, calendars, and cards at **Paper+Plus,** in the Mall (☎ 03/442-5296, fax 03/442-6396), open daily from 9am to 9pm. Look for toiletries, sunglasses, and such at **Wilkenson Pharmacy,** in the Mall (☎ 03/442 7313, fax 03/442-9256), open daily from 8:30am to 10pm. On **The Mall,** you can also buy casual clothing, spinning wheels, art supplies, and sheepskin rugs at **Alpine Artifacts** (☎ 03/442-8649). **Camera House,** 39 Beach St. (☎ 03/442-7644), sells film and other supplies and offers 1-hour processing.

The Mountaineer Shop, on the corner of Beach and Rees streets (☎ 03/442-7460), sells leather coats by Knights of New Zealand, oilskin coats, greenstone jewelry, and Coogi sweaters. They're open daily from 9am to 11pm.

Every other Saturday, the **Queenstown Art Council Craft Market** takes place in Earnslaw Park near the Steamer Wharf.

AFFORDABLE ACCOMMODATIONS

Queenstown is filled with accommodations, many that are well suited to budget travelers, despite the fact that prices are generally higher here than in other parts of New Zealand. However, the city is often filled with lots of visitors vying for these lower-cost lodgings, so try to reserve before you arrive here. If you do come without reservations, the **Travel & Visitor Centre,** in the Clocktower Centre at Shotover and Camp streets (☎ 03/442-4100, fax 03/442-8907, e-mail zqnvin@nzhost.co.nz), can help you find a place to lay your head.

The rates given below include the 12.5% GST.

Campgrounds & Cabins

✪ **Creeksyde Campervan Park,** Robins Road, P.O. Box 247, Queenstown (☎ 03/442-9447, fax 03/442-6621), is definitely the Mercedes of campgrounds. In a former life, it was a plant nursery, so there are plenty of trees around and room for 50 campervans, all with power outlets and water and waste hookups. The reception area is in a striking 12-sided building; Complimentary tea and coffee in the lounge in the evenings, a spa bath (great if you've spent the day skiing), bright baths (women get a hairdryer), a bath for the travelers with disabilities, kitchen, dining area, and complete laundry facilities are on the site. The charge is NZ$22 (US$15.40) for two for tent and van sites; tourist lodges are NZ$65 (US$45.50) for two adults, extra adult NZ$12 (US$8.40); lodge rooms are also available at NZ$40 (US$28) for two adults, extra adult NZ$10 (US$7); deluxe cabins are NZ$50 (US$35) for two adults, extra adult NZ$12 (US$8.40); and motel rooms are NZ$65 to $75 (US$45.50 to$52.50) for two adults; NZ$12 (US$8.40) for an extra adult. American Express, Japan Credit Bank, MasterCard, and Visa are accepted.

The **Queenstown Motor Park,** Man Street (P.O. Box 59), Queenstown (☎ 03/442-7252, fax 03/442-7253, e-mail kiwi@inq.co.nz), is about 1km (1/2 mile) from the post office and set on well-kept wooded grounds overlooking the lake. Mountain and lake views greet the eye on every path, and the camp itself sparkles with fresh paint on its airy kitchen, dining, and recreation blocks. There's a TV lounge, a provisions shop/take-out bar, a laundry with dryers, and a children's playground. Basic cabins—carpeted and heated, sleeping three or four in beds or bunks, and with a table and chairs rent for NZ$36 (US$25.20) for two people. Tourist flats with toilet, shower, and tea- and coffee-making facilities cost NZ$60 (US$42) for two. Motel units, fully self-contained two bedroom units (double bed and two twins) with TV, electric blankets and heaters, and telephone, are NZ$90 (US$63) for two. Leisure Lodges have a double bedroom, bunks recessed in hallway, double sleeper in living room, TV, full kitchen, and electric blankets rent for NZ$78 (US$54.60) for two. The 200 campsites and 300 caravan sites are NZ$10 (US$7) per adult, NZ$5 (US$3.50) per child under 14. American Express, Bankcard, MasterCard, and Visa are accepted. Be sure to reserve ahead if you're coming between December 24 and January 10.

Super-Cheap Sleeps

Bumbles

2 Brunswick St. (at Lake Esplanade), Queenstown. ☎ **03/442-6298.** 70 beds (none with bathrm). NZ$20 (US$14) per person double or twin (linens included); NZ$16 (US$11.20) dorm bed. No credit cards.

This lakeside hostel enjoys great views and a friendly atmosphere. There's room for 70, and everybody shares the big "self-cooking" kitchen (open from 7:30am to 10:30pm), the TV lounge, and laundry. Linens are available for rent. It's a 5-minute walk from the bus station and town center.

Goldfields Motel and Guesthouse

41 Frankton Rd., Queenstown. ☎ and fax **03/442-7211.** 4 rms (3 with bathrm), 8 units (all with bathrm). NZ$65 (US$45.50) double (including continental breakfast); NZ$70 (US$49) motel unit for 2 without kitchen, NZ$75 (US$52.50) motel unit for 2 with kitchen. Additional person NZ$10 (US$7) extra. AE, BC, DC, MC, V. The airport shuttle bus and the Shopper Bus stop at the gate.

At Goldfields, Bev Cooper offers units that sleep two or three; four have a full kitchen. All motel quarters are heated and have radios, TVs, showers, and electric blankets. Three of the four rooms in the modest guesthouse have private bathrooms. Guesthouse guests share a lounge where there are a TV and tea- and coffee-making facilities, and a continental breakfast is included in the guesthouse tariff. There's plenty of off-street parking and a guest laundry. This property is a 15-minute walk from town, and there's a great lake view.

✪ Wakatipu Lodge Queenstown YHA

80 Lake Esplanade, Queenstown. ☎ **03/442-8413.** Fax 03/442-6561. E-mail yhaqutn@avon. hindin.co.nz. 8 rms (2 with bathrm), 76 dormitory beds. NZ$20 (US$14) per person double or twin; NZ$18 (US$12.60) dorm bed. BC, JCB, MC, V.

Readers Recommend

The Queenstown Lodge, Sainsbury Road, Fernhill. ☎ **03/442-7107,** fax 03/442-6498. *"In Queenstown I was very impressed with the Queenstown Lodge. It was sort of like a backpackers' place—some rooms have four beds to a room, with no sink, but linens were supplied. That was NZ$20 (US$14) per night (with a restaurant and bar on the premises). Rooms with bathrooms also were available for NZ$45 (US$31.50). My backpackers' room had a great view of the lake. One note: There are lots of steps, so it's not a place for the disabled. I also liked the lodge because it was slightly out of town and away from the tourist-trap hubbub of Queenstown."*
—P. A. McCauley, Baltimore, Maryland, USA.

Brecman Lodge, 15 Man Street, Queenstown. ☎ **03/442-8908.** *"Pat & Kevin MacDonell operate this property. For clean, budget accommodation 1 block from the main street of Queenstown, it's good value."*

This hostel is across the street from the lake, a 10-minute walk from The Mall. The two-story lodge-type building is designed with many windows to take advantage of the beautiful view. There are 100 beds in 17 rooms, including 4 twin rooms and 4 family rooms, 2 with private facilities. The hostel provides good evening meals nightly year round, and there's a large communal kitchen. Other amenities include a laundry, drying room, and TV room. The hostel stays open all day.

For a Few Extra Bucks

✪ Alpine Village Motor Inn

325 Frankton Rd. (P.O. Box 211), Queenstown. ☎ **03/442-7795.** Fax 03/442-7738. 51 units (all with bathrm), chalets, and studio units. TV TEL. NZ$90 (US$63) double; NZ$100 (US$70) chalet for 2; NZ$125 (US$88) studio units for 2. Additional person NZ$15 (US$10.50) extra. AE, BC, DC, MC, V. The Shopper Bus provides transportation to and from town.

The Alpine Village is 5km (3 miles) from the center of Queenstown, but its scenic setting more than makes up for the drive. If you're not driving, there's a courtesy coach to and from town several times a day. Set right on the lake in wooded grounds, the Alpine Village offers A-frame chalets with breathtaking views of the lake and mountains on the far shore. They're furnished with tea and coffee makings and fridges, as well as central heating and electric blankets. In the main building are standard hotel rooms with the same amenities. Down on the lakefront are deluxe suites, certainly the stars of the complex. A laundry and tennis courts are provided for guests. One feature that keeps guests coming back again and again is the two indoor heated spa pools with a lake view. Equally popular are the lounge bar, where an inviting brick fireplace warms body and spirit, and the licensed restaurant with its superior menu and lovely lake view.

Amity Lodge

7 Melbourne St. (P.O. Box 371), Queenstown. ☎ **03/442-7288.** Fax 03/442-9433. 15 units (13 with bathrm). TV TEL. NZ$110 (US$77) double. Extra person NZ$15 (US$10.50). AE, BC, DC, MC, V.

Here the units sleep two to five people, two with access for the travelers with disabilites. All have a kitchen, tea- and coffee-making facilities, and a VCR. A guest laundry, a children's play area, and breakfast are available. You may not have a stunning view, but the surroundings and hosts are equally lovely.

Autoline Motel

Frankton Rd. and Dublin St. (P.O. Box 183), Queenstown. ☎ **03/442-8734.** Fax 03/442-8743. 11 units (all with bathrm). TV TEL. NZ$88–90 (US$61.60–$63) apt for 2. Additional person NZ$14 (US$9.80) extra. AE, BC, DC, MC, V. Courtesy-car service from the bus depot by arrangement.

This two-story motel has spacious one- and two-bedroom units sleeping two to six. All have nice views from their sundeck, but the end unit, no. 6, has the best lake view. Kitchens are fully equipped and have complete ranges. A radio, central heating, and electric blankets can be found in each unit. Additional facilities include an automatic laundry with dryer, a hot spa pool, a children's play area, a car wash, and covered off-street parking. The apartments are serviced daily. The Autoline is a short walk from shopping and even closer to the gardens.

Earnslaw Lodge

53 Frankton Rd., Queenstown. ☎ 03/442-8728. Fax 03/442-7376. 19 units (all with bathrm). TV TEL. NZ$112–$115 (US$78.40–$81) double. Additional person NZ$15 (US$10.50) extra. AE, BC, DC, MC, V.

This is one of the most inviting places you'll happen upon as you drive into town. It's modern, with a skylight in the inviting lobby/bar area. Five of the spacious units have a small kitchen; 14 have bay views (for the best views, ask for the upper level). A laundry and dining room are on the premesis, and breakfast is available on request. Tea- and coffee-making facilities and a unit accessible to wheelchairs are also available.

Author's note: Reader Patricia Downing of Los Angeles, California says "We had a great view from the upper level for 4 nights. It's also an easy walk to town. The manager, Greg, was very helpful with booking tours, but I felt the breakfasts were overpriced for average fare."

✪ Garden Court Motor Lodge

31 Frankton Rd., Queenstown. ☎ 03/442-9713. Fax 03/442-6468. 15 studios, 8 units (all with bathrm). TV TEL. NZ$116 (US$81.20) studio for 2, NZ$154 (US$107.80) apt for 2. Best Western discounts available. AE, BC, DC, MC, V.

The Garden Court offers eight two-level units, each with balconies, two TVs, and alpine views courtesy of picture windows. There are also 15 studios with kitchenettes. You can walk into town from here in 5 minutes. The hosts are Pauline Kelly and Ken Chisholm.

Larch Hill Bed and Breakfast

16 Panners Way, Queenstown. ☎ 03/442-7126. Fax 03/442-7128. E-mail walk@ing.co.nz. 3 rms (1 with bathrm), 1 flat (with bathrm). NZ$100 (US$70) double without bathrm, NZ$130 (US$91) double or flat with bathrm. Rates include breakfast. Dinner is available for NZ$35 (US$24.50) per person. AE, MC, V.

Located 3km (1.9 miles) outside of town, this is a good place for those with a rental car. The Shopper Bus also provides transfers. Paul and Micky Mathews of Overland Park, Kansas pointed me to this B&B with great views of the lake and mountains. The rooms are really nice; upstairs there's a king room and a twin room that share a bathroom (one room can have the bathroom to themselves for the higher rate). There's also a twin room with private bathroom and a self-contained flat with ensuite and kitchen downstairs. There is some traffic noise here, but it shouldn't be a problem unless you're a really light sleeper. The gardens are lovely.

Mountain View Lodge

Frankton Rd., Queenstown. ☎ 03/442-8246. Fax 03/442-7414. 57 units, 10 bunkrooms (all with bathrm). NZ$99 (US$69.30) units for 2 without kitchen, NZ$115 (US$80.50) unit for 2 with kitchen; NZ$60 (US$42) bunkroom for 2; NZ$80 (US$56) bunkroom for 4. AE, BC, DC, MC, V.

In a wooded hillside setting about a 15-minute walk from town, this lodge offers a wide range of accommodations, all of which have stunning lake and mountain views. There are nice motel units that sleep two to four and come with full kitchen, TV,

McFee's Waterfront Lodge, Shotover Street, Queenstown. ☎ 03/442-7400. *"Our motel was definitely the friendliest place in the center of town—if maybe a little too noisy. But for NZ$75 (US$52.50), with all facilities including laundry, it was fine for us."*

—Sue and Frank Thorn, Fallbrook, California, USA.

radio, heater, and electric blankets. Other accommodations come with everything except the kitchens (tea and coffee facilities only). A two-story building farther up the hill houses 10 rooms with heaters, each room with four bunks or a double bed with two bunks, bath, carpeting, and a table and four chairs in front of a window with a lovely view. A fully equipped kitchen is shared by all, and there's a TV lounge/bar, laundry, and children's playground. You supply cooking and eating utensils; they supply bedding. The Mountain View Lodge also has a licensed family-style restaurant on the premises. There are candles at night; windows look out to mountains and lakes.

One of the Mountain View's structures, the **Bottle House,** built in 1956, is known throughout New Zealand. Constructed entirely of 14,720 glass bottles set in sand-and-cement mortar, it serves as the motel office.

Trelawn Place

P.O. Box 117, Queenstown. ☎ and fax **03/442-9160.** Web site nz.com/webnz/bbnz/trelawn. 4 rms (all with bathrm), 1 cottage. NZ$125–$145 (US$84–$102) double; NZ$170 (US$119) cottage. Rates include breakfast. BC, MC, V.

Sitting on a spectacular bluff overlooking the Shotover River on the outskirts of town, this is the private home of Nery Howard. She provides not only double-occupancy rooms but also a very personal, friendly welcome that has won raves from readers—as has her cooking. Guests love the fishing trip and picnic lunch she arranges—according to her, the Shotover River provides "some of the best trout and salmon fishing in New Zealand." The self-contained stone cottage with roses around the door is perfect for honeymooners and families.

Worth a Splurge

✪ Queenstown House

69 Hallenstein St., Queenstown. ☎ **03/442-9043.** Fax 03/442-8755. 8 rms (all with bathrm). TV. NZ$185 (US$130) double. Rates include cooked breakfast. MC, V.

The big draws here are the convenient location, lake views, and comfortable quarters. Hostess Louise Kiely serves breakfast in the dining area from where there is a wonderful lake vista. This morning meal includes fresh fruit, homemade jams, yogurt, coffee, a variety of teas, and a choice of hot dishes. All rooms have either king or twin beds, their own bathroom, and lake view; there's also a laundry (free washing machine—small charge for dryer—or one day turn around on laundry service). From Queenstown House, it's a short downhill walk into town and a short uphill walk back. Louise invites her guests to enjoy predinner cheese and wine together every evening in the lounge, in front of the open fire in winter or in the courtyard in summer. Evening meals are available from NZ$20 (US$14) on request. No smoking permitted in the house. This is a really lovely place.

The Stone House

47 Hallenstein St., Queenstown. ☎ **03/442-9812.** Fax 03/441-8293. E-mail storey@xtra.co.nz. Web site: nz.com/Queenstown/StoneHouse/. 4 rms (all with bathrm). TV TEL. NZ$195 (US$137) double. Rates include breakfast. MC, V.

Happily removed from the hubbub, the Stone House sits on a hill above central Queenstown, providing a restful haven. Hosts Jo and Steve Weir are the owners of this lovingly restored home which was built in 1874. The interiors are very appealing: Laura Ashley and other English chintzes are featured on draperies, doonas (comforters), and shams, and the collections of ceramic mugs, jugs, and teapots are colorful and inviting. Three rooms have attached bathrooms, and one room has its bathroom across the hall. Jo and Steve will take guests fishing, walking, or picnicking for an extra charge. They also know the operators of many of the local attractions and are in a good position to make recommendations. Breakfast features homemade muffins and a great lake view. Sherry or wine is served in the parlor at "6-ish."

In Nearby Arrowtown

Speargrass Lodge

Speargrass Flat Rd. (R.D. 1), Queenstown. ☎ and fax **03/442-1417.** Web site nz.com/webnz/ bbnz/spear.htm. 4 rms (all with bathrm). NZ$105–$125 (US$73.50 –$87.50) double. 3-course dinner NZ$28 (US$19.60) extra. Rates include breakfast. JCB, MC, V.

Michael and Raewyn Fleck live on 8 acres of green hills from which there's a view of snowcapped Coronet Peak. They've arranged their 5,500-square-foot house so they can accommodate guests without impacting their family life. Each attractive room has an exterior door, electric blankets, and under-floor heating. One room has a bathtub; the rest, showers. Guests gather around a big round table for the evening meal; wine is available for purchase. (The hosts eat separately.) There are also a game rooms with a pool table and bar, a lounge with an open fire, and guest laundry. Speargrass Lodge is very close to Arrowtown and a 20-minute drive from Queenstown. There's no smoking in the lodge.

GREAT DEALS ON DINING

It won't be tough to find somewhere to eat in Queenstown, regardless of your budget— there are 104 restaurants and cafes in the city, and I've listed my favorites below.

If you drive out to Glenorchy and decide not to picnic, the **Glen-Roydon Lodge,** P.O. Box 27, Glenorchy (☎ and fax **03/442-9968**) serves inexpensive lunches in a relaxing setting.

SUPER-CHEAP EATS

✪ The Cow Pizza and Spaghetti House

Cow Lane. ☎ **03/442-8588.** Reservations not accepted. Most pizzas and main courses under NZ$15 (US$10.50). AE, BC, DC, MC, V. Daily noon–11pm. PIZZA/PASTA.

This cozy little stone building in the town center is at the end of a lane that got its name from the fact that cows were once driven this way each day to be milked. Inside, this place probably hasn't changed a whole lot since those early days— a smoke-darkened fireplace, wooden beams, lots of old farm memorabilia, and wooden benches and tables are features of the building. It's a friendly gathering spot for locals, and you'll probably rub elbows with them at the long tables here.

As for the menu, it was *designed* for budget travelers! I counted eight varieties of pizza (including a vegetarian version) and six spaghetti dishes—and the highest price on the menu is NZ$14.95 (US$10.47), unless you go for the extra-large pizza (don't, unless you're ordering for two or have an extra-large appetite), which can cost as much as NZ$21.95 (US$15.37). Soup, salad, homemade whole-meal bread, and ice-cream desserts are also offered. It's BYO. Take-out is available, but I strongly recommend that you eat right here—the Cow is a delightful experience.

Readers Recommend

Take Five Expresso and Juice Bar, Earnslaw Wharf. *"I lamented to our waitress at Solera Vino about our despair over New Zealand coffee; her response was instant sympathy and the name of this place where she insisted the coffee was great. She was right! We went there for coffee the next morning and again at lunch—they have super bagels also."*
— Dr. Alice Harting-Correa, St. Andrews, Fife, Scotland.

Berkels' Gourmet Burgers at 19 Shotover Street, Queenstown. ☎ **03/442-6950.** *"This is a fabulous place with good food and reasonable prices. They have a large range of burgers, all made on the chargrill and fresh as ordered. There is a large airy non-smoking sitting area and a bar. They're open until late and also have a takeaway and home delivery menu. Owners Susan and Mike Burke are a friendly, helpful couple and I recommend this eating place highly."*

*"Next door to Berkels' on Shotover Street is the Bakery with pies, rolls, breads, and lovely cakes etc. It is open 24-hours. Above the bakery is an Indian restaurant Little India Bistro and Tandoor, 11 Shotover Street, ☎ and fax **03/442-5335.** Sadly we were unable to eat there as they were completely booked out."*
—Jennie Fairlie, Broadbeach, QLD, Australia.

☻ Naff Caff

62 Shotover St. ☎ **03/442-8211.** Reservations not accepted. Coffee NZ$2–$2.75 (US$1.30–$1.93); lunch NZ$4–$5.50 (US$2.80–$3.90). No credit cards. Mon–Sat 8am–6pm. CAFE.

Coffee drinkers rejoice! Whether you want Vienna, borgia, latté, mega mucho, mella bella, flat white, double espresso, cappuccino, long black, or macchiato—you'll find it here. The Naff Caff is known to coffee drinkers New Zealand-wide because they roast and grind their own beans, serve the lattés in large bowls, and perform all the other rituals that devotees need. The casual atmosphere is also appealing: There's indoor and outdoor seating, and CDs provide background music. Besides the entrance on Shotover Street, another door faces Beach Street. No smoking here.

FOR A FEW EXTRA BUCKS

Avanti Restaurant & Bar

20 The Mall. ☎ **03/442-8503.** Reservations not required. Main courses NZ$9.50–$18.50 (US$6.70–$12.60). AE, DC, MC, V. Daily 7am–10pm. ITALIAN/NEW ZEALAND.

Fresh pasta is featured daily for lunch and dinner, and there's fresh fish on Wednesday. Any day's a good day for a continental breakfast. The bistro atmosphere is inviting, and in warm weather, there's courtyard dining with a view of the gondolas. Avanti is located in the town center and is fully licensed.

The Fishbone Bar & Grill

7 Beach St. ☎ and fax **03/442-6768.** Reservations not accepted. Main courses NZ$16.50–$24.50 (US$11.60 –$17.20); "kiddies' meals" NZ$7.50–$8.50 (US$5.30 –$6). AE, DC, MC, V. Daily noon–3pm and 5:30–10pm or later. SEAFOOD.

The colorful fish mobiles hanging from the ceiling and an open kitchen are part of the casual decor here, and daily specials are written on a chalkboard. These might include garlic-steamed mussels, oysters (natural or Kilpatrick), whitebait, prawns, or scampi. The scallops are sometimes poached and served with a Cointreau-cream sauce. Dollarwise diners might choose the fish and chips main course. Seating is at half a dozen booths and a dozen or so tables. It's fully licensed and you can bring your own wine, too.

✪ Giuseppe's Gourmet Pizza and Pasta Bar

155 Fernhill Rd., Richard's Park Lane, Fernhill. ☎ 03/442-5444. Fax 03/441-8047. Reservations recommended. Main courses NZ$11–$16 (US$7.70–$11.20). AE, DC, MC, V. Daily 6–10:30pm (later in summer). If you don't have a car, you'll need to pay NZ$5 (US$3.50) for a taxi or NZ$2 (US$1.40) bus fare from town. ITALIAN.

This spot is the favorite of many locals. It's in an unlikely location: a suburban shopping center, where you'd expect to see a fish-and-chips shop or a dairy—in fact, there's a dairy next door. The food here is—in short—*superb*. I'd start with the traditional bruschetta, followed by pasta topped with sun-dried tomato and fresh asparagus. You might, however, prefer Gino's bruschetta, with pickled eggplant, garlic, olive oil, and parsley. My favorite pizza is generously sprinkled with marinated lamb and fresh mushrooms. Giuseppe's is fully licensed, with many wines from Australia, Italy, France, and New Zealand available by the glass or bottle. You can also bring your own, but there's a small corkage fee. No smoking here.

HMS *Britannia*

The Mall. ☎ **03/442-9600.** Fax 03/442-6299. Reservations required. Main courses NZ$18–$29 (US$12.60–$20.30). AE, DC, MC, V. Daily 6:30–10pm. NEW ZEALAND.

This local favorite in the town center is designed like the interior of an 18th-century sailing ship, with nets and ropes hanging from the ceiling and lanterns and dripping candles giving off a warm glow. There may be more elegant restaurants in Queenstown, but none is more pleasant than this. Owner Doug Champion and his staff go overboard to provide painstaking service and a meal prepared to order. The menu features fresh lobster, mussels, fish, steak filet, and vegetarian dishes.

✪ Solera Vino

25 Beach St. ☎ **03/442-6082.** Fax 03/442-9585. Reservations recommended. Main courses NZ$16–$22 (US$11.20–$15.40). AE, BC, MC, V. Daily 6pm–late. MODERN NEW ZEALAND.

I felt as if I'd walked into a Spanish bodega when I crossed the threshold at Solera Vino. With the rough plaster walls, wooden tables, and rustic fireplaces, all that was missing was a flamenco guitarist. However, diners here don't think they're missing a thing, because the food is truly great! South Island salmon is prepared with fresh tomato, seasonal green vegetables, and fresh basil. Oven-baked rack of lamb is served on Provençal vegetables with a capsicum (green-pepper) rouille and marjoram part jus. Homemade vegetarian ravioli is served with a puré e of root vegetable, nut pesto, and sun-dried tomatoes in a coriander-lemongrass broth. The restaurant is licensed and offers nine beers as well as an extensive wine list. There are seven tables downstairs and eight upstairs. Ask to be seated with nonsmokers if that's important to you.

WORTH A SPLURGE

Boardwalk Seafood Restaurant

Steamer Wharf, Beach St., Queenstown. ☎ **03/442-5630.** Reservations advisable July to March. Main courses NZ$21.50–$28.50 (US$15.10–$20). AE, DC, MC, V. Daily 6–late. SEAFOOD.

"Fresh fish" sums up the specialty of the house at the Boardwalk. Owner, Tony Roberts says "it's all from New Zealand, except the giant prawns used as garnish, which we get from Australia and the tuna, which is from Samoa." Having eaten there recently I have no reason to doubt him. Tony came here 20 years ago for a ski holiday and never left. He also owns Minami Jujisei Restaurant and says "by owning two places I have better buying power for the seafood." Between the two, they use 250 to 300kg (550 to 660 lbs) of fresh New Zealand fish a week. I can personally recommend the smoked salmon soup. The Boardwalk is up a flight of stairs in the Steamer Wharf, the complex of trendy shops, next to where the TSS *Earnslaw* docks. The restaurant gets noisy at times; request a window table.

Minami Jujisei Restaurant

45 Beach St. ☎ **03/442-9854.** Fax 03/442-7008. Reservations required. Main courses NZ$19–$50 (US$13.30 –$35). AE, DC, JCB, MC, V. Daily noon–2pm and 6–10pm. JAPANESE.

If you have a yen for something Japanese, try this marvelous restaurant which was awarded Restaurant of the Region in 1995. The upstairs setting is a serene room with traditional decor; its kitchen is under the direction of Show Okamoto, a chef of distinction, and owner Tony Robertson will be happy to help you with your selection if you're not too sure about the dishes. Specialties include selections from the South Island's only sushi bar, plus ise-ebi (crayfish). There's a large choice of Japanese snacks and soups, plus three fixed-price meals of six courses and tea (tempura, sashimi, or steak). It's fully licensed.

Pot au Feu

24 Camp St. ☎ **03/442-8333.** Reservations recommended. Main courses NZ$21–$28 (US$14.70–$19.60). AE, MC, V. Daily 6–10pm. MEDITERRANEAN.

The ambience here is colonial: The restaurant consists of two rooms in what might have been an old house, and an interesting plate collection hangs on the walls. The food, however, is a Mediterranean treatment of fresh New Zealand produce. You might start with seafood soup flavored with sumac and coriander, and follow with hogget (mature lamb) loin roasted and served with a ratatouille of potatoes, courgettes (zucchini), mushrooms, and mint. Another popular main course is monkfish roasted with garlic, tomato, and fennel. The cervena (venison) medallions on a mustard-soy sauce are also popular.

Skyline Restaurant

Bob's Peak. ☎ **03/442-7860.** Fax 03/442-6391. Reservations recommended for lunch, required for dinner. Buffet lunch NZ$25 (US$17.50); dinner buffet NZ$35 (US$24.50). AE, BC, DC, MC, V. Daily noon–2pm and 6–9pm. Take the Skyline Gondola up Bob's Peak (NZ$12/US$8.40). NEW ZEALAND.

I have a real problem recommending a NZ$25 lunch buffet and a NZ$35 dinner buffet in a budget traveler's guidebook. On the other hand, you may feel that the Skyline Restaurant is worth a splurge. Personally, I don't like large lunches, so I'd eat my midday meal at the cafe here which is open from 9am to 6pm. Sandwiches, pies,

Readers Recommend

Pasta Pasta Cucina, 6 Brecon Street. ☎ **03/442-6762.** *"The pasta is made fresh on the premise daily, the service was very good, and the prices reasonable."*

McNeills Cottage Brewery, 14 Church Street. ☎ **03/442-9688.** *"Has a warm atmosphere and good food."*

—Patricia Downing, Los Angeles, California, USA.

Saguaro, upstairs in the Trust Bank Arcade, Beach Street. ☎ **03/442-8240.** *"We were given a recommendation of a Mexican restaurant in town. . . . We found it to be reasonable and had the best Mexican food I've eaten in a long time. I also sampled a delicious local wine: Gibbston Valley Chardonnay."*

—Meg Barth Gammon, Kailua, Hawaii, USA.

and hot meals are available from NZ$5 (US$3.50). If you want to make a night of it, the dinner buffet includes a carvery which features lamb, seafood, and other New Zealand specialties, and there is often live entertainment (usually a band that plays for dancing). The wraparound windows give you a fantastic panoramic view of the town and lake. You won't get a better view anywhere in the area, but you don't have to eat here to enjoy the vista. It's fully licensed.

QUEENSTOWN AFTER DARK

Eichardt's Tavern (☎ 03/442-8369), at the water end of The Mall, is sort of the Old Faithful of Queenstown's nightlife. **Wicked Willie's,** 24 Beach St. (☎ 03/442-7309), the pub at the Hotel Queenstown, is also popular, as is the **Casbah** (☎ 03/442-7853), a dance spot at 54 Shotover St.; **Chico's Restaurant** (☎ 03/442-8439) on The Mall is a cafe until 10pm, after which it becomes a popular watering hole. Live music is featured regularly at the **Skyline Restaurant** (see "Great Deals on Dining" above) on Bob's Peak, accessible only by gondola. Most folks who go up for dinner—and the fantastic view—stay and make a night of it. Another option is the dinner cruise on the **TSS** *Earnslaw* (☎ 03/442-7500 or 0800/656-503). Of course, all the stores are open at night, so you could shop, or drop into the **Naff Caff** (see "Great Deals on Dining" above) for a latté.

A SIDE TRIP TO MILFORD SOUND

If you're headed to Milford Sound from Queenstown, I recommend spending at least 1 day in Te Anau, and from here, move on towards the sound. Don't try to do Milford Sound directly from Queenstown—it's too far (unless you fly both ways, but then you'll miss Milford Road, which is quite pretty). Once in Te Anau, you can drive in and out of the sound, or bus in and fly out, or just stay overnight. I cover both Te Anau and Milford Sound in the next two sections of this chapter. That said, if time or budget still prevents these options, don't give up—you're not condemned to miss this very special part of New Zealand. InterCity and Mount Cook bus lines, and Fiordland Travel (see below) have day-long coach trips that include launch trips on the sound, and the option of flying one or both ways to Queenstown. **Fiordland Travel,** P.O. Box 1, Te Anau (☎ 0800/656-501 in New Zealand, or 03/249-7419; fax 03/249-7022), offers a bonus if you fly both ways—a free ticket for a TSS *Earnslaw* cruise.

Taking the coach in and flying out gives you an opportunity to see the scenery from two different perspectives while saving time—the bus takes 5 hours each way, including a half-hour break in Te Anau. Should weather conditions ground the plane at Milford, you can always take the coach back. I think it's nuts to consider driving round trip to Milford in 1 day (at least if you do the bus trip, you can sleep on the way back). The cost of the coach/fly trip with Fiordland Travel is NZ$299 (US$209.30) for adults and NZ$179.50 (US$125.65) for children; flying both ways costs NZ$265 (US$186) for adults and NZ$159 (US$111.30) for children.

All coach excursions to Milford Sound leave Queenstown between 7am and 8am, returning around 8pm, and fares average NZ$155 (US$109) for adults, NZ$77.50 (US$54.25) for children, inclusive of the launch trip. Lunch is available on most launch trips but not included in the ticket price; savvy budget travelers will bring their own.

Fiordland Travel also offers a great value deal called ✪ **"The Milford Backroad Adventure."** This 2-day trip from Queenstown begins with a cruise aboard the TSS *Earnslaw* across Lake Wakatipu to Walter Peak, followed by a coach trip to Milford Sound and a cruise to the Tasman Sea aboard the *Milford Wanderer* before anchoring for the night. Dinner and breakfast on board are included. This excursion allows time for a walk in Fiordland National Park and costs NZ$199 (US$139.30) for adults and NZ$99.50 (US$69.65) for children.

Fiordland Travel offers a 10% discount to auto club members on all trips, except overnight Milford trips, and accepts American Express, Bankcard, Carte Blanche, Diners Club, Japan Credit Bank, MasterCard, and Visa.

You can book through the Travel & Visitor Centre, the Fiordland Travel Centre at the Steamer Wharf, or the Mount Cook Travel Centre on Camp Street. I, personally, am quite fond of the Fiordland Travel trips, because of their superior (luxury-class) coaches, comfortable cruisers, and wonderfully informed drivers. They also furnish commentary tapes in four languages other than English, with a four-channel music system to soothe the return trip.

By the way, **Doubtful Sound** is a great day trip from Te Anau, but not a good trip to do from Queenstown. For more information on Doubtful Sound see "Te Anau" below.

EN ROUTE TO TE ANAU

It's a 172km (107-mile) drive from Queenstown, on good roads all the way. Follow Highway 6 to Kingston at the south end of Lake Wakatipu where you have the option of taking a ride on the historic *Kingston Flyer* (a pre-1930's passenger train pulled by steam engines). Trips depart twice a day at 10:15am and 4:15pm October 1 to the end of April. The round trip takes $1^1/_4$ hours and costs NZ$20 (US$14) per person. The train is owned and operated (on track which was set in 1878) by Tranz Rail. Continue on Highway 6 through Athol, where there are tearooms in the general store. Turn west onto Highway 94 over the summit of **Gorge Hill,** along the **Mararoa River** and through sheep and cattle country to **Te Anau,** the largest lake on the South Island.

2 Te Anau

172km (107 miles) SW of Queenstown; 116km (72 miles) S of Milford Sound

Lake Te Anau spreads its south, middle, and north branches like long fingers poking deep into the mountains that mark the beginning of the rugged and magnificent 3,000,000-acre World Heritage **Fiordland National Park,** New Zealand's largest and, indeed, one of the largest in the world. Within its boundaries, which enclose the whole of the South Island's southwest corner, lie incredibly steep mountain ranges, lakes, sounds, rivers, magnificent fiords, and huge chunks of mountainous terrain even now unexplored. In fact, one large section has been closed off from exploration after the discovery there in 1948 of one of the world's rarest birds, the flightless takahe. It had not been seen for nearly a century before, seldom even then, and was thought to be extinct. When a colony was found in the Murchison Mountains, the decision was made to protect them from human disturbance.

Lake Te Anau is a wonder in itself. Its eastern shoreline, where Te Anau township is located, is virtually treeless with about 30 inches of annual rainfall, while its western banks are covered by dense forest nurtured by more than 100 inches of rain each year. What attracts visitors to New Zealand's second largest lake, however, is both the opportunity for water sports and the proximity to Milford Sound, which is 116km (72 miles) away. The sound, which is actually a fiord, reaches $22^1/_2$km (14 miles) in from the Tasman Sea, flanked by sheer granite peaks traced by playful waterfalls that appear and disappear depending on the amount of rainfall. Its waters and the surrounding land have been kept in as nearly a primeval state as man could possibly manage without leaving it totally untouched. In fine weather or pouring rain, Milford Sound exudes a powerful sense of nature's pristine harmony and beauty.

ESSENTIALS
GETTING THERE & GETTING AROUND

BY PLANE   **Mount Cook Airline** provides daily service from Mount Cook and Queenstown.

BY COACH (BUS)   There is daily coach service between Te Anau and Christchurch, Dunedin, and Invercargill via **InterCity** and **Mount Cook Landline;** both lines also have daily service to Te Anau and Milford Sound from Queenstown.

BY CAR   From Queenstown, take Highway 6, then Highway 94 (see "En Route to Te Anau" above for details).

VISITOR INFORMATION

At the lake end of Milford Road sits the **Fiordland Visitor Information Centre,** Te Anau Terrace, P.O. Box 1, Te Anau (☎ **03/249-8900,** fax 03/249-7022, e-mail teuvin@nzhost.co.nz), which shares space with **Fiordland Travel,** P.O. Box 1, Te Anau (☎ **0800/656-501** in New Zealand, or 03/249-7419; fax 03/249-7022), is open daily from 8am to 6pm. Nearby, the **Fiordland National Park Visitor Centre,** on Lakefront Drive, P.O. Box 29, Te Anau (☎ **03/249-7921,** fax 03/ 249-7613), is a must for anyone contemplating short walks in the area or the well known multiday ones (Hollyford, Routeburn, Milford, Kepler, and Caples). It has a museum and audiovisual display. The center is open daily from 8am to 6pm during summer, 9:30am to 4:30pm during winter. The **telephone area code** (STD) for Te Anau is **03.**

A SPECIAL EVENT

Check ou the **Fiordland Summer Festival Weekend,** Te Anau (☎ **03/249-7959**). The festivities here include a celebrity debate, a rodeo, garden tours, and harness racing in the main street, as well as arts and crafts, food stalls, and street entertainment. The festival takes place early to mid-January.

ORIENTATION

Te Anau's main street is actually Highway 94, called **Milford Road** within the township. Stretched along each side you'll find the post office, restaurants, grocery stores, and most of the township's shops.

EXPLORING TE ANAU & THE SOUNDS

♥ **Lake cruises** are one of the main attractions in Te Anau; **Fiordland Travel,** Lakefront Drive (P.O. Box 1), Te Anau (☎ **0800/656-501** in New Zealand; fax 03/ 249-7022), operates the popular Te Anau-au Caves trip, which runs year round. The tour includes an underground boat ride into the glowworm grotto in the "living" cave, so called because it's still being formed. A crystal-clear river cascades down the cave tiers at the rate of 55,000 gallons per minute, creating frothy white falls. On the second level of the waterbed you'll see the glowworm grotto. In my opinion, the day trip is preferable to the evening, since the scenic 10-mile lake cruise begs to be enjoyed in daylight. The cost for adults is NZ$35 (US$24.50) and for children NZ$10 (US$7).

Another reason for coming to Te Anau is to go on to ♥ **Milford Sound** and ♥ **Doubtful Sound.** You can drive, fly, or take a coach tour to Milford Sound. Fiordland's half-day coach trip includes a cruise and costs NZ$85 (US$59.50), half price for children. For detailed information on Milford Sound, see the "Milford Sound" section later in this chapter).

The good value ✪ "**Milford Backroad Adventure**" offered by Fiordland Travel and described above in "A Side Trip to Milford Sound" costs NZ$153 (US$107.10) for adults and NZ$76.50 (US$53.55) for children when done from Te Anau. This includes coach transportation to Milford, cruise, accommodation, dinner, and breakfast on the *Milford Wanderer*.

Waterwings Airways Ltd., Lakefront Drive, P.O. Box 767, Queenstown, Te Anau (☎ **03/249-7405,** fax 03/442-3050), operates floatplane flights between Te Anau and Milford Sound. Their 1-hour and 10-minute (70-minute) scenic flight is a real delight, and costs NZ$154 (US$107.80) per adult, NZ$92 (US$64.40) per child. For NZ$131 (US$91.70) per adult, NZ$92 (US$64.04) per child, they'll take you on a 35-minute flight to Doubtful Sound. In addition, there's a 20-minute scenic flight around Te Anau, at NZ$66 (US$46.20) and NZ$40 (US$28), and one for 10 minutes that costs NZ$36 (US$25.20) and NZ$22 (US$15.40), respectively. One of their best offerings is the 1-hour combination Fly 'N Boat trip at a cost of NZ$84 (US$58.80) per adult, NZ$51 (US$35.70) per child; they'll take you down the Waiau River to Manapouri via jet boat, then bring you back by floatplane to Te Anau by way of the Hidden Lakes. They accept American Express, Bankcard, Diners Club, Japan Credit Bank, MasterCard, and Visa.

DOUBTFUL SOUND

Captain Cook was doubtful that it *was* a sound when he first saw it, thus the name, Doubtful Sound. And the name alone is intriguing enough to make you want to go there. It's not as famous as its neighbor to the north, Milford Sound, but where Milford is majestic, Doubtful is mysterious. Both are undeniably serene. Doubtful Sound is 10 times bigger than Milford, and while it can't boast Mitre Peak, its still waters mirror Commander Peak, which rises 4,000 feet in vertical splendor.

Another difference between Milford and Doubtful sounds is that at Milford you know civilization is nearby, with the airstrip and the hotel near the boat harbor. Doubtful is definitely more remote.

There's no way you can get to Doubtful Sound on your own. Fiordland Travel runs trips from Manapouri. These start with a boat ride across pristine Lake Manapouri and a coach to Deep Cove in Doubtful Sound—through lush forest and over Wilmot Pass, 2,208 feet above sea level, stopping along the way at the Manapouri Power Station, and spiraling downward 750 eerie feet to view the seven immense underground turbines. It's like delving into the underworld and is really interesting.

At Deep Cove Village, population of one—the Fiordland National Park conservation officer, you board the boat to explore the sound. This journey has several highlights including spotting dolphins, seals, and tiny penguins; getting close enough to waterfalls to feel the spray; and listening to the absolute silence when the captain shuts off the engine. You return to Te Anau the way you came, without the stop at the power station. Another high point is crossing Lake Manapouri again (especially at sunset) and watching as what looks like a wall created by the many islands in the lake magically opens as the boat draws near.

If you've never done either trip, I'd recommend Milford Sound for its sheer majesty and save Doubtful Sound as the highlight of your next trip.

Fiordland's Doubtful Sound trip from Manapouri costs NZ$155 (US$109) for adults and NZ$40 (US$28) for children. From Te Anau add about NZ$10 (US$7) more. Fiordland Travel offers a 10% discount to auto club members (except for the overnight Milford trip).

Author's notes: Don't feel compelled to buy one of their lunches; it's cheaper to pack your own picnic (go to the grocery store in Te Anau). Don't expect cloudless skies when you do the Doubtful Sound trip—if it were sunny you wouldn't see the mist enshroud the hundreds of waterfalls and the fiord. If you have to decide between splurging on the Doubtful Sound trip or flightseeing on the West Coast or at Mt. Cook, go with the flightseeing—it's more memorable.

THE MILFORD TRACK & OTHER WALKS

Most dedicated trampers consider the world-famous ✪ **Milford Track** the finest anywhere in the world. Four days are required to walk the 54km (33 miles) from Glade Jetty at Lake Te Anau's northern end to Sandfly Point on the western bank of Milford Sound. Other popular walks in this area are the **Hollyford Valley,** the **Routeburn,** and the **Kepler.** For information on these walks, see "Tramping" in chapter 4.

AFFORDABLE ACCOMMODATIONS

Between Christmas and the end of February, accommodations in Te Anau are tight; many rooms and places to stay are occupied by the week by Kiwi families on holiday. You should reserve as far ahead as possible or plan to rest your head outside the township. Other times of the year, there are usually ample accommodations available.

The rates given below include the 12.5% GST.

IN TE ANAU
Super-Cheap Sleeps
✪ Te Anau YHA

220–224 Milford Rd., Te Anau. ☎ and fax **03/249-7847.** 42 beds in 11 rooms (none with bathrm). NZ$18 (US$12.60) per person double or twin; NZ$16 ($11.20) dorm bed. MC, V.

This is a real standout, one of the most attractive hostels in the country. It adjoins a sheep meadow in a very central location and has 42 beds in six pine-paneled rooms with central heating, with plans to add more beds in the near future. A nicely equipped kitchen, a lounge (with a pot-belly stove), dining room, and laundry are available; in January, overflow accommodation is available. This is the ideal place to begin and end your Milford, Routeburn, Hollyford, Dusky, or Greenstone Track walks. They can also arrange discounted tours and sightseeing fees for YHA members.

For a Few Extra Bucks
Amber Court Motel

68 Quintin Dr., Te Anau. ☎ **03/249-7230.** Fax 03/249-7486. 9 units (all with bathrm). TV TEL. NZ$85 (US$59.50) double std rm, NZ$90 (US$63) studio, NZ$120 (US$84) 2-bedroom unit. Additional person NZ$15 (US$10.50) extra. AE, DC, MC, V. Courtesy-car service available.

This place is in a quiet in-town location, with one- and two-bedroom units that sleep two to eight. There's a guest laundry and—most unusual—a car wash. The hosts can arrange sightseeing reservations and will furnish a cooked breakfast at an extra charge.

Matai Lodge

42 Mokonui St., Te Anau. ☎ and fax **03/249-7360.** 7 rms (none with bathrm). NZ$74 (US$51.80) double; NZ$99 (US$69.30) triple. Rates include breakfast. AE, DC, MC, V. Closed June–Aug.

The Matai Lodge is only one block from the lakefront and has its rooms in a long block, with toilet and showers at one end. The rooms all have hot and cold running water, are tastefully decorated, and have heaters as well as electric blankets and comforters. The lounge is spacious, with comfortable seating, and there's a separate TV

Readers Recommend

The Cat's Whiskers Bed and Breakfast, 2 Lakefront Drive, Te Anau. ☎ 03/ 249-8112. *"My wife and I stayed 2 nights at this guest house and believe the accommodation and breakfast could be the best value in the South Island. We stayed in July and paid NZ$65 (US$45.50) double per night. The hosts, Irene and Terry Maher, make you feel very comfortable. They have three units, all with bathrooms."*
—B&J Hermann, Point Vernon, Queensland, Australia.

Author's Note: July is mid-winter when rates are at their lowest; the regular rate is NZ$95 (US$67) double bed and breakfast.

lounge. You're given several choices on the menu for the fully cooked breakfast. Host Richard Bevan is very helpful: He knows the area well and enjoys sharing sightseeing information with guests and booking tours, cruises, and the like. He will also store baggage for trampers. There is off-street parking for drivers. No smoking is permitted in the lodge.

✪ Shakespeare House

10 Dusky St., Te Anau. ☎ **03/249-7349**. Fax 03/249-7629. TV. 7 rms (all with bathrm), 1 motel unit. NZ$98 (US$68.60) double, NZ$140 (US$98) motel unit. Extra person NZ$20 (US$14). Rates include cooked or continental breakfast. MC, V. Lower off-season rates. Courtesy car transfers.

Thanks to reader Sandra Drake of Columbus, Ohio, for introducing me to Shakespeare House. While not posh, it is clean and well appointed. Don't be put off by the street-side appearance. The rooms are spacious and attractive. I particularly appreciated the king bed and excellent bed-side reading lights. Quarters bear Shakespearean names; we enjoyed "Rosalind," others include "Much Ado About Nothing," "Katharine," and "Mid-Summer Night's Dream." All rooms have tea- and coffee-making facilities and good firm beds (three have doubles, four have kings which can be made into twins). The two-bedroom motel unit has cooking facilities, a separate lounge, and sleeps five. Guests share a loggia where there are a fridge, brochures on area activities, and lots of chairs and plants. Hosts Margie & Jeff Henderson couldn't be nicer and will store luggage for trampers and let guests use their good laundry facilities.

Worth a Splurge

Te Anau Travelodge Hotel

64 Lakefront Dr. (P.O. Box 185), Te Anau. ☎ **03/249-7411**. Fax 03/249-7947. 112 rms (all with bath), 15 villa suites. MINIBAR TV TEL. NZ$112.50 (US$78.75) double; NZ$208 (US$145.60) villa suite for 2. AE, BC, DC, JCB, MC, V.

This resort hotel on the lakefront is the most deluxe place to stay in this area. Guest rooms all have tea- and coffee-making facilities, and hairdryers are available from reception. The villa suites consist of a lounge, bedroom, kitchen, and bathroom. On-premises amenities include two restaurants, three bars, a pool, spas, saunas, and two guest laundries.

IN NEARBY TE ANAU DOWNS

Te Anau Downs Motor Inn

Hwy. 94 (P.O. Box 19, Te Anau). ☎ **0800/500-805** in New Zealand, or 03/249-7811. Fax 03/249-7753.12 B&B rms, 20 motor inn units, 12 hotel rooms, 12 backpackers (all with bathrm). TV. NZ$42.50 (US$29.80) per person B&B room; NZ$89–$109 (US$62.30–$76.30) double in motor inn; additional person in motor inn NZ$17 (US$11.90) extra; NZ$70 (US$49) double in hotel room; NZ$38–$45 (US$26.60–$31.50) double in backpacker quarters. Best Western and AA discounts available. AE, DC, MC, V. Closed June–Aug.

Dave Moss, president of Best Western NZ, owns and operates this outstanding property on the road between Te Anau and Milford Sound. There are B&B rooms with private facilities and one-bedroom motor inn units that are neat and modern, with cooking and eating utensils, fridge, electric rangette, and color TV. There's a laundry available to all guests. Dave also runs a licensed restaurant with a local reputation for serving the largest and best roast dinner in the area at reasonable prices. It's located about 30km (19 miles) from Te Anau.

GREAT DEALS ON DINING

On our last trip to Te Anau I was pleasantly surprised to find that this former culinary wasteland had quite a few new restaurants. I think it's because of the increased popularity of the walks (tracks) that start here.

SUPER-CHEAP EATS

Pop-in Catering

In the Waterfront Merchants Complex, 92 Lakefront Dr. ☎ **03/249-7807.** Reservations not required. NZ$5–$9 (US$3.50–$6.30). No credit cards. Summer, daily 7am–8:30pm. Off-season, daily 7:30am–6pm. ICE CREAM/LIGHT MEALS.

Diagonally across from Fiordland Travel is this window-lined restaurant serving light meals at very moderate prices in a setting that overlooks the lake. A glass-walled conservatory affords 180° views. Everything is home-cooked and baked right on the premises. Sandwiches, meat pies, salad plates, barbecue, Kiwi-style chicken, venison, beef, and baked-on-the-premises pastries can meet just about any size hunger attack. It's fully licensed too.

FOR A FEW EXTRA BUCKS

Bailey's Restaurant, Cafe & Bar

In the Luxmore Resort Hotel, Milford Rd. ☎ **03/249-7526.** Reservations recommended. Dinner main courses NZ$13.50–$21.75 (US$9.50–$15.28). AE, MC, V. Daily 11am–the last person leaves. NEW ZEALAND.

Right in the center of town, Bailey's offers a range of food—from all-day breakfasts to morning and afternoon teas, to lunches of sandwiches, pies, and casseroles, to full à la carte dinners in the evenings. The dinner menu contains items such as pepper steak, rack of lamb, and blue cod fillet. It's fully licensed.

Henry's Family Restaurant

In the Te Anau Travelodge Hotel, 64 Lakefront Dr. ☎ **03/249-7411.** Reservations not required. Main courses NZ$15–$23 (US$10.50–$16.10); lunch NZ$8–$15 (US$5.60–$10.50). AE, BC, DC, JCB, MC, V. Daily noon–2pm and 5:30–9pm. NEW ZEALAND.

The lakefront setting is rustic and the food reasonably priced. The atmosphere is much like that of a frontier saloon, with a pot-belly stove and bare wooden tables. New Zealand specialties include Milford Sound crayfish, Fiordland venison, Steward Island salmon, and lamb. The restaurant is fully licensed.

For more elegant (and expensive) dinners, reserve at the Travelodge's **MacKinnon Room,** which specializes in local delicacies, including fresh crayfish. The Te Anau Travelodge Hotel can pack a very good **picnic lunch** for your Milford Sound day trip or tramping if you notify them the night before.

Hollyford Boulevard Bar & Grill

In Kiwi Country Complex, on the Milford Rd., Te Anau. ☎ **03/249-7334.** Fax 03/249-7884. Reservations advisable in summer. Main courses NZ$14.50–$21.95 (US$10.20–$15.37). DC, MC, V. Daily 8:30am–9:30pm (later in summer). ECLECTIC.

This popular cafe and bar has a contemporary decor. Menu items include vegetarian stir fry, chicken tetrazzini fettuccini, brandy pepper steak, tenderloin venison, and barbecued pork loins. Up until 6pm you can order off the menu or select from inexpensive sandwiches and cakes on the cafeteria shelves; after 6pm only menu items are available. Hollyford Boulevard is livelier and more casual than Keplers. It's fully licensed.

✪ Kepler's Family Restaurant

Corner of Mokonui St. and Milford Rd., Te Anau ☎ **03/249-7909**. Reservations advisable in summer. Main courses NZ$15–$24 (US$10.50–$16.80). AE, DC, MC, V. Daily 11am–2pm and 5:30–10pm summer, daily 5:30–9pm winter. ECLECTIC.

Kepler's impressed me with their quick service. After a long day, tired travel writers, like weary travelers, don't want to sit through a protracted meal. The decor is modern with wooden tables and chairs—the atmosphere is similar to an upscale hotel coffee shop. Menu items include kangaroo medallion steak, apricot and Camembert chicken, vegetarian pasta, and burgers. My husband and I both enjoyed a roast lamb dinner, served with three fresh vegetables; it was a great deal at only NZ$15/US$10.50 each. We each drank a complimentary glass of red wine because we'd picked coupons up at our accommodation.

3 Milford Sound

119km (74 miles) NE of Te Anau; 286km (177 miles) NW of Queenstown

No matter what time of year you arrive or what the weather is like, your memories of Milford Sound are bound to be very special. Its 14 nautical miles leading to the Tasman Sea are lined with mountain peaks that rise sharply to heights of 6,000 and 7,000 feet. Forsters fur seals sport on rocky shelves, dolphins play in waters that reach depths up to 2,000 feet, and its entrance is so concealed when viewed from the sea that Captain Cook sailed right by it without noticing when he was charting these waters some 200 years ago.

It rains a lot in Milford—some 300 inches annually, more than in any other one place in New Zealand. I personally don't mind the rain, for the sound, which is actually a fiord carved out by glacial action, shows yet another side of its nature under dripping skies—the trip out to the Tasman in the rain is as special in its own way as one when the sun is shining. On a fine day, when the sky is blue, the water reflects varying shades of green and blue and dark brown, the bush that flourishes even on sheer rock walls glows a deep, shiny green.

In summer, coaches pour in at the rate of 30 or more each day for launch cruises. That tide slows in other months, but the launches go out year round, rain or shine. The historic Mitre Peak Lodge (formerly the Milford Hotel) only provides accommodation to members of the guided Milford Track parties. The hotel dates from 1891, when Elizabeth Sutherland (wife of the sound's first settler) established a 12-room boardinghouse to accommodate seamen who called into the sound.

THE MILFORD ROAD

You'll be driving (or riding in a coach) through fascinating geographical, archeological, and historical country, through the **Eglinton and Hollyford valleys,** the **Homer Tunnel,** and down the majestic **Cleddau Gorge** to Milford Sound. To open your eyes to just what you're seeing, beyond the spectacular mountain scenery, take a tip from this dedicated Milford lover and contact the **Fiordland National Park Visitors Centre,** Lakefront Drive, P.O. Box 29, Te Anau (☎ **03/249-7921;** fax 03/249-7613), for information on **Fiordland National Park,** and ask specifically for their pamphlet **"The Road to Milford"** (NZ$1/US 70¢), which illuminates each mile of the way. It's a good idea, too, to arm yourself with insect repellent against sand flies, which can be murderous at Milford.

Highway 94 from Te Anau to Milford Sound leads north along the lake, with islands and wooded far shores on your left. The drive is, of necessity, a slow one as you wend your way through steep climbs between walls of solid rock and down through leafy glades. Keep an eye out for the keas, sometimes perched along the roadside trying to satisfy their insatiable curiosity about visitors to their domain. **Homer Tunnel,** about 101km (63 miles) along, is a major engineering marvel: a three–quarter-mile passageway first proposed in 1889 by William Homer, begun in 1935, and finally opened in 1940. It was, however, the summer of 1954 before a connecting road was completed and the first private automobile drove through. Incidentally, during winter months take those NO STOPPING—AVALANCHE ZONE signs very seriously. No matter how much you may want to stop for a photo, *don't!*—it could cost you your life.

Some 6km (4 miles) past the tunnel you'll see **"The Chasm"** signposted on a bridge (the sign is small, so keep a sharp eye out). By all means take the time to stop and walk the short trail back into the forest, where a railed platform lets you view a natural sculpture of smooth and craggy rocks along the riverbed of the **Cleddau River.** As the river rushes through, a sort of natural tiered fountain is formed by its waters pouring through rock apertures. The scenery is well worth the time and the short walk.

WHAT TO SEE & DO

To be fully appreciated, Milford Sound must be seen from the deck of one of the launches, with the skipper filling you in on every peak, cove, creature, and plant you pass. Fiordland Travel on Lakefront Drive, P.O. Box 1, Te Anau (☎ **0800/656-501** in New Zealand, or 03/249-7419; fax 03/249-7022) and Milford Sound Red Boat Cruises (☎ **0800/657-444** in New Zealand, or 03/249-7926; fax 03/249-8049), offer **cruise excursions.** These take you out into the Tasman where you see the shoreline close and understand how it is that the sound's entrance escaped Captain Cook's keen eye. Even in warm weather, a jacket or sweater will likely feel good out on the water, and if it should be raining, you'll be glad of a raincoat.

I've been out on Milford Sound in many different boats over the years, and my conclusion is that Fiordland Travel's *Milford Wanderer* is my favorite vessel. It's the only motor-sailor on the run, and the 2¹/₂-hour cruise costs NZ$45 (US$31.50) for adults and NZ$10 (US$7) for children. It operates from October through April. Fiordland's *Milford Haven* and *Milford Monarch* operate year round, and their excursions cost NZ$40 (US$28) for adults and NZ$10 (US$7) for children. A trip on Fiordland's MV *Friendship* costs NZ$39 (US$27.30) for adults or NZ$45 (US$31.50) with a stop at the Underwater Observatory.

Red Boat Cruises operate on the sound as well, their 1- hour and 45-minute trip costs NZ$39 (US$27.30) for adults NZ$45 (US$31.50) with a stop at the Underwater Observatory; children under 15 travel free of charge.

If you can stay over long enough, there are some marvelous **walks** from Milford Sound. Some climb into the peaks, others meander along the shore or up close to waterfalls. Ask at the Fiordland National Park Visitor Centre in Te Anau (see above). It's worth the effort to know this timeless place from the land as well as the water.

I find the tiny (2,650-foot-long) **airstrip** a constant source of fascination on every trip. The air controller here talks in more than 5,000 planes every year by radio, and accomplishes this task without the help of such safety devices as lights or radar.

The perfect safety record due to the fact that pilots must be rated specifically for this airfield, so they know what they're doing as they zoom down, dwarfed by those stupendous mountain peaks. I rather suspect, also, that careful monitoring of weather conditions and a watchful eye on all air traffic within radio range have a lot to do with that record. Among the clientele are scenic flights and farmers who drop down in their private planes. The airfield is a short (less than 5-minute) walk from the Mitre Peak Lodge.

On the other side of the airstrip, another short walk will bring you to the **fishing facilities** on the Cleddau River, an interesting and colorful sight, since there are nearly always a few of the fishing boats tied up in this safe anchorage.

Milford Sound Sea Kayaks, State Highway 94, P.O. Box 19, Milford Sound (☎ **03/249-8840,** fax 03/249-8094), offers an out of the ordinary way to see this famous sound and its abundant wildlife. Rosco Gaudin leads guided trips which depart twice daily. All equipment is provided. The most popular trip—in terms of weather and wildlife viewing—departs at 7:30am and returns between 12:30 and 1:30pm this costs NZ$69 (US$48.30) per person. There is also a 4-hour evening trip which departs at 3:30pm and costs NZ$45 (US$31.50). Rosco also does track pickup for people who have walked the Milford Track independently. This costs NZ$18 (US$12.60) per person. There's also a package which includes sailing across Lake Te Anau to the head of the track, walking the track, and then kayaking from the end of the track into Milford.

AFFORDABLE ACOMMODATIONS

Spending the night in Milford Sound is limited to a hostel and two on-the-water options. Only members of the guided walk group can stay at the Mitre Peak Lodge.

Milford Sound Lodge

Hwy 94 (Private Bag, Te Anau), Milford Sound, Fiordland. ☎ and fax **03/249-8071.** 23 rms (none with bathrm). NZ$20 (US$13) single; NZ$45 (US$29.25) double; NZ$18 (US$12.60) dorm bed; NZ$10 (US$7) campervan site. AE, BC, DC, MC, V.

This is the only accommodation at Milford Sound other than the boat options listed below. At this hostel you'll find simple, dormitory-type lodging in gorgeous surroundings just a short, beautiful mile from the sound. Basic rooms mostly hold four beds—nothing more in the way of furnishings—and the toilet-and-shower block is immaculate. There's also a big lounge with a fireplace, cooking facilities, a restaurant, and laundry facilities. Many hikers who walk the Milford Track stay here on their first night back—perhaps to prolong a too-rare close communion with nature in the wooded site. You'll get an early night's sleep—power is shut off at 10pm.

TWO OPTIONS ON THE WATER

It's possible to overnight in the Harrison Cove area of Milford Sound from October to April, on the *Milford Wanderer.* It sleeps up to 68 in bunk-style accommodations. Bedding is provided, and dinner and breakfast are included in the package: NZ$120 (US$84) for adults and NZ$60 (US$42) for children; for information contact Fiordland Travel (☎ **03/249-7416**).

The *Lady of the South Pacific* offers overnight cruises year round. The vessel offers two standards of accommodation (22 hotel-style cabins on A-deck and 8 two- or four-bed bunk rooms on B-deck, all with ensuite bathroom). The per person cost on A-deck is NZ$270 (US$189), and on B-deck it's NZ$192 (US$134.40). The experience includes a 3-hour cruise, welcome drink, a four-course dinner, lodging, and cooked breakfast. For information contact Milford Sound Red Boat Cruises (☎ **0800/657-444** in New Zealand, or 03/249-7926; fax 03/249-8049).

EN ROUTE TO DUNEDIN

The drive to Dunedin from Te Anau takes about 4¹/2 hours over good roads. Take Highway 94 across Gorge Hill into Lumsden, across the **Waimea Plains** to the milling center of **Gore,** through farmlands to **Clinton,** and across rolling downs to **Balclutha.** As you approach Balclutha, look for **Peggydale** (☎ **03/418-2345**), an ideal stopping point for tea, scones, sandwiches, or salad plates in the lovely Tea Kiosk. Peggydale handles a wide range of handcrafts—leather goods and sheepskin products (some made in their leathercraft shop), and handknits —even paintings by local artists. They're open daily from 8am to 5:30pm and will send you a mailorder catalog on request. From there, it's Highway 1 north along the coast past **Milton** to **Lookout Point,** where you'll get your first look at Dunedin. Along the way, you may want to stop in **Mossburn,** where **Wapiti Handcrafts Ltd.,** on the main street, makes and sells deerskin fashions.

WHERE TO STAY & EAT ON THE ROAD

Castlerock Cookhouse

Castlerock, R.D. 2, Lumsden 9661, Southland. ☎ and fax **03/248-7435.** 1 cottage (with bathrm). TV TEL. NZ$200 (US$140) double, NZ$320 (US$224) for 4. Extra person NZ$80 (US$56). Rate includes breakfast provisions. Dinner with wine NZ$30 (US$21) per person. MC, V.

This charming two-story cottage was built in 1872 and originally served as the cookhouse where meals for 60 station hands were prepared. It's situated on Castlerock Station, a 1,640 hectare (4,000 acre) farm, which has been in the Thomas family since 1862. Photographs of early station life, and the story of the cookhouse renovation are on display in the cottage. Hosts Juliet and David Thomas have created a modern, attractive hideaway with a country feel. Upstairs there are two bedrooms (a double and a twin) and full bathroom (with both bath and shower); downstairs a dining/living area with potbelly stove, separate lounge with open fire, a powder room, fully-equipped kitchen with modern appliances including a full size stove, microwave, fridge/freezer, and washing machine are the additional amentities. The sofa in the lounge opens to a double bed. There is also under-floor heating throughout. David will take you on a tour of the farm at no charge; other features include bicycles, bird watching, tennis court, farm animals, fishing (rods and a row boat are supplied), and walks. There's a pretty garden in front of the cottage which sits on the edge of a pond which is stocked with brown trout (catch and release only). Dinner is available in either the cookhouse or homestead. This is a convenient overnight stop if you're traveling from Te Anau to either Dunedin or Invercargill.

EN ROUTE TO INVERCARGILL

If Invercargill is your destination, you'll take Highway 94 only as far as **Lumsden,** then turn south on Highway 6 to ride through rolling farm and sheep country all the way down to Invercargill, 157km (102 miles) from Te Anau. Castlerock Cook House (see above) would be a good place to stay en route.

EN ROUTE TO MOUNT COOK

If Mount Cook is your next destination after exploring Fiordland, you'll need to head north on State Highway 6, turn east at **Frankton** (just outside Queenstown), and then pick up State Highway 8 at **Cromwell** and go north. The distance from Te Anau to Mount Cook is 433km (268 miles); the drive will take about 6¹/2 hours. If you start in Queenstown, you'll be covering 263km (163 miles), and the trip will take about 4 hours.

Cromwell's identity completely changed in 1992 when **Lake Dunstan** was formed by the massive Clyde Dam on the Clutha River. The original commercial center of the town is now under the new lake, as are more than 2,500 acres of productive orchards. The folks at **Cromwell & Districts Information Centre,** 47 The Mall, Cromwell (☎ **03/445-0212,** fax 03/445-1649), can fill you in on the details. They're open daily from 10am to 4pm.

WHERE TO STAY & EAT ON THE ROAD

✪ The Briars

Ahuriri Heights (P.O. Box 98), Omarama. ☎ **03/438-9615.** 2 rms (none with bathrm). NZ$70 (US$49) double. Rates include breakfast. No credit cards.

The Briars, about 2km (1 mile) north of Omarama and an hour from Mount Cook, is the perfect place to overnight en route to Mount Cook, especially if you leave Te Anau or Queenstown later than you expected. Marylou and Don Blue have a very attractive modern house high on a hill just off State Highway 8. From their living room window and the veranda is a good view of the Ben Mor Range. The decor includes some lovely antiques, lots of books, paintings of MacKensie Country scenery, and an impressive porcelain collection. The Blues have retired from farming and now enjoy gardening and tramping. The guest quarters are on a separate level, where two twin-bedded rooms share one bathroom.

4 Mount Cook

263km (163 miles) NE of Queenstown; 331km (199 miles) SW of Christchurch

Tiny Mount Cook Village is known the world over for its splendid alpine beauty and its remoteness. It sits within the 173,000 acres of **Mount Cook National Park,** some 2,510 feet above sea level and surrounded by 140 peaks over 7,000 feet high, 22 of which are over 10,000 feet. Most famous of all the Southern Alps is **Mount Cook/ Aorangi,** which soars 12,316 feet into the sky (it lost 60 feet in a 1991 avalanche). A full third of the park is permanent snow and ice, and the famed **Tasman Glacier** is the longest known outside of arctic regions—29km (18 miles) long and 3km (2 miles) wide. More difficult to get onto than either Fox or Franz Josef, it's still accessible for exhilarating downhill swoops on skis.

The park's most noted plant is the mountain buttercup, known as the Mount Cook lily, a pure-white blossom with thickly clustered petals and as many as 30 blooms to a stalk. There are, however, more than 300 species of native plants growing within park boundaries. Many have been marked by park staff so you can identify them as you walk. Bird sounds fill the air, most notably that of the mischievous kea, that curious little native parrot, which has clearly earned the nickname "Clown of the Snowline," and I strongly advise you to heed the "Do Not Feed" advice from park staff. Most animal life has been introduced—Himalayan thar and chamois. Hunting permits are issued by park staff.

ESSENTIALS
GETTING THERE

BY PLANE With regularly scheduled service, **Mount Cook Airline** has flights between Mount Cook and Queenstown and Te Anau.

BY COACH (BUS) There is daily coach service via **Mount Cook Landline** and **InterCity** between Mount Cook and Christchurch, Queenstown, and Timaru.

BY CAR Mount Cook can be reached via Highway 80.

ORIENTATION

A T-intersection at the end of the highway marks the entrance to Mount Cook Village. Turn left and you pass the Mt. Cook Travelodge, a modern motor hotel, and the youth hostel, post office, grocery shop, Alpine Guides Mountain Shop, and finally the DOC Visitor Information Centre. Turn right at the intersection, and you pass Mount Cook Chalets before reaching the elegant, peak-roofed internationally famous Hermitage Hotel.

VISITOR INFORMATION

At the **Department of Conservation Visitor Information Centre,** Mount Cook Field Centre, P.O. Box 5, Mouth Cook Village, South Canterbury (☎ 03/435-1818, fax 03/435-1080), is open daily from 8am to 5pm during summer and 8am to noon and 1 to 5pm during winter. Conservation officers can give you the latest information on weather, track, and road conditions. Trampers and mountaineers should check in and sign the intentions register. They can also fill you in on high-altitude huts, picnic grounds, and recommended walks in the area. **Alpine Guides (Mount Cook) Ltd.,** P.O. Box 20, Mount Cook (☎ 03/435-1834, fax 03/435-1898, e-mail mtcook@alpineguides.co.nz), can also provide a wealth of information on alpine activities, schedules, and fees. The **telephone area code** (STD) for Mount Cook is **03.**

WHAT TO SEE & DO

Clearly the mountains are the main attraction here. The Mt. Cook area is also the access point for the beautiful Tasman Glacier. If you missed the **scenic flights** at Fox and Franz Josef, you'll have another chance here. The planes lift off some 2,000 feet above sea level to begin an hour-long flight, which includes glimpses of Fox and Franz Josef and a 5-minute snow landing; the less expensive 40-minute flight surveys the Tasman Glacier only; and there are other options as well, with fares ranging from NZ$94 to NZ$300 (US$65.80 to US$210) for adults, NZ$71 to NZ$225 (US$49.70 to US$158) for children. Book through **Mount Cook Airline** (☎ 0800/800-737 nationwide, or 03/435-1849 locally). They also offer heliskiing and scenic helicopter tours.

Alpine Guides (Mount Cook) Ltd., P.O. Box 20, Mount Cook (☎ 03/435-1834, fax 03/435-1898, e-mail mtcook@alpineguides.co.nz), conducts 2-hour **coach excursions** to the Tasman Glacier for about NZ$28 (US$18.20) per person.

Skiers will undoubtedly head for the Tasman during the June-to-October ski season, but you should know in advance that **skiing** is neither inexpensive nor for novices. Skiing on the glacier involves two runs of about 11km (7 miles) each, with skiplanes returning you to the top after the first run and flying you out at the end of the day. Before you embark on the great adventure, you'll have to convince Apine Guides that you're reasonably good on skis. The day will run about NZ$595 (US$416.50). That's if the weather is right—it could run considerably higher if you have to wait for the weather to break, which could be a few days, and that means additional lodging, eating, and drinking expenses. Book through Mount Cook Airline or Alpine Guides.

That doesn't mean there aren't any no budget activities at Mount Cook. First of all, the sheer grandeur of the place costs nothing and is there for all. Park conservation officers will furnish a map of **easy walks,** which take anywhere from half an hour to half a day—no charge, and you'll commune with Mother Nature all the way. Individual booklets are available to explain the flora you'll be seeing.

Alpine Guides rents ski and climbing equipment and can furnish guides to take you **mountain climbing.** There's a 4-day hike, which leaves you at Fox Glacier via a transalpine crossing; a range of climbing experiences for those from novice to expert level; and special guided expeditions to the top of Mount Cook itself. These are not, however, budget activities. Alpine Guides can give you full details and make reservations.

AFFORDABLE ACCOMMODATIONS

Most accommodations—at any price—are owned by Southern Pacific Hotels, and the pickings are poor for budget travelers. One alternative, if you're driving, is to stay at nearby locations: Twizel, Fairlie, Tekapo, Omarama, and Kurow are under a 2-hour drive and have motels aplenty. Glentanner Park, 14 miles from Mount Cook Village, is a well-equipped motor camp. Needless to say, with such a shortage of rooms, advance reservations are an absolute necessity.

I used to recommend the Hermitage Hotel here as "Worth a Splurge," but this famous hostelry has fallen from grace. Until it has a major face-lift, I won't suggest you stay there.

The rates listed below include the 12.5% GST.

IN MOUNT COOK
Campgrounds & Cabins

Camping and caravaning are permitted in the park, but only at designated sites (*not* in the bush), which have water and toilets. If you use these facilities, remember that lighting fires is prohibited within park boundaries. Check with the park visitor information center for locations and conditions. Hikers and mountaineers have the use of 12 huts in the park, most of which have stoves, cooking and eating utensils, fuel, blankets, and radios with emergency lines. Only two of these are within reach of the casual tramper—the others are at high altitudes, and you'd need to be an experienced, expert climber to reach them. Fees for overnight use of the huts are about NZ$14 (US$9.80) per person, and arrangements and payment must be made at the Department of Conservation Visitor Information Centre.

Super-Cheap Sleeps
YHA Hostel

Bowen and Kitchener drives (P.O. Box 26), Mount Cook 8770. ☎ **03/435-1820.** 8 rms (none with bathrm), 49 beds in 7 dorm rms. NZ$25 (US$17.50) double; NZ$22 (US$15.40) twin; NZ$19 (US$13.30) dorm bed; rates quoted are for members. Non-members pay an additional NZ$4 (US$2.80). MC, V.

There are six twin rooms, two double rooms, and seven dorm rooms which sleep six to eight at this pretty alpine-style hostel in the village. Cooking facilities are good, and there are a large common room, a shop, and a sauna. Best of all, the large peaked window wall frames a fair share of that gorgeous snowcapped mountain scene. Reservations are essential during summer.

For a Few Extra Bucks
Mount Cook Chalets

Mount Cook Village (Private Bag, Mount Cook NP). ☎ **03/435-1809.** Fax 03/435-1879. 17 chalets (all with bathRM). TV. NZ$113 (US$79.10) chalet for up to 4. AE, DC, JCB, MC, V. Closed winter.

These chalets are A-frame prefab structures but are attractive, comfortable, and convenient, with several bright chairs in the felt-floored living area. There's a hotplate, fry pan, small fridge, bathroom facilities, and electric heaters. Two curtained-off

---

Readers Recommend
___

Glenbrook Sheep Station, 7 miles south of Twizel. ☎ **03/438-9407.** *"We had a very enjoyable farm stay at this sheep ranch. Penny and John have several cottages with full facilities; our unit had a TV. They have 25,000 acres with about 250,000 sheep. Penny took us for a four-wheel drive tour of the station in the morning. We had a great time, especially our kids. I highly recommend Glenbrook to your readers traveling with children. Penny recommended Hunter's for dinner, as we were too late for dinner at the station."*
—Jan Sokol, Portland, Oregon, USA.

---

sections hold two small bunks in each, and linen is provided. It's an efficient use of space, which manages to be pleasing to the eye as well. The complex, located in the village, includes parking space and a laundry with washers, dryers, and irons.

Worth a Splurge

Mt. Cook Travelodge

Mount Cook Village (Private Bag, Mount Cook NP). ☎ **03/435-1809.** Fax 03/435-1879. 57 rms (all with bathrm). TV TEL. NZ$191 (US$133.70) double. AE, DC, MC, V. Closed winter.

The Mt. Cook Travelodge is an attractive block of 57 rooms with nice decor, plus a convivial house bar that serves as a magnet for après-ski or aprés-sightseeing/flightseeing gatherings. The Wakefield Restaurant serves a buffet dinner for NZ$30.50 (US$21.40).

IN SURROUNDING TOWNS

Because of the scarcity of accommodations at Mount Cook, the town of **Twizel** (less than an hour's drive away) makes a good base.

High Country Holiday Lodge

P.O. Box 16, Twizel. ☎ **03/435-0671.** Fax 03/435-0747. 100 rms (some with bathrm), 9 motel units (all with bathrm). NZ$48 (US$33.60) double without bathrm, NZ$60 (US$42) double with bathrm; NZ$70 (US$49) double motel unit; N$15 (US$10.50) backpacker's bed. AE, BC, DC, MC, V.

The High Country Holiday Lodge is set amid lawns and shade trees just minutes away from shops, a skating rink, tennis courts, squash courts, a golf course, and pools. Nearby Lake Ruataniwha offers boating, jet skiing, windsurfing, and picnic areas. Incidentally, this area has some of the best fishing in the country, as well as excellent mountain tramping. The lodge holds single and double rooms and motel apartments, all serviced daily; the comfortable backpacker beds are in rooms with hot and cold running water, with centrally located bathroom facilities and a self-catering kitchen. The licensed restaurant/cafe is open all day.

Worth a Splurge

MacKenzie Country Inn

Ostler Rd., Twizel. ☎ **03/435-0869.** Fax 03/435-0857. 108 rms and motel units (all with bathrm). TV TEL. NZ$145 (US$102) double, NZ$168 (US$117.60) triple. AE, BC, DC, MC, V.

This attractive in-town hostelry offers serviced rooms and motel units with tea- and coffee-making facilities and a communal kitchen. On the premises are a licensed restaurant, a bistro, bars, a games room, and a guest laundry. Readers have commented on the "spacious rooms with fantastic views of Mount Cook."

Readers Recommend

Hunter's Cafe & Bar, 2 Market Place, Twizel. ☎ **03/435-0303.** *"Penny at Glenbrook recommended Hunter's for dinner, as we were too late for dinner at the station. The food is excellent at a reasonable price. The clam chowder and the grilled octopus were excellent. It has daily specials, a full bar, and is open late. I highly recommend it to your readers."*
—Jan Sokol, Portland, Oregon, USA.

GREAT DEALS ON DINING

In Mount Cook Village, budgeteers will gravitate to the **Mount Cook General Store,** which stocks grocery items.

At the **Wakefield Restaurant** in the **Travelodge,** buffet dinners cost NZ$30.50 (US$19.85).

MT. COOK AFTER DARK

The liveliest spot after dark is the **Tavern** in the village, as campers and hostelers come crowding in after a day on the slopes in all that mountain air. The **Snowline Bar** in the Hermitage Hotel is more elegant and features a wonderful mountain view. The house bar at the Mt. Cook Travelodge is the **Chamois Bar and Lounge.** That's most of Mount Cook Village's nightlife—and after a day amid so many of Mother Nature's wonders, it's likely to be enough!

EN ROUTE TO CHRISTCHURCH

Christchurch is about a 4-hour drive. Follow Highways 80 and 8 to **Fairlie,** about 150km (93 miles). At **Lake Tekapo,** take a minute to visit the **chapel,** whose altar is made from a large block of Oamaru stone and features a carved shepherd. The chapel was built of rock, wood, and stone from the area, and is dedicated to early settlers.

From Fairlie, Highway 79 takes you through a cute cafe **Geraldine,** and if it's lunchtime or teatime as you pass through, consider **Plums,** on the main road. Then go back to Highway 1, through the Canterbury Plains filled with grazing sheep, and across the level terrain, you'll see the spires of Canterbury's capital, **Christchurch,** long before you arrive.

WHERE TO STAY & EAT ON THE ROAD
✪ Poplar Downs Homestead
State Hwy. 8, Kimbell (R.D. 17, Fairlie). ☎ **03/685-8170.** Fax 03/685-8210. 2 rms (both with bathrm). NZ$150 (US$110) double. Rates include breakfast. 3-course dinner NZ$25 (US$17.50) extra per person. MC, V.

Robin and Shirley Sinclair live on 90 acres (1 1/2 hours from Mount Cook and 2 hours from Christchurch) where sheep graze and pretty gardens surround their homestead. One room has a king-size bed (which can convert to two twins) and bathroom with a shower; the other has a queen-size bed and a bathtub. Both open onto the garden. Occupants are treated to the finest bed and bath linens, terry robes, toiletries, an early-morning "cuppa" in bed, a cooked breakfast, and before-dinner drinks. Smoking is not permitted in the homestead.

13 Southland

The region you entered when you turned south at Lumsden extends as far northwest as Lake Manapouri and as far east as Balclutha. It is the country's coolest and rainiest region, yet the even spread of its rainfall is the very foundation of its economy, the raising of grass and grass seed, which, in turn, supports large numbers of sheep stations. Invercargill is New Zealand's southernmost city, the "capital" of Southland.

This area's coastline saw settlements of Maori (in limited numbers) and whalers, with frequent visits from sealers. From its waters have come those succulent Bluff oysters and crayfish (rock lobsters) you've devoured in your New Zealand travels. In fact, they account for about 90% of the value of fish landed in this area.

1 Invercargill

187km (116 miles) S of Queenstown; 221km (137 miles) SW of Dunedin

The first thing you'll notice about Invercargill is its flatness—a bump is likely to take on the dimensions of a "hill" in these parts. Actually, this flatness is due to the fact that a large part of the city was once boggy swampland. In its reclamation, town planners turned what could have been really dull terrain into a distinct advantage by creating wide, level thoroughfares and great city parks. Invercargill is a *spacious* city. Many of its broad, pleasant streets bear the names of Scottish rivers, revealing the home country of many of its early settlers.

Among its many attractions, perhaps primary, is its proximity to Stewart Island, the legendary anchor of Maui's canoe (which became, of course, the South Island, with the North Island seen as the huge fish he caught). Day-trips to Stewart Island are possible any day by air and several times a week by the ferry that runs from nearby Bluff.

ESSENTIALS
GETTING THERE & GETTING AROUND
BY PLANE   Both **Air New Zealand** (☎ **0800/737-000** in New Zealand) and **Ansett New Zealand** have service between Invercargill and Auckland and Wellington on the North Island; and Christchurch and Dunedin on the South Island.

Southland

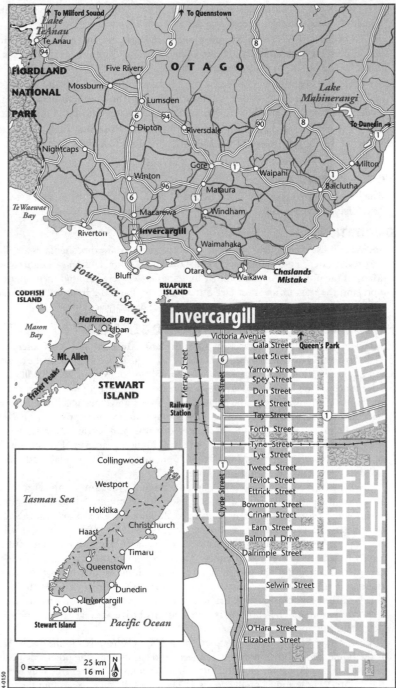

To Milford Sound
To Queenstown
Lake Te Anau
Te Anau
94

FIORDLAND

NATIONAL

PARK

Nightcaps

Te Waewae Bay

Riverton

Bluff

CODFISH ISLAND

Mason Bay

Halfmoon Bay
Oban

Mt. Allen

Fraser Peaks

STEWART ISLAND

Fouveaux Straits

Five Rivers

Mossburn

Lumsden

Dipton

Winton

Macarewa

Invercargill

Otara

Waikawa

O T A G O

6

8

Lake Mahinerangi

Riverdale

90

8

To Dunedin
1

Milton

Gore

Waipahi

Balclutha

1

Mataura

Windham

Waimahaka

Chaslands Mistake

RUAPUKE ISLAND

Invercargill

Victoria Avenue
Gala Street   Queen's Park
Loot Street
Yarrow Street
Spey Street
Don Street
Esk Street
Tay Street
Forth Street
Tyne Street
Eye Street
Tweed Street
Teviot Street
Ettrick Street
Bowmont Street
Crinan Street
Earn Street
Balmoral Drive
Dalrimple Street

Selwin Street

O'Hara Street
Elizabeth Street

Mersey Street
Dee Street
Clyde Street

Railway Station

6

1

1

Collingwood

Westport

Hokitika

Haast

Christchurch

Tasman Sea

Timaru

Queenstown

Dunedin

Invercargill

Oban

Stewart Island

Pacific Ocean

0   25 km
     16 mi

N

4-0150

349

BY TRAIN   The *Southerner* serves Invercargill and Christchurch, Dunedin, and Timaru Monday through Friday. The railway station is on Leven Street.

BY COACH (BUS)   Both **Mount Cook Landline** and **InterCity** have coach service between Invercargill and Christchurch, Dunedin, Queenstown, Te Anau, and Timaru. The bus depot is also on Leven Street.

BY CAR   Invercargill can be reached on Highway 6 from Queenstown or Highway 1 from Dunedin. See also, the information on the Southern Scenic Route under "En Route to Dunedin," at the end of the Invercargill section in this chapter.

BY TAXI   If you need a taxi while in Invercargill, call **Blue Star Taxis Ingill Ltd,** corner of Tay & Jed streets (☎ **03/218-6079**), or **Taxi Co,** 200 Clyde St. (☎ **03/214-4478**).

VISITOR INFORMATION

You'll find the **Invercargill Visitor Centre** in the Southland Museum and Art Gallery, Victoria Avenue (☎ **03/218-9753**). The **telephone area code** (STD) is **03.**

ORIENTATION

Invercargill's streets are laid out in neat grid patterns. Main thoroughfares are **Tay Street** (an extension of Highway 1) and **Dee Street** (an extension of Highway 6). Many of the principal shops and office buildings are centered around their intersection, and the **post office** is on Dee Street. **Queens Park** is a beautiful green oasis (200 acres) right in the center of town and the site of many activities.

EXPLORING INVERCARGILL: WHAT TO SEE & DO

Allow at least a full hour to visit the ✪ **Southland Museum and Art Gallery,** on Gala Street by the main entrance to Queens Park. The collections inside the Southern Hemisphere's largest pyramid include a multitude of exhibits, which will bring alive much of the history and natural resources of this area. In addition, there's a tuatarium, the only place in the country you can view live tuataras in a simulated natural setting. You can also see a multi-image audiovisual program on New Zealand's sub-Antarctic islands. In front of the museum, examine the section of fossilized forest from the Jurassic era some 160 million years ago. The museum is open Monday through Friday from 9am to 5pm and Saturday, Sunday, and public holidays from 1 to 5pm. Admission is free.

Two minutes from the city, **Queens Park** is just one (the largest) of Invercargill's parklands (a total of 2,975 acres) and might well keep you occupied for the better part of a day. Within its 200 acres are a rhododendron walk; an iris garden; a sunken rose garden; a grove of native and exotic trees; a wildlife sanctuary with wallabies, deer, and an aviary; a duck pond; a winter garden; an 18-hole golf course; tennis courts; and—perhaps most important of all—a cool, green retreat for the senses. A very special thing to look for is the beguiling children's fountain encircled by large bronze animal statues. Over the years this beautiful botanical reserve has seen duty as grazing land, a racecourse, and a sporting ground. The entrance is from Queens Drive at Gala Street. There's a delightful cafe for light refreshments.

Drive out to **Bluff,** Invercargill's port, some 27km (16¹⁄₂ miles) to the south. This is the home port for the Stewart Island ferry and the site (on the other side of the harbor at Tiwai Point) of the mammoth Tiwai Aluminum Smelter (the only one in the country) whose annual production is 313,000 tons. If you'd like to tour the complex, contact **Tiwai Smelter Tours,** NZ Aluminum Smelters Ltd., Private Bag,

Invercargill (☎ **03/218-5999,** fax 03/218-9747). You must be at least 12 years of age and wear long trousers or slacks, heavy footwear, and clothing that covers your arms. There's no charge, but usually tours are limited to one each week, so it pays to reserve well in advance.

There are two great **walks** in Bluff (ask the Visitor Centre in Invercargill for the "Foveaux Walk, Bluff" pamphlet). The **"Glory Walk"** (named for a sailing vessel, *England's Glory,* which was wrecked at Bluff) is about 1.5km (1 mile) long and passes through native bush and trees, which form a shady canopy overhead. Ferns and mosses add to the lush greenery. The **Sterling Point–Ocean Beach Walk** begins where Highway 1 ends at Foveaux Strait. It's almost 7km (4¹/₂ miles) long, following the coastline around Bluff Hill, with marvelous views of beaches, offshore islands, and surf breaking against coastal rocks. Parking facilities are provided at both ends of the walk, and you are asked to follow the signposts and to leave no litter in your footsteps.

AFFORDABLE ACCOMMODATIONS

You should have no trouble finding a place to lay your weary head in Invercargill. There are lots of good budget options. The rates given below include the 12.5% GST.

CABINS & CAMPGROUNDS

The **Invercargill Caravan Park,** 20 Victoria Ave., Invercargill (☎ **03/218-8787**), has two chalets and 21 cabins that sleep one to six people. On the premises are a kitchen, showers and toilets, a laundry, store, car wash, vehicle-storage area, and play area. There are facilities for the travelers with disabilities, plus 50 campsites and 40 caravan sites. Rates for bunks are NZ$10 (US$7) per person; cabins are NZ$24 to NZ$30 (US$16.80 to $21) for two; caravan sites run NZ$16 (US$11.20) for two; and tent sites, NZ$7.50 (US$5.30) per person. It's in a central location, 2 minutes from McDonald's.

SUPER-CHEAP SLEEPS

Gerrards Railway Hotel

1 Leven St., at Esk St., P.O. Box 380, Invercargill. ☎ **03/218-3406.** Fax 03/218-3003. 21 rms (12 with bathrm). NZ$40–$70 (US$28–$49) double without bath and with breakfast; NZ$80–$98 (US$56–$68.60) double with bath but without breakfast. AE, BC, DC, MC, V.

This interesting 1896 B&B hotel, across from the rail and bus stations, has a rosy-pink brick facade with white trim; the facade has had a face cleaning and the rooms have been redone, thanks to owners Keith and Margaret Gerrard. Though not fancy accommodations, they are comfortable, clean, and centrally located. Showers and toilets are conveniently located for those that share. Rooms with bathroom also have telephones and TVs. A guest TV lounge, cocktail bar, and moderately priced restaurant are available.

YHA Hostel

122 North Rd., Waikiwi, Invercargill. ☎ **03/215-9344.** 34 beds (no rooms with bathrm). NZ$15 (US$10.50) dorm bed. No credit cards.

The 34 beds here are in six rooms, and other facilities include showers and a kitchen. There's a barbecue/picnic area available for use during the day, and the resident manager can arrange reduced fares to Stewart Island on a standby basis. He can also advise about hostel-type accommodations on the island (there are tentative plans for a YHA hostel, but no timetable yet). The hostel is located on an extension of Dee Street, before it becomes Highway 6.

FOR A FEW EXTRA BUCKS

Ascot Park Hotel

Tay St. and Racecourse Rd., Invercargill. ☎ **03/217-6195.** Fax 03/217-7002. 69 rms (all with bathrm), 23 motel units (all with bathrm). TV TEL. NZ$145 (US$102) double; NZ$92 (US$64.40) double motel unit. AE, BC, DC, MC, V.

This is Invercargill's top spot, with hotel rates out of the reach of budget travelers; however, the motel units are affordable. Everyone shares the heated indoor pool, spa, two saunas, and solarium. A licensed restaurant is open daily. The complex is 4km (2¹/₂ miles) from the center of town.

Colonial Motor Inn

335–339 Tay St., Invercargill. ☎ **03/217-6058.** Fax 03/217-6118. 10 units (all with bathrm). TV TEL. NZ$80 (US$56) double. Additional adults NZ$14 (US$9.80) extra. AE, DC, MC, V.

There are one- and two-bedroom units with dining areas and fully equipped kitchens at the Colonial, 5 minutes from the city center. Other facilities include a guest laundry, room service, and off-street parking. Continental breakfast is available on request.

✪ Tayesta Motel

343 Tay St., Invercargill. ☎ **03/217-6074.** Fax 03/217-7075. 12 units (all with bathrm). TV TEL. NZ$86 (US$60.20) apt for 2. Additional person NZ$12 (US$8.40) extra. Best Western and auto club discounts available. AE, DC, MC, V.

This attractive one-story blue-and-white motel has one- and two-bedroom apartments, each with large picture windows in the lounge, a fully equipped kitchen, central heating, video, and a radio. There's a laundry, plus a play area with swings and sandpit. Continental or cooked breakfasts are available for a small charge. The Tayesta is located a mile from the city center.

GREAT DEALS ON DINING

Invercargill has numerous coffee shops offering good value. The coffee lounge in the **D.I.C. Department Store** has good morning and afternoon teas as well as light lunches, all inexpensive.

SUPER-CHEAP EATS

Gourmets Delight

37 Esk St. ☎ **03/214-9214.** Fax 03/214-9499. Reservations not required. Average lunch under NZ$8 (US$5.60); less for snacks. No credit cards. Mon–Thurs 7:30am–6pm, Fri 7am–10pm, Sat 7am–2am, Sun noon–9pm. LIGHT MEALS/SNACKS.

This is the place for quiche, baked potatoes with a variety of fillings, many different salads, nutritious hot meals, light lunches, carrot cake, muesli munch, soups, and cakes—all made daily on the premises and all very good. Try one of their traditional Kiwi roast meals. They also have takeout and are licensed. Incidentally, owner Peter Breayley and his staff are only too pleased to give advice on sightseeing in the city. It's located in the city center.

FOR A FEW EXTRA BUCKS

✪ Gerrards

In Gerrards Railway Hotel, 1 Leven St., at Esk St. ☎ **03/218-3406.** Fax 03/218-3003. Reservations recommended. Main courses NZ$20 (US$14); average lunch NZ$12 (US$8.40). AE, BC, DC, MC, V. Mon–Fri noon–2pm; daily 6:30–9pm. NEW ZEALAND/CONTINENTAL.

There's a bright cafe air about this restaurant, which is a great favorite with locals. The menu is a mixture of native New Zealand and continental dishes and includes coquilles St. Jacques and escalope de porc with mushrooms and brandy-cream sauce,

---

A Carvery Treat

Friday night in Invercargill means a carvery treat at the ✪ **Ascot Park Hotel** for residents as well as visitors— reservations are a very good idea (in fact, I heard about this feast way up on the North Island when I mentioned coming to Invercargill). The Ascot Park, on the corner of Racecourse Road and Tay Street (☎ **03/ 217-6195**), is a modern hotel of the first order, and the carvery is presented in an enormous room with different levels for tables. The spread is just about as enormous as the room, with every kind of seafood currently available, fresh salads, great roasts for non-seafood lovers, and luscious desserts. You'll see parties of locals chatting away with visitors, and there's a party atmosphere all through the place. The price is NZ$29 (US$20.30) for adults, and NZ$14.50 (US$10.15) children ages 5-12 for which you get full value, indeed.

---

local Bluff oysters, and fresh blue cod in a lemon-and-wine sauce. Service is friendly, and it's fully licensed. Gerrards is in the city center, opposite the rail and bus stations.

The Grand Hotel
76 Dee St. ☎ **03/218-8059.** Reservations recommended. Main courses NZ$14–$24 (US$9.80– $16.80). AE, DC, MC, V. Daily 7am–9pm. New Zealand.

This elegant hotel in the city center is a joy to go into, even if you don't eat. The lovely formal dining room serves seasonal dishes of mostly local ingredients, using many traditional recipes. If oysters are on the menu in any form, let that be your order—they'll be from Bluff and superior to any you've tasted before. It's fully licensed.

EN ROUTE TO DUNEDIN

You can drive from Invercargill to Dunedin in a little over 3 hours by way of Highway 1, through Gore, past farmlands and mile after mile of grazing sheep. It's a pleasant drive, and one I think you'll enjoy.

However, if you have a day to spend on the road, let me urge you to follow the Southern Scenic Route along Highway 92 and allow a full day to loiter along the way, rejoining Highway 1 at Balclutha. If you make this drive, the leaflet "Drive New Zealand's Southern Scenic Route" from the Visitor Centre in Invercargill is quite helpful because it details the reserves through which you'll pass.

The **Southern Scenic Route** takes you through a region of truly unusual character. There are great folds in the land that are covered with such a diversity of native forests. Beyond Chaslands, you'll be in one national forest reserve after another. Short detours will take you to the coast and golden sand beaches, prominent headlands, and fine bays.

Highway 92, let me hasten to add, is not paved its entire length—however, even unpaved portions are in good driving condition, albeit at a slower speed than the faster Highway 1. Picnic spots abound, so you can take along a packed lunch from Invercargill or plan to stop in the country pub in Owaka's only hotel for lunch (stop for refreshments even if you lunch elsewhere—it's an experience you wouldn't want to miss). One very special detour you might consider follows.

Just beyond Fortrose, follow the Fortrose-Otara road to the right, and when you pass the Otara School, look for the turnoff to **Waipapa Point.** The point is the entrance to Foveaux Strait, a treacherous waterway that has scuttled many a sailing vessel and that is now marked by a light, which was first used in 1884. Follow the Otara–Haldane road to Porpoise Bay; then turn right and drive a little over half a mile to the ✪ **Curio Bay Fossil Forest,** which is signposted. This sea-washed rock terrace dates back 160 *million* years and is the original floor of a Jurassic subtropical forest of kauri trees, conifers, and other trees that were growing at a time when grasses had not even evolved. At low tide, you can make out low stumps and fallen logs that have been petrified after being buried in volcanic ash, then raised when the sea level changed. You can then retrace your way around Porpoise Bay and follow the signs to Waikawa and continue north to rejoin Highway 92 and travel on to Chaslands.

If you'd like more information about this lovely part of a lovely country, contact the **Department of Conservation,** Owaka Field Centre, 20 Ryley St., Owaka (☎ and fax **03/415-8341**).

2 Stewart Island

30km (19 miles) SW of Bluff, across Foveaux Strait

Seen on the map, Stewart Island is not much more than a speck; when seen from the deck of the *Foveaux Express* or from the air, its magnitude will surprise you. There are actually 1,600km (975 miles) of coastline enclosing 1,680 sq km (625 square miles) of thick bush (most of it left in its natural state), bird sanctuary, and rugged mountains. Only a tiny stretch of that long coastline has been settled, and it's the little fishing town of **Oban** that will be your landfall. There are about 12 miles of paved road on the island, which are easily covered by the minibus tour, and many of the houses you see are the holiday "batch" or "crib" of Kiwis from the South Island who view Stewart Island as the perfect spot to escape the pressures of civilization. The population of Stewart Island is 690.

The pace here is quite unhurried—few cars, and friendly islanders more attuned to the tides and the running of cod and crayfish than to commerce—and the setting is a botanist's dream. The Maori called the island Rakiura, "heavenly glow," a name you'll find especially fitting if you are lucky enough to see the southern lights brighten its skies or to be here for one of its spectacular sunsets.

While its beauty and serenity can be glimpsed in the few hours of a day-trip, you might want to consider at least one overnight to explore its beaches, bush, and people, and to savor this very special place to the fullest. Incidentally, should you hear yourself or other visitors referred to as "loopies" by the islanders, not to worry—it's used with affection.

ESSENTIALS
GETTING THERE

BY PLANE The major transport to Stewart Island is via **Southern Air** (☎ **0800/ 658-876** in New Zealand, or 03/218-9129; fax 03/214-4681), which is based in Invercargill. Incidentally, during the 20-minute flight, the nine-seat Britten–Norman Islander provides breathtaking views of the coastline, the changing colors of the waters below, bush-clad islands, and Stewart Island itself, where you land on a paved runway and are minibused into Oban. Southern Air flies daily, almost every hour in the summer; there's a minimum of three flights a day, and extra ones are added upon demand. The airline schedules even allow for a day visit if you're pressed for time. The adult fare is NZ$68 (US$47.60) one way, NZ$123 (US$86.10) round trip; children pay half. The Golden Age fare for those over 60 is NZ$106 (US$74.20) round trip; and students can go standby for NZ$70 (US$49) round trip. Southern Air can also help you plan and book your entire Stewart Island holiday. They know the island well and are happy to arrange things to suit your preferences.

BY BOAT   You can go aboard the *Foveaux Express,* operated by Stewart Island Marine. During the winter it sails from Bluff daily at 9:30am and 4pm. From late August to late May, the boat departs Bluff daily at 9:30am and 5pm. The crossing takes 1 hour, and there is connecting bus service from Invercargill to Bluff. The round-trip fare is NZ$74 (US$51.80) for adults and NZ$37 (US$25.90) for children. For more information, call ☎ 03/212-7660 or fax 03/212-8377.

VISITOR INFORMATION

The town of **Oban** is located on Halfmoon Bay and consists of a general store, post office, travel office, craft shop, hotel, forestry office, a small museum, and the pier where the ferry docks. The **Stewart Island Visitor Information Centre** is on Main Road (☎ 03/219-1218; fax 03/219-1555). The **telephone area code** (STD) for Stewart Island is **03.**

EXPLORING STEWART ISLAND: WHAT TO SEE & DO

On the island, the only thing you really must not miss is the $1^{1}/_{2}$-hour ✪ **Sam and Billy the Bus** minibus tours available through **Stewart Island Travel** (☎ 03/219-1269). Sam will cover not only every one of those 20km (12 miles) of paved road, he'll give you a comprehensive history of Stewart Island—the whalers who settled here, the sealers who called in (it was, in fact, the mate of a sealer who gave his name to the island), the sawmill and mineral industries that came and went, and the development of the fishing industry—and will point out traces they left behind scattered around your route. He also knows the flora of the island (you'll learn, for instance, that there are 17 varieties of orchids on the island) and its animal population (no wild pigs or goats). You'll see many of the 18 good swimming beaches and hear details of the paua diving, which has proved so profitable for islanders (much of the colorful shell that went into those souvenirs you've seen around New Zealand came from Stewart Island). From **Observation Point** right to the road's end at **Thule Bay,** Sam gives you an insider's view of his home. And questions or comments are very much in order—it's an informal, happy hour of exchange: a perfect way to begin a stay of several days, an absolute essential if the day trip is all you will have. Sam also offers $2^{1}/_{2}$-hour Nature Excursions and 3- to 4-hour Twilight Tours. Check when booking for schedule and fare.

The **Rakiura Museum** in Halfmoon Bay (☎ 03/219-1049 or phone/fax 03/219-1126) features photos and exhibits that follow Stewart Island's history through its sailing, whaling, tin-mining, sawmilling, and fishing days. It also has shell and Maori artifact exhibits. It's open Monday through Saturday from 10am to noon and Sunday from noon to 2pm, with extended hours during the summer holidays (see the local notice board). Admission is NZ$1 (US 70¢) for adults and NZ50¢ (US 35¢) for children.

Visit the small **deer park** just across from Stewart Island Travel. Small Virginian (whitetail) and red deer are right at home in the enclosure and seem delighted to have visitors.

Next to the deer park is the office of the ✪ **Department of Conservation,** Main Road, P.O. Box 3, Stewart Island (☎ 03/219-1130, fax 03/219-1555), which has interesting displays of natural history, a video room where you can watch videos about Stewart Island, sub-Antarctic islands, and other natural history subjects. More important, the staff there can supply information on how best to spend your time on Stewart Island and details on many beautiful **walks** around Oban and farther afield. If you're interested in spending a few days on the island tramping, I suggest that you write ahead for their informative booklets on just what you'll need to bring and what you can expect. The **Rakiura Track** is a 3-day venture for those of moderate fitness; the North West Circuit is an 8- to 10-day trek for those who want a more strenuous tramp. There are recently upgraded tramping huts conveniently spaced along the tracks (ranging in size from 6 to 30 bunks), but they're packed in summer. A 2-night stay is the maximum at any one hut. The DOC office is open from Christmas to the end of February, from 8am to 7pm weekdays and from 9am to 7pm on weekends; the rest of the year, weekdays from 8am to 5pm and weekends from 10am to noon. If you find it closed, just ask locally—the conservation officer might have just popped out for a short spell.

Popular **short walks** around Oban are those to Golden Bay, Lonneckers, Lee Bay, Thule, Observation Point, and the lighthouse at Acker's Point. Ringarina Beach is a mecca for shell hounds (I have New Zealand friends who serve entrees in paua shells they've picked up on the beach here), but your finds will depend on whether the tides are right during your visit. If you're here on a day trip, be sure to check locally to be certain you can make it back from any walk you plan in time for the ferry or air return and be sure to bring insect repellent.

You can engage local boats for **fishing** or visiting nearby uninhabited islands at prices that are surprisingly low. Contact Stewart Island Travel.

AFFORDABLE ACCOMMODATIONS

Stewart Island Travel, P.O. Box 26, Halfmoon Bay, Stewart Island (☎ 03/219-1269; fax 03/219-1293 e-mail: Sam@southnet.co.nz), can send you a complete list of accommodations and prices, and can help you make reservations. Accommodations are extremely limited, and in summer they're booked months in advance, so if your plans include a visit here, contact them as soon as you have firm dates for your visit. It's sometimes possible to rent one of the holiday homes not currently in use.

SUPER-CHEAP SLEEPS

Shearwater Inn

Ayre St. (P.O. Box 25), Halfmoon Bay, Oban, Stewart Island. ☎ 03/219-1114. Fax 03/214-4681. 80 beds (none with bathrm). NZ$60 (US$42) double or twin; NZ$24 (US$16.80) dorm bed. Additional child NZ$10 (US$7) extra. MC, V.

When the Shearwater Inn complex opened in conjunction with Southern Air in 1989, it was the first major new accommodation on the island in 50 years. Situated right in the heart of Oban, near the post office, shops, and beach, it's an associate YHA hostel, and also has single, double, and family rooms. The 80 beds are in two-to four-bed rooms; there's a communal lounge with an open fireplace and TV; a kitchen (all utensils furnished); a licensed restaurant for moderately priced à la carte meals; and a courtyard used for barbecues. The inn provides wheelchair facilities.

FOR A FEW EXTRA BUCKS

Rakiura Motels

P.O. Box 96, Stewart Island. ☎ 03/219-1096. 5 units (all with bathrm). TV. NZ$80 (US$56) double. Additional person NZ$15 (US$10.50) extra per adult, NZ$10 (US$7) extra per child under 12. MC, V.

Elaine Hamilton offers self-contained motel units located about a mile from Oban. The units sleep up to six, are heated, and have kitchens and private bathrooms.

✪ South Sea Hotel

P.O. Box 52, Halfmoon Bay, Stewart Island. ☎ 03/219-1059. Fax 03/219-1120. 18 rms (none with bathrm). NZ$80 (US$56) double or twin. MC, V.

Captain Crayfish's South Sea Saturday Night

Of all the good times I've had in country pubs in New Zealand, one particularly enjoyable night in the public bar of the South Sea Hotel on Stewart Island stands out in my mind.

It was a Saturday evening and the pub was crowded with fishermen wearing their traditional patched overalls, heavy sweaters, and Stewart Island slippers (white gumboots). The local band, Captain Crayfish and the Wekas, was composed of a piano, an accordion, a trombone, and a tea chest (an instrument similar to a washtub bass, made of a carton box with a piece of rope attached to a broom handle). The musicians played simultaneously, but it didn't always seem as if they were playing the same tune—and no one seemed to mind.

The band took a break while the Kiwis' rugby match against Australia was broadcast on television. The home team won, and the crowd went wild.

Toward the end of the evening the trombone player conducted a sing-along—"Alouette" was the favorite, with "You Are My Sunshine" a close second. There was no dance floor, but that didn't stop a slippered local and a chubby woman in Nikes from doing a waltz.

I had planned to go to bed early, but halfway through the evening I realized I wouldn't have been able to sleep anyway. My room was right over the bar.

When the pub closed, I went upstairs and had the pleasure of drifting off to sleep with the sound of waves breaking on the beach directly across the road from the hotel.

The South Sea Hotel sounds like a place one would discover in Fiji, but only the name suggests a Polynesian resort. It never gets very warm on Stewart Island, and pesky sand flies often make sitting on the beach uncomfortable.

The rugged island is inhabited by commercial fishermen and their families. They live a basic existence and depend heavily on supplies and personnel that come by boat from Bluff. On a recent visit, I noticed that the community bulletin board outside the general store carried news of the impending arrival of a hairdresser from Invercargill.

The South Sea Hotel is the social center of the island. Birthdays are celebrated in the dining room, and the problems of the world are solved over a pint in the bar; cards and darts tournaments are held regularly to raise money for the local primary school. . . .

The two-story weatherboard hotel was built in 1927; its predecessor on the same site dated from the early 1900s. When the present hotel activated its liquor license in 1955, it broke a "drought" that had been in effect since the 1880s. It's hard to believe that Stewart Island was ever "dry," and there are plenty of stories about home-brewed beer and a secret whisky still.

I can only imagine the sigh of relief that issued from thirsty locals on the day the public bar opened its doors.

Stewart Island's only hotel (but not the only place to stay) sits in the curve of Halfmoon Bay, in the village center across from the water. Its public bar, bar/lounge (whose windows overlook the bay), and licensed restaurant are the center of much island activity, and even if you lodge elsewhere you're likely to find yourself in and out of the South Sea many times during your stay. The rooms all share the bathroom and toilet facilities down the hall, and there are six singles, two doubles, eight twins,

"While on Stewart Island I found two very clean, comfortable bed and breakfasts with lovely views over Halfmoon Bay, nice gardens, and most helpful and friendly people. A home away from home! "**The Nest,** P.O. Box 88, Halfmoon Bay, Stewart Island (☎ and fax **03/219-1310,** e-mail thenest@es.co.nz) and **Goomes B&B,** P.O. Box 36, Halfmoon Bay, Stewart Island, (☎ **03/219-1057).**

—Michaela Kammerer, Frankfurt, Germany.

Author's Note: The Nest offers en suite and private bathrooms and charges NZ$140 (US$98) double and NZ$25 (US$17.50) per person for dinner. Jeanette and Peter Goomes offer shared facilities and charge NZ$100 (US$70) double.

---

and two triples. This is the kind of charming, old-fashioned inn that seems exactly right for this island—the guest lounge, for example, has an open fire glowing on cool days, and the staff takes a personal interest in all guests (and casual visitors, too).

GREAT DEALS ON DINING

In addition to the listings below, the **Shearwater Inn** (see "Affordable Accommodations," above) has a good à la carte restaurant serving breakfast from 8 to 9am, and dinner from 6 to 9pm daily at reasonable prices. The South Sea Hotel can pack a **picnic lunch** if notified in ample time, and there's a **general store** where you can pick up picnic makings for a day in the bush. For light lunches, morning and afternoon teas, or take-aways, go to the **Travel Inn Tearooms,** adjacent to Stewart Island Travel in the village center.

✪ Annie Hansen's Dining Room

In the South Sea Hotel, Oban, Halfmoon Bay. ☎ **03/219-1059.** Average lunch NZ$15 (US$10.50); average dinner NZ$25 (US$17.50). MC, V. Daily 7am–10pm. SEAFOOD/NEW ZEALAND.

One of the best seafood meals I've had in New Zealand was in this large, pleasant waterfront dining room, named for a longtime owner of the hotel back in the early days of this century. My fish was truly fresh and cooked to perfection, and the salad bar was more extensive than I would have expected on an island where so much must be imported. The house specialty is freshly caught blue cod; crayfish and mutton bird are also on the menu when they're available. Homemade cheesecake is the favorite dessert. The service included a friendly chat about how best to spend my time on Stewart Island. Other main courses included beef, lamb, and chicken, and the manager tells me that they are constantly trying out traditional recipes, many of them brought by early Stewart Island settlers. The restaurant is fully licensed.

Dunedin 14

You won't find pipers in the streets of Dunedin, and the citizens of "New Edinburgh on the Antipodes" are quick to tell you they're *Kiwis,* not Scots. Still, one look at the stone Victorian architectural face of the city with its crown of up-reaching spires will tell you that the 344 settlers who arrived at the beautiful Upper Harbour in March 1848 could have come only from Scotland. And when you learn that Dunedin is the old Gaelic name for Edinburgh, that the city produces New Zealand's only domestic whisky and has the only kilt store in the country, and that the strains of a pipe band are common here, you surely won't be able to mistake its Scottish nature.

The other aura that's impossible to ignore is that created by the University of Otago. The 15,000 students and faculty members at this learned institution (which was patterned after Glasgow University) are much in evidence—giving the community an appealing academic/college-town atmosphere. The university's slate-roofed bluestone buildings hint of serious cerebral endeavors, but anyone who has visited Dunedin's pubs will assure you that these students know how to have fun, too.

Dunedin (pop. 110,000) is the South Island's second-largest city. The community's economy boomed in the 1860s when gold was discovered in Central Otago, and the city's (and the country's) future was forever impacted by the shipment of frozen meat that was sent to Britain from nearby Port Chalmers in 1882. Throughout its history, Dunedin has held on to its priorities of education, conservation of natural beauty, and humanitarian concerns.

A reader wrote recently, "Dunedin has a quiet charm. It's one of New Zealand's best-kept secrets." I couldn't agree more.

1 Orientation

ARRIVING

BY PLANE Both **Air New Zealand** and **Ansett New Zealand** provide air service between Dunedin and Auckland, Hamilton, and Wellington on the North Island; and Christchurch and Invercargill on the South Island.

The minibus **airport shuttle** (☎ **03/479-2481**) provides service for all flights, with hotel pickup and delivery, for a fare of NZ$10 (US$7). The airport is a full 30 minutes from the city, which makes a taxi prohibitive at fares of about NZ$45 (US$31.50).

Dunedin

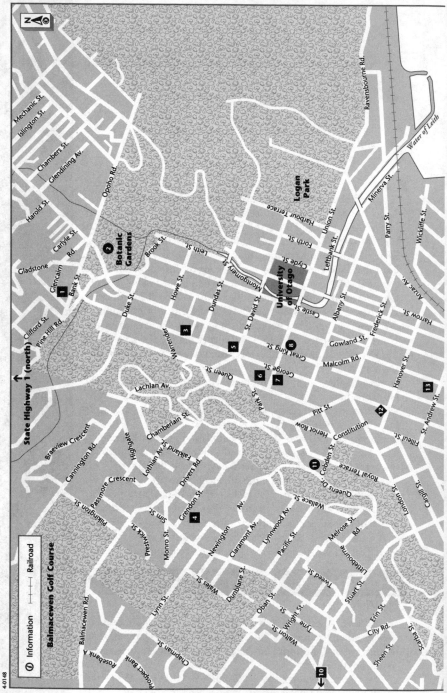

State Highway 1 (north)

Balmacewen Golf Course

⊙ Information

⊥⊤⊥ Railroad

Mechanic St.
Islington St.
Chambers St.
Glendining Av.
Harold St.
Carlyle St.
Gladstone
Glencairn Rd.
Bank St.
Pine Hill Rd.
Clifford St.
Opoho Rd.
Botanic Gardens
Brook St.
Duke St.
Howe St.
Leith St.
Dundas St.
Montgomery
Warrender
St. David St.
Great King St.
George St.
Queen St.
Park St.
Castle St.
University of Otago
Clyde St.
Forth St.
Harbour Terrace
Union St.
Leftbank St.
Albany St.
Gowland St.
Malcolm Rd.
Frederick St.
Hanover St.
Logan Park
Ravensbourne Rd.
Minerva St.
Parry St.
Wickliffe St.
Harrow St.
Anzac Av.
St. Andrew St.
Filleul St.
Pitt St.
Heriot Row
Constitution
Cobden St.
Royal Terrace
Queens Dr.
London St.
Lachlan Av.
Braeview Crescent
Cannington Rd.
Highgate
Chamberlain St.
Falkland Av.
Lothian Av.
Drivers Rd.
Wallace St.
Passmore Crescent
Pilkington St.
Prestwick St.
Sim St.
Crendon St.
Monro St.
Newington
Claremont Av.
Lynnwood Av.
Pacific St.
Melrose St.
Littlebourne Rd.
Rosebank A
Prospect Bank
Balmacewen Rd.
Lynn St.
Wales St.
Dunblane St.
Oban St.
Chapman St.
Walton St.
Tyne St.
Wright St.
Tweed St.
Stuart St.
Erin St.
Sheen St.
City Rd.
Scaife St.

Water of Leith

4-0148

360

ACCOMMODATIONS

Aaron Lodge 10
Aberdeen Motel 1
Alcala Motor Lodge 5
Arcadian Motel 27
Bentley's Hotel 13
Best Western Tourist Court 3
Farry's Motel 7
High Street Court Motel 23
Leviathan Hotel 19
Magnolia House 4
Sahara Guesthouse and Motel 6
Southern Cross Hotel 22
YHA Hostel 24

DINING

The Bank 16
Bell Pepper Blues 25
Best Cafe 18
Deli Cafe 22
Golden Harvest 12
High Tide 26
Joseph Mellor Restaurant 14
Palms Cafe 21
Potpourri 7
Terrace Cafe 15

ATTRACTIONS

Botanic Gardens 2
Dunedin Public Art Gallery 9
Olveston 11
Otago Museum 8
Otago Settler's Museum 20

Otago Harbour

Belleknowes
Golf Course

The Octagon

The Oval

Halsey St.
Frayatt St.
Sturdee St.
Jutland St.
Beauchop
Devon St.
Ward St.
Meson St.
Crosswell St.
Willis St.
Frayatt St.
Thomas Burns St.
Birch St.
Butler St.
Kitchener St.
French St.
Wharf St.
Strathallan St.
Oran St.
Portsmouth Dr.
Otaki St.
Turakina St.
Burlington St.
Moray Place
Dowling St.
Jetty St.
Police St.
Crawford St.
Cumberland St.
Wokesly
Gordon
Stuart St.
York Place
Tennyson St.
Rattray St.
Elm Row
Duncan St.
Macaggon St.
Princes St.
Hope St.
Stafford St.
Jervois St.
Manor Place
Lees St.
Melville St.
Carrell St.
Maitlands St.
Arthur St.
Russell St.
Canongate
Serpentine Av.
Alva St.
Cochrane
Patrick St.
Glen Rd.
Eglington Rd.
Haywood St.
Walter St.
South Rd.
Bridge St.
Brighton St.
Leckhampton
Murrayfield

←To Airport/State Highway 1 (south)

361

BY TRAIN   The *Southerner* train runs between Dunedin and Christchurch and Invercargill. The **railway station** (a sightseeing attraction; see "Exploring Dunedin: What to See & Do," later in this chapter) is at the foot of Stuart Street.

BY COACH (BUS)   **InterCity** and **Mount Cook Landline** provide coach service between Dunedin and Christchurch, Invercargill, Picton, Queenstown, Te Anau, and Timaru. The two lines have separate **bus terminals:** InterCity is at 599 Princes St. (☎ 03/477-8860), and Mount Cook, at 205 Saint Andrew St. (☎ 03/474-0674).

BY ALTERNATIVE COACH (BUS)   The Magic Traveller's Network includes Dunedin on their routes.

BY CAR   Dunedin can be reached via Highways 1 and 87. It's 336km (208 miles) south of Christchurch and 220km (136 miles) northeast of Invercargill.

VISITOR INFORMATION

The staff at the **Dunedin Visitor Centre,** 48 The Octagon (☎ 03/474-3300, fax 03/474-3311), will be happy to answer your questions. The office is normally open Monday through Friday from 8:30am to 5pm, and Saturday, Sunday, and public holidays from 9am to 5pm, with extended hours in summer. They can make lodging reservations and book all your sightseeing excursions and onward travel arrangements.

SPECIAL EVENTS

Dunedin is fun to visit any time of the year, but you'll be doubly blessed if you arrive during one of its special events. Probably the highlight of them all is the late-March ✪ **Scottish Week,** when the city breaks out with kilts, bagpipes, Scottish country dancing, and a host of other activities that reflect its heritage.

You might also enjoy its annual ✪ **Festival Week** in early February, with art and craft displays, a vintage-car rally, a family fun run, a street carnival, and—the highlight—a Festival Procession that features decorated floats, clowns, and bands. Then in early March the 1-day **Food and Wine Festival,** first celebrated in 1990, is held outdoors in the Woodhaugh Gardens. A large variety of Dunedin restaurants set up stalls and sell a selection of dishes from their menus; other activities include live music and entertainment, and cooking demonstrations. And the third week of October each year, **Rhododendron Week** celebrates the city's most famous floral asset by decking out just about every public space with the lovely blooms and hosting tours of private and public gardens in and around town. Information on Rhododendron Week is available from P.O. Box 5045, Dunedin (☎ 03/474-3300, fax 03/474-3451).

2 Getting Around

BY BUS   Most **city buses** (☎ 03/477-2224) leave from the vicinity of The Octagon. There's frequent bus service during the week, a little spotty on weekends. The fares are by zone and range from NZ$1.10 to NZ$1.80 (US 77¢ to US$1.26) per section, less for children. If you buy a packet of 10 tickets, you essentially get one ride free. The **Shopper Special** operates from 10am to 3pm and costs NZ$1.10 (US 77¢).

BY TAXI   Taxi stands can be found at The Octagon, at all terminals, and near the Chief Post Office (☎ 03/477-7777 or 03/477-1771).

BY CAR   A one-way street system makes driving easier than in most cities, all central streets have metered parking, and there's a municipal parking building near City

Impressions

We are in another country/Scotitanga/Where brass bands play, people fling to Scottish music in Moray Place, ladies of the Salvation Army palm ribboned tambourines, and smiles shiver and snap in the cold.
—Witi Ihimaera, *Deep South/Impressions of Another Country,* 1975

Dunedin is a place where it is front page headline if someone has a fire in their wardrobe.
—Dennis McEldowney, *Full of the Warm South,* 1983

The people here are Scots. They stopped here on their way home to heaven, thinking they had arrived.
—Mark Twain, writing about Dunedin.

Hall. The **Automobile Association** office is at 450 Moray Place (☎ **03/477-5945,** fax 03/477-9760). Central **gas (petrol) stations** include the Shell Kaikorai, 433 Stuart St. (☎ **03/477-8391**).

CITY LAYOUT

Most cities have a public square, but Dunedin has its eight-sided **Octagon,** a green, leafy park right at the hub of the city center that was totally remodeled in 1989 (be sure to notice the Writer's Walk on the upper side). Around its edges you'll find St. Paul's Anglican Cathedral and the City Hall. Within its confines is a statue of Scotland's beloved poet Robert Burns (whose nephew was Dunedin's first pastor) and park benches for foot-weary shoppers or brown-bagging lunchers. The Octagon divides the main street into **Princes Street** to the south and **George Street** to the north. One of my favorite things to do in Dunedin is to sit in The Octagon and watch the world go by.

The city center, at the head of **Otago Harbour,** is encircled by a 500-acre strip of land, the **Green Belt,** that has been, by edict of the founders, left in its natural state, never to be developed regardless of the city's growth. Thus it is that when driving to any of Dunedin's suburbs, you pass through forestland from which there are glimpses of the harbor.

FAST FACTS: DUNEDIN

Airlines   There is an **Air New Zealand** (☎ 03/477-5769) ticket office at the corner of The Octagon and Princes Street. The **Ansett New Zealand** office is at The Octagon and George Street (☎ **03/477-4146**).

Area Code   The telephone area code (STD) for Dunedin is **03.**

Automobile Association   The AA is at 450 Moray Place (☎ **03/477-5945,** or after hours 025/386-122; fax 03/477-9760) and is open Monday through Friday from 8:30am to 5pm.

Cameras & Film   Camera House, 115 George St. (☎ **03/479-2200**), provides 1-hour processing and other camera-related services.

Emergencies   For police, fire, and/or ambulance service, dial ☎ **111.**

Post Office   The Chief Post Office is at 283 Princes St., and there's another at 233 Moray Place.

Rest Rooms   If the need arises, there are good public rest rooms on Municipal Lane on the upper Octagon.

Shopping Hours   Stores are open Monday through Thursday from 9am to 5:30pm, Friday from 9am to 9pm, and Saturday from 10am to 1pm.

Taxis   See "Getting Around," earlier in this chapter.

3   Affordable Accommodations

Dunedin has many fine accommodations covering a range of prices. It also has, however, a large student population (with lots of visitors), so you'll need to reserve in advance if your visit coincides with graduation or another campus event.

The rates given below include the 12.5% GST.

IN TOWN
CAMPGROUNDS & CABINS

The **Aaron Lodge Motel and Holiday Park,** 162 Kaikorai Valley Rd. (near Brockville Road), Dunedin (☎ **03/476-4725,** fax 03/476-7925), is a whole complex of powered sites, tent sites, cabins, five tourist flats, and motel units on a main artery. Five motel units are in front (see the listing for the Aaron Lodge Motel below), and there are 15 standard cabins. Four- or five-berthed, all are spacious and have carpets, large wardrobes, a table and chairs, and electric heater. There are two modern kitchens, and TVs as well as showers and a laundry with dryer. Up the hill are eight two-berth cabins, a kitchen (crockery and cutlery provided), toilets, and showers are adjacent. A children's playground is located on the premises. There's also a supermarket adjacent. Rates for all cabins are NZ$30 to $33 (US$21 to US$23.10) double, NZ$5 (US$3.50) per child, NZ$10 (US$7) per extra adult. Tent and caravan sites are also available. The Aaron Lodge is owned and managed by Margaret and Lindsay McLeod and may be reached via the Bradford or Brockville bus from The Octagon. GST is included in all rates.

SUPER-CHEAP SLEEPS

Aaron Lodge Motel

162 Kaikorai Valley Rd., Dunedin. ☎ **03/476-4725.** Fax 03/476-7925. 5 units (all with bathrm). TV. NZ$65 (US$45.50) double. Additional person NZ$13 (US$91) extra per adult, NZ$8 (US$5.60) extra per child. AE, DC, MC, V.

Near Brockville Road, the Aaron Lodge offers one-bedroom units with heaters, radios, and electric blankets. All are nicely carpeted and well maintained.

Arcadian Motel

85–89 Musselburgh Rise, Dunedin. ☎ **03/455-0992.** Fax 03/455-0237. 4 studios, 7 units. TV TEL. NZ$60–$75 (US$42–$52.50) unit for 2. Additional person NZ$12 (US$8.40) extra per adult, NZ$8 (US$5.60) extra per child under 12. MC, V.

Units here include one-, two-, and three-bedroom accommodations, plus a bed-sitter (studio) in the old house on the property. All have full kitchens and comfortable furnishings. Guests have access to a full laundry. Markets, butchers, greengrocers, and a fish-and-chips shop are nearby. The Arcadian is within walking distance of St. Kilda Beach, and there's bus transportation nearby.

YHA Hostel

Stafford Gables, 71 Stafford St., Dunedin. ☎ and fax **03/474-1919.** 60 beds (none with bathrm). NZ$16 (US$11.20) per person dorm, NZ$19 (US$13.30) per person twin/double. Rates quoted are for members; non-members add NZ$4 (US$2.80). BC, MC, V. Limited off-street parking.

Dunedin's YHA hostel is housed in a grand old early-1900s mansion located right in the city center, near the Chief Post Office. It's also near food stores and a large supermarket. There are 60 beds in 21 rooms with high ceilings, carpeting, and attractive wallpaper, and ranging in size from twins, doubles, triples, and family rooms to dormitories. Three common rooms include a pool table and smoking room, and a TV and music room, and there are two dining rooms, a kitchen, and a coin-operated laundry. Twenty-four–hour access to the hostel for guests, off-street parking, a barbecue area, and a resident ghost (if you believe in such things) are other amenities.

FOR A FEW EXTRA BUCKS

Aberdeen Motel

46 Bank St. (at George St.), Dunedin. ☎ **03/473-0133.** Fax 03/473-0131. 18 units (all with bathrm). TV TEL. NZ$89 (US$62.30) double. Golden Chain discounts available. AE, DC, MC, V.

Ann and Neville Hollands are the thoughtful Aberdeen hosts who provide such little extras as a complimentary morning newspaper, a video on Dunedin attractions plus three Sky TV channels, and a collection of Dunedin restaurant menus. The attractive chalet-type units have one or two bedrooms, and some of the bedrooms are upstairs. You can order continental or cooked breakfasts to be delivered to your door, and if you choose to cook your own, you can buy the fixings at the supermarket a short walk away. Frequent bus service gets you into the city center and back home again. The motel is 2km (1 mile) from the city center, across from the Botanic Gardens.

Alcala Motor Lodge

George and St. David sts., Dunedin. ☎ and fax **03/477-9073.** Fax 03/477-4228. 23 units (all with bathrm). TV TEL. NZ$82 (US$57.40) double. Additional person NZ$14 (US$9.80) extra per adult, NZ$8 (US$5.60) extra per child. AE, BC, DC, JCB, MC, V.

This attractive Spanish-style complex is near the university and medical school, just a 20-minute walk from The Octagon. Each unit has a full kitchen, video, and radio; other facilities include a laundry, spa pool, and off-street parking. A cooked or continental breakfast is available at a small fee, and a licensed restaurant, shops, a hairdresser, and a service station are located close by.

Bentley's Hotel

137 St. Andrew St. (P.O. Box 5702), Dunedin. ☎ **03/477-0572.** Fax 03/477-0293. 39 units (all with bathrm). TV TEL. NZ$101–$135 (US$70.70–$95) double. AE, DC, MC, V.

The spacious units at Bentley's Hotel all come with private bathroom (bathtub or shower), and three are wheelchair-accessible. There are a guest laundry and a restaurant. It's located 2 blocks from The Octagon, at Cumberland Street.

Best Western Tourist Court

842 George St., Dunedin. ☎ **03/477-4270.** Fax 03/477-6035. 9 units (all with bath). TV TEL. NZ$84 (US$58.80) double. Additional person NZ$14 (US$9.80) extra. Best Western discounts available. AE, DC, MC, V.

Each of the spacious units here can sleep three to five and has a full kitchen, radio, central heat, and electric blankets. There's a guest laundry, and a continental breakfast can be ordered for a small fee. The units are exceptionally well appointed, each with an iron and ironing board. It's on a main bus line, but within easy walking distance of The Octagon.

✪ Farry's Motel

575 George St., Dunedin. ☎ **0800/109-333** in New Zealand, or 03/477-9333. Fax 03/477-9038. 15 units (all with bathrm). TV TEL. NZ$92 (US$64.40) double. Additional person NZ$16 (US$11.20) extra. AE, BC, DC, MC, V.

These units are tastefully furnished, with large picture windows in all lounges. Each is centrally heated and has a fully equipped kitchen, in-house video, Sky TV, and a radio. Standard units sleep up to four and special "executive suites" have private spa baths and videocassette movies. A guest laundry, a children's play area with swings and trampolines, and off-street parking are other features. A continental or cooked breakfast is available for a small charge. The motel is near city bus transportation, the university, and shopping.

✪ High Street Court Motel

193 High St., Dunedin. ☎ **0800/509-315** in New Zealand, or 03/477-9315. Fax 03/477-3366. 9 units (all with bathrm). TV TEL. NZ$89 (US$62.30) double. Additional person NZ$16 (US$11.20) extra. AE, BC, DC, JCB, MC, V.

With the same ownership and management as Farry's (above), this pretty place has a white-stucco facade with black wrought-iron trim. See the Farry's entry for the description of the rooms and facilities. A continental breakfast is available for a small charge. If you're on foot, it's an uphill hike from the city center. There's city bus transportation nearby.

Leviathan Hotel

27 Queens Gardens, Dunedin. ☎ **03/477-3160.** Fax 03/477-2385. 77 rms (all with bath), 6 suites. TV TEL. NZ$49–$84 (US$31.85–$54.60) single; NZ$59–NZ$93 (US$41.30–$65.10) double; NZ$119 (US$83.30) suite. AE, BC, DC, MC, V.

This three-story triangular hotel is a Dunedin landmark dating back to 1898. It's on a corner across from the Otago Settlers Museum, 1 block from the railway station, and within walking distance of the bus depot. The old building is in excellent condition and offers a high standard of central budget accommodations, plus fully equipped suites. The rooms are attractively decorated and furnished with built-in wardrobe, chest of drawers, and over-bed lights; all have electric heaters. Two family units sleep five. A games room with a pool table and two TV lounges are additional features. The elegant dining room serves meals in the moderate range. An elevator, hall telephones for guests, and off-street parking are also available.

✪ Magnolia House

18 Grendon St., Maori Hill, Dunedin. ☎ and fax **03/467-5999.** 3 rms (none with bathrm). TV TEL. NZ$75 (US$52.50) double. Rates include breakfast. No credit cards.

The suburban home of George and Joan Sutherland, Magnolia House is set on half an acre of sloping lawns and gardens, surrounded by native bush. The Victorian house, framed by a white picket fence at the lawn's edge, is quite spacious and graciously decorated, with a welcoming sitting room and a drawing room that holds a piano and opens onto a sun balcony. There's central heating throughout, and the bedrooms have fireplaces and antique furnishings. There are also two cats in residence and a no-smoking rule. The Sutherlands, who have lived in Dunedin for almost 30 years, are gracious hosts who enjoy helping guests plan their time in the city for the utmost enjoyment and provide a courtesy car upon request. There's city bus transportation nearby.

Sahara Guesthouse and Motel

619 George St., Dunedin. ☎ **03/477-6662.** Fax 03/479-2551. 10 rms (2 with bathrm), 10 units (all with bathrm). NZ$75–$79 (US$52.50–$55.30) double B&B; NZ$75 (US$52.60) unit for 2. AE, DC, MC, V.

This gabled brick guesthouse, which sports elaborate iron grillwork, is just a 5-minute walk from The Octagon and is on major bus routes. Built as a substantial family home back in 1863, it now holds nice-size rooms with hot and cold running water, with one to three twin beds, all immaculate and cheerful. Room 12 is especially bright, with a stained-glass window. Behind the house is a block of motel apartment units, four of which sleep up to five, all with kitchens, baths, telephones, color TVs, and use of laundry facilities. The home-style breakfast is a hearty one.

Readers Recommend

Castlewood Bed and Breakfast, 240 York Place, Dunedin. ☎ and fax **03/477-0526.** "Just back from an excellent holiday and thought I would point you in the direction of what we found was our best homestay in New Zealand. Castlewood is a wonderful venue with great hosts and excellent breakfasts (the muffins were yummy). Peter and Donna Mitchell are great hosts and made our stay in Dunedin the highlight of our trip."

—Tony George, Mt. Helena, Western Australia.

"We loved Castlewood Bed and Breakfast."

—Ami Jamael, Tokyo, Japan.

Albatross Inn B&B, 770 George St., Dunedin. ☎ **03/477-2727.** Fax 03/477-2108. "Both the rooms and breakfast were quite nice and it was only a 10 to 15 minute walk to town."

—Patricia Downing, Los Angeles, California, USA.

"Kerry and Nigel Kirland have eight ensuite rooms in an Edwardian house. The price is reasonable and it's very central."

—Jennie Fairlie, Broadbeach, QLD, Australia.

Jennie Fairlie also recommends **Manoro,** 84 London St., Dunedin. ☎ **03/477-8638.** Fax 03/474-1917. "Val and Bruce Duder have a grand old house, it's a NZ Historic Places Trust class 1 property with five ensuite bedrooms. There's also a guest coffee making galley, reading room, sun decks and city views. They are very nice, experienced hosts."

WORTH A SPLURGE

☼ Southern Cross Hotel

118 High St., Dunedin. ☎ **03/477-0752.** Fax 03/477-5776. 134 rms (all with bathrm), 8 suites. A/C MINIBAR TV TEL. NZ$141 (US$98.70) standard double; NZ$169 (US$118.30) premium or superior double; NZ$248 (US$173.60) suite. Lower weekend and corporate rates. Reservations can be made through Flag Inns. AE, DC, MC, V.

The Southern Cross is Dunedin's top hotel: It's got a great city-center location, attractive rooms, and an unusually personable staff. When I last stayed here, the Exchange Wing (formerly the adjacent State Insurance Building) had just opened, and I was impressed with its standard rooms (I liked these quarters more than the premium rooms). The Carlton Restaurant offers a full à la carte menu and flambé cooking. The Ports O' Call Bar & Grill is more casual, and the Deli Cafe is conveniently open very long hours. Four rooms are equipped for travelers with disabilities.

ON THE OTAGO PENINSULA

☼ Larnach Lodge

Larnach Castle, Otago Peninsula, P.O. Box 1350, Dunedin. ☎ **03/476-1616.** Fax 03/476-1574. 12 rms (all with bathrm), 40 beds in 6 rms (no rooms with bathrm). NZ$49 (US$34.30) double in stable stay, extra adult NZ$20 (US$14); NZ$120 (US$84) double in lodge, extra adult NZ$20 (US$14). AE, BC, DC, MC, V.

Larnach Castle dates from 1871, and when Margaret Barker bought it in 1967, it was in a sorry state. Now many years and much hard work later, it has been restored to its original glory; in addition to planting beautiful gardens, she and her family have converted the stables into a hostel and added a 12-room lodge to the grounds. Lodge

rooms have heaters, telephones, and coffee- and tea-making facilities, and, by the
time you get there, they'll all have bathrooms. My favorite room is upstairs in the
corner, but all quarters here have spectacular views over lush green hills rolling all
the way down to the harbor. Guests can dine in the castle and eat breakfast overlooking the grounds. House guests tour the castle for half price. Remember, it's
chilly on this windswept peninsula, so wear your woolies. It's 13km (8 miles) east
of Dunedin.

4 Great Deals on Dining

There's plenty of great budget dining in Dunedin, including lots of charming cafes.
Also, for quick, cheap eats, you can always swing by the **Golden Food Centre Court,**
251 George St., between St. Andrew and Hanover streets. It's part of a glass-enclosed
concentration of shops and has a variety of fast-food options.

If you're going to buy and bring your wine to dinner, head for **Robbie Burns
Shoppe,** 374 George St. (☎ 03/477-6355)—the markup is slight on New Zealand
wines; it's open Monday through Saturday from 9am to 10pm.

SUPER-CHEAP EATS

✪ The Bank

12 The Octagon. ☎ **03/477-4430.** Reservations not accepted. Lunch about NZ$6 (US$4.20).
AE, BC, DC, MC, V. Mon–Thurs 11:30am–11pm, Fri–Sat 11:30am–midnight. MODERN NEW
ZEALAND.

Until 1993 this really was a bank—the ANZ Bank. Now it's an attractive spot to have
a light meal, afternoon tea, or a drink. Large windows overlook the comings-and-
goings in The Octagon, and banknotes decorate the walls. Lunch choices include
quiche and salad, phyllo parcels, nachos with chiles, pita-bread basket with salad, or
a Kiwi version of a traditional ploughman's. The same buffet menu is in effect all
during the day until 9pm; after that only drinks, coffee, and desserts are offered. It's
fully licensed, with Guinness on tap.

Deli Cafe

In the Southern Cross Hotel, 118 High St. ☎ **03/477-0752.** Reservations not required. Main
courses NZ$7.50–$10.90 (US$5.30–$7.63). AE, DC, MC, V. Daily 6am–1am. DELI/ROASTS.

Ironically this great budget restaurant is in one of Dunedin's most luxurious hotels,
the Southern Cross (see "Affordable Accommodations," above). Located on street
level, it's bright, casual, and open long hours. It has the feel of a late-night diner, even
in the afternoon. Food is served cafeteria style and there's a smoking room upstairs.
You can get a snack for under NZ$5 (US$3.25), as well as roasts and other hot dishes.
It's fully licensed.

Potpourri

97 Lower Stuart St. ☎ **03/477-9983.** Reservations not accepted. Light lunches NZ$5–$6.50 (US$2.80–$4.55); 3-course dinner for NZ$10 (US$7). No credit cards. Mon–Fri 9am–8pm, Sat 10am–2pm. Closed 3 weeks at Christmas. VEGETARIAN.

Make Potpourri (locals pronounce it "Pot-*pour*-ee") one of your first choices for a meal because you'll probably want to return again and again. If you've been neglecting your vegetables while on the road, this is your chance to make up for it. Check the chalkboard for the quiche and main dish of the day or choose salads (you can order half portions), open-face sandwiches that come with three small salads, fresh scones and muffins, spanakopita with a half salad, and tacos. Good news for frozen yogurt lovers—it's available here. This is a non-alcoholic environment.

FOR A FEW EXTRA BUCKS

The Best Cafe

30 Stuart St. ☎ **03/477-8059.** Reservations not required. Main courses NZ$12–$15 (US$8.40–$10.75). BC, MC, V. Mon–Fri 11:30am–7pm. SEAFOOD/STEAK.

This friendly family-run cafe in the city center specializes in seafood served in downhome surroundings, complete with plastic tablecloths and a linoleum floor. Steaks and grills are also on the menu, and it has been welcoming families with children since 1937.

Golden Harvest Restaurant

In the Harvest Court Mall, 218 George St. ☎ **03/477-8333.** Fax 03/477-8888. Reservations not required. Main courses NZ$13.50–$35 (US$9.50–$24.50). AE, DC, MC, V. Daily 11:30am–2:30pm and 5:30pm–"late." CHINESE.

My cardinal rule for finding really good Chinese restaurants is to go where the Chinese go—and the large Chinese clientele at the Golden Harvest attests to its excellent ambience, food, and service. It's a pleasant place done in muted reds and greens, with an attractive lounge and bar, Chinese lanterns, and soft Chinese music. Specialties include pork filet Peking style on a sizzling plate, crispy chicken, sweet-and-sour choices, and other spicy dishes of the Orient. Le Ah Sew Hoy is the hostess and owner. It's fully licensed, or you can bring your own.

✪ High Tide

25 Kitchener St. ☎ **03/477-9784.** Reservations recommended. Main courses NZ$19.50 (US$13.70). AE, BC, DC, MC, V. Mon–Sat 6pm–"late." NEW ZEALAND.

If you have a penchant for sitting by the water and gazing out to sea, you'll feel right at home at this L-shaped restaurant in a former heliport building with a dozen large windows looking onto the harbor. Ceiling fans gently stir the air in this peaceful spot, where the chalkboard menu tempts with chicken, sirloin steak, lamb, pasta, fish, and seafood. If you want wine with dinner, you can bring your own. The High Tide is a short drive from the city center in an unlikely industrial area.

Joseph Mellor Restaurant

At the Otago Polytechnic, Tennyson St. at Upper Stuart St. ☎ **03/477-3014.** Reservations recommended. Three-course lunch NZ$7.50 (US$5.25); 4-course dinner NZ$17 (US$11.90). BC, MC, V. Tues–Thurs, lunch at noon and dinner at 6pm. (Call to confirm.) Closed all school vacations. NEW ZEALAND.

This is Dunedin's best-kept dining secret (I wouldn't know about it if long-time locals hadn't told me). The food is prepared by catering students under the watchful eye of their instructors. It's really good, but they keep their prices low because they need a constant flow of people to practice on. There's only one sitting for each meal, and I suggest you ring (phone) in advance to make sure there isn't a school holiday in effect. In addition to a good meal, you'll enjoy a harbor view and excellent service. It's fully licensed, or you can bring your own.

The Palms Cafe

18 Queens Gardens, Lower High St. at Dowling St. ☎ **03/477-6534.** Reservations recommended Sun–Fri, required Sat. Main courses NZ$18.50–$20 (US$13–$14). AE, BC, DC, MC, V. Mon–Fri from 5pm, Sat–Sun from 6pm. NEW ZEALAND.

This has got to be one of Dunedin's prettiest places to eat. Its window walls, ornate ceiling, and two intimate dining rooms make it romantic as well. The chalkboard menu usually lists an excellent chowder, while the main dishes might include lamb satay, vegetable quiche, or pan-baked flounder. There's a budget fixed-price menu on Monday through Friday from 5 to 6:30pm. It's strictly no-smoking and BYO.

○ Terrace Cafe

118 Moray Place. ☎ **03/474-0686.** Reservations recommended. Appetizers NZ$4.50–$8.50 (US$2.95–$5.55); main courses NZ$14–$17.50 (US$9.10–$11.40). MC, V. Tues–Sat 6pm–"late." MEDITERRANEAN/ETHNIC.

This little place is a real gem! By that, I don't mean that this is a spit-and-polish, take-yourself-seriously little gem—on the contrary, it's a down-to-earth, as-casual-or-as-dressy-as-you-feel sort of place that looks like a Victorian parlor. On cool nights, the fireplace glows with yet another inducement to relax as you enjoy a menu composed of great homemade soups (if they have pumpkin, you're in luck), main courses that might include deviled kidneys with bacon and mushrooms, fish curry, veal, chicken cooked in any one of a number of inventive ways, at least one vegetarian dish, Mediterranean and ethnic cuisine, crisp salads, and homemade desserts such as carrot cake or chocolate gâteau. Everything is fresh, and the service is friendly (as are your fellow diners—this has long been a Dunedin favorite). It's across from the Fortune Theatre. If you want wine with your meal, you have to bring your own.

WORTH A SPLURGE

Bell Pepper Blues

474 Princes St. ☎ and fax **03/474-0973.** E-mail bpepper@co.es.nz. Reservations recommended. Main courses NZ$20–$25 (US$14–$17.50); less expensive at lunch. AE, DC, MC, V. Mon–Sat 6:30–9pm. MODERN NEW ZEALAND.

Try to arrive here early enough to have a before-dinner drink in front of the open fire. Bell Pepper Blues has an inconspicuous exterior and an understated interior, but chef Michael Clydesdale offers this city's highest haute cuisine. Sample main courses include roast lamb rump flavored in olive oil with kafir lime leaves and garlic, served with crisp polenta and potato rosti; grilled fresh Marlborough salmon on linguine and wilted spinach; and baked tartlet of roast aubergine (eggplant) purée, avocados,

Readers Recommend

1908 Cafe, 7 Harington Point Road, Portobello, out on the end of the Otago Peninsula. ☎ 03/478-0801. "The food was great, incredibly reasonably priced, and a terrific stop for those hungry souls who go out to see the penguins at Penguin Place (also a great thing to do)."
—Katie Braun, Alameda, California, USA.

"On the return journey to Dunedin we were fortunate enough to stop at this wonderful restaurant. The building dates from 1908 and the food is wonderful. Bookings would be necessary."
—Jennie Fairlie, Broadbeach, QLD, Australia.

and spinach under a feta-and-cornbread crust. It's fully licensed, and you can't bring your own.

5 Exploring Dunedin: What to See & Do

The first thing you should do is stop by the visitor center; consider watching their half-hour color video *Dunedin Discovered,* which will give you a good overview of the region and of Dunedin's attractions. Also, pick up a sightseeing map and look for the ✪ "Walk the City" brochure (NZ$2.50/US$1.80) to guide you around the streets.

There are terrific scenic drives around the city and on the peninsula, and the visitor center has plenty of maps and brochures to show you where to go and what to look for on the road.

TAKING IN THE VIEWS

There are three very good lookout points from which to view the city and its environs: ✪ Mount Cargill Lookout, 8km (4³/₄ miles) from the city center (turn left at the end of George Street, then left on Pine Hill Road to its end, then right onto Cowan Road, which climbs to the summit); Centennial Lookout, or Signal Hill (turn onto Signal Hill Road from Opoho Road and drive 3km [1³/₄ miles], to the end of Signal Hill Road); and Bracken's Lookout (at the top of the Botanic Gardens).

OTHER HIGHLIGHTS

If you find yourself near Water and Princes streets, diagonally across from the Chief Post Office, you'll be standing on what was the waterfront back when the first settlers arrived in Dunedin and what had been a Māori landing spot for many years. Look for the bronze plaque that reads: "On this spot the pioneer settlers landed from a boat off the *John Wickliffe* on the 23rd day of March, 1848, to found the city and province." It's a good jumping-off point for your exploration of the city as it is today.

Now, for any bagpipe fanatics, let me suggest that you try to arrange to hear the lovely instruments while you're in this little bit of transported Scotland. You may be in town for a scheduled event at which they're featured, but if not, just take yourself to the Dunedin Visitor Centre, 48 The Octagon, or call ☎ 03/474-3300. They'll do their best to get you to a pipe-band rehearsal, if nothing else (which could turn out to be more fun than a formal performance). Also ask about attending an evensong choral service at St. Paul's Cathedral or a welcoming haggis ceremony.

According to the *Guinness Book of World Records,* Dunedin has the steepest street in the world, beating out San Francisco and alpine Switzerland. Just minutes from the city center, the little street begins gently, then rears skyward dramatically to come to a dead end on the hillside. It's quite an experience to walk up, and for the hale and hearty, there's a footpath with a railing on one side of the street, while on the opposite side, no fewer than 270 steps take you to the top. Steps or footpath, walking is your best way up—residents on the street groan when they see (or more likely, hear) a car attempting to climb the hill. Cars stall when you try to change gears; braking power is so much less when the car rolls backward that cars often careen backward down the hill, completely out of control; and gas tanks leak if a car is parked with fuel tanks pointed downward. So, as you *walk* up, remember that the view from the top of the city and harbor goes beyond spectacular. Just where will you find this hilly highlight? Its name is Baldwin Street, and you get there by taking the Normandy bus to North Road, and Baldwin is the tenth street on the right past the Botanic Gardens.

Dunedin's **railway station** is a marvelous old Flemish Renaissance–style edifice, designed by George A. Troup. He won the Institution of British Architects Award for his efforts and was later knighted, but never climbed to any position lofty enough to leave behind his affectionate local nickname, "Gingerbread George." Built of Kokonga basalt, with Oamaru limestone facings, the station's most prominent feature is its large square clock tower, but equally impressive are the Aberdeen granite pillars supporting arches of the colonnade across the front, the red Marseilles tiles on the roof, and the colorful mosaic floor in the massive foyer depicting a "puffing billy" engine and other bits of railroad life (more than 725,000 Royal Doulton porcelain squares). Look for a replica of Dunedin's coat-of-arms, stained-glass windows above the balcony (the engines on both look as if they're coming straight at you, no matter where you stand), and the plaque honoring New Zealand railway men who died in the 1914–1918 war.

The lovely **Botanic Garden** is at the northern end of George Street. Established in 1869, it's noted for masses of rhododendrons and azaleas (at their best from October to December). The rock garden, winter garden, and native kohai and rata trees are also noteworthy. Morning and afternoon teas, as well as hot snacks and buffet lunches, are available in the kiosk restaurant on the grounds. No matter how rushed your schedule, you owe yourself a stroll through this lovely, peaceful spot.

MUSEUMS, GALLERIES & AN HISTORIC HOME

✪ Otago Settlers Museum

220 Cumberland St. (postal address 31 Queens Gardens, Dunedin) ☎ 03/477-5052. Fax 03/477-8360. E-mail settler@es.co.nz. Admission NZ$4 (US$2.80) adults, NZ$3 (US$2.10) senior citizens, free for children. Additional charges for special exhibitions. Mon–Fri 10am–5pm, Sat–Sun and public holidays 1–5pm.

This museum provides a look back into the lives of Dunedin's first residents and follows the development of the city and province right up to the present. It's just down from the railway station in the city center. Look for the sole surviving gas streetlamp outside, one of many used on the city's major streets circa 1863. Inside are an exhibition on the Kai Tahu communities of Otago; a transport collection; three period rooms; *Josephine,* a double ended Fairlie steam engine, which pulled the first Dunedin–Port Chalmers express; a Penny Farthing Cycle you can actually ride (although you won't go anywhere since it's held by a frame and mounted on rollers— still fun, though); and all sorts of other relics of life in these parts many years ago. There are other hands-on exhibits, such as toys and mechanical musical instruments, and life in the 20th century is also vividly portrayed. In the Furniture Room, faded sepia photographs of early settlers peer down with stern visages at visitors—one has to wonder what they think of their progeny who wander through. The Archives and Research Department holds records of thousands of Otago families, and is open Monday through Friday for a charge of NZ$10 (US$6.50), which includes admission to the museum.

Otago Museum

Great King St. ☎ 03/477-2372. Fax 03/477-2372. Admission to Museum, free; Discovery World, NZ$6 (US$4.20) adults, NZ$3 (US$2.10) children, NZ$11–$14 (US$7.70–$9.80) families. Mon–Fri 10am–5pm, Sat–Sun 1–5pm. Closed: Good Friday and Christmas Day.

Established in 1868, this is one of New Zealand's most important museums, containing large ethnographic, natural history, and decorative-arts collections. Exhibits in the Maori Gallery focus on the culture of the southern Maori, as well as on Oceania in general. There's even a display showing a moa, the extinct giant bird of New Zealand. Guided tours are available on Saturday and Sunday at 2pm. The hands-on science center, Discovery World, is definitely cool for kids. There are a museum shop and a cafe on the premises.

Olveston
42 Royal Terrace. ☎ **03/477-3320.** Admission NZ$10 (US$7) adults, NZ$3 (US$2.10) children. Guided tour, daily at 9:30 and 10:45am, noon, and 1:30, 2:45, and 4pm.

Olveston is a "must see" of any Dunedin visit. It's one of the country's best-known stately homes, fully furnished, open to the public—and it's magnificent. The double brick house is Jacobean in style, faced with Oamaru stone and Moeraki gravel, surrounded by an acre of tree-shaded grounds. A much-traveled and very prosperous couple, the Theomins, built the 35-room home in 1904–1906 as a 25th-anniversary gift for each other, and it's as much a work of art as the multitude of art works within its walls. The house was bequeathed to Dunedin in 1966, and has been carefully maintained in virtually its original state. There are more than 250 pictures in a variety of media in Olveston, including those of some 37 New Zealand artists. The dining room's Regency table and Chippendale chairs are graced by a range of table settings allowing the variety of glass, porcelain, and silver, also seen in the butler's pantry, to be enjoyed by visitors. At every turn there is evidence of the comfort and convenience, as well as visual beauty, built into this home. Although reservations are not essential, they are given preference, and you can view the house only on a guided tour.

✪ Dunedin Public Art Gallery
The Octagon. ☎ **03/477-8770.** Nonresident admission NZ$4 (US$2.80) adults, NZ$3 (US$2.10) children; free to residents of Dunedin. Additional charges for special exhibitions. Mon–Fri 10am–5pm, Sat–Sun and holidays 11am–5pm.

Don't miss a visit to this art gallery, which holds a special collection of more than 40 works by Frances Hodgkins, Dunedin born and considered the finest painter ever produced by New Zealand. In addition, there's a fine collection of old masters that includes Gheeraerdts, Landini, Lorrain, and Monet, which was given to the gallery by the de Beer family, who have a long connection with Dunedin.

A SHORT DRIVE TO PORT CHALMERS
Half an hour's drive from the city on the northern shore of Otago Harbour lies historic **Port Chalmers.** It was from here in 1884 that a ship sailed for England with the country's first shipment of frozen meat, creating an important new industry for New Zealand. A bit of an artists' colony today, Port Chalmers has a visitor center and a small seafaring museum. This area is popular for salmon and trout fishing from October to April. Drive over by taking Oxford Road out of Dunedin through the rolling hills to Port Chalmers and return via the harbor road for completely different scenery. While you're in the town, drop into **Carey's Bay Pub,** where all the anglers go.

ON THE OTAGO PENINSULA
You really shouldn't leave Dunedin without exploring the 33km-(20-mile) long peninsula that curves around one side of the beautiful Otago (Oh-tah-go) Harbour. You can take one of the tours mentioned below or head out Portobello Road, which runs along the harbor. In addition to the places listed below, other sights you may want to visit include a **Maori church at Otakou** and an **aquarium** at the Portobello Marine Laboratory operated by the University of Otago near Quarantine Point (it's open on Saturday, Sunday, and holidays from noon to 4:30pm). The Visitor Centre can supply details.

You will also quite possibly be interested in the **yellow-eyed penguins** that can be seen at Southlight Wildlife near the Royal Albatross Colony. Admission is NZ$5

Readers Recommend

Penguin Place, ☎ 03/478-0286 or 03/474-3300. Fax 03/478-0257. "Home of the **Yellow-Eyed Penguin Conservation Reserve** was most interesting, and the fact that a couple of the young penguins were standing right beside the hides meant we were able to be a few inches from them. The cost of the tour was NZ$20 (US$14) each."

—Jennie Fairlie, Broadbeach, QLD, Australia.

Author's Note: Penguin Place is open for all-day viewing October through March, and the last 3 hours of the day April through September.

(US$3.50) for adults, free for children. Late afternoon is a good time to go; make arrangements through the visitor center.

THE HIGHLIGHTS

○ Royal Albatross Colony

Taiaroa Head. ☎ **03/478-0499.** Fax 03/478-0575. Admission to Albatross Centre, NZ$2 (US$1.40) adults. Two-hour tours, late-Nov to the end of Mar, NZ$27 (US$18.90); early Apr to mid-Sept, NZ$22 (US$15.40); mid-Sept to late Nov, NZ$17 (US$11.90) (dates are approximate, depending on birds' activity). Children are charged about half price; family discounts available. Open daily (hours vary seasonally). Closed Christmas Day.

The magnificent royal albatross, perhaps with an instinctive distrust of the habitations of humankind, chooses remote, uninhabited islands as nesting grounds. With the single exception, that is, of this mainland colony 33km (20 miles) from Dunedin. The first egg was found here in 1920; today the colony consists of more than 24 breeding pairs, as well as several non-breeding juvenile birds, each year. Unfortunatley, during the 1997 season the big birds made only ten nests, but none within the viewing area. It's only the second time in 25 years that this has happened, and everyone's keeping their fingers crossed for next season. Tours include an informative presentation on the birds, a video, a visit to the observatory, and a tour of the tunnel complex of the old Fort Taiaroa. These tours are popular during the late November to April period, so it is essential that you reserve in advance (either with the Visitor Centre on The Octagon or by calling the Albatross Colony directly).

Glenfalloch Woodland Garden

430 Portobello Rd. ☎ **03/476-1006.** Admission by donation requested. Daily dawn–dusk.

A good morning or afternoon tea stop on your Otago Peninsula excursion, Glenfalloch provides a microclimate on its grounds that allows plants to grow even in winter. At the 30-acre estate, allow time to wander through native bush, under English oaks (some as old as 200 to 300 years), and among magnificent and unusual rhododendrons and azaleas not to be found anywhere else in the country, fuchsias, and primroses. Full lunches as well as teas are available in the fully licensed Garden Chalet Restaurant, with strolling peacocks occasionally fanning their glorious plumage just outside.

○ Larnach Castle

Highcliff Rd. ☎ **03/476-1616.** Fax 03/476-1574. Admission NZ$10 (US$7) adults, NZ$3.50 (US$2.45) children. Daily 9am–5pm. Closed: Christmas Day. Take Portobello Road 2 miles north of Glenfalloch Woodland Garden and follow the signs inland.

This neo-Gothic mansion is right out of an old English movie, but much more grand than anything you've ever seen on film. William Larnach came from Australia in the late 1860s to found the first Bank of Otago. He began building the grandiose home (which he called "The Camp") in 1871 for his French heiress wife. It took 200 work-men 3 years to build the shell and a host of European master craftsmen another 12 years to complete the interior. Total cost: £125,000. Larnach's concept was to in-corporate the very best from every period of architecture, with the result that the hanging Georgian staircase lives happily with Italian marble fireplaces, English tiles, and colonial-style verandas. One of the most magnificent examples of master crafts-manship is the exquisite foyer ceiling, which took three craftsmen 6^1/$_2$ years to complete.

After rising to the post of M.P. but suffering a series of personal misfortunes, Larnach committed suicide in his typically dramatic fashion in the Parliament Build-ings in Wellington. (Larnach's first two wives died, and his younger third wife dealt him a fatal emotional blow by dallying with his son.) After his death, the farm around the castle was sold off and the Crown used the castle as a mental hospital. It is now the private home of the Barker family, who found it in a thoroughly dilapidated con-dition in 1967 and have spent the intervening years lovingly restoring it to its origi-nal glory. Pick up a printed guide at the reception area and wander as you choose, climbing the spiral staircase to battlements that look out onto panoramic views, and strolling through gardens and outbuildings. The stables now house hostel-type accommodations, and there are also comfortable accommodations in the lodge. Lunch and teas are available. *Author's note:* If your travel dollars are running short, you might decide to save the cost of admission to Larnach Castle and just enjoy the views on the way out, have tea, walk around the grounds, and savor only the exte-rior of this impressive structure.

ORGANIZED TOURS

Dunedin is blessed with excellent tour operators who provide enjoyable ways to do sightseeing the easy way. One word of advice, however: If possible, telephone or fax ahead to book, since—especially during summer—the tours are very popular, and if your time in town is limited, you may miss out on the one you most want.

COACH (BUS) TOURS

Newtons Coach Tours, P.O. Box 549, Dunedin (☎ **03/477-5577**), conducts ex-cellent tours of varying durations, all with knowledgeable guides providing valuable insight into the city's sightseeing highlights, along with the occasional human-interest anecdote to liven things up. All tours may be booked directly with Newtons or with the visitor center—*be sure to check exact departure times,* since they can vary from time to time. If requested, they will pick you up and drop you off at your hotel, motel, motor camp, or hostel.

Tour 1, this 1^1/$_2$-hour **City Sights** tour departs daily at 10am and 3:30pm from the visitor center. The fare for this double-decker bus ride is NZ$15 (US$10.50) for adults; children are charged NZ$8 (US$5.60).

Tour 2 departs the visitor center at noon for the Summit Road, Otago Peninsula, guided tour of Larnach Castle, and a visit to Glenfalloch Woodland Gardens. This is also a double-decker bus. Fares, including all admissions, are NZ$30 (US$21) for adults, NZ$15 (US$10.50) for children.

✪ **Tour 3,** departs at 2:30pm daily. Here you have three options: Tour 3A is a visit to the Royal Albatross Colony by sea; Tour 3B is a visit by land; Tour 3C is a tour of the yellow-eyed penguin conservation project. Adults pay NZ$49 (US$34.30); children are charged NZ$25 (US$17.50).

Tour 4, includes the Royal Albatross Colony and a tour of the yellow-eyed pen-guin conservation project. October 1 through April 30 tour departs at 2:30pm on the bus and returns by boat, May 1 through September 30 the tour departs at 12:30pm on the *Monarch* and returns via coach. The cost is NZ$87 (US$60.90) for adults and NZ$44 (US$30.80) for children.

Wild South, P.O. Box 963, Dunedin (☎ 03/454-3116, fax 03/454-3117), runs an unusual ✪ **Twilight Wildlife Conservation Experience,** with a maximum of 12 people. This is a 6-hour day trip that includes an introduction to Dunedin's history and visits to the Otago Peninsula Ornithological Section, peninsula beaches, and seal and penguin colonies. The tour includes a 2-hour visit to the Yellow-Eyed Penguin Conservation Reserve, a self-funded project for the world's rarest penguin. Viewing is from specially designed holes 5 to 10 meters (15 to 30 feet) away, which provides good photo opportunities. You'll have to call for exact departure times and for reservations. The fare is NZ$48 (US$33.60) per person (they offer a NZ$6 backpacker discount). For an additional NZ$20 (US$14) per person you can add a trip to the albatross colony by either land or sea.

CRUISES

To see Dunedin and the Otago Peninsula wildlife from the water, check with **Monarch Wildlife Cruises** at their waterfront office at the corner of Wharf and Fryatt streets, P.O. Box 102, Dunedin (☎ 0800/666-272 in New Zealand, or 03/477-4276; fax 03/477-4216), to see what they have to offer while you're there. They run a variety of interesting cruises, including viewing albatross, seals, and more. Their full Otago Harbour cruise from Dunedin takes 5 hours and includes Taiara Head wildlife, the wading birds, geology, and history for only NZ$45 (US$31.50) for adults. For an extra NZ$20 (US$14) you can include the yellow-eyed penguin land tour or an extra view of the albatross from land. If you're out on the Otago Peninsula you may join the One Hour Wellers Rock Cruise for NZ$20 (US$14) adults. For more details and reservations, contact the company directly or inquire at the visitor center. Dress warmly and bring your camera.

FOR CHOCOLATE LOVERS

The factory of ✪ **Cadbury Confectionery Ltd.** in Dunedin is among the very few in the world in which the complete chocolate-making process is performed under one roof. The tour begins with a 10-minute video on the company's history, which dates back to the early 1800s. As you're taken through the factory, you'll see the manufacturing process of several different chocolate products, with samples of each. Unfortunately, if one or more of those samples sparks off an appetite for more, you'll have to buy them through retail outlets, since the factory has no showroom or shop. The tours run Monday through Friday at 1:30pm and 2:30pm. It costs NZ$5 (US$3.50) for adults and NZ$2 (US$1.40) for children aged 5 to 12; they don't accept credit cards. Because of their immense popularity and a limit of 40 people per tour, *early booking is essential.* Children under 5 and the wearing of sandals are not permitted. To reserve, contact Cadbury Confectionery Ltd., 280 Cumberland St. (☎ 03/467-7800, fax 03/467-7893).

FOR WHISKY & BEER CONNOISSEURS

✪ **Wilsons Distillery Whisky Tours** take you behind the scenes in New Zealand's only whisky distillery (incidentally, while all other such spirits are "whiskey," in the case of scotch, it's always "whisky"). The tour begins with a short video describing the history of whisky making in Dunedin, with a detailed description of the distilling process from the original grains right through to the bottled product. You're then taken through the distillery to see that process in action, after which you're treated to a tasting in the distillery's visitor center, which has a number of whisky products, including crystal decanter sets and cherries in whisky, for sale. Each tour takes about 1¹/₂ hours and costs NZ$5 (US$3.50). All bookings must be made through the Dunedin Visitor Centre, 48 The Octagon (☎ 03/474-3300), which can also provide more detail and tour times.

Tours of **Speights Brewery,** 200 Rattray St. (☎ 03/477-9480), run only in the morning, usually at 10:30am, for the very good reason that the brewing process occurs only in the morning and an afternoon tour would be far less interesting. You're taken through the entire brewing process of Speights beer, "The Pride of the South," then presented with a sample of the end product. Tours run Monday through Thursday, take about 1¹/₂ hours, and cost NZ$5 (US$3.25). Book directly with the brewery.

A Train Trip to Taieri Gorge

The small jaunt to the Taieri Gorge is a terrific way to spend an afternoon if you're based in Dunedin. The spectacular Taieri Gorge has scenery easily on a par with the famed Silverton–Durango train in the U.S. state of Colorado. There are stops for picture taking and a fine commentary is provided along the way. Afternoon tea and snacks are available in the snack-bar car, as well as beer, wine, and spirits. Departures for the 4- to 5¹/₂-hour trips are from the Dunedin Railway Station, with varying schedules (for days of the week and times) throughout the year. Another popular option is to take the train one way and walk the Rail Trail, a 150km (93-mile) walking, horse trekking, and mountain bike route between Middlemarch and Clyde. The fare to Middlemarch is NZ$55 (US$38.50) for adults, and one school-age child rides free with each adult. The fare to Pukerangi is NZ$49 (US$34.30). Students get a 20% discount. Buy tickets at the railway station or the visitor center. Readers recommend riding in the "adults-only" car.

6 Outdoor Activities

CYCLING   If you want to tool around on a bike, you can rent one from **Browns,** Lower Stuart Street (☎ 03/477-7259). One of my best memories of Dunedin includes biking out to Larnach Castle—the views are truly breathtaking.

FISHING   Nearby Port Chalmers is known for its stellar salmon and trout fishing from October to April. See "A Short Drive to Port Chalmers," above.

GOLF   If you play golf, you might like to play at the **St. Clair Golf Club** (☎ 03/487-9201) or at the **Balmacewan** (pronounced "ball-mc-cue-en") course at the **Otago Golf Club** (☎ 03/467-2096 or 03/467-2099), the oldest course in the country.

SWIMMING   When the time comes for a break in all that sightseeing, the **Moana Pool,** at the corner of Littlebourne Road and Stuart Street (☎ 03/474-3513 for pool information, 03/477-7792 for water slides, 03/477-6592 for the cafe), can provide a refreshing hour or two. There's a 50-meter, eight-lane swimming pool, a diving pool, a learner's pool, and water slides. Those slides are fully enclosed tubes, and you can choose a leisurely ride in the slow tube or a more adventurous one in the fast tube. Other watery options are scuba instruction, aqua-fitness classes, underwater hockey, and water polo. On the less wet side, you can take advantage of the poolside circuit gym, sunbeds, and sauna. Plan lunch at the cafe, or in summer bring a picnic on the sun terrace, where there are barbecues, trampolines, and a children's play area. There's also Flippers Poolside Crèche (day-care center) for children under 5, which is open daily to give parents a bit of time off to enjoy all the above. Hours vary, so call ahead, and fees depend on the activities you choose.

7 Shopping

Dunedin offers excellent shopping. Stores are generally open Monday through Thursday from 9am to 5:30pm, Friday from 9am to 9pm, and Saturday from 10am to 1pm.

The **Golden Centre,** 251 George St., between St. Andrew and Hanover streets, is a glass-enclosed concentration of shops specializing in everything from leather to woolens to women's fashions to cosmetics to gifts and books. Basically, whatever you want or need, you'll probably find it here, including the **Golden Food Centre Court,** which boasts a variety of eating options. The **Carnegie Centre,** 110 Moray Place, was built in 1908 as the city's public library, and the impressive building now houses the **Carnegie Gallery,** featuring New Zealand contemporary art exhibits, the Abbey Road Bar & Cafe, and assorted craft shops and cultural service organizations.

Some of the cheapest spirits on sale can be purchased at the **Robbie Burns Shoppe,** 374 George St. (☎ 03/477-6355). The markup is slight on New Zealand wines; it's open Monday through Saturday from 9am to 10pm.

Dunedin has more than its fair share of gift shops, but one I can recommend is the ✪ **New Zealand Shop,** on The Octagon (☎ 03/477-3379) next to the visitor center (in the Civic Centre), with a fine collection of quality wool sweaters and other items, along with a large selection of T-shirts, gifts, and souvenirs; it's open daily in summer (normal shopping hours in winter) and will open just for you if you give them a call. Also worth a visit are the **Scottish Shop,** 187 George St. (☎ 0800/ 864-686 in New Zealand, ☎/fax 03/477-9965, e-mail scottish.shop@xtra.co.nz), which sells tartan ties as well as clan crest items; and **Helean Kiltmakers,** 8 Hocken St., Kenmure (☎ 03/453-0233). For leather and lambskin items, **Glendermid Limited,** 192 Castle St. (☎ 03/477-3655), is the leading specialist, with a wide selection of both.

The **Moray Gallery,** 32 Moray Place (☎ 03/477-8060), has an excellent selection of paintings, glassware, and pottery by New Zealand artists and craftspeople.

✪ **Hyndman's Ltd.,** 17 George St., in the Civic Centre (☎ 03/477-0174, fax 03/477-8175), was established back in 1906 and today stocks specialty books not readily found elsewhere, as well as a wide range of general-interest books. It's open Monday through Thursday from 9am to 5:30pm, Friday from 9am to 9pm, and Saturday from 10am to 1:30pm. American Express, Diners Club, MasterCard, and Visa are accepted.

Daniels Jewellers Ltd., 72 Princes St. (☎ 03/477-1923), has a wide variety of quality gifts, crystal, silverware, wooden items, leather items, pottery, Marlestone, diamond rings, gold, and silver. It's open Monday through Friday from 9:30am to 5pm.

8 Dunedin After Dark

As you might imagine, students from the University of Otago keep Dunedin's pub life lively—except, maybe, during exam week. The community also has two good live theaters and a multiscreen movie theater. For current schedules, check the Otago Daily Times.

THE PERFORMING ARTS

Fortune Theatre
At Stuart St. and Upper Moray Place. ☎ **03/477-8323.** Fax 03/477-6791. Tickets, NZ$22.50 (US$15.80) adults, NZ$15 (US$10.50) students with ID. AE, MC, V.

The Fortune, the world's southernmost professional live theater, is housed in a century-old bluestone building that was formerly Trinity Methodist Church. This theater presents the best of contemporary New Zealand and international plays in a nine-play season running from February to December.

Regent Theatre

On the Lower Octagon. ☎ 03/477-8597. Ticket prices vary depending on performance.

Another venue for live entertainment, the Regent Theatre hosts shows by international and New Zealand performers. Check the local newspaper for current schedules of concerts and plays.

THE BAR SCENE

In addition to the places listed below, The Bank (see "Great Deals on Dining," earlier in this chapter) is open Monday through Thursday until 11pm and Friday and Saturday until midnight.

The Albert Arms Tavern

387 George St. ☎ 03/477-8035.

This is Dunedin's "local"—popular with students and budget travelers for its cheery atmosphere and good-value pub meals. Monday night is Irish Band Night. The interior is Scottish tartan: Upstairs the decor includes a red-plaid rug, red upholstery on the chairs and booths, and green walls and ceiling. This upper level is where meals are served. The menu has been the same since 1971: chicken, or fish, or steak with chips for NZ$10 (US$7). The midday roast meal for NZ$5.50 (US$3.90) is an incredible deal. The Albert Arms, which dates from 1862, is across the street from the Robbie Burns (see below), so it's convenient to stop at both places. It's open daily from 11am to 11pm.

Bacchus Winebar

On the 1st Floor, 12 The Octagon. ☎ 03/474-0824.

British, Australian, and New Zealand readers will know that the "first floor" referred to in the address of this wine bar means one level above ground. However, since "first floor" is synonymous with "ground floor" in American and Canadian English, I need to point out to my compatriots that they'll have to climb a flight of stairs to find this spot.

This is a great place for a glass of wine or a light meal overlooking The Octagon. Domestic and imported wines are available by the glass or bottle. It's open Monday through Saturday from 11am to 11pm. Lunch is served Monday through Friday from 11am to 3pm; dinner is Monday through Saturday from 6 to 9pm. Smoking is not allowed.

Clarendon Hotel

28 MacLaggon St. ☎ 03/477-9095.

While pubs traditionally close at 11pm, the Clarendon Hotel stays open later. Here you'll find the upstairs Shamrox and Karaoke Bar open from 5pm until "late." Downstairs there's dance music and plenty of high spirits.

Heffs

244 King Edward St., South Dunedin. ☎ 03/455-1017.

I personally found this pub too smoky to be enjoyable, but it's very popular as a venue for live music and budget meals. If you go there, you'll find collections of spoons and mugs on display, as well as about 500 whisky jugs and Jim Beam bourbon bottles.

Robbie Burns Pub

370 George St. ☎ **03/479-2701.**

This is one of the oldest pubs in Dunedin, with a license dating from 1859. The "Poets Corner" near the door honors its namesake. There's a painting of Robbie Burns and friends and another of the poet at the opposite end of the bar. This attractive spot is popular with the university crowd. It's open Monday through Saturday from 11am to 11pm, and—as in most pubs—a handle (500ml) of beer will set you back NZ$3 (US$1.95).

MOVIES

Hoyts 6

33 The Octagon. ☎ **03/477-7019.** Tickets, NZ$10 (US$7).

There are six big screens at the Hoyts Cinema on The Octagon. You may even be able to see a recently released New Zealand film before it's shown overseas. My friends had talked about *Once Were Warriors* for more than a year before I could see it in California.

9 En Route to Christchurch

The 366km (227-mile) trip from Dunedin to Christchurch takes about 5 hours, but it's probably a good idea to slow down and look at a few things along the way.

SEEING THE BOULDERS IN MOERAKI

At Moeraki, about an hour's drive north of Dunedin, there's an unusual natural phenomenon that's worth looking at. On the beaches around this picturesque fishing village just south of Hampden, huge rounded **boulders** are scattered around as though some prehistoric giant had used them for a game of handball. The curious rocks were formed, according to scientists, by the gradual accumulation of lime about 60 million years ago, but the Maori have a different story. According to legend, one of the great migration canoes capsized nearby and large gourds and kumara seeds scattered on the beach and were turned to stone; they are known as *te kai-hinaki* (the food baskets). Now, maybe rocks don't sound like a sightseeing attraction to you, but some people find them fascinating. Incidentally, if you travel from Dunedin to Christchurch by rail or bus, you'll get a good view. If you happen to arrive shortly after noon, you may be able to buy fish straight from the fishing boats coming in about that time.

   If you're tempted to linger here for the night contact **Walter and Theresa Kiener,** R.D.2, Palmerston (☎ **03/439-4759**), who can provide a variety of accommodations, including flats, cabins, and caravan or sheltered tent sites—all at modest rates. Ask about the nearby penguin and seal colonies, which can be seen for free.

A QUICK STOP IN WAIANAKRUA

Some 85km (53 miles) north of Dunedin, you might want to stop at the **Mill House,** in Waianakrua (☎ **03/439-5515**), a handsome three-story stone building that was once a flour mill but is now a handsome restaurant-and-motel complex. The colonial-style dining room is beamed and attractively furnished, and the meals are reasonably priced. There's a wine license, and it's open Wednesday through Monday.

OAMARU: THE WHITE STONE CITY

Oamaru, 116km (72 miles) north of Dunedin, is another good place to stop. In the 1870s it claimed 8 hotels, 30 grog shops, and 14 brothels, but the importance of

Penguin Watching. In Oamaru there's a small section where the little blue penguins come in to shore for the night. I'm told they arrive at dusk and leave an hour before daybreak. A couple of people have fenced off the area and just recently built bleachers for the spectators. They are adorable, noisy little critters and well worth a night's stay in Oamaru to see.

—Lois Churchill, Elkland, Pennsylvania, USA.

Oamaru today is its architecture. Rightfully known as the "White Stone City," it's filled with impressive buildings made of gleaming-white limestone quarried in Weston, 6½km (4 miles) away (you can visit the **quarry** on Monday through Friday from 9am to 5pm—well worth the mini-excursion). Once you've walked along the main street and admired the architecture of the courthouse, bank, post office, and the fine Forrester Art Gallery, walk a little farther to the Harbour-Tyne Street **historic precinct** that the preservation-minded citizens of Oamaru have fought to save.

The **Oamaru Information Centre** is open Monday through Friday from 9am to 5pm and Saturday and Sunday from 10am to 4pm. The helpful staff can provide a map and show you how to get to the **basilica** and the **Waitaki Boys' School** to see more impressive examples of how the local limestone has been put to good use; and the local **Museum and Art Gallery,** which often features displays by local artists of the beautiful North Otago scenery. Ask at the information center about **architectural walks,** which can sometimes be organized for parties of two or more upon request, and about visits to the nearby colonies of yellow-eyed and blue penguins. You might want to save some time during your visit to Oamaru to stroll through the **Public Gardens,** especially Wonderland. For a quick bite, drop by one of the many coffee shops along the main street.

HAVING LUNCH IN ASHBURTON

In Ashburton, 87km (54 miles) south of Christchurch, the Ashford Cafe in the **Ashford Craft Village** makes a good lunch or tea stop. The shops in this complex are interesting, too. It's on the west side of State Highway 1 and open Monday through Friday from 9am to 5pm and Saturday from 10am to 4pm. The cafe closes at 4:30pm during the week and at 3:30pm on weekends.

15 Christchurch

Christchurch feels rather English, the way Dunedin feels Scottish—Gothic buildings built of solid stone are everywhere, modern glass-and-concrete structures scattered among them. There are also red buses, but not double-deckers. However, English trees, brought out by settlers as a bit of home, flourish along the banks of the Avon River. And cricket, that most English of all sports, is played by all Christchurch boys.

It is also a prosperous city—New Zealand's third largest after Auckland and Wellington, with a population of about 325,000. It enjoys an equitable climate (2,120 hours of sunshine annually), one of the best airports in the country, and sports arenas that outshine those in many other New Zealand cities. While still more conservative than most other places in New Zealand, Christchurch in recent years has become more vibrant and attractive to visitors. Mayor Vicki Buck gets the lion's share of the credit for the positive changes.

For the visitor, Christchurch offers a variety of restaurants and entertainment, as well as excellent accommodations and plenty of sightseeing attractions. Seattle and Christchurch are sister cities, by the way, so if you hail from Seattle, be sure to sign the Sister City Visitors Book at the information center.

In 1996 Christchurch was named "Friendliest City in the World" by the readers of *Condé Nast Traveler.* It was also voted No. 2 in the Ten Top Cities of the World in the January 1997 *Travel & Leisure* poll.

But most important, Christchurch is a budget-friendly destination. The area's parks and gardens are the highlights—and they're all free, as is strolling along the banks of the scenic Avon River. The excellent Robert McDougall Art Gallery and Canterbury Museum are also open to the public at no charge, and I could spend the better part of a day wandering through the historic Arts Centre, browsing in the shops and soaking up the ambience. And of course, you don't have to pay a dime to listen to the legendary Wizard of Christchurch rant and rave in Cathedral Square.

1 Orientation

ARRIVING

BY PLANE   Christchurch has frequent air service from all major centers via **Air New Zealand, Mount Cook Airlines, Air Nelson,** and **Ansett New Zealand.**

Christchurch International Airport is 10km (6 miles) from Cathedral Square, out Memorial Avenue. The **Visitor Information Centre,** in the domestic terminal, will book accommodations and transportation at no charge. A cafeteria and fully licensed (expensive) restaurant, car-rental desks, a bank with money-changing service, a bookshop, gift and souvenir shops, a flower shop, hairdressers for both men and women, showers, and a large duty-free shop are all available there.

The **airport coach** to Worcester Street (opposite the Christchurch–Canterbury Visitor Centre) costs NZ$3 (US$2.10); the **express bus** to the airport from hotels, motels, and backpacker lodgings costs NZ$7 (US$4.90). The **airport shuttle bus** runs regularly and picks up travelers from hotels, motels, and backpacker lodgings, for a fare of NZ$8 to $10 (US$5.60 to $7). Call ☎ **03/365-5655** anytime.

BY TRAIN There's train service to/from Christchurch via the *Southerner* (Dunedin, Invercargill), the *TranzAlpine* (Greymouth), and the *Coastal Pacific* (Picton). The **railway station** is on Clarence Street, in Addington. For train information, call ☎ **0800/802-802** toll free in New Zealand.

BY COACH (BUS) Two bus companies—**InterCity** and **Mount Cook Landline**—offer service between Christchurch and Dunedin, Fox and Franz Josef Glaciers, Greymouth, Invercargill, Mount Cook, Nelson, Picton, Queenstown, Te Anau, Timaru, and Wanaka. InterCity buses arrive at and depart from the corner of Fitzgerald and Moorhouse avenues; the Mount Cook terminal is at 40 Lichfield St. (☎ **03/379-0690**). For bus information, call ☎ **03/379-9020**.

BY ALTERNATIVE COACH (BUS) **Magic Traveller Network** and **Kiwi Experience** both provide service into Christchurch.

BY CAR If you're coming from the north, you'll arrive on State Highway 1. If you're driving up from Dunedin, via Ashburton, you'll also be on State Highway 1. However, if your approach is from the southwest, via Lake Tekapo and Geraldine, I suggest you take Highway 79 to Highway 77 to Highway 73; this will bring you into Christchurch through Mt. Hutt and over the scenic Rakaia River. Christchurch is 366km (227 miles) north of Dunedin, 350km (217 miles) south of Picton, and 254km (157 miles) southeast of Greymouth.

VISITOR INFORMATION

The **Christchurch–Canterbury Visitor Centre,** at the corner of Oxford Terrace and Worcester Boulevard (☎ **03/379-9629**, fax 03/377-2424), occupies a lovely 1886 redbrick building that was the first home of the Christchurch City Council. It's open Monday through Friday from 8:30am to 5pm and Saturday, Sunday, and holidays from 8:30am to 4pm (longer hours in summer). Be sure to pick up a copy of the *Christchurch and Canterbury Visitor's Guide,* a gold mine of information that's published by the Canterbury Tourism Council and distributed through hotels and the Visitor Centre. It not only gives up-to-date information on goings-on in the city, but also includes the surrounding area.

Christchurch

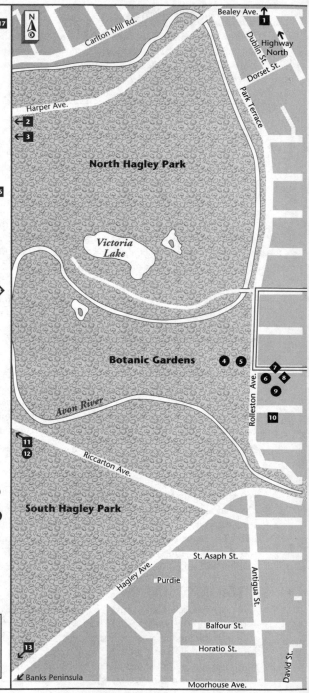

ACCOMMODATIONS
Alexandra Court Motel **17**
Cashmere House **37**
City Court Motel **18**
Cora Wilding
   YHA Hostel **31**
Diplomat Motel **1**
Fendalton House **2**
Foley Towers **24**
Hambledon
   Bed & Breakfast **14**
Pear Drop Inn **13**
Russley Park
   Motor Camp **11**
Turret House **16**
Windsor Private Hotel **26**
YMCA **10**

DINING
Boulevard
   Bakehouse Cafe **8**
Dux de Lux **29**
Hay's Cafe & Winebar **23**
Italia Caffè **34**
Le Café **7**
Main Street Cafe **19**
Michael's **34**
The Mythai **30**
Oxford on Avon **25**
Pedro's **28**
Strawberry Fare **20**
Tin Goose Bar
   & Whatever **22**
Via del Corso **33**

ATTRACTIONS
Air Force Museum **12**
Arts Centre **9**
Canterbury Museum **5**
Cathedral of the
   Blessed Sacrament **36**
Christchurch Casino **21**
Christchurch
   Cathedral **29**
Court Theatre **6**
Robert McDougall
   Art Gallery **4**

Information *ⓘ*
Pedestrian Mall ||||
Post Office ✉
Tramway ══

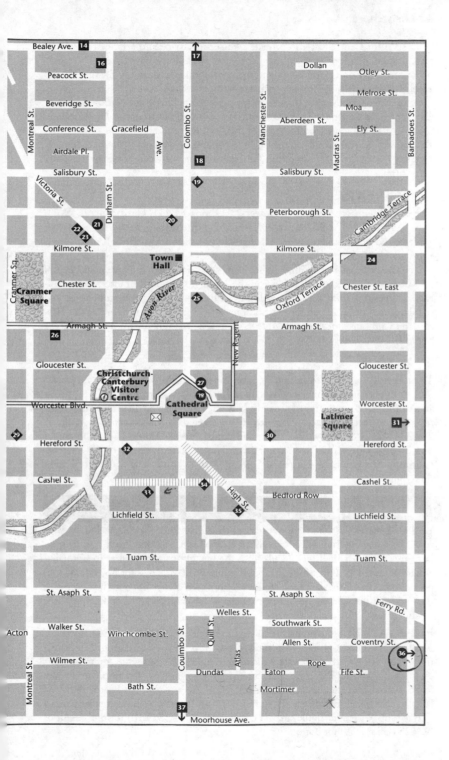

Bealey Ave. **14**

16

Peacock St.

Beveridge St.

Montreal St.

Conference St.   Gracefield

Airdale Pl.   Ave.

Colombo St.

17

Dollan   Otley St.

Melrose St.

Moa

Manchester St.   Aberdeen St.   Ely St.

Barbadoes St.

Salisbury St.   **18**

Victoria St.

Durham St.   **19**

Salisbury St.

21

22 **23**

20

Peterborough St.

Madras St.

Cambridge Terrace

Kilmore St.   Kilmore St.

Town Hall ■

24

Cranmer Sq.

Cranmer Square

Chester St.

Avon River

25

Oxford Terrace

Chester St. East

Armagh St.   Armagh St.

26

Gloucester St.

Christchurch-Canterbury Visitor Centre ⓘ

Worcester Blvd.

New Regent

27

28

Cathedral Square

Gloucester St.

Latimer Square

Worcester St.

31 →

29

Hereford St.

32

Cashel St.

33   ←

34

High St.

30

Hereford St.

Cashel St.

Bedford Row

35

Lichfield St.   Lichfield St.

Tuam St.   Tuam St.

St. Asaph St.

Acton

Walker St.

Wilmer St.

Winchcombe St.

Columbo St.

Quill St.

Atlas

Welles St.

St. Asaph St.

Southwark St.

Allen St.

Rope

Dundas   Eaton

Mortimer

Ferry Rd.

Coventry St.

Fife St.

36 →

Bath St.

37 ↓   Moorhouse Ave.

Montreal St.

The Visitor Centre can also provide sightseeing advice and arrange transportation, accommodations, and sightseeing reservations. They have an extensive supply of brochures on Christchurch and the surrounding Canterbury region. There's a well-stocked gift shop on the premises.

Before you leave the area, be sure to notice the **Kate Sheppard National Memorial,** which commemorates the centennial of women's suffrage in New Zealand (1893–1993). It's located on the bank of the Avon River adjacent to the center. New Zealand was the first country in the world to enfranchise women. If you have Internet access, you can get information on Christchurch at www.canterburypages.co.nz/ index.html.

SPECIAL EVENTS

The ✪ **Garden City Festival of Flowers,** P.O. Box 13-431, Christchurch (☎ **03/ 365-5403** or 03/379-9629, fax 03/366-2767), includes garden visits, floating gardens, and floral carpets in the "Garden City" of the South Island. It occurs mid-February for 10 days.

The **Canterbury A & P Show,** scheduled the second week in November (☎ **03/ 388-0846** or 03/379-9629), is held on the Addington Showgrounds. This agricultural and pastoral show is the South Island's largest and includes thoroughbred and standard-bred racing. Even those who don't attend watch the running of the New Zealand Cup horse race on TV. *Authors' note:* The last day of this 3-day show is a public holiday.

CITY LAYOUT

The center of things is **Cathedral Square,** the point from which to get your bearings. Above it rise the spires of Christchurch Cathedral, from whose Gothic tower you can look out over the flat, neatly laid out city. The **Avon River** runs lazily through the heart of the city, spanned by no fewer than 37 bridges as it wends its 24km (15-mile) course (west of Christchurch) to the sea. The graceful willows that line its banks are said to have come from Napoleon's grave site on St. Helena. **Colombo Street** bisects Cathedral Square north to south and is the city's main thoroughfare.

2 Getting Around

BY PUBLIC BUS   There are local buses that leave from Cathedral Square, with zoned fares ranging from NZ80¢ to NZ$4 (US56¢ to US$2.80). From 9am to 4pm, fares are reduced by half (get details from the bus information center in Cathedral Square or phone ☎ **03/366-8855**). You can buy an all-day pass for NZ$5/US$3.50 per person or NZ$10/US$7 for a family—there's even a 10% discount if you present their ad from the *Christchurch Visitors Guide,* which can be picked up for free at the visitor center.

BY PRIVATE BUS   The private **City Circuit Bus** (☎ **03/332-6012** or 025/ 346-940, fax 03/332-6598) offers transportation to the area's most popular attractions: The Plains Circuit goes to Willowbank, the Kiwi House, the Antarctic Centre, Air Force World, Riccarton Mall, and Mona Vale gardens. The Port Circuit goes to Ferrymead Historic Park, the Gondola, Lyttelton, and Sumner Beach. Both circuits start at the Christchurch–Canterbury Visitor Centre, at the corner of Oxford Terrace and Worcester Boulevard. The cost is NZ$13 (US$9.10) for one circuit or NZ$25 (US$17.50) for both.

BY TRAMWAY   In 1995 Christchurch's tramway (☎ **03/366-7830,** fax 03/ 366-7643) started running from Cathedral Square down Worcester Boulevard, along Rolleston Avenue, Armagh Street, New Regent Street, then back to Cathedral Square. Tickets can be purchased on board. Adult fare is NZ$5/US$3.50 for an hour, NZ$7/ US$4.90 for 4 hours, and NZ$10/US$7 for all day. Children under 15 are charged NZ$2/US$1.40 for an hour, NZ$3/US$2.10 for 4 hours, and NZ$7/US$4.90 for all day. Family fares are NZ$10/US$7 for an hour and NZ$15/US$10.50 for 4 hours.

BY TAXI   You'll find **taxi** stands at Cathedral Square and at all transport terminals. To call a cab, phone ☎ **03/379-9799, 03/377-5555,** or **03/379-5795.**

BY CAR   Getting behind the wheel of a car and driving isn't difficult; you only need to master the city's one-way street system. And since all on-street parking is metered, one of the following centrally located municipal parking buildings is your best bet: on Oxford Terrace near Worcester Boulevard, on Manchester Street near Gloucester Street, or on Lichfield Street near Durham. Check locally for the location of others. If you're traveling by rental car, there are several good self-guided drives to destinations such as Sumner Beach and the Port Hills. Pick up maps at the visitor information center.

BY BIKE   Bikers will find the city ideal cycling country, since most of the terrain is flat. Traffic may be a bit intimidating in the city center, but move out a bit and the bike will do just fine.

BY FOOT   Walking is the way to go as long as you're concentrating your sightseeing on the city center near Cathedral Square. To ramble through other, more far-flung sections, it's best to take a public bus and then hoof it.

FAST FACTS: Christchurch

Airlines   The Air New Zealand ticket office is at 702 Colombo St. (☎ **0800/ 737-000 in New Zealand,** or 03/353-4899); **Air New Zealand Link** and **Mount Cook Airline** (☎ **0800/800-737** in New Zealand); **Ansett New Zealand,** at 78 Worcester Blvd. (☎ **0800/800-146 in New Zealand,** or 03/371-1146); **Qantas,** at 119 Armagh St. (☎ **0800/808-767 in New Zealand,** or 03/374-7100); and **United Airlines,** at 152 Hereford (☎ **03/366-1736**).

American Express   The **American Express Foreign Exchange Service** at 78 Worcester St. (☎ **03/365-7366**) accepts mail for cardholders, issues and changes traveler's checks, and replaces lost or stolen traveler's checks and American Express cards.

Area Code   The telephone area code (STD) is **03.**

Baby-sitters   There's a child-care center (crèche) at 161 Tuam St. (☎ **03/ 365-6364**), open Monday through Friday from 8am to 5:30pm. Many hotels can furnish evening baby-sitters.

Currency Exchange   The ANZ Bank bureau de change, at the corner of Hereford and Colombo streets, in Cathedral Square (☎ **03/371-4714**), is open Monday through Friday from 8:30am to 4:30pm.

Doctors   For emergency referrals, contact **After Hours Surgery,** 931 Colombo St., at Bealey Avenue (☎ **03/365-7777**).

Emergencies   For police, fire, and/or ambulance emergency service, dial ☎ **111.**

Fax   Fax facilities are offered at the post office and at nearly all B&Bs, hotels, motels, and other lodging options. There's a commercial fax service at 148 Manchester St. (☎ **03/366-4829**).

Hospitals   Christchurch Hospital is at Oxford Terrace and Riccarton Avenue (☎ **03/364-0640**); ask for the Accident and Emergency Department.

Libraries   The public library is on the corner of Gloucester Street and Oxford Terrace (☎ **03/379-6914,** fax 03/365-1751, e-mail library@ccc.govt.nz), open Monday through Friday from 10am to 9pm, Saturday from 10am to 4pm, and Sunday from 1 to 6pm for reading only (no borrowing or reference service).

Post Office   There's a large, centrally located post office in Cathedral Square. Collect poste restante mail here. It's open 9am to 5pm Monday through Friday.

Services for Travelers with Disabilities   Contact **Disability Information Service,** 314 Worcester St., P.O. Box 32-074, Christchurch (☎ **03/366-6189,** fax 03/379-5939, e-mail disinfo@sirranet.co.nz), which is open Monday through Friday from 9am to 4:30pm.

3 Affordable Accommodations

Christchurch has the best selection of B&Bs in the country (picking the ones for this chapter was painful because there are so many good ones in the area). The savvy budget traveler will stay in one of these and enjoy a hearty morning meal as well as great hospitality. The city also has a host of other accommodations options, most of which are convenient to public transportation, a boon to those without a rental car.

The rates cited below include the 12.5% GST.

SUPER-CHEAP SLEEPS

✪ Alexandra Court Motel

960 Colombo St., Christchurch. ☎ **03/366-1855.** Fax 03/379-8796. 9 units (all with bathrm). TV TEL. NZ$102–$112 (US$71.40–$78.40) double. Extra person NZ$17 (US$11.90). Best Western discounts available. AE, DC, JCB, MC, V. Free off-street parking. Bus: 4.

Units at the Alexandra Court are spacious and nicely decorated and have outside patios. Bonus facilities here are in-room video, Sky TV, phones, and electric blankets. Also available are wakeup-call service, hair dryers, continental breakfasts, and fax service. One-bedroom units have both bathtub and shower, with an iron, ironing board, and radio. The guest laundry also holds a dryer. One-bedroom units can sleep up to four, those with two bedrooms will sleep six, and all have complete kitchens. There's at-your-own-door parking, with covered carports, at all except four units (there's covered parking space for them across the courtyard). Nearby are a golf course and a pool. The motel is a 15-minute walk from the city center.

Cora Wilding YHA Hostel

9 Evelyn Couzins Ave., Avebury Park, Richmond, Christchurch. ☎ **03/389-9199.** 40 beds in 6 rms (none with bathrm). NZ$15 (US$10.50) for members, NZ$19 (US$13.30) for nonmembers, NZ$18 (US$12.60) per person double. MC, V. Free off-street parking. Bus: 10.

This lovely old white mansion is on a tree-shaded residential street about 1 1/2 miles from Cathedral Square. It has stained-glass panels in the front door and is crowned by turrets and cupolas. There are six rooms sleeping 40 people total, all bright and cheerful, plus a comfortable lounge. To one side is a large parking area, and in the rear a children's playground. The laundry has coin-operated washers and dryers.

Foley Towers

208 Kilmore St., Christchurch. ☎ **03/366-9720.** Fax 03/379-3014. E-mail backpack@chch. planet.org.nz. 77 beds in 28 rms (7 rms with bathrm). NZ$15 (US$10.50) per person double without bathrm, NZ$18 (US$12.60) per person double with bathrm; NZ$12–$14 (US$8.40–$9.80) per person dorm bed. MC, V.

This comfortable two-story house is a short walk from Cathedral Square in the city center. Most rooms have under-floor heating, and there are two lounges, kitchens, and dining rooms, plus off-street parking and laundry facilities. Double-and twin-bedded rooms are quite basic, but attractive. Bed linen is not provided but can be hired for NZ$2 (US$1.40) per person per stay. This privately owned hostel is strictly nonsmoking, and children under 8 are not allowed.

✪ YMCA

12 Hereford St., Christchurch. ☎ **03/365-0502.** Fax 03/365-1386. 40 dorm beds, 147 rms (25 with bathrm), 2 units. NZ$37–$60 (US$25.90–$42) single; NZ$50–$85 (US$35–$59.50) double; NZ$100 (US$70) 1-bedroom unit for 4; NZ$105 (US$74) 2-bedroom unit for 6; NZ$17 (US$11.90) bunk. AE, BC, DC, MC, V. Free off-street parking.

This Y was the best find on my most recent visit to Christchurch. The location couldn't be better—across from The Arts Centre and steps from the Botanic Gardens. Each person in a 4-, 6-, or 10-bunk room gets a locker with a key. The more expensive singles and doubles have baths, telephones, TVs, and tea- and coffee-making facilities. Only the units have kitchens. Rooms in this 5-year-old building have contemporary decors, and the bathrooms are modern; half the rooms overlook the gardens, and 34 have balconies. There are both a dining room and a cafe on the premises. (I heard the food left something to be desired, but so what? There are several great places to eat in The Arts Centre.) The Y's gym, sauna, and aerobics class are available to guests at a discount.

FOR A FEW EXTRA BUCKS

Turret House

435 Durham St. N. (just off Bealey Ave.), Christchurch. ☎ **03/365-3900.** Fax 03/365-5601. 7 rms and suites (all with bathrm). NZ$85–$110 (US$59.50–$77) double; NZ$125 (US$88) triple; and NZ$140 (US$98) quad. Rates include continental breakfast. Lower off-season rates June through September. AE, BC, DC, MC, V. Free off-street parking.

Turret House, built in 1885, has been renovated. All the rooms have ensuite bathrooms, there's a nice guest lounge with a color TV, and the kitchen is available 24 hours a day for tea, coffee, and snacks. Owners Paddy and Justine Dogherty can provide fax service, laundry service, and baby-sitting. The hosts have created an environment which, while being historic, is also friendly and relaxed. All rooms are attractively decorated in styles that suit the era of the house but also have modern conveniences such as electric blankets, heaters, and hair dryers. One suite has a queen-size bed in one room and two single beds in another, accommodating four people comfortably. There's a nearby bus stop, and it's a 5-minute walk from the town center, park, and casino.

Windsor Hotel

52 Armagh St., Christchurch. ☎ **03/366-1503.** Fax 03/366-9796. 40 rms (none with bathrm). NZ$90 (US$63) double, NZ$15 (US$10.50) child 12 or under sharing with parents. Rates include breakfast. Discounts for groups of 3 or 4; children are charged half price. AE, BC, DC, JCB, MC, V. Free off-street parking.

Don Evans and Carol Healey, the charming—and caring—hosts, have built a devoted following over the years, primarily because of their personal interest in all guests. The carefully renovated, rambling old brick home has nicely decorated rooms (some with hot and cold running water). The hallways are heated for the trip to the conveniently placed bathrooms. The TV lounge holds lots of chairs and stacks of magazines. The outstanding breakfast often includes omelets or some other special item. Off-street parking is available. This guest house, centrally located off Cranmer Square, is located near a bus stop and on the tramway line.

MODERATELY PRICED OPTIONS

Diplomat Motel

127 Papanui Rd., Christchurch. ☎ **03/355-6009.** Fax 03/355-6007. 12 studios, 4 two-bedroom units (all with bathrm). TV TEL. NZ$96 (US$67.20) studio for 2; NZ$111–$126 (US$77.70–$88.20) 2-bedroom unit for 2. Extra person NZ$15 (US$10.50). Low-season and Best Western discounts available for direct bookings. AE, BC, DC, JCB, MC, V.

The attractive units here have cathedral ceilings with timbered rafters and are surrounded by landscaped grounds. Artwork is done by New Zealand artists and represents a wide range of styles. These two-bedroom units are spacious, with complete kitchens, queen-size beds, and a personal safe for your valuables. There's a nice spa, also, in a landscaped garden setting, as well as a guest laundry. Both cooked and continental breakfasts are available. Located about a mile from the city center on a city bus route, the Diplomat is a 3-minute walk from the Merivale Mall. French and German spoken.

✪ Fendalton House

50 Clifford Ave., Fendalton, Christchurch. ☎ **03/355-4298.** Fax 03/355-0959. 3 rms (all with bathrm). TV. NZ$110–$120 (US$77–$84) double. Rates include huge breakfast. MC, V. Limited free off-street parking.

Host Pam Rattray coddles her guests and serves the best breakfast in New Zealand—it's huge and may include homemade muesli, delicious homemade raspberry jam, yogurt, fresh fruit, waffles, pancakes, French toast, bacon and eggs, fresh croissants, and grapes off her own vine (not all of these everyday). It's hard to say whether I enjoyed the homemade raspberry jam or the hot-off-the-griddle pancakes more. All rooms have tea- and coffee-making facilities, terry robes, and decanters of sherry and port. Two of the rooms have king beds and one has a queen; one king room also has a single bed, as does the queen. In addition to a lounge with fireplace, there's a wonderful conservatory where grapes grow overhead. Concert radio ("Concert FM" 89.7) plays in the background throughout the day and adds to the homey, relaxing atmosphere. Pam is a wonderful host. In addition to the courtesies one might expect, she also provides complimentary beer and cold drinks in a guest fridge. There's a lovely swimming pool and spa in the back garden, and from here you can feed the wild ducks on the Wairarapa River. The river and the pool make Fendalton House a poor choice for those traveling with toddlers. Pam (a former science teacher) is absolutely wonderful about answering questions—even the 100+ this pesky travel writer asked—and is a font of information on the city's sights and dining options. It's a 5-minute drive or 20- to 30-minute walk to the city center from this nonsmoking B&B. Highly recommended.

✪ Hambledon Bed & Breakfast Inn

103 Bealey Ave., Christchurch. ☎ **03/379-0723.** Fax 03/379-0758. Web sites nz.com/webnz/ bbnz/hambldn.htm and www.canterburypages.co.nz/bnb/xhamble.html. 6 suites in the mansion, 4 rms in the gatehouse, 1 self-contained flat (all with bathrm). NZ$110–$165 (US$77–$116) double in the mansion; NZ$90 (US$63) double in gatehouse room; NZ$110 (US$77) double in flat. Mansion and Gatehouse rates include breakfast. MC, V. Free off-street parking.

This grand historic home is just a 10- to 15-minute walk from the city center. It was built in 1855 and includes a wonderful rimu and mahogany staircase and lead-light windows. The sea-foam and pastel tones compliment the rimu woodwork and paneling throughout. When Jo and Calvin Floyd bought the house, it was configured as nine separate apartments; now its 8,000 sq. ft. are divided into six spacious guest suites. Rooms in the mansion are furnished with antiques and collectibles and are stocked with books, magazines, tea- and coffee-making facilities, a small fridge, separate heaters, hair dryers, TVs, and telephones. This is a great place for three or four people traveling together, as several mansion rooms are two-bedroom, one-bathroom suites. The two-story, self-contained flat (apartment) in the coach house has a bathroom downstairs and a kitchen and bedroom upstairs—great quarters for long stay visitors. The gatehouse (built in 1955) offers great value. It lacks the grand historic ambience and spaciousness of the mansion, but provides charming quarters in the same convenient location with the same helpful hosts. Rooms in the gatehouse are attractive—three rooms have ensuites, the other a private bathroom; and a kitchen, lounge, and dining room are included—residents of the gatehouse gather in these shared spaces for meals and conversation, which makes this a very good place for single travelers. Laundry facilities are available (free wash, pay dry). This grand old Victorian gentleman's residence is a *very* special place. There's no smoking in any of the buildings.

WORTH A SPLURGE

Cashmere House

141 Hackthorne Rd., Cashmere Hills, Christchurch. ☎ and fax **03/332-7864.** 5 rms (3 with bathrm). NZ$190 (US$133) double without bathrm, NZ$$235 (US$165) double with bathrm. Rates include breakfast. BC, MC, V. Free off-street parking.

What a wonderful place! This 9,000-square-foot hillside mansion was built in 1928 and has more lead-light windows than I've ever seen in one place. There are also a charming conservatory with grand piano, a full-size billiard table in its own room, a lovely parlor with a fireplace, and a dining room with an expansive view of the whole city. Hosts Monty and Birgit Claxton couldn't be nicer or more helpful (Birgit speaks Swedish and German; Monty is a classic car buff). The five bedrooms vary in size, and occupants of the White and Rose rooms use private, but not attached, bathrooms. My favorite is East, where there's an antique king-size bed. Cashmere House, surrounded by lawn and gardens, is about a 15-minute drive from the city center. The historic Sign of the Takehe is nearby. Smoking is not permitted in the house, and Cashmere House is not suitable for children.

SLIGHTLY OUT OF TOWN

Pear Drop Inn

Hwy. 75, R.D. 2, Christchurch. ☎ and fax **03/329-6778.** 4 rms (2 with bathrm). NZ$75 (US$52.50) double. Rate includes breakfast. Dinner NZ$25 (US$17.50) per person. AE, MC, V.

Pear Drop Inn is 15 to 20 minutes by car from town on Highway 75 and easy to find. Staying on this 2¹/₂-acre property is just like staying with relies (relatives). Brenda

---

Readers Recommend

Croydon House. 63 Armagh St., Christchurch. ☎ and fax **03/366-5111.** *"Hosts Nita and Sigi have a well run establishment with reasonable prices in a very central location."*

The Grange Guesthouse, 56 Armagh St., Christchurch. ☎ **03/366-2850.** Fax 03/366-2850. *"Run by English mother and son, Paul and Marie Simpson. This is a Victorian mansion which they have refurbished with en suites."*
—Jennie Fairlie, Broadbeach, QLD, Australia.

Crocker is as friendly as hosts come, and this place has a homely (homey) feel to it. The grounds include fruit trees, flower gardens, lawns, a pond, and an extensive organic veggie garden. Eggs at breakfast are from Brenda's hens, and most of the food at dinner is homegrown, too; she bottles (cans) pears, walnuts, hazelnuts, plums, apples, and apricots. Two twin rooms downstairs share two toilets, two sinks, and one shower. The spacious upstairs room has ensuite facilities, a TV, queen and single bed, cot (crib), and tea- and coffee-making facilities. A piano and TV in the lounge, a conservatory for reading and conversation, and an outdoor spa are additional features. This place isn't posh, but the hospitality is very warm.

4 Great Deals on Dining

Christchurch's eating options tend to be clustered on Columbo Street north of Cathedral Square, on the Cashel Mall, and in New Regent Street. There are also several great dining spots in The Arts Centre—some of which are profiled below. In addition, you might like Annie's Wine Bar & Restaurant, ☎ and fax **03/365-0566,** where over 40 local wines are available.

SUPER-CHEAP EATS

In Italia Caffè

In the Guthrey Centre, 126 Cashel Mall. ☎ **03/365-5349.** Fax 03/384-0135. Reservations accepted but not required. Light meals NZ$3–$15 (US$2.10–$10.50). AE, BC, DC, MC, V. Mon–Thurs 8:30am–6:30pm, Fri 8:30am–10pm, Sat 8:30am–5:30pm. ITALIAN.

This pleasant little cafe in one of Christchurch's best city-center shopping malls is fully licensed and serves great wines (as well as mixed drinks, of course) to go with their terrific Italian dishes. The meats, cheeses, and salads were so delicious that I went back to sample the pasta. It was freshly made, and my dish came with a selection of napoletana (tomato, basil, and garlic), Bolognese (spicy beef and tomato), and carbonara (bacon, onion, cream, egg, and parmesan cheese) sauce. They also serve coffee, including Cappuccino and espresso. This place makes for a delightful lunch break or dinner at the end of a long shopping or sightseeing foray in the city center. Everything on the menu is available as take-away too.

Le Café

In The Arts Centre, Worcester Blvd. ☎ **03/366-7722.** Reservations only accepted for breakfast and dinner. Main courses NZ$6.50–$14 (US$4.55–$9.80). AE, MC, V. Sun–Thurs 7am–midnight, 24 hours on weekends. CAFE.

"Le Calf," as it's pronounced locally, is a great place for coffee and light meals. It's also a good spot for people-watching—its worn wooden tables, lead-light windows, and high ceilings attract a wide range of locals and visitors. Seating is inside or out; breakfast is served all day. Meals include open sandwiches on focaccia bread, ham and cheese croissants, a pasta of the day, stuffed baked potatoes, Thai chicken curry, and Greek country salad. Le Café's bakery, which is steps away, offers an even thriftier option. Here they make all the breads for Le Café, and there are a few tables where you can eat. The people-watching isn't as good, but it's less expensive (coffee at Le Café is NZ$3; at the bakery it's NZ$2). The aroma of fresh baking bread and budget prices make the bakery a good choice. However, Le Café has much better atmosphere and offers a more diverse menu.

✪ Oxford on Avon

794 Colombo St., on Oxford Terrace. ☎ **03/379-7148.** Reservations not accepted for dinner. Main courses NZ$12–$16 (US$8.40–$11.20); roast meal NZ$10.95 (US$7.67). AE, BC, DC, MC, V. Daily 6:30am–midnight. BISTRO/NEW ZEALAND.

The Daily Bagel, 197A Victoria St. ☎ **03/374-9905.** *"For Americans homesick for bagels this is the place to go. The owners of this little storefront learned their craft in Toronto and are doing a good job of spreading the gospel in this otherwise wonderful city."*
—Ira & Sharon Silverman, Rockville, Maryland, USA.

Il Felice, 56 Litchfield St. ☎ **03/366-7535.** *"Great food and service in this Italian restaurant and bar."*
—Jennie Fairlie, Broadbeach, QLD, Australia.

This fully licensed restaurant near the city center is in a 125-year-old building that for many years was a hotel and tavern. Nowadays it houses a complex of bars and a large restaurant that serves fish, roasts, grills, and salads at prices that make it truly one of Christchurch's best buys. Recent renovations have given birth to a tasteful garden bar built out onto the banks of the Avon—a terrific place to while away a sunny afternoon at the umbrella tables. Breakfast, lunch, dinner, and supper are served. The roast meals (usually lamb, beef, and one other choice) are especially good value. The bar upstairs is a disco, and there's a bottle shop on the premises.

Strawberry Fare Dessert Restaurant

114 Peterborough St. ☎ **03/365-4897.** Fax 03/365-4665. Reservations not required. Desserts NZ$7.50–$14 (US$5.25–$9.80); light meals NZ$10–$20 (US$7–$14). BC, MC, V. Sun–Thurs 10am–midnight, Fri–Sat 9am–midnight. DESSERTS/LIGHT MEALS.

For a dip into decadence, rush to Strawberry Fare and order a luscious dessert or a light meal. Desserts are their specialty, of course, but they also have an interesting selection of savory meals. Assuage that sweet tooth with such temptations as Death by Chocolate, Chocolate Mud Pie, or Devil's Dream Cake—or settle for a lunch such as salmon in phyllo or crunchy-topped chicken. Strawberry Fare is just off Colombo Street, set back from the street.

FOR A FEW EXTRA BUCKS

✪ Dux de Lux

In The Arts Centre, Montreal and Hereford sts. ☎ **03/366-6919.** Reservations not required. Main courses NZ$12 (US$8.40) at lunch, $15 (US$10.50) at dinner. AE, DC, MC, V. Daily 11:30am–11pm. VEGETARIAN/SEAFOOD/SALADS.

Dux de Lux, a favorite eating and meeting spot among Christchurch locals, is housed in one of the atmospheric old stone buildings that once comprised the University of Canterbury. It calls itself a gourmet vegetarian restaurant and serves such creative dishes as phyllo pastry stuffed with mushrooms, cottage cheese, and spinach or pumpkin-and-kumera roulade. For nonvegetarians, there's also a seafood bar. Hot main dishes come with a choice of salads and hot vegetables. There are two congenial dining rooms and a tree-filled courtyard with picnic tables. Service is cafeteria style, and if there's a line, it's worth the short wait. There's music on Thursday through Saturday nights. Licensed.

✪ Main Street Cafe & Bar

840 Columbo St., at Salisbury St. ☎ and fax **03/365-0421.** Light meal NZ$8 (US$5.60); main courses NZ$13–NZ$15 (US$9.10–10.50). AE, BC, DC, MC, V. Daily 10am–10:30pm. VEGETARIAN.

This is my kind of place. Enjoy healthy, wholesome food in relaxed surroundings—and it's licensed, so you can have a beer or wine with dinner. You order at the

---

👬 Family-Friendly Restaurants

Strawberry Fare *(see p. 393)*   Kids love this dessert restaurant where options for sweet tooths are endless.

Oxford on Avon *(see p. 392)*   The roast dinners here have a home-cooked taste that children enjoy. This is also a good spot for family breakfasts.

The Tin Goose Bar & Whatever *(see p. 394)*   The old-fashioned aircraft decor and informal, relaxed atmosphere make this a winner with kids. The menu includes family-friendly items such as French toast, burgers, and pasta.

---

counter: They usually offer half a dozen really interesting salads, such as cold rice with veggies, chick pea, carrot and sprout, and hummus. Typical main courses include cheesy bean casserole, chile yogurt vegetables, and spinach-and-mushroom lasagna. The homemade soups are especially tasty. The decor includes pastel-green walls with lavender trim hung with modern art. The bar stays open after food service stops. It's fully licensed, or you can bring your own. No smoking.

The Tin Goose Bar & Whatever

77 Victoria St. ☎ **03/365-2866**. Reservations accepted. Main courses NZ$10.50–$18.50 (US$7.40–$12.95). Mon–Fri 7am–late, Sat–Sun 8am–late. CAFE.

Aviation buffs will love this place named after the Ford Tri-motor aircraft, circa 1925. The exterior of the popular cafe is mottled gray, and the interior sports sky-blue walls with pictures of WWII fighters and bomber planes. The bar is shaped like an aircraft wing, and pump handles for dispensing beer are joysticks. Stop by and have a cup of tea (NZ$2.20/US$1.54), at the very least, just to enjoy the innovative interior. If you decide to stay for a meal, choices include Full Throttle Thai Chicken Curry, Squadron Leader Succulent Sirloin, and Spitfire Open Sami (sandwich). Breakfast, served all day, includes P-51 Scramble and Flack Jacket Stack (pancakes). I had heard that the music was perhaps a bit too loud, but found that it didn't intrude on our conversation when my friend and I ate there. I also appreciated the nice selection of wines available by the glass. The Tin Goose often has a DJ on Friday night.

MODERATELY PRICED OPTIONS

Hay's Cafe & Winebar

63 Victoria St. ☎ and fax **03/379-7501**. Reservations required on weekends, preferred all the time. Main courses NZ$18–$24.50 (US$12.60–$17.20). AE, DC, MC, V. Mon 8:30am–5:30pm, Tues–Sat 8:30am–10:30pm. PACIFIC RIM.

With 48 million sheep in the country, you'd think it would be easy to find lamb on restaurant menus. However, it won't take you long to find out that this isn't the case. Seems that this meat is considered "too common" to offer to visitors—until recently only farmstay and homestay guests could ever taste this delicious delicacy. Happily, a few restaurants have become aware that many visitors come to New Zealand to eat lamb—this cafe is one of them. Hay's is an award-winning place, located across from the casino. Hosts Celia and Allan Hay make all of their own bread and serve lamb, which comes from a farm in Pigeon Bay on the Banks Peninsula that Allan's family has owned since 1843. Favorite dishes include char-grilled lamb and vegetables with basil-pinenut jus; tender Inveralloch lamb with warm grape and chili salsa and kumera wedges; and braised lamb shanks and fennel with preserved lemons and saffron, on couscous. Vegetarian, fish, and chicken dishes are also on the menu, as are pizza and lighter fare. Paintings of Pigeon Bay line the walls. They also have a cooking school upstairs. (*Note:* For straightforward, cost-effective roast lamb dinners, the Oxford on Avon is a better choice.)

The Mythai

84 Hereford St. ☎ **03/365-1295.** Reservations required for dinner Fri–Sat. Main courses NZ$18–$20 (US$12.60–$14). AE, DC, MC, V. Mon–Fri 11am–3pm, daily 5–11pm. THAI.

You could walk right past this unpretentious little place in the city center, but that would be a real mistake if you like authentic Thai food. There's an extensive menu of chicken dishes; try the *pad gai benjarongdishes* (chicken with vegetables in peanut sauce), pork, beef, lamb, seafood, and vegetarian choices. The spicy fish cakes with a sauce of cucumber sweet chiles are outstanding among appetizers, as is the traditional dessert of *mythai gluay ghium* (banana with coconut sauce).

The Mythai is popular with office workers at lunch, but don't be put off if the place is crowded—there's a larger back dining room, and you seldom have to wait very long. It's a different story, however, for dinner on Friday and Saturday, when you could well be disappointed if you don't book ahead. It's BYO, and everything on the menu is available for take-out.

Via del Corso Trattoria

114 Cashel Mall, up 1 flight of stairs from the Cashel Mall. ☎ **03/377-5001.** Reservations recommended. Main courses NZ$18–$25 (US$12.60–$17.50). AE, DC, JCB, MC, V. Daily 6–10pm or later. PROVINCIAL ITALIAN.

You could easily miss this delightful eatery if I didn't tell you about it—the doorway on the ground level is not obvious. Once you get upstairs you'll notice the high ceiling and a sedate appearance, which don't seem to match the menu. Main courses include *Costolette Di Maiale Alle Mele* (panfried pork cutlets with rum and apples), *Quaglia Alla Casalinga* (braised quails wrapped in pancetta, served with julienne of spring vegetables), and the house specialty, *Coniglio Arrosto Con Polenta* (roasted rabbit served with polenta and red wine sauce).

WORTH A SPLURGE

✪ Michael's

178 High St. ☎ **03/366-0822.** Fax 03/365-1621. Reservations recommended. Main courses NZ$19–$27 (US$13.30–$18.90). AE, BC, DC, MC, V. Mon–Sat 6–10pm. MODERN NEW ZEALAND.

Michael's is praised by Christchurch's "foodies," many of whom have taken one of his cooking classes or belong to the Canterbury Gourmet Society, which gathers under his roof. The stylish dining room is adorned with antique furniture, long drapes, candlelit tables, and fine china and glassware. The sample main courses include lamb with sun-dried tomato and summer basil served on arugula salad with red-pepper dressing, wine-poached fish with julienne of vegetables, and smoked salmon with lemon herb-and-vermouth sauce. It's fully licensed, or you can bring your own wine.

Pedro's

143 Worcester St. ☎ **03/379-7668.** Reservations recommended. Main courses NZ$23 (US$16.10). AE, BC, JCB, MC, V. Tues–Sat 6:30–11pm. SPANISH.

Pedro's has been called the country's best Spanish restaurant. It's also very attractive: No bullfighter–poster-studded walls in this city-center restaurant though—instead, its tasteful decor is accented by an old Spanish sideboard, and the crockery is imported from Spain. Specialties include traditional paella (outstanding!), *langostinos à la plancha* (grilled king prawns), and *cerdo a la Navarra* (pork medallions in a sauce of tomatoes and red beans). Save room for lemon mousse or crema Catalana for dessert. If you want wine with dinner, you'll have to bring your own.

COFFEE, TEA & BREAKFAST SPOTS

There are several cafes on the Cashel Street Mall. You might try **Bardellis, Cafe Bleu,** or **Espresso 124.** In the same area is one of Christchurch's best food courts: Look for it upstairs in Shades Arcade.

One of the loveliest places for morning or afternoon tea is the **Sign of the Takahe,** a historic stone building on Dyers Pass Road overlooking the city in the Cashmere Hills. Cream tea is served from 10 to 11am and 2:30 to 3:30pm and costs NZ$6.50 (US$4.55); a Devonshire tea with clotted cream is also available for NZ$10 (US$7) per person. Buffet lunches in this impressive setting cost NZ$25 (US$17.50), and prices for à la carte dinners are off the charts. They accept American Express, Bankcard, Diners Club, Japan Credit Bank, MasterCard, and Visa.

Breakfast isn't a meal that many Kiwis eat outside their homes, so it's sometimes hard to find places that serve interesting ones. In Christchurch, you'll find good morning fare at **Oxford on Avon,** opposite the City Hall (it's served from 6:30 to 11am); **Strawberry Fare Dessert Restaurant,** 114 Peterborough St. (☎ 03/ 365-4897, fax 03/365-4665) open Sunday through Thursday, 10am to midnight, and Friday and Saturday, 9am to midnight; **Le Café** in The Arts Centre, Worcester Blvd. (☎ 03/366-7722); and **The Tin Goose Bar & Whatever,** 77 Victoria St. (☎ 03/365-2866), open Monday through Friday from 7am until late night, Saturday and Sunday, 8am to late night, and serves hearty breakfasts all day long.

Finally, the **Boulevard Bakehouse Cafe,** in The Arts Centre on Worcester Boulevard (☎ 03/377-2162), is a great spot to pick up sandwiches or other goodies for a picnic in the nearby Botanic Gardens. Or you could take your lunch up to Cathedral Square and eat while you listen to the Wizard rant and rave. This "beautiful-baking, great-coffee" spot is open daily from 8am to midnight, so you can go there after a play at the nearby Court Theatre, too.

5 What to See & Do in Christchurch

You may find news of free or inexpensive events by browsing through *The Press.* It was in this local daily newspaper that my husband, the car buff, learned that the annual British Car Days event would be happening during our visit.

THE TOP ATTRACTIONS

The hub of the city center is ✪ **Cathedral Square**—it will almost certainly be your orientation point, and it's great people-watching territory. Make a point of being in this area around 1pm, so you can listen to the **Wizard of Christchurch,** a colorful character (and actually a very learned individual) with very definite ideas about almost everything in the universe. If the Wizard's in town, you're in for some unusual entertainment, for which you won't be charged a cent. Christchurch treasures its "eccentrics and nutters," as the plaque outside the post office on Cathedral Square attests. It's in memory of another local character, the Bird Man.

More imposing architecturally than Christchurch Cathedral, below, is the magnificent **Cathedral of the Blessed Sacrament,** also called the basilica, on Barbados Street, about a 15-minute walk from Cathedral Square (or take bus no. 3J or 3K). Its classic revival architecture features colonnades, galleries, and an Italian mosaic floor, embellished with tapestries and bronzes. It's open daily from 8am to 4pm.

Cheap Thrills: What to See & Do for Free in Christchurch

- **Listening to the Wizard**   Be at Cathedral Square when the robed (black in winter, white in summer) Wizard of Christchurch is ranting and raving about anything from bureaucracy to religion to Americans—it's almost more fun to watch other people watch him in action.
- **Hanging Out at Mona Vale**   Take your travel journal or that stack of postcards you've been meaning to write to Mona Vale and sit on the bank of the Avon River or stretch out on one of the lawns. Take leftovers from breakfast to feed the ducks. The gardens here are gorgeous.
- **Browsing in the Canterbury Public Library**   There's so much to do, so little time: You can read the newspaper on the Internet; access your e-mail account and send faxes; find out what's going on locally from the notice boards; peruse the latest magazines and newspapers (including internationals); look at maps, tourist guides, and walkway books; brush up on New Zealand history; and possibly even meet some locals. The library is located on the corner of Gloucester Street and Oxford Terrace (☎ **03/379-6914,** fax 03/365-1751, e-mail library@ccc.govt.nz).
- **Shopping for Bargains at The Arts Centre Market**   It's up and running every weekend, and even if you don't buy any arts or crafts, you can browse among the Gothic arches and arcades and chat with the local artisans.
- **Strolling through the Botanic Gardens**   There's lots of room to wander here: 75 acres of trees, flower beds, and lawns. The gardens are encircled by a loop of the Avon River, and this peaceful stream, with its duck population, enhances the beauty of the plantings. Even if you're not into plants, this is a great place for a stroll among large majestic trees—many are more than 100 years old. You can even learn the names of all the exotic and indigenous plants, as most species are well labeled.
- **Watching the Punters**   No, we're not talking about football here. Sit on the bank of the Avon River and watch the local punters gracefully pushing passengers in their boats (punts). If you feel like splurging, hire a punt of your own. It'll cost about NZ$15 (US$9.75) per person for a 45-minute ride.
- **Touring the Canterbury Museum**   Check out the excellent display about Antarctica at this fine museum, along with the Hall of New Zealand birds; a prize-winning exhibit "Iwi Tawhito–Whenua Hou" (Ancient People–New Land) on New Zealand's early Maori settlers, and a gallery of Asian art.
- **Taking a Scenic Drive**   Pick up a brochure at the visitor center that describes local self-driving tours; my favorites include the "Garden Drive" and "Port Hills Drive."
- **Hearing the Cathedral Choir**   The choir gives a half-hour choral evensong at 5:15pm on Tuesday and Wednesday at the Christchurch Cathedral; the service is sung by the Boy Choristers on Friday at 4:30pm (except during school holidays).
- **Going for a Walk**   Several short and scenic self-guided walks are described in the "Christchurch Central City Walks" brochure available from the visitor information center. My favorite place to walk is in the Botanic Gardens, where in addition to magnificent trees and beds of perennials, you can feed the ducks swimming on the Avon.

Christchurch Cathedral ✓

Cathedral Sq. ☎ **03/366-0046.** Admission to Cathedral (and guided tours), free; tower, NZ$4 (US$2.80) adults, NZ$1.50 (US$1.50) children and students. There is a NZ$2 (US$1.40) fee to use your camera in the Cathedral. Mon–Sat from 8:30am, Sun from 7:30am. Guided tours given at 11am and 2pm.

Begun in 1864, just 14 years after the first settlers arrived, it was completed in 1904. The cathedral choir sings a half-hour choral evensong at 5:15pm on Tuesday and Wednesday, and the service is sung by the Boy Choristers on Friday at 4:30pm (except during school holidays). The cathedral is open for prayer weekdays, and holy communion is also celebrated daily. Climb the 133 steps in the 120-foot tower for a splendid panoramic view of the city and its environs.

○ Canterbury Museum

Rolleston Ave. ☎ **03/366-8379.** Free admission. Daily 9am–5pm. Free guided tours at 10:15 and 11:30am and 1:15 and 2:30pm. Closed Christmas Day.

The Canterbury Museum has an excellent permanent Antarctic discovery and heritage exhibit, which traces the exploration of the polar continent. Other interesting areas include the Hall of New Zealand birds, a prize-winning exhibit "Iwi Tawhito-Whenua Hou" on New Zealand's early Maori settlers, and a gallery of Asian art. Another exhibit depicts a pioneer-era Christchurch street. In the Maori section there's a display on the cutting and shaping of greenstone from raw rocks to polished adze. A series of new exhibits is planned through the year 2000.

Robert McDougall Art Gallery and Art Annex

Access via the Botanic Gardens. ☎ **03/365-0915.** Fax 03/365-3942. Free admission; charges apply to special exhibits. Daily 10am–4:30pm (Labour weekend through Easter 10am–5:30pm). Closed Good Friday and Christmas Day.

Among the Gallery's permanent collections are paintings, drawings, prints, sculptures, ceramics, and fiber arts by early and contemporary British, Australian, European, and New Zealand artists. There are also regular visiting and special-interest exhibitions from other places in New Zealand and abroad. The Art Annex presents the work of Canterbury artists working at the leading edge of contemporary art.

○ The Arts Centre ✓

Bounded by Worcester Blvd., Rolleston Ave., Hereford St., and Montreal St. ☎ **03/366-0989.** Free admission. Most craft and retail outlets daily 10am–4pm; market and food fair Sat–Sun and sometimes Friday in summer 10am–4pm; restaurant and cafe hours vary.

There's no way I can write about The Arts Centre without letting my prejudice show, so I might as well tell you up front that I love this place. Even if the wonderful old stone buildings were vacant, I'd like roaming among the Gothic arches and arcades and standing in the quadrangles that feel as if they're part of a "Masterpiece Theatre" set. The buildings were once the site of the University of Canterbury. They were constructed from 1876 to 1926 and coordinated by Samuel Hurst Seager's "grand design." The university left the space in 1975, and it now is home to several good eating spots (Dux de Lux, the Boulevard Bakehouse Cafe, and Le Café are described in "Great Deals on Dining," earlier in this chapter; Annie's Wine Bar & Restaurant is also very popular) and craft workshops. In addition, the **Court Theatre** is housed in the original Engineering Building and Hydraulics Lab, the **Academy Cinema** is in the old Boys' High Gym, and the **Southern Ballet** occupies the Electrical Engineering Lab and the Mechanical Engineering Lab. You may also be interested in seeing Rutherford's Den, which acknowledges Nobel Prize winner Ernest Lord Rutherford, who studied here from 1890 to 1894. Not surprisingly, The Arts Centre won a 1994 New Zealand Tourism Award.

✪ Botanic Gardens

Rolleston Ave. ☎ **03/366-1701.** Free admission; guided tours, NZ$4 (US$2.80). Grounds, daily 7am until 1 hour before sunset; conservatories, daily 10:15am–4pm; information center, Sept–Apr daily 10:15am–4pm, May–Aug daily 11am–3pm.

The world-renowned Christchurch Botanic Gardens are most easily accessed from Rolleston Avenue, but the 75 acres of trees, flower beds, and lawns spread out across Hagley Park and can also be approached via Riccarton Avenue. The gardens are encircled by a loop of the Avon River, and this peaceful stream, with its duck population, enhances the beauty of the plantings. Even if horticulture isn't of particular interest to you, this is a great place for a stroll among large majestic trees—many are more than 100 years old. And if you're a plant person, you'll want to visit the various special gardens and the conservatories (Cuningham House, Townend House, and Foweraker House). Twenty-minute guided tours on the "Toast Rack" tram leave from the Botanic Gardens Restaurant (☎ **03/366-5076**). An information center is adjacent.

✪ International Antarctic Centre

Orchard Rd., adjacent to the Christchurch International Airport. ☎ **03/358-9896.** Fax 03/353-7799. Admission NZ$12 (US$8.40) adults, NZ$6 (US$4.20) children 5–15, NZ$28 (US$19.60) family ticket. Free for children under 5. Oct–Mar, daily 9am–8pm; Apr–Sept, daily 9am–5:30pm. Closed Christmas Day. The center is a 20-minute drive from central Christchurch—I suggest that you take the airport bus.

I hope you won't be like me and allow only a short time for this fascinating center. Christchurch has long been the gateway to Antarctica, and finally there's a place where the public can share the experience of life on the frozen continent. Displays and sophisticated audiovisuals here tell about daily routines, the difficulty of access, the weather, the wonderful wildlife, and the ongoing scientific studies. They also tell of the various nations that maintain bases in Antarctica and the efforts to keep politics out of science. You can even experience what Antarctica actually feels like in the exhibit, which features real snow and ice with subzero temperatures. You can build a snowman, make a snowball, slide on the snow, and experience the effects of windchill. My spouse and I spent several hours and left wishing we had more time. There's a gift shop and a cafe on the premises. (Several readers have written to say how much they liked this attraction, and at least one has raved about the good food in the cafe.)

When you come out of the center, look across the street and note the **Operation Deep Freeze Base** on the edge of the airport. It is from here that the Antarctica-bound planes depart.

OTHER SIGHTSEEING HIGHLIGHTS

Head up on the **Christchurch Gondola** (☎ **03/384-4914**) for a 360° view of Christchurch and Lyttelton Harbour. With the displays and videos in the Time Tunnel, this is a good introduction into the city and surroundings. The top station of the cable car is 500 meters (1,500 feet) above the city, and you can stay and enjoy coffee and a snack or a meal before starting your descent. You can also mountain-bike down. The gondola is 15 minutes from town, but there's regular free shuttle service from the visitor center (10am, noon, 2, and 4pm during summer; noon, 2, and 4pm during winter). If you miss the shuttle, get a number 28 Lyttelton bus from Cathedral Square (NZ$1.90/US$1.33 return). **The Mountain Bike Adventure Co.** provides a gondola ride, map, bike, helmet, windbreaker, "and even brakes" for NZ$39 (US$27.30); rates are lower in the off-season. For information, call ☎ **03/329-9699.** The gondola operates daily from 10am to midnight from October 20 to April 30, noon to 10:30pm during the winter. The cost is NZ$12 (US$8.40) for adults and NZ$6 (US$4.20) for children with discounts for families, seniors, and students. There's no charge after 5pm if you're dining in the restaurant, which is open daily for lunch and dinner. The à la carte menu is really pricey, but there's an early-bird (5 to 6pm) set dinner for NZ$29.50 (US$20.70).

If your travel dollars are running short and you have a rental car, you can get the same view as provided by the gondola by following the Port Hills Drive detailed in the free brochure provided at the visitor information center.

Here's some other interesting sights to see:

Air Force World

Main South Rd., Wigram, Christchurch. ☎ **03/343-9532** or 03/343-9533. Admission NZ$9 (US$6.30) for adults, NZ$4 (US$2.80) for children. Open daily 10am–5pm. Closed Christmas Day. Take bus no. 8 or 25 from Cathedral Square.

This place is a must for aviation buffs, who will want to spend at least an hour or two here. It's located in Wigram Aerodrome, a 15-minute drive south of the city via Riccarton Road or Blenheim Road (both of which merge into Main South Road), where the Royal New Zealand Air Force was established in 1923. The aviation history of the country is depicted in dramatic re-creations, videos, and comprehensive displays of planes; exhibits such as the Bomber Command and Battle of Britain exhibits; and memorabilia. There's also a cafeteria overlooking the airfield, still in use by the RNZAF.

Ferrymead Historic Park

269 Bridle Path Rd., Heathcote. ☎ **03/384-1970.** Admission NZ$6 (US$4.20) adults, NZ$3 (US$2.10) children 5–15, NZ$1 (US70¢) children 3–5, free for children under 3; NZ$16 (US$11.20) family ticket. Daily 10am–4:30pm. Closed Christmas Day. Take Ferry Road east and make the first right turn after Heathcote Bridge (near the Christchurch Gondola). Bus: 3 from Cathedral Square.

The 8.2-hectare (20-acre) Ferrymead Historic Park holds a collection of things from the past, including Moorhouse Township (a late-Edwardian township complete with a church, a schoolhouse, a jail, an operating bakery, a print shop, a cooperage, and a livery stable), Hall of Firefighting, Hall of Transport, working exhibits, and lots more. There's a 1¹/₂km (1-mile) trolley link between the two main areas of the park, with restored electric trams from Dunedin and Christchurch, an 1881 Kitson steam tram, and a horse-drawn tram. The tram runs on weekends, and there is a small additional charge for riding it. *Author's note:* I would go here only if you're traveling with children.

Willowbank Wildlife Reserve

60 Hussey Rd. ☎ **03/359-6226.** Fax 03/359-6212. Admission NZ$10 (US$7) adults, NZ$4.50 (US$3.15) children; free (including a guide) with purchase of an evening meal costing NZ$32.50 (US$22.80). AE, BC, DC, JCB, MC, V. Daily 10am–10pm. Take Harewood Rd., turn right onto Gardiners Rd., and right again into Hussey Rd.; it's a 15-minute drive from the city.

This delightful natural park includes a zoo of exotic animals and a farmyard of endangered breeds, but it's the New Zealand Experience, featuring native birds, including the kiwi, that's of particular interest. Visitors who eat dinner here can see kiwis in their natural nighttime environment (floodlights help you). The fully licensed restaurant also serves morning and afternoon teas and lunch.

PARKS & GARDENS

Christchurch has the best gardens in the country—and that's saying something in this land of avid gardeners. The most impressive are Christchurch's **Botanic Gardens,** which are described separately under "The Top Attractions," above. There's also fierce competition every year between neighborhoods. To view some of the city's other glorious horticultural achievements, visit **Royds Street,** opposite Boys' High, which has won the competition for many years running. However, just about any street you stroll down will offer pretty patches of flowers. In February there are bus tours of the award-winning gardens.

If you like lawns and flowers, you won't want to miss ✪ **Mona Vale,** 63 Fendalton Rd., P.O. Box 8991, Riccarton (☎ **03/348-9659** or 03/348-9660, fax 03/348-7011), where 5.5 hectares (13.6 acres) of rolling lawns and flower beds surrounding a 100-year-old homestead are open to the public without charge. The Avon River flows along the border of Mona Vale, and punting is offered September through April. This costs NZ$12 (US$8.40) for 20 minutes, NZ$14 (US$9.80) for 30 minutes, and NZ$18 (US$12.60) for 45 minutes and is more interesting than punting in town because you have a view of private homes and gardens that enjoy river frontage. The restaurant in the homestead at Mona Vale can provide beverages and snacks to have on board and also offers morning tea, lunch, and afternoon tea. Frugal travelers will pack a picnic and enjoy it on the grounds. Mona Vale is a popular place to get married, with brides arriving by punt. If the urge strikes you while you're in Christchurch, the fee to hold your ceremony here is NZ$40 (US$28).

Gethsemane Gardens (☎ **03/326-5848**) is located about 8 miles from Christchurch on Clifton Hill in the seaside suburb of Sumner. I have my friend Helen Irvine to thank for this discovery. She's a local gardener and goes to Gethsemane regularly to buy plants. However, the big attraction here isn't the nursery; it's the 4 acres of English-style gardens planted and tended by Bev and Ken Loader. For NZ$2 (US$1.40) visitors can wander along garden paths with flowering beds on both sides. There's even a floral maze and a simple chapel constructed of wooden lattice and shade cloth. I'd match the ocean view through the window behind the altar here with any in the world. If you're thinking of getting married down under, you won't find a more beautiful site than this sweet little chapel surrounded by gorgeous gardens—the fee is NZ$100 (US$70). (For details on "Tying the Knot in New Zealand," see chapter 3.) Gethsemane is open daily from 9am to 5pm (closed Good Friday, Easter Sunday, ANZAC morning, and Christmas Day).

Stop by the Christchurch–Canterbury Visitor Centre and pick up a copy of the **Garden Drive** map which takes you from the city center to places of significance in Christchurch, through Hagley Park ending at the Botanic Gardens—there are 16 stops highlighted on this self-drive tour.

ORGANIZED TOURS

The Christchurch–Canterbury Visitor Centre, at the corner of Oxford Terrace and Worcester Boulevard (☎ **03/379-9629,** fax 03/377-2424), can book you on a 2-hour ✪ **guided city walk** (costing NZ$8/US$5.20), which leaves from their office at 9:45am and 1:45pm daily from October through April and 15 minutes later from the kiosk in Cathedral Square. From May through September, the tours are at 1pm and leave from the visitor center only.

COACH (BUS) TOURS

There are many good coach tours that cover the city and its surroundings, all of which may be booked through the visitor center, your hotel or motel, or directly with the tour operators. One of the best is that given by **Gray Line Tours** (☎ **03/343-3874**). It takes you to all the city highlights, and the afternoon tour takes the spectacular Summit Road to Lyttleton Harbour, with panoramas of snowcapped Alps, plains, and sea, and makes a stop at the baronial Sign of the Takahe for tea on the way back. The fare for adults is NZ$35 (US$24.50), half price for children. Gray Line also has day tours to **Akaroa** (see "Side Trips from Christchurch" below). Adults pay NZ$57/US$39.90; children are charged half fare.

While I think **Kaikoura** is too far to do as a day trip, there are daily bus tours to Kaikoura from Christchurch offered by Mount Cook Landline (☎ **03/379-0690,** fax 03/343-8053) and Gray Line (☎ **03/343-3874**); for more information on Kaikoura, see "En Route South" under "Picton" in chapter 11. There is also a rail excursion to Kaikoura; book at the railway station on Clarence Avenue in Addington (☎ **0800/802-802**).

Contact John Knox at **Ecotourism Australasia,** 55 Highsted Rd., Christchurch (☎ **03/359-6077,** fax 03/379-5150) for the **"Ultimate Insider Experience."** He provides escorted custom-tailored day trips, which can be to the homes of artists, Maori cultural sites, historical places, the Banks Peninsula, farms, fly-fishing spots, Kaikoura via the back road, vineyards, Authurs Pass for guided walks, horse trekking, or skiing. Meals and teas are often enjoyed at special places—in private homes and off the beaten path—for an additional fee. John is from Christchurch and studied environmental science in Brisbane, Australia. He's well connected to the best places and interesting people—not only in Christchurch but throughout New Zealand, Australia, and Fiji. His fee for this personal attention is NZ$185 (US$130) a day for two to three people; add NZ$60 (US$42) if he doesn't use your rental car or NZ$90 (US$63) if he uses a 4WD (for fishing or skiing). Extended trips of a week or two are billed at the same daily rate and don't include the cost of a rental car, accommodation, and meals.

A TRAIN TRIP TO GREYMOUTH

The ✪ *TranzAlpine* train trip to Arthurs Pass or Greymouth is another popular activity, and, while I think this train is great transportation to either of those places, I wouldn't do the round-trip as a day trip. If you do opt for the day trip, you can come back by bus and get a completely different view. The *TranzAlpine* is a great way of getting to Greymouth, but I think it makes more sense to spend the day there (see "Greymouth" in section 2, "Nelson & Beyond," in chapter 11) and then continue your journey north or south by car or by coach.

If you take the train, you'll cross the Canterbury Plains, go through the gorges of the Waimakariri River, and travel up into the beautiful Southern Alps.

Author's note: The best seat is by the window on the right side of the train in the direction of travel. Also, you might want to bring your own lunch rather than buy it on the train. The day-excursion fare is NZ$72 (US$50.40) to Arthurs Pass and NZ$99 (US$69.30) to Greymouth. If you take the Arthurs Pass option, you'll have 5 hours there before the train returns. If you go to Greymouth, you can take a short bus tour (NZ$5/US$3.50) before heading back to the east coast. For reservations and further information, call Tranz Scenic (☎ **0800/802-802** in New Zealand).

6 Outdoor Activities

BEACHES   Christchurch doesn't really promote its beaches, but there's a good one at **Sumner,** and you can take a No. 3 bus from Cathedral Square to get there (NZ$1.80/US$1.26). Sumner used to be a quiet seaside suburb but is now an up-and-coming area with good surfing, a safe swimming beach, and some appealing cafes. Lots of 20- to 30-somethings live in the area and hang out at the beach and in the trendy cafes.

BOATING   You won't be in Christchurch long before you notice the ✪ **punts,** maneuvered by young men in straw hats, on the Avon River. The way to get from the bank into one of those boats is to reserve a ride through the Visitor Centre. A 45-minute ride costs NZ$15 (US$9.75) per person or NZ$10 (US$6.50) for 20 minutes. Punting is also available on the Avon as it runs through Mona Vale (see "Parks & Gardens" above).

You can also take matters in hand and paddle your own canoe down the lovely Avon River. Canoes are for rent from **Antigua Boatsheds,** 2 Cambridge Terrace (☎ **03/366-5885,** fax 03/366-6768), as they have been from this same company for over a century. Prices for canoes are NZ$5 (US$3.50) per person per hour; for paddleboats, NZ$5 (US$3.50) per person per half hour. It's open daily from 9:30am to 6pm.

CYCLING   Christchurch's flat terrain invites cycling, and bike lanes are marked off in several parts of the city, including parks. Parking lots even provide bike racks. Join the bikers by renting from **Rent-a-Cycle,** 141 Gloucester St. (☎ **03/365-7589,** fax 03/389-1736), opposite the Coachman Inn. The price is NZ$2 (US$1.40) per hour or NZ$10 (US$7) per day for a single-speed bike, NZ$3 (US$2.10) per hour or NZ$15 (US$10.50) per day for a 3- or 10-speed bike, and NZ$5 (US$3.50) per hour or NZ$20 (US$14) per day for mountain bikes; discounts are given for weekly rentals, and cycle helmets are supplied. They don't accept credit cards. It's open daily from 10am to 6pm. There are other bike-rental shops, and the visitor center can supply a list of names and addresses, as well as brochures on cycling in Christchurch and its environs.

The Port Hills are a favorite place for mountain biking. **The Mountain Bike Adventure Co.** (☎ **03/329-9699**) makes it possible to take the Christchurch Gondola to the top and mountain bike down. The cost is NZ$39 (US$27.30) which includes the gondola ride up, map, bike, helmet, windbreaker, "and even brakes" (lower off-season rates). The gondola operates daily from 10am to midnight from October 20 to April 30, noon to 10:30pm during the winter. They will also just rent you a bike for the hour or the day.

GOLF   The Canterbury region boasts over 40 golf courses. The best known are **Russley,** 428 Memorial Ave. (near the airport; ☎ 03/358-4612), and **Shirley** in the suburb of Shirley (☎ **03/385-2738**). Russley Golf Club is parklike with its fairways lined by pine trees, while Shirley is more open but no less demanding.

SURFING   I have it on good authority that **Taylor's Mistake** in Sumner is a "primo" surfing area.

WALKING   If you prefer walking, Christchurch is the perfect place to do it; the visitor center can supply pamphlets mapping out scenic strolls—be sure to pick up **"The Christchurch Central City Walks"** brochure at the visitor center or follow your nose along the river or through the Botanic Gardens.

The Banks Peninsula Track is a 4-day, 35km (21.7 mile) walking experience that begins and ends in Akaroa. Trampers experience "four nights, four days, four beaches, four bays."

Arthurs Pass National Park, accessible by road and the *TranzAlpine* train, is another great area for tramping. It's 150km (93 miles) west of Christchurch. Walking and bird watching are popular activities here from November through March. In winter this is a popular area for skiing and snowboarding.

The 43km (27-mile) **Kaikoura Coast Track** offers an especially appealing and well-priced tramping option. This 3-day journey costs NZ$90 (US$63) per person and includes pack transfer and 3-nights' accommodation in farm cottages with full kitchens and bathrooms. For an extra NZ$30 (US$21) per person per day, breakfast, a picnic lunch, and an evening meal can be provided. For an extra charge of

NZ$6 (US$4.20) per person per night, all bed and bath linens are provided. The track starts 1¹/₂-hours' drive north of Christchurch. For further information contact Sally & David Handyside, "Medina," Parnassus R.D., North Canterbury (☎ 03/319-2715, fax 03/319-2724).

WINDSURFING   East Coast Windsurf, 1091 Ferry Rd., Christchurch (☎ 03/384-3788), on the water in Heathcote, hires windsurfers and can provide instruction. Sailing is done on the estuary; rentals cost NZ$20 to NZ$30 (US$14 to US$21) an hour.

SKIING AT NEARBY MT. HUTT

About 92km (57 miles) southwest of Christchurch and 34km (21 miles) north of the agricultural center of Ashburton, Methven lures those afflicted with downhill fever. It's the gateway to the **Mt. Hutt** ski area, which is blessed with a long season, often from late May through early November. Lift tickets cost NZ$50 (US$35) for adults and NZ$25 (US$17.50) for children; equipment rental runs NZ$25 (US$17.50) per day for adults and NZ$17 (US$11.90) per day for children. American Express, Bankcard, MasterCard, and Visa are accepted. For further information, call **Mt. Hutt** (☎ 03/302-8811); for a snow report, call ☎ 0900/99 SNO.

7 Shopping

There's good shopping in Christchurch, and I find prices here among the most reasonable in the country. For some of the best buys in New Zealand woolens and crafts, go by **The Arts Centre,** on Worcester Boulevard (☎ 03/366-0986), where the **Galleria** houses most of the permanent craft shops under one roof; it's open daily from 10am to 4pm. And don't forget about the ✪ **Public Market** held at The Arts Centre on Saturday and Sunday.

I also really like **Applied Art,** in Cashel Plaza, on Cashel Street near High Street (☎ and fax 03/377-2898), a gallery that sells the work of New Zealand–only artists. They are open Monday to Thursday from 9am to 5:30pm, Friday from 9am to 9pm, and Saturday from 10am to 4pm and accept American Express, Bankcard, Carte Blanche, Diners Club, Japan Credit Bank, MasterCard, and Visa. There's a **Regency Duty-free Shop** at 736 Colombo St. (☎ 03/379-1923), and **Ballantyne's Department Store,** on the corner of Colombo Street and City Mall (☎ 03/379-7400), is a good source for quality souvenirs. **Jumpers,** in the Shades Arcade, sells cute sweaters. Auto nuts are sure to find a trinket they'll need at **Fazazz, the Motorists Shop,** 82 Lichfield St. (☎ 03/365-5206). New Regent Street also has nice shops to browse.

8 Christchurch After Dark

For the latest news on nightlife, consult the "What's On" section of the *Tourist Times.*

THE PERFORMING ARTS

In addition to the venue described below, concerts, plays, and musical performances are often held in the **Town Hall,** on Kilmore Street (☎ 03/377-8899).

The Court Theatre

In The Arts Centre, Worcester Blvd. ☎ 03/366-6992. Fax 03/365-2793. E-mail court@chch.planet.co.nz. Tickets, NZ$24 (US$16.80) adults, NZ$19 (US$13.30) students, seniors, YHA cardholders, NZ$10 (US$7) children. AE, BC, DC, MC, V. Free parking available after 5:30pm.

This is quite possibly New Zealand's best theater. I've seen many plays here—ranging from Tom Stoppard to Shakespeare—and never been disappointed in the quality. Recent shows have included *She Stoops to Conquer, The Dining Room, Medea, Charley's Aunt,* and *I Hate Hamlet.* Performances are Monday through Wednesday and Friday and Saturday at 8pm, and Thursday at 6pm. The theater offers standby tickets on Monday, Tuesday, and Wednesday evenings (all unsold tickets are sold at a reduced price). Box office hours are Monday through Friday from 9am to 8:15pm and Saturday from 1 to 8:15pm. Highly recommended.

THE CLUB, MUSIC & BAR SCENE

Generally speaking, Christchurch's nightlife area is on Oxford Street between Cashel and Hereford streets.

If you want to dance, **The Palladium Nightclub,** on Chancery Lane opposite the library and near Cathedral Square (☎ **03/379-0572**), is a good choice. It's open nightly from 9pm until very late, and live bands play Thursday, Friday, and Saturday. Admission is free, except Thursday, Friday, and Saturday after 11pm when it's NZ$3 (US$1.95).

Jazz fans will want to head to **Kickin Jazz,** 633 Colombo St. (☎ **03/366-4662**), a lively spot that also serves good pizza.

New Zealand's answer to the Hard Rock Cafe is **Coyotes,** 126 Oxford Terrace, near the Bridge of Remembrance (☎ **03/366-6055,** fax 03/365-3720). This very popular place is known for its great music.

In addition to the places mentioned above, **Baileys 818 Night Club Restaurant & Bar,** 818 Colombo St. (☎ **03/366-6641**), in Cathedral Square sometimes has Irish bands and is popular with backpackers.

If your idea of a good night out involves drinking beer in a convivial atmosphere, get yourself over to **Dux de Lux** in The Arts Centre on the corner of Hereford and Montreal streets (☎ **03/366-6919**). They brew five beers in-house, including De Lux Lager, Nor'wester Pale Ale, Blue Duck Draught, Hereford Bitter, and Sou'wester Dark Stout. The mix of people here includes gays, university students, and yuppies. The Dux is also a great place to eat (see "Great Deals on Dining," earlier in this chapter).

MORE ENTERTAINMENT

SIGHTSEEING BY NIGHT

You can ride to the top of the **Christchurch Gondola** and have dinner with a knock-out view, or you can have dinner and a guided tour of the habitats of nocturnal animals at **Willowbank Wildlife Reserve.** See "Other Sightseeing Highlights," above.

MOVIES

Two cinemas in The Arts Centre, the **Academy** (☎ **03/366-0167**) and the **Cloisters,** show international and national art films. There's a Hoyts Multiscreen Theatre at 392 Moorhouse Ave. (☎ **03/366-6367**). Tickets cost NZ$9 to NZ$11 (US$6.30 to US$7.70).

A CASINO

Christchurch is home to New Zealand's first casino, the ✪ **Christchurch Casino,** Victoria Street (☎ **03/365-9999**), which opened at the end of 1994. This is a particularly attractive one, and features over 350 gaming machines, as well as blackjack, baccarat, minibaccarat, Caribbean stud poker, American roulette, keno, and sic bo. There's a buffet restaurant, the Grand Cafe, and a bar, the Canterbury Room. You must be 20 to enter the casino, and the dress code prohibits wearing denim, thongs, T-shirts, or active sportswear. It's open Monday through Wednesday from 11am to 3am and continuously from Thursday at 11am to Monday at 3am.

9 Side Trips from Christchurch

AKAROA

I went to Akaroa and the Banks Peninsula at the suggestion of a friend from Christchurch, and I agree with her that it's a lovely spot. This area has a beauty and charm all its own, and I urge you to experience it for yourself. You can drive or take **Intercity's French Connection** (☎ 03/379-9020) or the **Akaroa Shuttle** (☎ 0800/500-929) the 84km (52 miles) from Christchurch to Akaroa (sit on the right-hand side for the best views). Akaroa, with a population of a scant 800, is the southernmost French settlement in the world and New Zealand's only French inroad. In 1840 the French tried to establish a colony here, but England had just laid claim to the country in the Treaty of Waitangi. The original 63 French settlers loved the area so much, however, that they stayed on at the north end of town; French was spoken in that area until 1890. The English colonists who arrived in 1850 lived in the southern end, and to this day the street names reveal the dichotomy.

The Maori word *akaroa* means "long harbor," and the water is very much a constant reality here. If you spend any time at all, seduced by the delicate play of light and shadow on water and land alike, you may feel as if you've wandered into a watercolor painting. No wonder so many artists gravitate here.

Akaroa is known for its walnuts—it was the French who first brought the trees here. You can get a sense of much of Akaroa's character by wandering along **Rue Lavaud** and **Rue Balgueri.** Admire the charming wooden buildings and houses dating from the 19th century, including the cottages at the junction of Bruce Terrace and Aubrey Street. The old **French cemetery** is just off Rue Pompallier.

VISITOR INFORMATION

The **Akaroa Visitor Centre** and the local museum are located at 80 Rue Lavaud (☎ 03/304-8600). The **telephone area code** (STD) for Akaroa is **03.**

EXPLORING THE AREA

Experience Akaroa Harbour firsthand on the ✪ *Canterbury Cat,* which departs daily at 1:30pm year-round from the main wharf (☎ 03/304-7641, fax 03/304-7643). From November through March, there's also an 11am cruise. During the 2-hour cruise you'll spot penguins and dolphins (they're in residence November to April) and visit a salmon farm. Fares are NZ$27 (US$18.90) for adults, NZ$19 (US$13.30) for teens, NZ$13 (US$9.10) for children 5 to 12 years. For NZ$65 (US$45.50) you can swim with the dolphins from November to April (rate includes wet suit and hot drink after swim). The booking office is on the Main Wharf on Beach Road.

Akaroa's land-side attractions include its fine **museum,** the best place to start your visit, especially since it doubles as the town's visitor information center and can provide a good map; the **Langlois-Eteveneaux House,** part of the museum and probably the oldest in Canterbury, and the ✪ **lighthouse,** which was in service from 1880 to 1980, are additional attractions.

If you want to buy a book on the area or perhaps a woolen souvenir, go to ✪ **Pot Pourri,** 60 Rue Lavaud (☎ 03/304-7052), open from 10am to 5pm daily. I also like the **Picturesque Gallery,** 40 Rue Lavaud (☎ 03/304-7241).

Readers Recommend

Oinako Lodge, 99 Beach Rd., Akaroa (☎ **03/304-8787**). *"Judith and Trevor Jackson welcome guests to their historic mansion with lovely garden area and only 2-minute walk from town. They offer five bedrooms all with private bathroom, guest lounge, and dining room."*

—Jennie Fairlie, Broadbeach, QLD, Australia.

You can also take the **mail-run bus** (☎ **03/304-7207**) and experience the beauty of the Eastern Bays (the bus departs Akaroa at 8:30am and returns at 1:15pm); be assured that the driver will point out places of interest, in between delivering mail, milk, and passengers. The cost of this trip is NZ$20 (US$14).

Don't miss **Lake Ellsmere,** 111 square miles but only 6^1/$_2$ feet deep at its deepest part, and home to the Australian black swan, and **Lake Forsyth,** New Zealand's dramatic easternmost lake. Stop at the **Hilltop Tavern** for a view of Akaroa across the harbor.

Finally, the **Barrys Bay Traditional Cheese Factory,** Main Road (R.D. 2, Akaroa), Barrys Bay (☎ **03/304-5809,** fax 03/304-5814), makes a good stop on the road into Akaroa, between Hightop and Duvauchelle. Don & Jeanette Walker continue the tradition of cheese making, which dates back to 1844 on Banks Peninsula. There is a viewing gallery, and every second day from October to April you can watch cheese being made; it's open from 8am to 5pm.

OUTDOOR ACTIVITIES

The Banks Peninsula Track, P.O. Box 50, Akaroa (☎ **03/304-7612**), is a 4-day hike that begins and ends in Akaroa. Trampers can stay in backpacker hostels or B&Bs along the way. The 35km (21.7-mile) track crosses private farmland and a nature reserve and offers spectacular coastal views. Along the way there are swimming beaches, waterfalls, penguins, seals, Hectors dolphins, and terrain that varies from open pasture to beach forest. The track is open from the first of October to the end of April. Get details on the price of packages from the Banks Peninsula Track contact above.

AFFORDABLE ACCOMMODATIONS

For a little place, Akaroa has an impressive array of accommodations, including some of New Zealand's finest offerings of bed-and-breakfast and backpacker accommodation. No matter where you stay, you'll want to linger. The rates quoted below include 12.5% GST.

Glencarrig

7 Percy St., Akaroa. ☎ **03/304-7008.** Fax 03/304-7553. E-mail: glencarrig@bobparker.co.nz. 2 rms (both with bath). NZ$125 (US$88) double private bath, NZ$145 (US$102) double in king ensuite. Rates include breakfast. No credit cards.

Picturesque Glencarrig was built in 1853 by the first Anglican vicar in Akaroa for his wife and six children. You'll love the original timber work and the large farmhouse kitchen with its drying rack and Rayburn wood-burning stove that also runs the central heating. The lovely rooms all sport country decor, and two sitting rooms come with open fireplaces. The property, which sits prettily on 1^1/$_2$ acres a short walk from the town center, even has a stream and mill wheel on it, as well as a swimming pool. Hosts Bob Parker and Sally Omond enjoy looking after guests.

Kawatea Farmstay

Okains Bay, Banks Peninsula. ☎ and fax **03/304-8621.** 3 rms (1 with bath). NZ$75 (US$48.75) per person. Rates include dinner and breakfast. No credit cards.

Judy and Kerry Thacker are genuinely nice people and great hosts. Kerry is a fourth-generation New Zealander, and his family has been on the Banks Peninsula since 1850. Their 1,250-acre property provides an opportunity for guests to see a real working farm, with 1,000 sheep and 600 beef cattle. Depending on the time of year, you might be able to watch shearing or feed a lamb with a bottle. The historic homestead, built at the turn of the century, is another plus. Also within a couple of kilometers are a beach, a Maori museum, and a seal colony. My favorite room is upstairs, with its own bathroom.

Mount Vernon Lodge

Turn right off rue Balgueri, Akaroa. ☎ and fax **03/304-7180.** 6 rms (all with bath), 1 chalet, 2 cabins, 1 flat. NZ$40 (US$28) double; NZ$70 (US$49) cabin for 2; NZ$70 (US$49) chalet for 2; NZ$70 (US 49) apt for 2. NZ$15–$18 (US$10.50–$12.60) backpacker bed. Additional person NZ$10 (US$7) extra. MC, V. Courtesy transfers provided from Akaroa.

Put on your hiking shoes, for Mount Vernon Lodge has a premier site overlooking Akaroa Harbour, and it's no mean feat to get to it if you're on foot. The reward is a beautiful farmyard setting with well-maintained accommodations. Each room in the lodge has two levels with two beds on each level. There's a communal kitchen, lounge, barbecue area, and swimming pool. The lodge also has self-contained cabins and a cottage, as well as an A-frame chalet perfect for a couple who want to retreat from the world or for a family. It has a double bed looking out at the hills, three more beds upstairs, a tub and washing machine, a kitchen, and a TV. Horseback riding is available, and hiking is a given. This is a great place for families.

GREAT DEALS ON DINING

A popular place to sit and have breakfast or a "cuppa" is the **Akaroa Bakery,** on Beach Road. Here are a few other suggestions in the area:

✪ Astrolabe Cafe & Bar

71 Beach Rd., Akaroa. ☎ **03/304-7656.** Reservations recommended. Main courses NZ$14.50–$18.50 (US$10.20–$13); lunch NZ$10–$16.50 (US$7–$11.60). AE, BC, MC, V. Daily 10:30am–8pm (later in summer). Closed Wed in winter. ITALIAN/MODERN NEW ZEALAND.

The name of this restaurant comes from the first French ship to sail into the harbor here, but neither the cuisine nor the decor has a Gaelic flavor. Lunchtime options include pizza, calzone, focaccia sandwiches, and some interesting salads. Sample dinner main courses include grilled beef fillet, Akaroa salmon fillet, and lamb kebabs on couscous. The attractive modern decor is part of the reason for its popularity: Three walls are yellow, one is orange, and the high wood ceiling is green. Diners have the choice of sitting at the counter or at a table (the ones near the windows have a view). Focaccia is served on a wooden cutting board, and the soup arrives in huge white china bowls. It's licensed, so you can enjoy a Mac's Gold or DB Natural or choose from the wine list.

La Rue Restaurant

6 Rue Balgueri. ☎ **03/304-7658.** Reservations recommended. Main courses NZ$12–$14 (US$8.40–$9.80) at lunch, NZ$20 (US$14) at dinner. AE, BC, MC, V. Tues–Sun noon–2pm year-round; dinner daily from 6:30pm in summer, Tues–Sun in winter. SEAFOOD/NEW ZEALAND.

Overlooking Akaroa Harbour, La Rue is undoubtedly one of the best restaurants in town, and it has been a Taste New Zealand Award winner for 6 years running. The menu changes seasonally, always featuring seafood, with crayfish and Bluff oysters appearing in season. Lamb, venison, and pork dishes are also on the menu. It's fully licensed, or you can bring your own.

HANMER SPRINGS & OTHER SIDE TRIPS

Hanmer Springs, a 1¹/₂-hour drive northeast of Christchurch, offers hot pools for soaking, an 18-hole public golf course, and—yes, it's true—bungy jumping (☎ **03/315-7046**). Additional outdoor activities include jet boating and rafting (☎ **03/315-7323**), and horse trekking (☎ **03/315-7444**).

Arthurs Pass National Park is another day-trip possibility (see "Walking" in "Outdoor Activities" above). You can get there on the *TranzAlpine* train, on the Coast to Coast coach (☎ **0800/800-847** in New Zealand), or in your rental car.

See "En Route South" under "Picton" in chapter 11 for information on **Kaikoura,** where whale watching is the main draw. In my opinion, this picturesque little community is too far to go on a day trip, but if you disagree with me, you won't be the first. You may also be interested in the **Kaikoura Coast Track** (see "Walking" in "Outdoor Activities," above).

Appendix

air-conditioning refers to both heating and cooling the air

All Blacks New Zealand rugby team

bach North Island term for vacation house (plural: baches)

bath bathtub

bathroom where one bathes; bath

big bickies high salary

Biro ballpoint pen

biscuits/bickies cookies

bludge borrow

bonnet hood of car

boot trunk of car

Boxing Day the day after Christmas

bursary scholarship

bush forest

chemist shop drugstore

chilly bin Styrofoam cooler (U.S.), esky (Aus.)

Christmas crackers cylindrical party favors (U.S.), bon bon (Aus.)

coach long-distance bus

cocky farmer

college high school

cot crib (place where a baby or toddler sleeps)

crib South Island term for holiday house

cuppa cup of tea

cyclone hurricane

dairy convenience store

dinner the main meal of the day, can be the meal eaten in the middle of the day

doona comforter, quilt

duvet comforter, quilt

electric blankets in New Zealand they're found under the bottom sheet

en suite facilities attached bathroom

entree smallish first course, appetizer

fanny female genitalia; you'll shock Kiwis if you call the thing you wear around your waist a "fanny pack"

footpath sidewalk

freezing works slaughterhouse

gallops thoroughbred horse racing

get stuck in get started

as good as gold everything's OK

grizzle complain

grog booze

gumboots waterproof rubber boots (U.S.), Wellingtons (Britain)

hire rent

homely homey

hooker front-row rugby player

hotties hot-water bottles

housie Bingo

Parlez-vous Kiwi?

My lessons in Kiwi English began on my first trip to New Zealand, even before my plane had landed in Auckland.

"How about going to a hotel with me after we get into town?" queried my Kiwi seatmate.

"Would I *what?*" I shot back. I started giving him a piece of my mind, but, luckily, a nearby passenger intervened.

"If you'll excuse me," he said in a tone laced with détente, "I'm fluent in both Yank and Kiwi and I think I can straighten this out." He explained to me that in New Zealand *hotel* is synonymous with *pub* and my seatmate was only proposing we stop and have a drink. I accepted—both the drink and my first lesson in Kiwi.

My lesson continued as the gentleman and I drank our Lion Browns in Auckland's Albion Tavern: I learned that "to shout" has nothing to do with raising one's voice. "Hey, mate, it's your shout" is an invitation for your fellow guzzler to open his or her wallet, not mouth. I also learned that *blokes* often drink pints, handles, or scooners, but *birds* who request a 20-ounce mug of beer might get some sidelong glances.

Future lessons have helped me build my Kiwi vocabulary: When visiting friends at their home in Christchurch, I asked to use the bathroom. My hostess graciously showed me the way, but after I'd closed the door I realized the one piece of plumbing I urgently required was nowhere in sight. How was I to know that in New Zealand a *bathroom* is for bathing only and I should've asked for the *toilet?*

I expanded my vocabulary further during my brief career as a fruit picker on a South Island farm. When I was told it was time for a *smoko,* I replied, "Thanks, but I don't smoke." That brought peals of laughter from my Kiwi co-workers. Had they called it a coffee break I would've understood. It was on this same farm that I realized a *fine* day is one without rain and the small cottage I was living in was called a *crib.* (Had I been on the North Island it would've been called a *bach.*)

Unfortunately, not all my learning experiences have been pleasant. The farmer I was working for owned sheep as well as apple trees. One day he asked if I'd like to assist the shearer who was coming the next day. He said I could "pick dags." Though I had no idea what he was talking about, I happily jumped at the chance to pick something besides apples. I felt like a real fool when I realized what I'd agreed to do: The dictionary says a *dag* is a "dung-caked lock of wool around the hindquarters of a sheep"—but that isn't nearly descriptive enough.

While working as a waitress in one of Auckland's licensed restaurants, I had to master more Kiwi. When a customer ordered a *lemonade,* I correctly delivered a 7-Up. When someone requested *silverbeet,* I brought Swiss chard. I already knew that a diner ordering *chips* wanted french fries, but I added *kumara* (sweet potato), *silverside* (corned beef), *capiscum* (bell pepper), and *courgette* (zucchini) to my verbal repertoire.

However, I'll never forget the look on the face of one pompous businessman when I asked him if he needed a fresh napkin. While his dinner guests howled, one of the other waitresses explained that a *napkin* is what a baby wears (and *mums* change) and what I should've offered him was a fresh *serviette.*

It's been many years since that embarrassing incident, and now *I'm* the one who intervenes to smooth out potential international crises. Such was the case at a B&B in Napier when the proprietor asked a female compatriot, "Shall I knock you up in the morning?" As salacious as this sounded, he was only offering to wake her.

jandals   thongs (Aus.), flip-flops (Britain)

jersey   pullover sweater (U.S.), jumper (Aus.)

judder bars   speed bumps (U.S.), sleeping policeman (Britain)

jug   electric kettle or a pitcher

Kiwi   person from New Zealand; native bird of New Zealand

knickers   underwear, undies

knock up   wake up

LSZ   low-speed zone

lift   elevator

loo   toilet

lounge   living room

main course   entree

mate   friend

mossie   mosquito

nappy   diaper

Pakeha   anyone of European descent

panel beaters   body-repair shop

private facilities   private bathroom

pushchair   baby stroller

queue   line, waiting in line

rates   property taxes

return ticket   round-trip ticket

rug   blanket

serviette   napkin

shout   treat someone (usually refers to a meal or a drink), buy a round

single bed   twin bed

singlet   sleeveless undershirt

sister   nurse

smoko   morning or afternoon break

strides   trousers

ta   thank you

tea   beverage; also a light evening meal, supper; See also "dinner," above.

to call   to visit

to ring   to phone

togs   swimsuit (U.S.), cozzie (Aus.)

track   trail

trots   harness racing

uplift   pick up

varsity   university, college

wop wops   remote location, boon docks

Yank   American

A Glossary of Kiwi Menu Terms

Afghans   popular Kiwi cookies made with cornflakes and cocoa

ANZAC biscuits   cookies named for the Australia New Zealand Army Corps; they contain rolled oats and golden syrup

bangers   sausages

beetroot   beets

biscuits   cookies

blue vein   bleu cheese

capsicum   green or red bell pepper

chips   french-fried potatoes

chook   chicken

courgette   zucchini

Devonshire tea   morning or afternoon tea, plus scones with cream and jam

entree   appetizer

grilled   broiled

hogget   year-old lamb

jelly   gelatin dessert

kumara   Kiwi sweet potato

lemonade   7-Up

lollies   candy

main course   entree

milk shake   flavored milk

meat pie   a two-crust pie filled with stewed, cubed, or ground meat (usually beef) and gravy

Milo   a hot drink similar to Ovaltine

muesli   granola

pavlova   popular meringue dessert named after prima ballerina Anna Pavlova, served with whipped cream and fruit

pikelets   small pancakes served at tea time

pipis   clams

pudding   dessert in general, not necessarily pudding

roast dinner roast beef or leg of lamb served with potatoes and other vegetables that have been cooked with the meat
rock melon cantaloupe
saveloy a type of wiener
scone a biscuit served at tea time
silverbeet swiss chard
silverside a superior cut of corned beef
takeaway take-out
tamarillos tree tomatoes

tea the national beverage; also, colloquially, "dinner"
thick shake milkshake
tomato sauce ketchup
water biscuit cracker
Weetbix a breakfast cereal similar to Shredded Wheat "Everywhere the Queen's been there's Weetbix"
whitebait very tiny fish, served whole without being cleaned
white tea tea with milk

The Metric System

Length

1 millimeter (mm)	=	.04 inches (or less than 1/16 in.)
1 centimeter (cm)	=	.39 inches (or just under 1/2 in.)
1 meter (m)	=	.39 inches (or about 1.1 yards)
1 kilometer (km)	=	.62 miles (or about 2/3 of a mile)

To convert kilometers to miles, multiply the number of kilometers by .62. Also use to convert speeds from kilometers per hour (kmph) to miles per hour (m.p.h.).
To convert miles to kilometers, multiply the number of miles by 1.61. Also use to convert speeds from m.p.h. to kmph.

Capacity

1 liter (l)	=	33.92 fluid ounces	=	2.1 pints	=	1.06 quarts	=	.26 U.S.gallons
1 Imperial gallon							=	1.2 U.S. gallons

To convert liters to U.S. gallons, multiply the number of liters by .26.
To convert U.S. gallons to liters, multiply the number of gallons by 3.79.
To convert Imperial gallons to U.S. gallons, multiply the number of Imperial gallons by 1.2.
To convert U.S. gallons to Imperial gallons, multiply the number of U.S. gallons by .83.

Weight

1 gram (g)	=	.035 ounces (or about a paper clip's weight)			
1 kilogram (kg)	=	35.2 ounces	=	2.2 pounds	
1 metric ton	=			2,205 pounds	=	1.1 short ton

To convert kilograms to pounds, multiply the number of kilograms by 2.2.
To convert pounds to kilograms, multiply the number of pounds by .45.

Area

1 hectare (ha)	=	2.47 acres		
1 square kilometer (km²)	=	247 acres	=	.39 square miles

To convert hectares to acres, multiply the number of hectares by 2.47.
To convert acres to hectares, multiply the number of acres by .41.

To convert square kilometers to square miles, multiply the number of square kilometers by .39.

To convert square miles to square kilometers, multiply the number of square miles by 2.6.

Temperature

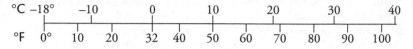

To convert degrees Fahrenheit to degrees Celsius, subtract 32 from °F, multiply by 5, then divide by 9 (example: 85°F — 32 × 5 ÷ 9 = 29.4°C).

To convert degrees Celsius to degrees Fahrenheit, multiply °C by 9, divide by 5, and add 32 (example: 20°C × 9 ÷ 5 + 32 = 68°F).

Index

Abel Tasman Coast Track, 4, 73, 75, 274, 275

Abel Tasman National Park, 4, 275, 282

Abseiling, 4, 164, 285, 310

Acacia Bay, 212

Accommodations, 9–10, 32–33, 37, 46–48

Agrodome Leisure Park (Ngongotaha), 179

Ahipara, 144, 149–50

Ahuriri Walk, 203

Air Force World (Christchurch), 400

Airlines, 35–36, 54–56, 57, 98, 387

Airports
Auckland International, 92-93
Wellington, 240

Air tours. See Flightseeing

Akaroa, 10, 403, 406–8

Akaroa Harbour, cruises, 406

Albatross, 7, 20, 269, 373–74, 376

American Express, 65–66, 98, 243, 317, 387

America's Cup, 3, 13, 92, 118, 122, 125, 130

Anaura Bay, 191

Anniversary Day Regatta, 43, 94, 118

Antarctica, 18, 25, 397

Antarctic Centre, International (Christchurch), 8, 399

Aorangi. See Mount Cook

Aquariums, 120, 201, 373

Arahura River, 293

Aranui Cave, 163

Aratiatia Falls, 213

Aratiatia Rapids, 212, 213, 215

Arikikapakapa Golf Course, 86, 181–82

Aroha Island Ecological Centre, 7, 143

Arrow River, 320

Arrowtown, 45, 313, 320, 328

Art Deco Weekend (Napier), 44, 200

Arthurs Pass National Park, 293, 402, 403, 409

Arts Centre (Christchurch), 397, 398, 404–5

Ashburton, 381

Atene Skyline Walk, 227

ATMs, 35

Auckland, 18, 64, 89–131
accommodations, 9, 10, 99
American Express, 65–66, 98
arriving in, 92–93
car rentals, 60, 61
for children, 105, 126
currency exchange, 98
emergencies, 99
Epsom, 95, 103
free activities, 96
gay men and lesbians, 13, 44, 51, 130, 131
harbor cruises, 98, 117, 122, 124, 125–26
Herne Bay, 95, 103
itineraries, suggested, 117
liquor stores, 129–30
Mission Bay, 95, 115
Mount Eden, 92, 95, 104, 118, 127
museums, 119–21
music, 96
neighborhoods, 95
nightlife, 13, 130–31
One Tree Hill, 7, 92, 118, 122, 127
panoramic views, 118
parks, 96, 118, 122
Parnell, 95, 113, 130
accommodations, 104–5
restaurants, 113–14
shopping, 96, 127–30
performing arts, 130
Ponsonby, 95, 112, 130, 131
restaurants, 112–13
post office, 99
pubs, 130–31
recreational activities, 84, 86, 126–27

Remuera, 95, 105–6
restaurants, 12, 110–17
sailing, 84, 127
shopping, 96, 127–30
sightseeing, 8, 117–26
special events, 43–46, 94
spectator sports, 127
Touristop, 93
tours, 124–26
transportation, 95, 97–98
traveling, 92–93
visitor information, 93–94
waterfront, 5, 92, 95, 96, 112

Auckland Art Gallery, 120–21

Auckland Domain, 8, 96, 122

Auckland International Airport, 92–93

Auckland Museum, 1–2, 8, 96, 119–20, 128

Auckland Regional Botanic Garden, 46, 94

Auckland Zoo, 121

Avon River, 2, 386, 397
punting, 397, 402–3

Balclutha, 342

Baldwin Street (Dunedin), 371

Ball, Murray, 5, 195

Balmacewan, golf, 86, 377

Banks Peninsula, 406

Banks Peninsula Track, 403, 407

Bark Bay, 275

Bason Botanical Reserve (Wanganui), 229

Bay of Islands, 3, 8, 18, 64, 136–53
accommodations, 145–50
beaches, 84, 137, 140
cruises, 144–45
fishing, 83, 137, 140
recreational activities, 83, 84, 85, 137, 140–41
restaurants, 150–52
sightseeing, 141–44
special events, 43, 45, 139
tours, 138, 144
traveling to, 137–38
visitor information, 139

Bay of Islands Arts Festival, 43, 139
Bay of Islands Maritime Park Headquarters and Visitors Centre (Russell), 142
Bay of Islands Wine and Food Festival, 45, 139
Bay of Plenty, 83, 85, 167–91
  beaches, 167, 168, 190
Bay View, 200
Beaches, 84, 133
  Bay of Islands, 84, 137, 140
  Bay of Plenty, 167, 168, 190
  Blaketown Beach, 288
  Christchurch, 402
  Cobden Beach, 288
  Golden Bay, 282
  Hahei Beach, 159
  Hawkes Bay, 200
  Hobson's Beach, 141
  Hot Water Beach, 2, 156
  Kaiteriteri Beach, 279
  Makarori Beach, 195
  Midway Beach, 195
  New Plymouth, 234
  Ninety-Mile Beach, 144, 145
  Ocean Beach, 168
  Ohope Beach, 190
  Piha Beach, 133
  Sterling Point-Ocean Beach Walk, 351
  Tahuna Beach, 274
  Te Mata Beach, 155
  Waikanae Beach, 195
  Wainui Beach, 195
  Westport, 284
Bed & breakfasts, 34, 37, 38, 39, 46, 47–48
Beehive (Wellington), 28, 255–56, 257
Beer and breweries, 30, 96, 195, 377
Bicycling, 87, 97, 126–27, 210, 214, 377, 403. See also Mountain biking
Birds, 19–20. See also specific birds
Bird watching, 6–7, 125
  Aroha Island Ecological Centre, 143
  Cape Kidnappers, 202
  Farewell Spit, 283

Kaikoura, 269
Kiwi House and Native Bird Centre (Otorohanga), 164
Miranda Shorebird Centre (Pokeno), 7, 135
Mount Bruce National Wildlife Centre, 260–61
Okarito Lagoon, 299
Royal Albatross Colony (Otago Peninsula), 374
Sea Bird Coast, 134–35
Sulphur Bay Wildlife Refuge, 177
Birkenhead, 95
Blackball, 290–91
Blackball Salami Company, 290
Blaketown Beach, 288
Blenheim, 266, 268
Blue Pools Track, 6
Bluff Hill, 199
Bluff Hill Walk, 203
Bluff (Invercargill), 350–51
Boating, 84–85, 181, 402–3. See also Canoeing; Jet boating; Kayaking; Punting; Rafting; Sailing
Boat tours and cruises. See Cruises
Books, recommended, 30–31
Botanical Reserve, Bason (Wanganui), 229
Botanic Garden, Auckland Regional, 46, 94
Botanic Gardens (Christchurch), 2, 397, 399
Botanic Gardens (Dunedin), 372
Botanic Gardens (Heathcote), 400
Botanic Gardens (Wellington), 254–55
Boulders in Moeraki, 380
Bracken's Lookout (Dunedin), 371
British settlers, 15, 25–27, 28, 136, 237, 254, 270
  Museum of New Zealand (Wellington), 2, 8, 251, 254, 255
Broadgreen House (Stoke), 274
Brunner, Lake, 6, 83, 286, 288
Buller River, 284
Bulls, 232–33
Bungy jumping, 4, 215, 318, 322, 409

Busby, James, 26–27, 141
Buses, 39, 57–59. See also specific bus companies
Bushwalking. See Hiking
Bushy Park (Wanganui), 229
Business hours, 66

Cadbury Confectionery Ltd. (Dunedin), 376
Calendar of events, 43–46. See also specific destinations
Cambridge, 13, 165–66
Cambridge Country Store, 13, 165
Cambridge Museum, 165
Campgrounds
  Auckland, 106–7
  Bay of Islands, 147
  Coromandel Peninsula, 157
  Dunedin, 364
  Fox Glacier, 305
  Franz Josef, 304
  Gisborne, 195–96
  Greymouth, 289
  Hawkes Bay, 204
  Hokitika, 296
  Invercargill, 351
  Mount Cook Village, 345
  Picton, 266
  Queenstown, 323–24
  Rotorua, 183
  Tongariro National Park, 224
  Wanganui, 230
  Wellington, 247
Canoeing, 3, 44, 84, 163, 164, 260, 299, 321
Canterbury Museum (Christchurch), 397, 398
Canterbury Plains, 347
Canterbury Public Library (Christchurch), 388, 397
Canyoning, 310
Cape Kidnappers, 7, 202
Cape Reinga, 143–44, 145
Cardrona Ski Field, 45, 86–87, 309, 310, 313, 321
Cardrona Snowboard Cup, 45, 309
Cardrona Valley, 309
Carew Falls Walk, 5, 288–89
Carterton, 260
Car travel, 60, 61–62. See also Car rentals
  buy-back plans, 61–62

East Cape Road, 189,
190–91
Milford Road, 2, 334,
339–40
rentals, 38, 60–61
Casinos, 14, 131, 405–6
Castlerock Station, 342
Cathedral Square
(Christchurch), 2, 386, 396,
397, 399
Cave rafting, 3, 285, 288
Cellier Le Brun (Renwick), 2,
30, 266
Centennial Lookout
(Dunedin), 371
Chard Farm Vineyard
(Queenstown), 318, 320
Chaslands, 354
"Chasm, The," 340
Children, 53
Auckland, accommoda-
tions, 105, 126
Christchurch, restaurants,
394
Children's discovery center, at
Auckland Museum, 8, 119,
126
Chinese Camp, Reconstructed
(Arrowtown), 320
Christchurch, 13, 18, 19, 64,
293, 347, 382–406
accommodations, 10,
388–92
currency exchange, 387
emergencies, 388
free activities, 397
nightlife, 14, 404–6
recreational activities,
402–4
restaurants, 12–13,
392–96
shopping, 404
sightseeing, 2, 8, 396–401
special events, 44, 46,
386
tours, 401–2
transportation, 386–87
traveling to, 382–83
visitor information, 383,
386
Wizard of, 2, 382, 396,
397
Christchurch Casino, 14,
405–6
Christchurch Cathedral, 397,
398

Christ Church Cathedral
(Nelson), 272–73
Christchurch Gondola,
399–400
Christchurch International
Airport, 383
Christ Church (Russell), 142
Clearview Winery (near
Havelock North), 30, 200,
207–8
Cleddau Gorge, 339, 340
Cleddau River, 340, 341
Clevedon, 44, 109–10
Clevedon Craft and Produce
Market, 128
CliffTop Walk, 269
Climate, 41–42, 72
Clinton, 342
Clinton River, 80, 81
Cloudy Bay (Blenheim), 2, 30,
266
Clutha River, 343
Clyde Dam, 313, 343
Coaches. See Buses
Coaltown (Westport), 285
Cobden Beach, 288
Colenso Orchard and Herb
Garden (Whitianga), 156–57
Collingwood, 283
Colville, 155
Cook, Captain James, 7, 21,
24–25, 136, 144, 191, 192,
194, 199, 237, 263, 287,
335, 339
Cook Strait, 19, 262
Wellington-Picton Inter-
Island Ferry, 63, 241,
257, 263
Cornwall Park (Auckland), 96,
122
Coromandel, 12, 154, 155–56,
158–62
Coromandel Craft Trail, 13,
154
Coromandel Forest Park,
155
Coromandel Peninsula, 13, 83,
153–62
Coronet Peak, 86, 87, 88, 318,
321
Court Theatre (Christchurch),
14, 398, 404–5
Crafts, 13, 43, 49, 128–29,
145, 154, 165, 178, 273,
275–76. See also Pottery;
Woodcrafts

Crater Lake, 222, 224
Craters of the Moon, 2,
212–15
Cricket, 45, 169
Cromwell, 342–43
Cross-country skiing, 310.
See also Skiing
Cruises
Auckland Harbor, 98, 117,
122, 124, 125–26
Bay of Islands, 144–45
Lake Rotorua, 181
Lake Taupo, 215–16
Lake Te Anau, 334
Lake Wakatipu, 318, 332
Marlborough Sounds, 264
Milford Sound, 340, 341
to New Zealand, 57
Otago Harbour, 376
Queen Charlotte Sound,
264
Tasman Sea, 332–33, 340
Wellington Harbor, 257
Cuisine. See Food and cuisine
Curio Bay Fossil Forest, 354
Currency, 35, 36
Customs requirements, 35
Cycling. See Bicycling

Dargaville, 152–53
Dargaville Maritime Museum,
153
Dart River, 4, 320–21
Darwin, Charles, 142
Deep Cove Village, 335
Deer, 22, 186, 226, 229,
355
Demon Trail, 78
Devonport, 12, 44, 95, 96,
107–9, 115–17, 124
Devonport Ferry, 98, 117, 122,
124, 126
Devonport Food & Wine
Festival, 44, 94
Devonport Museum and
Gardens, 124
Devonport Village Market,
124, 128
Diamond Lake, 310
Disabled travelers, 51, 98
Dog racing, in Auckland, 127
Dollar, New Zealand, 35, 36
Dolphins, 144, 265, 288,
406
swimming with, 3, 144,
145

Dolphin Watch Marlborough, 265

Doubtful Sound, 333, 334, 335–36

Dove Myer Robinson Park (Auckland), 122

Driving Creek Railway (Coromandel), 156

Dunedin, 18, 19, 353, 359–80
    accommodations, 364–68
    nightlife, 378–80
    recreational activities, 86, 377
    restaurants, 12, 368–71
    sightseeing, 2, 371–73
    special events, 45, 362
    traveling to, 359, 362

Dunedin Public Art Gallery, 2, 373

Dunstan, Lake, 313, 343

Durie Hill, 227

East Cape Lighthouse, 191

East Cape Road, 189, 190–91

Eastwoodhill Arboretum, 195

Eglinton Valley, 339

Egmont National Park, 5, 234, 235–36

Ellerslie Flower Show (Auckland), 46, 94

Elms Mission House (Tauranga), 169

Emergencies, 66, 72

Endeavour, 25, 136, 142, 191, 192

Entry requirements, 34–35

Evans Bay, 242

Ewelme Cottage (Auckland), 121

Fairlie, 347

Farewell Spit, 283

Farmer's market, in Auckland, 128

Farmstays, 9, 37, 38, 47, 53

Featherston, 260

Ferries, 39, 63, 98, 117, 122, 124, 126, 241, 257, 263

Ferrymead Historic Park (Heathcote), 400

Festivals, 43–46. *See also specific destinations*

Fiordland National Park, 19, 76, 300, 314, 333, 334–35, 339–40. *See also* Milford Track

Firth of Thames, 134, 135

Fishing, 6, 82–84. *See also* Trout fishing
    Bay of Islands, 83, 137, 140
    Bay of Plenty, 83
    Cleddau River, 341
    Coromandel Peninsula, 83
    equipment rental, 50
    Gisborne, 195
    guides, 83–84
    Lake Brunner, 6, 83, 288
    Lake Okareka, 181
    Lake Rotorua, 6, 83, 179, 181
    Lake Taupo, 6, 83, 210, 214
    Lake Te Anau, 6, 83
    Lake Wakatipu, 83, 321
    Nelson, 274
    Port Chalmers, 377
    Queenstown, 321
    Rakaia River, 83
    Stewart Island, 356
    Tauranga, 83
    Tekapo River, 6, 83
    Tongariro River, 6, 83, 221
    tours, 88, 145

Fletcher Challenge Marathon (Rotorua), 45, 174

Flightseeing, 3–4, 215, 344
    Mount Cook, 3–4, 302–3, 344

Flora and fauna, 19–22. *See also specific flora and fauna*

Food and cuisine, 29–30. *See also* Fruit; *and specific foodstuffs*
    Bay of Islands Wine and Food Festival, 45, 139
    ECNZ Wild Foods Festival (Hokitika), 44, 294
    hangi dinners, 8–9, 29, 188–89, 216
    Harvest Hawkes Bay Wine and Food Festival, 43, 200

Founder's Park Historical and Craft Village (Nelson), 273

Foveaux Strait, 353

Fox Glacier, 3–4, 5, 19, 300–303

Fox Glacier township, 300, 301, 303, 305–6, 306–7

Frankton, 342

Franz Josef Glacier, 3–4, 19, 299, 300–303

Franz Josef township, 300, 301, 303–6

Fruit orchards, 18, 40, 41, 140, 145, 149, 167, 169, 192, 199, 282

Fruit stands, 41, 145, 313

Fuller's Harbour Explorer, 98, 117, 125, 132, 145

Gannets, 7, 20, 64, 125, 133, 201, 202

Gay men and lesbians, 34, 51–52
    Auckland, 13, 44, 51, 94, 130, 131
    special events, 13, 44, 51, 94, 241
    Wellington, 44, 51, 241

Geothermal activity. *See* Hot springs; Thermal activity

Gethsemane Gardens (Christchurch), 401

Gibbston Valley Winery (Queenstown), 318, 320

Gisborne, 13–14, 192–98

Gisborne Museum & Arts Centre, 194

Glenfalloch Woodland Garden (Otago Peninsula), 374

Glenorchy, 321

Glenorchy Waterfront Reserve, 318

Glory Walk, 351

Glossary of terms, 29, 410, 412–13

Glowworm dells, 295, 303

Glowworm grottos, 334
    Waitomo Cave, 163–64

Golden Bay, 24, 282

Goldie, C. F., 8, 119

Gold mining, 153, 155–56, 284–87, 293, 314, 320

Golf, 3, 50, 85–86
    Auckland, 127
    Balmacewan, 86, 377
    Bay of Islands, 140
    Christchurch, 403
    Dunedin, 86, 377
    Purangi, 3, 156
    Queenstown, 321
    Rotorua, 86, 181–82
    Shirley, 86, 403
    Taupo, 86, 214, 216
    Wairakei, 86, 212, 214

Wanganui, 228
Wellington, 86, 257–58
Whataroa, 299
Gore, 342, 353
Gorge Hill, 333
Government Gardens
(Rotorua), 176–77, 181
Grand Traverse, 77, 78, 321
Great Barrier Island, 126
Greenstone River, 77
Greenstones, 49, 77, 119, 176,
262, 287, 293, 398
shopping for, 176, 182,
276, 289, 295–96, 323
Greenstone Valley Track,
77–78, 321
Grey, Zane, 83, 144
Greyhound racing, 49, 127
Greymouth, 3, 12, 283,
286–90, 292, 402
Grey River, 286
Gully, John, 273

Haast, 307
Haast Pass, 300–301, 307–8
Haast River, 307
Hagley Park (Christchurch), 2,
399, 401
Hahei Beach, 159
Halfmoon Bay (Stewart Island),
355, 356–58
Hamilton, 18, 162
Hang gliding, 69, 133, 322–23
Hangi dinners, 8–9, 29,
188–89, 216
Hanmer Springs, 409
Harris Mountains, 310
Harris Saddle, 5, 76
Haruru Falls, 145
Hastings, 193, 199, 200
Hatepe, 221
Hauraki Gulf, 3, 6, 84, 118,
125, 132, 136
Havelock North, 10, 14, 193,
199, 203, 205–6, 207
Hawea River, 309
Hawera, 235
Hawkes Bay, 18, 30, 43, 64,
193, 198–208
Hawkes Bay Exhibition Centre
(Hastings), 204
Hawkes Bay Museum (Napier),
202
Hawkes Crag, 284
Health concerns, 49, 51, 72
Heaphy Track, 5, 75, 283

Heathcote, 400, 404
Helicopter tours. See
Flightseeing
Helihiking, 4, 302–3, 307
Heliskiing, 4, 86, 310, 321,
344
Helisnowboarding, 87
Hell's Gate, 180
Herne Bay, 95, 103
Hibiscus Coast, 133–34
Hicks Bay, 190–91
Hidden Lakes, 335
Hiking, 69–82. See also
Helihiking
Abel Tasman Coast Track,
4, 73, 75, 274, 275
Ahuriri Walk, 203
Atene Skyline Walk, 227
Auckland, 127
Banks Peninsula Track,
403, 407
Bay of Islands, 140–41
Bluff Hill Walk, 203
Carew Falls Walk, 5,
288–89
CliffTop Walk, 269
Franz Josef, 302, 303
Greenstone Valley Track,
77–78, 321
Haast Pass, 307
Heaphy Track, 5, 75, 283
Hollyford Valley Track, 5,
78, 80, 336
Kahikatea Forest Walk,
295
Kaikoura, 269
Kaikoura Coast Track,
403–4, 409
Kepler Track, 73, 80,
336
Kerikeri River Walk, 5,
141, 143
Lake Kaniere Walkway,
295
Lake Matheson Walk, 303,
307
Maori Sacred Track, 180
Mercury Bay Walks, 156
Middle Hill Walk, 203
Milford Track, 5, 73–74,
75, 80–82, 88, 336, 339,
341
Motutara Walkway, 182
Mount Maunganui, 168
multiday walks, 4–5, 72,
73–74

Napier, 203
Okere Falls Track, 176,
182
Point Elizabeth Walkway,
288
Queen Charlotte Walkway,
4, 74–75, 265, 267
Queenstown, 321–22
Rakiura Track, 73, 356
Ridge Track, 224
Rob Roy Glacier Trek, 6,
310
Rotorua District, 182
Routeburn Track, 5, 6, 73,
75–77, 78, 321, 322, 336
safaris, 73, 88
safety tips, 72, 73
Shakespeare Walk, 274–75
Shoreline Walk, 269
short walks, 5–6, 73
Sterling Point-Ocean Beach
Walk, 351
Stewart Island, 73, 355–56,
356
Taupo, 212, 215
Taupo Walkways, 212, 215
Te Kuri Farm Walkway, 5,
195
Tongariro National Park,
224
Wanganui, 227
without a guide, 39, 72,
74
History, 22–27
Hobson's Beach, 141
Hodgkins, Frances, 2, 373
Hokianga Harbour, 152
Hokitika, 9, 44, 283, 286, 287,
289, 293–99
Hokitika Heritage Trail,
294
Hokitika River, 295
Holidays, 42–43
Hollyford Valley, 339
Hollyford Valley Track, 5, 78,
80, 336
Holly Lodge Estate Winery
(Wanganui), 228
Homer Tunnel, 339, 340
Homestays, 46–47
Honey, 40, 44, 49, 52, 129,
212, 216–17, 294
Honey Hive (Taupo), 216–17
Horotiu, 162
Horseback riding, 164, 215,
309

Horse racing, 43, 46, 94, 127, 165, 241

Hot springs, 133, 176, 177, 189, 214, 224. *See also* Thermal activity

Hot Water Beach, 2, 156

Howick Historical Village, 121

Huka Falls, 212, 213, 215

Huka River, 85

Hunter's Winery (Blenheim), 266

Information sources, 33–34

Insurance, 49

InterCity bus, 58–59, 93, 133, 137–38, 154, 163

International Antarctic Centre (Christchurch), 8, 399

Invercargill, 348–53

Isel House (Stoke), 274

Itineraries, suggested, 64–65

Jade Factory (Rotorua), 176, 182

Jerusalem Bay, 212

Jet boating, 4, 84–85, 165, 181, 210, 215, 229, 288, 299, 310, 320–23, 335, 409

Kahikatea Forest Walk, 295

Kahutara Canoes (Featherston), 260

Kaiaua, 135

Kaikoura, 3, 269–70, 409

Kaikoura Coast Track, 403–4, 409

Kaitaia, 144

Kaiteriteri, 275, 282

Kaiteriteri Beach, 279

Kaiti Hill Lookout, 7, 194

Kaituna River, 85, 176, 181, 182

Kakapah Point, 282

Kaniere, Lake, 295

Kapiti Coast, 233, 261

Kapiti Island, 233, 261

Katikati ("Mural Town"), 162

Kauri trees, 18, 19, 141, 152–53, 155, 354

Kawarau Gorge Suspension Bridge, 318, 322

Kawarau River, 85, 323

Kawau Island, 133

Kayaking, 3, 84, 140, 264–65, 309, 341

Kelburn Cable Car (Wellington), 254

Kelly Tarlton's Museum of Shipwrecks (Waitangi), 141

Kelly Tarlton's Southern Oceans Adventure (Auckland), 120, 126

Kemp House (Kerikeri), 142–43

Kenepuru Sound, 74

Kepler Track, 73, 80, 336

Kerikeri, 139–43, 145, 148–49, 151–52

Kerikeri River Walk, 5, 141, 143

Ketetahi Hot Springs, 224

Kimbell, 347

Kiwi bird, 7, 19–20, 121, 143, 203, 256, 260, 318, 400

Kiwi Experience, 39, 59, 174, 210, 241, 263, 272, 284, 287, 293, 300, 308, 316

Kiwifruit, 41, 47, 152, 169, 171–72, 179, 192, 282

Kiwifruit Country (Te Puke), 171–72

Kiwi House and Native Bird Centre (Otorohanga), 164

Kiwi House (Napier), 203

Kiwi House (Wellington Zoo), 256

Knight's Point View Point, 8, 307

Kowhai Park Playground (Wanganui), 228

Kuirau Park (Rotorua), 176, 182

Kumara, 291–92

Lady Knox Geyser, 180

Lake Brunner Lodge, 291–92

Lake Kaniere Scenic Reserve, 295

Lake Kaniere Walkway, 295

Lake Matheson Walk, 303, 307

Lakes District Museum (Arrowtown), 320

Language, 66, 411 glossary of terms, 29, 410, 412–13

Larnach Castle (Otago Peninsula), 374–75

Lesbians. *See* Gay men and lesbians

Lion Brewery (Auckland), 96

Literature, 30–31. *See also specific authors*

Lookout Point, 342

Lumsden, 342

Lyell, 284

Mackinnon Pass, 5, 80

Magazines, 67, 99

Magic Travellers Network, 39, 59, 168, 174, 241, 293, 300, 308

Mahia Peninsula, 193

Maitai River, 274–75

Makarora River, 309

Makarori Beach, 195

Manapouri, Lake, 335

Manapouri Power Station, 335

Mangonui, 144

Mansfield, Katherine, 28, 30, 31, 242 Birthplace (Wellington), 255

Manuka honey, 40, 44, 49, 52, 129, 212, 216–17, 294

Manutuke, 195

Maori culture, 141, 155, 167, 172, 194, 233, 373 art, 23, 49, 145 Auckland Museum, 1–2, 8, 96, 119–20, 128 best places to experience, 8–9 cultural performances, 119, 163, 189 *hangi* dinner, 8–9, 29, 188–89, 216 history of, 22–28, 136, 192, 209, 226, 237, 262 homestay, 145 language, 28–29, 142 legends, 20–21, 124, 136, 143, 155, 179, 181, 189–90, 203, 209–10, 223, 314, 380 literature, 31 meetinghouses, 119, 141, 188, 189, 190–91, 194 Museum of New Zealand (Wellington), 2, 8, 251, 254, 255 New Zealand Maori Arts and Crafts Institute (Rotorua), 178 Ohinemutu, 9, 176, 177–78, 189

One Tree Hill, 7, 92, 118, 122, 127
Otago Museum (Dunedin), 372–73
Te Papa Museum of New Zealand (Wellington), 2, 8, 251, 254, 255
tours, 8–9, 144
villages, 167, 189, 190, 191
Whanganui Regional Museum, 228
Maori Sacred Track, 180
Mapourika, Lake, 303
Marahau, 275
Mararoa River, 333
Marble Mountain, 282
Marineland (Napier), 201
Marine Parade (Napier), 199, 200, 201–3, 317
Maritime museums, 8, 120, 126, 142, 143, 194–95, 255, 273
Marlborough District, wineries, 2, 30, 266
Marlborough Sounds, 19, 64, 74–75, 84, 262, 263, 270
kayaking, 3, 84, 264–65
Marriages in New Zealand, 34
Martinborough, 43, 46, 241–42, 261
Masterton, 44, 241, 260
Matakohe Kauri Museum, 153
Matawai, 191
Matheson, Lake, 5, 300, 303
Matukituki River, 310
Measurements, metric, 413–14
Mercury Bay Walks, 156
Middle Hill Walk, 203
Midway Beach, 195
Milford Road, 2, 73, 334, 339–40
Milford Sound, 25, 64, 85, 332, 333–35, 339–41
cruises, 340, 341
kayaking, 84, 341
Milford Sound Lodge, 341
Milford Track, 5, 73–74, 75, 80–82, 88, 336, 339, 341
Millton Vineyard (Manutuke), 195
Milton, 342
Miranda Shorebird Centre (Pokeno), 7, 135
Mission Estate Winery (Napier), 200

Mitchell's Gully Gold Mine, 286
Mitchells Scenic Reserve, 288
Moana, 286, 291, 292
Moana Pool (Dunedin), 377
Moeraki, 380
Mohaka River, 85, 215
Mokoia Island (Lake Rotorua), 181
Mona Vale (Riccarton), 397, 401
Money, 35, 36
Money-saving tips, 32–33, 35–40, 38
Morere Springs Scenic Reserve, 198–99
Mossburn, 342
Motueka, 282
Motutaiko Island, 221
Motutara Walkway, 182
Mountain biking, 288, 309, 399, 403
Mountaineering, 69, 258, 303, 345
Mount Aorangi. See Mount Cook
Mount Aspiring National Park, 6, 76, 300, 308, 310, 321
Mount Bledisloe, 145
Mount Bruce National Wildlife Centre, 260–61
Mount Cargill Lookout, 371
Mount Cook, 19, 64, 300, 314, 342, 343–45
flightseeing, 3–4, 302–3, 344
skiing, 86, 344
Mount Cook Landline, 39, 58, 87
Mount Cook lily, 19, 343
Mount Cook National Park, 343
Mount Cook Village, 343–47
Mount Egmont, 5, 223, 234, 235
Mount Hot Pools, 168
Mount Hutt Ski Field, 86, 404
Mount Maunganui, 5, 85, 167, 168
Mount Mochau, 155
Mount Ngauruhoe, 18, 223, 224
Mount Ngongotaha, 180
Mount Ruapehu, 3, 18, 86, 222–25, 227

Mount Taranaki. See Mount Egmont
Mount Tarawera, 181
Mount Tasman, 300, 303
Mount Tauhara, 208, 209
Mount Te Aroha, 160
Mount Tongariro, 18, 223, 224
Mount Victoria (Wellington), 242, 254–55
Moutoa Gardens, 228
Mural Town (Katikati), 162
Murchison, 284
Murchison Mountains, 333
Muriwai Beach, 133
Murupara, 82
Museum of New Zealand (Wellington), 2, 8, 251, 254, 255
Museum of Shipwrecks, Kelly Tarlton's (Waitangi), 141
Museum of Transport and Technology (Auckland), 121

Napier, 30, 44, 193, 199–207
National Cricket Museum (Wellington), 45
National Library of New Zealand (Wellington), 256
National Maritime Museum, New Zealand (Auckland), 8, 120, 126
National parks
Abel Tasman, 4, 275, 282
Arthurs Pass, 293, 402, 403, 409
Egmont, 5, 234, 235–36
Fiordland, 76, 300, 314, 333, 334–35, 339–40
Mount Aspiring, 6, 76, 300, 308, 310, 321
Mount Cook, 343
Westland, 300, 301–3
Whanganui, 226, 227
Nature reserves and sanctuaries, 39
Glenorchy Waterfront Reserve, 318
Lake Kaniere Scenic Reserve, 295
Mitchells Scenic Reserve, 288
Morere Springs Scenic Reserve, 198–99
Nga Manu Sanctuary, 233

Nature reserves *(continued)*
  White Heron Sanctuary, 7, 299
  Willowbank Wildlife Reserve, 400
  Windsor Reserve, 44, 94, 115
Nelson, 262, 270–82
  accommodations, 10, 276–78, 280
  crafts, shopping for, 13, 275–76
  recreational activities, 274–75
  restaurants, 11, 280–82
  sights and activities, 272–74
Nelson Haven, 270
Nelson Provincial Museum (Stoke), 273–74
Newmans Coach Lines, 39, 52, 54, 58, 93, 163
New Plymouth, 64, 209, 234–36
Newspapers, 67, 99, 243
New Year's Eve (1999), 192, 194
New Zealand, Museum of (Wellington), 2, 8, 251, 254, 255
New Zealand, Te Papa Museum of (Wellington), 2, 8, 251, 254, 255
New Zealand Fighter Pilots Museum (Wanaka), 309
New Zealand Maori Arts and Crafts Institute (Rotorua), 178
New Zealand National Maritime Museum (Auckland), 8, 120, 126
New Zealand Rugby Museum (Palmerston North), 233
New Zealand Science Centre (Auckland), 121
Nga Manu Sanctuary, 233
Ngaruawahia River Regatta, 44, 163
Ngongotaha, 179
Ninety-Mile Beach, 144, 145
Northcote, 107
North Head Maritime Park (Devonport), 118
North Island, 18, 89–261
  itineraries, suggested, 64, 65
Northland, 18, 85, 138, 262

Oakura, 85
Oamaru, 380–81
Oban (Stewart Island), 354, 355–58
Ocean Beach, 168
Octagon (Dunedin), 363, 371
Ohakui, Lake, 186, 189
Ohinemutu, 9, 176, 177–78, 189
Ohope Beach, 190
Okareka, Lake, 181
Okarito Lagoon, 3, 299
Okato, 236
Okere Falls Track, 176, 182
Old St. Paul's Church (Wellington), 255, 256
Olveston (Dunedin), 373
Omarama, 6, 9–10, 343
Oneroa (Waiheke Island), 131, 132
One Tree Hill (Auckland), 7, 92, 118, 122, 127
Opotiki, 190
Orakei Korako Geyserland, 189, 213
Orewa, 133, 134
Otago Goldfields Heritage Trail, 322
Otago Harbour, 363, 373, 376
Otago Museum (Dunedin), 372–73
Otago Peninsula, 373–75
Otago Settlers Museum (Dunedin), 372
Otorohanga, 164–65
Outfitters, 87–88
Owaka, 354

Pacific Coast Highway, 64, 134–35
Package tours, 56
Paeroa, 155
Paihia, 13, 138–40, 144, 145, 147–48, 150–51, 152
Palmerston, 380
Palmerston North, 233
Papamoa, 170–71
Paparoa National Park, 286
Paragliding, 69, 133, 322–23
Parapara Hills, 226
Paraparaumu, 233
Paraparaumu Beach Golf Club (Wellington), 86, 257
Parliament Buildings (Wellington), 255–56
Parnell Rose Garden, 122

Parnell Village Shops, 13, 96, 104, 113, 114, 127
Passports, 34
Paua Shell Factory Shop (Carterton), 260
Pelorus Bridge, 270
Penguins, 20, 120, 140, 201, 269, 307, 335, 370, 373–74, 376, 380, 381, 406, 407
Pets, traveling with, 67
Picton, 3, 9, 262–69. *See also* Queen Charlotte Walkway
  ferries, 63, 241, 257, 263
Piha Beach, 133
Pihanga, 223
Pipiriki, 226
Pipiroa, 135
Pohaturoa Rock, 190
Poho-o-rawiri (Gisborne), 194
Pohutu Geyser, 178
Pohutukawa trees ("Christmas tree"), 19, 122, 132, 143, 155, 190
Point Elizabeth Walkway, 288
Pokeno, 135
Politics, 28
Polynesians, 22–23
Polynesian Spa (Rotorua), 177
Pompallier (Russell), 142
Port Chalmers, 373, 377
Port Hills, 403
Portobello Marine Laboratory, 373
Port Waikato, 85
Pottery, 13, 49, 124, 129, 145, 156, 274, 276, 296, 378
Poverty Bay, 25, 192, 193
Poverty Bay Flats, 198
Prince of Wales Feathers Geyser, 178
Puhoi, 2, 133
Puhoi Pub, 2, 133
Pukeiti Rhododendron Trust (New Plymouth), 235
Punakaiki Pancake Rocks, 286
Punting, Avon River, 397, 402–3
Purangi Golf & Country Club, 3, 156

Queen Charlotte Drive, 270
Queen Charlotte Sound, 74, 262, 263, 264
Queen Charlotte Walkway, 4, 74–75, 265, 267

Queens Park (Invercargill), 350
Queenstown, 45, 64, 314, 316–32. *See also* Greenstone Valley Track; Routeburn Track
  accommodations, 323–28
  bungy jumping, 4, 318, 322
  free activities, 318
  recreational activities, 4, 320–23
  restaurants, 11, 328–32
  sightseeing, 8, 317–20
  special events, 317
Queenstown Gardens, 318, 320
Queenstown Motor Museum, 320

Rabbit Island, 274
Rafting, 4, 85, 215, 309, 323
  cave, 3, 285, 288
Raglan, 165
Rainbow Falls, 5, 141, 143
Rainbow Farm (Rotorua), 179
Rainbow's End Adventure Park (Auckland), 126
Rainbow Springs (Rotorua), 179
Rainbow Warrior (shipwreck), 27, 85, 140, 153
Rainfall, average monthly, 41–42
Rakaia River, 83
Rakiura Museum (Stewart Island), 355
Rakiura Track, 73, 356
Rangitaiki River, 215
Rangitikei River, 84
Rangitoto Island, 92, 126, 132
Rapahoe, 288
Rapaura Watergardens (Thames), 155
Rappelling. *See* Abseiling
Raspberry farm, 228
Raukawa Falls, 226
Recreational activities. *See also specific activities*
  information sources, 69
  outfitters and tours, 87–88
  tips on, 39
Redwood Grove, 176, 181, 182
Remarkables, The, 8, 86, 88, 314, 321

Renwick, 266
Restaurants, 11–13
  glossary of terms, 412–13
  money-saving tips, 32, 33, 38
Rewa's Village (Kerikeri), 143
Rhododendrons, 40, 64, 209, 235, 236, 274, 350
Rhododendron Week (Dunedin), 45, 362
Richmond, 276, 279–80
Ridge Track, 224
Riwaka Valley, 282
Robbs Fruit Winery (Kerikeri), 151–52
Robert McDougall Art Gallery and Art Annex (Christchurch), 398
Rob Roy Glacier Trek, 6, 310
Rock climbing, 310
Rockhounding, 155
Ross, 299
Rotomahana, Lake, 180, 181
Rotorua, 8–9, 18, 64, 167, 172–89
  accommodations, 9, 183–87
  geothermal activity, 2, 64, 136, 167, 172, 176, 178, 180
  recreational activities, 86, 181–82
  restaurants, 11, 187–88
  special events, 45, 174
Rotorua, Lake, 45, 172, 174, 176, 181, 182, 183
  fishing, 6, 83, 179, 181
Rotorua Museum of Art and History, 177
Routeburn Track, 5, 6, 73, 75–77, 78, 321, 322, 336
Royal Albatross Colony (Otago Peninsula), 7, 374
Royal New Zealand Navy Museum (Devonport), 124
Royal spoonbills, 7, 299
Ruakuri cave, 163
Ruamahanga River, 260
Ruapehu Circuit, 73, 224
Rugby, 44, 127, 270
  New Zealand Rugby Museum (Palmerston North), 233
Russell, 13, 25, 138–39, 139–40, 142, 145–47, 150, 152

Russell Museum, 142
Russley Golf Club, 86, 403
Rutherford, Baron, 270

Sailing, 43, 84
  America's Cup, 3, 13, 92, 118, 122, 125, 130
  Auckland, 43, 94, 118, 127
  Picton, 265
St. Clair Golf Club, 86, 377
St. Faith's Anglican Church (Ohinemutu), 176, 177–78
St. Heliers, 5, 95, 96, 127
St. James Anglican Church (Franz Josef), 303
St. Paul's Anglican Memorial Church (Wanganui), 228
St. Stephen the Martyr (Opotiki), 190
Sandspit, 133
Savage, Michael Joseph, 7, 96, 118
Savage Memorial Park (Auckland), 7, 96, 118
School of Mines Museum (Coromandel), 155–56
Scuba diving, 85, 140
Sea Bird Coast (Pokeno), 7, 134–35
Senior citizen travelers, 52
Shakespeare Walk, 274–75
Shantytown (Greymouth), 287–88
Sheep, 21, 22, 254. *See also* Sweaters, shopping for
  Agrodome Leisure Park (Ngongotaha), 179
  Golden Shears (Masterton), 44, 241
  stations, 19, 262, 314, 346
Sheepskins, 13, 49, 129, 145, 179, 182, 203, 216, 256, 323, 342
Sheppard (Kate) National Memorial (Christchurch), 386
Shipwrecks, Kelly Tarlton's Museum of (Waitangi), 141
Shirley, 86, 403
Shopping, 40, 48–49. *See also specific items*
Shoreline Walk, 269
Shotover River, 314, 322, 323
  jet boating, 4, 85, 322
  rafting, 85, 323

Sightseeing tips, 39
Silverdale, 133–34
Single travelers, 52
Skiing, 86–87. *See also*
  Heliskiing
    Coronet Peak, 86, 87, 88,
      318, 321
    Mount Cook, 86, 344
    Mount Hutt Ski Field, 86,
      404
    Mount Ruapehu, 3, 86,
      224
    Temple Basin Ski Area, 87,
      293
    Tongariro National Park,
      3, 86, 224
    Treble Cone Ski Field, 45,
      86, 87, 308, 310, 321
    Wanaka Winter
      Wonderland, 45, 308–9
    Whakapapa Ski Area, 86,
      224
Skippers Canyon, 322
Skydiving, 1, 323
Skyline Gondola
  (Queenstown), 8, 317–18
Skyline Skyrides (Rotorua),
  180
Sky Tower (Auckland), 118,
  122
Smash Palace (Gisborne),
  13–14, 198
Snowboarding, 3, 45, 86–87,
  293, 308–9, 310, 313, 321
Somes Island, 257
Southern Alps, 19, 41, 50, 262,
  292–93, 294, 308, 343
Southern Lakes Ski Region,
  86–87
Southern Oceans Adventure,
  Kelly Tarlton's, 120
Southern Scenic Route, 353
South Island, 3, 18, 19,
  262–409
    itineraries, suggested, 64,
      65
Southland, 348–58
Southland Museum and Art
  Gallery (Invercargill), 350
Southlight Wildlife, 373
Southward Car Museum
  (Paraparaumu), 233, 261
South Westland World
  Heritage Visitor Centre, 307
Southwest New Zealand World
  Heritage Area, 300, 314

Special events, 43–46. *See also
  specific destinations*
Speights Brewery (Dunedin),
  377
Stables Colonial Museum and
  Waxworks (Napier), 201–2
Star of Canada Maritime
  Museum (Gisborne),
  194–95
Sterling Point–Ocean Beach
  Walk, 351
Stewart Island, 18, 19, 25, 73,
  85, 348, 350, 354–58
Stoke, 273–74
Stratford, 235–36
Stuart Landsborough's Puzzling
  World (Wanaka), 309
Student travelers, 53–54
Sulphur Bay Wildlife Refuge,
  177
Sumner, 85, 403
Sunshine Microbrewery
  (Gisborne), 195
Surfing, 85, 133, 168, 182,
  195, 234, 284, 288, 403
Suter Art Gallery (Nelson),
  273
Sutherland Falls, 80
Sweaters, shopping for, 13, 49,
  129, 216, 258, 276, 289,
  323, 378, 404

Tahuna Beach, 274
Tahunanui, 278–79
Taieri Gorge, 377
Tairua, 155
Takahe bird, 125, 333
Takaka, 282, 283
Takaka Hill, 282
Takapuna, 95
Tamaki Drive (Auckland), 5,
  96, 127
Tapu, 155
Taramea (Queenstown), 318
Taranaki Museum (New
  Plymouth), 234
Tarawera, Lake, 181
Tarlton, Kelly, 98, 115, 120,
  126, 141
Tasman, Abel, 24
Tasman Coast Track, Abel, 4,
  73, 75, 274, 275
Tasman Glacier, 4, 86, 343,
  344
Tasman National Park, Abel, 4,
  275, 282

Tasman Sea, 18, 294–95, 339
  cruises, 332–33, 340
Taupo, Lake, 4, 18, 209–12,
  214, 215–16, 221
    fishing, 6, 83, 210, 214
Taupo Hot Springs, 177, 214
Taupo township, 12, 209–21
    accommodations, 217–19
    restaurants, 12, 219–21
    sights and activities, 4, 9,
      212–15
Taupo Volcanic Plateau, 167
Taupo Walkways, 212, 215
Tauranga, 83, 167–72
Tauranga Historic Village (near
  Cameron), 169
Tawhiti Museum (Hawera),
  235
Taxes, 37, 40, 67, 99
Taylor's Mistake, 85, 403
Team New Zealand, 3, 118
Te Anau, Lake, 6, 80, 83, 332,
  333, 334, 336, 340
Te Anau-au Caves, 334
Te Anau Downs, 80, 337–38
Te Anau township, 11, 43,
  333–34, 336–37, 338–39.
  See also Greenstone Valley
  Track; Kepler Track;
  Routeburn Track
Te Araroa, 191
Te Aroha, 160
Te Awanga, 207–8
Ted Ashby (Auckland), 8,
  120
Te Kaha, 190
Tekapo, Lake, 347
Tekapo River, fishing, 6, 83
Te Kuri Farm Walkway, 5,
  195
Telephones, 40, 67–68
Te Mata Beach, 155
Te Mata Peak, 7, 203
Temperatures, average
  monthly, 41–42
Temple Basin Ski Area, 87,
  293
Tennis, 127, 258, 318, 320
Te Papa Museum of New
  Zealand (Wellington), 2, 8,
  251, 254, 255
Te Puke, 167, 171–72
Te Puke Vintage Auto Barn,
  172
Thames, 13, 155, 157–58, 160,
  161

Thermal activity, 18, 64, 86, 189, 209, 210, 212–13, 221, 262
  Craters of the Moon, 2, 212–15
  ECNZ Geothermal Information Centre (Wairakei), 212–13
  in Rotorua, 2, 167, 172, 174, 176–78, 180–81, 183
    Geothermal Wonderland Tour, 180–81
    Lakeside Thermal Holiday Park, 183
    Waikite Valley Thermal Pools, 176
    Whakarewarewa Thermal Reserve, 178
  Wairakei Geothermal Power Station, 2, 189, 212–13
  Waiwera Thermal Pools, 133
Thule Bay (Stewart Island), 355
Tikitiki Church, 191
Tiritiri Matangi Island, 6–7, 125
Tiwai Smelter Tours (Invercargill), 350–51
Todd's Valley (Nelson), 280
Tokaanu, 221
Tokaanu Pools, 214
Tokomaru Bay, 191
Tongariro Crossing, 73
Tongariro National Park, 3, 18, 86, 209, 221–25
Tongariro River, fishing, 6, 83, 221
Torrent Bay, 275
Tourist information, 33–34
Train travel, 39, 59–60. See also Tranz Scenic
Tramping. See Hiking
Tranz Scenic, 39, 52, 58, 59–60, 93, 163, 402
Traveling
  to New Zealand, 54–57
  within New Zealand, 39, 57–63
Travelpasses, 39, 58–59
Treaty House (Waitangi), 141

Treble Cone Ski Field, 45, 86, 87, 308, 310, 321
Trekking. See Hiking
Trounson Kauri Park, 152
Trout, 30
  fishing, 6, 82–83, 179, 181, 195, 214, 221, 274, 288
Trust Bank Ferry (Wellington), 257
Tuatara, 21, 121, 201, 256, 350
Tupare Garden (New Plymouth), 235
Turanganui River, 193
Turangi, 6, 221–22
Turoa, 3, 86, 87
Tutira, Lake, 198
Tuwhakairiora meetinghouse (Hicks Bay), 191
Twizel, 6, 346, 347

University of Otago (Dunedin), 359, 378
Upper Clutha River, 309, 310
Urupukapuka Island, 144

Valley of a Thousand Hills, 226
Victoria Park Market (Auckland), 110, 128
Vineyards. See Wine and vineyards
Virginia Lake, 228
Volcanic Activity Centre (Wairakei), 213

Waianakrua, 380
Waiau River, 335
Waihau Bay, 190
Waiheke Island, 3, 11, 84, 125, 126, 131–32
Waihi, 155, 185
Waikanae, 233–34
Waikanae Beach, 195
Waikato District, 162–66
Waikato River, 162, 163, 211, 212, 213, 215
Waikite Valley Thermal Pools, 176
Waimamaku, 153
Waimangu Volcanic Valley, 180, 181
Waimea Plains, 342
Wainui Beach, 195
Waioeka, 191

Waioeka Gorge, 191
Waiotapu Thermal Wonderland, 180
Waioweka Gorge, 189, 190
Waipapa Point, 353
Waipoua Kauri Forest, 152
Wairakei Geothermal Power Station, 2, 189, 212–13
Wairakei International Golf Course, 86, 212, 214
Wairakei Tourist Park, 212–17
Wairarapa, 260–61
Wairere Waterfall, 190
Wairoa River, rafting, 85, 215
Waitakere Ranges, 133
Waitangi, 139, 140, 141
  Treaty of (1840), 27, 28, 43, 89, 139, 141, 142, 145, 406
Waitangi Day, 139, 141
Waitemata Harbour, 92
Waitomo, 3, 162–65
Waitomo Cave, 3, 163–64
Waiwera, 133
Waiwera Thermal Pools, 133
Wakatipu, Lake, 314, 317, 321, 333
  cruises, 318, 332
  fishing, 83, 321
Wakatipu Basin, 322
Wakefield, William, 209, 226, 237, 270
Walking. See Hiking
Walter Peak, 332
Wanaka, 11, 308–12
Wanaka, Lake, 308
Wanaka Winter Wonderland, 45, 308–9
Wanganui, 11, 209, 226–32
Warkworth, 10, 133, 134
War Memorial Tower (Wanganui), 227
Water, drinking, 68, 72
Weather, 41–42, 72, 73
Web sites, 33–34
Weddings in New Zealand, 34
Weird and Wonderful (Auckland Museum), 8, 119, 126
Wellington, 18, 44, 237–59
  accommodations, 244–47
  Brooklyn, 242, 250
  embassies, 66, 243
  free activities, 255

Wellington *(continued)*
gay men and lesbians, 44, 51
harbor cruises, 257
Kelburn, 242, 251
libraries, 243
Mount Victoria, 242, 254–55
accommodations, 246–47
nightlife, 258–59
Oriental Bay, 242, 250
Parliament Buildings, 255–56
recreational activities, 86, 257–58
restaurants, 11, 12, 247–51
shopping, 258
sights and activities, 251–57
special events, 43, 44, 241–42
Thorndon, 242
accommodations, 246
restaurants, 250–51
tours, 256–57
transportation, 242–43, 244
traveling to, 240–41
visitor information, 241
Wellington Airport, 240
Wellington Cup Racing Meeting, 43, 241
Wellington Maritime Museum, 255
Wellington-Picton Inter-Island Ferry, 63, 241, 257, 263

Wellington Zoo, 256
West Coast Historical Museum (Hokitika), 294
Westland National Park, 300, 301–3
Westlands Water World (Hokitika), 295
Westport, 3, 4, 283–86
Whakapapa, 223–24
Whakapapa Ski Area, 86, 224
Whakarewarewa State Forest Park, 176, 182
Whakarewarewa Thermal Reserve, 178
Whakatane, 83, 167, 189–90
Whale watching, 3, 144, 269, 409
Whangamata, 155
Whangamomona Republic Day, 45, 227
Whanganui National Park, 226, 227
Whanganui Regional Museum, 228
Whanganui River, 223, 226, 227, 229–30
Whangaparaoa, 133, 190
Whangarei, 134
Whangarei Falls, 134
Wharerata Hills, 198
Whataroa, 9, 299–300
White herons, 7, 20, 299
White Heron Sanctuary, 7, 299
White Island, 190
White-water rafting. *See* Rafting

Whitianga, 9, 13, 83, 154, 155, 156–57, 159–60, 161
Whitianga Water Transport, 156
Wigram Aerodrome (Heathcote), 400
Willowbank Wildlife Reserve, 400
Wilmot Pass, 335
Wilsons Distillery Whisky (Dunedin), 376–77
Windsor Reserve (Devonport), 44, 94, 115
Windsurfing, 85, 182, 284, 404
Wine and vineyards, 2, 30, 132, 195, 228, 261, 274
festivals, 44, 45, 94, 139
Hawkes Bay, 30, 43, 200–201
Marlborough District, 2, 30, 266
Queenstown, 318, 320
Winter Garden (Auckland), 122
Wizard of Christchurch, 2, 382, 396, 397
Woodcrafts, 49, 182, 217
Wool sweaters, shopping for, 13, 49, 129, 216, 258, 276, 289, 323, 378, 404
World Dragon Boat Festival (Wellington), 44, 241
World Heritage Highway, 300–301

Yachting. *See* Sailing